Counseling Psychology

Third Edition

Counseling Psychology

Third Edition

Charles J. Gelso, Elizabeth Nutt Williams, and Bruce R. Fretz

American Psychological Association • Washington, DC

Second Printing, October 2015
Published by
American Psychological Association
750 First Street, NE
Washington, DC 20002
www.apa.org

To order
APA Order Department
P.O. Box 92984
Washington, DC 20090-2984
Tel: (800) 374-2721; Direct: (202) 336-5510
Fax: (202) 336-5502; TDD/TTY: (202) 336-6123
Online: www.apa.org/pubs/books
E-mail: order@apa.org

In the U.K., Europe, Africa, and the Middle East, copies may be ordered from
American Psychological Association
3 Henrietta Street
Covent Garden, London
WC2E 8LU England

Typeset in Meridien by Circle Graphics, Inc., Columbia, MD

Printer: Maple Press, York, PA
Cover Designer: Mercury Publishing Services, Inc., Rockville, MD

The opinions and statements published are the responsibility of the authors, and such opinions and statements do not necessarily represent the policies of the American Psychological Association.

Library of Congress Cataloging-in-Publication Data

Gelso, Charles J., 1941-
  Counseling psychology / Charles J. Gelso, Elizabeth Nutt Williams, and Bruce R. Fretz.
  — Third edition.
     pages cm
  Includes bibliographical references and index.
  ISBN 978-1-4338-1711-3 — ISBN 1-4338-1711-X 1. Counseling psychology.
2. Counseling psychology—Vocational guidance. I. Williams, Elizabeth Nutt.
II. Fretz, Bruce R., 1939- III. Title.

  BF636.6.G453 2014
  158.3—dc23
                                  2013039858

British Library Cataloguing-in-Publication Data

A CIP record is available from the British Library.

Printed in the United States of America
Third Edition

http://dx.doi.org/10.1037/14378-000

*This book is dedicated to the memory of Bruce Fretz,
an extraordinary friend, collaborator, mentor, and counseling
psychologist. His mind and enlightened views
are a part of every page.*

Contents

III

IV

Preface

Prior to the publication of the first edition of *Counseling Psychology* in 1992, the authors of the first two editions, Charlie Gelso and Bruce Fretz, had been troubled by the absence of a beginning text in our field. It appeared to us that every field within psychology had specialized books for students being introduced to the science and practice of the field—except the field that we studied, practiced, taught, and care most about—counseling psychology.

At that time, as is true still, there were numerous books on the activity of counseling, and such books were typically used as the texts in beginning courses in counseling psychology. As a result, some students and even some professionals confused counseling, the activity, with counseling psychology, the profession, mistakenly considering the two synonymous. There were no texts devoted exclusively to the field of counseling psychology.

So, the book filled a void in counseling psychology specifically and the field of psychology more generally. It also filled a personal need of ours as we taught advanced undergraduate and beginning graduate courses in counseling psychology. We have been heartened by how *Counseling Psychology* has been received by the field over the years and pleased by what we think the book has contributed.

New to This Edition

It would be an understatement to say that things have changed a lot since the appearance of the previous edition. Counseling psychology has made great strides as a science and a profession, and the specialty's place within the discipline of psychology is stronger than ever. Along with this strengthening of counseling psychology, major social, cultural, scientific, and professional changes have occurred since the publication of the second edition. It is clearly time for a new edition.

We have significantly restructured this edition. We have created chapters that emphasize the scientific foundations of the field. The field's historical focus on health, wellness, and optimum functioning is highlighted, as is the foundational area of vocational psychology. We describe the field's strong emphasis on diversity and social justice, including definitions and controversies across different social identities. The growing interest in the field in counseling and psychotherapy process and outcome research is also emphasized. These areas were certainly discussed in previous editions, but this new structure allowed us to highlight the scientific contributions of these foundational areas of counseling psychology.

Although we still include specific chapters on the therapy relationship, assessment, and career counseling, we added feminist multicultural counseling to the chapters on the major theoretical orientations in the field. Some important topics that had previously occupied their own chapters were merged with other chapters (e.g., the combining of topics related to psychotherapy "beyond the individual," the inclusion of consultation with vocational psychology). Unfortunately, space constraints prevented us from including chapters on other important topics (e.g., counseling supervision and prevention). It is our hope that this new structure and new edition reflect both the historically and currently important topics in the field, and that it is useful to both students of counseling psychology and experts who wish to update their broad perspective on the many facets of counseling psychology.

Features of This Text

This book is one of the few, if not the only, to provide a comprehensive overview of counseling psychology—its professional practices and issues, its interventions, its science and research, and its basic concepts. Although this text should prove useful to experienced counseling psychologists, as did its predecessors, our main focus in this edition is on the students commencing their study of counseling psychology, be they at the graduate or advanced undergraduate level.

The third edition is divided into four parts. In Part I, we introduce readers to the field of counseling psychology: its central values, defining features, and relationships to other specialties within and outside psychology; its historical background and development; and its ethical foundations.

In Part II, we present the scientific foundations of the field, from an overview of research paradigms in the field to the specific and historically defining research areas of the field: vocational psychology; health, wellness, and positive psychology; diversity and social justice; and counseling and psychotherapy process and outcome research.

In Part III, the focus is on the practice of counseling psychology. We introduce fundamental issues in individual counseling and psychotherapy, including a focus on the therapeutic relationship and the four primary theoretical perspectives in the field: psychoanalytic, cognitive-behavioral, humanistic, and feminist multicultural. Chapters in Part III also cover the topics of assessment; career counseling; and therapeutic work with couples, families, and groups.

Part IV contains the final chapter of the book, in which we describe many aspects related to training to become a counseling psychologist, from choosing graduate programs to surviving the dissertation to postgraduate training and specialty competencies.

Despite the book's fundamental purpose as a useful comprehensive text, portions of *Counseling Psychology* are also applicable to other courses in the field. For example, chapters in Parts I and II may be useful in research methods courses or courses on professional issues. Likewise, chapters in Part III could be incorporated into courses covering topics on the theories and techniques of counseling or psychotherapy or courses introducing the student to the counseling process.

We have entered a new phase with this third edition, with both growth and loss. Gelso and Fretz invited Libby Nutt Williams to join them as a third author. She, as someone interested in the concept of serendipity, found it meaningful that she began her graduate work in 1992, the year of the first edition of the book, and so was shaped as a professional by this very text. Her joining as an author provided a new perspective, and the three of us had a wonderful time working together. However, not long after beginning work on the revisions, our dear colleague Bruce Fretz passed away. Still, Bruce's presence was with us throughout the process, as he left his indelible mark on so much of this third edition.

Acknowledgments

We would like to thank Ellen Lockwood and Christina Torres for scanning old chapters into current electronic form and ensuring the revision process would be a smooth one. We also wish to thank Jeff Barnett and

Brad Johnson for consulting on our coverage of ethical dilemmas and controversies. We are indebted to Donna Gozelanczyk for her meticulous proofreading of several chapters, including chapters in which the scanning process did strange things and created, shall we say, unusual symbols in the document! APA Senior Acquisitions Editor Susan Reynolds believed in our work and provided wonderful support during the process.

We also thank our partners and children, who give us support and joy.

THE SCOPE AND GOALS OF COUNSELING PSYCHOLOGY

I

An Introduction to Counseling Psychology

1

This book is devoted to counseling psychology, one of the major specialties within the broad science and profession of psychology. In this book we explore what counseling psychology is about: its themes, its history and areas of growth, its focus on science and practice, and its contributions to the field of psychology. We examine the foundations of counseling psychology, including the vital areas of ethics and cultural competence. We highlight unique areas in which counseling psychologists have provided cutting-edge research, such as in vocational psychology and social justice issues, as well as the ways in which counseling psychologists have contributed to the more general areas of psychotherapy and counseling. The profession of counseling psychology is wide and varied. We hope to give a sense of its breadth while still highlighting those essential elements of counseling psychology that give it its unique focus within psychology.

On a personal note, this book has been written by counseling psychologists who have a deep and abiding love for

http://dx.doi.org/10.1037/14378-001
Counseling Psychology, Third Edition, by C. J. Gelso, E. N. Williams, and B. R. Fretz

the field. You will not get a wholly impartial picture of the specialty and its issues and practices, simply because we, the authors, are steeped in the field, value it, and are strongly committed to its growth and development. We believe that counseling psychology has something special to offer to both its practitioners and the public, and you will certainly detect this viewpoint in the pages to come. Nonetheless, we have done our best to present the facts of the specialty in as clear, fair, and objective a way as possible.

In a general introduction to the specialty of counseling psychology and its development, three concepts are highly pertinent: definitions, diversity, and distinctiveness. From the start, the field has emphasized the need to clarify its identity; to distinguish itself from other specialties and fields within and outside of psychology; and to develop, retain, and honor diversity.

Defining Features of Counseling Psychology

Roles and themes that serve to bring together the diverse and sometimes disparate elements and activities of the profession of counseling psychology and to differentiate it from related fields and specialties within and outside of psychology have always existed.

PRIMARY ROLES

Throughout the history of counseling psychology, three roles have remained central: the remedial, the preventive, and the developmental. (Probably the first to articulate them systematically were Jordaan, Myers, Layton, & Morgan, in 1968.) The individual importance of these roles has varied over time, yet all three have been significant in lending counseling psychology self-definition.

The *remedial* role entails working with individuals or groups to assist them in remedying problems of one kind or another. As noted by Kagan et al. (1988), remedial interventions may include personal–social counseling or psychotherapy at an individual, couples (e.g., marriage counseling), or group level. Crisis intervention and various therapeutic services for students requiring assistance with unresolved life events are additional examples of work at the remedial level. Often, when students think about becoming a counseling psychologist, they think of this remedial role first and articulate it as a desire to help others. Yet, in many ways, the other two roles are more foundational to counseling psychology and might, if done extremely well, lead to a reduction in need for remediation.

The *preventive* role is one in which the counseling psychologist seeks to "anticipate, circumvent, and, if possible, forestall difficulties that may arise in the future" (Jordaan et al., 1968, p. 1). Preventive interventions may focus on psychoeducational programs intended to forestall the development of problems or events, such as classes or workshops at a university counseling center designed to impact students, residence hall counselors, and university personnel (Kagan et al., 1988). They may also entail individual prevention strategies (such as for drug relapse prevention). In a business or industrial setting, the preventive role is exemplified by consultations held with the company on matters such as team building, supervisor–staff relationships, management assessment and development, and communication enhancement across departments. Although prevention programs may differ in setting, the key feature is to help clients make changes in their personal and interpersonal environments to minimize the occurrence of problems (Fretz, 1985) and forestall remedial work. Counseling psychologists remain at the forefront of prevention (Hage & Romano, 2010). For example, John Romano, Sally Hage, and others have developed prevention guidelines for psychologists for the American Psychological Association (APA, 2013).

The third general role of the counseling psychologist is referred to as the *educative–developmental* role, the purpose of which is to "help individuals to plan, obtain, and derive maximum benefits from the kinds of experiences which will enable them to discover and develop their potentialities" (Jordaan et al., 1968, p. 1). Examples of the educative–developmental role might include various skill training interventions, couples groups formed to enhance relationships, growth groups, and various workshops or seminars. Another example might be a study skills class for college students aimed at making good students even more effective (rather than remedying ineffective academic behavior). In the developmental role, the focus is on enhancement. We counseling psychologists teach skills or enhance attitudes that facilitate dealing with inevitable, everyday problems and that maximize effectiveness or satisfaction. The distinction between the developmental and preventive roles is often subtle—a matter of degree rather than kind. The key feature of the developmental role is that when performing it, counseling psychologists are going beyond prevention and are involved in enhancement.

We have been addressing the three general roles of the counseling psychologist as if each activity involved only one of the roles. Thus, the reader might now think, for example, that individual therapy or counseling is remedial, consultation with residence hall counselors is preventive, and couples enhancement workshops are developmental. This separation is far from fully accurate. Most or perhaps all activities combine the three roles in one way or another. The difference is the point of emphasis. For example, when the counseling psychologist is working in individual counseling with a client suffering from anxiety that interferes with job performance, the primary role may be remedial, but the preventive and developmental roles will also be present. The counselor seeks to prevent more debilitating disorders and to actualize the client's potential. Indeed, one of the distinguishing features of the counseling psychologist is his or her consistent attention to the three roles.

CENTRAL VALUES

The three primary roles discussed above, along with five unifying themes, were initially proposed by Gelso and Fretz (1992) to define the specialty of counseling psychology. These five unifying themes emphasized (a) assets and strengths; (b) person–environment interactions; (c) educational and career development; (d) brief interactions; and (e) intact personalities. Since the early 1990s a number of authors have attempted to further examine, clarify, and refine the definition of counseling psychology (Howard, 1992; Scheel et al., 2011; Whalen et al., 2004). The continuous attempts to make clear the identity of counseling psychologists emanate in part from external pressures to clarify the role as a specialty in psychology. Another reason for this continued self-exploration is that the field is still growing and developing. Such explorations themselves also fit with identity as psychologists and counselors.

So, in the last 20 years, other authors have added themes, values, and features to the five unifying themes proposed by Gelso and Fretz (1992, 2001) as being critical to counseling psychology. For example, Howard (1992) took an ethnographic look at what counseling psychologists value (e.g., "diversity is good," p. 425). In 2004, Whalen et al. suggested a similar but modified version of the themes put forward by Gelso and Fretz based on counseling practice with feminist multicultural perspectives with emphasis on client strengths, hygiology (or health and optimal functioning), life-span development, vocational development, persons-in-environments, and prevention/education. In 2008, Goodyear et al. surveyed counseling psychologists and determined that the profession may be experiencing ideal/real self-dissonance. They noted that, although "the specialty's 'ideal self' is one in which career counseling, prevention, and the promotion of client strengths are central" (Goodyear et al., 2008, p. 242), their data suggested a reduction in the involvement of counseling psychologists in vocational counseling and a greater tendency to specialize or engage in more focused activities.

In 2009, Packard provided a review of previous discussions of the core values of counseling psychology and proposed a list of nine core values for counseling psychology. He also included a discussion of the three "enduring goals" that the Society for Counseling Psychology's executive committee approved in January 2005 as a strategic focus for 2006–2010. The goals focused on (a) diversity; (b) strength-based, developmental, and contextual approaches; and (c) the integration of science and practice.

Most recently, Scheel et al. (2011) noted that what "fundamentally distinguishes counseling psychology from other subdisciplines within psychology (e.g., school or clinical) is the term *counseling*" (p. 674). They found a noticeable decline in counseling-related articles in the *Journal of Counseling Psychology* and *The Counseling Psychologist*, with a growing focus instead on social justice and cultural competence. They also proposed that "the trend for the publication of counseling research to move away from the counseling flagship journals cannot be good news for our identity" (Scheel et al., 2011, p. 687). Others, however, have celebrated the growing focus of the field on multiculturalism and social justice initiatives (Pope-Davis, Coleman, Liu, & Toporek, 2003; Toporek, Gerstein, Fouad, Roysircar, & Israel, 2006).

When these various perspectives are pulled together, a list of five overarching and enduring central values of counseling psychology emerges:

1. An emphasis on a person's strengths and optimal functioning;
2. A focus on the whole person, with particular emphasis on life-span development and vocational growth;
3. A commitment to advocacy and social justice, maintaining an ongoing awareness of the importance of environmental context and culture;
4. A concentration on brief, educational, and preventive counseling interventions; and
5. A dedication to the scientist–practitioner model.

Strengths and Optimal Functioning

The first defining value is the focus on people's assets and strengths and on positive mental health, regardless of the degree of disturbance. We have stated this value first because it is primary in the identity of counseling psychologists and has often run contrary to the ways in which mental health is viewed, both historically and in the public. Thankfully, it is now more than a century since persons with mental illness were seen as possessed by demons and hopelessly incurable. In the mid-19th century, what is now known as the *mental health movement* became well established. Under the leadership of Dorothea Dix (1802–1887) in 1848, New Jersey built a hospital (rather than an insane asylum) for the mentally ill. At this point in history, the mental health movement sought to provide more humanitarian custodial care for the mentally ill; there was still little expectation for cures. Several decades later, a new level of understanding concerning the role of assets and strengths in working with mental problems was reached via the work of Clifford Beers (1876–1943). His book, *A Mind That Found Itself* (Beers, 1908), represents a critical turning point in the public's awareness that persons with mental problems could recover and that, even in the depths of depression or other problems, they had strengths that could be utilized to help them make that recovery.

Another major step forward in mental health ideology was the establishment of a psychological clinic by Lightner Witmer at the University of Pennsylvania early in the 20th century. His clinic was devoted to working with children who had learning or behavioral problems in contrast to those as yet described as insane or mentally disturbed. Such a clinic helped the public understand that persons other than those identified as mentally ill could be helped by therapeutic intervention. In one sense, Witmer's clinic is the precursor of thousands of mental health clinics and counseling centers that now exist throughout this country. Although the clinic's operations were largely remedial, the concept that children could be helped to function more effectively served to lead counseling psychology to focus more on potential development of the individual rather than on deficits that must be overcome.

Counseling psychologists have long held the viewpoint that people with mental health problems have the potential for moving beyond their difficulties; that is, they were not incurable. In a classic paper by Super (1955), this emphasis on assets was referred to as a focus on hygiology (or health) rather than on psychopathology (or sickness). Super noted that even when working with the severely disturbed, the counseling psychologist tended to look for strengths and build on them. The underlying assumption is that even profoundly disturbed persons have strengths, assets, and coping abilities and that it is valuable to work with these.

Tied to this emphasis on the positive is a point of view characterized by hopefulness and optimism, based on the belief that

> individuals can change, can lead satisfying lives, can be self-directing, and can find ways of using their resources, even though these may have been impaired by incapacitating attitudes and feelings, slow maturation, cultural deprivation, lack of opportunity, illness, injury, or old age. (Jordaan et al., 1968, p. 2)

How is this philosophical emphasis on the positive, and on assets and strengths, put into practice? In part, it is an assumption and attitude that counseling psychologists carry with them and convey to their clients. In addition, the focus on strengths is operationalized in numerous ways. When counseling psychologists engage in career counseling with a very disturbed client, they are expressing the belief that the client has coping abilities that can be built upon that will allow him or her to make use of the counseling. When counseling psychologists work in an inpatient setting and develop an empathy training program for disturbed patients, they are building on these patients' resources. And when counseling psychologists empirically study healthy aspects of personality, they are expressing their involvement in this central value. The reader is encouraged to think of other examples of how this emphasis on strengths may be manifested. Suffice it to say for now that, whenever the counseling psychologist is functioning in the educative–developmental role, she or he is focusing on strengths and assets.

In fact, this focus on optimal functioning provides an important value for counseling psychologists: an emphasis on health and positive coping skills. Although it appears that greater numbers of counseling psychologists have increasingly worked with more disturbed clients (Corazzini, 1997; Goodyear et al., 2008), it is also true that counseling psychologists (relative to practitioners in other fields, such as clinical psychology and psychiatry) more often work with clients who are closer to the normal range of functioning (Hayes, 1997). Despite great variability in the range of clients with whom counseling psychologists work, practitioners often deal with clients who have "problems in living" (Szasz, 1960, p. 113); for example, counseling psychologists often help clients with a wide range of concerns, from improving interpersonal relations to making career plans to fostering resilience in the face of difficult life circumstances. What underlies these counseling approaches is a firm belief in the power of the positive (Snyder, Lopez, & Pedrotti, 2011), or that helping clients discover and develop their strengths will be curative and transformative. Thus, in comparison to those with other psychology specialties, such as clinical psychology, counseling psychologists are less interested in diagnosing and treating the "illness" and more interested in helping clients use their assets to resolve their problems.

When considering the range of interventions offered by counseling psychologists and when contrasting counseling psychology with other fields (e.g., clinical psychology, psychiatry), one can easily see that counseling psychology devotes relatively more of its energy to issues of psychological health and wellness (e.g., Lightsey, 1996), rather than focus on illness and disease. Given the wide range of clients served and the interventions offered, the preventive and developmental roles discussed earlier fit quite naturally into the work of the counseling psychologist.

Life-Span Development and Vocational Growth

The second central value of counseling psychology is an emphasis on the whole person, with special emphasis on life-span development and vocational growth. It was only in the 1960s and afterward that the profession of counseling psychology, and indeed psychology at large, began to fully recognize the distinctive importance and relevance of developmental stage models produced by Piaget (1952), Erikson (1959), Vygotsky (1978), Maccoby (1980), and Kohlberg (1984). During the past 50 years, counseling psychologists have given increasing attention to developmental models for the understanding they provide about normal developmental crises and transitions, as well as about opportunities for growth (Juntunen, 2002).

The translation of these theoretical concepts into the work of counseling psychologists allows for a unique focus on an individual's needs across the life span, from childhood (Werner & Smith, 1982) to older adulthood (Rowe & Kahn, 1998). Such a focus also allows for emphasis on changes in life status, such as adaptation to transition (Gibson & Brown, 1992) as well as intervention strategies for coping with transitions (Brammer & Abrego, 1981) and with stress (Matheny, Aycock, Pugh, Curlette, & Cannella, 1986). Such changes and transitions do not always require counseling or psychotherapy, but they are part of the experiences of the whole person and therefore are part of what counseling psychologists study, research, and apply.

Similarly, in the career development area, counseling psychologists both study vocational choice and development and provide services to enhance career development and treat vocational problems. Career counseling and development, at the heart of counseling psychology since the early vocational guidance movement in the mid-20th century, allow for the focus on the whole person perspective so highly valued in counseling psychology (Fitzgerald & Osipow, 1986; Richardson, 2012; Robitschek & Woodson, 2006). In today's technological age, with literally thousands of jobs to choose from, many requiring highly specialized training, understanding that over 100 years ago the majority of young people did not really consider career choices may be difficult. Most followed in a parent's occupational footsteps, whether that be farmer, bootmaker, or seamstress. As many new and different jobs were created by the Industrial Revolution, people increasingly realized not only that there were there career choices to be made but also that certain kinds of work required specific skills and training.

The social reformer Frank Parsons saw the need to develop what would today be called a career counseling service. In 1908 he established his vocations bureau in Boston to guide individuals through a three-step process he developed, which still serves as the foundation of most current career counseling. Parsons's three steps involve acquisition of

> (1) a clear understanding of [oneself], [one's] aptitudes, abilities, interests, ambitions, resources, limitations and their causes; (2) a knowledge of the requirements and conditions of success, advantages and disadvantages, compensation, opportunities, and prospects in different lines of work; (3) true reasoning on the relations of these two groups of facts. (Parsons, 1909, p. 5)

The vocational guidance movement quickly incorporated much of the psychometric tradition as a way of providing information about individual aptitudes, abilities, and interests. In subsequent years, the need for occupational classification of literally millions of men in the two world wars was answered in large part by the methods of the vocational guidance and psychometric movements.

Of even greater significance for the development of counseling psychology was the response of these movements to the American Depression in the 1930s:

> The economic depression of the 1930's added a new current to the stream of history. Large-scale unemployment highlighted vocational guidance as a job-placement activity as well as an educational function. The Minnesota Employment Stabilization Research Institute experimented with psychological tests, occupational information, and retraining as methods of getting adult workers back into the active labor force. Then many private and public vocational counseling centers, together with the United States Employment Service, quickly took over the research and counseling methods developed in this pioneer project. (Super, 1955, pp. 3–4)

The historical emphasis on career development remains a strong part of counseling psychology, but the field has moved a long way from more simple occupational assessment. Recent areas of focus within the vocational realm continue to show counseling psychology's commitment to understanding individuals and their vocational experiences within the context of their broader lives and across cultures (Arulmani, 2009; Flores, Hsieh, & Chiao, 2011; Vespia, Fitzpatrick, Fouad, Kantamneni, & Chen, 2010). In Chapters 5 and 15 in this volume we further examine the importance of vocational and career issues within counseling psychology.

Social Justice and Multicultural Awareness

The third central value of counseling psychology is a commitment to advocacy and social justice with an emphasis on person–environment interactions (rather than an exclusive focus on either the person or the environment) and with specific attention to cultural contexts. Since its inception, counseling psychology has carefully considered the impact and role of the situation in the client's life (whether the client is an individual, group, organization, etc.). Consequently, theories that have placed an extreme emphasis on *intrapsychic* explanations of behavior have not on the whole been attractive to counseling psychologists. The interest in person–environment transactions has been evident in the attention paid over the years to activities such as consultation, outreach, and environmental modification (Gallessich, 1985; Howard, 1993; Ivey, 1979; Meade, Hamilton, & Yuen, 1982). Although the specialty has been criticized in the past for not paying enough attention to the environment portion of the person–environment interaction in actual practice (as opposed to writing about practice; see Ivey, 1979), recent years have seen an explosion of research, interest, and commitment to multiculturalism and social justice (Ponterotto, Casas, Suzuki, & Alexander, 2001; Toporek et al., 2006) that makes clear counseling psychology's commitment to cultural and environmental context in scholarship and in practice.

To understand the importance of culture and person–environment interactions in counseling psychology, one needs to acknowledge the impact of three particular historical elements in the growth of the profession: psychology's orientation toward measurement, the discovery of the critical role of environment, and the way in which cultural context and competence have become a predominant force in the profession. One of the first tasks of early psychologists (and still a major task of psychologists today) was to develop means of measuring psychological processes and behaviors, now referred to as *psychometrics*. Psychology's roots in the area of measurement may be traced back to the work of Galton (1822–1911) and his quest for understanding differences among people by applying quantitative methods. J. M. Cattel (1860–1944) continued this study of individual differences, using much of what he had learned in Wilhelm Wundt's (1832–1920) laboratory established in Leipzig in 1879. Shortly thereafter, Binet (1857–1911), in France, established the first intelligence test, further expanding the measurement of differences in persons.

The combination of these psychometric developments with the vocational guidance movement, previously described, helped launch psychology as a profession in the first half of the 20th century. Even in the days of mass testing during World War I and the postwar boom years of the 1920s, there were those who were beginning to see that limits existed to what could be accomplished through measurement of differences only in persons. In 1935 Lewin provided his now classic explication of the concept that behavior is a function of both the person and the environment. In Lewin's view, predictions of what persons will do, no matter how much information one has about aptitudes or skills, will always be limited unless information about the environments in which persons function is also considered.

Psychologists have increasingly come to understand that they cannot simply ask questions such as "What kind of person will succeed as a dentist?" and "Which kind of client problem will benefit from psychotherapy?" outside of an environmental context. One type of individual may be an effective leader of one kind of organization (environment) but not of another. The critical factor is the *interaction* between the person and the environment. Not only do environments affect persons but persons also affect environments. (See Claiborn and Lichtenberg, 1989, for an elaboration of the history of interactional thought in psychology and more specifically within counseling psychology.)

In recent years, counseling psychologists have used their historical perspective on the importance of understanding the dynamic interplay between the person and the environment to fuel an explosion of research on the importance of the cultural context of an individual (Ponterotto et al., 2001; Sue & Sue, 2008). Counseling psychologists have been crucial in the development of multicultural counseling assessment (Suzuki & Ponterotto, 2008), competencies (Pope-Davis et al., 2003), and guidelines (APA, 2003a). Counseling psychologists have provided a strong voice in the literature for advocacy and social justice (Toporek et al., 2006), reinforcing these central values and helping other areas of psychology and human services understand their importance as well. We address these topics in more depth in Chapters 6 and 14 in this volume.

Brief, Educational, and Preventive Interventions

The fourth central value of counseling psychology is an emphasis on relatively brief interventions. Counseling psychologists typically view counseling as one of their primary activities, and this intervention is, by definition, relatively brief. To clarify what we mean by the term *brief*, we contrast what we call *counseling* with a closely related term, *psychotherapy*. Some psychologists view these two terms as representing the same process, but we think the terms can be differentiated, at least in the extreme, and that it is useful to do so.

Although exact numbers (e.g., numbers of counseling sessions) are of course arbitrary, we think of interventions up to about 12 to 15 sessions as constituting counseling or psychotherapy, in the sense that either term is fitting. However, interventions beyond that point are typically deemed psychotherapy, or *therapy* as it is commonly called. In further differentiating counseling and therapy, we subscribe to the model suggested by Brammer, Abrego, and Shostrom (1993). In that model, at the extreme ends of the continuum, the two activities differ. At one extreme, work that is supportive, seeks to educate, and focuses on situational problems and problem solving at a conscious level, with normal individuals, is aptly called counseling. At the other end of the continuum, interventions that seek to reconstruct personality, include depth analysis, and analytically focus on subconscious processes with more troubled individuals are best labeled psychotherapy. In the broad middle range of this continuum, when the interventions contain a mixture of the factors just described, the terms *counseling* and *psychotherapy* imply one and the same process.

Having discussed the terms *counseling* and *psychotherapy*, let us now return to the issue of duration of treatment. We have said that counseling psychologists view counseling as defined here as a central part of their work (cf. Fitzgerald & Osipow, 1986; Scheel et al., 2011). Further, although counseling psychologists certainly conduct long-term psychotherapy, the kind of psychotherapy that has been seen as central to the counseling psychology tends to be short term. (The reader is referred to Leona Tyler's 1961 discussion of brief therapy as especially suited to counseling psychology.) Again, although exact figures would be arbitrary, interventions of up to 6 months' duration would generally be considered short-term therapy.

Until the 1930s, treatments based on humanitarian (not to be confused with humanistic) viewpoints emanating from the late-19th-century mental health movement were limited largely to the psychoanalytic perspective and were lengthy and intensive. E. G. Williamson and Carl Rogers then developed very different perspectives on counseling and psychotherapy. As a leading figure in the development of college student personnel services, Williamson (1939) dealt with the full range of problems of personal living and other nonacademic problems that students bring to large universities. He developed a process of focused, goal-oriented counseling to help students adjust to their environment. In addition to writing (see *How to Counsel Students*), he served as mentor for several generations of counseling psychologists who further researched and developed his brief, active, focused counseling in the various university counseling centers established across the country after World War II to meet the educational, vocational, and personal counseling needs of the thousands of veterans then returning to college.

During the same period, mostly as a reaction against his psychodynamic training in child clinical psychology, Carl Rogers developed his phenomenological, client-centered approach to counseling. His now classic book on counseling and psychotherapy (Rogers, 1942) had a tremendous impact on shifting the focus of the then-emerging specialty of counseling psychology from assessment and diagnosis to counseling and psychotherapy. Evidence that such a shift had taken place was clearly manifested in the decade after Rogers's book was published: "The early 1950's saw the publication of ten books on counseling methods and only three had retained their exclusive diagnostic and assessment emphases" (Whiteley, 1984b, p. 5).

In more recent years, many social and economic factors have combined to create a climate in which short-term treatment is strongly favored and, in fact, is mandated by many managed-care companies. Although we do not see brief therapy as a panacea or indeed as always appropriate (see Seligman, 1995), it often is a highly effective format (Gelso, 1992; Steenbarger, 1992). Given their long-standing focus on relatively brief treatments, counseling psychologists are in a good position to work successfully within the current climate, while also working to change the climate toward one in which each client receives the most suitable treatment, be it short term or longer term. Such an emphasis on brief treatments has gone hand in hand with the previously discussed roles of counseling psychologists in educational–developmental work (such as applied work within college counseling centers) and prevention (Hage et al., 2007; Romano & Hage, 2000).

The Scientist–Practitioner Model

Although the other four central values remain stable and there is little disagreement within the field, the fifth central value of counseling psychology has remained somewhat contentious. Despite continued debate, counseling psychology has maintained and reaffirmed its dedication to the scientist–practitioner model over the last 60 years (Vespia & Sauer, 2006). As discussed more fully in Chapter 4 in this volume, counseling psychologists continue to learn in graduate school how to be both scientists and practitioners and how to integrate those perspectives in all of their professional roles.

The term *scientist–practitioner* was introduced in 1949 at the Boulder Conference on Graduate Education in Clinical Psychology (Raimy, 1950). The goal of the conference was to establish principles for doctoral education in clinical psychology. The conference may be best known for its endorsement of the importance of both science and practice, known today as the *Boulder model.* Counseling psychology, a newly established discipline in 1946, had its first major conference—the Northwestern Conference—soon after in 1951. The Division of Counseling and Guidance (now the Society of Counseling Psychology) convened the Northwestern Conference and endorsed the scientist–practitioner model as a primary tenet in the training of counseling psychologists (Blair, 2010). The model was again endorsed within counseling psychology's Model Training Program (Murdock, Alcorn, Heesacker, & Stoltenberg, 1998) nearly 50 years later. In the years and conferences between, the scientist–practitioner model continued to be endorsed.

Yet, the model is not without its critics (see the overview in Stoltenberg, Kashubeck-West, Biever, Patterson, & Welch, 2000). Again, external pressures raised the issue for continuous debate. By the 1970s, there were increased calls for psychologists to be seen as health care professionals (Heppner, Casas, Carter, & Stone, 2000). Schools of professional psychology began popping up, with even some traditional university settings embracing the Doctor of Psychology (PsyD) degree, which deemphasized research and put its primary emphasis on applied professional training. In addition, external pressures related to licensure and third-party insurance reimbursements as well as criteria for being eligible for inclusion in the National Register of Health Service Providers in Psychology pushed counseling psychologists to align even more strongly with the term *psychology* and its scientific basis (as opposed to its historical roots in counseling and guidance). At the same time, the broader profession of psychology was itself undergoing a massive split between science and practice. Some members of the APA split apart to become the American Psychological Society in 1988 (called the Association for Psychological Science since 2006). Again, counseling psychology, however, reaffirmed its commitment to both science and practice (i.e., the scientist–practitioner model) at its third national conference in 1987 in Atlanta, Georgia.

The friction between science and practice continues, with concerns over the definitions of "empirically validated techniques" (Task Force on the Promotion and Dissemination of Psychological Procedures, 1995) and counseling psychology's ambivalence regarding the medical model (Wampold, 2003) and what some view as its emphasis on logical positivism (Blair, 2010). There have been some notable attempts, however, at integration of science and practice, such as growing emphasis on practice research networks (see Castonguay et al., 2010; Locke et al., 2011). Despite some conflict inherent within the paradigms of science and practice, the scientist–practitioner model endures in counseling psychology, in part as an acknowledgment of the importance attributed to the synergy between science and practice and in part as an acknowledgment of our roots in both counseling and psychology. Although counseling psychologists do not usually experience a 50–50 split in their time devoted to science and practice (Gelso, 1979b; Neimeyer, Saferstein, & Rice, 2005; Watkins, Lopez, Campbell, & Himmell, 1986), they tend to blend the perspectives in all they do. For example, counseling psychologists conduct research on counseling and psychotherapy and apply research findings to their counseling work (Williams & Hill, 2001). As Naomi Meara noted in her Division 17 presidential address, "being a scientist–practitioner or a practitioner–scientist is less a matter of what we do and more a matter of how we think" (Meara, 1990, p. 161). In 1993, Gelso proposed his research training environment method for enhancing scientist–practitioner training, and in 1997 Stricker suggested that the scientist–practitioner model was experiencing a "resurgence" (p. 444). In 2000, Stoltenberg et al. reiterated that "the scientist–practitioner is 'core' to the identity of counseling psychology" (p. 629), compared with other models, such as the practitioner–scholar model.

Although some have expressed concern that the scientist–practitioner model does not clearly differentiate counseling psychology from clinical psychology, counseling psychology's emphasis on the model has remained a central aspect of the field's identity, particularly in resistance to a pull toward professionalization (Vespia & Sauer, 2006). It appears that Brown and Lent's (1984) specific definition of counseling psychology, as "an applied psychological discipline devoted to scientifically generating, applying, and disseminating knowledge on the remediation and prevention of vocational, educational, and personal adjustment difficulties" (p. ix), still stands and stands in support of the scientist–practitioner model.

A PERSPECTIVE ON DEFINITION AND IDENTITY

From what we have presented thus far, one can see that counseling psychology is that specialty within psychology that tends to focus on research, assessment, and interventions on and with clients who have relatively intact personalities (i.e., people who are not profoundly disturbed but instead are closer to the "normal range") rather than on typically treated clients, for example, by psychiatrists or clinical psychologists. Also, the specialty tends to pay close attention to the assets and psychological strengths of individuals, even when those persons are profoundly disturbed. The central interventions of the specialty tend to be brief and varied (e.g., counseling, therapy, guidance, training, consultation, outreach, teaching). Throughout the life of counseling psychology, particular attention has been paid to person–environment interactions, to multicultural contexts, and to educational and vocational development and environments.

It is important to stress that the roles and values discussed in the preceding sections represent central tendencies. In particular, although the central values help solidify counseling psychology's identity and clarify its distinctiveness in relation to other fields within and outside of psychology, one must understand that there is great variability around these central tendencies and that probably few, if any, individual counseling psychologists fit each theme perfectly in their career. In fact, individual practitioners vary greatly regarding the extent to which and the ways in which the themes fit their practice. One practitioner may, for example, do mostly long-term therapy with deeply troubled clients, but she may still consider herself a practicing counseling psychologist because she pays close attention to the healthy aspects of her clients' personalities, does a good deal of career counseling within the context of her psychotherapy, and is very attentive to the person–environment interactions in her clients' development. Another counseling psychologist may work largely with relatively healthy clients, conducting a variety of workshops and consulting with business organizations on, for example, how to improve the leadership sensitivity to worker concerns and find ways of reducing violence in the workplace. His work is largely within a preventive and developmental framework.

Given the above complexity, what determines whether one is a counseling psychologist and whether one is doing counseling psychology?

Just as in any field or profession, the answer to such questions must be complex. (We describe these issues more in Chapter 17 in this volume.) We offer that whether one is a counseling psychologist is determined by the interaction of the five central values in one's professional life. Given proper credentialing in the specialty, the practitioner may perform a wide range of activities and be legitimately considered a counseling psychologist doing the work of counseling psychology.

Counseling Psychology and Other Specialties and Fields

We discuss in the following the ways in which counseling psychology is similar to and different from other specialties within psychology (e.g., clinical psychology) and other professions outside of psychology (e.g., mental health counseling).

DISTINCTIVENESS AND OVERLAP WITHIN PSYCHOLOGY

In 1995, the APA established the Commission for the Recognition of Specialties and Proficiencies in Professional Psychology (CRSPPP). Counseling psychology was formally recognized as a unique specialty in 1999 by CRSPPP (Heppner et al., 2000). Of the applied specialties, some overlap considerably with each other and with counseling psychology. These specialties are referred to as "applied" because each seeks, in its own way, to apply principles of psychology to the solution of human problems. The lack of clear and concise boundaries among the specialties is inevitable because they rely essentially on the same training and education in fundamental areas of psychology. Further, they employ similar assessment and intervention procedures in their attempts to solve human problems. At the same time, each specialty has distinctive foci.

The specialty most often compared to counseling psychology is that of clinical psychology. The latter is the largest of the applied specialties in psychology. Despite much overlap in training, job activities, and job settings of counseling and clinical psychologists, there are notable differences. Historically as well as currently, clinical psychology has concerned itself with the study and treatment of abnormal or maladaptive behavior (Garfield, 1985). Although clinical psychologists do not ignore people's assets or strengths, relatively greater attention has typically been paid to underlying pathology than to health (Norcross, Sayette, Mayne, Karg, & Turkson, 1998). Perhaps as a consequence, clinical psychologists have tended to implement treatments of longer duration, more often called psychotherapy (of a longer term nature) than counseling. Attention to educational and vocational development and environments has not been a central part of the clinical psychologist's work. Because of the focus on psychopathology, clinical psychologists are much more likely than counseling psychologists to be found in work settings that focus on the severely disturbed (e.g., inpatient psychiatric settings and mental hospitals); they are much less likely to be found in educational settings (e.g., university counseling centers; Gaddy, Charlot-Swilley, Nelson, & Reich, 1995; Strauss, 1997).

Although significant differences remain between counseling and clinical psychology (Neimeyer, Taylor, Wear, & Buyukgoze-Kavas, 2011) and will likely continue to remain (Norcross et al., 1998), the two specialties have moved closer over the years. In the 1980s, for example, Garfield (1985) noted that clinical psychologists were more likely than in past years to work with the less disturbed and pay attention to assets. Likewise, as we noted previously, counseling psychologists increasingly conduct longer term psychotherapy.

Counseling psychology is also at times compared with industrial/ organizational (I/O) psychology. Siegel (1985) defined I/O psychology as "the science of behavior applied to persons in industrial and other organizations. Its objective is to enhance organizational effectiveness" (p. 207). Moreover, I/O psychologists, as Siegel noted, are centrally involved, in one way or another, in the assessment and enhancement of employee, supervisory, and managerial performance. As Tenopyr (1997) noted, the traditional core of activities of the industrial psychologist revolves around personnel selection; appraisal of employees' job performance; job analysis to determine what the job duties are and what employee knowledge, abilities, and skills are necessary to do each job; and the development of assessment centers, which are "collections of simulated work situations in which employees are observed to determine job abilities" (Tenopyr, 1997, p. 186). There are important differences between the traditional industrial and the organizational roles of the I/O psychologist. Tenopyr indicated that the industrial role emphasizes the assessment and improvement of individual behavior (e.g., work performance), whereas the organizational role focuses on whole organizations (e.g., a company's purchasing department). The organizational role may be subsumed under a newer subfield of I/O psychology called "organizational development" (Tenopyr, 1997). In comparisons of I/O and counseling psychology, a major area of overlap becomes evident: the concern with career and vocational development and environments. Counseling psychologists study career development in all settings and have sought to develop theories of what makes people gravitate toward certain fields, what interferes with their deciding on a suitable career path, and which treatments facilitate career development. I/O psychologists are more interested in the work and worker-performance aspect of career functioning. When working within business and industrial settings, the two types of psychologists perform similar functions. The differences are a matter of degree rather than kind. Overall, the counseling psychologist is more likely to work with individuals in a counseling context, whereas the I/O psychologist is more inclined to study and intervene at a broader organizational level. The counseling psychologist is probably more invested in overall individual emotional adjustment; the I/O psychologist is probably more invested in organizational as well as individual work performance and its impediments. Like the counseling psychologist, the I/O psychologist deals with relatively intact personalities and is concerned in a very basic way with person–environment interactions. Both specialties are involved in organizational consulting. The counseling psychologist, on the whole, however, is basically more involved in therapeutic interventions, again at the individual level.

Another specialty that overlaps with counseling psychology is *school psychology*. In 1985, Bennett established the definition of school psychology as "the application of knowledge and skills to the prevention or solution of problems children face in learning what society deems essential for success" (p. 129). Bennett went on to note the overlap between school psychology on the one hand and counseling, clinical, and industrial/organizational psychology on the other, but she stressed that their key difference lies in the concern of school psychologists for children, adolescents, and college students "in their world of work, the school setting." School psychologists do consultation, counseling, and assessment with students, parents, and teachers, with the aim of furthering the educational process: For example, they often help teachers identify ways to help children learn more effectively, and they work directly with children to help the children develop more effective skills for emotional regulation.

The overlap between counseling and school psychologists is especially great when counseling psychologists work in elementary and secondary schools (more typically the setting for the school psychologist) and when school psychologists work in higher education (more typically the setting for the counseling psychologist; Brabeck, Walsh, Kenny, & Comilang, 1997). Even in these settings, the school psychologist is more likely to be involved in educational and psychological assessment of students (e.g., to determine which factors are impeding effective learning), whereas the counseling psychologist is more often involved in counseling efforts with students and families and with developing prevention programs related to bullying, poverty, and retention (Espelage & Poteat, 2012b; Kenny & Walsh-Blair, 2012).

In attempting to define themselves and their specialty, counseling psychologists have most often focused on the similarities and differences between themselves and clinical, I/O, and school psychologists. Perhaps this is because of the overlap in the work of counseling/psychotherapy, career/work consultation, and education, activities that hold broad appeal to the various specialties (as well as to other fields). At the same time, each specialty differs from every other one in certain ways. To be sure, no specialty in applied psychology can lay exclusive claim to a given activity (e.g., counseling, consulting) or setting. Yet, each has its particular areas of emphasis, its particular foci, and settings in which it is more often found than are other specialties.

In comparing counseling psychology to other fields and specialties within and outside of psychology, one should keep in mind the central values of counseling psychology as discussed earlier: (a) an emphasis on a person's strengths and optimal functioning; (b) a focus on the whole person, with particular emphasis on life span development and vocational growth; (c) a commitment to advocacy and social justice, maintaining ongoing awareness of the importance of environmental context and culture; (d) a concentration on brief, educational, and preventive counseling interventions; and (e) a dedication to the scientist–practitioner model. The emphasis on these core values gives the specialty of counseling psychology its distinctiveness, although not in a simple, linear way. Counseling psychology's distinctiveness derives from its embodiment of all five of the central values. Although the specialties that we have summarized (and others; e.g., clinical neuropsychology, family psychology) overlap with counseling psychology on one or more of these themes, taken together, no other specialty reflects these themes to nearly the extent that counseling psychology does.

COUNSELING PSYCHOLOGY AND FIELDS OUTSIDE OF PSYCHOLOGY

A number of fields outside of psychology are involved in activities similar to those of counseling psychology, but a fundamental difference exists between these fields and counseling psychology. Counseling psychologists, from the beginnings of the specialty, have been psychologists first and "counselors" second. That is, professionals in this specialty are trained in basic areas of psychology and seek to apply theories and principles of psychology to their professional activities and interventions. The three fields outside of psychology proper that are most closely related to counseling psychology are psychiatric social work, psychiatry, and the general counseling profession (often referred to as counselor education or mental health counseling).

Psychiatric social workers generally complete a 2-year master's degree program, referred to as a master of social work (MSW) degree. Ordinarily, the 1st year of their program is academic, and the 2nd entails closely supervised work in an agency. Many psychiatric social workers, such as counseling psychologists and others, conduct counseling and psychotherapy and are often found in private practice settings. In hospital and clinic settings, psychiatric social workers work on health care teams. They may specialize in the intake process, consult with other agencies, do family counseling, and develop social histories on patients (Brammer et al., 1993). Professionals with MSWs rarely conduct research, do not perform psychological testing, and do little educational and vocational counseling.

Psychiatrists are physicians (medical doctors) who have gone on to specialize in psychiatry. This specialty is concerned with the diagnosis and treatment of severe emotional disorders and in this way is probably most closely related to clinical psychology among the applied psychology specialties. As medical doctors, psychiatrists are responsible for medical–psychological interventions, such as the prescription of drugs. They overlap with counseling psychologists and a number of other specialists in conducting counseling and psychotherapy. The brand of therapy they conduct is often the same as or similar to that conducted by counseling psychologists, although psychiatrists are more likely to take a psychodynamic and psychoanalytic perspective in their work than are counseling psychologists.

The final field we shall cover is perhaps the most similar of all to counseling psychology. The counseling profession (also termed counselor education or mental health counseling) probably adheres to many of the same central values as does counseling psychology. Counselors are found in a wide range of job settings and may function as school counselors, rehabilitation counselors, employment counselors, college counselors, or community counselors. Many counseling positions require a master's degree rather than a doctorate. Typically, master's-level training programs in counseling are accredited via the Council for Accreditation of Counseling and Related Educational Programs (CACREP). Although some common roots certainly exist with counseling and guidance, counseling psychology has an ambivalent relationship with master's-level training (see McPherson et al., 2000, for an overview).

In addition, counseling psychology, to a greater extent than the general counseling profession, subscribes to the scientist–practitioner model of training and practice. Because of this, the counseling psychologist receives more training in research and the scientific aspects of psychology.

Also, the counseling psychologist is extensively trained as a psychologist, with required graduate-level coursework in several core areas (e.g., assessment, biopsychology, learning) of the discipline of psychology. In contrast, although students who pursue degrees in counseling may take many psychology courses, expectations about which psychology courses they take, as well as how many, vary greatly between training programs. The combination of extensive study in the discipline of psychology with acquisition of the skills needed to be both a psychological practitioner and a scholarly investigator provides counseling psychologists with a broader array of competencies and career choices.

Summary

Counseling psychology, a specialty within the science and profession of psychology, has established itself firmly as a distinct profession that exhibits growth, strength, and vitality. Throughout the history of counseling psychology three roles have been most central: the remedial, the preventive, and the developmental. Carried out in various settings, the three roles are combined in most activities performed by counseling psychologists.

One can distinguish five central values in counseling psychology: (a) an emphasis on a person's strengths and optimal functioning; (b) a focus on the whole person, with particular emphasis on life span development and vocational growth; (c) a commitment to advocacy and social justice, maintaining ongoing awareness of the importance of environmental context and culture; (d) a concentration on brief, educational, and preventive counseling interventions; and (e) a dedication to the scientist–practitioner model. These values help bring together the diverse aspects of the specialty and clarify how counseling psychology is differentiated from other specialties within and outside of psychology. Despite their defining character, the five values represent no more than central tendencies. Counseling psychology practitioners differ considerably in the extent to which they subscribe to each particular theme.

Comparing and contrasting counseling psychology to other applied specialties within psychology, such as clinical psychology, industrial/organizational psychology, and school psychology, serves to delineate the unique characteristics of each. Likewise, common ground can be found between counseling psychology and fields outside of psychology, such as social work, psychiatry, and the general counseling profession, though substantial differences exist.

History of Counseling Psychology

2

A n interesting exercise for a beginning counseling psychologist is to trace the academic heritage of his or her instructor
or advisor. The specialty of counseling psychology is sufficiently young that it is usually possible to find out who one's
advisor's advisor was, his or her advisor, and so forth, back at
least to the formal beginnings of the specialty in the 1940s.
(In many cases, the lineage can be traced back to some of
the progenitors in the first half of the century and, in a few
cases, back even to the 19th century.) As Alex Haley (1976)
illustrated in his work on the roots of African Americans,
understanding heritage gives deeper and even new meaning to life in the present. To examine the roots of counseling
psychology, in this chapter we describe both its establishment as a profession in the 1940s and how the profession
has matured over time. Finally, we describe the continuities
and changes of recent years that have resulted in a vigorous
profession of counseling psychology for the 21st century and
beyond.

http://dx.doi.org/10.1037/14378-002
Counseling Psychology, Third Edition, by C. J. Gelso, E. N. Williams, and
B. R. Fretz

The History and Development of the Profession

In this section we shall see how and, most important from our perspective, why counseling psychology became an identifiable profession in the years immediately following World War II. Some of the factors leading to the creation of the profession during that time continue to contribute to its present vitality. (Note that, from this point forward, the terms *profession* and *specialty* are used interchangeably. The term *specialty* usually denotes a specific discipline within the profession of psychology. Yet, in most ways, the level of autonomy and organization of the various specialties allows them to be classified as professions.) Table 2.1 lists key events in the profession's history.

THE 1940s AND 1950s

Sociologists studying professions specify that, to constitute a profession, a group of workers must form governing organizations that establish educational and service standards and thereby create the conditions necessary for autonomous functioning. The beginning autonomous organizational steps for counseling psychology were set in motion during the 1940s, even though the official written record of many of these initial steps did not appear until the early 1950s.

The beginnings of organized counseling psychology can be found in the "psychological foxholes" (Scott, 1980) of World War II. During that time, almost every person with any training as a psychologist became involved in some way with assessment activities, either for selection and training of military personnel or for psychological diagnosis of military casualties. Thus, there were collections of psychologists in every major military installation throughout the country and sometimes even abroad. During the war years, an increasing number of psychologists who were involved in selection and training began to see the need for an organization that would respond to their specific interests, outside the realm of psychiatric hospitals.

In the rapidly expanding divisional structure of the American Psychological Association (APA) immediately following World War II, these interests became represented by a new division, Division 17 (Counseling and Guidance). Founded in 1946 by E. G. Williamson and John Darley, it joined the increasing number of applied divisions then being added to the APA; for example, those of clinical psychology, consulting psychology, industrial psychology, educational psychology, and school psychology. In 1951, Division 17 decided to change its name to the Division of Counseling Psychology, which was formally established

TABLE 2.1

Key Events in the History of Counseling Psychology

Year	Event
1946	Division 17: Division of Counseling and Guidance in the American Psychological Association (APA) established
1949	Boulder Conference: Scientist–practitioner model adopted by clinical psychology
1951	Division 17 changed its name to Division of Counseling Psychology
	First counseling psychology conference held: Northwestern University (Chicago), scientist–practitioner model endorsed
1954	*Journal of Counseling Psychology* founded
1964	*The Counseling Psychologist* established
	Second counseling psychology conference held: Greyston (at the Greyston Conference Center at Teachers College, Columbia University, in New York City)
1973	Vail Conference: General conference about training in psychology
1974	National Register of Health Service Providers formed
1975	Council of Counseling Psychology Training Programs founded
1987	Third counseling psychology conference held: Atlanta, Georgia
1988	American Psychological Society founded (Association for Psychological Science since 2006)
1999	Counseling psychology recognized as a specialty by APA's Commission for the Recognition of Specialties and Proficiencies in Professional Psychology
2001	Fourth counseling psychology conference: Houston, Texas
2003	Division 17 changed its name to the Society of Counseling Psychology
2008	Fifth counseling psychology conference: Chicago, Illinois (Creating the Future: Counseling Psychologists in a Changing World)

in 1952 (APA, 1952). Whiteley (1980) has provided extensive original source material and descriptions (Whiteley, 1984a, 1984b) of the details of these early organizational developments, including meeting places, agenda, persons involved, and so forth.

Let us raise a twofold question not often addressed in these historical descriptions: Why did persons interested in counseling choose to affiliate with psychology, and why did psychology choose to include counseling? Many prospective counselors still choose to practice outside the profession of psychology. Others have felt the need for a connection to the empirical and psychometric traditions of psychology. It is this grafting of counseling onto empirical roots that helps explain the greater commitment of counseling psychologists, as compared to counselors in general, to the scientist–practitioner model of training and functioning. Indeed, with the Boulder Conference in 1949, the scientist–practitioner model was adopted by clinical psychology. Counseling psychology formally endorsed the model in 1951 at the first national conference for counseling psychology (described in more detail subsequently).

On the other side of the coin, why did psychology include counseling as a division? As already noted, in the beginning, clinical psychologists concentrated on assessment and diagnosis primarily in psychiatric hospitals; the focus on counseling and therapy did not develop for *any* psychologists until the 1950s. Industrial psychology began as the study of what is known today as human factors and engineering psychology. (The emphasis on organizational behavior now seen in industrial/organizational [I/O] psychology was largely a development in the 1960s.) The emergence of counseling psychology filled a perceived vacuum within psychology between industrial psychology and clinical psychology: the study and treatment of normal personality functioning and development, which was not yet represented by any applied division.

Despite the overlaps and shared heritage with generic counseling on the one hand and other applied psychology fields on the other, counseling psychology has continued to be linked to both in the 70 years of its history. During that time, probably more than half of those who identified themselves as counseling psychologists have also maintained membership in either a major counseling organization (e.g., American Counseling Association, formerly known as the American Personnel and Guidance Association) or a more clinically oriented psychology division (e.g., APA Division 12, Clinical Psychology, or Division 29, Psychotherapy). Although these dual associations have sometimes caused tensions, the maintenance of breadth of perspectives is one of the sources of the profession's vitality. As suggested in Moore's (1970) sociological study of professions,

> The plight of the professional is that extreme specialization radically narrows those significant others with whom he can carry on job-centered social discourse. Here, once more, the importance of identification with a broader calling is apparent, even if common interests are in some measure nostalgic rather than strictly contemporary. (p. 83)

Another perspective on this post–World War II emergence of counseling psychology was provided by Schmidt (1977) in his examination of why the specialty developed and has remained strongest in the United States. Schmidt drew a parallel between our society's commitment to change—specifically, change wrought through scientific technology— and counseling psychology as a process of change that builds on the empirical findings of the science of psychology. Schmidt also noted the high degree of mobility in our culture coupled with the emphasis on achieving self-improvement. Counseling psychologists have provided both the social support needed for coping with changing environments and the technical assistance needed for launching personal careers. After World War II, millions of veterans, who had been dislocated for several years from their home communities, were expected to forge ahead in new careers for which they typically had little or no preparation. From this perspective, in 1945–1950, counseling psychology was a profession "waiting to happen."

In the 1950s, counseling psychology began to demonstrate its ability to stand and be recognized as an independent entity. The exciting times of "let's get organized" had to give way to a period of sustained development that would establish the foundation of systematic knowledge needed to maintain a profession. The first of these major steps was addressed in 1951 by the Northwestern Conference, the first major conference for the profession of counseling psychology. Key leaders of the Division of Counseling and Guidance met at Northwestern University on August 29–30, 1951; they prepared formal definitions of the roles and functions of counseling psychologists. They proposed standards for practicum training, research training, and the content of core psychology courses. Final versions of these statements were originally published in the *American Psychologist* (APA, 1952) and were reprinted in Whiteley's (1980) *The History of Counseling Psychology.*

Although subsequent conferences have addressed many of the same definitional and curriculum issues and innumerable position papers have been published about these topics, it is of interest to reread many of those original statements for their timelessness. Surveys of the actual training practices and employment locations of counseling psychologists have documented a number of changes over the years, but the applicability of many of the initial statements is truly remarkable. Consider the following definition of roles and functions:

> The professional goal of the counseling psychologist is to foster the psychological development of the individual. This includes all people on the adjustment continuum from those who function at tolerable levels of adequacy to those suffering from more severe psychological disturbances. (APA, 1952, p. 175)

The impetus for setting training standards at the very beginning of the specialty derived mostly from the interests of the Veterans Administration (VA) in employing counseling psychologists. The VA had created the job title of counseling psychologist to function in the Division of Medicine and Neurology, outside of the psychiatric division where clinical psychologists normally practiced, in order to provide counseling services for the full range of general medical and surgical patients. The standards of training and practice established at the Northwestern Conference were used to set VA employment standards. The VA has remained, throughout the history of counseling psychology, a major employer of counseling psychologists. The same training standards also served as the foundation for the creation of a diplomate in counseling psychology from the then newly created American Board of Examiners in Professional Psychology and in the establishment of program accreditation procedures by the APA Doctoral Education Committee.

Hammering out these position statements led the pioneers of counseling psychology to realize their increasing connections to the discipline of psychology; as previously noted, in 1951 the decision to change the discipline's title from "counseling and guidance" to "counseling psychology" was formalized (APA, 1952).

Through the wisdom and initiative (though some colleagues of the time probably thought foolhardiness) of four young counseling psychologists—Milton E. Hahn, Harold G. Seashore, Donald E. Super, and C. Gilbert Wrenn—in 1954 the *Journal of Counseling Psychology*, a major new empirical journal, was launched to address publication needs in the same areas that the division of counseling and guidance had been established to fill. The idea of putting a journal into practice, of course, required considerable funds. Wrenn described the journal's economic origins as follows:

> We established a list of probable stockholders who would represent various dimensions in counseling, each to be asked to buy a limited number of shares at $50 a share. None was to have over ten shares even if he was foolish enough to want to risk that much money . . . for it was clearly stated that this was a risk investment. . . . The response was remarkable. I found an early list of 28 prospects . . . there were 19 of the 28 who had become stockholders—and I am not even sure that we invited all on this particular list! (Wrenn, 1966, p. 486)

The first volume of the *Journal of Counseling Psychology* was published in 1954; it has since become the most important empirical journal in counseling psychology. Because of the excellence it achieved over its first decade of publication, it was actively sought by the APA for inclusion in its set of journals and has been published by the APA since 1967. The journal is today one of the most selective of the APA publications and is the third most subscribed to APA journal after *Health Psychology* and *Professional Psychology: Research and Practice* (http://www.apa.org/pubs/journals/features/2012-statistics.pdf). A fascinating perspective on the journal's first 25 years, including its antecedent social and political conditions (1946–1956) as well as its subsequent impact on the profession of counseling psychology, was prepared by Pepinsky, Hill-Frederick, and Epperson (1978). Other outstanding achievements of the *Journal of Counseling Psychology* can be found in four articles commissioned by the journal in recognition of the centennial of the APA in 1992. The purpose of these articles was to provide

> critical examination of how knowledge in certain core areas of psychology has been used by counseling psychologists, how counseling psychologists have transformed and modified that knowledge for their purposes, and what has been the impact, if any, of counseling psychologists' knowledge base on these core areas of scientific psychology. (Richardson & Patton, 1992, p. 3)

A survey of articles in the *Journal of Counseling Psychology* (1999–2011) shows the profession's enduring interests in counseling (18% of articles) and in vocational issues (13%), as well as growing interest in cultural diversity (39% of articles). The growth in time represented in the *Journal of Counseling Psychology* highlights the growth of the profession, started in the 1940s and 1950s and continuing today.

THE 1960s AND 1970s

Barely before the ink was dry on some of the documents of the 1950s that created counseling psychology as an organized and autonomous profession, some writers were raising questions about the identity of the specialty. The 1960s and early 1970s were a time of significant self-doubt among the leadership in the profession. Growth leveled off both in membership of the division and in number of accredited programs.

Whiteley (1980) brought to light previously unpublished papers that had been written in the early 1960s regarding the "decline" of counseling psychology (Berg, Pepinsky, & Shoben, 1980) and another concluding that counseling psychology "presently has only a weak potential for growth" (Tiedeman, 1980, p. 126). Other articles during this period cited low-level prestige of counseling psychologists compared with clinical psychologists. The strains were not just around declining growth but also about future directions. Because the 1950s had seen an increase in the counseling and psychotherapy activities of both counseling and clinical psychologists, some counseling psychologists were proposing that it was time for a merger of these specialties. Others, vehemently opposed to the remedial therapeutic emphasis in clinical psychology, identified more with the emergence of community psychology and its emphasis on prevention and developmental activities. For almost every paper that criticized the profession, members of the profession arose to prepare counterarguments (e.g., Tyler, Tiedeman, & Wrenn, 1980).

The division responded by organizing a second conference to reexamine its self-definition and the standards it had originally set at the Northwestern Conference in 1951. In the Greyston Conference of 1964 (held at the Greyston Conference Center at Teachers College, Columbia University, in New York City), many concerns were aired extensively. The majority of participants endorsed the Northwestern statements. Recognizing changing times and contexts, the conference included the following statement in the introduction to its specific recommendations:

> The conferees further recognize that counseling psychologists have significant overlapping interests with the related specialties of clinical, educational, industrial or personnel, and school psychology. The great majority, but not all, subscribe to the statement that counseling psychology has a special substance and

emphases requiring preparation in a number of didactic as well as practicum courses that are not necessarily included in the preparation of other psychologists. This special substance consists of the educational and vocational and, less distinctively, the familial and community environments of the individual, of the psychology of normal development, and of the psychology of the physically, emotionally, and mentally handicapped; the special emphases are on the appraisal and use of assets for furthering individual development in the existing or changing environment. (Thompson & Super, 1964, pp. 3–4)

Perhaps these publicly manifested aspects of self-doubt and confusion were hiding, or at least overshadowing, the ongoing accomplishments of counseling psychologists that were building upon the foundations established in previous decades. Both theoretical and empirical developments in the area of career psychology were expanding and growing with considerable practical impact (for example, new assessment instruments and new types of interventions). Research on how to train counselors to provide the necessary and sufficient conditions in psychotherapy was building so rapidly that, by the end of the 1960s, counseling psychology researchers were among those who were most often identified (Bergin & Garfield, 1971) for research on training.

Continuing the linkage with mainstream psychology, developments in experimental analysis of behavior were being translated into counseling theory and practice, most notably by Krumboltz and Thoresen (1969). Perhaps the clearest manifestation of the continued growth of the conceptual as well as empirical expertise of the profession was the establishment in 1969 of *The Counseling Psychologist*, a journal dedicated to stimulating professional dialogue about important theoretical and conceptual issues of the day. John Whiteley, founder and first editor (1969–1984), developed the format of having each issue dedicated to one or sometimes several major conceptual articles on a single topic, followed by a set of reactions from other counseling psychologists and professionals. The topics of the journal serve as a quick survey of the major topical interests of each decade, from early issues on client-centered, behavioral, and vocational counseling to more recent issues on wellness, multicultural counseling, qualitative research, and social-cognitive models of training. Heppner (1999) listed the journal's articles from 1969 to 1999, highlighting the historic focus in counseling psychology on counseling and vocational issues. Flores, Rooney, Heppner, Browne, and Wei (1999) also noted the evolving interests in counseling psychology to include cultural diversity. Indeed, a survey of articles from 2000 and 2011 shows most articles from *The Counseling Psychologist* (35%) have been focused on multicultural issues, including issues of race, gender, sexual orientation, and international themes. In contrast, fewer than 10% of articles from 2000 to 2011 focused on vocational issues, again highlighting the shifts and changes in the profession.

By the 1970s, although the identity problem of counseling psychology was still not fully resolved (are any of us absolutely sure of who we are?), the character of the identity issue shifted from pessimism about whether the field should exist to how it should be defined in relation to others. The task of the 1970s seems to have been to find out how counseling psychology would relate to all of those other professions with which it shares so many aspects.

In terms of the number of APA-approved training programs, the beginning of the 1970s saw the nadir of the profession. However, in the last few decades of the 20th century, the growth in number of accredited programs was phenomenal by any standard. Significant developments in the setting of standards for credentials in professional psychology were a major factor in this growth. With an increasing number of states developing procedures for the licensing of psychologists in the 1960s, plus the more widespread inclusion of mental health benefits in health insurance policies, a series of questions was raised for all of psychology about which kinds of training qualified persons for licensure as psychologists as well as for providing health care service. The Vail Conference was held in 1973 on training in psychology, and other conferences, such as those sponsored by the National Register of Health Services Providers in Psychology and the APA, resulted in greater specifications regarding the curriculum and the identity of the programs. In 1975, the Council of Counseling Psychology Training Programs (CCPTP) was founded.

Most important for counseling psychology, the developing standards recognized that psychological training might take place in a variety of settings other than psychology departments; for example, colleges of education, colleges of business and management, colleges of medicine, or freestanding schools of psychology. The formal recognition that psychology programs could exist in colleges of education (long the home of many programs in counseling and guidance), coupled with the new requirement for identification of the programs as *psychology* programs (if the graduates were to be eligible for licensing as psychologists), had an immediate impact on many programs that were formerly identified as "counseling and guidance" but that had for years graduated persons who considered themselves trained as counseling psychologists.

Many programs moved as expeditiously as possible to make whatever changes were necessary to their curriculum, faculty, and resources to receive accreditation by the APA. This rapid growth brought new political strength. At the end of the 1970s, counseling psychology was regaining, within the APA, some of the representation and leadership roles that it had had in the 1950s but that had waned over the

1960s and early 1970s. The leadership of the Division of Counseling Psychology and the CCPTP directors found themselves, for the first time in the profession's history, in continual dialogue with the leaders of clinical, school, and I/O psychology as well as professional leaders in the American Personnel and Guidance Association, for the purpose of developing an understanding of both overlapping and distinctive roles. Heppner, Casas, Carter, and Stone (2000) interviewed, in the late 1990s, many of the persons involved in the leadership of these various organizations; they provided not only historical facts but also intriguing perspectives on the pertinent political developments in professional psychology during the 1970s and 1980s.

THE 1980s AND 1990s

The 1980s began with the publication of two collections of papers, one set looking to the year 2000 (Whiteley & Fretz, 1980), the other to "The Coming Decade" (Whiteley, Kagan, Harmon, Fretz, & Tanney, 1984). Both sets of papers addressed how the profession would develop for coming generations of counseling psychologists.

The most tangible indicators of the emerging maturity of counseling psychology were the publication of the profession's first comprehensive handbooks, *Handbook of Counseling Psychology* (Brown & Lent, 1984) and *Handbook of Vocational Psychology* (Walsh & Osipow, 1983), and the beginning of two book series, *Advances in Vocational Psychology*, edited by Walsh and Osipow, and the Brooks/Cole series in *Counseling Psychology*, edited by Whiteley and Resnikoff.

Also during this decade, three reviews of counseling psychology published in the *Annual Review of Psychology* (Borgen, 1984; Gelso & Fassinger, 1990; Osipow, 1987) covered a broad array of topics, indicating the growing diversity of the field. Borgen (1984) noted that "the discipline teems with vitality and resolve" (p. 597). Osipow (1987) examined its strengths, especially in the areas of career counseling and vocational developments. Gelso and Fassinger (1990) applauded the accomplishments of the 1980s, observing that many of the methodological and conceptual recommendations of earlier reviewers and critics had been incorporated by researchers.

Two firsts, again reflecting the confidence that comes with maturity, enabled the profession to look at some nontraditional research methodologies. For the first time ever, the *Journal of Counseling Psychology* published a special issue dedicated entirely to the topic of research design (October 1987). *The Counseling Psychologist* also published (in January 1989) a special issue on alternative research paradigms, with special attention to the teaching of them. Another first occurred at the beginning of the 1990s: The first textbook solely dedicated to the field of counseling psychology (of which you are now reading the third edition) was published in 1992 by Gelso and Fretz. Not only was it the first text in the field, it remains the only one dedicated entirely to counseling psychology as a whole.

The emerging maturity of the profession was also indicated in the recognition accorded counseling psychology by other specialties and organizations. At some time during the 1980s, almost every major board and committee in the APA was chaired by a counseling psychologist, as were the boards of related credentialing organizations; for example, the National Register of Health Service Providers in Psychology, the American Board of Professional Psychology, and the American Association of State Psychology Boards. During the early years of counseling psychology, only a few counseling psychologists had been involved in leadership roles of the APA; they served in key positions such as executive officer (John Darley) or as president of the APA (Leona Tyler). By the late 1970s a number of critical issues had emerged regarding licensing, specialty definitions, and other such topics. It then became vital for the voice of counseling psychologists to be more fully heard within the profession of psychology as well as in health care and educational institutions. By 1998, seven of the 14 members of the APA Board of Directors had received their doctoral training in counseling psychology programs (Heppner et al., 2000). By 1999, an unprecedented number of counseling psychologists was serving in the APA Council of Representatives, the APA's primary legislative body. These counseling psychologists had been elected by a broad range of colleagues outside of counseling psychology, in a wide range of divisions and state associations. More and more counseling psychologists began serving in the highest levels of organizations and government outside of psychology. For example, the first psychologist elected to the U.S. Congress (Ted Strickland, who became governor of Ohio in 2007) is a counseling psychologist. Counseling psychologists in such leadership roles can bring to these major social agencies the understandings of the profession regarding individual differences in strengths and assets, person–environment interactions, and ways to encompass cultural diversity.

With such enthusiasm and leadership among counseling psychologists, the field responded to long-standing calls for a third national conference on counseling psychology. The Georgia Conference was held in April 1987. Although it had less government and foundation support than either of the prior conferences, this working conference was attended by over 180 psychologists. They formed five task groups to prepare recommendations in the areas of training and accreditation; research; organizational and political structures; public image; and professional practice in various settings. Each group's recommendations for the development of the profession may be found in the July 1988 issue of *The Counseling Psychologist*.

Rude, Weissberg, and Gazda (1988) summarized the common themes of the conference discussions as follows:

> First, we are scientist–practitioners. . . . Discussion[s] of identity . . . include counseling psychology's emphasis on "positive mental health . . . adaptive strategies . . . empowerment of individuals." . . . Also mentioned was what might be termed the counseling psychologist's *scope of vision*, the attention to promotion of mental health at the level of groups and systems as well as individuals, to development across the entire life span, to adjustment and satisfaction in vocational as well as personal spheres, and to prevention and enhancement as well as remediation. (pp. 425–426)

Rude et al.'s (1988) closing observation was the reaffirmation, seen in all the task groups, of the importance of viewing people and behavior in the context of cultural variables such as ethnicity, gender, age, and sexual orientation. The conference participants promoted a diversity of roles but remained passionately committed to the viability of the core themes of counseling psychology.

By the end of the 1980s, a sense of meaningfulness in what had been accomplished permitted greater receptivity to diversification within the profession in terms of work setting, theoretical orientation, gender, race, lifestyle, and so forth. Rather than fighting the problems of diversity and feeling compelled to choose to go one way or the other (e.g., remedial/therapeutic vs. developmental/educational), counseling psychologists were embracing diversity and finding strength in it. Naomi Meara, president of the Division of Counseling Psychology for 1989, chose the theme "unified diversity" for the annual convention (Meara, 1990). Even though counseling psychologists engage in many different roles in many different settings, they share a unity of perspective and ideology. What had emerged was an even more vigorous and rigorous "clearly identified psychological specialty whose scientist–practitioners engage in a wide variety of activities including research, education and training; and a full range of psychological services in the areas of assessment, treatment, and evaluation" (Meara & Myers, 1998).

Moving beyond an identity-development, inward-searching perspective, the end of the 1980s and beginning of the 1990s also brought on greater perspective for the ways counseling psychology fit in with the broader profession of psychology. Significant political changes were occurring at the national level with regard to psychology. For example, several members of the APA, unhappy with the association's growing focus on applied and clinical issues, split off to form the American Psychological Society in 1988 (known since 2006 as the Association for Psychological Science). In part as a response to counseling psychology's growth and relationship to the broader APA organization, the Division of Counseling Psychology underwent a reorganization in 1992 under

President Bruce Fretz in which the current vice presidential structure was created (Delgado-Romero, Lau, & Shullman, 2012; Heppner et al., 2000). In addition to a presidential trio (president, president-elect, and past president), five vice presidents oversaw specific areas: Diversity and Public Interest, Education and Training, Professional Practice, Scientific Affairs, and Communication (added in 2006). The vice presidencies were created to facilitate more proactive leadership of the division within the APA as well as to support professional development for Division 17 members. The new structure also provided for sections, special interest groups, and special task groups. Sections were to be reserved for those interest groups that could enroll and sustain a significant number of members and provide their own programs and conferences. The new structure has been successful beyond anyone's expectation. Within 5 years of the establishment of this new structure, six interest groups had met the stringent criteria for becoming a section: Counseling Health Psychology; Ethnic and Racial Diversity; Independent Practice of Counseling Psychology; Lesbian, Gay, and Bisexual Awareness (now Lesbian, Gay, Bisexual and Transgender Issues); Society for Vocational Psychology; and Section on Women (now the Section for the Advancement of Women). As of this writing, there are a total of 13 sections with an additional nine special interest groups ranging from Adoption to Religious and Spiritual Issues to Military Issues in Counseling Psychology. Although "it is doubtful that the early leaders of the division could have foreseen the multifaceted, complex, efficient, and well-managed organization that has resulted from their initiatives" (Meara & Myers, 1998, p. 19), we are indebted to them for their foresight, vision, and clarity about the purpose of counseling psychology.

Also significant for the profession in the 1990s was the recognition of counseling psychology as a specialty by the APA's Commission for the Recognition of Specialties and Proficiencies in Professional Psychology (CRSPPP) in 1999. In 1986, the APA Council endorsed a resolution to expand the scope of accreditation of professional education and training programs in psychology beyond those areas that had historically been considered specialties (e.g., clinical, counseling and school psychology). The result of the ensuing Task Force on the Scope and Criteria for Accreditation was the establishment of CRSPPP in 1995 (Heppner et al., 2000). CRSPPP required that existing specialties apply for redesignation as a specialty, engaging in a process in which the specialty verified its distinctiveness in scope and focus. During this time, confusion arose over the differences between clinical and counseling psychology and the use of the term *clinical* to apply broadly and in more generic ways. In 1997 APA President Norm Abeles appointed a task force to examine this issue. A new term (*health service psychologist*) emerged from the process and was inclusive of a number of specialties (e.g., clinical, counseling, and school psychology). In 1998, the APA Council accepted the archival definitions created by these specialties, which firmly established "their historical place as specialties in the field" (Heppner et al., 2000, p. 17). (See APA, 1999, published in *The Counseling Psychologist*, for the archival description of counseling psychology.)

COUNSELING PSYCHOLOGY IN THE 21ST CENTURY

The new century brought on many changes for counseling psychology as well as a reaffirmation of the field's central values. Of significance near the turn of the century, the Division of Counseling Psychology changed its name in 2003 to the Society of Counseling Psychology (SCP). We focus here on three particular areas of impact on counseling psychology in the last dozen years: leadership within Division 17 and the APA; the development of practice guidelines; and the impact of conferences where counseling psychologists have gathered to move forward an agenda of inclusiveness and strength-based vision.

SCP Leadership

In 2000, Division 17 President Jean Carter became the first full-time practitioner to be president of the division, making clear the profession's commitment to practice issues. Her theme was "New Traditions for a New Millennium," and she established the Council of the Specialty of Counseling Psychology to protect and promote counseling psychology within the APA and external organizations. Her plan succeeded well, as there are currently numerous counseling psychologists at every level of committee service in the APA. Several other presidential themes since the turn of the century have both addressed the profession's foundational central values and looked ahead to the future of counseling psychology. Most notably, there has been a continuing focus on multiculturalism, with a strong emphasis on diversity and social justice (e.g., Tania Israel's focus on "Exploring Privilege" in 2010–2011). There has also been a growing focus on globalization, with inclusion of counseling psychologists outside of the United States (see below for a description of the 2008 International Counseling Psychology Conference) and a refocus on issues of prevention (e.g., Andy Horne's 2012–2013 theme, "Addressing Tomorrow's Needs Today: Promotion, Prevention, and Beyond in Counseling Psychology").

Finally, concerns have again been raised about the future of counseling psychology and a desire to ensure support for future leaders. As an example, a new Leadership Academy was established for early career professionals as part of Barry Chung's "Future of Counseling Psychology Campaign" (2011–2012). The most recent three presidential themes as of the writing of this text are listed here as examples. All of the presidential themes can be reviewed in the SCP *Newsletter*, accessible on the SCP website (see http://www.div17.org).

In recent years, counseling psychologists have moved into greater positions of leadership within the APA. It is quite telling, for example, that two of the three most recent APA presidents at the time of writing this revision have been counseling psychologists: Carol Goodheart, 2010, and Melba Vasquez, 2011. With such strong leadership, along with a name change in 2003 to the Society of Counseling Psychology, the profession has matured from attempting to define itself to focusing on promoting the core values of counseling psychology at the national and international levels. We will be excited to see what is in store for counseling psychology in the decades ahead.

Practice Guidelines

The SCP and APA presidents clearly have provided leadership and vision for counseling psychology and psychology more broadly, but the membership also has exhibited a great deal of visionary leadership. One way their energy and advocacy have been evidenced is with the participation of Division 17 members in the creation of practice guidelines with the APA. A number of practice guidelines have been passed by the APA Council since the turn of the century. The practice guidelines are designed as a practical tool to help practitioners develop and maintain their competencies and as an educational tool to help practitioners develop new competencies.

In 2000 (APA, 2000), the *Guidelines for Psychological Practice With Lesbian, Gay, and Bisexual Clients* was adopted by the APA (with an update adopted in 2011; see APA, 2012b). Although the project was primarily conducted by Division 44, Division 17 members were involved at every level of the process. In 2002, Divisions 17 and 45 led the process for the adoption of the *Guidelines for Multicultural Education, Training, Practice, and Organizational Change for Psychologists* (see APA, 2003a). In 2004, Division 17 members participated in the *Guidelines for Psychological Practice With Older Adults* (see APA, 2004a). In 2007, the APA Council adopted the *Guidelines for Psychological Practice With Girls and Women*, led by an interdivisional task force between Division 17 and 35 (see APA, 2007b). Most recently, as of this writing, *Guidelines for Assessment of and Intervention With Persons With Disabilities* passed the APA Council in 2011 (see APA, 2012a), also with the participation of Division 17 members. Very clearly, the advocacy efforts of Division 17 members have had a tremendous impact on the field and on the guidance given to practitioners on a diverse set of competencies.

Conferences

Counseling psychology has continued to evolve in focus, as evidenced by its most recent conferences. The National Multicultural Conference and Summit (NMCS) was established at a meeting in Newport Beach, California, in 1999 and has occurred as a biennial conference since that time. The conference is cosponsored by four divisions of the APA: 17 (Society of Counseling Psychology), 35 (Society for the Psychology of Women), 44 (the Society for the Psychological Study of Lesbian, Gay, Bisexual, and Transgender Issues), and 45 (Society for the Psychological Study of Ethnic Minority Issues).

In 2001, the fourth national conference was held in Houston, Texas (see Fouad et al., 2004, for an overview of the conference), in collaboration with the CCPTP. The theme of the conference was "Counseling Psychologists: Making a Difference." The conference was designed to help create a proactive agenda for the profession and to push forward work being done on competencies for effective practice (Fouad et al., 2004). Norine Johnson, APA president in 2001, opened the conference with a talk entitled "Building a Healthy World: A Vision for Counseling Psychology." There were keynotes, symposia, poster sessions, and a town hall meeting. The primary focus of the conference was the creation of several social action groups, on topics ranging from community violence to homelessness to racism to the moral challenge of managed care. Each group developed specific recommendations and led the profession in a greater commitment to social justice and social change.

In 2006, the Society of Counseling Psychology cosponsored the APA Expert Summit on Immigration in San Antonio, Texas (entitled Global Realities: Intersections and Transitions). And in 2008, counseling psychology held its fifth conference (and first international conference) in Chicago, entitled Creating the Future: Counseling Psychologists in a Changing World. The conference, like its predecessors, included keynote addresses, symposia, and roundtable discussions but focused on enhancing collaboration among different counseling psychologists (e.g., practitioners, academics, early career professionals, midcareer professionals, and students) from all over the world. Twenty-one working groups provided a small, interactive group experience for participants. The outcome was very successful, with over 1,400 counseling psychologists representing 40 countries drawn to attend (Forrest, 2008). The fifth conference positioned the profession well to move beyond a self-focus, beyond an American focus, and into full collaboration with counseling psychologists all over the world.

Summary

Although the formal, written history of counseling psychology is now just entering the 21st century, the roots of the profession lie in sociocultural and disciplinary developments of the late 19th and early 20th centuries. Counseling psychology was formally founded in 1946 by E. G. Williamson and John Darley as the Division of Counseling and Guidance (Division 17) of the American Psychological Association (APA). The name of Division 17 was officially changed to the Division of Counseling Psychology in 1952, and the *Journal of Counseling Psychology* was established in 1954. Counseling psychology spent its early years in self-definition, wrestling to combine its dual affiliations to the field of counseling and the field of psychology. It also established its emphasis on the scientist–practitioner model at the Boulder Conference in 1949, later reiterated at counseling psychology's first national conference (the Northwestern Conference, 1951).

In 1964, the Division 17 journal, *The Counseling Psychologist*, was established and the profession held its second national conference (the Greyston Conference), which firmly established counseling psychology as a grounded and vibrant profession. In the 1970s, that sense of identity grew as the CCPTP was founded in 1975. In the 1980s, counseling psychology held its third national conference (the Georgia Conference, 1987) and began producing handbooks (e.g., Brown & Lent, 1984; Walsh & Osipow, 1983), establishing the growing maturity of the field. By 1999, counseling psychology was recognized as a specialty by the CRSPPP.

At the start of the 21st century, the leadership of Division 17, renamed the Society of Counseling Psychology (SCP) in 2003, evidenced a strong focus on multiculturalism, globalization, and attention to the future of the field. Counseling psychologists were active in shaping the broader field of practicing psychology through development of practice guidelines (for girls and women; lesbian, gay, and bisexual clients; multicultural education, training, research, practice, and organizational change; older adults; and persons with disabilities). And counseling psychology held its fourth (Houston, 2001) and fifth (Chicago, 2008) conferences. The Chicago Conference in 2008 was also the division's first international conference. The continuity of counseling psychology, which relies on its five central values (strength and optimal functioning; focus on development and vocational growth; commitment to social justice and multiculturalism; concentration on brief, educational, and preventive interventions; and adherence to the scientist–practitioner model), has provided a strong base from which the field has grown. Now nearly 70 years old, the field of counseling psychology is more energized, more committed to advancing the needs of all people, and more dedicated to leading psychology into the next decades of research, practice, and service.

Ethical Values of Counseling Psychologists

3

W hat does it require to be an ethical psychologist? We deliberately examine ethical issues, principles, and standards before presenting the fundamentals of counseling and research in later chapters. Fully attending to the well-being of clients is more than a matter of using good counseling techniques. What are psychologists' professional obligations beyond using good techniques? Are there rules governing what psychologists can and cannot do? Should and should not do? This chapter is designed not only to acquaint readers with current ethical standards that are to be observed by all psychologists but also to give readers an appreciation of the limits of such codes in resolving all ethical situations and in ensuring that all professionals act in ways that are beneficial to clients, colleagues, and society.

Why are ethical standards needed? On what basis have the current standards been chosen? Are these standards sufficient for adequate protection of the public and the promotion of human welfare? The major issues underlying these questions

http://dx.doi.org/10.1037/14378-003
Counseling Psychology, Third Edition, by C. J. Gelso, E. N. Williams, and B. R. Fretz

are identified in the first section of this chapter. The chapter's second section provides an overview of the 2002 *Ethical Principles of Psychologists and Code of Conduct* of the American Psychological Association (APA), highlighting ways in which the code has changed over time.

In the third section, we provide examples and commentary on behaviors that represent possible violations of the APA Ethics Code. Our examples are drawn from among the least sensational violations of ethics; they have been chosen to increase sensitivity beyond the media-emphasized ones, such as sexual exploitation and clear breaches of confidentiality. The fourth section explores the concept of ethical dilemmas compared to specific behaviors that can be identified as "ethical" or "unethical." These situations present difficult challenges to psychologists, because there can be no simple right or wrong action to take in such situations. They include two of the more controversial ethical issues to have arisen for psychologists in the last decade. Some of the problems and difficulties that have been discovered regarding psychologists' implementation of ethical standards and codes of conduct are examined in the chapter's final section.

It is our hope that integration of the theoretical, applied, and empirical contexts of these sections will enable readers to achieve the aspirations of Meara, Schmidt, and Day (1996) in their treatise on virtue ethics:

> Reflections upon and increased understanding of the moral domain (its theories, principles, virtues, and other constructs) in the context of professional codes, changing mores, multicultural communities, and intellectual and technological advances provide ways to improve one's ethical decisions, policies, and character. (p. 70)

Evolving Discourse on Ethics

Most of the major service professions in society have developed codes of ethics that mandate some behaviors and forbid others. Because a profession is by definition a group that has "expertise and competence not readily available to the general public" (Biggs & Blocher, 1987, p. 3), the public usually is not very knowledgeable about what constitutes competent professional behavior. The concept of being professional thus includes a trust that members will monitor their own and other members' professional behavior so that competent services are provided to the public. Notice both elements: Professionals are to be competent in their services, and it is their responsibility to see that fellow professionals provide competent services. When persons contact a physician, attorney, or psychologist, they typically do not know what is best for them (other than that they need help); otherwise, they would not be contacting a professional. It can be argued that the marketplace principle *caveat emptor* (let the buyer beware) does not apply to human services as it does to products like clothes or refrigerators. Counseling psychologists, like all mental health professionals, have supreme responsibility to the public trust. Persons seeking help from them are troubled and vulnerable and, consequently, are especially subject to exploitation and manipulation. Client trust is one of the most valuable commodities of the profession, but too often ethics are considered only after a problem arises.

The need for some set of standards for professional ethics has been widely recognized by most professionals; however, the development of such codes has proved to be quite controversial. (For reviews of the history of the developments of the APA's ethical standards, see Joyce & Rankin, 2010; Knapp & VandeCreek, 2003; Pope & Vetter, 1992.) Since the publication of the APA's first ethics code in 1953, there have been 10 revisions (1959; 1963; 1968; 1977; 1979; 1981; 1990; 1992; 2002; Barnett & Lorenc, 2003), including the most recent update to Standards 1.02 and 1.03 (discussed subsequently) in the 2010 revision. Despite the existence of the Ethics Code, plus an APA committee to monitor ethical compliance since 1938, there was an increase in cases brought before the APA Ethics Committee until the number peaked in 1995. Since 1995, possibly due in part to the fact that ethics training had become a common part of doctoral education (Welfel, 1992), there has been a steady decline in active ethics cases before the APA Ethics Committee (APA, 2003b, 2007c, 2012c). Although a decrease in cases brought before the Ethics Committee is likely good news, it remains critical for psychologists not only to understand the Ethics Code but to be able to apply it across diverse and complex professional situations. Otherwise, they risk possible harm to those they serve as well as erosion of the public trust (Meara et al., 1996).

> Effective self-regulation entails more than clearly written, widely disseminated, frequently taught and strictly enforced ethical codes. What appears to be necessary is a membership capable of making sophisticated judgments about which course of action may be ethical in situations in which no one behavior seems entirely ethical or unethical. (Welfel & Lipsitz, 1984, p. 31)

Thus, what more is necessary beyond a code of ethics? Beginning in the 1980s, an ever increasing number of psychologists began attending to both the conceptual and the implementation issues for developing a profession that could gain and maintain the full trust of the public (Kitchener, 2000; Meara et al., 1996; Urofsky, Engels, & Engebretson, 2009). Many of the conceptual controversies that arose can be tied to basic philosophical issues about the nature of humans. Attempts to increase understanding of what is needed for the profession to be more ethical by counseling psychologists such as Biggs and Blocher (1987), Jordan and Meara (1990), and Meara et al. (1996) have called upon both classic philosophers (e.g., Aristotle and Kant) and more contemporary writers on moral development (e.g., Kohlberg and Gilligan). Contrasts of philosophical dialectics, such as deontological and teleological principles, absolutism, and relativism, underlie many of the contemporary controversies.

> Psychologists have certainly become more daring in questioning the value base of their work, but their commitment to articulating moral visions remains tenuous at best. Psychologists find themselves in the paradoxical position of talking more about values and knowing less about what to do. (Prilleltensky, 1997, p. 517)

At the most fundamental level, an ethical psychologist understands what it means to be a moral person. Yet, when current APA ethical standards are presented later in this chapter, it will be evident that the standards address quite specific behaviors, often listing behaviors in which psychologists should not engage. For example, "psychologists do not engage in sexual harassment" (APA, 2002, p. 1064) and "psychologists do not engage in sexual intimacies with current therapy clients/patients" (APA, 2002, p. 1073). As the introduction to the standards indicates, "the Ethical Standards set forth enforceable rules for conduct as psychologists" (APA, 2002, p. 1061). Although such enforceable standards are important in setting minimum thresholds of acceptable behavior and making it more possible to legally enforce the standards if any psychologists violate them, such very specific statements leave unaddressed at least two major problems. One of these problems relates to *ethical dilemmas*, which are not the result of a psychologist's inappropriate actions but rather most often arise from conflicts among what a client desires; a counselor's values, laws, or regulations; and injustices in the client's environment. Ways of coping with such dilemmas are provided in a major section later in this chapter.

The other issue not addressed by existing standards is that of the character of psychologists. Kitchener (2000) cited the metaphor of putting good seed in bad soil; will ethical training of a flawed character result in a deformed sense of ethical behavior?

For most of the 20th century, character was virtually ignored as an aspect of being ethical, but in the past few decades almost all major writers have devoted far more attention to the topic (Beauchamp & Childress, 1994; Kitchener, 2000; Meara et al., 1996; Urofsky et al., 2009). Meara et al. (1996) proposed that the best way to enhance the ethical standing of the profession of psychology is by increasing the attention given to character and virtue: "Virtue ethics focus on the ideal rather than the obligatory and on the character of the agent or professional rather than on the solving of specific ethical dilemmas" (Meara et al., 1996, p. 47). In this provocative treatise published in *The Counseling Psychologist*, they identified the virtues that should serve as the fundamental foundation of a psychologist's ethical behavior. Meara et al. described four virtues: prudence, integrity, respectfulness, and benevolence. Although none of these writers or others claimed these four to be an exclusive set of pertinent virtues, they are the most widely supported ones. How may each of these be defined?

> Prudence . . . involves appropriate restraint or caution, deliberate reflection upon which moral action to take, an understanding of the long-range consequences of the choice made, acting with due regard for one's vision of what is morally good, and a knowledge of how present circumstances relate to that good or goal. (Meara et al., 1996, p. 39)

For a definition of integrity, Meara et al. (1996) turned to Beauchamp and Childress: "Moral integrity, then, is the character trait of a coherent integration of reasonable stable, justifiable moral values, together with active fidelity to those values in judgment and in action" (Beauchamp & Childress, 1994, p. 473). Regarding respectfulness, Meara et al. (1996) wrote,

> Respectfulness means that we, as professional psychologists, respect (i.e., provide special attention, deference, or regard to) individuals or communities on and in the terms they themselves (not the professionals) define. The critical question is how others wish to be respected. (p. 44)

They followed their definition with examples of what it means to be respectful of clients who may come from a culture quite different from that of the counselor. Finally, regarding benevolence, they suggested that

> to label an individual as benevolent means that [that] person can be distinguished by wanting to do good. . . . We believe that benevolence is important if psychologists and the profession of psychology are going to achieve the goal of contributing to the common good. (Meara et al., 1996, p. 45)

Thus, benevolence not only involves actions concerning clients but also speaks to the profession's social responsibility. "Prudence and integrity are most closely related to the goal of competence. . . . Respectfulness and benevolence further the goals of developing a psychology sensitive to multiculturalism and providing for the common good" (Meara et al., 1996, p. 47).

Should the criteria for selection as a graduate student in psychology include assessment of character? If so, how is it to be assessed? How much of each virtue is needed? These questions are difficult to answer. Can a person without high amounts of such virtue learn to become an ethical psychologist? Are there risks of a "deformed" sense of ethics if training is provided to one without virtue? Although such questions have not been definitively addressed, counseling psychologists strive to be virtuous as well as to follow the *Ethical Principles of Psychologists and Code of Conduct* set forth by the APA.

The APA Ethics Code

There have been a number of revisions of the APA Ethics Code since its first edition in 1953. Some have been extensive, whereas others have been more minor. The last significant revision of the Ethics Code was in 2002. The most recent update (to Sections 1.02 and 1.03) in 2010 is discussed in a later section of this chapter.

The 2002 *Ethical Principles of Psychologists and Code of Conduct* (APA, 2002) includes an introduction, a preamble, five general principles that are aspirational in nature, and 10 enforceable ethical standards.

The five general principles reflect the desire for psychologists to operate with an attitude of ethics, a model of moral reasoning similar to Kitchener's principle ethics (Kitchener, 1984). Principle A (Beneficence and Nonmaleficence) suggests that psychologists should promote the welfare of those with whom they interact in professional settings and avoid doing harm. Although simple at the surface level, these aspirational principles often come into conflict, particularly when one considers the complex contexts in which psychologists work (including "virtual" contexts of the Internet, which are discussed later). Principle B (Fidelity and Responsibility) asserts that psychologists "keep their promises, tell the truth, and honor their obligations" (Knapp & VandeCreek, 2004, p. 250). Principle C (Integrity) states that psychologists "seek to promote accuracy, honesty, and truthfulness in the science, teaching, and practice of psychology" (APA, 2002, p. 1062). It also reminds psychologists that acting with integrity prohibits theft, cheating, fraud, or intentional misrepresentations. Principle D (Justice) reminds psychologists to be fair in all their endeavors and to exercise reasonable judgment at all times. Finally, Principle E (Respect for People's Rights and Dignity) highlights the psychologist's respect for individual rights and the dignity of all people, from all backgrounds and cultures, and the need for psychologists to guard against biases. Although aspirational in nature, these five guiding principles set the tone for what it means to be an ethical psychologist.

The 10 ethical standards that follow provide more explicit directions about ethical behavior and are enforceable by the APA. We provide a brief overview here, with greater elaboration in the following section:

- Section 1 (Resolving Ethical Issues) gives direction to psychologists on how to manage conflicts that arise among ethics and law, regulations, organizational demands, and other governing authorities.

- Section 2 (Competence) seeks to ensure that psychologists do not practice outside the boundaries of their competence, as indicated by their "education, training, supervised experience, consultation, or professional experience" (APA, 2002, p. 1063), while allowing for some leniency in emergency situations.

- Section 3 (Human Relations) covers a lot of ground, with attention to avoiding discrimination, harassment, multiple relationships, conflicts of interest, and exploitative relationships. It also spells out the best practices for informed consent in multiple settings (e.g., research, assessment, therapy, consultation).

- Section 4 (Privacy and Confidentiality) emphasizes the importance of confidentiality and trust in psychological activities while also discussing the limits of confidentiality and other aspects of privacy to which psychologists must attend.

- Section 5 (Advertising and Other Public Representations) reminds psychologists, particularly in modern times when electronic media is so pervasive, to stay vigilant about what they print, claim, or advertise and thereby avoid "false, deceptive, or fraudulent" representations (APA, 2002, p. 1067).

- Section 6 (Record Keeping and Fees) helps psychologists create, maintain, and dispose of records in the most protective and ethical manner possible. It also provides direction with regard to managing fees, referrals, and correspondence with payors (such as insurance companies).

- Section 7 (Education and Training) promotes accuracy in teaching and provides clear protections for students in training programs (with regard to assessment of performance, disclosure of personal information, and program requirements for personal therapy).

- Section 8 (Research and Publication) makes clear the need for institutional approval for research, as well as informed consent, debriefing, and the humane care of animals. It also overviews critical research processes and includes cautions about inducements and deception in research, avoidance of plagiarism, and appropriate management of issues of publication credit.

- Section 9 (Assessment) provides updated information about what psychologists can share (e.g., test data) and must protect (e.g., test materials). It clarifies the ways in which psychologists may use assessment data and the precautions for best practices (e.g., not using obsolete tests, maintaining test security).

- Section 10 (Therapy) overviews ethical behaviors in individual, couples/family, and group therapeutic settings. In particular, the code clearly prohibits sexual intimacies with clients and relatives of clients and cautions psychologists regarding termination and interruption of therapeutic services.

The 2002 Code of Ethics is only 14 pages in length, but it packs in a great deal of information meant to be useful to psychologists. For it to be useful, psychologists must be aware of the code, must have read it carefully, and must be prepared to apply the code to their professional activities. As applying the code is often more difficult to achieve than it sounds, we provide some illustrations of unethical behaviors next to help readers contemplate the nuances of the ethics code.

Illustrations of Unethical Behaviors

As we have noted, every psychologist is expected to be fully acquainted and willing to comply with the APA's *Ethical Principles of Psychologists and Code of Conduct* (2002). These standards may be applied to psychologists, as well as students of psychology, by state psychology boards, courts, and other public bodies. In this section, each of the 10 parts of the APA's ethical standards is illustrated by one or more examples of a violation. After the violation is stated, an abbreviated quotation from the most applicable standard and pertinent commentary are provided. (The three-digit number by the cited standard is the reference number in the 2002 APA Code of Conduct. Some of the violations provided could be cited as violations of several standards; however, in order to keep the discussion of each violation concisely focused, we present only one key standard with each of the violations.)

As noted earlier, we have deliberately avoided choosing the most highly sensationalized and publicized violations, such as predatory sexual relationships and fraudulent billing (e.g., a psychologist billing an insurance company for a greater fee and/or number of sessions than was provided to an insured client); rather, we have chosen examples that reflect the ethical problems typically created by impulsive and unthinking (or at least poorly thought through) actions by psychologists, by far the most prevalent source of ethical violations (Bersoff, 2008). Because we can explore only a few of the 89 standards in this chapter, readers are encouraged to become acquainted with numerous other examples of ethical violations and dilemmas found in publications such as those by Knapp, Gottlieb, Handelsman, and VandeCreek (2012); Koocher and Keith-Spiegel (2008); and Pope and Vasquez (2010). An acquaintance with a broad range of such examples is critical to increasing one's sensitivity to the presence of ethical situations.

1. RESOLVING ETHICAL ISSUES

Violation: Psychologist A becomes aware that a colleague, Psychologist B, frequently invites his clients to go out to dinner with him and, on several occasions, invited them to go on weekend trips with him. Psychologist A speaks with Psychologist B and indicates concern about B's violation of the standard (3.05) regarding multiple relationships. B argues that taking these clients out is part of the treatment they need for learning how to develop effective friendships. Subsequently, Psychologist A hears from several different sources that B engages in sexual relations with some of these clients. Psychologist A takes no further action after initial expression of concern to B.

> 1.05. *Reporting Ethical Violations:* If an apparent ethical violation has substantially harmed or is likely to substantially harm a person or organization and is not appropriate for informal resolution under Standard 1.04, Informal Resolution of Ethical Violations, or is not resolved properly in that fashion, psychologists take further action appropriate to the situation. Such action might include referral to state or national committees on professional ethics, to state licensing boards, or to the appropriate institutional authorities. (APA, 2002, p. 1063)

Psychologists are often reluctant to take the step of reporting violations to ethics committees or licensing boards, even though they know an ethical violation has been committed. Like Psychologist A, they more willingly attempt an informal resolution, but when that fails, they hesitate to take the next step because of its potential for long-lasting complications in working relationships and possible legal ramifications. Yet, it must be clearly noted, such inaction is derived from self-protection rather than protection of the welfare of clients of psychologists. Therefore, not reporting a known ethical violation is actually an ethical violation in itself and can result in censure or more severe penalties if the psychologist who failed to report the violation does not cooperate with licensing boards' and/or ethics committees' inquiries about a colleague's unethical behavior.

2. COMPETENCE

Violation: Psychologist C accepts and begins working in a position at a mental health clinic where many of her clients are children from a Native American community. Psychologist C has had no prior experience or training in working with Native Americans or with children.

> 2.01. *Boundaries of Competence:* (b) Where scientific or professional knowledge in the discipline of psychology establishes that an understanding of factors associated with age, gender, gender identity, race, ethnicity, culture, national origin, religion, sexual orientation,

disability, language, or socioeconomic status is essential for effective implementation of their services or research, psychologists have or obtain the training, experience, consultation, or supervision necessary to ensure the competence of their services, or they make appropriate referrals, except as provided in Standard 2.02, Providing Services in Emergencies. (APA, 2002, p. 1064)

Psychologist C could have ethically accepted this position if she arranged to seek supervision of her work until she had completed appropriate training. We cover additional issues of culturally competent practice in Chapter 14. However, it is important to note that not only is it preferable to be culturally competent but that it is an ethical obligation to work within the boundaries of one's competence or seek additional training to expand one's areas of expertise.

Violation: Psychologist D, who was in the midst of litigation regarding divorcing his wife of 12 years and seeking custody of their four children, began canceling nearly 40% of his scheduled appointments week after week, saying some unexpected developments precluded him from coming to the office. Some clients whom he did see were overheard telling other clients that Psychologist D seemed very preoccupied and had fallen asleep during some of their recent sessions.

2.06. *Personal Problems and Conflicts:* (b) When psychologists become aware of personal problems that may interfere with their performing work-related duties adequately, they take appropriate measures, such as obtaining professional consultation or assistance, and determine whether they should limit, suspend, or terminate their work-related duties. (APA, 2002, p. 1064)

Psychologists are people, too! They do at times encounter difficulties in their personal lives and/or become overburdened with their workloads. Fortunately, a number of research articles and continuing education programs have focused on ways to prevent and ameliorate some of the stresses inherent in professional roles as psychologists (Coster & Schwebel, 1997; Myers et al., 2012; Orlinsky & Rønnestad, 2005), focusing on the rewards the work brings as well as the stresses. In particular, Sherman and Thelen (1998) recommended that training programs "should be proactive in preparing trainees for coping effectively distress and impairment" (p. 84).

3. HUMAN RELATIONS

Violation: Psychologist E is asked by the chief executive officer (CEO) of the company that employs him to provide psychological evaluations of several candidates being considered for promotion to a vice presidency. The CEO indicates that the only persons he wants evaluated, from among all those nominated, are the men because he will not consider any women as vice-presidential candidates. Psychologist E agrees to conduct psychological evaluations only on the men.

> 3.01. *Unfair Discrimination:* In their work-related activities, psychologists do not engage in unfair discrimination based on age, gender, gender identity, race, ethnicity, culture, national origin, religion, sexual orientation, disability, socioeconomic status, or any basis proscribed by law. (APA, 2002, p. 1064)

Psychologist E, by agreeing to test only the male nominees, colluded in discriminatory actions against women, even though there are a number of alternatives, within both the ethical obligations and legal rights of the psychologist, that the psychologist could have chosen rather than collude with the CEO's discriminatory action.

Violation: Psychology Professor F, well known for her research and practice with victims of sexual abuse, is asked by one of her advisees to become her primary internship supervisor as well. The intern will be working on her dissertation during the internship. Professor F agrees to serve as both dissertation advisor and clinical supervisor.

> 3.05. *Multiple Relationships:* (a) A psychologist refrains from entering into a multiple relationship if the multiple relationship could reasonably be expected to impair the psychologist's objectivity, competence, or effectiveness in performing his or her functions as a psychologist, or otherwise risks exploitation or harm to the person with whom the professional relationship exists. Multiple relationships that would not reasonably be expected to cause impairment or risk exploitation or harm are not unethical. (APA, 2002, p. 1065)

Although there is apparent logic in the intern wanting supervision from an established expert in her area of both research and practice, such dual roles are fraught with dangers to the objective performances of both the professor and the intern and, perhaps more important, to the quality of their working relationship (Barnett, 2008). Because the psychologist would need to be in an evaluative role in two very different contexts (i.e., evaluating the dissertation, evaluating the intern's performance), conflicts could well arise in one area, "spill over" into evaluation or performance in the other area, and result in harm. Slimp and Burian (1994) identified the many, often regrettable, consequences of the prevalence of multiple role relationships that occur in internships. There may be cases where specialized expertise and/or rural locations make such dual relationships almost unavoidable or where such multiple relationships would not risk harm (and are therefore not unethical), but such relationships should be entered into only after the superiors of both parties in the relationship (e.g., director of internship, chair of psychology department) have all been informed of and given their consent to the establishment of a dual relationship.

4. PRIVACY AND CONFIDENTIALITY

Violation: Psychologist G shows the counseling center receptionist the results of a test he has recently given to one of his clients, noting that the client obtained the highest IQ score he had ever seen.

> 4.04. *Minimizing Intrusion on Privacy:* (b) Psychologists discuss confidential information obtained in their work only for appropriate scientific or professional purposes and only with persons clearly concerned with such matters. (APA, 2002, p. 1066)

Though the psychologist might have thought he was not sharing anything damaging but rather something quite complimentary, any information obtained in professional relationships is to be treated confidentially. Sharing such information, with the identity of the client not concealed, is always limited to those with a "need to know" even if it is complimentary, humorous, or particularly instructive.

Violation: Psychologist H was asked by an accounting firm president to provide substance abuse counseling to one of the firm's junior executives. After 3 months of treatment have been completed, the firm president requests treatment records before he will make payment for the psychologist's services. Psychologist H refuses to provide records but does provide a progress report prepared in consultation with the client. The president finds this unacceptable and has the firm's attorney issue a subpoena for the records; Psychologist H then submits the record to the firm's president.

> 4.05. *Disclosures:* (b) Psychologists disclose confidential information without the consent of the individual only as mandated by law, or where permitted by law for a valid purpose, such as to (1) provide needed professional services; (2) obtain appropriate professional consultations; (3) protect the client/patient, psychologist, or others from harm; or (4) obtain payment for services from a client/patient, in which instance disclosure is limited to the minimum that is necessary to achieve the purpose. (APA, 2002, p. 1066)

Why was Psychologist H's action an ethical violation when a subpoena had been issued? This example provides the opportunity to make two vital distinctions: One, there is a difference between a court order and a subpoena; any lawyer may request a subpoena (Stromberg, 1993). Two, privilege belongs to the patient, not to the psychologist; therefore, even in response to a subpoena the psychologist needs to consult the client (and possibly the client's attorney) before responding to the subpoena. Even though the president of the firm believed he was entitled to the records because he was paying for the therapy, he could not really justifiably request more than evidence that treatment was necessary and being provided. Additional communications between the therapist and the client remain privileged communications (Glosoff, Herlihy, & Spence, 2000; Knapp & VandeCreek, 1997).

5. ADVERTISING AND OTHER PUBLIC REPRESENTATIONS

Violation: A popular radio announcer tells Psychologist J how impressed she is with the progress her son has made in the program the psychologist developed for children with mild learning disabilities. Psychologist J tells her that he would be happy to waive any fees for her son's further participation if she would talk about the "good results" from his program on some of her radio programs.

> 5.05. *Testimonials:* Psychologists do not solicit testimonials from current therapy clients/patients or other persons who because of their particular circumstances are vulnerable to undue influence. (APA, 2002, p. 1067)

If Psychologist J wanted some publicity for his program, he should have followed the usual procedures for purchasing advertising time on the radio. It would not have been inappropriate for Psychologist J to ask the radio announcer how best to arrange for such a purchase, but any further involvement of the announcer would be inappropriate in accordance with standards regarding both multiple relationships and advertising.

6. RECORD KEEPING AND FEES

Psychologist K has completed her internship and is moving across the country to take a new job. She has closed out all of her client files at the counseling center and successfully completed terminations with all of her clients. She throws out all of her case notes but does not go through each piece of paper to ensure that no identifying information is included.

> 6.02. *Maintenance, Dissemination, and Disposal of Confidential Records of Professional and Scientific Work:* (a) Psychologists maintain confidentiality in creating, storing, accessing, transferring, and disposing of records under their control, whether these are written, automated, or in any other medium. (APA, 2002, p. 1067)

Psychologist K has completed her clinical work at her internship site and left appropriate records with the site, but she should have removed identifying information from her notes before disposing of them. She should have considered shredding her paper notes and ensuring that she did not have remaining digital files on her computer.

7. EDUCATION AND TRAINING

A student has entered a doctoral program in counseling psychology. As part of the training program, students are required to participate in individual therapy. The training director hands the student a list of individuals who teach in the program who are willing to see graduate students for a small fee and asks the student to initiate treatment by the middle of the semester.

> 7.05. *Mandatory Individual or Group Therapy:* (a) When individual or group therapy is a program or course requirement, psychologists responsible for that program allow students in undergraduate and graduate programs the option of selecting such therapy from practitioners unaffiliated with the program. (APA, 2002, p. 1069)

Although it is not unethical for a program to require mandatory individual or group therapy for its students, it is unethical not to allow students to choose their own therapist from among practitioners not affiliated with the program. At a minimum, such a procedure leaves room for problematic and harmful multiple relationships and does not respect the privacy of the student.

8. RESEARCH AND PUBLICATION

Violation: Psychologist L invites students to take part in an experiment she describes as an investigation of various modes of group discussion. Once students have begun participating in the experiment, leaders in some of the groups urge them to reveal their most pressing personal problem; those participants who are reluctant to do so are assured "we're all friends here who want to help one another."

> 8.07. *Deception in Research:* (b) Psychologists do not deceive prospective participants about research that is reasonably expected to cause physical pain or severe emotional distress. (APA, 2002, p. 1070)

Psychologist L neither fully informed students nor took safeguards to protect their welfare when they were essentially manipulated into revealing personal problems to others in their groups. There are only a very limited number of circumstances, as outlined in Sections (a) and (c) of Standard 8.07, in which deception is permitted in research.

Violation: Psychologist M asks a graduate student to work with him on developing a research project, then has the graduate student collect the data, run the analyses, and prepare a report of the results. When Psychologist M prepares a manuscript for publication based on the research report, he lists himself as sole author and acknowledges the contribution of the graduate student only in a footnote.

> 8.12. *Publication Credit:* (b) Principle authorship and other publication credits accurately reflect the relative scientific or professional contributions of the individuals involved, regardless of their relative status. (APA, 2002, p. 1070)

The involvement of the graduate student in almost all phases of the research, as well as the primary responsibility for data collection, analyses, and reporting, merits at least coauthorship credit, possibly even primary authorship. Psychologist M should have made clear from the outset of their working relationship how the work of the graduate student would be recognized and stated that the level of this recognition would be relative to the student's contributions to the research.

9. ASSESSMENT

Violation: Psychology Professor N, who teaches career development at a community college with 60% minority students, 30% of whom have English as a second language, offers them the opportunity to come in and use his personal computer to take a computer-assisted academic aptitude test developed for and normed with traditional university students. The students receive a sheet interpreting their results, which the professor tells them can be of use in helping them decide whether they have the ability for education beyond the community college level. They do not have any further contact with Professor N to discuss the results.

> 9.02. *Use of Assessments:* (b) Psychologists use assessment instruments whose validity and reliability have been established for use with members of the population tested. (APA, 2002, p. 1071)

Not only did Psychologist N use an assessment instrument that was developed on a population that differed radically from the one he was teaching, he did not meet with the students to discuss how their results might well have been affected by their ethnic and language background. These results were at best of dubious value regarding any assessment of the students' potential for continuing education.

10. THERAPY

Violation: Psychologist O is asked by the president of the company that employs him to provide employee Jones with some counseling to "get him out of his plateau." Psychologist O invites employee Jones to have coffee with him in his office and subsequently continues to invite him in for "coffee," during which time the psychologist shapes the sessions into ever more personal counseling sessions.

> 10.01. *Informed Consent:* (a) Psychologists inform clients/patients as early as is feasible in the therapeutic relationship about the nature and anticipated course of therapy, fees, involvement of third parties, and limits of confidentiality. (APA, 2002, p. 1072)

By Psychologist O not making clear to employee Jones that he had been requested to be of assistance to him, he was actually deceiving Jones regarding his (the psychologist's) intent when inviting him for coffee. Such deception would almost inevitably lead to an eventual betrayal of trust with damaging implications for the client, the psychologist, and the profession of psychology.

Ethical Dilemmas

We use the term *ethical dilemmas* to describe those situations in which taking any action or even taking no action will violate at least one or more ethical principles.

In this section we explore the kinds of ethical dilemmas that are all too often encountered in the everyday practice of psychology (Bersoff, 2008). We then explore the most useful approaches to analyzing and then taking action in these difficult situations. Consider the following situations:

A. A client tells the counselor that he wants to commit suicide and has a plan to do it, but he does not want the counselor to tell anyone. The client has thought about it carefully and has decided that this is his "best" choice. He refuses all the counselor's attempts to have him consider alternatives. Sensing the counselor's concern and suspecting that she might commit him, he threatens to sue for breach of confidentiality if she tells anyone about his plans. (This scenario assumes that the counselor and the client have not previously discussed limits to confidentiality.)

B. The only female counselor in a rural county's mental health center has a list of eight persons who have been waiting up to 3 months for counseling. A new client comes to the clinic in a highly agitated state of depression and insists on seeing a female counselor because "no men are to be trusted." The female counselor suspects that if this client is not treated promptly, she is at risk for either a psychotic breakdown or a possible suicide. Yet, if the counselor begins seeing her at this time, she would be making other clients, who were referred earlier though are less disturbed, wait several more weeks or months. There are no practical referral resources available because the next nearest female counselor is 125 miles away.

C. The following example is from Kitchener (1984):

> The counseling psychologist concerned with the increase in cases of bulimia reported in university counseling centers decides to compare the effects of a cognitive behavioral intervention with a pharmacological treatment in a controlled study. He considers using a wait-list control group and a placebo group but is aware that the use of the placebo group will involve deceiving subjects, and the use of a wait-list group will involve refusing some individuals treatment for several months. (p. 43)

In both counseling and research settings, counseling psychologists often find themselves between a rock and a hard place. Although such situations typically get far less media attention than ethical violations such as dual relationships, misrepresentation of credentials, and inappropriate public statements, it is the dilemmas, rather than the violations, that help us most clearly understand the limitations of ethical codes in solving ethical problems.

Kitchener (1984, 2000) has usefully articulated the relationship of existing ethical standards to "principle ethics" when faced with these dilemmas. In her "decision tree," a psychologist would first ask whether the current APA ethical standards indicate how one should proceed. For most of the dilemmas, like those cited above, two or more conflicting courses of action would be recommended. How can we simultaneously respect a client's wishes if that means allowing a client to harm himself, herself, or others? Kitchener (1984, 2000) has provided counseling psychologists who confront such dilemmas with a very useful explication of principle ethics. She described not only how principle ethics underlie the development of APA ethical standards but also the necessity of returning to these fundamental principles to determine how to proceed when ethical dilemmas present themselves. By understanding these basic principles, psychologists gain a better understanding of what ethical values are in conflict and can therefore make a more informed choice about when and why there may be a need to violate any given ethical standard. Kitchener's (1984) description of five basic principles, drawn from earlier versions of the work of Beauchamp and Childress (1994), remains the most concise presentation of a set of principles highly pertinent for psychologists and is therefore presented here. Extensive material on the definition, origins, and usefulness of each of these principles may be found in Kitchener's most recent book (Kitchener & Anderson, 2011).

> *Autonomy* . . . includes the right to act as an autonomous agent, to make one's own decision, to develop one's own values . . . [and] includes respecting the rights of others to make autonomous choices, even when we believe they are mistaken, as long as their choices do not infringe on the rights of others.
>
> *Nonmaleficence* . . . not causing harm to others, includes both not inflicting intentional harm nor engaging in actions which risk harming others. . . . Seeing nonmaleficence as fundamental suggests that if we must choose between harming someone and benefiting that person, another, or society, our stronger obligation, other things being equal, would be to avoid harm.
>
> *Beneficence*. . . . Doing good to others is critical to ethical issues in psychology and especially counseling psychology. . . . The term "helping profession" underlines this obligation.
>
> *Justice*. . . . In order to live together with minimal strife, people must develop rules and procedures for adjudicating claims and services in a fair manner. . . . Considerations of equal need are particularly relevant to the issue of how to distribute scarce psychological services.

> *Fidelity* . . . involves questions of "faithfulness," promise-keeping, and loyalty. Issues of fidelity arise when individuals enter into some kind of a voluntary relationship (e.g., counselor–client, husband–wife, supervisor–supervisee). . . . The issue of fidelity seems especially critical in psychology because issues like truthfulness and loyalty are basic to trust. . . . It is particularly vital to client–counselor, research–participant, supervisor–supervisee, and/or consultant–consultee relationships. All are dependent on honest communication and the assumption that the contract on which the relationship was initiated obliges both parties to fulfill certain functions. (Kitchener, 1984, pp. 46–51)

The example of the suicidal client at the beginning of this section represents a conflict between the principles of autonomy and beneficence. If interventions are made to protect him from harming himself, his dignity and worth as an autonomous person have been "violated" because his wishes to act in accordance with his own plan are not being honored by the psychologist. On the other hand, if no effort is made to intervene, there is great risk that the welfare of the client will not be protected, assuming "protecting the welfare" means keeping him from suicide. As Beauchamp and Childress (1994) noted, in our society principles of beneficence usually outweigh those of autonomy in these dilemmas, the justification for this being that clients are being protected from harms that would result from their illness, immaturity, or psychological incapacitation rather than a fully rational, mature judgment.

In the example concerning the highly agitated, depressed woman, a conflict between the principles of justice and nonmaleficence is illustrated. Because the principle of justice is based on the presumption that all people are equally deserving, one could argue that treatment of them should be on a "first come, first served" basis. However, in this case, not to provide treatment to the agitated client seems to contribute to potential harm to the client (i.e., to maleficence). Ideally, in a just society, there would be adequate resources for all individuals. However, such availability of resources is all too rare, especially in rural settings, and this kind of dilemma is an almost daily occurrence. University counseling centers often find themselves in similar situations near the end of semester, when huge waiting lists may develop because there are far more clients wanting services than the staff can provide. At such times, many agencies develop some policies that recognize that some needs are greater than others; distribution of services then is based on this differential assessment of needs, thereby redefining the basis of justice.

In the third example, concerning research on bulimia, the conflict is between the principle of nonmaleficence (do no harm by eliminating the waiting list and so avoid refusing some individuals treatment for several months) and the principle of beneficence (the research potentially could make significant contributions to determining the most effective treatment for bulimia). Making decisions about research projects, as well as about whether to use any given treatment when there is little or no research to support its benefits, has to include, in the reasoning process, a careful consideration of whether the potential benefits of the research project outweigh the "costs" suffered by those treated with placebos or not treated at all (if on a waiting list).

These examples are just a few of the many illustrations that could be offered in how to use principle ethics when confronted with an ethical dilemma. Which principles can be honored and which ones must be "violated"? Such an analysis is critical in accomplishing the third step in Rest's (1984) model of moral behavior; that is, selecting, from among competing values the one on which to act. In the final section of this chapter we return to the fourth step of Rest's model: that of executing and implementing what one intends to do.

ETHICAL DILEMMAS CREATED BY LAWS

The passage of a number of laws in recent decades has added to the complexity and urgency of several types of ethical dilemmas. Many states now have laws regarding "duty to warn or protect"; that is, if a client discusses in therapy the intent to cause harm to another person through actions such as assault or infection with the virus that causes AIDS, the psychologist must take appropriate action to protect the intended victim. "Duty to report" laws require, for example, that when a psychologist has any firsthand knowledge of child abuse, such abuse must be reported to appropriate social service authorities.

In one sense, such laws create ethical dilemmas because if the psychologist fulfills legal obligations, client confidentiality will be breached. In addition, reporting offenses can at times create serious ruptures in the client–counselor relationship. However, in another sense, although the laws create a perceived dilemma, they prescribe exactly what must be done. The laws are clear that confidentiality must give way to protection, and autonomy must be sacrificed for beneficence.

The nature of laws regarding duty to warn and duty to report varies greatly from state to state, so psychologists need to become familiar with these kinds of laws in any states in which they practice. Failure of the psychologist to act expeditiously when confronted with these situations can lead to the imposition of criminal penalties against the psychologist or a situation in which the psychologist is a defendant in a civil suit. Pabian, Welfel, and Beebe (2009) found, unfortunately, that psychologists were quite misinformed about the laws in their own state, despite having confidence that they understood the laws. We encourage readers to become informed about the laws and best practices in the field. A number of useful books are available, such as Werth, Welfel, and Benjamin's

(2009) *The Duty to Protect*. Even with such knowledge, however, the difficulty of navigating ethical dilemmas, particularly in those cases where ethics and law collide, should be acknowledged. A clear answer is not always obvious or available in legal documents or precedents. Thus, psychologists must have a working knowledge of ethical principles such that they can use that knowledge to help them make decisions when the answers are not clearly delineated.

ETHICAL DILEMMAS CREATED BY PERSONAL VALUES

Some ethical dilemmas occur primarily because all counseling psychologists have their own set of personal values, some of which may conflict with those of their clients. Each of us had an upbringing that provided us with cultural norms, some derived from ethnic backgrounds, some from religious backgrounds. These values affect not only personal views about how we should manage our own lives with respect to such issues as what constitutes masculinity, femininity, sexual relationships, appropriate roles within a marriage, parenting behaviors, and the like but also the range of options we can comfortably consider with our clients. During the first half of the 20th century, proponents of both traditional Freudian analytic and Rogerian client-centered perspectives argued that therapy and counseling needed to be value free. After years of struggle to keep therapy neutral, there was a growing consensus, best captured by Corey, Corey, and Callanan (1979):

> Since we believe that counselors' values do inevitably affect the therapeutic process, we also think it's important for counselors to be willing to express their values openly when they are relevant to the questions that come up in their sessions with clients. (p. 85)

Can one be an effective therapist for a client who wishes to have an abortion if one believes that abortion is always wrong? Can one be an effective therapist for a gay client who wishes to pursue an interracial adoption when one believes children should not be raised by gay parents and/or only should be raised by parents of their own race? The issue is clearly not whether it is acceptable for psychologists to have such personal views: The introduction to the APA Ethics Code (APA, 2002) clearly states, "This Ethics Code applies only to psychologists' activities that are part of their scientific, educational, or professional roles as psychologists" (p. 1061). Thus, the issue is how to be sure that our personal values do not interfere with the welfare of our clients. The first challenge for us is to be fully conscious of the values we hold. This challenge is greater than many of us realize until we have been confronted with instances in which we have many implicit values that conflict with the values of, for example, those of persons from other cultures, religions, and worldviews (see Chapter 14 in this volume). The second challenge is the one noted above by Corey et al. (1979): a willingness to express these values openly with the client and explore together how they affect the therapeutic relationship and the options for the client to consider, including the option of working with another therapist who may feel more comfortable and effective in aiding the client explore all available options.

ETHICAL DILEMMAS THAT REMAIN IN DEBATE AT THE BROADER SOCIAL LEVEL

Two issues in the past decade have received a great deal of attention from psychologists and others. Both are related to specific societal changes and raise a number of ethical concerns and dilemmas. We present them here as a way for you to think through and sharpen your own ethical beliefs and critical thinking skills.

Military Psychologists' Participation in Interrogations

Few issues have created as much controversy and concern as the role of psychologists in military interrogations. After the terrorist attacks at the World Trade Center in New York and the Pentagon in Washington, DC and the downing of United Airlines Flight 93 in Shanksville, Pennsylvania, on September 11, 2001, the United States and the world grew ever more concerned about preventing future terrorist attacks. Governments set about to gather up those suspected of participating in terrorist organizations and detained these people at various locations. In the wake of 9/11, there were reports of detainee abuses at Abu Ghraib prison, Iraq; Bagram Airbase Detention Center, Afghanistan; and Guantanamo Bay Naval Base, Cuba. These disturbing reports opened questions about the roles of psychologists at some of these locations who had participated in interrogations of detainees or "enemy combatants" (Abeles, 2010). The concern was primarily that some of the strategies used in interrogations had tipped the scale into abuse and torture. Some (see Kalbeitzer, 2009) suggested that there was evidence that psychologists played key roles in interrogations, such as by reverse engineering the Survival, Evasion, Resistance and Escape (SERE) training (Soldz, 2008; i.e., using the principles learned in SERE training to break through resistance and defenses of those being detained). Others (see James, 2008) suggested that psychologists' roles had been limited and that "no illegal or unethical behavior by DoD [Department of Defense] psychologists supporting interrogations has been discovered" (Greene & Banks, 2009, p. 29). Although debate over the evidence of any specific wrongdoing by military psychologists continues, the debate itself may have begun to erode the public's confidence in psychologists. We attempt to overview here not the political debate or the presentation of facts but rather the ethical issues that have been raised.

One ethical concern that has been raised centers around the wording of the 2002 APA Ethics Code. When the 1992 Ethics Code was revised (approved on August 21, 2002), the wording in the introduction provided what Pope (2011) has called rejection of international law and the Nuremberg Ethic. The Nuremberg "defense" was so named when Nazi defendants after World War II claimed they were just "following orders" or "obeying the law." The Nuremberg Trials clearly established that "people who chose to violate fundamental ethical responsibilities could not avoid responsibility by blaming laws, orders, or regulations" (Pope, 2011, p. 153). Pope (2011) further suggested, somewhat controversially, that "APA's post–9-11 ethics code rejected the historic Nuremberg Ethic" (p. 153), such that when faced with a conflict between ethics and law, "psychologists may adhere to the requirements of the law, regulations, or other governing authority" (p. 153). Although the 2002 code (Section 1.02) was written prior to the events of 9/11 and based substantially on legal dilemmas faced by school and forensic psychologists, in 2010, the APA revised the 2002 Ethics Code, Sections 1.02 and 1.03, including what had previously been only aspirational language and thus making clear that "under no circumstances" can the language in the Ethics Code be used to justify the violation of human rights (see APA, 2010, p. 493).

> 1.02 Conflicts Between Ethics and Law, Regulations, or Other Governing Legal Authority. If psychologists' ethical responsibilities conflict with law, regulations, or other governing legal authority, psychologists clarify the nature of the conflict, make known their commitment to the Ethics Code, and take reasonable steps to resolve the conflict consistent with the General Principles and Ethical Standards of the Ethics Code. Under no circumstances may this standard be used to justify or defend violating human rights.

> 1.03 Conflicts Between Ethics and Organization Demands. If demands of an organization with psychologists are affiliated or for whom they are working are in conflict with this Ethics Code, psychologists clarify the nature of the conflict, make known their commitment to the Ethics Code, and take reasonable steps to resolve the conflict consistent with the General Principles and Ethical Standards of the Ethics Code. Under no circumstances may this standard be used to justify or defend violating human rights.

Leading up to this change in the Ethics Code, the APA Council of Representatives passed a resolution that established the APA's position against torture (APA, 2006) and a member referendum passed in 2008 that stated that psychologists would be prohibited from working in detention settings in which there are violations of international law or the U.S. Constitution unless they were working directly in protecting human rights or providing psychological treatment (Abeles, 2010). Although the resolution was passed by the membership, it is not part of the enforceable standards of the Ethics Code (Pope, 2011), as it remains outside of the written Code of Ethics.

Probably the most controversial issue within the concern over psychologists' roles in interrogations, however, is what is known as the PENS Report. In 2003, the APA established a Task Force on Psychological Ethics and National Security (PENS; Greene & Banks, 2009). The report produced by the PENS Task Force was approved by the APA Board of Directors on July 1, 2005. The primary task force recommendation was that "psychologists do not engage in, direct, support, facilitate, or offer training in torture or other cruel, inhuman, or degrading treatment" and that psychologists "have an ethical responsibility to be alert to and report any such acts to appropriate authorities" (PENS Report; APA, 2005, p. 1). In fact, it has been noted that the "whistleblower" for the abuses at Guantanamo Bay was a psychologist, Michael Gelles, who was a member of the PENS Task Force (Abeles, 2010).

Although the APA's position against torture seems clear, it is still true that military psychologists often are faced with competing ethical demands. Johnson and Kennedy (2010) noted the "sobering sense of responsibility" (p. 298) that military psychologists hold, as they are both military officers (and so obligated to the authority of the Department of Defense) and psychologists (and so obligated to the APA ethical code and professional guidelines). As Jeffrey, Rankin, and Jeffrey (1992) noted, military psychologists must serve "two masters." Psychologists working with the military also participate in a number of other roles (e.g., assessment of fitness for duty, evaluation of personnel qualifications, and leadership or organizational screening and training). It is also important to understand that psychologists working in nonmilitary settings have historically been involved in interrogations (such as in police training, prison settings, and within the judicial system as expert witnesses and forensic experts; Johnson, 2002). What has been most controversial, perhaps, is the concern that psychologists might misunderstand their role in interrogations (either military or nonmilitary). In our view, it is incumbent upon the psychologist to remember always that their roles involve ensuring well-being and humane treatment.

This particular ethical issue (when there is conflict among a psychologist's different roles and responsibilities) highlights the dilemmas psychologists are faced with in conducting their jobs, upholding the ethics code, and protecting the people with whom they interact. It is noteworthy that in August 2013, APA's Council of Representatives voted to consolidate all of APA policy on this matter into a single, more forceful resolution that rescinded some of the earlier policies, including the

PENS report (APA, 2013). We urge psychologists who are dealing with complex ethical issues to uphold the APA Ethics Code, consult with experts as needed, and adhere to a sense of personal morality such as that described by Kitchener's (2000) principle ethics.

Psychologists and Telehealth

Another controversial issue has arisen and intensified in the past decade: that of psychologists providing services to clients via electronic means (e.g., landlines, smartphones, e-mail, chat rooms, videoconferencing, websites). Although these emerging technologies have made the provision of psychological services more efficient and convenient, they also have created additional ethical dilemmas (Barnett & O'Leary, 1997; Ragusea & VandeCreek, 2003). Barnett and Scheetz (2003) summarized some of the known recommendations for ethical practice with the earliest electronic technologies. For example, they reminded us to use passwords and encryption software for confidential information we store on our computers; to place phone numbers on speed dial to prevent misdialed faxes; to be aware that cell phone frequencies may be picked up by some radios and baby monitors, rendering private conversations public; and to find out who has access to voicemail messages before leaving a message for a client. Similarly, Collins (2007) overviewed possible ethical concerns that can arise with e-mail and listserv messages, such as messages being subpoenaed. She noted that "listserv communications are admissible as evidence in court" (p. 693) and that it may be the owner of the server (company or institution) that may be subpoenaed, not just the individuals who sent or received the messages. Others have discussed the ethics of online research (e.g., Mathy, Kerr, & Haydin, 2003) and online assessment (e.g., Barak, 2003).

What is clear is that despite the benefits of electronic devices in service provision (e.g., with agoraphobics, in rural settings, for contact between in-person sessions), there are a number of ethical concerns of which to be aware. *Telehealth*, or the use of electronic devices in service provision (Nickelson, 1998), has been growing in popularity. Nearly a third of the world's population and more than three quarters of the population in the United States are Internet users (Internet World Stats, 2011). Similarly, Salaway, Caruso, Nelson, and Ellison (2008) reported that 85.2% of undergraduates participate in social networking (on sites such as Facebook, LinkedIn, and Twitter). These numbers appear to be growing, even among a group that Prensky (2001) earlier referred to as "digital immigrants." For example, DigitalBuzzBlog (2011) has claimed that more than 30% of Facebook users are over age 35. Each year that passes brings additional "digital natives" to the population—those who were born at a time when the Internet and similar technologies were already in existence and being used widely. So, over time, more and more clients and therapists will be those from the digital native category, making it almost impossible to imagine not using these technologies in both personal and professional lives.

Some of the matters that have gained attention (and will likely gain more over the years) are the ways in which clients "google" their therapists before meeting with them and the effect of unwanted or unplanned self-disclosures (Lehavot, Barnett, & Powers, 2010), appropriate (and not appropriate) times to employ interventions via technology, inadvertent threats to confidentiality (e.g., via hackers; Maheu, 2001), and issues regarding the provision of services across state lines and into different jurisdictions than where the therapist remains and is licensed (Koocher & Morray, 2000). Barnett and Scheetz (2003) provided additional cautions for those who plan to provide services via telephone, e-mail, or interactive video conferencing, including using comprehensive informed consent procedures, planning ahead for emergency procedures, working to ensure confidentiality (e.g., by using encryption) as well as knowing the true identity of the person with whom you are interacting electronically, and being familiar with the applicable laws (e.g., duty to warn, mandatory reporting) in the jurisdictions the in which psychologist is working.

Overall, the issue of the ethics of telehealth is a rapidly changing, ever expanding topic. As for all practice issues, psychologists are urged to become familiar with the relevant ethical and legal issues, know how to apply the 2002 APA Ethics Code, and always act with the best interests of clients and the public good in mind.

Implementing Ethical Decisions

Recall that Rest's (1984) fourth component of moral behavior is the execution and implementation of what one decides is the ethical course of action. This statement may fall into the category of "easier said than done." It may be easier on us not to report others' inappropriate professional behaviors; we can avoid possible confrontations and the time and emotional turmoil it takes to make the complaint. T. S. Smith, McGuire, Abbott, and Blau (1991) were among the first to study the factors that influenced ethical compliance. One of their key findings was that compliance was far more likely when laws and ethical standards applied to the situation (e.g., in cases of sex with clients, child abuse reporting, insurance fraud). One of the implications, however, of Smith et al.'s findings (regarding greater compliance when laws are involved) is that even more laws are developing over time, rather than the profession focusing on being self-regulating. Having an increased number of professional behaviors subject to laws also leads to greater distrust of the profession of psychology as well as to increased legal and malpractice costs for all psychologists. It would clearly be desirable to have more voluntary compliance with existing standards, so that additional laws do not become necessary. To that end, several researchers, such as Cottone and Clause (2000), have provided helpful overviews of different ethical decision-making models to help psychologists with difficult ethical dilemmas.

Summary

So, we ask again, what does it require to be an ethical psychologist? Knowledge such as we have presented in this chapter has proved necessary but not quite sufficient for the highest of public perception as a fully trustworthy, self-monitoring profession. As professionals serving persons in troubled and turbulent situations, counseling psychologists need to keep ethical considerations at the highest level of awareness. Psychologists, along with philosophers and biomedical ethicists, have an ongoing discourse about how best to ensure that the public is well served by our professions. There is healthy debate in psychology and other mental health fields about the roles of character (virtues) and training in achieving the goal of being a more fully trusted profession by the public. Continued research on the development of more effective training programs is needed to improve psychologists' identification of ethical situations and then choice and implementation of appropriate actions.

Our purpose in providing illustrations of the major sections of the current APA ethical standards has been to sensitize readers to the frequent ethical implications of many professional behaviors. Many ethical violations result from behaviors that are carried out with good intentions. Violations often result simply from psychologists not giving full consideration to the ethical implications of their behaviors.

Ethical dilemmas are situations that are not easily responded to with only the APA code of ethical standards. These dilemmas occur in situations in which honoring one ethical standard unavoidably results in violation of one or more other principles. For example, a counselor's wanting to maintain confidentiality about a client's communications in counseling sessions about a wish to kill someone might lead to significant bodily harm to another person. Psychologists' understanding and use of principle ethics, applicable laws, and personal values is the primary way to deal with these dilemmas. Finally, implementation of and compliance with ethical standards often require that psychologists recognize the weight of responsibility, even though that responsibility may bring stress to oneself and to collegial relationships.

THE SCIENCE OF
COUNSELING PSYCHOLOGY II

Research Strategies and Paradigms of Counseling Psychologists

4

n the following chapters we focus on the topics of science and research in counseling psychology. Chapter 4, on research strategies and paradigms, is divided into four sections. In the first, the concept of "scientist" within the scientist–practitioner model is explored. We seek to answer the question "What does the 'scientist' part of the scientist–practitioner model really mean?" Different levels of "being a scientist" are examined.

Whereas the first section tends toward the philosophical, the second and third sections are more practical. Our aim is to help the reader understand approaches to counseling psychology research and some key issues in research. We have intentionally sought to go beyond the beginning survey course, gearing the material to the student or professional with some background in psychological research but little or no background in counseling psychology research. The second section presents four typically quantitative research strategies commonly used in counseling psychology research.

http://dx.doi.org/10.1037/14378-004
Counseling Psychology, Third Edition, by C. J. Gelso, E. N. Williams, and B. R. Fretz

We focus on qualitative methodologies in counseling psychology in the third section.

The chapter concludes with a perspective on research in counseling psychology and a discussion of the relevance of research to practice. In this final section, Gelso's "bubble hypothesis" is suggested as a useful way of thinking about the advantages and disadvantages of different research strategies and of the many decisions the researcher must make about the methods used in any given study. We also explore the concept of research relevance, with an emphasis on what the counseling psychology practitioner should and should not expect from research. Finally, some often ignored complexities of the idea of relevance are explored, and ways in which research can be highly relevant to practice are discussed.

The "Scientist" Part of the Scientist–Practitioner Model: What Does It Mean?

We have discussed the scientist–practitioner model of training and practice in counseling psychology (see Chapter 1). We noted that from the beginnings of the specialty, this model has been seen as crucial to sound progress in understanding of all of the activities in which counseling psychologists are involved (e.g., counseling, assessment, consultation) and the phenomena that counseling psychologists study (e.g., career development, prevention).

Within the scientist–practitioner model, students are trained (more precisely, educated) so that they will be scientists as well as professional practitioners. And a vital element of this scientific training is learning how to conduct scientific research. Because research is so vital in this model and in the field, before proceeding further, we shall offer answers to the questions "Why, in fact, is scientific research so important to counseling psychology?" and "Why not just practice what we believe to be true from our personal experiences with clients and human beings more generally?"

Without the benefits of scientific checks and rigorous scientific tests of our favorite hypotheses, we counseling psychologists run the risk of creating magical solutions or cures that are more products of our fantasies and personal needs than of reality. Along the same line, without scientific research and theory, we shall very likely develop treatment approaches that are only products of our biases and prejudices. In the last analysis, counseling practice, in the absence of controlled tests of the efficacy of that practice, is doomed to limited effectiveness at best and harmfulness at worst. Research allows us to check whether our beliefs and theories hold up under controlled conditions and, just as important, whether we are in fact having the effects (e.g., on our clients) that we think and hope we are. In this way, science helps us to continually improve practice.

Along with helping the counseling psychologist check and study his or her theory and treatments, scientific research can have a still more proactive effect. Not only can we find out if our research hypotheses hold up under controlled conditions, we can also create new knowledge and theories through research. Research findings virtually always lead to new directions for the researchers, suggest new ideas and theories, and point to ways in which treatments may be modified so as to become more effective. In these ways, scientific research and the findings emanating from it are always exciting. At least a portion of what turns up is almost always new!

Do the above formulations imply that all counseling psychologists should be involved in science and research? Should the counseling psychologist who, for example, is working full time as a private practitioner make empirical research a part of his or her workday? Is it enough for the practitioner to think scientifically or to be a consumer (i.e., reader of) rather than a producer of scientific theory and research? These important questions lead us to a discussion of what the scientist part of the scientist–practitioner model really means.

Although the scientist–practitioner model has been around for a long time, disagreement about what the terms of the model mean and how they are to be actualized, both in graduate education and in the worklives of counseling psychologists (or psychologists in other specialties), is not uncommon. Defining just what is meant by being a scientist within this model is more complicated than it might first appear. Thus, there are several meanings to the concept of "scientist" and several ways in which the concept is manifested in practice.

From the time of the Northwestern Conference in 1951, some have suggested that, at a minimum, "being scientific" means having the "ability to review and make use of the results of research" (American Psychological Association, 1952, p. 179). Thus, the counseling practitioner should be able to understand research and apply research findings to his or her practice. We might view this as the first level, or minimal level, of functioning as a scientist–practitioner.

A second way in which the counseling psychologist is to be a scientist is in the way he or she goes about thinking of practice as well as the manner in which he or she conducts counseling psychology practice. With respect to thinking, the practitioner follows what is perhaps the most fundamental tenet of the scientific attitude: Think critically and be sufficiently skeptical. Thus, one is to think critically about theories, one's own and others, rather than just accept them. Also, when one reads research studies, one is to think critically. When new approaches are suggested in the literature, the practitioner does not simply swallow them; he or she is duly skeptical. After careful examination, approaches may be tried out tentatively.

In terms of the manner in which the practitioner conducts his or her practice—for example, in working with clients—a scientific process is followed. In counseling, the counselor sifts through material the client presents and forms hypotheses about (a) the nature of the client's problem, (b) how best to intervene, and (c) the ways in which the client might respond to various interventions. The counselor then puts these hypotheses to the test in practice, and the hypotheses are subsequently revised as a result of the client's response. These steps continually recycle throughout the therapeutic work.

This adherence to a critical thinking style and to a scientific process in one's work may be viewed as a second level of functioning within the scientist–practitioner model. The scientific process, as used in counseling, was systematically articulated many years ago by Pepinsky and Pepinsky (1954) and has been an important part of the scientist–practitioner model since then (see Howard, 1986, for an interesting version of the "counselor as personal scientist" model). Many scholars in the specialty believe that the scientist part of the scientist–practitioner model means or ought to mean much more than being able to review research, apply research findings to practice, and carry out one's practice in a scientific way. In effect, they call for a third level of functioning within the scientist–practitioner model. Whiteley (1984b) advocated a more demanding view of the scientist–professional model of training. He suggested that at a minimum, training at the doctoral level in counseling psychology should teach students to "formulate hypotheses, and to conduct original inquiry" (p. 46) as well as to review and make use of research.

In fact, at the doctoral level, students are now and have always been taught to formulate hypotheses and conduct original inquiry. What Whiteley and others were implying is not only that students should be taught this aspect of science, but that there should also be an expectation that they actually do empirical research as part of their subsequent careers, regardless of whether they are in academic settings, independent practice settings, or other settings. In this sense, being a scientist–practitioner means being involved in research as well as counseling practice throughout one's career, although individual counseling psychologists will of course differ greatly in just how much of their work time is devoted to research.

In sum, the concept of "scientist" within the scientist–practitioner model refers to each of the three levels just discussed (see Heppner,

Wampold, & Kivlighan, 2008). Although the counseling psychologist functions as scientist at each and any level, we suggest that the field will benefit most if the individual actualizes all three levels. The counseling psychologist must be able to understand research and be able to apply it to practice, although, as shall be proposed later in this chapter, the application of research to practice will rarely if ever be direct. The counseling psychologist should also think scientifically and carry out practice in a scientific fashion. Finally, if the field and our clients are to profit maximally, the counseling psychologist should conduct scholarly work as part of his or her career. Note that we here use the term *scholarly work* rather than *research, empirical research,* or *science.* Scholarly work is the broadest and most inclusive of these terms, and, as we shall see, expecting that counseling psychologists will do scholarly work is more realistic than expecting that they will do empirical research, regardless of their work settings (Carter, 2006). To make sense of this suggestion, we first need to clarify further our use of the terms research, science, and scholarly work.

RESEARCH, SCIENCE, AND SCHOLARLY WORK

As part of the Third National Conference on Counseling Psychology (referred to as the Georgia Conference), the Committee on Research (Gelso et al., 1988) grappled with the similarities and differences among three related concepts: research, science, and scholarly work. Too often these terms are used interchangeably and without clarification in the counseling psychology literature. In discussing the scientist–practitioner model and the role of research in counseling psychology, authors need to differentiate them.

As noted by Gelso et al. (1988), empirical research is done within the broader context of science. In such research, the investigator ordinarily imposes controls so that his or her observations will lead to nonbiased conclusions about the phenomena under study. Usually, but not always, there is a degree of quantification in counseling psychology research. The purpose of research, as discussed by Gelso et al. (1988), is to contribute to a body of knowledge that, together with theory, constitutes the scientific endeavor.

Note here that theory, as well as research, is part of the scientific endeavor. Too often in counseling psychology and other specialties and fields, the fact that theory and research go hand in hand in science is forgotten (Gelso, 2006). In producing hypotheses, theories provide the subject matter that research studies seek to test (of course, theories themselves vary greatly in how formally, coherently, and comprehensively they are stated). In turn, research results serve to revise and refine theoretical hypotheses. This reciprocal process has been referred to as "the cycle of scientific work" (Strong, 1991, p. 208).

Of the three concepts (research, science, and scholarly work), science is the hardest to define clearly and simply. That is because science is many things. Not only does science consist of theory and research, as discussed above, but it can also be seen as an attitude, a method, and a set of techniques. (For clear and interesting elaborations, see Heppner et al., 2008; Howard, 1985; Rychlak, 1968.) For present purposes, science may be viewed as an attitude and method that place a premium on controlled observations, precise definitions, and repeatability or replicability. The scientist controls variables to rule out competing explanations; he or she clearly defines terms, operations, and procedures so that other scientists may understand what is meant and are able to replicate the investigation. In order for a scientific theory or research finding to be accepted as valid, the events or phenomena being observed must be replicable. The value placed on control, precision, and replicability in science applies to both scientific theory and scientific research.

As indicated by Gelso et al. (1988), scholarly work or activity is the most general of the three concepts (research, science, and scholarly work). It includes intellectual activities that may go well beyond what we ordinarily consider as science (e.g., philosophical inquiry, historical analysis, thoughtful but nonquantified and minimally controlled analyses of counseling cases). We may define scholarly work as a disciplined and thoughtful search for knowledge and understanding. Although it may not include the degree of control, precision, and replicability characteristic of science, the search for knowledge inherent in scholarly work is nonetheless disciplined.

SCHOLARLY WORK AND THE COUNSELING PSYCHOLOGIST

A key point to this discussion of research, science, and scholarly work is that when we discuss the scientist side of the scientist–practitioner model in counseling psychology (and other applied specialties in psychology), we are concerned first and foremost with training effective scholars. Such individuals thoughtfully and creatively seek to understand phenomena in counseling psychology, seek to understand deeply, and communicate that understanding to others (for example, in written papers and conference presentations). It is within this intellectual context, as Gelso et al. (1988) proposed, that we promote students' functioning as scientists and empirical researchers.

Let us now return to the discussion of what ought to be expected from the scientist side of the scientist–practitioner model. To recapitulate, we looked at three ways in which being a scientist within the model is manifested: (a) reviewing and applying research findings to one's practice; (b) thinking scientifically and carrying out one's work scientifically; and (c) actually doing research as part of one's career, regardless of one's job setting.

The expectation that the counseling psychologist be able to review and apply research is the least demanding of the three approaches, whereas the expectation that he or she actually do research is the most demanding. Is this latter expectation realistic and viable? Perhaps, though it may be difficult to accomplish. As affirmed by many observers (e.g., Gelso, 1979a, 1979b, 1993; Gelso & Lent, 2000; Heppner et al., 2008; Magoon & Holland, 1984; Scheel et al., 2011; Whiteley, 1984b), there is, and probably will always be, an ongoing need for more and better research in counseling psychology. Faculty who train counseling psychologists should do everything possible in the training situation to promote students continuing their research after obtaining the doctorate.

It is also true that many counseling psychologists are in work settings (e.g., community mental health settings, private practice settings) in which carrying out empirical research is extraordinarily difficult. Also, some counseling psychologists (no matter how inspiring or competent their doctoral training) simply do not have the inclination or perhaps enough of the kinds of abilities needed to do empirical research. Many of these people can do very effective scholarly and scientific work other than empirical research. Thus, for example, developing theories and treatment approaches and publishing these in the professional literature can be highly scholarly and can contribute significantly to science as well as good practice. One who writes conceptual articles that are clinical theory papers, hypotheses developed from individual cases, and so forth effectively satisfies the dictates of the scientist side of the scientist–professional model. Such activities are more viable than empirical research in some settings.

Another way in which practitioners may be able to participate more fully in doing empirical research is with the practice-research network (or PRN). As a response to the idea of "empirical imperialism" (see Lampropoulos et al., 2002) in which the empirical findings of a few (researchers) dictate the evidence-based practice of the many (practitioners), a new strategy has emerged to rely more heavily on the experience of practitioners in designing and implementing useful clinical research. In the PRNs now being developed (Castonguay, Locke, & Hayes, 2011), a fully collaborative relationship between researchers and practitioners results in both "scientifically rigorous and clinically relevant research" (Castonguay et al., 2011, p. 107).

The Pennsylvania Psychological Association launched what is possibly the first PRN study (see Borkovec, Echemendia, Ragusea, & Ruiz, 2001). In a follow-up study, considered to be the first PRN process study of its kind, Castonguay et al. (2010) examined helpful and hindering events in psychotherapy sessions in an attempt to replicate previous findings (Llewelyn, 1988). Although only one of Llewelyn's (1988) findings was replicated (the clients' perceptions of the helpfulness of problem solution), Castonguay et al. suggested that they had more confidence in their study's findings due to the benefits of a larger sample and more statistical analysis and to the collaborative nature of the paradigm (i.e., both researchers and practitioners devised the research questions, methods, and analyses). We expect to see more PRN studies in the future (e.g., Andrews, Twig, Minami, & Johnson, 2011), as the strategy allows for a different window through which research questions are seen and also allows psychologists to participate more fully in the scientist–practitioner model.

In summary, scholarly and scientific work should be part of the counseling psychologist's job activity, regardless of job setting. The particular kind of such work that is done will depend on a host of factors, most notably, the job demands and facilities of the specific setting and the inclinations and abilities of the individual counseling psychologist. In regard to setting, those who work in university settings, especially in academic departments, will have the most favorable climate and the most concretely facilitative environment for the conduct of empirical research. Those who work in private practice and other agency-type settings will typically have the fewest practical and psychological facilities for doing research. Unless they are exceptionally motivated and/or are able to collaborate with colleagues in more favorable settings (e.g., universities), research will not get done. But again, scholarly work can and should be contributed by counseling psychologists in all settings.

Investigative Styles: A Typology for Quantitative Research

Although we have been discussing scholarly activities that are viable alternatives to research within the scientist–practitioner model, the fact that empirical research has always held a highly prominent place in counseling psychology should be underscored. The next section of this chapter is devoted to a key research issue in the field: a classification of quantitative research approaches. The student of research methodology knows that there are a great many key issues in counseling psychology research, as well as in psychological research in general. One could devote many pages to topics such as selection of criteria, use of control groups, reliability and validity of measurements and instruments, and statistical issues. Rather than examine topics such as these in a superficial manner (as would be necessary in a book that covers the entire specialty of counseling psychology), we have chosen to focus on the research approaches that seem fundamental to understanding counseling psychology research. (Heppner et al.'s 2008 book on counseling research provides a comprehensive treatment of the entire range of counseling research issues.)

In the present section, we discuss a way of classifying quantitative methodologies that should aid the reader in understanding counseling psychology research generally. As one of the authors had earlier suggested (Gelso, 1979a, 1979b) and as has been empirically verified (Ponterotto, 1988; Scherman & Doan, 1985), one can classify most quantitative research in counseling psychology into four basic types or approaches. Each of these four types has its own advantages and disadvantages, and it is important for the student of counseling psychology research to understand these.

To arrive at the four types of research in question, it is useful to think of counseling research as existing along two basic dimensions. One of these dimensions reflects the degree to which the experimenter or researcher controls or manipulates the independent variable (the variable or variables that are considered to have the experimental effect). As shown in Table 4.1, studies can be divided into those that are manipulative (high control of the independent variable) and those that are nonmanipulative (low control).

Note that in Table 4.1 this dimension of degree of control is termed an internal validity question. That is because the extent to which the researchers manipulate or control the independent variable relates very closely to the internal validity of the study; that is, how clearly they can say that the variable(s) they presume to be producing the experimental effect, and not other variables, are the ones that are in fact having that effect.

TABLE 4.1

A System for Categorizing Types of Research

		Degree of control of independent variable (internal validity question)	
		A Manipulative (high control)	B Nonmanipulative (low control)
	A Laboratory	Type AA Experimental analogue	Type AB Correlational analogue
Setting (external validity question)	B Field	Type BA Experimental field	Type BB Correlational field

Note. From "Research in Counseling: Methodological and Professional Issues," by C. J. Gelso, 1979, *The Counseling Psychologist, 8*(3), p. 13. Copyright 1979 by Charles J. Gelso. Reprinted with permission.

The second dimension of counseling psychology research is labeled Setting in Table 4.1. As shown, there are basically two settings: the laboratory and the field. Laboratory studies are usually simulations of the activity they are studying, whereas in field studies, the researcher examines the actual activity (e.g., counseling) in its natural setting.

Whereas the first dimension, as discussed above, related directly to internal validity, this second dimension relates to external validity—the extent to which one can generalize the findings from this particular study and this particular sample to the actual activity and population of interest. For example, if one studied career counseling with a sample of college students, the question of external validity would ask to what extent the findings could be generalized to career counseling, as practiced outside of the experiment (for example, in actual college counseling centers). In general, studies done in field settings are high on external validity (one can generalize from them), whereas those done in laboratory settings contain some problems with external validity. These issues shall be explored more fully as we examine the types of research below. The reader is referred to Cook and Campbell (1979) for a classic work on internal and external validity issues in research and Heppner et al. (2008) for a more recent discussion.

As evidenced in Table 4.1, when one combines the two levels of the degree of control dimension (manipulative and nonmanipulative) with the two levels of the setting dimension (laboratory and field), four types of quantitative research, or investigative styles, result. Before examining how each of these operates in counseling psychology research, we must underscore that categorization systems such as these are inevitably simplifications. In the real world of counseling psychology research, studies usually vary in the extent to which they represent a given type, and studies often are mixtures of the four types. Yet, such simplifications can be very useful in understanding the strengths and weaknesses of different approaches.

RESEARCH STRATEGY AA: THE EXPERIMENTAL ANALOGUE

The first investigative style, the experimental analogue, is considered experimental because the researcher has full control over the independent variable (in counseling, for example, the treatment, who gets it, and when). The researcher controls the independent variable (IV), ordinarily through assigning participants to different treatments randomly and determining when the treatments are offered. Thus, for example, in an experimental analogue study on counseling, the researcher may randomly assign college students who are seeking course credit for their participation to different types of 30-minute treatments and perhaps to a control group for which treatment is not given. The groups receiving different treatments are compared to each other and with the treatment control group. Alternatively, the researcher may conduct what is called a within-subjects experiment in which the participant gets each of two or more different treatments, with the order in which he or she receives them being determined randomly (called *counterbalancing order*).

If assignment to groups was random and if all treatments were offered at equivalent times, the researcher is in a good position to conclude that the experimental effects were due to the treatments and not to other, extraneous variables. Such a conclusion is likewise warranted if the client or participant received each treatment and the order in which they were offered was alternated among participants. In other words, the experimental control allows for strong causal inferences. If the researcher manipulates IVs in a highly controlled situation and finds changes in the dependent variables (those being affected) that follow the manipulation, he or she can safely conclude that it was the IV that had the effect.

So far we have been discussing how the experimental analogue is experimental. These comments reflect general thinking in psychology and other fields about what constitutes an experiment and what kinds of conclusions an experiment permits. The experimental analogue, however, is also an analogue of something we are interested in studying. That is, the analogue does not study the activity directly in a real-life situation; rather, it studies the activity by analogy, in one way or another, by approximating or simulating the activity.

Analogue research within counseling psychology most often studies an intervention. This intervention may be any of a wide range of activities or treatments in which the counseling psychologist is involved. Some examples of these are counseling, psychotherapy, consultation, guidance, assessment, supervision, training, and teaching. Again, the intervention is studied not as it actually is or naturally occurs but instead as it is approximated by the researcher. Also, it should be understood that the typical analogue examines some aspect of the intervention rather than the entire intervention.

In the context of a given intervention, the experimenter may study the effects of any of an almost infinite array of independent variables and an equally wide range of dependent variables. Among the manifold aspects of counseling, for example, one can study the effects of (a) counselor techniques, behavior, personality, appearance, intentions, or style; (b) numerous client characteristics; and (c) different kinds or characteristics of treatments. In a like manner, the researcher may examine the effects of such variables on various client and counselor behaviors, perceptions, reactions, and so on. Here we can look at how the independent variable (or variables) affects some aspect of the client's behavior, some aspect of the counselor's behavior, some aspect of their interaction, or all these. Typically, the IV is manipulated by using an audiovisual design in which the participant is presented with a stimulus tape or film of a counselor, client, or both. (In some designs, the participant meets an actual person, a confederate or actor, who exhibits predetermined behaviors or characteristics.) The researcher has complete control over what transpires on the tape or film.

An example of an audiovisual analogue is an experiment by Yeh and Hayes (2011). These experimenters wanted to better understand the differential effects of therapist self-disclosures (specifically of more and less resolved countertransference issues, a topic covered in more depth in Chapter 11) on perceptions of the therapist and the quality of the therapy session. College student–participants were assigned to two different conditions: one in which the therapist disclosed unresolved personal issues and one in which the therapist disclosed more resolved issues. The students logged onto a website (using a secure password) to watch the 12-minute video and then answer a number of surveys about the therapist and the therapy. In particular, Yeh and Hayes assessed participants' perceptions of the therapist's trustworthiness, expertness, attractiveness, and the extent to which participants believed the therapist provided hope to the client and was similar to the client (i.e., universality). They also measured the students' perceptions of the session's depth (i.e., whether the session stayed at a superficial level or delved into deeper material) and smoothness (i.e., how smooth or difficult the session seemed).

The assessment included what is called a *manipulation check*, in which the researchers ask a question (in this case, "Did the therapist make any statements revealing personal information during the session?" and "Was the information that the therapist revealed based on personal difficulties with which he still struggles?") in order to be sure that their intended manipulation of the independent variable (here, the disclosure of resolved or unresolved personal issues) was indeed perceived by the participants. Yeh and Hayes (2011) found that disclosures of resolved personal issues were associated with perceptions of the therapist as more trustworthy and attractive and as better at providing hope. Yet, there was no difference in perceived expertise of the therapist or in the perceived depth and smoothness of the session when the therapist revealed resolved or unresolved conflicts. These findings support other research in the field that suggests that therapist self-disclosures in general are well received by clients.

Evaluation of the Experimental Analogue in Counseling Psychology Research

The laboratory analogue has a number of strengths and weaknesses that must be kept in mind when conducting and reviewing research. On the positive side, it permits precise control of variables in a tightly controlled setting. The researcher is able to isolate some very specific variables for study, as in the Yeh and Hayes (2011) study of therapist self-disclosure.

Not only can specific variables be isolated and tightly controlled, but the experimenter can manipulate variables to an extent that is not possible in actual counseling. Thus, in actual counseling conducted in, for example, a counseling center, the researcher could not possibly have counselors limit or modify their behavior with clients in a way that prohibits them from doing the best job possible. Contrary to the Yeh and Hayes (2011) experiment, for example, actual therapists are unlikely to self-disclose in any particular session; nor would researchers be privy to which disclosures are of resolved issues and which are related to unresolved ones. The researcher cannot manipulate variables as freely in the real world of counseling because of ethical considerations. Ethics must of course always be an issue in considering experimental control (see also Chapter 3).

Probably the most fundamental strength of the experimental analogue is that because it tightly controls and manipulates, it allows for strong causal inferences. If an experimental effect occurs, we can have a high degree of confidence that the effect was a function of the independent variable(s) and was not due to other extraneous factors.

As in all research strategies, though, all is not methodologically well with the analogue. In a certain way, its very strengths are its weaknesses. In isolating specific variables and in rigorously controlling them, we violate nature, so to speak. To isolate a variable, we must pull that variable out of its natural context. Again using the Yeh and Hayes (2011) experiment as an example, type of self-disclosure was the only response that varied in the taped vignettes, as the other responses (e.g., open-ended questions, minimal encouragers) were scripted to be identical. This response was carefully isolated and was manipulated in that different participants heard different kinds of self-disclosures. When we isolate variables in an analogue, the effects of that variable may be assessed in and of themselves, but we cannot know if they would occur in a like fashion in the real world. In this way, internal validity is enhanced at the expense of external validity.

To maximize experimental control, laboratory research inevitably simplifies the phenomena it studies. As implied above, the whole package is not studied but only its contents. The question about this is always "Have we simplified too much, such that the findings are not really relevant to the treatment we sought to study?" In counseling psychology there is currently a great deal of sensitivity to this issue, and analogue researchers are seeking to develop simulations that are as realistic as possible.

Despite attempts to make analogues as realistic as possible, it should be clear, there will always be an artificiality to them by their very nature.

Because of artificiality and the attendant problems of generalizing analogue results to real counseling, the ultimate usefulness of the laboratory analogue has come under scrutiny in recent years. The merits of this approach have been debated, hotly at times (e.g., Forsyth & Strong, 1986; Gelso, 1979a, 1979b; Gelso & Fassinger, 1990; Goldman, 1979; Heppner et al., 2008; Stone, 1984). Some believe that research by analogy is not of particular value and might best be done away with or conducted only under very special circumstances. Indeed, whereas in past years many experimental analogues appeared in leading counseling research journals (Scherman & Doan, 1985), the number has reduced rather dramatically in recent years. Scheel et al. (2011) examined research articles in the journals *The Counseling Psychologist* and the *Journal of Counseling Psychology* from 1979 to 2008 and found a steady drop over time in published analogue studies.

We believe there is still a valuable place for the experimental analogue in counseling psychology research. It is one's research question, above all, that should dictate the research approach taken (Heppner et al., 2008), and for some questions, the experimental analogue is an excellent strategy. For many questions, an analogue experiment is the best approach, and for some it is the only viable method. Some studies, again because of the questions being asked, require the tight control and precision allowed for by the analogue. In the Yeh and Hayes (2011) example, because self-disclosure is infrequently used by counselors, it would make no sense to study session after session of therapy in hopes that one could catch an example of therapist self-disclosure. Also, for ethical reasons, there are many important questions that simply could not be studied in real-life counseling. For example, studying the impact of poorly delivered clinical interventions would not be morally sound with actual clients. Moreover, as long as their inherent limitations are appreciated and efforts are made to produce sound simulations and enhance their realism, experimental analogues will continue to serve an important role in the counseling psychology research literature.

RESEARCH STRATEGY AB: THE CORRELATIONAL ANALOGUE

The correlational analogue, the second research approach, is similar to the experimental analogue in that it is an approximation or simulation of some intervention situation. Also, the correlational analogue does not ordinarily occur in a real-life intervention setting but rather in a laboratory setting that itself is a simulation of the natural intervention setting.

It should be noted that even when the correlational analogue (or the experimental one, for that matter) occurs in a natural setting—for example, a university counseling center office—it is still an analogue. That is because, although the actual physical setting may be naturalistic, real-life counseling as it typically occurs is not being investigated.

The correlational analogue is unlike the experimental analogue in that the design is correlational rather than experimental. It is correlational in nature because independent variables are not manipulated; random assignment (e.g., of participants to treatments) does not occur. Essentially, the researcher does not have full control of who receives which experimental condition at what time. What does happen in the correlational analogue is that the researcher examines how two or more variables are related to one another in a controlled context. An almost infinite array of variables may be studied in this manner, although it is important that the selection of variables be guided by some theory or sound reasoning (and preferably both).

It must be underscored here that the AB strategy's correlational aspect in no way relates to the type of statistics used to analyze the data in a study. One may use correlational statistics (e.g., correlation coefficients) in experiments; likewise, one may examine the differences between means for different groups in a correlational study. Correlational and group difference statistics are essentially interchangeable mathematically. Our use of the terms *correlational* and *experimental* pertains strictly to the experimental operations used, to the extent to which variables are isolated, manipulated, and controlled.

The fact that the AB strategy is correlational has profound implications for what we may conclude about the findings. That is, we may conclude that variables are systematically interrelated, but we cannot draw strong causal inferences. We cannot know what causes what. For example, if a researcher finds that, after a 30-minute interview, degree of counselor empathy is closely related to whether or not interviewees would want to be counseled by that person (should they desire counseling), we cannot know that empathy caused the wish to see the counselor. It is equally plausible that participants who would want to be counseled possess qualities with which counselors easily empathize.

The axiom that "correlation does not imply causation" underlies an interesting paradox in psychological research. As a result of correlational findings, we cannot infer causality based on our methodology. Yet, we can and, in many cases, should theorize about what causes what, and, further, we can use correlational research to test theories about what causes what. In testing the theory, for example, that counselor empathy is causally related to the client's wish to be counseled by the counselor in question, a correlational study will support the theory in that, if we find the hypothesized relationship, the theory has escaped disconfirmation (a relationship was, in fact, found to exist).

Let us examine an example of a correlational analogue. Williams and Fauth (2005) invited licensed therapists and advanced doctoral students to provide one session of counseling with undergraduate students who had volunteered to be clients. The student "clients" presented real issues related to academic, emotional, or relationship concerns. The sessions were held in the laboratory and videotaped, and they were followed by a videotape-assisted process review (Hill et al., 1994). Williams and Fauth (2005) were interested in studying the therapists' experiences of in-session self-awareness (defined as "therapists' momentary recognition of and attention to their immediate thoughts, emotions, physiological responses, and behaviors during a therapy session," p. 374) and their use of particular strategies to manage hindering self-awareness. They also wanted to extend the current research to examine how self-awareness, an internal and personal experience, might manifest affectively or interpersonally in session and how clients responded.

The therapists and clients completed a number of measures, and a research team transcribed and coded the sessions. Williams and Fauth (2005) found that therapists did report moderate levels of in-session self-awareness and that they typically used basic techniques (e.g., question, reflection) to redirect themselves to focus on the client. However, there were no significant differences among the effectiveness of different management strategies. Williams and Fauth were surprised to find that therapists' in-session self-awareness was related to more positive client reactions, greater levels of therapist exhilaration, and lower levels of therapist stress. They suggested that the results might relate to their measurement of self-awareness; therapists rated their self-awareness on a continuum from hindering to helpful. However, it may be that even negative self-awareness (e.g., self-criticism) might be rated as helpful to the therapist. Without an experimental design, Williams and Fauth were not able to manipulate the variables in question and so could not draw strong conclusions about what caused what. They suggested that future studies tease apart the valence (e.g., negative or positive) of the self-awareness in addition to the perceived helpfulness.

In order to address covert issues in therapy (e.g., therapist self-awareness, client perceptions of the therapist), process researchers typically have used a postsession video recall strategy (see also Chapter 8). When they videotape sessions (and then have the therapists, clients, and sometimes observers review them), a laboratory setting is usually needed, thus creating a therapy analogue. However, because they allow sessions to unfold as naturally as possible, without manipulating the independent variable or randomly assigning participants to conditions, the correlational strategy is employed. Thus, the correlational analogue allows researchers to study phenomena to which they would not otherwise have access. However, it limits the researchers' ability to make causal inferences about their findings.

Evaluation of the Correlational Analogue in Counseling Psychology Research

The correlational analogue generally is not discussed as a research strategy or approach in itself. Writers sometimes mistakenly assume that analogues are by definition experimental. This assumption confuses control of the context of a study with control of the independent variables. As we have seen, the correlational analogue is indeed one of the approaches to counseling psychology research.

In terms of limitations, the correlational analogue, as an analogue of an intervention or situation, shares many of the problems of the experimental analogue, such as artificiality and external validity (generalizability). On the other hand, because researchers are not isolating and manipulating specific independent variables, the correlational analogue may be more realistic than the experimental analogue.

An example may help clarify how this increased realism is possible. Suppose you wanted to study in a laboratory context the relationship of counselor expertness to clients' self-exploration. In an experiment, you might arrange for counselor–confederates to behave in expert or inexpert ways. Client–participants would be assigned randomly to the expert or inexpert condition and asked to discuss some role-played problem in a 30-minute interview. This study is low in realism because counselors are required to behave in arranged ways and clients are asked to role-play. In fact, in experiments such as this, the "inexpert" counselor has been required to behave so ineffectually that she or he was less expert than would be conceivable in the real world (even granting that some counseling can be pretty awful). Now, contrast this with a correlational analogue in which, during a 30-minute session, counselors behave naturally while students recruited to participate in a counseling study discuss a real problem (which is ethically permissible because the counselors are doing their best; see Chapter 3 for a discussion of ethics in research). Trained raters could evaluate expertness and these ratings could be related to participants' self-exploration during the session (using whatever statistics best fit the specifics of the study). This approach is correlational in that the independent variable (counselor expertness) is not manipulated and what transpires obviously is a more realistic approximation of counseling than in the experiment.

The trade-off for the increased realism that is permitted in the correlational analogue is the inability in this strategy to make strong causal inferences. The correlational analogue is ordinarily far more controlled than the correlational field study (discussed later), but it is nonetheless correlational.

At this point in time, few studies appearing in counseling journals are correlational analogues. Yet, the AB strategy has some strengths that make it highly valuable. It allows for greater control (e.g., of the context) than the field study, greater realism than the experimental analogue, and perhaps greater convenience than any other strategy. Finally, although correlational analogues are not frequently used in and of themselves, correlational components are often incorporated into experiments. Thus, many studies have a correlational and an experimental component. Ruelas, Atkinson, and Ramos-Sanchez (1998), for example, did an interesting study that examined Mexican American and European American students' evaluations of counselors' effectiveness under four experimental conditions. These four conditions varied in terms of how much responsibility counselors attributed to clients for causing and for quitting their cigarette smoking habit. Each student read one of the four contrived transcripts in which counselors differed from one another in these responsibility attributions. The correlational component in this study was the Mexican American students' adherence to both Mexican and North American values, attitudes, and behavior (called *acculturation*). It was found that the four experimental conditions (varied on responsibility attributed to the client) did not differ in their effect on participants' evaluations of the counselor. However, Mexican American students' evaluations of the counselor were positively related to adherence to Mexican values, attitudes, and behavior (the correlational component). The more the participants adhered to Mexican values and so forth, the more positive were their perceptions of the counselor under all of the experimental conditions.

Incorporating a correlational component into an experimental analogue can be a powerful way of taking advantage of the strengths of both approaches. The advantages of this procedure have been discussed in greater detail in Heppner et al. (2008).

RESEARCH STRATEGY BA: THE FIELD EXPERIMENT

The third type of investigative style is called the *field experiment*. As shown in Table 4.1, the Type BA study is manipulative; the researcher has full control (or nearly so) over the independent variable—who gets which experimental treatment when. Random assignment of participants to groups or treatments occurs.

The term *field* implies that the intervention being observed is the real-life activity itself. For example, if one is interested in studying the effects of consultation, the field experiment would examine actual consultation. Typically, the term *field* also implies that the study occurs in the natural setting of the intervention. In counseling psychology research, that setting might be a counseling center, a community clinic, or a classroom. The basic feature of the field experiment, as we use this term, though, is that the real-life activity under study is being carried out (rather than an approximation of it) in a context that is not artificial.

In counseling psychology research, the field experiment usually investigates the effects of some intervention(s). When the Type BA study does look at the effects of interventions, it is called an *outcome study*. Such outcome studies will frequently compare the effects of an intervention on participants randomly assigned to one or more treatment groups and a control group, to treatment groups and more than one control group, or to treatment groups with no control groups. There are many methodological and ethical issues surrounding the use of control groups in experimental field research in counseling psychology; these are described in Chapter 8. Because of some of the methodological and ethical issues in the use of traditional control groups, alternative methods of forming and carrying out controls have been suggested and deserve consideration: established treatments as quasi-controls, time-abbreviated waiting periods as controls, and approximations of random assignments to control groups (see Gelso, 1979b).

As an example of the BA research strategy, Worthington et al. (1997) conducted an experiment in which a certain type of couples–marital counseling was evaluated. The treatment was called strategic hope-focused relationship enrichment counseling (SHRC). This counseling seeks to help couples enhance intimacy, resolve differences, and make commitments. Couples were assigned randomly to five weekly sessions of SHRC or to a control group in which participants completed three written assignments with no feedback but with a promise of treatment after the study ended. The counselors received special training in SHRC and followed the guidelines prescribed in a manual. Directly after counseling ended and 3 weeks later, couples receiving SHRC reported greater changes in satisfaction with their relationship (based on several measures) than did those in the control condition. The degree of positive change in the counseled couples was as much as that found in prior studies in which the counseling was of longer duration. One of the elements of this study that makes it a *field experiment* was the random assignment of participants to different experimental conditions (e.g., a treatment and a control group). Although random assignment is a key feature of an experiment, it is quite difficult to do in the field. Thus, more quasi-experimental field studies than true field experiments are typically found in the counseling literature.

As an example of a quasi-experimental field study, Chien, Fischer, and Biller (2006) used a pretest–posttest design to assess the effectiveness of a 12-week career training course. (It is considered "quasi" experimental because they did not randomly assign participants to classes, though they did check for initial differences between groups as part of the data analysis.) In particular, they were interested in examining the impact of a metacognitive approach used in planned happenstance theory (Mitchell, Levin, & Krumboltz, 1999). To test the approach in the field, Chien et al. chose four classes at a Taiwanese college. Two of the classes, one in the daytime and one in the evening, were classified as the "treatment groups" that participated in a 12-week career course emphasizing metacognition. There were two control groups; one was a daytime no-treatment control group, and one was a nighttime comparison group where students were in a career class that did not include a focus on metacognition.

Because the design was quasi-experimental (no random assignment), Chien et al. (2006) tested for initial differences between groups. As they found unequal pretest means on the measures, they conducted their analysis on gain scores (the pretest scores subtracted from the posttest scores). They found that the treatment groups gain scores were significantly different, with the treatment group showing more positive self-perceptions at the end of the course. The treatment groups also showed greater gains in motivation, time management, problem solving, and metacognitive competency. Chien et al. did note that there were also gains made by the comparison group (also receiving career development information) as compared to the control group. Despite some mixed results, they suggested that there were "notable gains" specific to the treatment groups trained in metacognitive approaches.

Evaluation of the Field Experiment in Counseling Psychology Research

Because it is a controlled experiment in a field setting, the BA research strategy combines scientific rigor with clinical relevance. The clinical relevance is high or at least is capable of being high, because the BA strategy investigates actual interventions or other phenomena in field settings in which these activities occur. As implied earlier, field experiments (and quasi-experiments) can be especially effective strategies if they incorporate additional independent variables; that is, IVs additional to the primary treatment variable. These variables are in practice often aspects of the client, the counselor, the intervention, the intervention situation, and so forth. No one experiment can look at more than a few factors, but the inclusion of one or more in addition to the main independent variable allows the experiment to move toward addressing the "who, what, when, where" questions that are so important.

Despite its positive features, the BA strategy is not without its limitations. A major difficulty is that field experiments are simply very hard to do. There are many practical problems in carrying out controlled experimentation in a field setting. For example, if a researcher plans to do an intervention study in a university counseling center, assigning clients randomly to different treatment groups, pretesting clients, posttesting clients, following them up, and perhaps assigning clients to control group conditions all create concerns in the agency setting. Not only are ethics an ever present issue, but if the experiment is not well organized, the research can create administrative difficulties in agency settings. This is a reason why one more typically sees quasi-experimental designs, in which there has been no random assignment.

In addition to being difficult to accomplish in many applied settings, the field experiment is limited in that it tends to examine global variables. When actual interventions are offered to recipients who are in an actual client role, inspecting specific variables that are elements of the treatment often is not possible. For example, in the Yeh and Hayes (2011) analogue experiment discussed earlier, the researchers could readily isolate one specific counseling technique (self-disclosure) for examination. In a field experiment, however, it would not be possible to offer counseling to clients, with the implicit promise that counselors are doing their very best, and then provide a treatment that was only a fraction of the promised intervention. Because field experiments ordinarily examine global variables, and laboratory studies are able to inspect specific variables (in a more precise manner), it can be extremely valuable for researchers to use both approaches in studying particular phenomena. In this manner, investigative styles can be combined to most effectively advance knowledge.

Because of the field's emphasis on studying phenomena in their natural settings (Gelso & Fassinger, 1990), we had forecast in the first edition of this book (Gelso & Fretz, 1992) that the percentage of field experiments in counseling psychology would remain high. However, that has not been the case. Much like the counseling analogue, field studies in counseling have decreased over time (Scheel et al., 2011), a finding particularly true for the experimental field study.

RESEARCH STRATEGY BB: THE CORRELATIONAL FIELD STUDY

What are the defining features of the correlational field study? Its most basic elements are that it is nonmanipulative and occurs in a field setting. The researcher does not seek to control the "when" and "to whom" of exposure to experimental conditions; no random assignment to treatments is attempted. As regards setting, the BB strategy takes place in the setting in which the phenomena being studied naturally occur; there is no attempt to simulate treatments, situations, or both. Overall, the correlational field study aims to look at relationships between and among variables as they occur naturally.

As we noted in examining the correlational analogue strategy, the fact that the BB strategy is correlational has nothing whatsoever to do with the kinds of statistics used to analyze the data. The researcher conducting a correlational field study may analyze his or her data with correlational statistics (e.g., correlation coefficients) or difference statistics (e.g., analysis of variance). Again, the key in the BB strategy is that the researcher studies the relationships between and among variables, as they occur naturally.

Whereas the three research strategies discussed earlier typically (though not always) examine the effects of some intervention (e.g., counseling, consultation, training, supervision) or elements of an intervention, the correlational field study may or may not focus on interventions. It may and often does study the interrelationships and among characteristics of the person (for example, between personality and behavior, thoughts and feelings, interests and choices, and so forth).

In attempting to understand the BB research strategy, one needs to examine its connection to what is usually called *naturalistic research*. It is common for observers of the research scene to view correlational field research and naturalistic research as one and the same, almost by definition. This view is incorrect. Although naturalistic research is invariably correlational field research, the reverse may or may not be true. What are the characteristics of naturalistic research? In a classic paper, Tunnell (1977) clarified that there are three independent dimensions of naturalness: natural behavior (part of the person's existing behavior and not instigated by the researcher), natural setting, and natural treatment (an event the participant would have experienced with or without the research).

Artificiality can occur along any of the three dimensions pointed to by Tunnell (1997). Consider the fairly common practice in correlational field research of testing participants at several points. To begin with, when we use a test of our making, we are imposing categories on the participant's responses, and that intrudes on naturalness (i.e., categories prevent participants from responding as they would naturally). The process of repeatedly testing participants also intrudes on the natural flow of behavior. So, a correlational field study may be very "nonnaturalistic" in certain ways, or it may be fully naturalistic.

As in the correlational analogue, the correlational aspect of the BB strategy has consequences for what we may conclude about its findings. For example, although we may conclude that the variables are systematically interrelated, we cannot conclude, on methodological grounds, that they are causally related. Also as noted earlier, however, we certainly may and should make causal interpretations on theoretical and subject matter grounds.

Let us now look at an example of a study using the Type BB strategy. Kasper, Hill, and Kivlighan (2008) examined *therapist immediacy* (defined as a focus on the here-and-now therapeutic relationship) in a case study. They intensively studied the case of a 24-year-old woman who received 15 sessions of counseling for which a duration limit was established at the beginning of the work. The client, called "Lily," was involved in extensive testing as part of the research. She took a battery of psychological tests before counseling, completed measures both before and after each session, and completed posttesting at 1 week and 4 months after ending counseling. Lily also participated in a 50-minute interview with the first author 1 week after the final session to discuss her reactions to the study. The therapist ("Dr. N") also completed measures after each session and participated in an interview 2 weeks after the final session to discuss his reactions to the study. All sessions were transcribed and rated by trained judges on immediacy and client involvement.

Kasper et al. (2008) found that therapist immediacy seemed to stimulate client immediacy, in that the therapist helped Lily express her feelings and feel emotionally closer to the therapist. They did note, though, that therapist immediacy "sometimes made the client feel pressured to respond, awkward, vulnerable, challenged, and hurt" (p. 293), thus acknowledging the complexity of immediacy. Just because there was evidence that immediacy generally evoked greater client expressiveness, it can sometimes have negative effects.

Although Kasper et al. (2008) is a field study in that "therapy as usual" was studied with no interventions or restrictions (with a client seeking treatment from a practicing psychologist), survey research is perhaps more typical of the BB strategy. For example, Dunkle and Friedlander (1996) hypothesized on the basis of prior theory and research that certain personality characteristics, as well as therapists' level of counseling experience, would be related to the clients' assessments of the quality of the working alliance between therapist and client. Seventy-three therapists completed measures of self-directed hostility, the quality of their social support network, and their degree of comfort with intimacy; one client of each therapist completed a measure of the quality of their working alliance. As predicted, the greater the self-directed hostility in therapists, the weaker their working alliance with their clients; on the other hand, the stronger social support networks and greater comfort with interpersonal closeness in these therapists were indicative of better working alliances. Contrary to prediction, therapists' level of counseling experience was not related to the strength of therapists' working alliances. Because of the correlational methodology, Dunkle and Friedlander were careful not to draw conclusions about what caused what, but they did offer interesting ideas about how the therapist factors (e.g., self-directed hostility) might contribute to poorer alliances.

Evaluation of the Correlational Field Study in Counseling Psychology Research

The Type BB approach has many strengths. More than any strategy, the correlational field study allows for the simultaneous study of many variables. At the same time, this strategy permits a relative lack of interference with natural processes of the phenomena being studied. Kiesler (1971) summed up the strengths nicely by stating that this type of research "represents a more comprehensive strategy, potentially dealing with multiple variables, thus bowing toward the admitted complexity of real-life events" (p. 55).

Perhaps the main overall strength of the correlational field study is its external validity. This is especially true when the BB strategy moves toward the naturalistic side of the continuum. The more we study natural behavior and events in natural settings, the more clearly we can generalize the results to the real world, which is, after all, what our theories are about. On the negative side, external validity is usually gained at an expense, and that expense is *internal validity*. In the correlational field study, as indicated, we cannot determine what is causing what on methodological grounds.

Qualitative Research Methodologies in Counseling Psychology

In earlier editions of this text, we included qualitative methodologies with correlational field studies. However, there are some notable differences in the research paradigms and philosophies of the two approaches, such as the use of statistics (in quantitative designs) and linguistics (in qualitative designs) and the "purpose" of the research (e.g., to test hypotheses in quantitative designs and to explore constructs that emerge from the data in qualitative designs). These paradigm differences have been referred to as *postpositivist* (quantitative focus on establishing approximation to a universal truth through the use of probabilistic statistics) and *constructivist* (qualitative focus on allowing ideas to emerge from the participants' views without intervention, a priori hypotheses, or statistical analysis). (See Ponterotto, 2005, for an excellent review of the terminologies used and assumptions made in different research paradigms.) Thus, in this edition of the text, we include qualitative methodologies as a separate category altogether.

Over the past several decades in counseling psychology, there has been a gradually building dissatisfaction with traditional research approaches and a corresponding interest in alternatives to traditional approaches (Borgen, 1984; Gelso & Fassinger, 1990; Haverkamp, Morrow, & Ponterotto, 2005; Heppner et al., 2008; Hill, 2012). Few of the advocates of qualitative approaches suggest that traditional methods are not valuable. They suggest that different approaches are needed to supplement, not supplant, traditional methods. McLeod (2011) explained that "the primary aim of qualitative research is to develop an understanding of how the social world is constructed" (p. 3). The idea that knowledge is "constructed" is what made qualitative research "alternative" at a time when traditional views in psychological research (e.g., postpositivist) held that the concept of "truth" could be found and approximated. When constructivist theorists began to challenge assumptions of "truth" (Neimeyer, 1993), the alternative or qualitative movement was launched, though the tenets of constructivism can be traced back to Kant's philosophy in 1781 (Ponterotto, 2005).

The 1980s was marked by numbers of conceptual papers advocating alternative approaches in counseling research (e.g., Hoshmand, 1989; Howard, 1984, 1985; Neimeyer & Resnikoff, 1982; Patton, 1984; Polkinghorne, 1984). By the 1990s actual research studies using qualitative methods began to appear in leading counseling journals, and such methods have since become both more valued and more common (Haverkamp et al., 2005; McLeod, 2011). O'Neill (2002) even went so far as to say that "qualitative research may (and perhaps should) replace the hegemony of quantitative methods in psychology" (p. 193). Although most researchers are not looking to replace one approach with the other, some have called for a balance in research methodologies where both qualitative and quantitative approaches are used and work together to ensure methodological pluralism (Haverkamp et al., 2005).

There are many specific approaches to research that can be grouped under the qualitative category (see Morrow & Smith, 2000), such as discourse analysis, grounded theory, and phenomenological approaches. A particular qualitative approach that is now in wide use in counseling psychology is the consensual qualitative research (CQR) method devised by Hill, Thompson, and Williams (1997; extended in 2005 by Hill et al., and again in 2012 by Hill). Well over 50 CQR studies have been published, and more than 50 doctoral dissertations have used the methodology in counseling psychology.

Hill (2012) overviewed the key components of CQR. She noted that the approach is inductive rather than deductive, in that the data analysis uses a *bottom-up* rather than a *top-down* approach. That is, researchers do not create hypotheses to test but rather allow results to emerge from the data in sometimes unexpected ways. CQR also uses open-ended questions in interviews to allow for the most data-rich responses possible. Although this approach makes it harder to code results (and the analysis takes considerably longer than in traditional quantitative studies), the results are never predetermined; nor are responses reduced to numbers (e.g., responses on a Likert scale). As such, CQR relies on words rather than numbers and highlights the importance of context. For example, have you ever filled out a traditional survey that asked you to rate your responses on a 1 to 5 scale (from *strongly disagree* to *strongly agree*)? And have you ever been frustrated, wishing you could explain the nuances of your response to the researcher? As a researcher, have you ever had the experience of participants creating new numbers (a rating of 3.5 when only whole numbers were offered) or writing explanatory responses in the margins? We rarely include these responses in typical quantitative research analyses. In qualitative research, however, we want to understand and include the nuances and full explanations of a participant's response.

Another difference with traditional quantitative research is that qualitative research, like CQR, uses small sample sizes of typically around 12 to 15 participants (Hill & Williams, 2012). Having a small sample allows researchers to use an interview method (which would be prohibitive with larger samples) and allows researchers to collect more in-depth data for each participant. Having a lot of data, however, can be challenging when research teams get to the analysis stage. How much does one include? How can researchers be sure they are not leaving out important information? We are traditionally trained to summarize and come to one point of conclusion in our empirical work. However, qualitative research demands that the researchers honor multiple viewpoints and resist coming to one "universal" conclusion. To reach these varied conclusions, CQR relies on consensus among research team members, a truly integral part of the method. The team works to honor the meaning of the participants' words while balancing their own expectations and worldviews and the different power dynamics often found in research teams. The strategies needed to help balance the participant and researcher voices are a critical issue. In doing so, CQR seeks to enhance the trustworthiness of the data analysis by attending to the integrity of the data (have the researchers provided enough information to the reader?), examining issues of reflexivity and subjectivity (i.e., the tension between what the participants said and how the researchers interpreted what they heard), and ensuring clarity in communicating results (Williams & Morrow, 2009). Finally, CQR researchers continually return to the original data to ensure clarity and accuracy (of representing the participants' views).

An early example of a qualitative study using the CQR method is that by Hayes et al. (1998). These researchers wanted to find out the causes and triggers of therapist countertransference (CT) and how CT is manifested during counseling sessions. In order to do so, Hayes et al. studied transcripts of eight expert therapists' responses to questions about their CT that were asked after each therapist completed sessions of time limited therapy. After reading these transcripts, Hayes et al. selected all instances of CT (defined as therapist's reactions stemming from his or her unresolved intrapsychic conflicts). The researchers found that CT occurred in 80% of the sessions that were studied, and, using a consensus method, they also determined that virtually all specific CT reactions could be placed into three general domains: the *origins* of CT in the therapists' lives; the *triggers*, or the events in therapy that elicited CT; and CT *manifestations*, or how CT was exhibited by the therapist in the hour. These findings were arrived at by the research team's reading transcripts, reaching consensus on what responses represented CT, and also coming to agreement on how therapists' responses about CT could be categorized. Most important, rather than determining which categories of CT to study in advance, as is typical of quantitative research, the investigators allowed the categories to be determined by their therapist–participants' responses to open-ended questions about their CT during sessions. Thus, these categories emerged from the data rather than from the investigators' hypotheses.

A more recent example of a CQR study is a study by Tuason, Güss, and Carroll (2012) on the experiences of displaced survivors of Hurricane Katrina in 2005. Tuason et al. chose to use a qualitative approach so as to allow participants the opportunity to tell their stories, "without prompts or premeditated hypotheses" (p. 289), about the experiences of having left their homes after a disaster and relocating to a new area. The hope was to provide insight into the physical, emotional, and spiritual challenges faced by displaced survivors, illuminated by the voices of the survivors themselves. Tuason et al. interviewed nine participants who had relocated from New Orleans after Hurricane Katrina. General categories identified (meaning those true for all participants) included feeling forced to start over, experiencing financial hardship, needing to fight for resources, and recognizing the need for self-reliance. Participants also reported losing trust in the government, experiencing inadequate health care, feeling isolated, and having a new appreciation for life. Their findings supported past research in which displaced survivors experienced heightened levels of stress (Madrid et al., 2008) and reported that the greatest challenge had been the task of rebuilding their lives (Zwiebach, Rhodes, & Roemer, 2010). The findings of the qualitative study, however, gave poignant voice to the survivors who had experienced such loss and devastation.

So why is qualitative research so useful? We have given two examples to illustrate the ways that qualitative research (specifically in these examples the CQR method) allows concepts to emerge from the data (without presupposing a theoretical framework), allows researchers to access internal thoughts and feelings, and encourages people in specific situations to share their voices, perspectives, and ideas. Although there are limitations (e.g., inability to control variables) as with any research strategy, qualitative research allows one to explore new ideas (that do not yet have a long track record of quantitative research behind them) and to expand on nuances found in traditional studies. It is our contention that qualitative and quantitative approaches to research create a strong balance to seeking explanations in counseling psychology and that both are necessary for a full and productive research environment.

The Bubble Hypothesis and the Search for Clinical Relevance

In this final section of the chapter, we offer a perspective on psychological research in general and counseling psychology research in particular. The aim is to clarify how each and every piece of research or, more broadly, approach to research possesses inevitable weaknesses and, especially, to demonstrate the inevitable connection between the weaknesses and strengths of all studies and research approaches. In addition to presenting this research perspective, the final section explores the issue of the relevance of research to counseling practice: the ways in which research may be relevant, the costs of relevance, and the consumer's role in making research relevant to practice. These issues are presented to show that the concept of relevance is complex and that the problem of perceived low relevance of research to practice does not have simple solutions.

One need be involved in only a tiny amount of research to begin to see what is so obvious to the experienced scientist—that each and every study is highly imperfect and that each contains some inevitable flaws. Each broad research approach also has strengths and weaknesses. Although one begins to see the inevitability of this with a little experience, what may be less clear is that weaknesses cannot be eliminated and that each attempted solution to methodological problems and shortcomings in itself causes another set of problems.

As a way of illuminating the phenomena discussed in the above paragraph, Gelso (1979a, 1979b) coined the term *bubble hypothesis*. This concept likens the research process to a sticker on a car windshield. Once a bubble appears in the sticker, it is impossible to eliminate it. Pressing the bubble simply causes it to pop up in another place. Each attempted solution causes a problem to appear elsewhere.

In order to clarify how the bubble hypothesis operates in counseling research, Gelso (1979a) offered two propositions:

a. Immutable trade-offs exist with respect to the choices the researcher must make in each and every phase of the research process. These trade-offs are most apparent in critical general areas such as the basic selection of a design, the choice of criteria, sampling procedures, decisions about the scope of the project, etc.

b. Solutions to problems of design themselves create problems, such that the partially subjective, partially objective choices as regards matters of design need to be based on formulations about which problems are least (and most) injurious to the research endeavor, the generation of knowledge in which the investigator is most interested. (p. 62)

In effect, every choice we make with respect to how we design a study entails a trade-off; every decision we make to solve one or a set of methodological problems, in itself, causes another problem or set of problems. Consider how the bubble hypothesis might apply to the strengths and weaknesses of each of the four investigative styles already discussed.

As but one example of the application of the bubble hypothesis to the general area of research methodology, one can examine what has been called the "rigor-relevance issue" in counseling psychology research (Gelso, 1985). The term *rigor* usually implies that a study is tightly controlled, or high on internal validity. That is, the design of the study allows an ample degree of certainty that the independent variables, rather than other, extraneous variables, are what produce the changes in the dependent variables. In other words, we have a good idea of what is causing what. Of the four research strategies discussed earlier, the AA strategy—the experimental analogue—is strongest in terms of internal validity.

In the experimental analogue, the researcher attains rigorous control at the expense of relevance. The greater the control, the less the operations of the study reflect what happens in real life (i.e., the less natural the procedures). In other words, we researchers attain internal validity at the expense of external validity.

To solve the problem of low external validity (low generalizability to the real world of whichever phenomenon we study), we can conduct a fully naturalistic version of the correlational field study. Obviously, in this case we have the greatest possible external validity, because nothing is tampered with by the experimenter. He or she simply observes and records what is happening, for example, in counseling. As discussed earlier, this external validity is gained at a cost. We now have proportionately reduced the ability to make sound causal inferences about what is causing what.

The reader is encouraged to think through how these trade-offs exist with respect to other aspects of methodology. In so doing, he or she may begin to wonder if we counseling psychologists can ever advance knowledge and improve our research techniques. As all research is flawed, should we just give up and settle for inferior studies? How is knowledge advanced if problems are inevitable in every study and approach?

Our answers to the above questions are optimistic and positive. Despite the inevitable limitations, we can and should design studies to answer most effectively the questions being asked. Even in the face of the bubble hypothesis, knowledge may indeed be advanced by studying topics from a variety of vantage points, each with its own sets of problems. To use an example discussed earlier, in studying the effects of the therapist countertransference, a number of different analogue studies (e.g., the Yeh & Hayes, 2011, analogue experiment) may be combined with a qualitative approach (e.g., Hayes et al., 1998), each with its own set of methodological problems. Convergent findings from these studies (again, each with its own set of weaknesses) allow us to have confidence that knowledge has been advanced reliably. The key concepts here are *continued study* (or programmatic research, as it is called), the use of a *variety of methods*, and the *convergence of findings under conditions of methodological diversity*.

In recent years, great concern has been expressed in counseling psychology and other applied psychology specialties that our research is not sufficiently relevant to our practice. Some critics have attacked research, especially experimental research, as being irrelevant because of an obsession with control and quantification (Goldman, 1978, 1979). Others have proposed that the problem of is low relevance because traditional research models view humans as passive recipients of stimuli, whereas counseling practitioners see humans as active agents whose goals, plans, and intentions determine their behavior (see Howard, 1985). This profound difference in the image of humans held by scientists versus practitioners, according to Howard and others, makes for a poor fit between science and practice and, thus, the low relevance of research to practice.

The belief that research should be highly relevant to practice is perhaps most clearly expressed in what was called the "test of relevance" a number of years ago by one of the leading researchers in the field (Krumboltz, 1968). According to Krumboltz's (1968) test of relevance, for any piece of research to be worthwhile, it must have an effect on what counselors do in their practice. Research that does not affect what counselors do is seen as "academic calisthenics" (Krumboltz & Mitchell, 1979, p. 50), and, by implication, probably should not be published in counseling psychology journals.

Although there is debate within the field as to just how relevant research typically is to practice (Castonguay, 2011; Cohen, Sargent, & Sechrest, 1986; Heppner & Anderson, 1985; Williams & Hill, 2001) and how relevant it ought to be, most researchers and practitioners do believe those in the field should continually work on relating research to practice.

In seeking to make research relevant to counseling psychology practice, however, we encounter certain difficulties that must be understood. In fact, we may be faced with a dilemma in the search to enhance clinical relevance. The kind of research that is most clearly relevant has been discussed by Gelso (1985) as *experience-near research*. In experience-near research, the questions being studied closely approximate those raised in practice (e.g., in counseling); the theory from which the research originates closely approximates the counselor's experience of what goes on in counseling; the methodology of the research closely approximates counseling; and the constructs being studied closely approximate those used in practice. Examples of the most experience-near research are the uncontrolled and unquantified case study in counseling, the variety of qualitative methodologies employed in counseling research (e.g., grounded theory), and counseling itself as a research method (as is popular in psychoanalysis, where analysis itself is seen as a research model).

The problem with experience-near research, and the source of the dilemma noted above, is that as we move more in that direction we become increasingly less sure of what causes what in the research and of how the findings generalize to other samples. This loss of certainty occurs because of the lack of control and quantification and because experience-near research tends to focus on the individual (as in the case study). *Experience-far research*, on the other hand, is better controlled and does allow for clearer explanations about what causes what. (The tightly controlled experimental analogue tends to be the prototype of the experience-far study.) Yet, as we move in the direction of experience-far research, perceived relevance is diminished. The research tends to capture less of the fullness, richness, and vitality of the intervention experience. We again are faced with the bubble hypothesis; experience-near (relevant) and experience-far (rigorous) research both have costs. And we cannot optimally advance knowledge and improve practice by simply doing research that has the greatest perceived relevance (experience-near research).

Despite these inevitable limitations, research can still be profoundly important to practice. It can help the practitioner think more clearly and in a less biased way about his or her practice and organize his or her ever-changing personal theory about whatever processes in which he or she is involved (e.g., consultation, teaching, therapy). In this way research is relevant, but it is indirectly rather than directly relevant to practice. One should not expect to apply research findings, even those based on experience-near research, directly to one's practice. Rather, findings help one refine one's theory of practice and think more clearly about that practice. When the issue of relevance is considered in this way, experience-far research is seen as highly relevant (indirectly) to practice.

In addition, research can be made relevant to practice only if the practitioner is an active agent in the process. All too frequently consumers of research expect to be able to read journals and have the relevance of the research strike them, without having to actively work at seeing the relevance. This passive approach is doomed to failure. If the reader is going to be able to use empirical research in practice, he or she must approach the reading with the notion of finding what is relevant. That is, the reader needs to take the attitude that he or she is going to look for what is relevant and actively think about how a given study may apply to practice. When one takes this active approach to reading research, it is striking to see just how many applications most pieces of research have.

Summary

Scientific research is vitally important to counseling psychology. It allows us to test our theories and improve them. Without scientific research, we would simply be acting out our biases in counseling psychology practice, and in the final analysis such practice would be ineffectual. Within the scientist–practitioner model, three levels of being a scientist have been explored: (a) reviewing and applying research findings to one's practice, (b) thinking and carrying out one's work scientifically, and (c) doing research as part of one's career.

In terms of counseling psychology research strategies, four prominent *quantitative strategies* have been explored in depth. These four strategies result from combining two dimensions: setting (field or laboratory) and degree of control of the independent variable (high or low control). The resulting strategies are labeled (a) the experimental analogue, (b) the correlational analogue, (c) the experimental field study, and (d) the correlational field study. Each of these four strategies has notable advantages and disadvantages. Combining strategies in certain ways may advance knowledge in the field maximally.

Qualitative methodologies also have been explored. Issues unique to qualitative research were described, such as the use of small sample sizes, the use of words rather than numbers, and attention to context (of both the participants and the researchers). In particular, consensual qualitative research was highlighted with examples from early and recent studies. As a bottom-line principle, the approach that should be taken in a given study is determined by the research questions the investigator seeks to answer.

Gelso's bubble hypothesis serves as a way of clarifying the inevitable advantages and disadvantages of every research strategy and of demonstrating how each decision the researcher makes about the design of a study contains a cost. The most basic features of this perspective on research are that inevitable trade-offs exist about choices the researcher must make at all stages of research and that solutions to problems of design create other problems. In effect, all studies are flawed to some extent. Knowledge is most powerfully advanced by the continuing study of a given topic through the use of a variety of methods, each with different methodological limitations.

Vocational Theory and Research

Milestones and New Frontiers

5

R esearch in vocational psychology not only is vast and ever growing, it is also the oldest and most distinctive area of research endeavor associated with counseling psychology. As described in Chapter 1, the origins of formal study of vocational behavior and counseling go back to 1909 with Parsons's development of a "vocations bureau." Growing out of societal changes related to industrialization and manufacturing (from a more agricultural society), advances in measurement and assessment, and the need to develop qualification criteria for military jobs during World War I (Walsh & Savickas, 2005), vocational psychology found its place in the study of the individual and the fit between the individual and the environment (Larson, 2012). In the 1930s and 1940s, while industrial psychologists moved to study industry itself (e.g., worker productivity, employee selection criteria), vocational psychologists (who formally became counseling psychologists in 1946) sought to study the needs and career choices of the

http://dx.doi.org/10.1037/14378-005
Counseling Psychology, Third Edition, by C. J. Gelso, E. N. Williams, and B. R. Fretz

individual. Thus, the focus of vocational psychology from its beginnings has been on the central values of counseling psychology:

1. an emphasis on an individual's strengths and optimal functioning;
2. a focus on the whole person over the course of the life span;
3. an ongoing awareness of the importance of environmental context;
4. a concentration on brief, educational, and preventive counseling interventions; and
5. a dedication to the scientist–practitioner model.

Yet, though programs of research and counseling related to vocational behavior are located primarily in counseling psychology programs, this unique location does not signify that counseling psychologists are the only professionals attending to career issues. Vocational psychology shares endeavors mostly with industrial/organizational (I/O) psychology. Further, the study of vocational behavior brings counseling psychologists into interdisciplinary contact with sociologists and economists. These professions often focus also on "world-of-work" problems, using approaches and methodologies common to their own specialties, though more typically from the systems or industry perspective and less so with the perspective of the individual.

This chapter explores the exciting developments that seem to be emerging from what we view as expansions and shifts in the paradigms that have previously been employed in the study of vocational behavior. These changes have occurred as counseling psychologists have experienced sociocultural and economic changes in the world of work and as researchers articulated and reflected on the inadequacies of earlier theoretical developments. These new developments hold great potential for advances in both the theory and the practice of vocational psychology, helping the field address some ongoing and some new important social and individual problems related to the world of work. We thus review in this chapter changing forces in the world of work, emerging theories of vocational behavior, and research on life span issues of particular interest to counseling psychologists (e.g., the school to work transition, adjustment to work, work–family balance, job satisfaction and health, retirement planning).

The Changing World of Work

At the very beginnings of career psychology (Parsons, 1909), the focus of counselors' work with industries was to select appropriately skilled workers. After World War II, counseling psychologists, along with I/O psychologists, became increasingly involved with industry and business in studying and intervening to improve levels of worker satisfaction and adjustment. I/O psychologists focused largely on *organizations* and how to get them to change in ways that would make employees more productive and satisfied. Counseling psychologists, on the other hand, focused more on *employees* to empower them to make changes in their worklife that suited each of their own complex roles and needs (Gerstein & Shullman, 1992).

Beginning in the 1960s, several changes in society and the workforce brought greatly expanded roles for counseling psychologists in the workplace. With an expanding economy but limited expansion in the workforce (the demographic bubble of "baby boomers" was still in school and college), companies increasingly turned to psychologists for assistance in selecting and training managers and executives. Committing errors in such selections is extremely costly, and the established role of psychologists in improving selection processes during World War II made them attractive to leaders of industry who were faced with selection problems. Counseling psychologists therefore gained roles in executive screening and coaching; from these beginnings the first career development centers emerged in some larger industries as places where employees could both complete assessments of themselves and participate in leadership development workshops that would prepare them for advancement. Although some employees might use such training to move to better positions in other companies, many companies felt that the in-house career development opportunities provided both employer and employee a better opportunity to determine advancement potential of employees and was therefore cost effective. The civil rights movement of the 1960s also brought new roles for counseling psychologists in the workplace. The "old-boy network" way of hiring and promoting no longer was acceptable. Psychologists were first called on for their assessment skills in designing and implementing equal employment opportunity programs. Now, industries more often seek the help of psychologists in designing and implementing human relations management programs that can help both employees and employers cope more effectively with issues of discrimination, harassment, and other forms of grievances.

Yet other roles for counseling psychologists in workplace settings emerged with the development in the 1970s of outplacement programs and employee assistance programs. These developments evolved quite differently. Outplacement programs and their close relative, preretirement programs, were initially a result of the combination of a sudden downturn in the economy in the early 1970s, along with extreme cutbacks in the aerospace and defense industries after the Vietnam War came to a close and men had landed on the moon. Suddenly, thousands of America's best and brightest engineers and the like, who had been hired by defense and aerospace industries directly out of college and had therefore never even really applied for a job, were facing unemployment in an economy that had few jobs for persons whose only career experience was in aerospace or defense. Many governmental agencies and large aerospace companies then developed programs to assist these employees in creating effective career plans and strategies to "translate" their prior work experience into résumés that would help them obtain new employment. Such programs had to deal not only with the realities of helping these persons make self-assessments and implement job searches but also with how to incorporate strategies for dealing with the psychological consequences of becoming unemployed (Mallinckrodt & Fretz, 1988). Pickman (1994) detailed the history, development, and offering of outplacement programs. Such programs have proved popular with soon-to-be-terminated employees as a kind of reasonable, "good-faith" effort by the terminating employer. Because such programs are not needed in good economic times, most companies now outsource such services, using them only in times when the economy and/or mergers require downsizing and a consequent dismissal of many long-term employees. Most counseling psychologists who practice as consultants to business and industry are able to offer individual and/or group outplacement counseling.

Preretirement programs are a close relative of outplacement in that they often were supported by companies in order to encourage early retirement of current employees. "Early out" retirement options remain one of the most attractive ways companies have of reducing their workforce. Today, such programs are seldom company run; rather, when a company, for whatever reason, needs to reduce the number of employees, it may offer older workers early retirement. To accomplish this, it contracts with consultants, such as counseling psychologists, who design and offer preretirement programs. We review many of the conceptual and research issues in counseling psychologists' work with retirement later in the chapter.

The development and evolution of employee assistance programs (EAPs) has been quite different from that of outplacement. EAPs emerged largely in the 1970s as company-run programs to reduce the direct and indirect costs of treating alcohol and substance abusers. Not only is it expensive to pay for such treatment in hospital or outpatient programs, but the employee has even more frequent absenteeism from work than that caused directly by substance abuse. Although severe cases still must be referred to hospital-based programs, many preventive, remedial, and follow-up services to hospital-based programs can be offered in the work setting. The employee can then achieve better attendance and also have a ready place to turn to for help during the workday and maintain the perception that the workplace does care about his or her situation. Such immediate accessibility to and perception of support are components of psychological services for anyone struggling with substance addiction.

The fact that employers perceived a value to the treatment of a problem in workplace setting, even when the problem was not totally related to the work environment, was a major breakthrough. Workplace treatment now went beyond simply emergency care for workplace injuries. In the relatively small number of published studies, the effects of EAPs are supported by a reasonable body of literature of significant results for both employees (better psychological functioning) and employers (lower direct and indirect costs for care of and performance by employees who are substance abusers; Myers & Cairo, 1992). Although many employee assistance programs initially employed primarily master's-level substance abuse counselors, as services have expanded in some EAPs, opportunities for doctoral-level psychologists providing a wide range of assessment and counseling services have increased.

In some cases employers have been quite ambivalent about a continued expansion of EAPs into "comprehensive mental health" facilities for reasons of both cost and company image. On the other hand, employers are far more enthusiastic about an interesting evolution in the 1990s: the emergence of occupational health psychology, with its more narrow focus on job-related stress. There is clear evidence that such stress leads to increased job turnover and negative mental health outcomes (Humphrey, Nahrgang, & Morgeson, 2007; Podsakoff, LePine, & LePine, 2007). New training programs in occupational health psychology have been developed as a direct outcome of collaboration between the National Institute for Occupational Safety and Health and the American Psychological Association. Several universities were funded to offer graduate-level curricula on the application of psychology to improving the quality of worklife and protecting and promoting the safety, health, and well-being of workers. Of the programs, the one most closely integrated with counseling psychology is at the University of Minnesota. Students in the University of Minnesota counseling psychology program have been able to minor in occupational health psychology and take courses and training in collaboration with the Industrial Relations Center of the Carlson School of Management, the School of Kinesiology and Leisure Studies, and the Center for Research on Girls and Women in Sport. Further description of the rationale for and the development of occupational health psychology training and service programs can be found in a special section of the journal *Professional Psychology: Research and Practice* (1999, Vol. 30, pp. 117–142).

In the 1990s, counseling psychologists began a number of research programs related to the components of programs for preventing stress in the workplace (Kagan, Kagan, & Watson, 1995; Roberts & Geller, 1995) and developmental programs for improved coping with occupational stress (Bowman & Stern, 1995). More recently, vocational psychologists have focused on developing interventions for those who are most at risk (e.g., those with fewer coping resources, higher perceived stress, and a strong personal emphasis on work as a central role in their lives; McKee-Ryan, Song, Wanberg, & Kinicki, 2005). The changing stressors in the job market, including the impact of globalization, layoffs, downsizing (Gysbers, Heppner, & Johnston, 2009), and the economic crisis of 2008 and beyond, suggest that counseling psychologists who have been trained in understanding how to intervene in career settings to reduce occupational stress will continue to have many opportunities in the coming years to assist workers and those seeking work.

In the past 30 years, one of the biggest changes in the world of work to affect counseling psychologists has been in the area of consultation. By the 1990s, as globalization of the economy required some severe cutbacks in services, in-house career development services were largely abandoned and replaced with outsourcing. A number of counseling psychologists who were once employed in industry-based career development centers simply shifted to individual or small partnership consulting practices (which we discuss in more detail below). These consulting practices offer a variety of services, ranging from executive development to human relations to stress management training for those managing mergers and acquisitions—what some psychologists have called "marriage counseling" for businesses. However, consultants may be found in a wide range of locations and roles, such as working with parents or teachers on understanding ways to enhance child development and classroom management strategies, creating a staff development plan for a company, or helping a university design new residential and student services programs. As consultation is typically an *indirect* service, meaning that the consultant works with a person, group, or system that will then apply the information directly to individuals, consultants share knowledge in ways that help the consultees apply the knowledge in service of the end clients.

Today, counseling psychologists continue to engage in various types of consultation (Cooper & Shullman, 2012), including mental health consultation, behavioral consultation, school consultation, and organizational consultation. *Mental health consultation* refers to situations in which consultants provide mental health information, such as to physicians, ministers, residence life staff, police officers, and teachers who may need to have a better understanding of the mental health needs and challenges of those with whom they have direct contact. In *behavioral consultation*, psychologists help consultees understand and apply basic behavioral principles (see Chapter 12) to specific situations. In *school consultation*, consultants help teachers directly (such as with learning strategies or classroom management) or help schools improve systemwide functioning. *Organizational consulting* focuses on interpersonal issues and organizational policies and processes to improve effectiveness in some area. One might find consultants in the education and training arena, program development, or problem-solving scenarios. As

Cooper and Shullman (2012) noted, "consulting psychology is a major area of psychological practice" (p. 853), one that covers a wide variety of roles and locations. Counseling psychology's focus on vocational psychology provides a training advantage for those interested in consulting work (Shullman, 2002).

Perhaps the biggest workforce change in recent years affecting vocational psychology has been the widespread availability and use of the Internet and social networking sites. An entire field, web-enabled career information and counseling (Osborn, Dikel, & Sampson, 2011), has emerged to address the issues that have arisen from the sheer volume of career information now accessible on the web. Some "virtual career centers" now provide services that are completely online. The use of online assessment instruments has long been a part of modern career counseling. For example, a computer-assisted guidance system, DISCOVER, was long a staple of career development centers. Although DISCOVER has been decommissioned, the publisher, ACT (originally called American College Testing but now referred to simply as ACT), is providing a new version, the ACT Profile, that includes many of the same features (including a revised interest inventory, abilities inventory, and values inventory). The features and approach are consistent with the past, but the new ACT Profile includes updated graphics and changes in how the end user accesses the information. ACT launched the new Profile in 2013. There are, of course, other web-based assessment programs out there (such as Focus) and some free access to established assessments, such as the Self-Directed Search (Holland, 1994). Probably the biggest change in this arena of technology has been the use of social networking sites (SNS) in the delivery of career services. Old-fashioned networking has been virtually replaced (pun intended) by SNS, weblogs, and "tweets"; however, the concept is the same—network with people to get the word out about a job search. Because this area appears to be ever changing, we direct the reader to check for regular updates, such as through the National Career Development Association's text *The Internet: A Tool for Career Planning* (Osborn et al., 2011).

Twenty-First-Century Frontiers: Paradigmatic Shifts and Expansions

We believe that when the centennial history of counseling psychology is written in the late 2040s, the beginning of the 21st century will be identified as a time of important expansions of theory and shifts in paradigms used for the study of vocational psychology. Before proceeding with an exploration of these shifts, we must explain what is meant by *paradigm* and the what, how, and why of paradigmatic shifts. Borgen (1992) provided an excellent description of the broader scientific issues in identifying paradigms and their impact. Citing Kuhn as the originator of the importance of paradigms, Borgen quoted Kuhn's (1970) definition of paradigms: "These I take to be universally recognized scientific achievements that for a time provide model problems and solutions to a community of practitioners" (p. viii). Kuhn noted that when there is a realization that things have gone wrong, or at least that there are some seemingly unremediable deficiencies in present models, scientists begin to "shift" to other sets of models or viewpoints to see if better predictions and understandings can be obtained.

Borgen (1992) chose to speak of *expanding* paradigms because he felt that many counseling psychologists were not abandoning traditional models but rather were using new theories and statistical techniques to make new analyses of old problems. Our next sections provide examples of paradigm shifts and expansions in the field, emphasizing theory developments related to foundational career theories (see Chapter 15).

PERSON–ENVIRONMENT RECIPROCITY AND THE ROLE OF PERSONALITY

Walsh and Chartrand (1994) captured the essence of the need for an expansion of the person–environment interaction paradigm: "The theories of career choice and development tend to say a great deal about selection or occupational fit, but very little about evoking, cognitively restructuring, and manipulating processes" (p. 193). Although those who adhered to trait-oriented theories (see Chapter 15 for a more detailed description) were among the first to recognize that there were interactions between persons and environments, the focus has long been simply on how one can use that interaction to achieve better fits between persons and jobs. What is needed is greater attention to the fact that work environments are dynamic, not static, and often change because of the nature of the individuals who have entered them (Schneider, 2008). And, probably just as often, individuals change because they learn new things about themselves as they seek to adjust to a work environment that is not a natural fit for them. In short, persons affect environments, just as environments affect persons. A good fit at any given time may well become less of a good fit if either the person or the environment changes.

As examples of the last sentence, consider what would happen to a work environment that generally attracts very hands-on, task-oriented people if suddenly there was an influx of people who were much more engaged by social and interpersonal issues. It is possible that there would be increased interactions between individuals, a greater willingness to be self-disclosing, and a greater tolerance for at least a little less preciseness. If the original task-oriented environment changes in that way, when a new task-oriented person enters that environment, the fit may not feel as "right" as it might have in the prior environment. So, the people changed the environment. On the other side of the coin is how environments can change the people in them. For example, many psychologists who are very high on "social" interests (e.g., those who tend to gravitate toward careers in counseling) have found in establishing private practices that they need to learn much more about what it means to run a business (something typically thought to be an "enterprising" trait). If a thriving practice has been established, those psychologists might take great pleasure in their learned business acumen and look for additional ways to increase their business-related skills. It could reasonably be predicted that they might at some future time show increased enterprising scores on interest measures (see Chapter 15). In short, their work environment had the power not just to change their behaviors or alter their skill sets but also to change their pattern of interests.

We have used the word *reciprocity* in the heading for this section to recognize that these changes are bidirectional. There is at least a growing appreciation of this reciprocal influence apparent in many career development theories in which causal affects going both ways between sets of variables have been explicitly included (Staggs, Larson, & Borgen, 2007). These expansions of theory generally reflect the use of newer statistical modeling techniques. Counseling psychologists are now beginning to understand that making predictions about vocational behavior requires an understanding of ongoing dynamic changes in both individuals and environments, each affecting the other. Although we even now may be able to achieve reasonably good predictions for a group of individuals, the dynamics of reciprocity will mean that making predictions about any given individual will always be less than perfect. In addition, though there is evidence that individuals tend to express stable interests over time (Low & Rounds, 2006), there is also evidence that interests do interact with the environment to produce changes (Betz, 2006; G. D. Gottfredson, 1999).

One of the most recent shifts in the person–environment theories has been the research into personality and temperament. Although interests relate to one's attraction to an environment or particular activities, personality traits and temperament seem more related to how one interacts with an environment (Low & Rounds, 2006). Several meta-analyses (Barrick, Mount, & Gupta, 2003; Larson, Rottinghaus, & Borgen, 2002; Staggs et al., 2007) have linked Holland's six interests (see Chapter 15) with the Big Five personality traits (neuroticism, agreeableness, conscientiousness, extraversion, and openness; McCrae & Costa, 1999, 2008). Larson et al. (2002), for example, found several stable relationships across these dimensions, including artistic and investigative interests with openness, enterprising and social interests with extraversion, and social interests with agreeableness. Barrick et al. (2003) found very similar relationships, with the addition of a relationship between conventional interests and conscientiousness. As Larson (2012) noted that "interests have been one of the most researched constructs in vocational psychology" (p. 162), we have little doubt that we will continue to see emerging theories, empirical advances, and continuing paradigm shifts in the trait-factor/person–environment approaches to vocational behavior.

CONSTRUCTIVISM AND ADVANCES IN DEVELOPMENTAL THEORY

Throughout the first and second thirds of the 20th century, social sciences, including psychology, relied primarily on the scientific paradigm of logical positivism (the paradigm that has so well served the physical sciences, such as physics and chemistry): Develop theories with logical proofs, then collect empirical data and determine whether the data support or refute the theory. However, in the social sciences there is general agreement that logical positivism has not resulted in theories that are nearly as productive and supportable as those in the physical sciences. During the last third of the 20th century, those social scientists who studied the philosophy of science and reviewed alternative paradigms increasingly turned to constructivism. Numerous monographs and books have been published in recent decades describing and illustrating constructivism. D. Brown, Brooks, and Associates (1996) concisely summarized the major propositions:

1. All aspects of the universe are interconnected; it is impossible to separate figure from ground, subject from object, people from their environments.
2. There are no absolutes; thus, human functioning cannot be reduced to laws or principles, and cause and effect cannot be inferred.
3. Human behavior can only be understood in the context in which it occurs.
4. The subjective frame of reference of human beings is the only legitimate source of knowledge. Events occur outside human beings. As individuals understand their environments and participate in these events, they define themselves and their environments. (p. 10)

A careful reading of these propositions makes evident the attractiveness of a constructivist approach to the study of vocational psychology. In one sense, constructivism is an elaboration and broad expansion of Rogers's phenomenological views (see Chapter 13); that is, persons' subjective perspectives of self and environment guide behavior. Yet, for vocational psychology, it was Super's foundational developmental theory of career choice and development (see Chapter 15) that provided the impetus for a constructivist paradigm shift in the field. In particular, as an outgrowth of Super's theory, career construction theory emerged (Savickas, 2002, 2005).

In this theoretical approach, people's unique narratives about the meaning they apply to work experiences give us an understanding of how they have "constructed" their careers. Counselors elicit these narratives or stories from an individual, looking for evidence of three primary constructs: vocational personality, life themes, and career adaptability. The concept of vocational personality relates back to earlier models of person–environment fit; in other words, how well does a person's interests, values, skills, and needs fit with the chosen occupational environment (Savickas, 2005). A person's life themes give information about the way a chosen occupation reflects the person's self-concept. Finally, career adaptability references the ways in which people construct the notion of career, from their behaviors and attitudes to their ability to cope with tasks, transitions, and difficulties (Savickas, 2005). Savickas (2002) presented a number of propositions to be tested, though more empirical research is needed (Larson, 2012). Career construction theory represents a paradigm shift for the field in that it introduces the necessary component of inherent subjectivity in career development, rather than looking for more objective "answers" to help guide career choices. Particularly in the fast-paced and rapidly shifting environment of today's workforce, helping individuals make meaning of their varying career experiences will become only more important.

THE SOCIAL–COGNITIVE REVOLUTION

In 1991, Borgen noted that "the cognitive revolution has quietly overtaken vocational psychology" (p. 279). Lent, Brown, and Hackett (1996) emphasized that "accompanying this quiet cognitive revolution has been an equally important trend toward viewing people as active agents in, or shapers of, their career development" (p. 373). Building upon both the social learning theory of Krumboltz (see Chapter 15) and the self-efficacy research on women's career development (Hackett & Betz, 1981), Lent, Brown, and Hackett (1994, 2000) developed a comprehensive model of career development that addresses interest development, vocational choice, and vocational performance.

Central to Lent et al.'s (1996) theory are the three primary variables from general social-cognitive theory: self-efficacy (Can I do this?), outcome expectations (If I do this, what will be the result or outcome?), and personal goals. As they explained, "By setting personal goals, people help to organize, guide, and sustain their own behavior. . . . Though environmental events and personal history undoubtedly help shape behavior . . . it is also motivated or animated, in part, by people's self-directed goals" (pp. 381–382). Their model also incorporates Bandura's (1986) triadic reciprocity; that is, fully bidirectional causal relationships between personal attributes, external environmental factors, and overt behavior. As an illustration of this reciprocity, consider Lent et al.'s model of how interests develop: When an individual believes he or she is interested in something, some intention is made to select and practice that activity. The actual performance attainment affects what individuals tell themselves about their skills and abilities. "Whether new interest emerges depends less on simple exposure and past reinforcement experiences than on how people read their competence (self-efficacy) at the activity and on their prospective expectations about obtaining prized versus nonvalued outcomes" (Lent et al., 1996, p. 385). In their models of choice and performance, like their model of interest development, a key component is always the feedback loop of not only what happens but also what conclusions the person draws from what happens (see Figure 5.1).

The specificity of the model, combined with statistical modeling techniques that can identify bidirectional causality, allows for more sophisticated hypotheses about the development of vocational behavior than do any of the other models we have reviewed in this chapter. Recent meta-analyses have confirmed that there is a strong relationship between self-efficacy and interests (e.g., Rottinghaus, Larson, & Borgen,

FIGURE 5.1

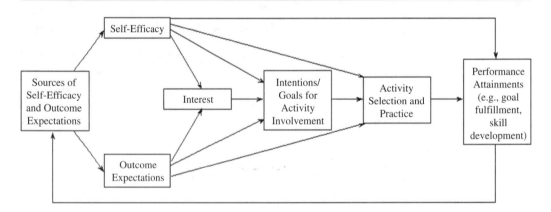

How basic career interests develop over time. This model highlights cognitive and behavioral influences during childhood and adolescence. From "Toward a Unifying Social Cognitive Theory of Career and Academic Interest, Choice, and Performance," by R. W. Lent, S. D. Brown, and G. Hackett, 1994, *Journal of Vocational Behavior, 45*, p. 88. Copyright 1994 by Academic Press. Reprinted with permission.

2003). For example, those who feel efficacious about their scientific abilities are likely to be interested in math and science (STEM) careers. Other studies have also supported the model's prediction that self-efficacy will be related to academic major (Larson, Wei, Wu, Borgen, & Bailey, 2007) and career choice (Betz et al., 2003). Research also supports the relationship between self-efficacy and outcome expectations (Ali, McWhirter, & Chronister, 2005) and between self-efficacy and occupational choice (Gore & Leuwerke, 2000). In 1992, Hackett and Lent suggested that the research clearly supported the proposition that self-efficacy has had unique and additive statistical power, over that of abilities and interests, in explaining variance in both development of interests and job performance. For example, if persons of lower levels of aptitude for a particular task are divided into groups of those who have higher versus lower perceptions of self-efficacy, those who possess higher levels will be found to perform better, even though their aptitude is no greater than that of the other group. For counselors, the most important data show that self-efficacy can be improved with "self-regulatory skills training programs" that provide ways of attaining better performance outcomes and of drawing more appropriate conclusions from those performances. When self-efficacy is improved, job performance improves (Lent et al., 1996).

Yet, the complexities of triadic, bidirectional interactions make it extremely difficult to create a generalized model that can predict the particular direction any one individual—or even group of individuals—will take in choosing or changing his or her vocational behavior. One might assume on the basis of the research, for example, that counseling psychologists should help individuals to increase their self-efficacy related to their work. However, ethnic minorities with long histories of realistic conclusions about discrimination may not respond to programs to increase self-efficacy without attention also paid to removing real barriers to success, such as institutional racism (see Chapter 6). Another potential problem with the idea that we should attempt to increase career self-efficacy is that there is evidence that persons who develop inflated senses of self-efficacy may create problems for themselves and/ or others (Silvia, 2003). There is much yet to be learned about the best educational and counseling strategies for modifying self-efficacy in efficient and effective ways that will enhance career choice and development. Yet, of all the theories reviewed in this chapter, this approach seems to have the greatest potential for more "giant steps forward" in career education and career interventions.

Theoretical advances continue to emerge. As Larson (2012) noted, "vocational psychology's vision is a mosaic with diverse viewpoints" (p. 168). We look forward to seeing more of the developing theory in vocational psychology as we move closer to counseling psychology's centennial.

Vocational Research Addressing the Developmental Needs of the Whole Person

In addition to seeing developments in vocational theories over time, we have seen greater attention paid in recent years to specific vocational issues that relate to the developmental needs of people at various life stages. We overview here those research areas highlighted by counseling psychologists that relate to the school-to-work transition, work adjustment, work–life balance, and retirement planning.

THE SCHOOL-TO-WORK TRANSITION MOVEMENT

Counseling psychologists have had a long-standing role in schools (Espelage & Poteat, 2012a), particularly in the area of the development of career education programs. Such programs were expanded rapidly in the 1960s as one way of responding to the challenge of the Russians being the first in space with their successful launching of *Sputnik*. America felt challenged to identify and channel its best students into greater achievement. The "Great Society" concepts of then-President Lyndon Johnson also included helping all students identify and realize their potential. Numerous counseling psychologists were involved in the design, implementation, and evaluation of career education programs throughout the 1960s and 1970s. Then, as noted earlier in this section, the narrowing of focus in public education to basic academic skills (i.e., the reduction or elimination of art, music, career education, etc.) resulted in significant restrictions in the continuation and development of such programs. Gysbers (1997) provided a review of the smaller but significant continuation of such concepts in some ongoing comprehensive guidance programs. In most recent years, we have again seen a strong governmental push in the K–12 school system with federal government mandates such as the 2001 No Child Left Behind Act and the U.S. Department of Education's Race to the Top program of 2009. We have also seen a new focus on emerging adulthood (age 18–25) in the literature (Arnett, 2000, 2004).

One of the long-extant criticisms of career education programs has been their focus on college-bound youths. The very concept of "career" hardly applies to the experience of all students, many of whom move right from high school years, often even before finishing high school, into the workforce. As the workforce became even more technological and service oriented and fewer jobs were available in unskilled or semi-skilled manufacturing plants, students who were not college bound were increasingly found to be unemployed, floundering in whatever jobs they did get, switching jobs frequently, and rarely finding chances for advancement. The discrepancies in pay for college graduates compared with high school graduates have steadily widened in recent years; when current pay rates are adjusted for inflation, contemporary high school graduates actually make less than high school graduates of their parents' generation. Concerns with these potentially costly social trends—costly to individuals in terms of their mental health, to society in terms of unemployment and welfare payments—led the federal government to pass, in 1994, the School-to-Work Opportunities Act. The purpose of this act was to support the development of partnerships between industries and schools so that high school students would receive more coursework and experience directly related to the kinds of work they might enter after graduating from high school. Ideally, such programs will result in students receiving, at graduation, a "skill certificate verifying that they have mastered occupational skills . . . [to] be used in any state to obtain employment" (Worthington & Juntunen, 1997, p. 331).

There are significant challenges for counseling psychologists who work with these work-bound, as compared to college-bound, youths. Modest changes in career education programs do not tend to address the issues of this culturally diverse, often discouraged, and poor population (Blustein et al., 2002). As Fouad (1997) described, many of the participants in such programs are irregular in their school attendance and continue that pattern of irregular attendance in the workplace. Several programs have been developed in the last decade to reenvision the type of psychoeducational model that might be most useful to students from economically disadvantaged backgrounds. For example, Kenny, Bower, Perry, Blustein, and Amtzis (2004) developed the Tools for Tomorrow program for use in high schools. The program was designed to enhance self-awareness, foster career exploration and goal setting, and help students make connections between their high school educational experiences and their future career goals. Research has suggested that students who internalize the importance of a connection between school and work are more likely to work hard in school and thereby realize their career ambitions (Solberg, Howard, Blustein, & Close, 2002).

Blustein et al. (2010) conducted a consensual qualitative research (CQR; C. E. Hill et al., 2005) study with 32 students (more than 90% of whom were persons of color, primarily Caribbean American, African American, and Latino/a) in an urban high school. Half of the students had participated in the Tools for Tomorrow program; half of the students were in ninth grade, and the other half were in 12th grade. Blustein et al. framed an interview protocol informed by the career construction theory discussed earlier in this chapter (Savickas, 2005). They wanted to examine how the students understood the relationship between school and work and how they understood the role of race and ethnicity both in society's expectations of them and in their own perceptions of their future success. They found that all of the students in the Tools for Tomorrow program endorsed a connection between work and school but that this endorsement was also typical of the entire sample. Students were aware both of the important role education played in future career success and of the obstacles racism puts in their path. Blustein et al. noted that "faith in the value of education is robust among our sample" (p. 253), a finding consistent with other research showing that students of all races and socioeconomic backgrounds have internalized the important connection between school and work and that they want to do well academically (Cokley, 2003; Tyson, Darity, & Castellino, 2005).

In recent years there has also been a resurgent interest in the college experience, with particular programs designed to address the college-to-career transition. Yang and Gysbers (2007) noted that "career search is one of the most important tasks that graduating college students face. For many of these students, this is the first time that they will look for a full-time job or a career path that will become a part of their identity" (p. 157). Yang and Gysbers found a negative relationship between career search self-efficacy and distress, a finding that is not surprising. We have spoken with numerous undergraduates who find the job search process to be "a full-time job" and one that causes great ambivalence and worry. The students most at risk for increased stress and decreased feelings of efficacy were those who were least ready for a career transition, least confident, and in need of the most support.

In 2010, Murphy, Blustein, Bohlig, and Platt conducted a CQR study (C. E. Hill et al., 2005) with eight college graduates to look at the importance of career adaptability in the difficulties of today's workforce (Blustein, 2006). Surprisingly, the participants did not report any relationship between their sense of well-being and the difficulties of their college-to-work transition. They also emphasized the importance of social support, particularly by mothers, in enhancing or diminishing the success of their transition. Finally, consistent with the literature on resilience in young adulthood (Masten et al., 2004), participants reported feeling optimistic even after adapting to a disappointing work environment. Their responses clearly indicate that today's college graduates see career as a long process, not firmly established by one's first job.

Although counseling psychologists and other professionals continue to implement college-to-career and school-to-work-to-life programs (Lapan, Turner, & Pierce, 2012; Solberg et al., 2002), the opportunities also continue to be broad in scope and professionally challenging. This is a frontier that encompasses the preventive, developmental, and remedial roles of counseling psychologists on every one of the central values of the profession: focus on strengths and optimal functioning; focus on the whole person; commitment to advocacy and social justice;

concentration on brief, educational, and preventive interventions; and dedication to the scientist–practitioner model.

ADJUSTMENT TO WORK

Once an individual has chosen an area of work, counseling psychologists often turn their attention to how well that individual adjusts to different work demands and opportunities. Probably the best known theory in this area is the theory of work adjustment (Dawis & Lofquist, 1984). The theory of work adjustment grew out of research begun in 1959 that investigated the work adjustment of vocational rehabilitation clients. That focus on rehabilitation clients led to a greater emphasis on longer range issues of *adjustment* compared to a shorter term focus on vocational *choice*. On the basis of results from their initial studies, Dawis, England, and Lofquist (1964) presented a theory that had as its primary focus the proposition that tenure (length of stay on a job) would be predicted by a combination of satisfaction (worker's self-reported job satisfaction) and satisfactoriness (e.g., supervisor's ratings of employee as performing satisfactorily) and, most important, how the two interacted: Greater job satisfaction would lead to higher ratings of satisfactoriness, and higher ratings of satisfactoriness would lead to greater job satisfaction. Note that, as in Holland's theory (see Chapter 15), which was being developed independently at the same time, Dawis et al. shifted the focus from simply looking at person–worker characteristics to an *interaction* of the person and the work environment. The most current outgrowth of theory is called *person–environment correspondence theory* (Dawis, 2005).

By 1978, Dawis and colleagues felt they had sufficient data regarding the proposed interactions and their effects to redefine work adjustment "as a symmetric, circular process in which both person and environment attempt to achieve and maintain an acceptable level of satisfaction" (Dawis, 1996, p. 79). In this statement, then, achieving and maintaining some correspondence becomes a driving force causing changes in environments as well as individual workers. Paying attention to how, when, and why work environments change is a unique aspect of this theory and a critical component of emerging new conceptualizations of reciprocity of person–environment interactions (discussed earlier in this chapter).

The theory propounded by Dawis et al. makes extensive use of measures of abilities to assess the individual side of the person–environment fit. Examination of limits in much of their initial data led the theory's authors to go beyond an assessment of abilities and include an assessment of what they sometimes call needs, other times, using the learning terminology that had emerged in the 1960s, "reinforcer requirements." Dawis and colleagues developed the Minnesota Importance Questionnaire (Weiss, Dawis, Lofquist, Gay, & Hendel, 1975), in which 20 classes of "reinforcer requirements" cluster around six values: achievement, comfort (freedom from stress), status, altruism, safety, and autonomy. Although the measure has not been used extensively outside of its use in testing work adjustment theory, it has withstood several years of empirical investigation supporting its factor structure and validity in understanding what workers deem important.

On the environmental side of the equation, Dawis, Dohm, Lofquist, Chartrand, and Due (1987) developed the Minnesota Occupational Classification System. The classifications of that system have been incorporated into a computerized software program that, after data entry, examines an individual's abilities and values and generates a list of the occupations that yield "correspondence" between the individual and the job. Recall that this correspondence is the key to tenure in a job.

The theory of work adjustment contains some of the most explicitly stated hypotheses and well-operationalized constructs of any of the vocational theories (Betz, 2008). Although this theory has not attracted nearly as many researchers as has Holland's, partly because of the need for assessments of individuals and environments more extensive than Holland's Self-Directed Search, it is, however, an attractive theory for I/O psychologists and for counseling psychologists working in industry. Empirical data from industrial settings do support the importance of fit between the person and the environment for achieving both satisfaction and satisfactoriness. There is also a growing body of research results supporting their proposition that as a worker remains longer on a particular job, that worker will change in ways that are more correspondent (congruent) with that work environment (Dawis, 2005).

Much of the research regarding the theory of work satisfaction has received less critical peer review than the research on many of the other career theories (Walsh & Savickas, 2005). Many of the theory's propositions have yet to be empirically tested (Larson, 2012). In related research on job satisfaction, however, strong progress has been made, particularly within the I/O literature. A number of meta-analyses have suggested a strong relationship between person–environment fit and job satisfaction (Verquer, Beehr, & Wagner, 2003), with some analyses focused on what prevents job satisfaction, such as workload, time pressure, organizational politics, and concerns about job security (Podsakoff et al., 2007). Lent (2008) reviewed various sources and measures of job satisfaction, suggesting that future research focus on integrative models and longitudinal designs. As long as the theory of work adjustment remains focused on the "what" of adjustment, rather than on the "how" (i.e., the process by which clients can attain adjustment), use of the theory by counselors will be comparatively limited. Finally, the range of persons studied has been relatively restricted, especially compared to the cultural diversity now characterizing the workforce of the United States, though there is evidence that that might be changing (see Lyons, Brenner, & Fassinger, 2005; Lyons & O'Brien, 2006).

WORK–LIFE BALANCE

One particular aspect of work adjustment that has received a great deal of attention in the literature is that of work–life balance. (As an aside, the second author found it ironic that as she sat down to begin writing this section, she was trying to figure out how to dedicate time to writing, then get to her child's elementary school for a function there, and then to the office and back in the amount of time allotted in the day. Yes, work–life balance remains a critical and current issue for many!) Early work in women's career development, particularly in the 1980s (Astin, 1984; Betz & Fitzgerald, 1987; Farmer, 1985), examined barriers to women's advancement that included work–family conflict (Greenhaus & Beutell, 1985). More recent research in the 1990s and in the 21st century has moved toward looking at gender (including roles played by both men and women), rather than specifically women per se (Betz, 2008; Fitzgerald, Fassinger, & Betz, 1995), and has focused more on the positive aspects of managing multiple roles (Ormerod, Joseph, Weitzman, & Winterrowd, 2012). Thus, a previous focus on work–family conflict has turned more toward examining work–life balance or work–life interface (Gilbert & Rader, 2008; Ormerod et al., 2012; Whiston, Campbell, & Maffini, 2012).

Frone (2003) reviewed the work–family literature, noting the progression of various theories that have impacted the field. For example, early models included the *segmentation* model, which suggested that work and family roles are in separate spheres and so do not impact one another. However, as Blustein (2001) has aptly noted, people rarely experience work and family as separate and unrelated domains. Competing *spillover* models suggested an entirely different story whereby work and family roles do influence each other, such as work conflicting with family (e.g., an important presentation that has required a great deal of effort and time is rescheduled during a child's band performance) or family conflicting with work (e.g., a parent needs to cancel an important meeting because he needs to stay home with a sick child). Even more recently, *integrative* models emphasize the reciprocal nature of the roles we hold in work and family, acknowledging that the impact is often bidirectional.

Past research examining the impact of the roles on one another has, as previously noted, primarily focused on work–family conflict. Carlson (1999), for example, overviewed several ways in which work–family conflict manifests itself. One might experience time-based conflicts, where one feels there is not enough time to focus on both family and work roles adequately. One might also experience strain-based conflicts; for example, a father might find it difficult to attend to and complete his work for the day after receiving a call from the school about a problem a teacher had with his child. Behavior-based conflicts also occur when whatever type of behavior or action is called for from one role is incompatible with the other role. For example, a mother might be expected to be available to come into work at a moment's notice, which conflicts with her scheduled time as the coach of her child's soccer team. Such required flexibility (work) and required constancy (family) may make for difficult situations and increased stress. A number of meta-analyses have found negative impacts of work–family conflict, including lower levels of life satisfaction and higher levels of distress (Allen, Herst, Bruck, & Sutton, 2000; Byron, 2005).

Although counseling psychologists may indeed be called upon to help individuals manage situations involving work–family conflict, more positive, recent perspectives on work and family have also suggested, in line with counseling psychology's focus on strengths and assets, that people may actually benefit from the multiple work and home roles. In 2006, Greenhaus and Powell offered the work–family enrichment theory that views work and family roles not only as integrative but also as potentially positive rather than conflictual. For example, if one is experiencing a great deal of stress in one role, the other role might provide respite or a buffer from the stress. Different roles also provide different support systems and perspectives (Barnett & Hyde, 2001). Indeed, research supports the idea that work–life interface can provide greater life and relationship satisfaction (Eby, Maher, & Butts, 2010). Recent theories have also taken into account the changing definitions of family (Perrone, 2005; Schultheiss, 2006), going beyond the heteronormative assumptions of one father and one mother as the parents. Family roles in the literature have also expanded to acknowledge that many workers have family responsibilities involving children but also involving the care of an older parent (Beauregard, Ozbilgin, & Belle, 2009). In addition, the definition of "life" (going beyond the concept of "family") has expanded to include other nonwork factors, such as community volunteerism and social contact with friends (Voydanoff, 2005). Thus, in the past decade, we have seen great changes in the earlier theories and assumptions about the relationship between work and life, along with full alterations in the definitions and policy implications.

In terms of policies, Slan-Jerusalim and Chen (2009) noted that a number of organizations now offer specific initiatives for helping workers manage work–family conflict (S. E. Anderson, Coffey, & Byerly, 2002).

However, they also noted that these initiatives are not always effective, because they focus at the organizational rather than individual level (Rosin & Korabik, 2002) and are often structured to attend to immediate rather than long-term conflicts (Lobel, 1999). Slan-Jerusalim and Chen suggested, as a result, that career counseling may be an important factor specifically in work–family conflict situations. Gilbert and Rader (2008) suggested that counselors may need to help individuals address their views of fairness and work on issues of communication and mutual support. For example, those who perceive their partner as doing "too little" at home (i.e., feel that there is inequity in their home roles) may experience lower relationship satisfaction (Stanley, Markham, & Whitton, 2002). Yet, a counselor might "help the client renegotiate previously unspoken rules about who does what in the household" (Gilbert & Rader, 2008, p. 434). A counselor may also need to help clients examine their gender role socialization and how such socialization impacts current life choices (see also Chapter 14).

In a similar vein, Jackson, Wright, and Perrone-McGovern (2010) suggested that L. S. Gottfredson's (1981, 1996) theory of circumscription and compromise might be "particularly useful" (p. 159) in helping clients understand the role of gender and gender socialization, particularly in work–family interface. Gottfredson (1996) wanted to "solve an apparent puzzle: why do people of both sexes and of different races and social classes tend to differ, even in childhood, in the kind and quality of jobs they wish for?" (p. 179). Her theory therefore emphasizes the most public, social aspects of self (gender, social class, intelligence) rather than the more private, personal elements (values, personality, plans for family) that are the principle focus of other theories (Gottfredson, 2005). She defined *circumscription* as the "progressive elimination of unacceptable alternatives to create a social space (zone of acceptable alternatives)" (p. 187). She defined *compromise* as "the process by which youngsters begin to relinquish their most preferred alternatives for less compatible but more accessible ones" (Gottfredson, 1996, p. 187). Her incorporation of a sociological perspective into career choice and development has been provocative and seminal. The empirical evidence in support of the theory is rapidly accumulating (see Coogan & Chen, 2007). In particular, empirical data support the propositions that the processes of circumscription and compromise regularly occur at an early age. As it has been well established that gender socialization also occurs early in childhood (Crawford & Unger, 2004), Gottfredson's theory can help us understand both how gendered work (and home) roles can develop and also how we might be able to intervene earlier in life to expand individuals' options and attitudes. Lapan and Jingeleski (1992) suggested that interventions must begin well before junior high school years if the range of career choices of female students is to be maximized.

RETIREMENT PLANNING

In the past decade there has been a strong resurgence of interest in retirement in the psychology literature (Shultz & Wang, 2011). Society is clearly aging (Vacha-Haase, Hill, & Bermingham, 2012), and counseling psychology is well poised to make significant contributions to the literature on retirement (Vacha-Haase & Duffy, 2012). On the basis of the central values in counseling psychology on the focus on strengths and assets and the focus on the whole person with both life span and vocational emphases, counseling psychologists have helped shift the perspective of aging from one of disease and decline to one of great heterogeneity where there is extensive variability in the aging experiences of individuals. This change in focus from aging as a chronic disease to "normal aging" has prompted new research on successful aging (Rowe & Kahn, 1998), which emphasizes optimal conditions and engagement. Vacha-Haase et al. (2012) noted that successful agers are now characterized by "(a) active engagement with life, (b) absence or avoidance of disease or risk factors for disease, and (c) maintenance of high levels of physical and cognitive functioning" (p. 492). Thus, contemporary views of aging (Charles & Carstensen, 2010; R. Hill, 2005) continue to focus on the positive aspects of aging.

Though Fretz (1993) called for greater attention to issues of aging in counseling psychology, Werth, Kopera-Frye, Blevins, and Bossick (2003) found there was "disturbingly little representation of older adults in the literature being reported in counseling psychology's two premiere journals" (p. 803) at the end of the 20th century. Although this trend seems to be continuing on the whole (Vacha-Haase et al., 2012), it is in the area vocational psychology and retirement planning that counseling psychologists can make the most difference. Several large studies (e.g., Mermin, Johnson, & Murphy, 2007; Topa, Moriano, Depolo, Alcover, & Morales, 2009) have suggested that the baby boomers had a high likelihood of working longer and delaying retirement. This has become even more likely with economic crisis in 2008 and the devastating effects of unethical and illegal maneuvers that have cost many workers their retirement savings (Barlett & Steele, 2012), such as the Enron scandal in 2001 (Healy & Palepu, 2003). In addition, more and more aging adults are entering what has been referred to as "bridge employment"—taking a job "postcareer" but preretirement (D. A. Jones & McIntosh, 2010).

Thus, the need for vocational research and career psychology applications is growing in importance in this area. Simon and Osipow (1996) suggested the use of a constructivist approach (described earlier in the chapter) to help clients recognize their enduring "vocational scripts" and help them use those scripts in retirement planning. Of particular importance, Simon and Osipow noted the need to help clients determine how to preserve their vocational script even during times of tremendous change and transition. In contrast, Harper and Shoffner (2004) suggested using a theory of work adjustment approach (also reviewed earlier in this chapter) to help clients find positive individual–environment correspondence in retirement. Adjusting to retirement also involves examining other sources of satisfaction beyond the traditional career. For example, Hansen, Dik, and Zhou (2008) emphasized the need to consider individuals' leisure interests as an important part of career and life planning. They investigated the factor structure of leisure interests of college students, working adults, and retirees. Although there were notable differences between the structure of leisure interests and Holland's vocational interests, there were surprising similarities in the structure of interests across the three cohorts. They suggest that the assessment of leisure interests might be a fruitful avenue to explore for helping individuals identify new leisure pursuits, develop greater social contacts, and develop additional skills, all things that might be very helpful in retirement planning. Given the importance of a life span perspective in counseling psychology, we anticipate we will see more research of this type in the coming years.

Although covering all the issues in vocational psychology in one chapter would not be possible, given the vast amount of information, theory, and empirical work in the field, we have given the reader an overview of some of the recent developments in the field and the areas of new endeavor in which counseling psychologists remain on the cutting edge. We look forward to seeing the additional changes in vocational theory and research, a vibrant area in counseling psychology, in the coming decades.

Summary

We have described in this chapter the changing world of work and new opportunities for counseling psychologists in the workplace and in schools. In workplace settings, there is a wide variety of opportunities ranging from career development offices to employee assistance programs to newly funded training and service programs in occupational health psychology. We overviewed the importance of consultation to counseling psychology and the changes in work environments and vocational psychology related to technology advances, the Internet, and social media.

We next reviewed that concurrent with the advances described there was a growing awareness of significant shortcomings in the applicability of much career theory and research to the diversity of workers in contemporary society. By the beginning of the 21st century, innovative thinkers and researchers in career psychology had established the foundations for expanding traditional strategies as well as incorporating shifts to new ways of looking at the world of work. We described how and why strategies to study person–environment interactions should be expanded, paying greater attention to how we can change work environments as well as to how work environments change people. We reviewed the emerging themes of constructivism and career constructivist theory. We also reviewed the social–cognitive "revolution" in counseling psychology, emphasizing the application of self-efficacy theory to career choice and development.

In our final section, we overviewed four important stages in career development and vocational psychology. First, we reviewed the research in the school-to-work and college-to-career literatures. Next, we examined the foundational theory and recent updates to the Dawis's theory of work adjustment. We then explored the changing definitions and trends in the work–family balance literature, noting the recent trend toward more inclusive and more positive framing of research and policy. Finally, we ended with an exploration of the growing area of retirement planning, noting vocational psychology's long-standing connection with life span research.

We believe that counseling psychologists, by combining the advances from the past 70 years with the new and expanded paradigms reviewed in this chapter, will be well poised to address both societal and individual issues in the world of work in the 21st century.

Diversity and Social Justice 6

An explosion of literature occurred in the 1990s in counseling psychology on issues related to social justice and attention to diversity that has continued into the 21st century. Issues specific to culturally competent counseling (with emphasis on feminist therapy and multicultural counseling) are covered in Chapter 14. This chapter focuses on the many ways in which counseling psychologists are addressing the complexities of diverse social identities in their research and advocating for changes in social structures, availability of resources, and accessibility of opportunities for all people.

Overviewing all social identities in one chapter is not possible, so we focus on those that have generated the most research by counseling psychologists (race/ethnicity, gender, and sexual orientation) before moving on to discuss social justice efforts in counseling psychology. For information on additional social identities not covered specifically in this chapter, we urge the reader to see that provided in the *APA Handbook of Counseling Psychology* (Fouad, Carter, &

http://dx.doi.org/10.1037/14378-006
Counseling Psychology, Third Edition, by C. J. Gelso, E. N. Williams, and B. R. Fretz

Subich, 2012), the *Oxford Handbook of Counseling Psychology* (Altmaier & Hansen, 2012), and the *Oxford Handbook of Feminist Multicultural Counseling Psychology* (Enns & Williams, 2012). There are excellent chapters on aging (Vacha-Haase & Duffy, 2012; Vacha-Haase, Hill, & Bermingham, 2012), disability issues (Olkin, 2012; Palombi, 2012), and social class (Liu, 2012; Smith, Appio, & Chang, 2012), among others. From a review of this literature, prospective counseling psychologists should then comprehend the range and kinds of competencies that must be developed and implemented to ensure ethical and competent research and practice in the culturally diverse world of the 21st century.

Definitions

Given the shifting paradigms and changing demographics in United States today, multiculturalism has become the "fourth force" in American psychology (Pedersen, 1999), complementing the earlier three forces of the 20th century (described in Chapters 11, 12, and 13); that is, the psychodynamic, cognitive–behavioral, and humanistic–experiential explanations of human behavior. One piece of evidence for multiculturalism's central role within counseling psychology, in particular, is the proportion of articles published in *The Counseling Psychologist*, the primary conceptual journal of the specialty, on issues of multicultural practice and training, diversity, and social justice. By the 1990s, training in and practice of multicultural counseling were more frequently than any other topic the focus of major contributions to *The Counseling Psychologist* (Jackson, 1995). The trend continues today. Although many counseling psychologists remain concerned that more progress is needed to have a truly multicultural profession, this continuing emphasis in *The Counseling Psychologist*, along with the election of many more culturally diverse leaders in the profession in the past several decades; the emergence of the Section for the Advancement of Women, the Section on Racial and Ethnic Diversity, and the Lesbian, Gay, Bisexual, and Transgendered Issues Section in Division 17 (Society of Counseling Psychology); and the growing literature on diversity and social justice issues all indicate that the concept of diversity has moved from being a topic for minority groups in particular to a critical professional issue that requires the attention of all counseling psychologists. In fact, cultural competency is viewed as critical to effective and ethical practice for all psychologists (American Psychological Association [APA], 2003a).

Even with the emphasis on cultural competency for all in the profession, defining what is meant by the terms *cultural* and *multicultural* has proved difficult. In particular, what (or really who) is included when using the terms *multicultural, cultural diversity*, and *minority* is a point of contention. There are ongoing controversies in response to this question, with some counseling psychologists passionately arguing one position, and other counseling psychologists just as passionately arguing for a contrasting position. In this section we explore these various positions and why there are such strong feelings about how the terms are used. Understanding these definitional concerns provides some of the fundamentals that counseling psychologists need to begin to explore regarding their own culture as well as the culture or cultures of those with whom they work in their research and practice.

We also think it is important for the reader to be familiar with the definitions of culture, race, ethnicity, multiculturalism, and diversity set forth in the *Guidelines on Multicultural Education, Training, Research, Practice, and Organizational Change for Psychologists*, the practice guidelines approved as APA policy in 2003. APA (2003a) defined *culture* as "the belief systems and value orientations that influence customs, norms, practices, and social institutions" (p. 380). Included in this definition are both psychological processes, such as language and caretaking practices specific to particular cultures, and organizational processes, including particular experiences with media and educational systems. All people have a unique cultural, racial, and ethnic heritage that defines their particular worldview. Our worldview comprises our learned beliefs, values, and traditions (such as spiritual or religious practices). Although there is evidence of some "universal phenomena" (APA, 2003a, p. 380), culture is generally seen as dynamic, changing over time with different sociopolitical, historical, and economic changes in the world.

APA (2003a) defined *race* as "the category to which others assign individuals on the basis of physical characteristics, such as skin color or hair type, and the generalizations and stereotypes made as a result," and *ethnicity* as "the acceptance of the group mores and practices of one's culture of origin and the concomitant sense of belonging" (p. 380). The idea that race is not biologically determined but rather socially constructed has been a point of contention among psychologists for some time (see Levin, 1995; Phinney, 1996; Rushton, 1995; Yee, Fairchild, Weizmann, & Wyatt, 1993). Although there is no truly consensual definition of race (Helms & Cook, 1999), it is clear that we all act as if race were a clearly defined construct. It has also been clear that people often confuse and conflate the concepts of race and ethnicity (Helms & Talleyrand, 1997).

Why is there such confusion in meaning for the words *race* and *ethnicity?* Opposing viewpoints are maintained by different counseling psychologists as well as psychologists from many other specialties. We address issues of defining race first: When Yee et al. (1993) published their article "Addressing Psychology's Problems With Race," it was soon followed by eight diverse and passionate reactions (see pp. 40–47 in *The American Psychologist*, January 1995). Some argued that race should no longer be a categorical variable in psychology, and others argued just as strongly but for incredibly diverse reasons, from the biological to the psychological, that even more concerted attention should be paid to race as a variable in psychological research and practice. There is much evidence that what is labeled race in many studies may not be defined reliably: Is race self-defined by those being studied or counseled, and, if so, what is the race given by someone with an Asian American father and an African American mother? Or is race determined by some biological marker, such as skin color or eye shape, and, if so, how reliable are the categorizations when, for example, someone has naturally blond hair and what are called Mongoloid facial features (Rushton, 1995)? In addition, race is sometimes confounded with social class as a descriptive and/or explanatory variable. This questionable reliability of how race is determined is one reason some have argued for the elimination of race as a category for further study.

On the other side of this argument are authors such as Eisenman (1995) and Helms (1992), who have provided persuasive arguments that eliminating race as a category for study would actually lead to more racial discrimination and to less awareness on the part of the majority about their own ongoing contributions to discrimination. Their strong concerns about why race needs continued focused attention in psychologists' research and practice apply not only to the continuance of race as a category but also to its differentiation from ethnicity.

Similarly, Phinney (1996) attempted to address much of the messiness in the use of the word *ethnicity:* "Ethnicity is a complex multidimensional construct that, by itself explains little" (p. 918). She used the term *ethnic group* to refer only to members of nondominant groups of non-European origin and encompassed race within that definition because her definition of *ethnic group* referred almost exclusively to persons of color (e.g., African Americans, Asian and Pacific Islanders, Americans, Latinos, Native Americans). "The term race is avoided because of wide disagreement on its meanings and usage for psychology. . . . Biologists find more differences within so-called racial groups than between them" (Phinney, 1996, p. 918). Phinney's focus did allow her to build a case for recognizing that ethnicity, as a category of psychological study, confounded issues of ethnicity as culture, ethnicity as identity, and ethnicity as minority status. We explore in the next section the idea that all people have a cultural background and racial identity. What varies tremendously is the strength, salience, and meaning of culture and racial identity for each of us.

In response to Phinney's (1996) distinctions, Helms and Talleyrand (1997) argued that "race is not ethnicity." However poorly race might be defined, they found it a less fuzzy construct than ethnicity, which "seemingly has no real meaning apart from its status as a proxy for racial classification or immigrant status" (p. 1246). Some years before Phinney's work, Cook and Helms (1988) recognized that when words like diversity and ethnicity were being used, the primary focus was on visible racial ethnic groups, the same groups Phinney encompassed in her attempts to clarify what we mean by American ethnic groups. There may also be a tendency for some people to defer to ethnic identity as a way to avoid discussing race. For example, a person might feel at ease discussing her Polish heritage but might feel awkward describing what it means to be a White person in the United States.

Despite the lack of consensus in the definitions of race and ethnicity, both terms have been used to define the concept of the term *minority* in the United States. Originally, the term was designated for non-White persons in the United States who represented, statistically speaking, a smaller proportion of the people in the country and who "because of physical or cultural characteristics are singled out from the others in society in which they live for differential and unequal treatment" (Wirth, 1945, p. 347). The term continues to be used even though changing U.S. demographics have meant that in many geographic areas, racial and ethnic groups are no longer statistical minorities and have in fact become the majority. Although most often associated with racial/ethnic categories, the term minority has also been applied to other social categories. As the scope of definition minority expanded, the word became something of a misnomer: For example, women were labeled a minority even though they were not a statistical minority even in 1960s. Thus, in the 1970s the term *culturally disadvantaged* came into vogue. Yet, the *disadvantaged* part of this term had for many implications of deficiency, even its use was well intentioned to indicate that such individuals had been deprived of many of the opportunities enjoyed by other citizens. Therefore, *culturally disadvantaged* was quickly replaced by *culturally diverse*, which remains one of the most frequently used terms today (Sue & Sue, 2012).

For similar reasons, the 1960s term *minority counseling* evolved into *cross-cultural counseling*. There were two important implications in this evolution. First, the issues to be considered went beyond those of a majority group counselor working with a minority group client; that is, there were issues to be considered when counselors and clients came from different minorities, or when the counselor was from a minority group. Second, "by shifting the focus away from minority groups exclusively, these terms challenged majority group counselors to become aware of the role that their own cultural assumptions played in their interactions with clients" (Jackson, 1995, p. 11).

In the 1980s, the term *cross-cultural counseling* evolved into *multicultural counseling* for at least two reasons. First, *cross-cultural* had long been a sociological term referring to the study of international ethnic groups, and its use therefore led to some confusion when the primary focus was intended to be on American ethnic groups. The word *multicultural* came into use to distinguish a focus on American ethnic groups as compared to cultures from other countries. Second, because so many counselors and clients belonged to more than one culturally diverse group (e.g., Asian American hearing-impaired male, fundamentalist Christian female, biracial bisexual male, African American female), the term *multicultural* made clear that the issues from more than two cultures could often be involved in the research and practice of counseling psychologists.

The terms *multicultural* and *diversity* are often used interchangeably. However, as Liu and Pope-Davis (2003) noted,

> As much as people may want to construe diversity and multiculturalism to be opposite sides of the same coin, it is probably more accurate to state that diversity and multiculturalism represent different denominations and have different currency depending on the context. (p. 91)

Liu and Pope-Davis went on to note that power is an essential element in understanding multiculturalism (e.g., power obtained, held, lost, recovered, even unacknowledged), whereas diversity refers more directly to "individuals' social identities" (APA, 2003a, p. 380), including gender, race/ethnicity, sexual orientation, socioeconomic class, ability/disability status, and age. Although the APA (2003a) acknowledged that the definition of multiculturalism includes a "broad scope" of individuals' identities (p. 380), it focused its attention for the purposes of the *Guidelines* on "interactions between racial/ethnic groups in the United States" (p. 380). Thus, the *Guidelines* themselves acknowledge the difficulty psychologists have had in agreeing whether multiculturalism really includes all social identities (gender, sexual orientation, etc.) or whether it is more appropriately reserved for a focus on race and ethnicity.

Jackson (1995) defined multicultural counseling as "counseling that takes place between or among individuals from different cultural backgrounds" (p. 3). Jackson's broad definition of multicultural counseling is commonly used, even if it is controversial. In its broadest sense, then, multicultural counseling includes an African American male counseling an African American female, an Asian American counseling a Hispanic, a visually impaired counselor counseling a wheelchair-bound client, a heterosexual counseling a bisexual, and an Anglo 25-year-old counseling an Anglo 85-year-old. What is the concern with inclusiveness of the definition beyond race/ethnicity? Helms (1994) said it best: "A decided disadvantage of the all-inclusive, pluralistic, or multicultural perspective was that it permitted the mental health specialties to shift their attention away from an analysis of the impact of racial factors on therapy process"

(p. 162). As we have noted, the roots of the attention now given to multiculturalism are found largely in the civil rights movements of the late 1950s to early 1970s. The identification of discrimination, oppression, and neglect of basic health, education, and welfare services experienced by African Americans in particular led, especially in the 1960s, to "a composite consideration of the mental health concerns of members of various racial (e.g., Asians and Blacks), cultural (e.g., Latinos and women), and ethnic groups (e.g., Native American tribes or nations)" (Helms, 1994, p. 162). Significant concerns remain that many of the unique and potent issues regarding race in U.S. society receive insufficient attention when the word *multicultural* is so broadly encompassing.

On the positive side of this broad definition of multiculturalism, however, is a growing realization, in the society at large and especially in the mental health professions, that numerous individuals from many backgrounds experience discrimination in striving for educational and work opportunities as well as incur the painful psychological effects of societal oppression, all on the basis only of their group membership (e.g., age, ethnicity, gender, sexual orientation, social class, religious beliefs, physical disability). Perhaps, as suggested by Liu and Pope-Davis (2003), attention has shifted from whether to include more social identities in the term multiculturalism to the importance of acknowledging the impacts of power, oppression, and discrimination when exploring any of the social identities we claim. So, although it is important to continue to work to enhance diversity (acknowledgment and inclusion of people of all social identities), it is simply not enough. We counseling psychologists must be vigilant that our attention to issues of diversity does not "act like an invisible shield" (Liu & Pope-Davis, 2003, p. 100), allowing us to ignore the more difficult elements of multiculturalism (such as acknowledgment of privilege and oppression and the difficulties associated with advocating for social change). As such, we turn our attention now to an overview of specific research in the major social identities identified by counseling psychologists.

Race and Ethnicity

There have been several notable areas of research on race and ethnicity in counseling psychology in the past several decades. We focus our discussion in this chapter on racism and color-blind racial attitudes, issues of acculturation and immigration, and racial identity theories. *Racism* can be defined as "any behavior or pattern of behavior that tends to systematically deny access to opportunities or privileges to members of one racial group while perpetuating access to opportunities and privileges to members of another racial group" (Ridley, 1995, p. 28). Ridley's (1995) definition emphasizes behaviors and the systemic nature of oppression. When people consider racism, they may focus on overt behaviors (while ignoring the systematic issues). Although there are certainly overt actions that are racist (in fact, extremist hate groups grew "explosively" in 2011 for the 3rd straight year in the United States; Southern Poverty Law Center, 2012), modern racism (see Dovidio, Gaertner, Kawakami, & Hodson, 2002) is often more subtle and goes beyond the individual and individual action.

In 1967 Carmichael and Hamilton introduced the term *institutional racism*, acknowledging that racism is perpetuated via social and political structures. In 1999, Thompson and Neville offered a new definition, expanding beyond the structural aspects of racism:

> Racism consists of two interlocking dimensions: (a) an institutional [structural] mechanism of domination and (b) a corresponding ideological belief that justifies the oppression of people whose physical features and cultural patterns differ from those of the politically and socially dominant group—Whites. (p. 163)

Neville, Spanierman, and Lewis (2012) linked the structural concept of racism to White privilege. They noted that White privilege "consists of greater access to resources, normative assumptions of self-worth, and escaping penalties such as being discriminated against on the basis of race" (p. 335). This unearned and invisible social power is manifested at both macro (e.g., higher salaries, access to new technologies) and micro (e.g., personal sense of entitlement) levels (Neville, Worthington, & Spanierman, 2001) and is often unacknowledged by those who hold the privilege. For example, White people often struggle with acknowledging racism because it can create feelings of guilt and typically runs counter to an individual's sense of self as a good person (e.g., I'm a good person; I couldn't possibly be racist). It is perhaps easier to deny individual and overt racism (e.g., I don't personally harass individuals who are different than me and I don't make racist jokes, therefore I am not racist) than to really seek to understand the more structural elements of racism (e.g., I benefit from privileges simply based on the color of my skin). Keeping a focus only on the individual level also obscures the interpersonal or intergroup elements of racism that have been referred to as *microaggressions*. Sue et al. (2007) defined *microaggressions* as "brief and commonplace daily verbal, behavioral, or environmental indignities, whether intentional or unintentional, that communicate hostile, derogatory, or negative racial slights and insults toward people of color" (p. 271). Because racial biases can exist outside of conscious awareness (Dovidio et al., 2002), people can be unaware of the ways in which they have engaged in microassaults (e.g., racial slurs), insults (e.g., insensitive comments), or invalidations (e.g., ignoring someone's racial or cultural heritage; Sue et al. 2007).

Neville et al. (2012) showed in their expanded model of racism (see Figure 6.1) the ways in which our expressions of racism (cultural, institutional, individual, interpersonal, and color-blind racial ideology) have psychological and health impacts (e.g., racial disparities, psychological costs). Cultural expressions of racism, for example, are exemplified in what different groups in society hold as beautiful, moral, and desirable, what is essentially both ideal and normative. Perhaps one of the most extreme examples of how cultural racism was enacted was the Nazi Party push in the 1940s to eradicate anyone not blue-eyed, blond, and "German" (ignoring the fact that Jewish Germans were also, of course, German). Less extreme, perhaps, but still poignant examples of cultural racism include perceptions of what is "normal" or "good" in modern society, including which celebrities are deemed "beautiful" and what pieces of history make it into children's textbooks in the

FIGURE 6.1

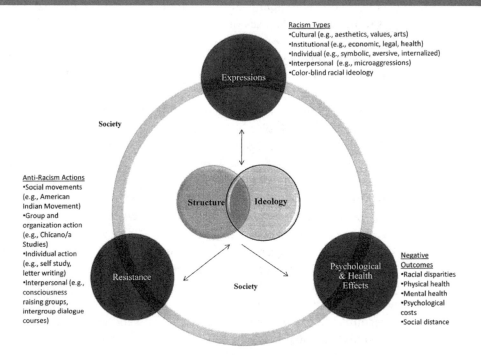

Expanded psychosocial model of racism. From *APA Handbook of Counseling Psychology* (p. 336), by N. A. Fouad, J. A. Carter, and L. M. Subich (Eds.), 2012, Washington, DC: American Psychological Association. Copyright 2012 by the American Psychological Association.

K–12 system in the United States. For example, in September 2013, when Nina Davuluri from Syracuse, New York, was the first woman of Indian American descent to be crowned Miss America, social networking sites lit up with racist comments, inaccurately suggesting that she was Arab, Muslim, connected to the terrorist group al Qaeda, and essentially "not American" on the basis of her ethnicity (http://www.cnn.com/2013/09/16/showbiz/miss-america-racist-reactions/).

Neville et al. (2012) pointed out that institutional racism includes policies and practices that disadvantage certain racial–ethnic groups. For example, discriminatory practices and differential resource allocation have been identified as factors in explaining the findings that minority ethnic groups in the United States (e.g., Black, Latino) show lower educational attainment (National Center for Educational Statistics, 2010) and lower wages (Bureau of Labor Statistics, U.S. Department of Labor, 2010) than do Whites. Neville et al. also overviewed the impact of several forms of individual racism, such as symbolic racism, aversive racism (see also Chapter 14), and laissez-faire racism. They noted that "in contrast to old-fashioned racism, symbolic racism does not rely on the concept of biological inferiority, but instead it relies on logics of cultural deprivation and cultural inferiority" (p. 341). Laissez-faire racism, in contrast, focuses on resource allocations (e.g., entitlement to status and resources of one group), emphasizes a zero-sum perspective (Radloff, 2007; e.g., if the other group gets additional resources, I will lose resources), and resists efforts to alter policies and practices that more equitably distribute social resources.

In addition, Neville has led a groundswell of research in the past decade on issues of color-blind racial ideology (see Neville, 2009; Neville, Awad, Brooks, Flores, & Bluemel, 2013; Neville, Lilly, Duran, Lee, & Browne, 2000; Neville, Spanierman, & Doan, 2006). Color-blind racial ideology minimizes the notion that racism exists (e.g., the claims that we are in a "postracial" America now that there is a Black president) and instead frames issues as "race-neutral" (e.g., we are in a postracial world, so affirmative action is no longer needed). Those who adopt color-blind attitudes often express that it is a positive stance (e.g., I don't notice skin color, I treat everyone the same). Although this certainly sounds positive (particularly the behavior noted, treating people equally), the claim that one does not "notice" skin color does not adequately take into account the ways in which race, ethnicity, and culture are important both to individuals and at a societal level. Neville et al. (2012) suggested instead that we learn to resist and disrupt racism, choosing to increase awareness of power, privilege, and oppression and participate in difficult intergroup dialogues about race. (See also Utsey, Ponterotto, & Porter, 2008, for an overview of methodological advances in the study of racism and suggested strategies for reducing prejudice and racism.)

The racial disparities that persist today among ethnic groups in the United States (e.g., access to health care, level of wages, educational opportunities) also touch on the concepts of immigration and acculturation. There are more immigrants to the United States each year than to all other countries combined (Segal, Elliott, & Mayadas, 2010). In addition to the 38 million legal immigrants in the United States (U.S. Census, 2010), there are an estimated 12 million undocumented immigrants (Yakushko & Morgan, 2012). Because there are nearly 315 million people living in the United States (according to the U.S. Census; see http://www.census.gov/main/www/popclock.htlml), immigrants make up about 12% of the population. Thus, it is incumbent on counseling psychologists to gain knowledge about issues of specific import to immigrant groups.

Immigrating to a new country can be a stressful event (Yakushko, Watson, & Thompson, 2008). For example, arrivals in a new country may encounter language difficulties, economic stress, discrimination, and loss of social support (Levitt, Lane, & Levitt, 2005). One particular form of discrimination that immigrants face is *xenophobia*, defined by Yakushko (2009) as "a form of attitudinal, affective, and behavioral prejudice toward immigrants and those perceived as foreign" (p. 43). One example of xenophobia in the United States was the reaction to people of Arab descent after the terrorist attacks on September 11, 2001. Immigrants (or in this case more broadly anyone perceived as being of Arab descent and therefore "foreign") were targeted as potential terrorists, seen as a source of concern, and blamed for any number of issues from economic problems to overpopulation.

These stressors can make the transition to living in a new country quite challenging (Chung, Bemak, Ortiz, & Sandoval-Perez, 2008). The process of adopting the behaviors and cultural traditions of a new culture is called *acculturation* (Merluzzi & Hegde, 2003). Lecca, Quervalú, Nunes, and Gonzales (1998) suggested that there are five levels of acculturation: (a) traditional (where the individual adheres to his or her original culture), (b) acculturated (where the individual identifies with the new dominant culture), (c) bicultural (where the individual identifies with both the original and adopted cultures), (d) marginality (where both cultures are rejected), and (e) transitional (where the individual is considered bicultural but questions the traditions and values of the original culture). This list should make clear that there is not one particular pathway that immigrants travel during the assimilation process.

Although early studies of acculturation led to the development of the alternative term *biculturalism*, LaFromboise, Coleman, and Gerton (1993) suggested that counseling psychologists use the term *second culture acquisition* instead. Their research suggested at least five different levels of second culture acquisition, with persons at each level having quite different feelings about and reactions to the dominant culture.

Their five levels are assimilation, acculturation, alternation, multiculturalism, and fusion. At the highest level of LaFromboise et al.'s continuum, persons interested in fusion endeavor to see how some unique factors in their own culture might be combined with some elements of the dominant culture to enhance quality of life for members of either or both cultures. For example, are there healing practices in some Native American or African American cultures that would enhance the quality of traditional Western medicine? Are there spiritual traditions in some cultures that can help Anglos make their lives less stressful and depressing? Over the past few decades, studies of acculturation (including biculturalism and second culture acquisition) of Hispanics, Native Americans, Asian Americans, and recently arrived immigrant groups have resulted in the identification of the varied and often unique coping strategies used by these individuals. From these studies, various schemas for coping with diversity have been conceptualized (e.g., Coleman, 1995), and measures have been developed for assessing the type of acculturation in which individuals are engaged (see Paniagua, 1998).

Those working with immigrants should not make assumptions about whether the process has been primarily positive or primarily negative. However, it is helpful to assess a number of variables to determine how individuals feel about their transitions, including number of generations in the family that have been in the adopted country, language fluency issues for the individual and other immediate family members, and community resources available to help with transitional issues. As issues of immigration take center stage in American politics, with state-level changes to providing access to undocumented students (see http://dreamact.info/), the importance of understanding the acculturation process, including assimilation difficulties, will become even more central for counseling psychologists.

Just as one cannot presume to know how a person feels about his or her acculturation status, one cannot know how salient an individual's race or ethnicity is to him or her (Yakushko, Davidson, & Williams, 2009). For example, one cannot assume that a White woman's race is of minimal importance to her, just as one cannot assume a Black man identifies as African American. Thus, one additional way that researchers in counseling psychology have added to the discussion about race and ethnicity is in highlighting the concept that race means different things to different people at different times in their lives. In other words, we all have a developing sense of ourselves as racial beings, a concept that has been referred to as *racial identity*. How we conceive of ourselves as racial beings may have more impact on the counseling relationship and counseling effectiveness than simply our externally viewed characteristics.

Early research in the area of race and ethnicity treated different racial–ethnic groups as having strong within-group homogeneity, with similar attitudes, values, and experiences (Quintana, Chew, & Schell, 2012). With the introduction of the concept of *racial identity*, counseling psychologists began to explore the complexities of our racial self-perceptions (though we also note that the clear and steplike structure of many racial identity models might lead some to develop an oversimplified understanding of these complexities). Ponterotto and Park-Taylor (2007) suggested that the theories of racial identity that have had the most influence on research in counseling psychology are Cross's (1971, 1991) model of psychological nigrescence and Helms's (1984, 1992) White identity model.

Cross's model (revised in 1991) posits four overall stages (with substages in each). The *pre-encounter* stage includes three identity clusters: assimilation, miseducation, and self-hatred (Cokley, 2002). In the pre-encounter stage, individuals do not find race very salient or have internalized negative stereotypes about their race (e.g., lazy, violent). In the second stage, termed the *encounter* stage, the individual encounters discrimination or racism and consequently becomes aware of race in a new way. The *immersion/emersion* stage, the third stage, involves an extremely positive perspective on one's race (e.g., Black is beautiful) in the intense Black involvement substage and an extremely negative view of White culture in the anti-White substage. With the *internalization* stage comes a positive racial identity, which can be more in the Black nationalism category (a pro-Black focus of identity that highlights an African perspective) or the multiculturalist inclusive category (a positive Black identity that also embraces the importance and salience of other social identity categories, such as gender and sexual orientation). Cross's original (1971) and revised (1991) models have prompted an enormous amount of research over the past 40 years in counseling psychology.

The trend in racial identity research over the past 20 years has been to expand the number of underlying dimensions of each model. Quintana et al. (2012) explained that most models of racial or ethnic identity development include affective dimensions (e.g., positive self-regard), the development of psychological and interpersonal connections (e.g., belongingness), and exploration and commitment to an identity (a process similar to the identity formation models proposed in the 1960s; Erickson, 1968; Marcia, 1966). Quintana et al. noted that "formation of positive and strong ethnic and racial identity" (p. 462) is an important and normative part of development for minority children and adolescents.

Racial identity development has been proposed as an important process for White children, adolescents, and adults as well. Helms (1992) created a theory of White racial identity development whereby individuals progress through six stages: *contact* (where an individual lacks awareness of him- or herself as a racial being), *disintegration* (where an individual is propelled into race consciousness and experiences confusion), *reintegration* (where an individual begins to idealize White culture), *pseudo-independence* (where an individual attains a more balanced perspective on race but continues to intellectualize racial issues), *immersion/emersion* (where an individual begins to redefine race consciousness and understand racism), and *autonomy* (where an individual internalizes a nonracist positive racial identity). There are many similarities between this model and racial identity models for ethnic minorities (e.g., the progression to an internalized positive sense of self and rejection of racism), but there are some obvious differences as well. For example, it is virtually impossible for a racial–ethnic minority member in the United States to be unaware of him- or herself as a racial being even from a very early age, and that discrimination is often a trigger for ethnic minority racial identity exploration (Quintana, 2007).

Racial identity models have proved useful for the field, such as by launching a focus on multicultural counseling competency (Burkard, Ponterotto, Reynolds, & Alfonso, 1999), but there is strong evidence that ethnic identity development is correlated with a person's academic achievement (Costigan, Koryzma, Hua, & Chance, 2010) and sense of well-being (Rivas-Drake, Hughes, & Way, 2009). The advances in conceptualizations and measures of racial identity and acculturation have been major contributions of counseling psychologists in helping counselors from all backgrounds understand the heterogeneity of attitudes and behaviors related to culture-specific information.

Sex and Gender

Much as counseling psychologists have made contributions to the understanding of race, ethnicity, and racism, they have also made considerable contributions to the study of sex, gender, and sexism. And, just as in defining race and ethnicity, counseling psychologists have not always been clear about the definitions of sex and gender (Unger, 1979). *Sex* is typically a biological term used to define people based on their constellation of genes, hormones, and internal and external genitalia (Mintz & O'Neil, 1990; Wiesemann, 2011). Although we typically sort people into two sex categories (male and female), not all people fall clearly into these two dominant categories. This issue is gaining greater attention in counseling psychology (Schweizer, Brunner, Schützmann, Schönbucher, & Richter-Apelt, 2009). For example, those with androgen insensitivity syndrome are born with both an X and a Y chromosome (typically male) but because the body is insensitive to testosterone, development becomes more typically female (Gough, Weyman, Alderson, Butler, & Stoner, 2008). The currently recognized categories of sex include male, female, and intersex. In contrast to the use of biological markers, *gender* is more typically defined as behaviors, expectations, and roles defined by society as masculine, feminine, or androgynous (Mintz & O'Neil, 1990). Thus, gender is considered a social, not a biological, construct and has been the topic of study in counseling psychology for many decades (Farmer, 1985; Gilbert & Waldroop, 1978; Niemann, 2001; O'Neil, 2008; Pyant & Yanico, 1991).

Sexism can be defined as "negative attitudes, beliefs, and behaviors that devalue, denigrate, stigmatize, or restrict females" (Szymanski & Moffitt, 2012, p. 361). Examples of the impact of sexism include inequities in salaries between men and women, sexual objectification of women in the media, and beliefs that women are more emotional than men. There are many variations of sexism, including both hostile or overt forms of sexism (allowing or encouraging differential treatment of women and men, believing that women are less competent than men) and what has been called "benevolent" sexism (Glick & Fiske, 1996), where men take on protective (and patronizing) attitudes toward women. Like racism, sexism has serious consequences on women's psychological health (Klonoff, Landrine, & Campbell, 2000; Moradi & Funderburk, 2006) as well as on their lived experience (e.g., their economic status, ability to control their own reproductive health, and safety from violence). Although the impacts on women are more common and more extreme, sexism also impacts men in negative ways (Swim, Hyers, Cohen, & Ferguson, 2001).

The literatures in counseling psychology on the psychology of women (see Moradi & Yoder, 2012) and the psychology of men (see O'Neil, 2012) are vast. Thus, we focus our attention in this section on three specific issues that have garnered a great deal of attention from counseling psychologists in recent years: men's gender role conflict, the effects of objectification of women's bodies, and the impact of violence against women.

The psychology of men (O'Neil, 2012) emerged in the past 30 years following the men's liberation movement (Pleck & Pleck, 1980). O'Neil (2012) noted that counseling psychology was one of the first divisions of the APA to recognize the psychology of men with Skovholt, Gormally, Schauble, and Davis's (1978) special issue in *The Counseling Psychologist* entitled "Counseling Men." In 1995, the Society for the Psychological Study of Men and Masculinity officially became a division of the APA (Division 51). Mintz and Tager (2012) noted that "the vast majority of

Division 51 presidents (e.g., Gary Brooks, Glenn Good, Mark Kiselica, Sam Cochran, John Robertson, Fred Rabinowitz, Chris Kilmartin, Jay Wade, Aaron Rochlen) were trained as counseling psychologists" (p. 323). It is clear that counseling psychologists have led the way in defining this ever-growing field.

To date, the best defined theoretical concept in this field is that of men's gender role conflict (O'Neil, 1981, 2008). O'Neil (2012) defined gender role conflict (GRC) as "the psychological state in which socialized gender roles have negative consequences" such that "rigid, sexist, or restrictive gender role result in restriction of a person's human potential or the restriction of another person's potential" (p. 381). GRC occurs when men display "rigid and restrictive adherence to traditional masculine roles or failure to adhere to masculine roles" (Szymanski & Ikizler, 2013, p. 211). O'Neil (2012) overviewed the four domains of GRC as (a) cognitive (how we think about gender); (b) affective (how we feel about gender); (c) behavioral (our responses and interactions based on our gender roles); and (d) unconscious (the ways in which gender roles that are outside of our awareness can still impact our behavior and create conflict).

Four patterns of GRC have emerged in the literature. The first pattern is that of success–power–competition, reflecting the attitude that success is gained through competition and acquisition of power. The second pattern is restrictive emotionality. Men high in gender role conflict demonstrate fear of expressing emotion. The third pattern is restrictive affectionate behavior between men, making it uncomfortable for some men to touch other men and express their thoughts and feelings to them. The final pattern is conflict between work and family relations, which can result in stress, overwork, and difficulty in relaxing.

These patterns can result in a variety of negative health, psychological, and interpersonal outcomes for men (O'Neil, 2008). In particular, Szymanski and Ikizler (2013) found, for sexual minority men, that gender role conflict occurring between work and family relationships was associated with higher levels of depression. Jones and Heesacker (2012), however, found that the expression of gender role conflict could be manipulated with exposure to short videos (e.g., stand-up comedian clips about the masculine norm that men should not cry). They suggested that this manipulation provides evidence that gender role expression is context dependent and possibly transient. In particular, they emphasized the need to examine "microcontexts" to better understand the variability in gendered behavior and its consequences. Counseling psychologists, whose central values include attention to environmental and contextual detail, are well suited to pursue these additional avenues in understanding masculine gender roles in general and male gender role conflict in particular.

Counseling psychologists have also made significant contributions to the literature on the objectification of women. Just as men can experience a fear of femininity, women appear to be conditioned in American society to fear not being feminine enough. Sexual objectification of women is considered a form of "everyday sexism" (Enns, 2012b) in which the value of girls and women is equated with standards of beauty that are, on the whole, unattainable (Moradi & Yoder, 2012). Girls and women are socialized to view themselves with an observer's gaze and to evaluate themselves on their external appearance. If they fall short of the ideal (which is typical because the ideal seems too often to represent perfection), girls and women often experience shame and anxiety (Moradi & Huang, 2008). As a consequence, women are nearly always dissatisfied with their bodies in some way and, as a result, experience greater mental health problems in certain diagnostic categories, such as depression, sexual dysfunction, and eating disorders (Fredrickson & Roberts, 1997).

The media have played a significant role in delivering images of women and conveying cultural stereotypes that shape societal values and attitudes. Television, in particular, at the end of the 20th century, often presented those idealized versions of women by overemphasizing youth, thinness, and sexuality (Fouts & Burggraf, 2000). Now, images go beyond television, movies, advertising, and magazines and have entered our daily consciousness via the Internet, smartphones, and tablets. As images are everywhere, we tend not to analyze them one by one. However, an accumulation of these stereotyped images can have a strong impact on one's beliefs and attitudes (Blaine & McElroy, 2002; Botta, 2003; Monro & Huon, 2005). As Kashubeck-West and Tagger (2012) pointed out, this body dissatisfaction is so prevalent among women that it has been referred to as *normative discontent* since the 1980s (Rodin, Silberstein, & Striegel-Moore, 1985) and starts very early in elementary school girls (Kashubeck-West, Saunders, & Coker, 2012). Sadly, not only is there evidence that girls and women feel unhappy with their bodies, but, given social pressures to express their dissatisfaction to their peers, they may also feel they *should* feel unhappy (Salk & Engeln-Maddox, 2011).

One especially troubling consequence of this overattention to body image in girls and women is the incidence of eating disorders in the United States (Kashubeck-West & Mintz, 2001). Although body dissatisfaction may be normative for females in the United States, it is still somewhat rare to be diagnosed with a full-blown disorder such as anorexia nervosa or bulimia nervosa (estimated to be diagnosed in 1%–2% of the population, according to the *Diagnostic and Statistical Manual for Mental Disorders;* 4th ed., text revision; *DSM–IV–TR;* American Psychiatric Association, 2000). However, some categories (such as binge eating disorder) appear to be growing in prevalence (Hudson, Hiripi, Pope, & Kessler, 2007). A number of treatment approaches have been developed, and significant progress has been made in successful treatment of eating disorders (Wilson, Grilo, & Vitousek, 2007), particularly for the treatment of bulimia, which has responded well to cognitive–behavioral therapy (Wilson, 2005). However, anorexia remains "impressively resistant" to most treatments (Kashubeck-West & Tagger, 2012, p. 399). Some promising new approaches reviewed by Kashubeck-West and Tagger (2012) include acceptance and commitment therapy (Hayes, Strosahl, & Wilson, 1999), dialectical behavior therapy (Linehan, 1993), and mindfulness-based stress reduction (Kabat-Zinn, 1990). Because one of the central values of counseling psychology is prevention, it is no surprise that counseling psychologists are looking for ways to prevent eating disorders before remedial (and often emergency) treatment is needed. Mussell, Binford, and Fulkerson (2000), for example, stressed the importance of understanding an individual's sociocultural context when examining the risk factors and prevention strategies.

Counseling psychologists have also done a great deal of work on the issue of violence against women, from the trauma impacts women experience to advocacy efforts focused on both treatment and prevention. Approximately 15% of women in the United States will experience rape or sexual assault in their lifetime (Rozee & Koss, 2001), and approximately 25% will experience assault by an intimate partner (Browne, 1993). When abuse (such as incest) occurs during childhood, there is a high likelihood of some kind of revictimization later in life (Courtois, 2011). Courtois (2012) called the scope of gender-based victimization "truly sobering and as horrifying as it is tragic" (p. 376).

These forms of traumatic violence have significant impact on women's well-being, increasing feelings of helplessness, depression, and anxiety (Goodman, Koss, & Russo, 1993). In particular, scholars in counseling psychology such as Christine Courtois (1988, 2012) identified a constellation of response to sexual violence as posttraumatic syndromes (e.g., rape trauma syndrome, battered woman syndrome). However, the diagnosis of posttraumatic stress disorder (PTSD in the *DSM–IV–TR;* American Psychiatric Association, 2000) is not always a good fit, particularly because the disorder was originally designated from studies of men in combat (Courtois, 2012). In 1992, Herman introduced the conceptualization of complex PTSD/disorders of extreme stress not otherwise specified (CPTSD/DESNOS) for victims of sexual violence; however, complex PTSD was not included in the *DSM* as a freestanding diagnosis even in the latest revision (*DSM–5;* American Psychiatric Association, 2013).

Women may be more likely to speak to a family member than a professional about their abuse (Goodman, Dutton, Weinfurt, & Cook, 2003), but there are excellent programs designed by counseling psychologists to help survivors of abuse. Courtois (2012), for example, overviewed a treatment plan that involves three phases: (a) safety, stabilization, and skill building; (b) integration of traumatic memories with emotions; and (c) reintegration and life reconsolidation. Although traditional counseling and therapy remediation models are critical, Goodman and colleagues have argued for more community-based and social networking-based interventions in addressing issues of intimate partner violence (IPV), including rape and domestic violence. Goodman and Smyth (2011) stated that "the antidomestic violence movement has had less success in reaching one of its own primary goals: that of making IPV a problem of the community rather than a problem between two individuals" (p. 79).

The social justice orientation of counseling psychologists provides an avenue for focusing on both the individual needs of the survivors of violence and the systemic societal elements that sustain the existence of such violence. As Bell and Goodman (2006) pointed out, "Many of the traditional professional activities of counseling psychology—including program design and evaluation, research, and consultation—can be fruitfully applied to shape policy and popular thinking" (p. 158). One example of this type of social justice advocacy by counseling psychologists is the work by Epstein, Bell, and Goodman (2003), who helped build the Victim Informed Prosecution Project in Maryland as a way to help the criminal justice system take into account the victim's perspective (not just a focus on prosecuting the offender). Chronister and Aldarondo (2012) overviewed a number of other community-based interventions, such as victim shelter programs, transitional housing programs, and empowerment programs, that should be considered the primary approach "to address systemic factors that contribute to the oppression of women and children and reinforce the use of violence in our families and society" (p. 136). As counseling psychology has moved more intentionally over the past decade into social justice efforts, the central values of counseling psychology (where we emphasize individual strengths, the whole and diverse person, environmental context and advocacy efforts, prevention and education, and a balance between science and practice; see Chapter 1) will serve us well, allowing us to participate in remedial healing needs of individuals, preventative approaches to ensuring mental health, and systemic efforts to produce broader social changes.

Sexual Orientation

As with our discussion of race–ethnicity and sex–gender, we begin our discussion of sexual orientation research in counseling psychology with definitions and "isms." We recognize the pull toward binary discourse

(Fassinger, 2000) when discussing sexual orientation. Humans have often used two opposing categories to describe a construct (e.g., male–female, gay–straight), which misses the complexities and the realities of those constructs (Smith, Shin, & Officer, 2012). There has also been an expansion of the "acronym umbrella" (Moradi, Mohr, Worthington, & Fassinger, 2009) including, for example, lesbian, gay, bisexual, transgender, queer, questioning, and ally (LGBTQQA). Terminology, too, is changing at a rapid rate (Morrow, 2012). Morrow gave the example that "some heterosexual people prefer not to be called 'straight' because of the implications that such an identity is rigid, giving rise to the slogan, 'Straight but Not Narrow' espoused by some progressive heterosexual people" (p. 412). Thus, we caution against the unexamined use of terms and hope to provide insight into where terminology stands in the sexual orientation literature at this time.

Chung, Szymanski, and Markle (2012) defined *sexual orientation* as "a person's affective or emotional and physical or sexual attractions toward males and females" (p. 426). *Sexual identity* (or, more accurately, sexual orientation identity; Morrow, 2012) refers to how a person consciously self-identifies or self-labels with regard to his or her sexual orientation (e.g., lesbian, gay, bisexual, queer, homosexual, heterosexual, asexual, metrosexual, polyamorous, bicurious; Chung et al., 2012; Worthington & Reynolds, 2009). Worthington and Reynolds (2009) pointed out that there is a long history of acknowledging the complexities of defining sexual orientation (Kinsey, Pomeroy, & Martin, 1948; Kinsey, Pomeroy, Martin, & Gebhard, 1953; Sell, 1997; Weinrich & Klein, 2002). Similarly, Chung et al. (2012) noted that "it would be overly simplistic to describe a person's sexual orientation using categories such as heterosexual, homosexual (gay or lesbian), or bisexual" (p. 426). Worthington and Reynolds (2009) suggested, on the basis of their review of the literature, that "there may be more sexual orientation subgroups than is commonly assumed" (p. 46) and that cluster analysis be used to identify subgroups within groups of lesbian, gay, bisexual, and heterosexual groups.

Likewise, the concept of *homophobia* has been reanalyzed. Historically, the term homophobia has been used to describe a fear, or phobic reaction, toward sexual and gender minorities. Examples of this kind of discrimination abound, from the everyday expressions of crude jokes to violent hate crimes involving physical brutality or death. Although these oppressive and vicious behaviors do exist, the term itself has come into question. Because "the term interferes with a contextual understanding of heterosexist oppression by tacitly locating prejudice toward sexual and gender minorities within the individual," L. C. Smith, Shin, and Officer (2012), like others (see Dermer, Smith, & Barto, 2010; Herek, 2004; Schiffman, Delucia-Waack, & Gerrity, 2006), "advocate suspending use of the term" (p. 392). They suggested, instead, the use of the terms *heterosexism* and *heteronormativity*. Heteronormativity refers to the insidious cultural messages, assumptions, and narratives that perpetuate the privileging of heterosexuality (Chin, 2004). Similarly, heterosexism refers to behaviors and processes that systemically privilege heterosexuality as both normative and ideal (Chesir-Teran, 2003) and disadvantage sexual minorities even in the absence of overt acts of discrimination (Herek, 2004). L. C. Smith et al. (2012) preferred the use of the term *heterosexism* to *homophobia* because, much like the terms *racism* and *sexism*, it "may be used to convey systemic as well as individual moral culpability" (p. 394).

The research on heterosexism has focused on three main areas (Szymanski & Moffitt, 2012): (a) attitudes and behaviors toward sexual minorities, (b) individual's experiences as the target of heterosexism, and (c) internalized heterosexism. Counseling psychologists have established a strong link between attitudes and behaviors, such that those with traditional gender-role attitudes and authoritarian views are linked with negative attitudes toward sexual minorities, which are, in turn, linked with heterosexist behaviors (Goodman & Moradi, 2008). In particular, thrill-seeking heterosexual boys and men who feel the need to assert their heterosexuality, particularly among peers, are more likely than others to exhibit antihomosexual behaviors (Franklin, 1998, 2000). The ways in which heterosexism is experienced by individuals are wide reaching, from child abuse at the hands of parents, to verbal harassment, to hate crimes (Szymanski & Moffitt, 2012). Herek (2008) reported that approximately 20% of sexual minorities report being victims of hate crimes, which is related to higher levels of depression and anxiety (Herek, Gillis, & Cogan, 1999). Psychological distress is also related to higher levels of internalized heterosexism (Szymanski, Kashubeck-West, & Meyer, 2008).

Although much of the literature has documented the concerns, consequences, and treatment of the effects of discrimination and heterosexism, another large body of literature in the field is dedicated to the more positive identity development process for lesbian, gay, bisexual, and transgendered individuals. In fact, Croteau et al. (2008) referred to sexual identity theory as counseling psychology's "most studied concept" in the sexual minority literature (p. 196). Sexual identity development is the process of becoming aware of one's sexual orientation, embracing one's identity, and disclosing one's sexual orientation even in the face of heteronormativity (Chung et al., 2012; Croteau et al., 2008).

A number of models of sexual identity development have been proposed over the years. The two earliest models (Cass, 1979; Coleman, 1982) were somewhat similar to the early racial identity models, where individuals moved from lack of awareness or confusion to a positive, integrated identity. For example, Cass (1979) proposed that individuals move through six stages of identity development, beginning with identity confusion and concluding at the highest level with identity synthesis. Cass's stage theory exemplifies the *coming out* process, in which one moves from hiding one's sexual orientation to disclosing that information to others (Chung et al., 2012). Typically, coming out is thought of as a two-step process where one comes out to oneself (e.g., the early stages in the Cass model) and then intentionally comes out to others (e.g., the final stages in Cass's model).

However, the early models have been criticized for being overly simplistic and linear and for not sufficiently addressing contextual issues (Chung & Singh, 2009; Fassinger & Arseneau, 2007). They were also criticized as being more applicable to gay men and less so for lesbians, bisexuals, and transgendered individuals (Lev, 2007; Potoczniak, 2007; Rust, 2003; Savin-Williams, 2001; Sophie, 1986). Contemporary models are more contextualized and inclusive, and they integrate issues of race–ethnicity (Morrow, 2012). For example, McCarn and Fassinger (1996) proposed a model for lesbians that conceptualized two separate developmental phases: individual sexual identity and group membership identity. The model does not, for example, view coming out to others as the most integrated and positive step in identity, thus acknowledging that one might have a strong and positive sexual identity but choose not to disclose it publicly because of the very real risk of discrimination. Both aspects of identity development (individual and group membership), however, progress through different processes, including awareness, exploration, commitment, and synthesis. Similarly, models of bisexual identity development have matured from considering bisexuality to be "transitional" (not a mature point of identity in and of itself) to viewing bisexuality as a "mature state of identity flux" (Rust, 2007, p. 4). Diamond (2008), in underscoring the fluid nature of sexual orientation, proposed a model in which women's bisexuality is considered a stable pattern (of attraction to both sexes) that varies in its expression (e.g., choosing a same-sex or other-sex partner) based on contextual (e.g., situational and interpersonal) variables. Research suggests that women are more likely than men to identify as bisexual (Sheets & Mohr, 2009) and that the experiences of bisexual identity development are different for men and women (Brown, 2002).

Most recently, attention has been turned to transgender identity development. The term *transgender* encompasses individuals with a wide variety of nonconformist expressions of gender, including most typically transvestites (e.g., cross-dressers) and transsexuals (e.g., individuals whose gender identity is different from their biological sex; Carroll, Gilroy, & Ryan, 2002). Lev (2007) proposed a model for transgender identity development that included six stages: (a) awareness, (b) seeking information/reaching out, (c) disclosure to significant others, (d) identity exploration, (e) exploration of transitions, and (f) integration/ acceptance (including post-transition issues).

Less research has been done on transgendered identity development. The topic is receiving much more attention now, even in popular culture with the HBO movie *Normal* (in 2003) and the independent film *Transamerica* (in 2005), for which actor Felicity Huffman was nominated for an Academy Award.

Another topic of growing importance in the field is that of marriage and parenting in gay and lesbian communities (Croteau et al., 2008). The issue of same-sex marriage remains a heated political debate, but several states have passed laws legalizing same-sex marriages. In the 2012 election, for example, Maryland was one of the first states (along with Maine and Washington) to legalize same-sex marriage by popular vote (Linskey, 2012). In addition, on June 26, 2013, the Supreme Court struck down the federal Defense of Marriage Act (1996) and rejected a ban on same-sex marriage in California. Despite these recent changes, same-sex marriage is still not legally recognized in most states. Such laws and policies make it difficult for same-sex couples in many ways, including having access to health care and keeping custody of children from previous heterosexual unions (Morrow, 2012). In addition, there are distinct challenges for same-sex couples who want to have children (Patterson, 2009). Not only are there challenges in deciding how to have biological children (e.g., heterosexual intercourse, artificial insemination, surrogacy), there are also societal challenges that families face, such as the belief that children might be harmed by having two parents of the same sex. The APA, (2012b) made clear that "the adjustment, development, and psychological well-being of children is unrelated to parental sexual orientation" (p. 3). As Haldeman (2012) pointed out, the APA has also clearly opposed discrimination based on sexual orientation in cases of "adoption, child custody and visitation, foster care, and reproductive health services" (APA, 2004b, p. 1).

Beyond the federal and state laws and the advocacy efforts of the APA, Haldeman (2012) noted that "counseling psychology, with its emphasis on clarifying personal values and activating health behaviors, is an excellent lens though which to view the evolution of family structures" (p. 105). Counseling psychologists are well equipped, on the basis of the central values of counseling psychology (see Chapter 1), to further the research and the advocacy efforts in this area for both adults and children. Szymanski and Hilton (2012) suggested several treatment strategies for counseling psychologists. For example, they emphasized the role of counseling psychologists in facilitating sexual identity development and the coming out process and attending to heterosexism and other forms of oppression. Given counseling psychology's emphasis on individual development and on contextual issues, attendance to both the individual and social advocacy issues in this area is both critical and well within the expectations of a trained counseling psychologist. Because counseling psychology also emphasizes a client's strengths and assets, Szymanski and Hilton (2012) emphasized building on clients' strengths and developing skills for coping with oppression. At the broader level, Szymanski and Hilton suggested instituting inclusive organizational policies and practices and engaging in political and legislative action. The interplay between attention to the individual (e.g., building on strengths and attending to developmental issues) and to sociocultural processes and structures that impact the individual (e.g., paying attention to contextual factors and empowering clients to advocate for social changes) is at the heart of the social justice commitment of counseling psychology.

Social Justice in Counseling Psychology

In a call to the profession, Fouad, Gerstein, and Toporek (2006) stated that "it is critical that more counseling psychologists develop a sophisticated understanding of social justice, social action, and advocacy" (p. 2). In addition, Williams and Enns (2012) noted that "beyond understanding, we are called to action, activism, and advocacy" (p. 486), staying true to our counseling psychology roots. Fouad et al. (2006) overviewed the early advocacy efforts of counseling psychologists, including their commitment to ensuring equity in work and vocational issues. Counseling psychology is now experiencing a resurgence and renewed commitment to social justice issues (Fouad & Prince, 2012; Goodman et al., 2004; Speight & Vera, 2004).

Vasquez (2012) defined *social justice* as the goal "to decrease human suffering and to promote human values of equality and justice" (p. 337), noting that fairness and justice are guiding moral principles for psychologists (Kitchener & Anderson, 2011; see also Chapter 3). Although counseling psychologists often work at the individual level to promote personal empowerment and well-being, the focus in social justice is also on creating change at institutional, systemic, and structural levels (e.g., in economics, environmental issues, government, and politics). To address the various levels, counseling psychologists may need to step out of their comfort zones, including the therapy room, the classroom, and research laboratories. More counseling psychologists are being trained in social justice models now (e.g.,

McWhirter & McWhirter, 2007), allowing opportunities for students to be exposed to issues of injustice, to develop a deepening commitment to social justice, and to develop necessary skills (Caldwell & Vera, 2010).

Toporek and Liu (2001) suggested that counseling psychologists focus on four areas of social justice: (a) awareness of interdisciplinary connections (e.g., ensuring knowledge of related research outside of counseling psychology and outside of psychology on the whole), (b) commitment to cultural competence (which we cover in depth in Chapter 14), (c) acceptance of complex roles (e.g., from empowering individuals to broader social advocacy efforts), and (d) knowledge of social justice resources (e.g., financial or legal resources). Adopted as advocacy competencies by the American Counseling Association (Lewis, Arnold, House, & Toporek, 2002), their suggestions also included focusing on community collaboration and public communication among other ways that counselors can participate more directly in social justice efforts. Counseling psychologists have long been involved in social justice efforts, including prevention efforts in schools (Roysircar, 2006), homelessness (Campbell & Durrah, 2012), health care (Chwalisz, 2012), poverty (L. Smith, Appio, & Change, 2012), legislation and public policy (Shullan, Celeste, & Stickland, 2006), and international–transnational efforts (Horne & Aurora, 2012).

Norsworthy, Abrams, and Lindlau (2012) interviewed counseling psychologists about their personal journeys and their development as agents of social change. Examples of individual counseling psychologist efforts at the community level include Sue Morrow's work on women's and lesbian, gay, and bisexual rights and Laura Palmer's work with the Child Abuse Network. At the professional organizational level, Norsworthy et al. cited the work of Carol Enns, Roberta Nutt, and Joy Rice on the *Guidelines for Practice With Girls and Women* (APA, 2007b) and Melba Vasquez's work as APA president on ethics and social justice issues, and they cited work in the academy by Dawn Szymanski with a Safe Zone program for lesbian, gay, bisexual, and transgendered (LGBT) college students and Lisa Goodman's First Year Experience program for graduate students at Boston College. At the political/legal and international levels, the work of Sharon Horne (on LGBT civil rights at the local and state levels and her work in transnational contexts) and that of Kathryn Norsworthy (with her advocacy for domestic partner benefits at the state level and her international work in Asia) were highlighted. These are merely a few examples of the many counseling psychologists working for social justice efforts at each of these levels, including other examples highlighted earlier in this chapter. We expect the next decade to bring about even greater examples of social justice work in counseling psychology.

Summary

Counseling psychology has long been a leader in issues of diversity and social justice. With the growing emphasis on multiculturalism and the recognition of issues of power, privilege, discrimination, and oppression, counseling psychologists are engaged in a great deal of research and advocacy efforts related to our various social identities. We have focused on the three that have generated, to date, the most research: race–ethnicity, sex–gender, and sexual orientation.

We provided an overview of the definitions of and the controversies over the terms diversity and multiculturalism, race and ethnicity, sex and gender, sexual orientation and sexual identity. We also overviewed several isms: racism, sexism, and heterosexism. These "isms" and others not fully covered in the chapter (e.g., ageism, classism) are critical for counseling psychologists to understand. The nuances and complexities in these terms demand a profession that both understands and stays current with the dynamic interplay among these issues.

With regard to race and ethnicity, we focused on three main issues: racism, acculturation and immigration, and racial identity theories. We reviewed the literature on color-blind racial ideology and micro-aggressions (see also Chapter 14). We noted the growing importance of knowledge about immigration issues, given changing demographics and political issues in the United States. And we overviewed the racial identity theories that have had the most impact on the field: Cross's (1971, 1991) model of psychological nigrescence and Helms's (1984, 1992) model of White racial identity.

In the section on sex and gender, we reviewed a small portion of the literatures in the psychology of men and women. We reviewed in particular men's gender role conflict and the consequences of objectification of women. We also reviewed information about violence against women. As with race and ethnicity, the contributions counseling psychologists have made to the literature on women and men's psychology cannot be adequately covered as part of one chapter. However, our aim has been to introduce the reader to topics of importance and to underscore the role of counseling psychologists as researchers, theorists, and social justice advocates.

We also covered topics around sexual orientation, emphasizing, as with the other sections, the difficulties we have encountered defining and researching such complex issues. We focused on issues of heterosexism, sexual identity development models, and marriage and parenting issues. The changes in focus and research methodology over time are quite apparent, with an increasing sophistication in addressing these topics. In the current political and social climate, a greater acceptance of sexual minorities and more difficult political challenges are both apparent. These broad sociopolitical issues impact individuals and, as such, are important for counseling psychologists to understand. But, as counseling psychologists also consider social justice a central value, the broader, systemic issues are also part of the repertoire of what counseling psychologists address (in advocacy, in research, in direct political action).

We conclude with a discussion of social justice in counseling psychology. We highlight the definition Vasquez (2012) suggested: making efforts to decrease human suffering and promote equality and justice. Thus, counseling psychologists balance their roles of the remediative (in reducing suffering) and preventive (in efforts to ensure equitable treatment, opportunities, and access to resources for all) areas, making them well suited for social justice work. We review a number of examples of social justice work in counseling psychology, again recognizing that it is just a small percentage of the actual work being done in the field. We hope that by reading this chapter readers feel well introduced to these issues and compelled to seek out additional information on their own.

Working With Strengths
Counseling Psychology's Calling

7

The focus on strengths and its sister concept, optimal functioning, has been an ingrained part of counseling psychology from the beginning (Walsh, 2003). As we have indicated in Chapter 1, in fact, attention to strengths and optimal function has been an overarching and enduring central value of the specialty over the decades. This orientation may have been most pointedly captured in Donald Super's (1955) brief statement emphasizing counseling psychology's focus on hygiology (or health) rather than psychopathology (or sickness), even when working with the severely disturbed. Thus, the counseling psychologist was said to look for people's strengths and build on them, taking the stance that even profoundly troubled persons have strengths, assets, and coping abilities, and that it is valuable to work with these. This point of view, characterized by hopefulness and optimism, was based on the belief that

> individuals can change, can lead satisfying lives, can be self-directing, and can find ways of using their resources, even though they may have been impaired

http://dx.doi.org/10.1037/14378-007
Counseling Psychology, Third Edition, by C. J. Gelso, E. N. Williams, and B. R. Fretz

by incapacitating attitudes and feelings, slow maturation, cultural deprivation, lack of opportunity, illness, injury, or old age. (Jordaan, Myers, Layton, & Morgan, 1968, p. 2)

As discussed in Chapter 1, the focus on strengths and optimal functioning is evidenced in the developmental, preventive, and remedial roles that counseling psychologists take in their work. However, this focus on strengths is most notable in the developmental role, where, to use the phrase coined by Menninger, Mayman, and Pruyser (1963), we may seek to help clients be "weller than well" (p. 401).

Although this deep philosophical commitment may be seen in the precursors of counseling psychology in the first half of the 20th century, continuing into the second half (Lopez et al., 2006), Gelso and Woodhouse (2003) pointed out that during a 15- to 20-year period beginning in the 1950s, conceptions of positive mental health and human strengths were developing at a particularly fast pace. This focus was witnessed powerfully in the work of the Joint Commission on Mental Illness and Mental Health (1961). Jahoda's (1958) reflection on the Commission's work captures what was happening:

We commonly use "mental health" as a term interchangeable with "mental illness," in the same euphemistic way that "public health" generally refers to the prevention and control of disease by mass methods. The behavioral scientists who have joined the mental health team and are making increasingly important contributions to the mental health movement have expressed dissatisfaction with a primary focus on "sick behavior." They argue that a new and broader perspective is needed if interest in mental health, as a positive force, is to be made conceptually clear and practically useful. (p. ix)

During this period, important conceptualizations of high-level functioning were developed; for example, Rogers's (1962) fully functioning person, Allport's (1963) mature personality, Heath's (1964) reasonable adventurer, and Maslow's (1970) self-actualized person. Although these models were not developed by counseling psychologists, they had a great bearing on the specialty, and counseling psychologists sought to incorporate them into their work. For example, Foreman (1966) did one of the few studies on optimal functioning at the time by comparing college students who functioned psychologically at an especially high level, called "zestfuls," with those with "normal" mental health. At the theoretical level, Blocher (1966, 1974), a counseling psychologist, developed his psychology of effectiveness. Blocher was critical of earlier models of well-functioning because they seemed to depict "idealized paragons of virtue rather than flesh-and-blood human beings" (1966, p. 97). He theorized a set of five characteristics of effective personalities: consistency, commitment, control, competence, and creativity. These qualities were presumed to be strengths of real people instead of idealizations.

As Gelso and Woodhouse (2003) have noted, around the latter part of the time period of these publications, the human potential movement was in full force. Phrases such as "make love, not war" and "rehabilitate rather than incarcerate" were frequently heard. But by around the mid-1970s, work on optimal functioning and strengths, with a few notable exceptions (see subsequent paragraphs in this chapter), seemed to come to a halt. Gelso and Woodhouse suggested that

> no doubt, complex social-cultural-economic factors were at the root of this movement toward the positive. Such factors were also the likely culprits in the movement coming to an end. The post-Vietnam cynicism along with a major economic downturn ushered in a far more conservative era. Positive mental health and attention to human strengths slowly faded from much of the consciousness of psychology. (pp. 172–173)

Although the focus on strengths continued as a philosophical part of counseling psychology and some research continued on positive traits, little theory on optimal functioning or the use of strengths emerged in this post-Vietnam time period. In fact, by the early 1990s, in their review of the contributions of developmental and personality psychology to counseling psychology and vice versa, Gelso and Fassinger (1992) considered the study of the healthy or effective self to represent counseling psychology's unfulfilled promise.

The inattention to the positive was soon to change again, and the impetus for the change came from outside counseling psychology. During his presidency of the American Psychological Association in the late 1990s, Martin Seligman vigorously promoted the study of strengths and coined the term *positive psychology*. Seligman lamented what he viewed as psychology's inattention to the positive and overattention to the study of deficit. In his seminal paper with Csikszentmihalyi, he noted,

> At this juncture, the social and behavioral sciences can play an enormously important role. They can articulate a vision of the good life that is empirically sound while being understandable and attractive. They can show what actions lead to well-being, to positive individuals, and to thriving communities. Psychology should be able to document what kinds of families result in children who flourish, what work settings support the greatest satisfaction among workers, what policies result in the strongest civic engagement, and how people's lives can be most worth living.
>
> Yet psychologists have scant knowledge of what makes life worth living. They have come to understand quite a bit about how people survive and endure under conditions of adversity. . . . However, psychologists know very little about how normal people flourish under more benign conditions. Psychology has, since World War II, become largely about healing. It concentrates on repairing damage within a disease model of human functioning. The almost exclusive attention to pathology

neglects the fulfilled individual and the thriving community. The aim of positive psychology is to begin to catalyze a change in the focus of psychology from preoccupation only with repairing the worst things in life to also building positive qualities. (Seligman & Csikszentmihalyi, 2000, p. 5)

In this statement, Seligman and Csikszentmihalyi (2000) seemed to ignore the history described earlier; nor did they incorporate counseling psychology's long-standing orientation toward strengths or the contributions it had by that time made to the study of strengths, optimal functioning, and the use of strengths in treatment. However, Seligman's singular pursuit of what he termed *positive psychology* served to reinvigorate science and practice on these topics, in and outside of counseling psychology.

In the remainder of this chapter, we explore positive psychology and its role in counseling psychology; counseling psychology's recent contributions to the study and use of strengths in psychological interventions; and the field of counseling health psychology, which also attends to positive development.

Positive Psychology and Counseling Psychology

The term *positive psychology* has been used in a range of ways and, according to Lopez and Edwards (2008), with little precision. Lopez and Edwards noted that in a scan of 855 references on PsycINFO and 10.3 million hits in a Google search, the term has been used to describe a philosophy, a science, a movement, a practice, and a professional specialty. They offered a reasonable working definition of the concept as "the scientific and practical pursuit of optimal human functioning" (Lopez & Edwards, 2008, p. 87). Positive psychology may be seen as encompassing three domains: (a) positive subjective experience (e.g., positive emotions such as joy and pleasure), (b) positive individual traits (e.g., character strengths and virtues), and (c) positive institutions and communities that enable the first two domains (Seligman & Csikszentmihalyi, 2000). In recent years, progress has been made in studying the first two of these. For example, Lopez and Edwards (2008) noted that positive subjective experiences of attachment, flow, spirituality, mindfulness, joy, contentment, interest, and, in particular, happiness have been studied. Lopez and Edwards also indicated that in the area of positive individual traits, "hope, optimism, self-efficacy, emotional intelligence, wisdom, and courage, and more generally, human strengths, have received the most attention from social scientists" (p. 87).

Levels of Theory and Research on Positive Experiences, Strength, and Optimal Functioning

In considering how strengths and optimal functioning may be studied by counseling psychologists, we may consider four levels of research and theory, ranging from broad theories to conceptualizations about individual positive traits and affective experiences. Work at each of these levels is valuable.

The first and broadest level consists of theories of optimal human functioning that are universal and, as such, cut across time and culture. Thus, we may theorize about constellations of strengths and virtues that are universal, and theory can be framed on how these qualities interact with one another, how they were developed, how they may be facilitated, and how they affect people's lives. The aforementioned theories of the fully functioning person (Rogers, 1962), the self-actualized person (Maslow, 1970), the mature personality (Allport, 1963), and the effective personality (Blocher, 1966) are examples of such broad theorizing.

More than four decades ago, R. W. White (1973), one of the leading theoreticians in the area of strengths and ego psychology (see Chapter 11), cautioned counseling psychologists that theories at the broad level of the healthy personality were problematic for two main reasons. First, such theories seemed aligned with the medical model, and second, and more important, the construction of a long list of positive traits overlooks the reality that each person develops an individualized life pattern. Within this pattern, no one can have all the qualities on the list because some are negatively related to others. For example, the qualities that make for a great physician may be the opposite of those that make for a good friend or romantic partner. White argued instead for the study of specific qualities that are implicated in effectiveness (e.g., a sense of competence).

White's reasoning may have had an effect because since his treatise was published, theories have not emerged in counseling psychology at the broad level of the healthy personality. Yet, as Cattell (1973) noted in his response to White's viewpoint, there is likely a common core to all forms of maturity that cut across all fairly complex cultures: Certain traits that are necessary for survival and success (e.g., intelligence, capacity to control impulses and work for more remote gains, foresight, dependability).

Gelso and Fassinger (1992) suggested that theory and research would be useful on the effective or healthy personality (or, we would add, optimal functioning) at both the universal level and a second level. This second level includes more situation-specific or culture-specific theorizing. At this level, for example, one could develop theories of optimal functioning within ethnicities, racial groups, or, more broadly, cultural groups; the similarities and differences between such groups could also be theorized about and studied. Similarly, the focus could be on personality and developmental factors as they relate to optimal function in particular domains (e.g., in work, health, or relationships).

With regard to these two levels, probably the major area in which counseling psychologists have theorized about and studied effective functioning is that of career choice and development (Robitschek & Woodson, 2006; Savickas, 2003). These authors have underscored theories and research within the vocational psychology domain of counseling psychology that embody a focus on positive development or optimal functioning. They suggested that vocational counseling psychologists have historically emphasized the positive aspects of development and have been the cornerstone of counseling psychology's emphasis on building strengths in people.

At a third level, counseling psychologists study individual traits or qualities that are generally positive or adaptive. These include the character strengths and virtues that were noted by Seligman and Csikszentmihalyi (2000) and that we have pointed to earlier by Lopez and Edwards (2008). It is at this level that counseling psychologists appear to have done the most work. Just a few examples of qualities and traits focused on in counseling psychology research and theory over the years are self-efficacy (Hackett & Betz, 1981), effective problem solving (Heppner & Krauskopf, 1987), security of attachment (Woodhouse, Schlosser, Ligiero, Crook, & Gelso, 2003), resilience (Arbona & Coleman, 2008), adaptability of career decision making (Gadassi, Gati, & Dayan, 2012), and work satisfaction (Lent, 2008). Gelso and Fassinger (1992) suggested that work at this level of specific, individual traits or qualities would be maximally useful if it were placed within a broader theoretical framework of healthy or effective personality and functioning. Although this may be so, work at the level of individual positive qualities, in itself, can be highly valuable.

The fourth and final level of theorizing and research in which counseling psychologists are involved is that of positive affects and experiences. Although some work has been done within counseling psychology at this level, Lopez and Edwards (2008) stated that work in this area has been dominated by debates about what constitutes personal happiness and emerging theories about happiness.

We have not mentioned research on Seligman and Csikszentmihalyi's (2008) third domain, that of positive communities and organizations that foster positive traits–qualities and positive affects–experiences. Gable and Haidt (2005) noted that this domain has not attracted as much attention as the domains of positive traits and positive affects. It is a fruitful area for counseling and other psychologists to address.

Strength-Based Interventions

Counseling psychologists have long paid attention to ways of attending to, using, and fostering clients' strengths in counseling and psychotherapy. However, until recent years, there was little explicit writing about just how therapists actually worked with strengths or sought to foster them. It was not until the 21st century that the field began to theorize about and study how strengths are attended to and used in its interventions. In recent years, clinical and theoretical discussions have taken place on how strengths may be used in existing theoretical approaches (Chapters 11–14) and on new approaches that are specifically strength focused.

ATTENTION TO STRENGTHS

We might begin by addressing the question of to what extent counseling psychologists and psychologists in related specialties such as clinical psychology actually attend to clients' strengths in their work, in both their assessment and treatment. Two recent studies point to the fact that therapists do appear to pay close attention and capitalize on clients' strengths in therapy. For example, in a qualitative study, Scheel, Davis, and Henderson (2013) conducted interviews with eight therapists in order to get a picture of how and the extent to which they attended to clients' strengths during treatment. These therapists identified with a range of theoretical orientations. As part of the study, the participants were asked to rate the importance in their work of a strength focus and the importance of a problem focus. On a 10-point scale, ranging from 1 (*not at all important*) to 10 (*extremely important*), therapists' mean ratings for Strength Focus was 8.88, whereas the rating for Problem Focus was 8.13. Thus, it appears that this small, theoretically diverse sample of therapists viewed a strength focus as very important in their work.

Scheel and his collaborators (Scheel et al., 2013) also unexpectedly found that instead of seeing deficits and strengths as two ends of a continuum, the therapists in their study sought to give equal attention to both. These therapists viewed problems and strengths on two different continua, which made it possible to concentrate on problems and strengths at the same time.

Harbin, Gelso, and Pérez Rojas (2013) studied a large sample ($N = 225$) of therapists with a wide range of counseling experience and theoretical orientations. Similar to Scheel et al.'s (2013) small-sample study, Harbin et al. found that therapists place a great deal of importance on work with clients' strengths. And the importance ratings were high for the three factors of treatment that were examined: (a) therapists' use of positive psychology theory in considering how to work with strengths, (b) therapists' assessment of strengths, and (c) therapists' bringing clients' attention to and supporting changes clients have made in therapy. The degree of importance therapists placed on work with strengths was related to their theoretical orientation. The more therapists identified with cognitive–behavioral, humanistic–experiential, and feminist–multicultural theoretical orientations (see Chapters 12, 13, and 14), the greater the importance they placed on working with strengths. However, the degree of identification with a psychoanalytic–psychodynamic orientation was generally unrelated to the importance therapists placed on work with strengths.

Finally, these ratings of importance were substantially related to therapists' reports of the degree to which they actually worked with strengths of the most recent client they saw. Thus, it appears that importance ratings do get translated into what therapists actually do (or at least say they do) with actual clients. Overall, it does appear that psychotherapists as a group at this point in time are paying attention to their clients' strengths, including when making assessments, drawing on positive psychology theories, and supporting clients' growth in treatment.

ATTENTION TO STRENGTHS IN EXISTING THEORETICAL APPROACHES

Within existing approaches to therapy, strengths may be addressed when assessing the client and during the process of providing treatment. Assessment may occur particularly in the early phase of treatment but also continues throughout the counseling process.

Assessing Strengths

The positive psychology movement has been criticized for an overemphasis on the positive. Virtually anyone who writes about attention to strengths in therapy also will mention the importance of taking clients' vulnerabilities or psychopathology seriously. Still, there tends to be such a strong emphasis on the positive that the reader may be left with the question "just how do these therapists work with psychopathology in addition to strengths?" Counselors obviously cannot simply ignore their clients' psychopathology. Clients seek treatment because in one way or another they are in pain, and they have problems, conflicts, or disorders they want to deal with and resolve. It is important that therapists assess both strengths and deficits. In fact, it is not enough to ask about the strengths and weaknesses in the client, for the counselor also needs information on the resources and deficiencies in the client's environment. Wright and Lopez (2002) provided a useful framework in their Four Front Approach. Psychologists are asked to consider four questions of human functioning: (a) What are the strengths and assets of this individual, (b) what are the deficiencies and undermining characteristics of the person, (c) what resources and opportunities exist in the individual's environment, and (d) what are the lacks or destructive factors in the environment? As Lopez, Edwards, Magyar-Moe, Pedrotti, and Ryder (2003) suggested, this Four Front Approach can serve as a useful reminder and guide to look more complexly at human behavior and situations. Lopez et al. also underscored the importance of exploring a client's cultural backgrounds when making assessments of strengths and vulnerabilities of the person and the opportunities and deficits in the environment.

Assessing strengths (and vulnerabilities) usually occurs in the context of what is termed case conceptualizations. Here, the counselor early in treatment develops a conceptualization of the client; his or her presenting problems, background, personality or behavioral patterns; and how he or she is likely to work as a client. Gelso and Woodhouse (2003) enumerated key strengths-related questions to address as part of this conceptualization.

- In what areas of life does the client do well?
- What are the client's internal–psychological assets?
- How adaptable is the client? What is his or her ability to observe himself or herself and his or her psychological processes?
- What is the client's capacity for self-understanding?
- What are the client's relationship strengths?
- What are the client's vocational-career strengths and assets?
- What social supports does the client have?

Gelso and Woodhouse (2003) also noted that which questions are to be asked should be tailored to the individual client, and the questions may be addressed during counseling sessions, through psychological testing, or both. In addition, it is important that the counselor consider clients' strengths within the therapy session, as well as more generally. For example, what aspects of the treatment process does the client do well in? Is the client able to form a sound working alliance with the counselor? Can the client experience feelings in the session? Does he or she have the ability to maintain some degree of control over affects and impulses? Although these assessment-oriented questions may occur most often early in counseling, assessment is also an ongoing process (Chapter 10) and as such occurs throughout counseling.

Strengths During Treatment

Each of the major theoretical orientations has a vision of psychological health, effective functioning, and how strengths ought to be addressed in therapy. At times these visions are spelled out, but more often than not they are implicit and vague. Gelso and Woodhouse (2003) provided a range of examples of how therapists may attend to strengths during counseling, focusing on what the therapist actually does that makes use of and builds on the client's strengths. These tactics may be used across theoretical orientations. The tactics, along with case examples provided by Gelso and Woodhouse, are described in the following.

Pointing Out Strengths

Other than the work of Wachtel (1993, 2011), little has been written about just how to comment on clients' strengths in a way that promotes therapeutic progress. At times, simply pointing out clients' strengths may be very helpful. For example, a 1st-year college student was having trouble adjusting to college life and making friends. This client attended college far from her home, and she lost regular contact with her friends from high school. A campus housing shortage left her in an unusually isolated living situation. When her counselor noted to her the social skills that had allowed her to make friends in high school, the client explored what was happening in her life that, in her words, influenced what her counselor and she dubbed "forgetting her social skills." By using this phrase, the therapist was affirming what actually were her very strong social skills, even though at the time, they did not seem apparent to the client.

It can also be useful to notice strengths that are in the early stages of development. The therapist can point to this developing strength, and this can facilitate the client's owning it and exploring what it feels like to have this strength. For example, a client had significant difficulty expressing his expectations in relationships. In a particular session, he seemed emotionally flat, and the therapist pointed this out. The client shared that he wished the therapist challenged him more on topics he avoided. The therapist asked what it felt like to express this expectation. For this client, the awareness that he was able to do what he had previously felt was undoable helped build a belief in his capacity to do so and foster further exploration.

Wachtel (1993) has pointed out that the process of building strengths is aided by the therapist's commenting on small steps in the right direction. Wachtel used as an example a female client who came to treatment with problems dating men. The therapist had noted that the client had been very disparaging of the men she dated. When this client described a time when she was assertive without being disparaging, the therapist commented,

> I notice you didn't say to him that you earned more than he did, only that you earned a good living. I think that's important to notice, because it's an instance of where you communicated clearly, directly, and yet without threatening him or being excessively competitive. (Wachtel, 1993, p. 117)

The goal had been to build on the capacity she had shown to communicate more effectively, while not the more problematic ways the client communicated with men. At times, it is important to look carefully for positives. For example, with a very troubled client who was unable to experience or explore her feelings, it was helpful to note when she took small steps toward opening up. Over time, her capacity to experience her inner world grew. At times, when no strengths are apparent, the therapist may need to wait and watch for signs of strength.

There are some key factors for the therapist to consider when attempting to notice and point out strengths. Four of the main factors are (a) strengths at times are shown in avoiding old negative behaviors rather than exhibiting new positive behavior, (b) strengths may emerge within the therapeutic relationship that are not evidenced in other areas of the clients life, (c) it may be useful to help the client focus awareness on the body experience of positive affects, and (d) nonverbal responses to clients' strengths (e.g., showing pleasure at a client's progress) can also be valuable.

It should also be noted that at times it is best that the counselor *not* explicitly comment on clients' strengths. For example, one of the authors did long-term therapy with a client whose negative feelings, including painful ones, had been dismissed by her parents throughout childhood. She experienced her therapist's attention to positives as a recapitulation of the dismissive attitude she lived through as a child. Only in the latter phase of this work was the client able to hear comments on her positives as helpful rather than dismissive.

Positive Reframing

One way therapists can bring hidden strengths to light is through reframing apparent weaknesses as strengths to be explored, as in the following example:

> One client had been in twice-a-week therapy for 15 months. This client complained about her inability to deal with graduate school issues with authority figures. She was adamant that she had no control over consistently turning in her papers late. She felt helpless about this pattern of late papers, was continually in conflict with her advisor about this problem, and was deeply anxious about being asked to leave her program. The therapist hoped to help the client realize the strength underlying this defensive pattern, and pointed out that the fact that she was consistently choosing to turn in her papers two days late showed that she did, in fact, have considerable control over her papers. The therapist suggested that with this strength, the client could use the same control to turn in her papers at any time she chose. The client was able to make use of this positive reframe, and suddenly realized that she did have a choice in when to

turn in her papers. She explored the ways in which this pattern reflected a dynamic of rebellion against her mother. The client would passively rebel against her mother by being late, and the mother would respond by being very upset. The client realized that a similar dynamic was being enacted with her advisor. Once these issues were explored, the client no longer continued in the same pattern of lateness. She began to call on her strength to choose, and was able to turn in her assignments on time. (Gelso & Woodhouse, 2003, p. 188)

When reframing apparent weaknesses as strengths, therapists need to be careful that they genuinely believe that what they are addressing actually is a strength. Reframing can easily come across as a kind of trickery or as the therapist not wanting to see the client's pain, which can be experienced as an empathic failure that, in turn, creates ruptures in the working alliance.

Attending to Strengths Embedded in Defenses

Defenses are ordinarily thought of as things to be worked through, resolved, and done away with. In this sense, defenses represent undesirable self-protections that may have been needed at earlier times in one's life but that have outlived their usefulness. However, strengths are often embedded in defenses, and it is helpful to notice and work with these strengths. The therapist can openly express appreciation of a client's strength, even when the therapist and client work together to soften or resolve the defense. An example from the practice of one of the authors was therapy with a client, an attorney, who tended to intellectualize as a way of avoiding painful feelings. However, embedded in this defense was a strength—the ability to think deeply, clearly, and rationally. This person enjoyed using his mind, and his training as an attorney facilitated the sharpness of intellect. He used his intellect in adaptive, nondefensive ways to further his understanding, as well as in defensive ways to avoid his more delicate and threatening feelings. Throughout the work, the therapist appreciated and in fact enjoyed this client's ability to think well. This valuing helped the client feel appreciated and allowed him to move toward opening up his feelings rather than defending against pain, while also maintaining his ability to think through problems.

Finding strengths within weaknesses or defenses can at times be a profound experience for clients. Gelso and Woodhouse (2003) provided examples of this. The key may be for the therapist to ask him- or herself what the strengths are in an individual client's defenses. This frame of mind can also help clients understand that defenses were created for good reasons and that, at the time of their creation, they themselves represented strengths.

Interpreting Strengths in a Cultural Context

Strengths, as well as vulnerabilities, must always be understood and interpreted within the context of the client's cultural background (Constantine & Sue, 2006). Indeed, all cultures possess strengths as well as vulnerabilities, and these must be understood as part of assessing and treating any client. It is important that the student of counseling psychology become familiar with a range of cultures, especially the cultures of which one's clients are a part. Ethnicity and race reflect culture, or at least one aspect of culture, and it is important for therapists to understand the cultural components of their clients' race and ethnicity. McGoldrick, Giordano, and Garcia-Preto (2005) have provided wonderful summaries of the family backgrounds and organizations of 54 different racial/ethnic groups in the United States (e.g., African American families, Slavic families, Korean families), and readings such as this can be invaluable for the student of counseling psychology.

There can be great complexity in the conceptualization of strengths within a cultural context. An example of such complexity was the client who was an international student from South Korea. The work with this client, who had many psychological strengths, revolved around her conflicts with her mother. The mother wanted her either to return to Korea to join the family business or to invite the mother to come to live with her in the United States. Given her strong cultural value around filial piety in the face of her wish to start her own business in the United States without her mother, the client was in great conflict. Her Korean friends pressured her to do as her mother asked, but her American friends pressed her to be assertive and "do your own thing." This represents a clash of cultural values (filial piety vs. individualism), which was being played out internally in the client. As work around this conflict evolved, the client revealed that the mother had been highly abusive both physically and verbally throughout the client's childhood and even when she worked in her mother's business as a young adult. The therapist helped the client explore the ways in which the mother's behavior was inconsistent with her cultural values around good mothering. This facilitated the client's coming to see how her wish to be independent of the mother made sense, and the client came to see this wish as a strength, even though on the surface it was culturally inconsistent. In this case, independence from the mother was not seen as a strength just because it is a valued trait in the United States. The client and therapist took Korean cultural values into account and examined how the realities of the client's life influenced the meaning she made of adherence or nonadherence to cultural norms. The take-home message in this case is that therapists must carefully consider culture when interpreting strengths, and they must be equally carefully not to promote, however subtly, one set of cultural values over another when assessing what is a strength and what is a weakness.

WHAT DO THERAPISTS ACTUALLY DO?

We have cited recent evidence that therapists actually do pay attention to clients' strengths and work to build strengths in their psychotherapy (Harbin et al., 2013; Scheel et al., 2013). But what about their specific methods of working with strengths? In the aforementioned study by Scheel and his collaborators, eight therapists were intensively interviewed about what they did in their sessions that represented working with strengths. These investigators noted that their therapists clearly identified strength-based assessments and therapist behaviors in their sessions. These behaviors strongly fit the ones described above. Thus, Scheel et al. (2013) noted that their therapists' enactments "included asking directly about client strengths or pointing out client strengths, finding strengths embedded in deficits or defenses, using positive reframing, and contextual [e.g., cultural] interpretation of strengths" (p. 422). These investigators underscored that

> the use of client strengths was more than being encouraging and pursuing positives. It was an authentic process in which therapists genuinely believed in the client and trusted that the therapeutic process would uncover positives the client could value. Meanings were formed about strengths by the therapist listening and reframing. Resilience, hope, self-efficacy, and empowerment were linked as strength-oriented concepts in therapy. The client's investment in therapy and the therapeutic alliance became strengths upon which to build and generalize beyond the therapeutic context. (Scheel et al., 2013, p. 421)

Thus, there is some beginning support for the assessment and counseling behaviors pointed to by Gelso and Woodhouse (2003). Research is now clearly needed on the extent to which various strength-oriented assessment and treatment techniques are effective.

STRENGTH-ORIENTED PSYCHOTHERAPIES

In the last section we examined strengths-oriented assessment and intervention techniques that could be integrated into any theoretical orientation and that apparently are used considerably by practicing therapists with a wide range of orientations. However, there are therapeutic approaches that are themselves strength based, and some have existed for many years. Examples of such treatments are Ivey's developmental therapy (Ivey, 1986; Ivey, Ivey, Myers, & Sweeney, 2005) and treatments stemming from couple and family therapy (see Chapter 16), such as solution-focused therapy and narrative therapy. In recent years, and probably stimulated a great deal by Seligman's leadership in calling for a psychology of the positive (e.g., Seligman, 2002; Seligman & Csikszentmihalyi, 2000), new psychological therapies specifically focused on strengths have been developed by counseling psychologists. The two that have received the greatest attention are Smith's (2006) strength-based counseling for adolescents and Wong's (2006) strength-centered therapy. We describe these approaches below.

Strength-Based Counseling (SBC)

In one of the most extensive explorations of the use of strengths in counseling psychology and therapy, E. J. Smith (2006) presented a series of 12 theoretical propositions underlying SBC. Her theory is generally focused on adolescents, with a particular emphasis on at-risk teenagers. As a philosophical and theoretical backdrop to her theory of counseling, Smith wrote,

> The strength perspective requires psychologists to learn that regardless of how poor, downtrodden, or sick the clients may be, they have survived, and in some instances they have thrived, sometimes under the worst of circumstances. . . . People have summoned their strengths when all else seemed lost, and they have coped. The psychologist searches for what people have rather than what they do not have, what people can do rather than what they cannot do, and how they have been successful rather than how they have failed. (p. 38)

Smith theorized 10 stages of SBC that may be summarized as follows:

Stage 1: *Creating the therapeutic alliance.* The counselor builds a relationship with clients by helping them to identify and marshal strengths and competencies to confront their difficulties and adversities.

Stage 2: *Identifying strengths.* The therapist teaches clients to narrate their life stories from the perspective of psychological strengths. Telling one's story, seeing oneself as a survivor, and making sense of one's life tends to have a powerful and positive effect on the client.

Stage 3: *Assessing presenting problems.* Although SBC is solution oriented, counselors must develop a clear understanding of the client's perceptions of the problems, their causes, and their consequences.

Stage 4: *Encouraging and instilling hope.* Smith uses the term *encouragement counseling* to capture the fact that the counselor is strongly oriented toward positive reinforcement (Chapter 12) from the beginning of treatment and throughout. Hope is called the cornerstone of the treatment, and techniques are given for instilling hope.

Stage 5. *Framing solutions.* The strength-based counselor is solution focused and uses a variety of techniques to help create solutions to problems. Techniques are drawn from solution-focused therapy (see Chapter 16).

Stage 6. *Building strength and competence.* The counselor attends to and makes use of the client's external assets (supports and love from family) and internal assets. The counselor seeks to nurture a sense of focus, purpose, and centeredness.

Stage 7. *Empowering.* The process of recognizing and promoting the client's competent functioning. The therapist helps clients activate resources within themselves and within their communities.

Stage 8. *Changing.* Change is a process, and Smith used the concept of "change talk" to capture counselors' focus on helping understand the changes clients need to make to improve their lives, as well as the inner strengths and outer resources they have to help them make those changes. Particular focus is given to changing meaning and reframing so that positives are seen in experiences previously experienced as exclusively negative.

Stage 9. *Building resilience.* The counselor works to help clients develop resilience, which will fortify them from a repeat of the same problem or similar problems.

Stage 10. *Evaluating and terminating.* Counselor and client honor the progress the client has made. They assess the extent to which progress occurred on the client's goals and what client strengths and environmental resources were brought to bear in facilitating the client's achievement of goals. Assessment of the need for further counseling is made.

As the reader has likely noted, the discussion of stages of counseling is quite general. This is a promising theory, and greater specificity and research evaluation will help further refine the theory. More work is needed in specifying just what goes on during sessions and what the therapist does at each step in the process. Smith (2006) provided a helpful case presentation that gives the reader a sense of how her treatment works. Further articulation can make this a highly valuable theory.

Strength-Centered Therapy (ST)

This second recent strength-based approach was developed by Wong (2006), and it seeks to integrate positive psychology theory with postmodern, social constructionist philosophy. As part of the process, strength-centered therapy pays close attention to how political, systemic, and cultural factors structure the meanings clients attach to character strength. What is considered virtuous, as well as the salience of particular character strengths, varies across cultures. Wong conceptualized ST as unfolding in four phases:

Explicitizing Phase

In the initial phase of ST, the therapist focuses on explicitly identifying character strengths. The therapist tentatively points out his or her perceptions of the client's strengths and/or seeks the client's perceptions. The therapist also might reflect on the client's presenting concerns in terms of strengths without negating painful experiences. During this phase the therapist might use reframing as described previously, invite one or two friends of the client to sessions during which they might be asked to offer their perceptions of the client's strengths, and employ other techniques aimed at highlighting strengths, while being careful that this not be done at the expense of the client's freedom to explore the negative.

Envisioning Phase

During this second phase of ST, therapists facilitate the clients' envisioning of the character strengths they wish to develop, as well as the ways in which they can use the strengths identified during the explicitizing phase to help attain their goals. Clients may be asked directly what strengths they want to develop or what strengths will help them meet their goals. An emphasis is on stating these strengths in their positive form, rather than in terms of characteristics to avoid. Clients are encouraged to elaborate the meanings of the strengths they want to develop. For example, if the client wants to develop greater ambition, he or she might be asked to envision a day in his or her future life (e.g., 5 years from now) as an ambitious person.

Empowering Phase

This third phase entails clients experiencing empowerment in the development of their desired character strengths. Empowerment is more likely to occur when clients have the chance to actually use the desired character strength. Wong used the example of a client whose goal it is to cultivate gratitude. This client might begin the habit of describing five things he is grateful for each week in a journal. Clients are also asked who can support them in their efforts to develop the particular strength. Also explored is the reality that the client needs to use judgment as to when and the extent to which a given strength is to be used. This is so because, true to its social constructionist roots, ST pays attention to context and situation as determinants of the appropriateness of behavior.

Evolving Phase

This final phase is most salient during the termination stage of counseling. The term *evolving* implies that the growth process for character strengths is never ending, and it continues long after therapy comes to an end. The therapist and client, during this ending phase, review and celebrate positive changes that have been made by the client, especially as these changes reflect character strengths. The therapist and client also seek to identify areas for further growth. In this sense, ST is like most other therapies in that therapist and client look back at where they have come and look forward to what is needed and hoped for in the future. The difference is that in ST, there is a particular focus on character strengths and how they have developed and facilitated the client's goals. Again, the client may be asked to share areas of growth from the perspective of his or her significant others.

Like Smith's strength-based counseling, Wong's ST is a promising approach that is highly compatible with the enduring central values of counseling psychology. Wong has discussed the need for research on this treatment approach, in terms of how its effectiveness compares with that of other approaches, as well as the clients and problems to which it is best suited. He noted that qualitative designs will also be helpful in studying ST. Finally, Wong noted that the therapist who is effective in using ST is likely to possess the character strength of encouragement. Encouraging therapists may be best at communicating genuine belief and faith in the client and his or her potentials.

A PERSPECTIVE ON STRENGTHS IN THERAPY AND STRENGTH-BASED THERAPIES

In the second decade of the 21st century, after seeming to stray from its roots, counseling psychology is clearly moving toward actualization of its historical emphasis on the positive. This progress is evidenced in the interventions it uses, ranging from psychotherapy to brief, structured interventions aimed at fostering strengths, such as Lopez, Tree, Bowers, and Burns's (2004) strength mentoring. Further theoretical refinements are now needed in terms of approaches to treatment and particular strength-based techniques. There have been promising empirical efforts. For example, Seligman, Rashid, and Parks (2006) developed and empirically studied positive psychotherapy, a manualized set of exercises aimed at alleviating depression. They found this strength-based, brief (up to 14 sessions) treatment to be superior to treatment-as-usual and medication in reducing depression. This is an excellent beginning, and it will be exciting to see what the next decade brings by way of development of strength-based treatments and techniques and the empirical scrutiny of such interventions.

Counseling Psychology and Health

The broader field of psychology has been involved in the study and treatment of the psychological antecedents and consequences of health problems for many years. Chwalisz and Obasi (2008) noted that professional psychologists' earliest health-related roles included helping patients and their families cope with the emotional turmoil and disability related to medical illnesses and conditions. This kind of work was conducted from a traditional mental health perspective, with an emphasis on psychopathology and remediation. Chwalisz and Obasi also suggested that things have changed vastly in the medical field, and these shifts have brought about changes in the health care system in terms of how health problems are to be dealt with. For example, medical advances have eliminated some life-threatening illnesses (e.g., tuberculosis), but many chronic diseases and medical conditions including heart disease, diabetes, and arthritis still exist. Such chronic lifestyle diseases require new ways of conceptualizing health care and of responding to immense increases in costs.

The kinds of changes just described necessitate a shift from an exclusive focus on remediation to a greater emphasis on prevention and public health. In addition, a shift is occurring in health science, from a biomedical model of health and disease to a biopsychosocial model (Chwalisz & Obasi, 2008). Researchers are also now finding genetic bases for at-risk behaviors and, just as important, that these behaviors can be modified and health outcomes improved through psychological treatments.

Given these major shifts in our understanding of health, what prevents health problems, and what facilitates good health, counseling psychology has had an increasingly fitting role to play within the context of health psychology. In fact, a field of counseling health psychology has developed. From its beginnings, counseling psychology has been deeply invested in the health and well-being of people. Whiteley (1984a) has pointed out that, in the field's early years, counseling psychologists worked with other health care professionals in Veterans Administration hospitals in serving the comprehensive, health care needs of returning military people. However, Chwalisz (2012) explained that during the past half century

the range of populations, health issues, and intervention targets and levels has expanded, and counseling psychologists have moved into a much broader range of health care and other professional settings. The basic interdisciplinary nature of counseling health psychology remains the same, however, and counseling psychologists have brought their unique identities and strengths to those interdisciplinary settings. (p. 207)

In their review of counseling psychologists in the health arena, Raque-Bogdan, Torrey, Lewis, and Borges (2013) summarized additional figures that bespeak counseling psychology's increased involvement in matters of health. These investigators noted that the estimated number of counseling psychologists working in hospital settings has quadrupled over the course of three decades; the percentage of counseling psychology graduates taking positions in Veterans Administration medical centers had nearly tripled from 4.7% to 14% between 1995 and 2005; and the percentage of counseling graduates in general hospitals rose from 5.6% to 9% during essentially the same period. In these settings and additional ones, counseling psychologists are providing assessment and treatment in such areas as pain management, eating disorders, heart disease, neuropsychology, infertility, chronic disease, and life-threatening illnesses (Raque-Bogdan et al., 2013).

It appears that doctoral training in counseling psychology increasingly includes the option of graduate study related to health psychology. For example, in their survey of counseling psychology doctoral programs, Nicholas and Stern (2011) discovered that, in program websites, over two thirds of the doctoral programs described faculty involvement in health psychology. Even more to the point, Raque-Bogdan et al. (2013) found that 41% of the doctoral programs in counseling psychology that they studied offered students the opportunity to pursue a minor, a concentration, or a track in health psychology; training directors of these programs reported that approximately 16% of their graduates pursued positions in health psychology.

What Is Counseling Health Psychology?

In the health psychology activities enumerated above, counseling psychologists may do essentially the same work as other psychologists, such as clinical psychologists, when working with health-related problems. However, counseling psychologists bring a particular attitude and skill set to their work revolving around the focus on strengths, well-being, and optimal human functioning. They also bring a particular emphasis on going beyond remediation to addressing the important roles of prevention and development in the area of health. To these contributions, we would add that counseling psychologists' attention to diversity, social justice, and multiculturalism tends to infuse their work on health disparities among certain ethnic/cultural groups and the goals of prevention and development for all groups.

Counseling health psychology is a very young field, especially when one considers that it was as recent as 1985 that Thoresen and Eagleston (1985) introduced counseling psychology to the emerging field of health psychology (Chwalisz, 2012). What is counseling health psychology? And what do counseling health psychologists bring to the table that is distinctive in the health psychology area? The section on Counseling Health Psychology of Division 17 (Society of Counseling Psychology) of the American Psychological Association tells us that counseling health psychologists are

> dedicated to the science and practice of counseling psychology in health related contexts either through research with medical, rehabilitation, or related populations, direct service to individuals across their lifespan (e.g., prevention, adjustment to and recuperation from illness, healthy lifestyle changes, psychological concomitants of medical illnesses), teaching and training of graduate students or the education of other health care professionals, or involvement with health policy. (Section on Counseling Health Psychology of Division 17, 2005)

Thus, it appears that counseling health psychologists do a lot of the same things that other health psychologists do. What is likely to distinguish counseling health psychologists from others is their application of the overarching and enduring central values of the field of counseling psychology to their work as counseling health psychologists, in addition to their greater focus on prevention and development than other psychologists. This is a key point made by Chwalisz (2012), herself a leading counseling health psychologist. She noted that counseling health psychologists have made especially notable contributions in areas springing from their core values. For example, Chwalisz underscored important contributions in the areas of (a) resilience in managing stressful events and environments and the effects of stress and resilience on health; (b) gender, ethnicity, and other cultural dimensions of health and illness; (c) interventions and treatment factors aimed at fostering wellness and healthy development.

Chwalisz (2012) concluded her extensive review by noting that

> most of all, counseling psychologists are doing health psychology, although they may not be conceptualizing their work in that manner. Thus, even greater gains in the nation's health might be possible with a slight shift in perspective of all counseling psychologists. (p. 227)

The years ahead will be telling ones for counseling psychology, as related to matters of health and wellness, and for the young field of counseling health psychology. We expect that this branch of counseling psychology will continue to grow and develop, constructing its own theories, obtaining grant support for its research, and vigorously studying interventions that foster good health and prevent illness. For excellent reviews of the current status and contributions of counseling psychology related to health, the reader is referred to Chwalisz (2012), Chwalisz and Obasi (2008), Tucker et al. (2007), and Buki and Selem (2012).

Summary

From its beginnings, counseling psychology has had as one of its most fundamental values the focus on peoples' strength, well-being, and optimal functioning. This value appeared in theoretical and empirical writings in its early history in the middle of the 20th century. However, attention to strengths and optimal functioning seemed to diminish in the counseling psychology literature to the extent that, in the latter part of the 20th century, Gelso and Fassinger (1992) considered this an area of counseling psychology's unfulfilled promise. The positive psychology movement appeared to produce a turnaround, and since the turn of the century, there has been a renewed interest in the psychology of the positive and the attention of strengths in psychological treatments.

Several assessment questions and therapy tactics for attending to and fostering strengths were described. Questions around clients' personal and environmental strengths were enumerated. Counseling strategies that were discussed were pointing out strengths, including ones that are just emerging and steps in the right direction; positive reframing; attending to strengths embedded in defenses and vulnerabilities; and interpreting strengths within a cultural context. Two strength focused therapies were also summarized: Smith's (2006) strength-based counseling and Wong's (2006) strength-centered therapy. Beginning evidence indicates that practicing therapists do pay attention to strengths in their therapy, and most of the ways in which they do that are consistent with techniques noted in this chapter.

Another area in which attention to strengths and well-being is now being addressed in counseling psychology is research and practice related to physical health: how to enhance health, create healthy lifestyles, and prevent illness. The field of counseling health psychology is now in its earliest stages and is becoming an important part of counseling psychology in general.

Analyzing the Techniques, Processes, and Outcomes of Counseling and Psychotherapy

8

W hy should one do research on counseling and psychotherapy? A modern answer might be that we counseling psychologists need to have evidence of our effectiveness so that insurance companies will continue to pay for counseling services. Although that is certainly true, a more abiding answer is that it matters. We need to know that what we say that is helpful, therapeutic, or curative is actually effective and that we are indeed helping people in distress; providing symptom relief; and assisting people in making positive, affirming changes in themselves and their lives.

On the surface, this seems like a relatively straightforward question to answer. Did your treatment help someone? As you will see in this chapter, the answers to that question are anything but straightforward. Hence you will see an entire field of research dedicated to answering it in a variety of ways. We focus in this chapter on psychotherapy research findings. We also include a detailed discussion of the techniques of therapy because much of the research on psychotherapy has focused on what therapists do in counseling to effect change.

http://dx.doi.org/10.1037/14378-008
Counseling Psychology, Third Edition, by C. J. Gelso, E. N. Williams, and B. R. Fretz

Before we begin to discuss the details of the research, however, there are a few terms with which we think the reader should be familiar: process research and outcome research. One key way of differentiating counseling research pertains to whether the focus is on the process of one or more interventions or on the effect or outcome of the intervention. The distinction between process and outcome has had a long history in the area of counseling or therapy research (Hill & Corbett, 1993; Hill & Williams, 2000). In this section, we clarify the distinction and summarize some central findings and issues in the area of counseling outcomes.

Process generally refers to what happens during an intervention (e.g., counseling, therapy), usually in terms of counselor behaviors, client behaviors, and the interaction between client and counselor (Hill & Corbett, 1993; Lambert & Hill, 1994). As Hill and Corbett (1993) clarified, the behavior being studied can be either overt (e.g., what can be observed by others, such as movements or verbal statements) or covert (e.g., that which cannot be directly observed, such as thoughts, internal reactions, inner experiences). Studies of the process of counseling have been occurring for decades (see Robinson, 1950), and a large literature has developed (Hill & Williams, 2000; Scheel & Conoley, 2012).

Whereas process research focuses on what goes on (e.g., during a counseling hour), *outcome* research examines the results or effects of particular treatments. The researcher may study outcomes that represent a step toward the changes that are desired and/or the desired effects themselves. An example of a step toward the desired change might be the client's expressing feelings more openly during sessions at the end of treatment than the beginning. Outcomes at this level may be referred to as *proximate* outcomes, because they approximate a desired effect but do not actually measure that effect. Outcomes that actually measure the effect that is sought can be referred to as *distal* or *ultimate* outcomes (e.g., specific behavior change being sought, increase in appropriate expression of feeling outside of treatment). Finally, outcome measurement usually occurs directly after treatment ends and at follow-up. Such follow-ups may take place anywhere from a few weeks to many months to, at times, years after the intervention ends.

Outcome Research

Eysenck (1952) conducted what is considered to be the first attempt at examining evidence of psychotherapy effectiveness (Heesacker & Lichtenberg, 2012). His paper is infamous in the psychotherapy community because he suggested not only that psychotherapy was ineffective but that it might actually be counterproductive or harmful. As you can imagine, those who conducted psychotherapy strongly disagreed. First, there was a barrage of critiques about Eysenck's methodology in the late 1950s and early 1960s, resulting in the emergence of several major psychotherapy research programs (such as Lester Luborsky's Penn Psychotherapy Research Project, Hans Strupp's Vanderbilt studies, and David Shapiro's Sheffield Project, to name just a few) and a number of American Psychological Association (APA) conferences that highlighted psychotherapy research in 1958, 1961, and 1966 (Muran, Castonguay, & Strauss, 2010). In 1963, the journal *Psychotherapy* was launched, followed by the establishment of Division 29 (Psychotherapy) of the APA (Williams, Barnett, & Canter, 2013). In 1970, David Orlinsky and Kenneth Howard held the first meeting of the newly formed Society for Psychotherapy Research (SPR) in Chicago. To this day, the SPR remains the major international organization for psychotherapy researchers.

Thus began a wave of research that continues today to look into the question of therapy's effectiveness. In general, these studies contradicted Eysenck's findings, suggesting that psychotherapy is indeed helpful. (We highly recommend that the reader review the March 2013 special issue of the journal *Psychotherapy*, which reprints a series of papers between Strupp and Eysenck in which they debated the "outcome problem in psychotherapy." This issue also includes a number of articles that address the current state of outcome research in therapy.) To summarize a large body of research evidence, researchers sometimes use a strategy called *meta-analysis*. A meta-analysis is a statistical procedure in which numerous empirical studies are examined to seek a common effect size. In other words, across studies, what is the overall effect of the construct in question? Rather than summarize what the studies have found in words, meta-analysis allows for a mathematical and statistical answer to the general finding across studies. The first meta-analysis to look at the outcome of psychotherapy was by M. L. Smith and Glass (1977). They analyzed the results of 375 studies, arriving at an overall effect size of .68 suggesting that on average, psychotherapy is beneficial. Specifically, compared with nontreatment controls, clients in therapy improved more than 75% of the control group members. So, as in Eysenck's study, some people in the control group improved without counseling (called *spontaneous remission*). However, those in counseling improved in greater numbers, showing evidence of positive therapeutic outcomes.

As continuing research firmly established the effectiveness of psychotherapy, researchers turned to examining the differential effectiveness of various psychotherapeutic approaches. Chapters 11 to 14 overview the major theoretical approaches to counseling and psychotherapy: psychoanalytic and psychodynamic approaches, humanistic and experiential approaches, cognitive and behavioral approaches, and feminist and multicultural approaches. Although training of psychotherapists has become more integrative over time (Boswell, Nelson, Nordberg, McAleavey, & Castonguay, 2010; Norcross & Halgin, 2005), initially (and still sometimes today) psychologists were trained in a particular approach to the exclusion of other approaches. That led, in part, to suggestions that one type of therapy was more effective than other types. As you might imagine, the research on this issue soon followed. The overarching finding, to the consternation of practitioners and researchers alike, was that there were no significant differences, on the whole, between different therapy approaches. Luborksy, Singer, and Luborsky (1975) referred to this finding as the Dodo Bird hypothesis, based on Lewis Carroll's book *Alice in Wonderland*, where the Dodo Bird claims after a race that "everybody has won, and all must have prizes" (Carroll, 1865/2001, p. 18).

Again, outcome researchers adjusted their lens and began asking "what treatment, by whom, is most effective for this individual with that specific problem, and under which set of circumstances?" (Paul, 1967, p. 111). Another wave of psychotherapy research began to address these nuances and interactions in terms of both outcomes and process, resulting in more influential research programs in the 1980s and 1990s at major universities throughout the world (Muran et al., 2010).

If we now know that therapy in general is effective, why is there a growing and vibrant field of psychotherapy research today? We mentioned at the start of this chapter that the question "Did your treatment help someone?" is more complex than it looks and has not been sufficiently answered. How would a researcher begin to study psychotherapy and answer this question? First, what is the treatment? You could start by noting the theoretical orientation of the practitioner (see Chapters 11–14). If you know that the therapists in your study are all cognitive–behavioral, do you have enough information? Not likely. What else might be pertinent about the treatment? Researchers consider such questions as the following: How long was a treatment (e.g., number of sessions, time spent in therapy in months)? How often did the client and counselor meet (e.g., once a week, twice weekly, once a month). How long was each session (e.g., the typical 50-minute hour, 30 minutes, 2 hours)? What modality of the treatment was used (e.g., individual therapy, couples therapy, group therapy)? Who was the therapist (e.g., demographic characteristics of therapist, such as age, gender, race)? Do these personal characteristics have impact? How competent is the therapist at delivering the treatment? How do you know? If therapists say they are providing cognitive–behavioral therapy, how do you know they are? What elements define the treatment? What elements of that treatment are shared in common by other treatments? Ok, that's a lot so far. Perhaps you are starting to see the complications.

How about the "someone" in the question? Who is the client? What are the client's personal characteristics? What kind of concern or problem is the client seeking help for? Would the treatment for this person with depression look the same as the treatment for this person with career confusion? How insightful is the client or how resistant? And what do we mean by "help"? How will we know if the treatment helped the client? Do we take the client's word (self-report), the therapist's word (self-report), an observer's report (observation)? Do we use surveys? Do we use behavior measures? Would we get different answers if we used different measures? When should we give the measures? During the session, immediately following the session, 2 weeks later, 6 months later? If we find that we "helped" immediately following the session, do we know if that helpful effect lasted?

Okay, it's complicated. We don't mean to scare anyone off from psychotherapy research. In fact, *we* are psychotherapy researchers and so have a deep passion for the field. We find that the unpackaging of the simple question of helpfulness of therapy is fascinating. It's a puzzle that we (and many others) are simply impassioned to solve, particularly because the results of this work have such important implications for those who receive psychotherapy. Let's assume for a moment that we haven't frightened you away from therapy research. How might you take on some of these elements of therapy in order to create research designs that address the question?

To help you consider this question, we focus here on three primary areas of research that attempt to answer questions about the outcome of therapy: efficacy versus effectiveness, empirically supported treatments, and common factors across therapeutic treatments.

EFFICACY VERSUS EFFECTIVENESS

As we learned in Chapter 4, do we take our research questions to the lab or go out into the field? This question of approach has been referred to as the *efficacy versus effectiveness controversy* in the literature (Nathan, 2007). *Efficacy studies* are those that allow researchers a high degree of control over conditions and variables such as the type of treatment, the length of treatment, and the presenting problem of the client. In efficacy studies, researchers employ random assignment of participants to different conditions (such as a treatment condition and a no-treatment control), and those conditions are typically highly structured or standardized. Although high in internal validity, efficacy studies have been criticized for being lower in external validity, or their generalizability to actual therapy (Shean, 2012). That is where effectiveness studies come into play.

Effectiveness studies are those that use naturalistic models (e.g., field studies) to examine an aspect of therapy as it occurs in actual practice. As you might imagine, a challenge for effectiveness researchers is accessing a population willing to be studied in the context of actual counseling. Effectiveness studies are also "messy" in terms of lack of control over what happens in the therapy and who the clients are. The researcher must take the setting "as is." However, this type of research shows us what really happens in therapy and thus is not limited in its generalizability the way efficacy studies are.

To give you a comparison of these types of research, we contrast here two approaches to exploring the outcomes for the treatment of depression. In the first example, an efficacy study, Connolly Gibbons et al. (2012) examined brief psychodynamic treatment for depression in a community mental health setting. Connolly Gibbons et al. compared 40 patients in which approximately half were randomly assigned to receive supportive–expressive (SE) dynamic therapy whereas the other half were assigned to receive treatment as usual over 12 weeks. The therapists in the SE condition were recruited from the community mental health setting and were trained in relationship focus, alliance building, socialization strategies, educational techniques, and cultural sensitivity. The results of the comparison indicated that the clients in the SE condition showed greater symptom improvement, with effect sizes comparable to those reported for cognitive therapy compared with treatment as usual (see Simons et al., 2010). Their study, although including a treatment-as-usual component, employed an efficacy approach in that clients were randomly assigned to treatment conditions that were structured (both types of treatment were limited to 12 weeks, and the SE condition employed a manualized approach ensuring standardization of the treatment). Using a manualized approach is a common strategy for randomized control trials (or RCTs), a typical form of efficacy study (Maltzman, 2012).

In contrast, Blais et al. (2013), although also studying treatment as usual for depression, employed an effectiveness strategy. Effectiveness approaches were highlighted in 1995 by Seligman, who called for greater attention to studies of treatment in the naturalistic environment that do not employ random assignment or use control groups. Blais et al. examined the experiences of 1,322 patients receiving treatment for depression in an academic medical center. Although they did not assign patients to treatments, they did gather information about the type of treatment received (e.g., individual psychotherapy, pharmacotherapy, or a combined treatment). They found that on average all treatments produced improvement and that the rates of change were similar across treatment groups. Thus, they established a strong argument for the effectiveness of psychotherapy (and pharmacotherapy) for the treatment of depression under real-world conditions.

Both Connolly Gibbons et al. (2012) and Blais et al. (2013) provided useful and interesting information about the treatment of depression.

Both have made important contributions to the psychotherapy research literature. What differs primarily is their particular approach: efficacy versus effectiveness. It is our contention that both efficacy and effectiveness studies are important, allowing us to move the "bubble" of our research limitations (see Chapter 4) and examine the same topic with a different lens.

EMPIRICALLY SUPPORTED TREATMENTS DEBATE

In recent years, the counseling and psychotherapy field has been faced with a deep paradox in the area of counseling outcomes. On the one hand, it has become clear that counseling and therapy, on the whole, are efficacious. This fact has been repeatedly supported over many years (Lambert, 2013). Additionally, research evidence supports the idea that on the whole, the established theoretical approaches to counseling (e.g., psychoanalytic, humanistic, cognitive–behavioral) seem to be about equally effective (Wampold et al., 1997). Thus, it appears that (a) counseling in general is effective and (b) the established treatments do not differ in their general efficacy.

On the other hand, a movement has occurred that assumes that some treatments are more demonstrably effective than others and that seeks to select and publicly list these specific treatments. The empirically supported treatments (EST) movement (Chambless & Ollendick, 2001) has sought to create a list of specific treatments that have been found through research to be effective for clients with specific disorders, with the idea that those treatments would receive priority in graduate training and insurance reimbursements.

This movement was spawned partly by the wish to present to governmental agencies and insurance companies lists of psychological treatments of proven effectiveness and also partly by the fear that psychotherapy would be left out of rapidly emerging practice guidelines in favor of psychopharmacological agents that are no more effective (Elliott, 1998). Division 12 (Clinical Psychology) of the APA established a task force to create the list (Chambless, 1996; Task Force on the Promotion and Dissemination of Psychological Procedures, 1995). Although it may seem obviously worthwhile to spell out which of our treatments have been validated by research, the effort to create a list has been deeply controversial.

The sources of the controversy are many (Bohart, 2000; Lampropoulos, 2000), but some of the arguments against the creation of a list of validated treatments seem most telling. The most fundamental arguments focus on the criteria used for validation. First, the criteria for validating treatments had initially required that these treatments be manualized. Thus, therapists would conduct treatment according to a written manual, which many believe inhibits creative advances and ultimately hinders effectiveness. As Blatt (1995) suggested,

> We run the risk that treatment manuals can become mechanistic cookbooks which do violence to the complexities of the therapeutic encounter. To put it another way, painting by numbers may produce a painting, but it is not a work of art. Nor is it a way to inspire students to become artists or to teach them the subtleties of painting. (p. 75)

A second fundamental difficulty with the list was that the criteria required the use of specific treatments. This would tend to disfavor the efforts to provide theoretically integrative treatment. Third, the criteria clearly favored treatments and studies that addressed specific client problems or diagnoses. Many therapies, for example, those that were humanistically and psychodynamically based, were not developed to treat specific problems and are not studied in the context of specific client problems or disorders. In other words, these therapies seek to treat a range of problems and diagnostic groupings. The requirement that treatments be validated for specific problems also ignores the fact of "comorbidity" (i.e., most clients do not have single, specific problems).

Given the criteria for "validation," it is not surprising that the large majority of treatments on the original list produced by the task force fit clearly within the behavioral and cognitive approaches. These approaches fit very well with the criteria. A consequence of the particular criteria used for validation has been that a number of major theory-based treatments that have been empirically supported in studies using criteria relevant to those theories may never get on the list.

The movement toward listing and publicizing the psychological treatments that have been empirically supported has continued, but it has also shifted over time. For example, it is becoming more common now to refer to "evidence-based practice" (Carter & Goodheart, 2012) rather than empirically supported (or its precursor, empirically validated) treatments. We are encouraged by these semantic changes because the earliest terms implied a degree of definitiveness that is scientifically unwarranted. More important, the criteria for support or validation continue to be broadened and further refined to allow for a wider range of types of research, as well as client selection and treatment approaches that allow for fairer evaluation of many different theories.

Division 17 has been actively involved in formulating a counseling psychology perspective on identifying empirically supported interventions (Wampold, Lichtenberg, & Waehler, 2002) and evidence-based practice (Wampold & Bhati, 2004) for some time. In particular, Wampold and Bhati (2004) cautioned that evidence-based movements (both those labeled as EBPs, or empirically based practice, and those labeled as ESTs), although important in many ways, have tended to overemphasize theoretical and treatment differences (e.g., cognitive–behavioral therapy compared with placebo control in a randomized, double-blind study) and underemphasize other factors in psychotherapy that contribute to outcome, such as the psychotherapeutic relationship (see Chapter 9) and other "common factors" (discussed in detail in our next section). They suggested that our historical reliance on the medical model (and its emphasis on Food and Drug Administration rules for approving drugs) has led to a research approach to psychotherapy grounded in a flawed logic—that we could ever create such a double-blind placebo design. Kirsch (2005) suggested that "placebo psychotherapy" is an oxymoron because "it is impossible to devise a meaningful placebo control for psychotherapy" (p. 800). As Wampold and Bhati pointed out, a psychotherapy placebo is not "inert" (as would be expected in a drug trial) but is "indistinguishable from the active treatment" (p. 566). They also emphasized that research on psychotherapy can never be truly blind because "quite obviously, the psychologist must be aware of the treatment being delivered" (p. 566).

Borkovec and Sibrava (2005) have called for an abandonment of the placebo condition in psychotherapy research. They instead called researchers to attend more fully to basic knowledge (e.g., causal conditions that can be established with experimental methods; see Chapter 4) and less so to practical questions (e.g., which therapies are most effective?) because, they argued, these practical questions are "not directly answerable by scientific methods" (Borkovec & Sibrava, 2005, p. 807). Given the problems with the use of a psychotherapy placebo (including ethical issues), they suggested instead a refocusing on other designs available to the psychotherapy researcher. For example, they noted that dismantling and additive designs (where one systematically removes or adds specific psychotherapeutic elements to assess their impact on outcome) have been very useful in establishing active ingredients of psychotherapies (e.g., Newman, Castonguay, Borkovec, Fisher, & Nordberg, 2008). In particular, they suggested that parametric designs (where levels of a construct, such as duration, are compared within a treatment type) and catalytic designs (where interactions among treatment effects are examined) may be the most powerful research designs at our disposal.

On the whole, the shift in psychotherapy research within counseling psychology has underscored one of the central values of our field: the emphasis on the whole person. Rather than take a medical model approach, counseling psychology psychotherapy research has placed greater emphasis on examining the underlying "person" factors and how they relate to the "environment" of counseling. In particular, as Wampold and Bhati (2004) suggested, psychotherapy research needs to attend to factors of the therapist and client, their relationship, and those "common factors" that impact outcome across treatments. Thus, we now turn our attention to the research on common factors.

COMMON FACTORS APPROACH

Despite the empirically supported treatment movement, most studies across different therapeutic orientations have shown very few differences in outcome. Thus, attention has turned to looking at what factors are "pantheoretical" (Grawe, 1997) and common to all therapies. A great deal of work has looked at the common factors (Wampold, 2001) that impact therapy regardless of theoretical approach. With this common factor perspective, a number of different categories have been studied. One area of common factors that are somewhat understudied and yet critical to psychotherapeutic success (Bohart & Tallman, 2010) includes client factors, such as hope, motivation, and involvement. Norcross and Lambert (2006) suggested that client factors, particularly severity of distress, account a significant amount of variance in outcomes.

Common factors associated with the therapist include constructs such as empathy (Norcross, 2010) and management of countertransference or self-focused attention (Williams, Hayes, & Fauth, 2008). An interesting therapist factor that has not been studied as much is the impact of the individual therapy, or *therapist effect*. Wampold (2006) suggested that therapist effects may outweigh the impact of the therapeutic working alliance (described in Chapter 9). In other words, "some psychotherapists consistently produce better outcomes than others" (Wampold, 2006, p. 205). Some researchers have looked into what makes master therapists effective (e.g., Jennings & Skovholt, 1999; Skovholt & Jennings, 2004) and have found that master therapists value cognitive complexity, possess strong relationship skills, and attend to their own emotional well-being in ways that create an emotionally receptive environment for their clients. These findings support the research that suggests that the psychotherapeutic relationship is indeed a key curative factor in therapy. They also suggest that becoming a master therapist is not just "an accumulation of time and experience" (Jennings & Skovholt, 1999, p. 9); rather, master therapists can be identified as those who are "voracious learners" and who are open to feedback, are self-aware, and demonstrate maturity regardless of experience level. The findings also suggest ways in which therapists may not be masters; examples include highly skilled and intelligent therapists who lack emotional maturity or self-insight and highly insightful therapists who are less comfortable with ambiguity and complexity. Indeed, there appears to be growing interest in the person of the therapist as a research topic, one that we will cover in the section on process research.

Finally, a tremendous amount of research has been conducted on the therapeutic relationship as a common factor across treatment modalities and orientations. As one key instance, a significant amount of research has looked at attachment style (Bowlby, 1973) as a factor associated with positive therapy outcome. For example, Mallinckrodt,

Porter, and Kivlighan (2005) found that secure attachment styles were associated with greater client exploration in therapy. In contrast, avoidant attachment has been linked with difficulty forming a strong therapeutic relationship (see Fuertes et al., 2007; Marmarosh et al., 2009). (See Chapter 9 for more information about the therapeutic relationship, including the working alliance, the real relationship, transference, and countertransference.)

Researchers have also studied ruptures and repairs in the therapeutic alliance between the therapist and client. Safran, Muran, Samstag, and Stevens (2001) suggested that taking a nondefensive stance can be an effective way to repair a problem with the alliance. Repairing ruptures in the alliance is important because unaddressed ruptures can lead to termination or slowed progress in therapy (Gelso & Samstag, 2008). For example, Hill, Nutt-Williams, Heaton, Thompson, and Rhodes (1996) found that therapists were often surprised by unilateral termination after an impasse and found themselves struggling with self-doubt and ruminating thoughts in the aftermath. They tended not to recall a specific rupture event but suggested that ruptures occur when there are pervasive problems in the therapeutic relationship. Hill and Williams (2000) suggested that research on both ruptures and impasses is important to helping us understand when therapy doesn't work. Of note, there has been a resurgence of interest in the ways in which psychotherapy is not always effective (echoing Eysenck's early criticism; see Lilienfeld, 2007). Barlow (2010) called for greater attention to the negative effects of psychotherapy as a way to ameliorate the effects of harm and to better understand the causes of harm. Castonguay, Boswell, Constantino, Goldfried, and Hill (2010) emphasized the need to understand harmful effects in order to improve the training of psychotherapists.

As you can see, the research on psychotherapy outcomes is extensive. It has not dimmed in interest or productivity in the last 60-plus years. Although numerous unanswered questions remain, we do have evidence of therapy's effectiveness across theoretical approaches and a growing body of evidence about what makes all of these diverse approaches efficacious.

Process Research and the Techniques of Counseling

Now that we hope to have convinced you that we *can* study the outcome of therapy, we have just as much (if not more) to learn about what actually happens in the room. Before discussing the findings uncovered by process research, we describe the range of techniques used in counseling.

In so doing, we are not seeking to provide the student with a cookbook on how counseling should proceed. Rather, the aim is to give an overall picture of the kinds of responses counselors make to clients in an effort to promote positive change. We particularly like Harper and Bruce-Sanford's (1989) definition of *technique* as "a defined tool or method that is employed by the counselor in order to facilitate effective counseling or positive behavior change in the client" (p. 42). Implied in this definition is the idea that techniques are deliberate. That is, they are verbal and nonverbal responses made by the counselor with the conscious intent of fostering certain behavioral or internal reactions in the client. As Brammer, Abrego, and Shostrom (1993) reminded us, the value of techniques is very limited unless the counselor has a good understanding of the therapeutic goals for which he or she is striving, of the basic attitudes that are central to counseling, and of the theoretical assumptions to which the techniques are tied (see Chapters 11–14). In essence, the use of techniques without a broader understanding of counseling will be ineffectual in the long run. Brammer et al. (1993) brought this point home when they noted, "One characteristic of a charlatan is blind adherence to pat techniques applied indiscriminately to all clients" (p. 111).

Counselor techniques can be divided into three general levels or categories (see Table 8.1). The first two categories (nonverbal and verbal behavior) contain the most specific and observable levels of counselor technique. Techniques at these levels are not necessarily derived from particular theories of counseling (e.g., open questions, which come under the heading Verbal Behavior and are used in all theories). In this chapter, we focus on these first two levels of technique. The third category

TABLE 8.1

Classification of Counselor Techniques

Level or category	Definition	Example
Level 1: Nonverbal behavior	Behavior not expressed through formal language	Facial expression, eye movements, body language, non-language sounds, touch, silence
Level 2: Verbal behavior	Classes of verbal responses counselors make with clients	Minimal encourager, approval, information, direct guidance, questions, paraphrase, interpretation, confrontation, disclosure
Level 3: General strategies	Border procedures usually	Empty chair technique, systematic desensitization, free association

tends to contain more abstract and general variables that must be inferred from behavior but that may not be directly observable. These variables are often derived from particular theories of counseling. For example, the "empty-chair technique" derives from gestalt therapy. These Level 3 general strategies are examined in Chapters 11–13.

NONVERBAL BEHAVIOR

Imagine yourself in counseling with a psychologist whose actual words to you seem to convey caring, interest, and respect as you relate some emotionally painful experiences. At the same time, this counselor looks out the window rather than at you most of the time, speaks in a flat and emotionless tone of voice, sits with arms folded while leaning back in an easy chair, and when sitting up frequently taps his or her foot. Despite the counselor's positive words, you would not have to be a psychologist yourself to feel that something was wrong here and to feel hurt by the psychologist's nonverbal responses. You probably would not stay around for counseling very long unless this changed. (We hope not!)

Although this example may seem extreme, we have observed counselors whose nonverbal behavior was quite inconsistent with their verbal behavior, something that can vastly and negatively impact the success of counseling. Effective counselors are aware that they are always communicating with clients through a wide range of nonverbal mechanisms, realizing that they, as well as their clients, cannot *not* communicate messages and cues nonverbally. These counselors pay attention to their own and their clients' nonverbal behavior and are able to read such behavior effectively. As discussed by Hill (2009), nonverbal behavior can be divided into several categories (see Table 8.2). Among the most common and important are paralanguage, facial expression, kinesics, eye contact, and proxemics. When such behavior pertains to the counselor's

---

TABLE 8.2

Categories of Nonverbal Behaviors in Counseling

Category	Definition
Paralanguage	How things are said rather than what is said.
Facial expression	Facial movements that communicate meaning and intent.
Kinesics	Body movements other than facial expression and eye movements. "Touch" is a form of kinesics.
Eye contact	Extent to which participants look at each other and how they look at each other.
Proxemics	How space is structured and used; for example, seating distance between counselor and client.

reactions, it is often referred to as *attending behavior* (how the counselor physically orients himself or herself to the client).

Paralanguage pertains to how things are said rather than what is said. Paralinguistic cues qualify how a word or verbal message is sent or received. For example, the flat and emotionless voice tone used by the counselor described at the beginning of this section was a paralinguistic cue, qualifying as it did the counselor's verbal expression of interest, caring, and respect; making that expression, in effect, less believable to the client. In addition to voice tone, paralanguage includes spacing of words, emphasis, inflection (loudness and pitch), pauses, various nonlanguage sounds (e.g., moans, yells), and nonwords ("uh," "ah"). These nonwords are sometimes referred to as *minimal encouragers* (Hill, 2009). The minimal encourager is a short utterance (e.g., "Mm-hm," "I see," "Okay") that may show simple acknowledgment, agreement, or understanding. It usually reflects acceptance of the client and encourages the client to continue talking. In this sense, it aims to facilitate the client's exploration and convey acceptance. As a caution, phrases like "mm-hm" can at times be used too frequently, so that the flow of the session is impeded by the seemingly constant use of "encouragers."

Facial expression is another area of nonverbal behavior. Counseling is typically done face-to-face; thus, the face itself features prominently in what is occurring between counselor and client. Even if our paralanguage (how we say things) is matched to the words we are using, facial expression is a key factor in how the meaning of the message may be received. Counselors, in fact, often point to a mismatch of spoken language and facial expression in their clients (e.g., a client who is smiling while relaying a traumatic and painful experience) as a way to explore the meaning of a client's story. Counselors' facial expressions, too, communicate to the client; for example, smiles, frowns, and blank stares may convey interest, concern, and inattentiveness. Although we wouldn't want a novice counselor to be overly concerned about his or her facial expressions, we do encourage counselors to adopt a relaxed and comfortable expression.

Kinesics pertains to body movements other than facial expression and eye movements. In the example used to begin our discussion of nonverbal behavior, the counselor's leaning back, arm folding, and foot tapping were body movements that fit this category. Ekman and Friesen (1969) categorized body movements into four types. *Emblems* are movements that can clearly substitute for words; for example, waving good-bye. *Illustrators* are movements that occur at the same time as speech and serve to clarify visually what is being said; for example, dropping one's head in cupped hands to indicate sadness. *Regulators* monitor the flow of verbal interaction; for example, head nods, shifts in posture. Finally, *adaptors* are body movements without conscious communicative purpose, although they are often indicators of inner thoughts and feelings;

for example, head scratching, foot tapping, biting one's lips. Research in counseling psychology has long established the impact body movements can have in counseling; for example, approximately 50 years ago Fretz (1966) found that counselors' forward body lean and direct body orientation were related to positive evaluations of counseling by clients. How the counselor uses his or her body in counseling communicates something to the client (whether he or she means to or not!).

An area of nonverbal behavior that is often classified under kinesics is that of *touch* in counseling. This may well be the most controversial of the nonverbal topics (Bonitz, 2008). Some therapists maintain that touch should never occur in counseling or therapy, with the possible exception of handshakes, for example, upon meeting, after initial sessions, before or after vacations, or at termination. Similarly, many counselors have a conservative view about touching clients, believing that this nonverbal behavior should be engaged in with great caution. The concern about physical contact is that it may overstimulate clients' dependency, arouse sexual impulses or fears of the counselor's sexual motivations, and move the counseling away from being a "talking cure" and toward physical acting-out. Within this conservative viewpoint, some counselors do believe that certain kinds of physical contact with clients are appropriate and even helpful in certain, specific situations. For example, in moments of crisis or great emotional pain, touching the client's hand can helpfully communicate concern and provide comfort (Hunter & Struve, 1998).

Eye contact and *proxemics* are also important and somewhat complicated categories of nonverbal behavior. For example, the extent to which clients and therapists look at each other, and how they look at each other, may have significant impact on the strength of the therapeutic relationship. Although early research showed that counselor eye contact was related to clients' positive ratings of their counselors (Lee, Uhlemann, & Haase, 1985), the construct is more complicated than it first appears. Have you ever noticed whether you look directly at people while you speak or while they are speaking? Do you assume that "rules" for eye contact are similar for most people? How do you feel if you are speaking to someone and he or she is not looking at you? Miscommunication can arise when there is a mismatch in expected eye contact. As just one of many examples, Hill (2009) noted the impact of cultural factors on eye contact behavior. She noted that White middle-class North Americans tend to maintain eye contact while listening but look away when speaking. Conversely, African Americans tend to maintain eye contact when speaking but look away when listening. Further, Brammer and MacDonald (1996) noted that sustained eye contact is considered a sign of disrespect by some Native American groups. The cultural scripts around eye contact are clearly complex. Similarly, there are different cultural scripts about how close we should be to another person in different contexts (i.e., proxemics). For example, early research (E. T. Hall, 1963) established that there are different distance zones among White middle-class Americans for different types of communication: intimate (0–18 inches), personal (1.5–4 feet), social (4–12 feet), and public (12 feet or more). For those from different ethnic groups, from different socioeconomic groups, or from other countries, the distances for those types of communication may vary quite a bit and can impact how comfortable or uncomfortable they all feel.

As stated earlier, there is no "cookbook" on the right way to be a counselor. Our best advice is to become familiar with the multicultural research (see Chapter 6) and try to be as genuine, relaxed, and comfortable as you can be in a counseling session, while staying attuned to the different nonverbal needs and preferences of your clients. We also suggest paying close attention to your own nonverbal behavior and communicating a sense of involvement with and interest in the client and what he or she is sharing. Hill (2009) emphasized that each counselor–client dyad may establish its own set of rules for nonverbal behavior and that one must study each dyad individually rather than try to establish a universal set of nonverbal qualities applicable to all.

VERBAL BEHAVIOR

Although it is clear that nonverbal behaviors have communicative power unto themselves, much of what goes on between counselor and client is at a verbal level. One of the most useful approaches to understanding counselor verbal behavior is what is often called the *response modes* approach. Here, the focus is on the grammatical structure of the counselor's verbal response, rather than on the content. Thus, for example, we classify counselor responses into categories or types, such as reflection, advice, question, and interpretation, and we look at how these types relate to a wide range of other variables in counseling. For the most part, when observing a counseling session, the observer can readily and reliably (with a little training) classify virtually all of the counselor's responses by using a response modes approach. Because of this, and because counselors must typically learn the different response modes as part of their training, we shall focus the remainder of this section on these responses.

Hill and Williams (2000) noted that there are more than 30 measures of or systems for classifying counselor response modes. Although there are naturally variations among the systems, there appear to be more similarities than differences. Using a slight modification of the classification system developed by Hill (1985, 1986) and revised by Hill and O'Brien (1999), we look at individual counselor responses in this section (see Table 8.3). Before describing and giving examples of each response mode,

TABLE 8.3

Counselor Techniques in Terms of Response Modes

Response mode	Definition	Example
Directives		
Approval	Agreement with/support of client	"That was a really effective response."
Provide information	Provision of facts, opinions, data, resources	"Dr. Gelsomini in Zoology would be a good source of info."
Direct guidance	Offering directions, suggestions, or advice	"I think it might be helpful to share your feelings with Ralph."
Information seeking		
Closed question	Questions requiring one- to two-word answer	"Are you sad?"
Open question	Questions fostering exploration	"How do you feel?"
Complex counselor responses		
Paraphrase	Summary of what client has communicated. Several kinds.	"You feel hurt by your friend's response."
Interpretation	Statement of connections, hidden causes, underlying themes in client's material	"You seem to react to Jane as your father reacted to you."
Confrontation	Response that challenges client	"You say you want friends, but you avoid returning phone calls and other approaches."
Self-disclosure	Revelation to client of facts about or feelings of the therapist	"I feel happy about how you have grown."

we note that Hill (2009) referred to these modes as *helping skills* because verbal techniques such as these are indeed aimed at helping clients. Hill also separated helping skills into what she suggested are the three key stages of therapy: exploration, insight, and action. In the real world of counseling, these stages are not always sequential, and even when they are, they may recycle one or more times. Still, the stages make good clinical sense in that as therapy progresses, the therapist seeks to facilitate, first, the exploration of the problem, including the client's feelings and thoughts. Once the client explores sufficiently, the aim becomes understanding the problem or gaining insight into the problem. Finally, when sufficient exploration and insight have occurred, the therapist moves toward helping the client toward taking action to solve the problem. However, we want to emphasize that things are not as tidy in practice as they appear in theory.

Silence

Before discussing other categories of verbal behavior, we wanted to begin with the absence of verbal behavior: silence. It is probably safe to say that beginning counselors undervalue silence. It makes them anxious, as they feel they must be *saying* something. In fact, silence may be filled with meaning. Silence may facilitate counselor and client emotional connection, or it may indicate that something is awry in the working alliance. In general we like to differentiate useful silence (where it is clear that the client is processing or experiencing important thoughts and feelings) from "empty silences" (which serve no therapeutic purpose). Using silence as a technique, the therapist purposefully allows the client time to think, process ideas, and absorb feelings. In an empty silence, little positive is going on and the client typically shows signs of anxiety, such as fidgeting. It is our contention that if silence is not being used purposefully, extensive silences should be avoided. What is "extensive," however, is debatable. Beginning counselors often think that a silence has gone on for ages when in fact it may have been only a few seconds. As always, use your best judgment and try to apply techniques with purpose and care.

Directives

With regard to actual verbal behaviors, the broad category of directives involves directing the client to do something. In using directives, the counselor may try to get the client to continue what he or she is already doing (approval) or provide information or guidance regarding what the client should do. When the therapist uses the response mode of *approval*, he or she may be offering support, explicit approval of some aspect of the client or the client's behavior, reassurance, and/or reinforcement. Sympathy also fits this category, although counseling educators and theorists generally agree that offering sympathy is not a desirable counseling response, except under unusual circumstances. Responses within the response mode of approval may be very short (e.g., "Very good"), or they may be longer ("I think you did the right thing").

There is evidence in the therapy literature that it is helpful to show approval of and support for the client as a person and in a general way (see Hill, 1989, 1990), but counseling can also be too supportive. One can be so supportive that the client's own strengths are not being marshaled. Also, as with all techniques, it is crucial that we differentiate effective from ineffective use. Well-timed support or reassurance can indeed move the client forward, whereas certain kinds of reassurance offered in certain ways may be experienced as hollow and may impede client growth. For example, implying that "everything will be okay" is often experienced as a lack of empathy, and such reassurances may interfere with the client's working through affects that need to be lived and experienced.

The second response mode under directives is called *providing information*. Counselor responses that fall into this category supply information to the client in the form of facts, data, opinion, or resources. The information that is given may be related to the counseling process, the counselor's behavior, or counseling arrangements such as meeting time, place, fee, and so forth. The provision of information in counseling can be quite important. For example, it is quite appropriate to answer requests for direct information or facts. At the same time, the counselor can become too involved in being an expert information giver, forgetting the fact that simple information rarely has an impact on underlying feelings and attitudes. The counselor also needs to be sensitive to the possibility that the client seeks information as a way of avoiding self-exploration and possibly painful feelings.

The third response mode under directives is *direct guidance*. This involves directions, suggestions, or advice offered by the counselor. One can think of direct guidance as being of two kinds: that which offers advice or directions within the session, and that which does so outside the session. The following are examples of direct guidance within the session.

Counselor (CO): Relax right now and take a deep breath.

CO: I would like you to tell me whatever crosses your mind when you think about your mother. Try not to edit and don't worry about how irrational or silly you may feel it sounds.

Examples of direct guidance regarding behavior outside the session include the following:

CO: I really think it would be a good idea to talk this over with Jim.

CO: I think you should talk with your math professor about why you had problems with the exam last week.

CO: As homewolrk, I would like you to keep a record of how many times you feel anxious during each day, and of what was occurring at those moments.

The use of direct guidance, especially in the form of advice to the client regarding behavior outside the counselor's office, has always been a controversial issue. Many counselors do not believe advice should be given except in extraordinary circumstances, whereas in the therapies that are more "directive," advice is viewed as a desirable element of the process. In our view, the first step in responding to a request for advice should be to explore what the client thinks about the situation being discussed, what alternatives have been considered, and what the client's hopes and fears are regarding the conflict situation:

> *CO:* I realize that you are terribly concerned about this. Perhaps if you can tell me the various alternatives you have considered and how you feel about them, we may be able to arrive at something that makes sense to you. (from Benjamin, 1987, p. 234)

Often, such an exploration eliminates the need for advice from the counselor. The client is able to follow his or her own dictates.

Information Seeking

Counselor responses used to elicit information of some sort from the client are classified as *information seeking*. In general, there are two counselor response modes here: *closed questions* and *open questions*.

Closed questions are used by the counselor to gather data and typically request a one- or two-word answer, a "yes" or "no" or a confirmation. Here are some examples:

> *Client (CL):* I just don't think I am studying enough in geometry. The problem is more the time I'm putting in than my study skills.
>
> *CO:* How many hours a night do you study for geometry on the average?
>
> *CL:* Jane and I finally got away for a weekend without the kids.
>
> *CO:* Did you have a good time?

Open questions, rather than delimiting the client's response, seek client exploration or clarification. Usually, one is not looking for a specific and short answer when asking an open question. If we use the client statements as given above, here are examples of open questions:

> *CL:* I just don't think I am studying enough in geometry. The problem is more the time I'm putting in than my study skills.
>
> *CO:* What do you think gets in the way of your studying more?
>
> *CL:* Jane and I finally got away for a weekend without the kids.
>
> *CO:* What was the experience like for you?

As you can see from these responses, the counselor, when using open questions, is seeking to facilitate exploration by the client. This exploration may pertain to the client's feelings, thoughts, behavior, personality dynamics, and/or expectations about counseling.

Although both open and closed questions have their place among counseling techniques and may be helpful at times, many of those who write about technique believe that closed questions, in particular, may be overused (e.g., Benjamin, 1987; Hill, 2009; Ivey, Ivey, & Zalaquett, 2010). We have observed therapist trainees who tend to ask many closed questions in therapy sessions with the hope of helping the client explore. Unfortunately, asking one closed question after another tends to impede exploration rather than facilitate it. As Benjamin (1987) said, "The open question may widen and deepen contact; the closed question may circumscribe it. In short, the former may open wide the door to good rapport; the latter usually keeps it shut" (p. 136).

Complex Counselor Responses

In Hill's (1985) classification system, called the Counselor Verbal Response Modes Category System, the four complex counselor response modes or techniques include paraphrase, interpretation, confrontation, and self-disclosure. These four response modes are complex in that they are more abstract than the other modes, and each of them may be divided into two or more subtypes. Also, their effectiveness depends greatly on complex and often subtle issues of timing, precise phrasing, and sensitivity to the client's dynamics and feeling states at the moment as well as more generally. Because of these considerations, the four complex techniques are more difficult to learn, and certainly more difficult to master, by counselors. Let us examine each of these techniques.

Paraphrase

The technique of paraphrase may be divided into four kinds of responses that have much in common with each other: restatements, reflections, nonverbal referents, and summaries. All four basically paraphrase, mirror, or summarize what the client has communicated to the counselor, either at the verbal or the nonverbal level. The counselor does not add his or her perspective to the communication but rather gives back to the client what the counselor hears the client expressing.

When the counselor verbalizes a restatement, she or he essentially restates or rephrases what the client has said, usually using similar but fewer words. In a good restatement, the counselor's expression is clearer and more concrete than the client's, and this fosters the client's examination of what he or she is expressing.

> CL: I just don't know if I have produced enough to be
> promoted to the next level at the university; and if I'm

> CL: not, I'll have to begin looking around for what I can find; for another job.
>
> CO: You're not sure if you'll make the cut and may need to find a new job.
>
> CL: It has just seemed like one thing after another this year. There was my wife's illness, and then Heather's accident was almost more than I could take. Now my 8-year-old son has to have this operation. I just wonder if it will ever end.
>
> CO: It just seems like the problems never stop and you're wondering if they ever will.

In contrast to a restatement, a *reflection* rephrases the client's expression with explicit attention to the feelings involved in that statement. These feelings may have been stated by the client, or they may be implicit. In the latter case, the feelings are inferred by the counselor from the client's nonverbal behavior or from his or her total communication. To reflect feelings that are unstated, the counselor must listen empathically. When reflecting, the therapist does not add his or her own viewpoint, as would be so with interpretation, a technique we examine later. Instead, the reflecting counselor brings to the surface those feelings underneath the client's words. The counselor in this sense is a mirror to the deeper feelings the client may be struggling to explore. The exchange below exemplifies this sort of reflection.

> CL: It's hard to talk about this stuff or even to think about it. I mean, I've been complaining about not having a relationship for a long time, and now that there's a possibility, what do I do?
>
> CO: It's upsetting to see how fearful and avoiding you are of just what you thought you wanted.
>
> CL: That's for sure. I just don't know if John is the person for me. He seems too nice, and yet he has everything I should want. I just don't know.
>
> CO: You're feeling confused about whether you want John or should want John.
>
> CL: Yes, but as I think about it, that's the way I've always been. When someone cares about me and is good to me, I move away; when someone doesn't want me, I want them. What a mess this is. Will I ever improve?
>
> CO: You feel discouraged, wondering if you will ever connect when the other person cares.

The *nonverbal referent* is similar to reflection and restatement but points to the client's nonverbal behavior as an indication of his or her feelings. *Nonverbals* here may refer to body posture, facial expression, tone of voice, gestures, and so forth.

CL: I don't know what's wrong. I should be happy with Sally's attention but I'm not.

CO: Your face has a sad expression as you talk about this.

CL: But, darn it, I do care about John, despite his craziness and social discomfort.

CO: Your voice was very soft as you said that.

CL: I feel happy in this relationship for the first time ever.

CO: Your voice sounds alive when you say that.

The final kind of paraphrase is called a *summary*, which verbalizes the major themes in what the client has expressed. The summary may cover a part of a session, the entire session, or the treatment as a whole.

CO: It looks like the basic issue you've been struggling with today is your fear of relationships and how you avoid involvements that are good for you.

CO: In sum, you've spent several weeks sorting through what you want and have come to realize engineering isn't it. You are now focusing on management and feel really good about that.

As a general technique, the four types of paraphrase have a long history in counseling and therapy. Beginning in the 1940s, paraphrase became a prominent verbal technique, when what was called *nondirective therapy* (later *client-centered therapy*, then *person-centered therapy*; see Chapter 12) became popular. But even therapists who are not client centered or are nondirective with their clients use paraphrase. Each of the four types of paraphrases may be of significant help to clients. They show the client that the therapist is listening and enable the client to continue exploration and often communicate the counselor's empathic understanding to the client. Paraphrases also let therapists check out their understanding of what clients are saying. On the other hand, as with all techniques, paraphrase can be misused. Continual use of restatement can be an irritant to the client, especially if the counselor approaches exact restatement of the client's verbalizations. Egan (1998) referred to merely repeating what the client has said as "parroting" and viewed this as a parody of empathy. He stated that "mere repetition carries no sense of real understanding of, no sense of being with, the client. Since real understanding is in some way 'processed' by you, since it passes through you, it should convey some part of yourself" (pp. 96–97). We agree with Egan that the effective counselor is always looking for the core of what is being expressed—that he or she becomes highly expert at finding that core and communicating it to the client. This kind of response is more likely to be *reflection* than *restatement*.

Interpretation

Of the complex counselor responses, interpretation is probably the most complex. It requires greater skillfulness, in our view, and may have the greatest potential for both moving the client forward and interfering with progress. Whereas paraphrase techniques stay with the client and give back to him or her what the therapist hears in that client's expression, interpretations go beyond what the client has stated or recognized. An interpretation usually offers new meaning and points to the causes underlying the client's actions and feelings. Here the therapist's frame of reference emerges as the therapist reframes the client's material in terms of his or her view of what is happening. This seeks to help the client see things from a new perspective and in a new way.

The complex nature of interpretation is underscored by the fact that this response encompasses several different types. In Hill's (1985, 1986) category system, for example, five types are described.

A common type of interpretation establishes connections between seemingly isolated statements, problems, or events. For example, to a client who has been discussing his fear of giving speeches, his low self-esteem, and his problems with relationships, the counselor may eventually point out how all three problems are interconnected and, further, how this client's excessive standards and expectations of himself appear to underlie each problem.

A second type of interpretation points out themes or patterns in the client's behavior or feelings. An example of this type might occur in response to the client who continues to become disenchanted with jobs after having high hopes initially. The counselor might note, "Each time it seems that you feel very excited about the possibilities of a job, and then when you see the inevitable problems, you turn away." The counselor might follow this interpretation with an open question about what the meaning of this pattern might be, or the counselor can provide a further interpretation, assuming of course that the client has provided enough material (e.g., "Based on what we have been talking about, I suspect that your turning away is a way of dealing with your fear of failing"). This follow-up statement demonstrates how the skilled therapist can connect two or more different types of interpretations within the same response.

The last interpretation above pointed to the client's underlying defense ("turning away") against anxiety (fear of failure). This type of interpretation falls within the third type discussed by Hill (1985); that is, interpretation of defenses, resistance, or transference. Interpretation of transference is probably the central technique in psychoanalytic treatment (see Chapter 11). Here the therapist points out how the client's perceptions of the therapist's feelings, behavior, or attitudes are based on past relationships, usually with father or mother. In an effort to help the client gain insight, the counselor shows the client how she or he is reacting to and perceiving this counselor as if she or he were a significant person in the client's childhood. For example,

> CL: I just can't seem to talk to you comfortably about being gay. It's as if you are sitting there and quietly judging me, thinking I'm not masculine. Even though you seem accepting of me, I can't trust that, and have this fear that you are critical of me as a person. I half expect you to start yelling at me, to really explode.
>
> CO: As I listen to you I'm struck with how you are seeing me as so similar to the way your father was. It's as if you're putting father into me.

The fourth type of interpretation relates present events, experiences, or feelings to the past. When making this type of interpretation, the therapist aims to help the client see how present problems and conflicts are causally linked to the past. We say to the client, in effect, "You are misperceiving the present or behaving in ways that hurt you or others in the present because of these issues or experiences in your past." For example,

> CL: I don't know—I just seem to avoid men who are good for me and get hooked up with these jerks who abuse me. And I turn into such a nag. Nag, nag, nag—I nag so much that I'll turn them into jerks even if they aren't to begin with. I just don't know why I do these things.
>
> CO: It seems like you consistently get into, and create, situations that are just like your mother and father's relationship when you were a child.

The fifth and final type of interpretation in Hill's (1985) system entails giving a new framework to feelings, behaviors, or problems. Counselors use this technique to provide clients with a fresh, new way of looking at some aspect of themselves and their lives. Hill exemplified this process as follows:

> CL: He just never does anything around the house, and he goes out drinking with the guys all the time. I get stuck taking care of the kids and doing everything around the house.
>
> CO: He seems to be saving you from any decision about what you are going to do with your life and your career.

We began the discussion of interpretation by noting how complex this technique is and how, more than most techniques, it can be for better or worse: It can help or harm the client. Probably more than with any technique, the issues of depth and timing are absolutely crucial in determining whether an interpretation has its desired effect. Throughout psychoanalytic theory, for example, one finds a great sensitivity to the use of interpretations that are only slightly ahead of the client's level of insight, enabling the client to take a short step forward in understanding. In this sense, the "good interpretation" is never a depth interpretation, or at least it is never so deep that it does not make contact with the client's awareness. In terms of timing, an effective interpretation must be made when the client can absorb it—can take it in, so to speak. No matter how accurate or well stated an interpretation may be, if it is ill timed, the client's response will not be what the therapist is hoping for: one of insight and awareness. Recent reviews of research (Hill, 2009; Hill & Williams, 2000; Levy & Scala, 2012) do in fact clearly support the importance of interpretations being well timed and of moderate depth. This topic is discussed in the section on process research.

Confrontation

The next technique to be discussed is controversial because for many therapists and clients it conjures up the image of attacking and being attacked. In fact, *confrontation* may be gentle as well as aggressive. Although some confrontations may be explicitly hostile, we believe the most effective ones are embedded in a caring relationship and are neither hostile nor attacking.

Confrontation may be seen as any therapist response that challenges the client's behavior. The challenge most often focuses on discrepancies or contradictions in the client's behavior, thoughts, or feelings. Challenges may also focus on distortions, evasions, games, tricks, excuse making, and smoke screens in which clients involve themselves and that ultimately keep them from solving their problems.

The kind of confrontation that focuses on discrepancies or contradictions usually has two parts. In the first part, the therapist states or refers to some aspect of the client's behavior; in the second part, which often begins with a "but," the discrepancy is presented. Note that, unlike interpretations, confrontations do not state the cause of the discrepancy.

An example of confronting a discrepancy between the client's words and behavior (or between verbal and nonverbal behavior) might be

> *CL:* I've been looking forward to coming to this session today because I get so much out of our work together.
>
> *CO:* You say this but you were 15 minutes late and have been sitting silently with your arms folded. [The counselor might follow up this confrontation with an open question, e.g., "What do you make of this difference between what you've expressed and your behavior?"]

A slight modification of a case noted by Egan (1986) provides a good example of confronting distortions. Eric, a young gay male, blames his problems on an older brother who seduced him during his early years of high school:

> CO: Eric, every time we begin to talk about your sexual behavior, you bring up your brother.
>
> CL: That's where it all began!
>
> CO: Your brother's not around anymore. . . . Tell me what Eric wants. But tell me as it is.
>
> CL: I want people to leave me alone.
>
> CO: I don't believe it because I don't think you believe it. . . . Be honest with yourself.
>
> CL: I want some one person to care about me. But that's deep down inside me. . . . What I seem to want up front is to punish people and make them punish me.

As discussed with respect to interpretation, confrontation can be for better or worse. Research studies clearly point to the fact that confrontation can stir up client defensiveness and make clients feel misunderstood (Hill & Williams, 2000). Yet there is also evidence that confrontations can lead to arousal and make clients more receptive to change (Hill, 1989). As we reflect on the research, as well as our own counseling experiences, we conclude that a key part of being sensitively empathic and skillful as a therapist is knowing when and how to confront clients, as well as sensing which clients may be helpfully confronted. In general, confrontations work best in the context of a trusting relationship wherein the client feels understood and cared about. We also find Egan's (1986, pp. 227–228) guidelines useful in thinking about the do's and don'ts of effective confrontation:

1. *Avoid labeling.* Derogatory labels, in particular, make clients feel put down and increase resistance to feedback.
2. *Describe the situation and the relevant behaviors.* Rather than label, describe the context and self-limiting behaviors as specifically and accurately as possible. Even when you do this, don't dump everything on the client at once. You are not trying to build a case for a trial!
3. *Describe the impact or consequence of the behavior.* Point out how relevant parties (e.g., the counselor, client, significant others) are affected by the behavior in terms of both emotions and behavior.
4. *Help clients identify what they need to do to manage the problem.* Showing clients alternatives or, even better, helping them explore alternatives can be valuable when you challenge some aspect of their behavior.

Self-Disclosure and Immediacy

The final technique to be discussed is controversial. The merits and liabilities of self-disclosure have been debated for many years in the counseling and therapy literature. Generally, humanistic counselors (see Chapter 12) believe therapist self-disclosure can be a very helpful way of facilitating a genuine I–thou relationship between counselor and client. When counselors self-disclose, they take themselves off the therapist pedestal and show themselves to be human beings, just like clients.

In general, self-disclosure may be divided into *involving statements* and *disclosing statements* (McCarthy & Betz, 1978). In the involving disclosure, the counselor communicates to the client his or her feelings or perceptions, usually (but not always) in the moment, and about the client and/or relationship. When such disclosures are of feelings and thoughts in the present, they are often referred to as *immediacy*. Examples of such statements might be "Sometimes, like right now, it's real hard to know how to respond to you in a way that would feel helpful"; or "I feel sad as I listen to your continual attacks on yourself"; or "I feel like we have had a good relationship, and although I know we must end now, it's a loss for me as well." Disclosing statements reveal something about the counselor or his or her life that does not directly relate to the client or the relationship. These disclosures may be facts about the therapist; similarities between the therapist and client, including how they feel; or therapeutic strategies used by the therapist. Examples of disclosing statements in these different categories might be "If someone responded to me that way, I, too, would have a lot of feelings—anger, helplessness, and so on" (disclosure of similarities in feelings); "I understand because I have two teenagers also" (disclosure of similarities); "One of the things that has worked well in my practice and my life has been to listen carefully and not interrupt" (disclosure of strategy); "I got my degree in counseling psychology from the University of Maryland and have been practicing for 20 years" (disclosure of facts).

In addition to making the division between involving and disclosing types of self-disclosure, we can make a further distinction: Self-disclosures may be either *positive* or *negative*. Positive disclosures are reassuring in that they support, reinforce, or legitimize the client's perspective; for example, "I, too, feel very good about our work and our relationship" (Hill, Mahalik, & Thompson, 1989). The negative disclosure, on the other hand, tends to be challenging in that it confronts the client's perspective, way of thinking, or behavior; for example, "You say it's okay, but if someone responded to me in that way, I'd feel pretty upset" (see Hill et al., 1989).

Because the decision to self-disclose or not can be a difficult one, we review some of the research on disclosures in the next section. Yet, we offer this caution before we move on: Just because research has found a particular response mode or technique to be effective does not mean that the more it is used the better will be the counseling. Conversely, because some techniques have been shown to be minimally effective does not imply that they should not be used at all. The patterning of techniques may well be as important if not even more important than the particular techniques used.

WHAT PROCESS RESEARCH TELLS US

Now that we have reviewed a range of therapist techniques, we hope you are wondering how we know what works to promote positive change in counseling. And so we return to our discussion of psychotherapy research, focusing now on the process of counseling. What are the effects of different specific techniques therapists use? When therapists intend to do something in the session, do their techniques follow from that intention? How is it perceived by the client? What is going on beneath the surface, from therapists' attention, countertransference, and self-talk to clients' reactions and secrets they keep?

Carl Rogers was credited with bringing a true empirical study to the process of psychotherapy. Rogers used a wide variety of methods to understand recorded sessions of therapy in the 1940s (Muran et al., 2010). He also mentored a long list of well-known process researchers who continued his work and made creative and unique contributions of their own. Thus, much work has been done to examine what therapists actually *do* in a therapy session. For example, several years ago, Hill (1982) suggested that researchers could analyze counseling and psychotherapy at six levels, from the most observable (and easily rated) to more abstract and inferential categories. She listed (a) ancillary behaviors (e.g., behaviors that can be examined using physiological measures), (b) response modes (e.g., verbal utterances), (c) content (e.g., topic of discussion), (d) ratings of behavior (e.g., ratings of client involvement), (e) covert behaviors (e.g., therapist intentions or client internal reactions), and (f) clinical strategies (e.g., specific interventions). We focus here on one of the more easily observed categories (response modes or therapist verbal behavior) and on one of the more difficult to study (covert behaviors of both therapists and clients).

Therapist Response Modes

We overviewed various therapist response modes in the previous section. A typical way to study response modes is by coding transcriptions of therapy sessions that have been video- or audiotaped. In this chapter, we focus on the findings in five categories derived from Hill's original (1978) system: directives, interpretation, self-disclosure, questions, and paraphrase.

Those just learning about counseling often assume that therapists should be giving advice and solving problems (and that this can happen efficiently in one or two sessions!). However, for many reasons, the best therapy avoids doling out advice and seeks instead to help clients discover their own answers. As such, the research on therapist directives has been quite mixed. Because client resistance has been strongly linked with poor outcome (Beutler, Rocco, Moleiro, & Talebi, 2000), some researchers have suggested that directiveness may not be particularly helpful as it is linked with resistance (Bischoff & Tracey, 1995). Use of directives with clients high in resistance (Beutler, Harwood, Michelson, Song, & Holman, 2011) has resulted in poor outcomes. In contrast, giving assignments for work outside of sessions (Bennett-Levy, 2003) and engaging in experiential confrontation in session may more effective (T. Strong & Zeman, 2010). Thus, directiveness may be an effective strategy when used with particular (e.g., less resistant) clients in particular ways (e.g., homework assignments).

In contrast, there is more consistent evidence for the effectiveness of *interpretation* as an intervention. Interpretation is used when a therapist goes beyond the client's current level of understanding, drawing connections, pointing out themes or patterns, and helping the client establish a new frame of reference. Although therapists typically use interpretation in modest amounts (e.g., 6%–8% of their verbal statements; Auletta et al., 2012; Hill et al., 1988), clients respond well to a therapist's attentiveness and can successfully use interpretations to elaborate on their own perspectives (Peräkylä, 2010). It appears that a variety of theoretical orientations effectively use interpretation (Gazzola & Stalikas, 2004). Although accurate interpretations (Crits-Christoph, Barber, & Kurcias, 1993), delivered to clients who are "ready" to hear them (Joyce, Duncan, & Piper, 1995), have been shown to be quite effective, transference interpretations in particular have been more controversial. Some research has suggested that transference interpretations have been experienced quite negatively by some clients (Bateman & Fonagy, 2004) and have been associated with less positive therapeutic outcomes (Crits-Christoph & Connolly Gibbons, 2001; Ryum, Stiles, Svartberg, & McCullough, 2010); however, Levy and Scala (2012) have suggested that transference interpretations may be quite effective for certain individuals. Their findings beautifully demonstrate that as research advances to studying better questions, what once seemed to be true may no longer be seen as fully accurate. Thus, the research again suggests a complex understanding of when to use a particular intervention to maximize therapeutic effectiveness.

As previously noted, a fairly controversial therapist verbal response mode is that of *self-disclosure* (Farber, 2006). How much of the therapist should be known to the client? How much self-disclosure is appropriate, and when does it cross the line out of therapy and into a more reciprocal relationship? If a therapist chooses to self-disclose, the research suggests, the best likelihood of success may be with disclosures that are about issues the therapist has resolved (Yeh & Hayes, 2011) and done in the context of therapeutic immediacy (Hill, 2009; Knox & Hill, 2003). Of interest, therapists tend not to like using self-disclosure, whereas clients often find it to be the most helpful of a therapist's interventions (Audet & Everall, 2003). In particular, using Hill's (2004) model of therapist immediacy, Mayotte-Blum et al. (2012) suggested that such self-disclosures are associated with better treatment outcomes. Gelso and Palma (2011) suggested that it is important to consider the strength of the working alliance when deciding whether or not to self-disclose to a client. Gelso and Palma, in overviewing the considerations posited by Henretty and Levitt (2010; e.g., to what, what, when, why, and how), also cautioned that researchers should focus on identifying the "optimal amount" of self-disclosure because "well-timed and infrequent usage" (Gelso & Palma, 2011, p. 347) may be a way to enhance the effectiveness of the technique.

Another verbal technique that gets mixed reviews from clients and therapists is that of *questions*. Clients tend not to like questions, though asking questions is by all accounts one of the most common therapist techniques used (Goates-Jones, Hill, Stahl, & Doschek, 2009; Hill et al., 1988). Therapists typically use questions as a way to gather information and help the client explore or discuss a topic in more depth. Overuse of questions, particularly closed questions (which typically require a simple yes or no type of response), however, may be related to negative perceptions of the therapist's skill or empathy (Hill & O'Brien, 1999). In Hill's (1989) intensive study of eight psychotherapy cases in which highly experienced therapists conducted the therapy, clients typically gave low helpfulness ratings to closed questions. This technique created a feeling in the clients of being interviewed rather than being invited to become emotionally involved in a therapeutic relationship. Open questions, on the other hand, have been found to be useful in encouraging clients to talk longer and more deeply about their feelings, thoughts, and problems (Hill, 2009). Yet, among Hill's (1989) eight cases, though some clients apparently liked the challenge involved in open questions, others experienced them as too threatening. It appears that the effectiveness of open questions depends on many factors: for example, how well timed the questions are, whether the client is ready for them, the issues with which the client is dealing, and of course the specific nature of the questions being asked.

As a final category, *paraphrase* has yielded helpful information. Clients may not always appreciate a good restatement or reflection of feeling (perhaps misunderstanding the therapist's intention, typically to help the client clarify their thoughts or emotions, and instead seeing the technique as a type of unskilled parroting of information). Not only are paraphrase responses used often in therapy (up to 31% of a therapist's response), they are positively related to other aspects of the therapy process, such as client collaboration and emotional experiencing (Williams, 2002). Similarly, Iwakabe, Rogan, and Stalikas (2000) found that in sessions where therapists focused on immediate expressions of feeling, there were higher levels of alliance between therapist and client. Although clients rarely express negative reactions to paraphrase (Cooper, 2008), students sometimes question its effectiveness. (They are quite aware of the media portrayals of therapists who don't really listen but just repeat what a client has said. By the way, these media stereotypes drive us crazy, but they do make for great discussion starters in our classes.) It is our belief that a really good paraphrase (well-timed, accurate, introduced in a way that conveys caring and attentiveness) can be a very powerful technique.

The research on therapist verbal techniques has a strong base and provides practitioners with useful and important information. However, as with research on nonverbal communication (Hill & Williams, 2000), there appears to be a decrease in research in this area. We wonder if the methodologies available to us have limited our current creativity. For example, although interesting, it is not terribly useful to know the frequency of use of particular techniques. We are more interested in the complexities and nuances of these techniques, and this, as such, is a measurement conundrum. Some very interesting work on microanalytic sequential analysis has been done (Elliott, 2010), and we feel that this is an area of investigation in need of reinvigoration.

Research on Covert Processes

It is important to examine what (and how) therapists respond to clients during a session, but it is also fascinating to uncover what is going on beneath the surface. Although difficult to do, studying covert processes has proven to be very informative (and surprising). A typical way to study covert reactions is to video- or audiotape a counseling session and then have clients and therapists participate in an immediate post-session recall. In this recall session, the tape is played back and stopped at particular points (such as predetermined time intervals or after a therapist speaking turn). Clients and therapists complete measures at each time the tape is stopped. For example, clients might be writing down what their internal reaction had been at that moment in the session or how helpful they found the therapist right then, and therapists might be rating their own sense of helpfulness and writing down what kinds of self-statements they had been making to themselves. One inherent difficulty with this kind of research is that it is retrospective. Does the client remember what she was really experiencing at that moment in the session, or has her perspective been altered by the subsequent moments in the session or even by the research process itself? Does the therapist actually remember what he was saying to himself, or is he responding with his current thoughts? The alternative to this kind of post-session recall, of course, would be to interrupt the actual session to complete measures in vivo (or find some way to introduce an unobtrusive measure, such as galvanic skin response). Yet, to interrupt the session alters the counseling itself, and sometimes physiological measures do not get at the kinds of research questions being asked (such as about therapist self-talk).

Despite these research difficulties, several interesting studies have provided great insight into what is actually happening during a counseling session. In this section, we overview two particular areas of research: client reactions and therapist self-focused attention. Hill, Thompson, Cogar, and Denman (1993) suggested that there were three categories of *covert client reactions:* hidden reactions, things left unsaid, and secrets. Although Farber and Hall (2002) found that clients disclosed a moderate amount to their therapists, Farber (2003) also suggested that about 50% of clients keep secrets from their therapists. D. A. Hall and Farber (2001) found that sexual issues were the most difficult ones for clients to share with their therapists. Kelly (1998) suggested that keeping secrets may actually be facilitative (as it was associated with a reduction in symptoms), but Hill, Gelso, and Mohr (2000) disagreed, noting that clients say they in fact hide very little from their therapists. Subsequently, Kelly and Yuan (2009) found evidence that contradicted Kelly's (1998) earlier assertions. Kelly and Yuan found that secret keeping was related to poorer therapeutic alliance. Clients in general hold very little back, but there are times they choose to withhold information from the therapist, particularly with regard to sexual matters. Although such as withholding of a secret *might* be associated with feeling less anxious in the moment, the keeping of secrets in therapy does not seem like a strategy for long-term successful outcomes.

In terms of the covert reactions of the therapists, one area of particular interest to us has been the kinds of internal reactions therapists experience and, ultimately, must manage. When counselors work with clients, how aware are they of their own thoughts, feelings, and reactions in the moment? To what extent does such awareness facilitate therapy, and to what extent does it potentially hinder therapy? Are therapists ever overly self-aware? The term *self-awareness* has often been defined as a type of self-insight or self-knowledge (Williams et al., 2008) and has thus been seen as a very positive quality. Williams and colleagues, however, were interested in the definition of self-awareness to describe momentary states of heightened self-focus (Williams & Fauth, 2005), which might be either facilitative or hindering during therapy. To clarify the use of the terms in the research, Williams et al. (2008) suggested that the term *therapist self-focused attention* be used when researchers wish to study states of self-directed attention, such as therapist self-talk and hindering self-awareness.

So, what do therapists think about when they are in a counseling session? One would hope and presume they are thinking about the client or other processes related to the therapy. But it also is quite expected that therapists might entertain other thoughts, perhaps wholly unrelated to the session at hand. Early research on therapist self-talk created classifications of therapist self-talk as either facilitative or distractive (Borders, Fong-Beyette, & Cron, 1988; Fuqua, Newman, Anderson, & Johnson, 1986; Morran, 1986; Morran, Kurpius, & Brack, 1989). Thus, some thoughts (such as those focused on the client) might assist the therapy, whereas other thoughts (such as worrying about a nagging car repair or remembering that you need to update your LinkedIn profile to reflect a newly acquired skill) might be a distraction to the therapist or be hindering in some other way. Hiebert, Uhlemann, Marshall, and Lee (1998) found that counselor anxiety was associated with negative self-talk. Similarly, Nutt-Williams and Hill (1996) found that negative self-talk was related to therapists' perceptions that their clients were reacting negatively and found them unhelpful.

To test whether these perceptions therapists held might be accurate, Williams (2003) assessed the perspectives of both therapists and clients using a post-session recall design. Williams found that as therapists rated themselves as more self-aware in the moment, clients did in fact rate them as less helpful, suggesting there may be a distraction factor. In other similar studies, however, therapist self-awareness was related to more positive helpfulness ratings. Thus, the role of therapist self-focused attention is "both intriguing and seemingly complex" (Williams et al., 2008). Therapists do report a variety of in-session thoughts, including feeling bored or worrying about external matters (Williams, Polster, Grizzard, Rockenbaugh, & Judge, 2003), suggesting that perhaps what makes self-awareness helpful at times is the ability to manage distracting or hindering self-focused attention. A number of studies have begun to examine such management strategies (Gelso & Hayes, 2007; Williams & Fauth, 2005; Williams, Hurley, O'Brien, & de Gregorio, 2003), including a growing interest in therapist mindfulness (Bruce, Shapiro, Constantino, & Manber, 2010; Ryan, Safran, Doran, & Muran, 2012).

We hope that at this point the reader has a good understanding of why the question "Did your treatment help someone?" is so complicated. Not only can we study the observable behaviors occurring (or not occurring) in the treatment room, but we can research the reactions that exist beneath the surface. We often have a sense that the typical 50-minute therapy hour is simply busy. We could (and expect that many will) spend years researching what we can observe in therapy (e.g., what happens when therapists alter an aspect of their nonverbal behaviors during sessions?) as well as the covert experiences of clients and therapists (e.g., what is the impact of reminding therapists about insurance forms they need to fill out before they go into a counseling session?). In the end, we know that the exciting advancements in the study of psychotherapy will improve our training methods, support practitioners in their work, and help us find better ways to help the individuals who seek therapeutic assistance.

Summary

In this chapter we have reviewed the history of research that has established the effectiveness of counseling and psychotherapy. We overviewed Eysenck's (1952) provocative critique of therapy and the subsequent meta-analyses that contradicted his findings (e.g., M. L. Smith & Glass, 1977). We introduced the reader to the Dodo Bird hypothesis (Luborsky et al., 1975), suggesting the surprise finding that although therapy is effective, no one type of therapy is necessarily any more effective than any other. Given the complexities of outcome research, we discussed the ways in which researchers choose to establish efficacy (using greater laboratory control) and effectiveness (maximizing generalizability of findings to treatment as usual). We also reviewed the empirically supported treatment and evidence-based practice movements, noting the limitations of highly structured, manualized strategies to establish efficacy of treatment across theoretical orientations. Finally, we overviewed the shift from examining differences across treatments to looking for the common curative factors in psychotherapy. Clearly, a large body of evidence has accumulated to suggest that therapy can be highly effective, even if we are still unsure of the mechanisms of change.

One possible mechanism of change is what the therapists actually do in the treatment hour. We reviewed the basic nonverbal and verbal techniques employed by therapists regardless of theoretical orientation. The concept of "technique" was defined as a tool or method used by the therapist to facilitate positive change in the client. In this chapter, we have focused on two levels of technique: nonverbal behavior and verbal behavior. Nonverbal behavior consists of *paralinguistics, facial expressions, kinesics, visual behavior,* and *proxemics.* The effective therapist is aware that he or she is always communicating nonverbally and that the client, too, is doing so. It is important that therapists be aware of their nonverbal behavior and seek to understand it and use it in a way that displays the therapist's interest and involvement in the work.

Therapist verbal behavior was described through the therapist *response modes approach*. This approach focuses on the grammatical structure of verbal responses, rather than the content. Such response modes are usually what we mean by the term *verbal technique* in therapy. Hill's (1985) system of classifying response modes was used to distinguish a number of these modes: *silence, approval, providing information, direct guidance, open and closed questions, paraphrase, interpretation, confrontation,* and *self-disclosure*.

We concluded the chapter with an overview of just some of the research findings in process research. We focused on what we have learned about the usage of particular verbal response modes, such as research on directives, interpretation, self-disclosure, questions, and paraphrase. We also discussed the analysis of covert processes, those we are unable to directly observe. For example, research has established that approximately half of clients report keeping secrets from their therapists but that such secret keeping may be harmful to the therapeutic alliance. We also examined covert therapist experiences, with a particular focus on therapist self-focused attention, self-talk, and mindfulness. We hope that the reader is inspired both to practice the techniques and strategies overviewed in this chapter and to study the fascinating nuances of psychotherapy.

THE PRACTICE OF COUNSELING PSYCHOLOGY

The Therapeutic Relationship 9

W hen the beginning student first considers what personal counseling or psychotherapy is all about, he or she probably focuses on what psychologists view as technical factors. That is, the student thinks of psychotherapy techniques and procedures applied by an expert. The application of techniques, in fact, is only a part of the psychotherapy equation (see Chapter 8). The "other part," the relationship that develops between therapist and client, is at least as important (see empirically based reviews in Norcross, 2011).

Although there has been a great deal of debate over the years about which of these two parts (the therapeutic relationship vs. therapist techniques) is more important (Gelso, 2005), most current thinking in counseling psychology supports the view that the therapeutic relationship and techniques act in concert, that one cannot exist without the other, and that both together are what psychotherapy is all about (Goldfried & Davila, 2005; Hill, 2005; Norcross & Lambert, 2011). This is the viewpoint reflected in the present chapter.

http://dx.doi.org/10.1037/14378-009
Counseling Psychology, Third Edition, by C. J. Gelso, E. N. Williams, and B. R. Fretz

We discussed the research on therapist verbal techniques in Chapter 8. Now we begin an exploration of the therapist–client relationship in counseling; what is meant by the relationship; and what are called "facilitative conditions" that, when present to a high degree, appear to promote constructive change in clients.

The Importance of the Relationship

> Human beings are social animals. They live through a series of interrelationships, forming and being formed by interactions with other people. Much of what people come to feel and be is directly and indirectly related to the quality of the associations they have had with others. . . . If relationships help to form troubled lives (in the natural environment), then new relationships are needed to help change troubled lives. The relationship that develops between patient and psychotherapist can be especially powerful in stimulating personality change. Despite the long history of successful and unsuccessful relationships the patient has had, the relationship that develops with the therapist, *quite apart from the techniques the therapist uses* [emphasis added], can facilitate the patient's growth. (Lambert, 1983, p. 1)

On the basis of years of both empirical research and counseling experience, the great majority of professionals who practice counseling, as well as those who study it, would agree with Lambert's (1983) statement that the counselor–client relationship is very important. Still, there are wide differences of opinion as to just how important the therapeutic relationship is to successful counseling. Some see the counselor–client relationship as the sine qua non of effective intervention (Duncan, Miller, Wampold, & Hubble, 2010; Norcross, 2011). Others go even further. They suggest that certain relationship conditions are all that is needed for successful therapy. These conditions are both necessary and sufficient for constructive behavior and personality change (see Patterson, 1984).

On the other side of the ledger, few, if any, therapists view the relationship as unimportant. However, a sizable cluster of therapists, mostly aligned with behavior therapy or cognitive behavior therapy, view the counselor–client relationship as important but running a rather weak second to counselor techniques in terms of what promotes client change. At about the midpoint on this continuum of importance is probably the therapist who views the relationship as very important and who sees a good relationship between therapist and client as a necessary factor for positive change but not a sufficient factor. Other factors, such as counselor techniques and client characteristics, are also important.

As we discuss later in greater detail, conceptions of the role and importance of the therapeutic relationship seem to follow closely one's theoretical orientation. (We review in detail four foundational theoretical orientations to counseling in Chapters 11, 12, 13, and 14.) In terms of the way in which the relationship affects clients and client change, Prochaska and Norcross (2010) suggested that the counselor–client relationship can be seen as (a) one of the preconditions for therapy to proceed (as in rational–emotive or perhaps behavior therapy), (b) an essential process that itself produces change (as in certain humanistic approaches), or (c) a primary source of content to be talked about and processed in therapy (as in most of the psychodynamically oriented approaches). In feminist multicultural approaches, the therapeutic relationship is a critical element in considering the sharing of power with the client (such as using the therapist's first name) and in establishing a safe environment in which clients can address issues of race, ethnicity, gender, and sexual orientation (see Chapter 14). In terms of importance, in the humanistically oriented approaches, such as person-centered therapy, existential therapy, and gestalt therapy, the relationship is central to client change. This is also the case in most of the psychodynamically oriented therapies (e.g., Freudian analysis, neo-analytic approaches, Adlerian therapy). Thus, although the humanistic and psychodynamic therapies work within the counselor–client relationship in different ways, both view it as deeply important.

In the learning-based approaches (behavior therapy, cognitive therapy, rational–emotive therapy, etc.), views of importance appear to range from those few who contend the relationship to be unimportant to those who see it as moderately important. Some learning-oriented therapists do indeed view the relationship as more central to change than we have implied (see Lejuez, Hopko, Levine, Gholkar, & Collins, 2005), but the general tendency is for learning-oriented therapists to view relationship factors as second in importance to counselor techniques.

The Therapeutic Relationship Defined

Although the relationship has been a key construct in theory, practice, and research for many years, little effort has gone into defining just what a therapeutic relationship is and how relationship factors may be differentiated from nonrelationship factors. The inattention to definition is most surprising on the part of theories placing the relationship at the center of change. For example, in relationship-oriented therapies such as client-centered therapy (now called person-centered therapy; see Chapter 13), no more effort seems to have been put into matters of definition than in other approaches in which the relationship is not so crucial. These relationship approaches most often discuss so-called relationship conditions that are necessary and/or sufficient for positive change to take place. The conditions represent qualities and/or behaviors in the therapist, and the client's role essentially is to perceive or take in the conditions. For example, from the time of Rogers's (1957) famous statement about the necessary and sufficient conditions for positive change in therapy, virtually all client-centered therapists have viewed empathic understanding on the part of the counselor as one of these conditions. Thus, if constructive change is to take place, the counselor must empathically understand the client (as defined later in the chapter), and the client is to perceive the counselor's empathy.

Although therapist-offered conditions may be quite important, perhaps even necessary, they do not help us much in attempting to define what a relationship is and is not. Along with being conditions that contribute to a relationship rather than necessary elements of a relationship, they are one-sided. Therapist-offered conditions minimize the role of the client in the relationship and do not incorporate the reciprocal interaction and influence that must be part of a dyadic relationship.

A definition that does capture the reciprocal nature of relationships has been offered by Gelso and Carter (1985, 1994) and Gelso and Hayes (1998). This definition is simple and general: The relationship is the feelings and attitudes that counseling participants have toward one another and the manner in which these are expressed. In this definition, the techniques used by the counselor that come from his or her theory may be influenced by and influence the relationship, but these techniques do not define the relationship. For example, the interpretations offered by the psychoanalytic therapist are techniques, and they are prescribed by that therapist's theory of counseling (i.e., psychoanalytic theory of therapy). Likewise, when the behavior therapist uses conditioning techniques, one could not say that is the relationship. This therapist is following the dictates of his or her theory of counseling.

The differentiation between relationship and technical factors in therapy can be useful in helping us understand this highly complex enterprise. Yet, more often than is probably recognized, relationship factors color and give shape to how technical factors are actualized in counseling (Gelso & Carter, 1985, 1994; Gelso & Hayes, 1998). Thus, often subtle feelings and attitudes the counseling participants hold toward one another will strongly influence just how they enact their theoretically prescribed roles. On the counselor's side, for example, if the counselor is psychoanalytically oriented and thus places a premium on the technique called interpretation, how and what that counselor feels toward the client will influence the nature, depth, frequency, length, and content of the interpretations that are offered. Even when the counselor is astute in his or her ability to understand his or her own feelings and not let them interfere with the work, these feelings must color the interpretations.

Not only does the relationship influence how the counseling participants enact their theoretically prescribed roles, these roles also affect the relationship. For example, whether the counselor primarily reflects feelings, interprets, gives advice, or engages in conditioning exercises will each affect the relationship differently. Also, it goes without saying that the manner in which these roles are enacted both is affected by the emerging relationship and influences and alters that relationship.

In sum, then, although relationship and technical factors can be thought of as two elements of any therapeutic encounter, the two are highly interdependent. Each affects the other to a marked degree. In terms of the relationship, it often emerges silently, as the participants' feelings and attitudes toward one another develop. The therapist and client each do what they are supposed to do, according to the counselor's theory and the client's needs and compatibility with that theory. Ordinarily, the relationship comes to the fore either when something goes awry (e.g., when negative feelings arise) or when something special happens (e.g., the client feels especially moved by a feeling expressed by the counselor or vice versa).

Components of Therapeutic Relationships

For many years, psychologists have theorized about the therapeutic relationship as a global entity. More recently, however, theorists have come to believe it useful to break the overall relationship into its key elements (Gelso, 2009; Horvath, 2009; Norcross, 2011). It has been reasoned that the study of the elements or components of the global relationship will better help psychologists to study and understand how the relationship works during counseling.

Actually, from the time of Sigmund Freud's early writing (Freud, 1912/1959), at least some psychoanalysts have theorized about different dimensions of therapeutic relationships. Although in psychoanalysis the transference element of the relationship has always garnered the greatest interest, from Freud on, a number of analysts have proposed that there is more of interest to analysis than the transference relationship. Freud himself believed that there were two significant components to analytic relationships. The first was the transference proper, or the neurotic transference. This component needed to be analyzed and worked through. Juxtaposed with this neurotic transference, however, were what Freud called the "friendly" and "affectionate" feelings of the analysand toward the analyst, and he felt them to be essential to successful analysis.

It remained for Ralph Greenson (1967) to theorize that analytic relationships could be divided into three parts: the working alliance, transference, and the real relationship. Greenson's writing has had an important impact within psychoanalysis. Gelso and Carter (1985) extended Greenson's propositions to essentially all theoretical approaches (not only psychoanalysis). In a pantheoretical statement, they proposed that "all therapeutic relationships consist of these three components [working alliance, transference, real relationship], although the salience and importance of each part during counseling or therapy will vary according to the theoretical perspective of the therapist and the particulars of a given therapy" (p. 161).

In the remainder of this section we examine these three components of therapeutic relationships. In our discussion, we draw heavily on the initial conceptions of Gelso and Carter (1985) and subsequent revisions (Gelso, 2014; Gelso & Carter, 1994; Gelso & Hayes, 1998; Gelso & Samstag, 2008). Before we begin our discussion, it should be underscored that although we discuss the three components as separate constructs, they are in fact quite interrelated in counseling practice. The way in which they operate together is explored at the end of this discussion. The three theorized components of the counseling relationship, along with their definitions, are presented in Table 9.1.

THE WORKING ALLIANCE

Over the past several decades the working alliance (also called the *helping alliance*, the *working relationship*, and the *therapeutic alliance*) has

---

TABLE 9.1

Components of the Counseling Relationship

Component	Summary description
Working alliance	Joining of client's reasonable/observing side with counselor's working side.
Client transference	Client experience of therapist involving feelings and perceptions belonging rightfully to early significant relationships.
Therapist countertransference	Therapist reaction based on his or her unresolved conflicts and vulnerability.
Real relationship	Genuine and realistic part of counselor–client relationship.

been empirically investigated more than perhaps any other construct pertaining to the counselor–client relationship. A number of measures have been developed to study the alliance (see Horvath, Del Re, Flückiger, & Symonds, 2011), and it has been clearly documented that this alliance is a key part of the therapy relationship (Gelso, 2014; Horvath et al., 2011).

What is the working alliance? What are its ingredients? What counselor and client characteristics and behaviors facilitate or inhibit its development? Following the thinking of Gelso and Hayes (1998), we may consider the working alliance as the alignment or joining together of the client's reasonable and observing side (the *reasonable/observing ego* in psychoanalytic terms) with the counselor's working or "therapizing" side (the counselor's observing ego applied to the counseling) for the purpose of facilitating the work of counseling. This definition is based on the notion that two rather disparate qualities exist in human personality. The first is that which permits us to stand back and reasonably observe phenomena, including ourselves and our own functioning, motives, and feelings. This is the side that could be seen as the reasonable/observing ego. The second quality allows us to experience and feel unreflectively and may be viewed as the experiencing side of the ego or the experiencing ego.

In therapies that may be considered expressive or insight-oriented treatments (e.g., psychodynamic and humanistic therapies) and perhaps in feminist multicultural, behavioral, and cognitive therapies as well, the client needs to be able to oscillate between the experiencing and observing sides of his or her personality. Thus, the client needs to be able to feel and experience and then look and reflect upon those feelings and experiences.

Once again, in the working alliance the reasonable sides of the counselor and client join together so that both individuals can carry out their roles in the work successfully. Both counselor and client share a reasonable belief that this experience will be worthwhile for the client, and because of this, both are committed to their collaboration in the work.

What makes the working alliance so important? Not only does it reflect the participants' commitment to the work and an intent to collaborate, it also allows the client to continue in the work during difficult times. For example, if and when the client's defenses and negative transference reactions push the client in the direction of discontinuing counseling, it is the working alliance that allows him or her to stand back from these feelings and recognize them as defensively based. Thus, although the alliance is always important during the counseling experience, it is especially important during difficult times between the counselor and client.

Probably the most seminal theoretical statement about the working alliance as it operates across diverse forms of psychotherapy has been offered by Edward Bordin (1979). Bordin proposed that the alliance consists of three parts: agreement between counselor and client on the goals of counseling, agreement about the tasks of the work, and the emotional bond that forms between the participants. Agreement on goals implies that the participants share the goals of the work, regardless of whether this agreement is explicitly stated or indeed whether the goals themselves are explicitly stated. Agreement on tasks implies that therapist and client also share a view of how those goals may best be attained. It is important here to understand that Bordin was not talking about tasks as structured work tasks. Rather, he was referring to any of the in-therapy or extra-therapy role behaviors expected of the participants. For example, in most forms of therapy an expected client task is for that client to talk about himself or herself and to express feelings. In analysis, the in-therapy task is for the analysand to free-associate, whereas in most structural treatments, a frequent task is for the client to carry out homework assignments. In any event, if the alliance is to be strong, client and counselor need to reach sound agreements on the value of the main tasks of a given therapy. Last but not least, an attachment is needed between counselor and client if the alliance is to be strong.

In our way of thinking about a working alliance, agreement on tasks and goals and bonding contribute to the strength of the alliance. In turn, the strength of the alliance facilitates agreement on tasks and goals as well as on emotional attachment. Thus, there is a reciprocal causal relationship between alliance and the three dimensions discussed by Bordin (1979). Implicit in this reciprocal relationship is the fact that the working alliance exists on a continuum, ranging from weak or nonexistent to very strong. Bonding and agreement on tasks and goals also exist on continua, varying in the same way as does the working alliance.

As should be clear by now, the working alliance is interactive in that both the counselor and the client contribute to it. With regard to the counselor's contribution, we would expect a number of qualities and behaviors to be important. The counselor's professional concern, compassion, and willingness to persist in the work seem highly pertinent. Also, the well-known "facilitative conditions" of empathic understanding, unconditional positive regard, and congruence (to be discussed later in this chapter) would appear to be vital to a strong alliance. Just as is the case with the client, if the alliance is to be strong, the counselor must make use of his or her reasonable or observing side so that the feelings he or she experiences toward the client may be used appropriately. Counselors experience a range of emotional reactions to clients, and it is imperative that they use their reasonable/observing capacities to understand these reactions. Then, as a bottom line, they must try to use their emotional reactions in the service of the client, to the client's benefit, and not in antitherapeutic ways.

The therapist qualities described in the above paragraph come into play particularly when what has been termed a rupture occurs in the working alliance. Alliance ruptures have been defined as a tension or breakdown in the collaboration between the therapist and client. They can be caused by misunderstanding on the part of the therapist, pushing the client in ways for which the client does not feel ready, or by negative projections from the client based on past relationships (see discussion of transference later in this chapter). It is important that the therapist be sensitive to such ruptures, face them nondefensively, and empathically grasp the client's feelings. Research evidence suggests that at least some minor ruptures are almost inevitable, and, indeed, ruptures that are effectively explored actually tend to have a positive effect. This positive effect results from, for example, clients gaining understanding of their difficulties in relationships and how to resolve them (see Safran, Muran, & Eubanks-Carter, 2011; Samstag, Muran, & Safran, 2004).

In terms of the client's contribution to the working alliance, probably the most essential feature is a capacity to trust. Without this, there can be no healthy bonding, no positive attachment. As uncovered in a study by Gaston, Marmar, Thompson, and Gallagher (1988), client defensiveness or resistance tends to affect the alliance negatively, at least in brief therapy (analytic, behavioral, and cognitive) with depressed elderly patients. Perhaps most basically, though, the client must have a strong enough, reasonable, observing side, or ego, to allow him or her to stand back and observe what is transpiring in him or her and in the work.

Gelso and Carter (1994) and Gelso and Hayes (1998) presented a series of theoretical propositions about how the alliance operates in and affects the process and outcome of therapy. These propositions are aimed at facilitating both counseling practice and research. Gelso and Hayes's (1998) work, along with Horvath and Greenberg's (1994) book-length treatment of the working alliance and Horvath et al.'s (2011) major review of alliance research, should be consulted by the reader who is interested in studying this construct further. In terms of research support, probably the clearest finding at this early stage of empirical investigation is that the strength of alliance, as measured within the first few sessions of counseling or therapy, is related to a wide variety of measures of outcome. The stronger the alliance in the first few sessions, the more positive are the results of counseling. The working alliance appears to be equally important in work with children, adolescents, adults, couples, and families (Friedlander, Escudero, Heatherington, & Diamond, 2011; Horvath et al., 2011; Shirk & Karver, 2011). This finding appears quite robust because it holds up for both brief and longer term therapy, for counseling from a range of theoretical perspectives (analytic, behavioral, cognitive, humanistic, gestalt, etc.), and with several different types of alliance measures.

In sum, the findings do appear to support the proposition that it is quite important to establish a sound working alliance very early in counseling. This formation of an early alliance is especially important in briefer counseling, in which the counselor does not have the luxury of time to devote to the gradual cultivation of an alliance. On the basis of our own counseling experiences, we would go even further and suggest that the greatest attention needs to be given to promoting this aspect of the total relationship. Without an alliance, it is hard to imagine the work of therapy being done with much ultimate effectiveness.

According to Horvath and his collaborators (Horvath et al., 2011), two concepts are fundamental to any conception of the working alliance: *collaboration* and *consensus*. With regard to collaboration, counselor and client must invest in the work jointly. If this sense of collaborativeness is not strong at the beginning of counseling, it is necessary that it develop as the work unfolds. With regard to consensus, it is essential that counselor and client come together and agree, explicitly or implicitly, on what their work together should focus on and what their therapeutic tasks should be. These two elements—collaboration and consensus—are common across modern conceptions of the working alliance that cut across theoretical orientation.

Just what constitutes a sound or sufficiently strong working alliance may depend on a host of factors. For example, interventions that are more emotionally demanding on the client may require a stronger alliance than less demanding treatments. Also, the alliance may need to be especially strong during certain critical points in the therapy; for example, when negative transference or certain resistances threaten the work or when the client feels particularly vulnerable. Finally, certain aspects of the alliance may need to be stronger at certain times in the work. An example of the latter may be that early in the work the agreement on tasks may be essential, whereas later in the counseling the bonding aspect may be more important.

In summary, over the past several decades, theory and research have addressed how the alliance operates in different approaches to therapy and how it affects the counseling process and outcomes. Research suggests that the working alliance is one of the key elements of therapy, perhaps the very foundation of the therapy relationship.

THE TRANSFERENCE CONFIGURATION

The second component of the therapeutic relationship actually consists of two elements: client transference and therapist countertransference. We first define and discuss transference and then examine the therapist's countertransference.

Transference

Many consider transference to be Freud's most significant discovery. Despite its centrality in psychoanalytic theory, transference (and countertransference) may be considered to be a part of all therapeutic encounters and to be a component of all therapeutic relationships. In fact, as Freud (1912/1959) clearly formulated, transference can be seen as occurring in all human relationships. For example, in their extensive social psychological program of research, Andersen and her collaborators (see Andersen & Przybylinski, 2012) have shown convincingly how a wide range of transference reactions occurs in everyday life and relationships. Thus, transference is a natural human tendency that becomes magnified and intensified in therapeutic relationships because of the nature of such relationships. That is, because therapeutic interactions focus on help giving, with one person seeking to provide conditions for psychological growth in another, the tendency to experience and manifest transference reactions becomes heightened.

Just what is transference? In the classical Freudian view, transference is seen as the reliving of oedipal issues in the therapy relationship. The therapist is reacted to as if he or she were any or all of the participants in the client's early oedipal situation, most often the client's mother and/or father. Because of the exclusive focus on the oedipal context, this definition is quite narrow and restrictive, and it of course requires that the therapist share the psychoanalytic view of the critical importance of the Oedipus complex in human development.

When we view transference as an element of all therapeutic relationships, a broader conception of this construct is in order. Such a conception, in keeping with more current thought, has been offered by Gelso and Bhatia (2012, p. 385). *Transference is defined as the client's experience of the therapist that is shaped by the client's own psychological structures and past involving carryover and displacement onto the therapist of feelings, attitudes, and behaviors belonging rightfully in earlier significant relationships.* To the extent that the client's reactions to the counselor are transference based, the client is responding to the counselor as if the counselor represented aspects of the transference source; for example, mother, father, sibling. It is important to understand that the client does not really think or believe that the therapist is mother, father, or sibling when transference occurs. Rather, the client transfers significant aspects of the parents' reactions toward him or her from earlier times onto the therapist, such that the therapist is erroneously assumed to be exhibiting those reactions (e.g., motives, attitudes).

In transference situations such as these, the client may react to the therapist as if the therapist does not like him or her, is being critical, will abandon him or her, is not trustworthy, is perfect, is wonderful, and so on. In other words, an almost infinite array of affects, characteristics, motives, and behaviors may be attributed to the counselor erroneously. Inspection of these client perceptions, sometimes over long periods of time, usually reveals them to be displacements from earlier significant relationships. Examples of transference reactions from cases actually worked with by one of the authors are given in the following.

▪ Case 1: Over many sessions, this client felt sure that the therapist could give her solutions to her life problems, which in fact were profound. She felt that the therapist really knew the solutions but was withholding them. He was not giving her her fair share— what she deserved to have. Because of this she experienced a chronic sense of deep anger toward the therapist. During one session in which she angrily criticized and pleaded with the therapist to "tell her," he pointed out the bitterness in her request and how her feelings must echo feelings from long ago. She responded by tearfully expressing how she never got her share from her parents, how she was never taken care of. This interaction was a critical step in the work toward her coming to understand her transference and work through the conflicts underlying them.

▪ Case 2: Even though the client experienced the therapist's empathy and concern in an ongoing way, during periods of the work he responded to the therapist as a critical, demanding, and deeply attacking figure. The sound working alliance and the client's strong observing ego helped him stand back from these feelings and come to grips with where they were coming from. A good bit of the work centered on the client's conflicts with a highly critical, demanding father and the effects of this relationship on his self-concept and relationships with others.

▪ Case 3: During the early weeks of a long counseling experience, this client, among other things, could never break silences by offering new material. Her mind would go blank. She feared and fully expected that the therapist would feel critical of her initiating new topics and of any material she might initiate, despite the reality of the treatment situation; that is, her initiation was welcomed. A significant proportion of the counseling focused on this client's injurious relationship with her mother, a deeply narcissistic woman who had few boundaries, and whose needs this client had to constantly attend to. In close relationships, this client consistently carried with her a sense that the only way she could be cared about was if she, in effect, denied any of her needs and attended to the other's. She became a stranger to her own needs, and much of the counseling aimed at helping her learn about what she wanted and needed and psychically disengage from the often unconscious entanglement with her mother.

Just as in all counseling relationships, in these three cases there were many transference elements. We have presented what may be seen as single strands of these transferences so as to clarify how transference reactions may occur in counseling. As a way of further clarifying this complex concept, the following rules of thumb about transference may be useful.

1. *Transference is always an error.* By definition, the perceptions the client has of the counselor, when transference based, are, to an important extent, erroneous. They represent displacements that were appropriate (not an error) to other relationships, from another time and place. It needs to be stated here that by no means are all perceptions the client has of the counselor erroneous. Nor are all experiences of the counselor based on misperceptions. It is important for the counselor to understand which reactions are realistic and which are based on transference.

   There is at least an element of reality, too, in all transference reactions. Often, something in the therapeutic relationship serves as a trigger for transference (e.g., something the therapist says or does, verbally or nonverbally). Fundamentally, though, the client is experiencing the therapist and the relationship in a way that does not befit the therapist and his or her behavior but instead echoes relationships and issues from the client's earlier life.

2. *Transference may be positive or negative.* The misperceptions that are part of transference reactions are just as likely to be positive as negative. Thus, the client may project positive attitudes onto the counselor, based on needs tied to past conflictual relationships. For example, because of the client's deprivations with a parent, the client may need to see the counselor as more loving or powerful than is realistically the case. Because counselors' feelings are most often positive and because the counseling role is a positive one, positive transferences are often more difficult to appreciate as transferences than are negative transferences.

3. *The emergence of transference in the counseling is facilitated by the therapist's neutrality and ambiguity.* The concept of neutrality is one of the most misunderstood in all of the psychotherapy and counseling literature. By neutrality we do not mean bland

indifference or lack of caring. Instead, we refer to the therapist's not taking sides and not imposing his or her values and beliefs on the client. Ambiguity is a similar but not identical concept. It refers to the tendency not to present a clear picture of one's feelings, life, and attitudes. Counselors as well as theoretical approaches to counseling vary widely in the extent to which they endorse the concept of ambiguity.

In any event, it is generally agreed that counselor ambiguity and neutrality create an environment in which transference is more likely to develop and emerge fully. This is not to say that transference does not occur in active therapies, where the therapist is very open about his or her values and may take sides. It occurs there, too, but ambiguity and neutrality allow it to develop and come into the open more fully and in a way that many counselors believe to be less "contaminated" (by the reality of the counselor). It must be added that the extent to which transference should be encouraged to develop and emerge is not nearly agreed on by counselors. Theories vary widely on this point.

4. *Transference is not conscious.* Although the client's feelings toward the counselor may be fully conscious, the fact that they are displacements from earlier relationships is not. Some approaches to counseling (especially those that are psychodynamically based) seek to make them conscious, with the aim of resolving or correcting transference distortions.

5. *Transferences are most likely to occur in areas of greatest unresolved conflict with significant others earlier in one's life.* The final rule of thumb implies that humans are more likely to misperceive the present based on the past (i.e., erroneously project the past into the present) in areas in which there were significant unresolved conflicts in past important relationships. Thus, for example, if a central area of unresolved conflict in one's childhood had to do with dependency, issues around dependency are likely to be evidenced in the transference relationship with the therapist.

It should be reiterated that what we have presented above are rules of thumb about the operation of transference in counseling and therapy. Some of these are a basic part of the definition of transference (e.g., it is not conscious); others have never been tested in a rigorous scientific manner. The concept of transference (and countertransference, as will be discussed next) is one of the most complex in psychology today, and it has been extremely difficult to develop methods of studying it scientifically. That is because theoretical propositions that incorporate unconscious processes are not easily tested with traditional scientific methods. In recent years, though, empirical research has begun to develop. A number of methods of studying transference have emerged, including both quantitative and qualitative methods. Some of these methods make use of therapists' judgments, whereas others use judgments made by raters based on audio- or videotapes of sessions. More recently, methods of assessing transference from clients' perspective have been developed (see Gelso & Samstag, 2008, and Kivlighan, 2002, for a description of these methods). An important body of research has also accrued on how to better deal with transference in therapy (Levy & Scala, 2012).

How does transference operate in different forms of therapy? How is it handled, and how should it be dealt with by the counselor? We refer the reader to subsequent chapters of this book (Chapters 11, 12, and 13) and to Gelso and Hayes (1998) for detailed discussion of these complex questions. For now, suffice it to say that although we propose that transference is a component of the therapy relationship in all forms of counseling, some approaches more than others provide conditions allowing the transference to develop more fully and then work with these reactions with the aim of helping the client gain insight into them. Generally, the psychoanalytically based approaches do this. Other approaches pay less attention to transference.

In general, transference will develop and become manifest to a greater extent in therapies that view it as central and aim to work with transference reactions. At the same time, there is evidence that it does occur even in therapies in which it is viewed as unimportant (see Gelso & Bhatia's 2012 review of research on the occurrence of transference in nonanalytic therapy). Counselors of all theoretical persuasions should be trained to at least recognize signs of transference and to deal with transference issues when they are interfering with progress. As Gelso and Hayes (1998) discussed, therapists can do this and still remain faithful to the theoretical approaches they are practicing. For example, the behavior therapist can help the client understand transference difficulties that are negatively affecting the counseling, without violating any principles of behavior therapy.

Countertransference: The Counselor's Transference

Given that the client–counselor relationship is a two-way street, involving contributions from both participants, it is important to look at the counselor's contributions to the transference configuration. As implied earlier, the counselor can behave in ways that evoke certain transference reactions; by so doing, the counselor will contribute to the client's transference. But it is important to note that the counselor also contributes his or her own transference reactions, and these are called *countertransference*.

Just as we propose that client transference occurs in all therapy, so too is countertransference seen as universal. No matter how emotionally mature the counselor and how effectively he or she has overcome inevitable conflicts, the counselor is a human being and as such will have areas of unresolved conflict. These sore spots contain the issues that are likely to develop into countertransference reactions. This occurs when material presented by the client touches areas of unresolved conflict in the counselor. The universal nature of countertransference has been documented empirically (Hayes et al., 1998).

The above discussion may seem to imply that there is some agreed-upon definition of countertransference. Actually, this construct has been one of the most confused and confusing ones in the history of psychology (and of psychoanalysis). A wide array of definitions can be found in the literature. These range from the broadest, called the *totalistic* definition, to the narrowest, called the *classical* definition. The totalistic definition of countertransference views this phenomenon as including virtually all of the counselor's emotional reactions to the client. Thus, realistic reactions, not based on particular conflicts within the counselor, will be seen as countertransference, just as will conflict-based reactions.

The classical definition of countertransference is the "counselor's transference to the client's transference." This is very narrow in that only client transference reactions and not reactions that are nontransferential can be the trigger for countertransference. An intermediate definition may be the most useful one. *Countertransference* can thus be defined as the counselor's transference to the client's material—to the transference and nontransference communications presented by the client. As Langs (1974) suggested, countertransference may be seen as

> one aspect of those responses to the patient which, while prompted by some event within the therapy or the therapist's real life, are primarily based on his past significant relationships; basically they gratify his needs rather than the patient's therapeutic endeavors. (p. 298)

Is countertransference therapeutic or antitherapeutic? Does it hinder or help progress in counseling? The answers to these questions depend on whether countertransference is considered an overt behavior or an internal experience in the counselor. Earlier writing, usually in psychoanalysis, appeared to focus on external behavior, what the analyst *did* with the client based on internal conflicts in the work. When viewed as an external behavior, countertransference is something to be controlled and ideally to be worked through, because it is important that therapists not act out their own conflicts with and on their clients. Such acting out may take numerous forms. For example, the counselor who, because of his or her unresolved issues, becomes angry, submissive, or unresponsive is likely acting out countertransference.

In recent times, countertransference has more often been viewed as an internal experience in the counselor (Gelso & Hayes, 2007). When seen as an internal experience (rather than as a behavior that is acted out with the client), countertransference can be extremely helpful to counseling if it is understood and effectively managed by the counselor (see review of empirical studies by Hayes, Gelso, & Hummel, 2011). For example, if the counselor uses his or her internal countertransference-based experiences to better understand the impact of the client on him or her and on others, this can greatly benefit the work. Doing so requires that the counselor be willing to focus on his or her feelings toward the client when these are experienced as conflictual. It also requires that the counselor be willing and able to try to understand where these feelings come from in his or her own life, a task that can be anxiety provoking but extremely important.

In summary, like transference, countertransference is seen as a component of all therapy relationships. The countertransference experience can be for better or worse, depending on the counselor's willingness to inspect his or her own experience and the roots of his or her conflict based reactions to clients. Also, as is the case with transference, countertransference had been ignored by researchers for many years. Over the past 2 decades, however, a sound body of research has accrued suggesting the adverse effects of countertransference when it is acted out in the session by therapists and the positive effects that occur when countertransference is understood and effectively managed (Gelso & Hayes, 2007; Hayes et al., 2011).

THE REAL RELATIONSHIP

Coexisting in an interrelated way with the working alliance and transference components of the counseling relationship is a third component. Following the lead of the classical psychoanalyst Ralph Greenson (1967), authors have labeled this component the "real relationship" (Gelso, 2009, 2011; Gelso & Carter, 1985, 1994; Gelso & Hayes, 1998). Although we use the term *real relationship*, this term can be confusing, implying as it does that relationships vary in how "real" they are. All relationships are of course real in the sense that they actually exist; it is probably safe to say that none exists any more than others.

The real relationship may be seen as the personal relationship between a therapist and a client, and it is conceptualized as having two main elements: genuineness and realistic perceptions. Counseling relationships are seen as having a strong real relationship if both participants were highly genuine and perceived each other in a realistic (undistorted) way. The concept of "genuineness" has been central in counseling and therapy for many years, especially in the humanistic therapies (e.g., person-centered, gestalt). When genuineness is discussed in the counseling literature, what is usually being referred to is the *therapist's* genuineness; especially in the humanistic approaches, therapist genuineness is seen as an important facilitative factor.

What is meant by *genuineness?* We define it as the ability and willingness to be what one truly is in the relationship, to be honest, open, and authentic. As noted above, the counseling literature has tended to focus on therapist genuineness and in this sense has neglected the fact that the relationship goes two ways. In order for the relationship to be high in genuineness, both parties must be open, honest, and authentic, or at least they must work to express these qualities with each other. As Greenberg (1985) put it, in a genuine relationship, the two participants in the counseling situation are "stubbornly attempting to dispense with appearances and reveal themselves as they truly are in the moment" (p. 254). Along a similar vein, a relationship that is highly genuine would tend to be what is often described as an *I–thou relationship.* To follow Greenberg's (1985) thinking further, the genuine involvement in an I–thou relationship is seen as "the attempt for people to break down barriers between inside and outside, between image and experience, and to communicate intimately their moment-to-moment inner experience" (p. 254).

Because the roles differ in the relationship for the counselor and client, however, their expression of genuineness is quite different. From the client's side, he or she is expected to try to express feelings, thoughts, and inner experience essentially at all times, although it is of course not expected that the client will always be successful at accurately expressing these inner qualities. In this sense, though, the client is expected to be genuine, or struggle to be so, throughout the work.

The counselor's contribution to a genuine relationship is more complicated than the client's role. No approach to counseling and therapy would advise the counselor to say whatever is on his or her mind and express or act out his or her feelings unreflectively. As Greenberg (1985) pointed out, "The relationship is therefore not a strictly mutual I–thou relationship in which the counselor is equally acknowledged and confirmed by the client in an ongoing fashion" (p. 255). The counselor puts many of his or her needs aside and is in the service of the client's needs and growth during the time of the work. Returning to the issue of genuineness, the extent and ways in which the counselor should be open, honest, and authentic must depend on what is best for a given client at a given point in the work. In this sense, the counselor must practice a kind of "controlled spontaneity"—expressing what he or she feels, what is on his or her mind, after reflecting on what is best for the client and deciding that expression of this feeling would be appropriate.

In summary, the counselor pays close attention to the client and his or her expressions. The counselor thinks about what is going on in the work, in the client, in himself or herself, and in the relationship. At certain points the counselor may express his or her feelings toward and about the client. It must be emphasized, however, that our comments do not imply that the counselor ought to be disingenuous or dishonest at any point. Although whether and how particular feelings ought to be directly expressed is open to debate, we would contend that there is no place in counseling for counselor dishonesty or disingenuousness.

The second aspect of the real relationship is *realistic perceptions*. Here the participants perceive each other in a realistic and accurate way, undistorted by transference experiences or other defenses. From the first moment of contact, at least some of the therapeutic relationship contains such realistic perceptions on the part of *both* client and counselor. We emphasize the word *both* here because some theoretical approaches (particularly those psychoanalytically based) appear to imply that, whereas the therapist's perceptions may be mostly realistic from the beginning of the work, all or nearly all of the client's perceptions are transference based. On the contrary, not only does the client perceive or "subceive" aspects of the counselor realistically, but this realistic or accurate picture builds and increases throughout the work. Also, as transference distortions are worked through (whether or not they are interpreted to the client as such), realistic perceptions take their place, at least in part.

All therapists communicate their personhood in numerous ways, from their office decor to their attire and general appearance to their sense of humor to the questions they ask, and so forth. And even clients with very strong transference proclivities and tendencies to distort will be able to perceive the counselor realistically to an extent.

How important is it for the real relationship to be positive, for participants to experience genuine and realistic positive feelings and thoughts toward one another? Evidence indicates that a positive real relationship, on the whole, is beneficial from the beginning of counseling. Even when clients experience some negative reactions, which they certainly do in effective counseling, it is important that the overall tone of the relationship be positive. The research evidence summarized by Gelso (2011) and Gelso et al. (2012) suggests that from the perspective of clients and therapists, in more successful therapy the real relationship is strong from the beginning, and it tends to strengthen further as work progresses. Although promising, research on the real or personal relationship is at an earlier stage than research on working alliance or transference/countertransference. Now that reliable and valid measures of the real relationship have been developed by Gelso et al. (2005) and Kelley, Gelso, Fuertes, Marmarosh, and Lanier (2010), research is expected to increase in the years ahead.

A PERSPECTIVE ON RELATIONSHIP COMPONENTS

We noted in the beginning of this section that the three components of the therapeutic relationship are interrelated in practice. We conclude this section by discussing how they are interrelated and how they might be expected to operate together in counseling.

Early in counseling, the working alliance is especially important. The reasonable sides of the counselor and client will need to join together, to bond, so that the value of working together can be appreciated, and emotional threats to the emerging relationship can be looked at without destroying what has begun to build. The counselor and client must also come to agree—implicitly or explicitly—on the goals and tasks of counseling, as discussed earlier. Utmost attention needs to be given to the cultivation of this alliance early in counseling. Initial positive transference and a positive real relationship aid considerably in alliance development. Even though transference reactions are displacements from earlier relationships (i.e., errors, as described earlier), if they are positive, they can help create warm, friendly feelings that serve to solidify the working bond between counseling participants. In a like manner, if each participant feels positively toward the other, who is seen realistically and who has genuinely expressed himself or herself, the working alliance will be strengthened. In this way, genuine and realistic caring, which itself creates and is part of a personal, emotional bond, also furthers the working bond of the alliance.

In turn, when the working alliance is sound, the client is able to experience negative feelings toward the counselor in the transference relationship without these feelings injuring the work. In fact, the strength of the alliance allows one to work through the negative transferences and thus further strengthen the total relationship. On the other hand, when negative transference develops early in the work and before a strong working alliance has had a chance to develop, it is important, perhaps essential, that these feelings be explored and their transference roots uncovered. Without this, the alliance may be irreparably damaged by the negative transference, and the relationship may end or stagnate. (See Horwitz's 1974 examination of such phenomena based on a 20-year process outcome study done at the Menninger Clinic.) When such negative transference is explored and understood, the result is better and more successful counseling (Gelso & Bhatia, 2012; Levy & Scala, 2012). We should note here, though, that negative transference is not always present to a significant degree and is not always an important part of treatment (Gelso, Kivlighan, Wine, Jones, & Friedman, 1997; Patton, Kivlighan, & Multon, 1997).

As counselor and client continue to work together and their alliance strengthens, we would expect the real relationship to strengthen. The client is able to be increasingly genuine and to perceive the counselor more realistically. The working alliance facilitates this and is thus a factor in the strengthening of the real relationship, just as the real relationship affects the working alliance.

What is the developmental course of the three components during counseling? As indicated earlier, the working alliance is most salient early in the relationship. After the early phase, when it becomes established to a satisfactory degree, the alliance tends to fade into the background, only coming to the fore when needed (e.g., when the relationship is threatened by negative feelings that may result from transference). There is also emerging evidence indicating that in successful counseling, the working alliance declines in strength for a period. That is, after being initially strong, the alliance will weaken as the counselor begins to focus on the client's resistances or basic emotional issues. Subsequently, the alliance will again strengthen. This high–low–high pattern does not appear to occur in less successful counseling, but it may recycle or recur in successful cases in the form of alliance ruptures and repairs.

The real relationship, on the other hand, tends to be positive from the beginning and in the sense that the therapist and client seem to "click" with each other personally. As we have said, this real relationship may well build throughout the relationship, becoming most salient in the later phases of the work, when the participants come to know each other most deeply, have become increasingly genuine, and perceive each other most realistically. Transference continues throughout counseling but is increasingly understood by the client (Gelso et al., 1997; Graff & Luborsky, 1977; Patton et al., 1997), at least in therapies that focus on these transference reactions. In therapies that do not, we would expect the transferences to become less salient as other phenomena are attended to—unless these transferences are injurious to the work. In such cases, they need to be dealt with and resolved, or the effects can be irreparably damaging.

In summary, each component of the counseling relationship develops in its own way, although each is also interdependent. Additional theory and research are needed to further our understanding of the course of development of the various components in both successful and unsuccessful counseling.

Facilitative Conditions and the Therapy Relationship

At several points in this chapter, reference has been made to therapist-offered conditions, necessary and sufficient conditions, and relationship conditions. All of these references pertain to a set of conditions initially

TABLE 9.2

Rogers's Necessary and Sufficient Conditions for Constructive Change in Counseling

1. Two persons are in psychological contact.
2. The first, whom we shall term the client, is in a state of incongruence, being vulnerable or anxious.
3. The second person, whom we shall term the therapist, is congruent or integrated in the relationship.
4. The therapist experiences unconditional positive regard for the client.
5. The therapist experiences an empathic understanding of the client's internal frame of reference and endeavors to communicate this experience to the client.
6. The communication to the client of the therapist's empathic understanding and unconditional positive regard is to a minimal degree achieved.

    No other conditions are necessary. If these six conditions exist, and continue over a period of time, this is sufficient. The process of constructive personality change will follow. [emphasis added]

Note. From "The Necessary and Sufficient Conditions of Therapeutic Personality Change," by C. R. Rogers, 1957, *Journal of Consulting Psychology*, 21, p. 96. Copyright 1957 by the American Psychological Association.

formulated nearly six decades ago by Rogers (1957), the founder of client-centered therapy, which is now known as *person-centered therapy* (see Chapter 13). Rogers's original theoretical statement was one of the most influential in the history of counseling psychology. It has generated an enormous amount of research and has had a profound effect on counseling practice.

As a preface to his famous statement, Rogers (1957) asked, "Is it possible to state, in terms which are clearly definable and measurable, the psychological conditions that are *both necessary and sufficient* [emphasis added] to bring about constructive personality change?" (p. 95). Rogers answered his question by stating the six conditions presented in Table 9.2.

According to these conditions, the client needs to be in contact with the counselor and needs to be in a state (i.e., incongruence, anxiety, vulnerability) that makes him or her receptive to help. The client also must perceive or take in what the counselor has to offer. Despite the importance of these client contributions, though, the features of Rogers's statement that have been given the greatest attention over the years are Items 3, 4, and 5 in Table 9.2, the three therapist-offered conditions. As implied in Rogers's own work, as well as the research of many others, the three therapist-offered conditions, or the relationship conditions, constitute the bulk of his theoretical statement.

Before discussing each of the three conditions, we clarify our preference for the term *facilitative conditions*. Research evidence accumulated over many years indicates that the three conditions are not sufficient, in the sense that other factors are also involved in successful therapy

(Lambert, 2013; Norcross, 2011). Also, it is conceivable that for at least some clients in some treatments, positive change may occur when the conditions are at a low level. Yet, as shall be elaborated, the conditions generally are important for successful counseling and do seem to facilitate positive change in clients.

EMPATHIC UNDERSTANDING

Of the three facilitative conditions, empathic understanding has the greatest appeal theoretically and clinically, and it has received the greatest amount of empirical support in terms of being associated with positive counseling outcomes (Elliott, Bohart, Watson, & Greenberg, 2011). Indeed, it is hard to envision effective counseling if the counselor is not able to empathize with the client and his or her issues. Therapists from virtually every theoretical orientation have noted the importance of empathy (see, e.g., Eagle & Wolitzky's 1997 in-depth discussion of the importance of empathy in psychoanalysis and Linehan's 1997 discussion of its role in cognitive–behavior therapy). In describing his view of empathy, Rogers (1957) told us,

> To sense the client's private world as if it were your own, but without ever losing the "as if" quality—this is empathy, and this seems essential to therapy. To sense the client's anger, fear, or confusion as if it were your own, yet without your own anger, fear, or confusion getting bound up in it, is the condition we are attempting to describe. When the client's world is this clear to the therapist, and he moves about in it freely, then he can communicate his understanding of what is clearly known to the client and can also voice meanings in the client's experience of which the client is scarcely aware. (p. 98)

Shortly after Rogers made his seminal statement, G. T. Barrett-Lennard (1962), who had studied with Rogers, published an inventory that sought to measure empathic understanding and the other therapist-offered conditions from the vantage point of the client receiving counseling. Over the years, Barrett-Lennard has done careful and important research on the Relationship Inventory and revised it several times (see Barrett-Lennard, 1986). Because of that, the Relationship Inventory continues to be the most effective method of measuring the facilitative conditions in a manner that is true to Rogers's theory. Some items from the RI will help clarify the meaning of empathy. Pluses indicate high and minuses indicate low empathy.

(+) He appreciates exactly how the things I experience feel to me.
(−) He may understand my words but doesn't see the way I feel.
(−) Sometimes he thinks I feel a certain way, because that's the way he feels.
(+) He realizes what I mean even when I have difficulty saying it.

In Rogers's initial definition and many of his subsequent writings (e.g., Rogers, 1975), he stressed that empathy and the other conditions were *attitudes and subjective experiences with the therapist*. Yet, over a long period of time what Rogers and many others (see Bozarth, 1984, 1997) had seen as "a way of being" was reduced and narrowed to a trainable skill.

As part of this development, it appeared that empathy became almost equated with the counseling technique called reflection of feeling, in which the counselor paraphrases or reflects back to the client the feelings involved in what the client has just communicated. Bozarth (1997) pointed out that many in the counseling field came to believe that reflection of feeling is empathy and empathy is reflection of feeling.

Although the technique of reflection may aid the counselor in expressing his or her empathy, equating the two oversimplifies and excessively narrows the concept of empathy. In his thoughtful clarification of why empathy and reflection must be differentiated, Bozarth (1984) presented the following multiple-choice item, asking his reader to indicate which statement is the most empathic: (1) I'm having strong sexual feelings toward you; (2) When I took my Volkswagen engine out, the car rolled down the hill, hit the rabbit pen, etc., etc.; (3) You feel as though you have lost contact with the physical world. The third response is a standard reflection of feeling, but Bozarth presented compelling case data to show how Alternatives 1 and 2 were highly empathic. For example, in Alternative 2, the client experienced an intense and painful communication block in one session. She began the next session by asking the therapist, "What have you been doing?" He responded by telling her a nearly session-long story about his car. She later expressed appreciation that the therapist did not try to force her to reconfront her struggle; she needed a respite from it. She also described how the session helped her identify the core of her difficulties.

The above shows how nonreflective responses can be empathic. On the other side of the ledger, reflections, even accurate ones, may signify a lack of empathy. One of the authors vividly recalls an instance when a colleague accurately reflected another colleague's underlying feelings during a meeting, resulting in the recipient tearfully and, to her, shamefully breaking down. This colleague, at that time, neither needed nor wanted someone to illuminate her underlying feelings, and doing so was a deeply unempathic act, although it entailed an accurate reflection of feeling.

There are many ways in which one can become empathic. As Hackney (1978) recommended, the counselor needs to "experience the feeling, first, comprehend it as best you can, then react to it" (p. 37). Modes of being empathic can and should be based on who the therapist is as a person, who the client is as a person, the therapist–client interactions, and probably some other factors (see Elliott et al., 2011).

In essence, empathy is subjectively experienced and is best expressed in a way that fits the counseling participants and their relationship. Numerous responses (silence, reflection of feeling, interpretation, storytelling, etc.) may express empathy.

Gladstein (1983) pointed out that several conceptualizations of empathy seem to include some common stages. First, empathy is experienced emotionally, through a process of identification with the client. This is not complete identification. Rather, it is a process in which the counselor to some extent experiences what the client feels and yet maintains the necessary separateness. Second, there is cognitive activity, in which the counselor consciously sifts through the client's expressions and considers their meanings to the client. Third, there is a communication of that empathy to the client. Finally, there exists the client's "sense and perception of the degree to which the therapist is attuned and actually 'with' him, or her, in immediate personal understanding" (Barrett-Lennard, 1986, p. 446). It is useful to conceptualize the stages of empathy as recycling throughout the encounter.

For example, Elliott, Bohart, Watson, and Greenberg, all leading researchers and theoreticians in the area of empathy, have delineated four useful forms of a therapist's responding to and carrying forward the meaning of the client's communication (Elliott et al., 2011). These are (a) empathic understanding responses, which are similar to reflection of feeling (discussed in Chapter 8) and convey understanding of the client's experience; (b) empathic affirmations, which are attempts to validate the client's perspective (e.g., "yeah, it's really hard being pulled in a thousand directions and there hasn't been any time for you. No wonder it feels like things are a great mess"); (c) empathic evocations, which seek to bring the client's experience alive using rich, concrete, evocative language (e.g., "it's like being caught in a whirlpool, as if it is hard to keep your boat from being sucked under"); and (d) empathic conjectures, which get at what is implicit in the client's words but not yet explicitly spoken (e.g., "just a continual sense of being intruded on. I suppose that makes you feel invaded"). In summary, Elliott et al. (2011) stated that "empathic therapists assist clients to symbolize their experience in words, and track their emotional responses, so that clients can deepen their experience and reflexively examine their feelings, values, and goals. . . . Therapists attend to what is not, or what is on the periphery of awareness as well as that which is said and is in focal awareness" (p. 48).

UNCONDITIONAL POSITIVE REGARD

Of the three facilitative conditions, unconditional positive regard is the most controversial and perhaps also the most complex. At various points in the history of this construct, it has been viewed as synonymous with any and all of the following: warmth, nonpossessive warmth, acceptance, unconditional acceptance, respect, regard, and caring. In his original theoretical statement, Rogers (1957) discussed unconditional positive regard in this way:

> To the extent that the therapist finds himself experiencing a warm acceptance of each aspect of the client's experience as being a part of that client, he is experiencing unconditional positive regard. . . . It means that there are no *conditions* of acceptance, no feeling of "I like you only *if* you are thus and so." It means a prizing of the person. . . . It is at the opposite pole from a selective evaluating attitude—"You are bad in these ways, good in those." It involves as much feeling of acceptance for the client's expression of negative, "bad," painful, fearful, defensive, abnormal feelings as for his expression of "good," positive, mature, confident, social feelings, as much acceptance of ways in which he is inconsistent as of ways in which he is consistent. . . . It means a caring for the client as a *separate* person, with permission to have his own feelings, his own experiences. (p. 98)

As can be seen from Rogers's original definition, virtually all of the terms that have been used interchangeably with *unconditional positive regard* are included in his formulation. As Lietaer (1984) pointed out, some of the controversy and ambivalence surrounding the concept of unconditional positive regard is due to the fact that Rogers did not elaborate much further or at least did not examine some of the problems with the concept.

The controversy surrounding the concept of unconditional positive regard most basically relates to the notion that the therapist can be unconditional in his or her reactions to clients. Critics maintain that it is unrealistic to expect a therapist to experience any feelings toward a client without conditions. In this way, the concept of unconditionality runs into conflicts with the third facilitative condition, genuineness, or congruence. Except in extremely rare circumstances, critics argue, one cannot be unconditionally positive in one's regard for the client and genuine or congruent—simply because unconditionality is not possible.

On the other hand Lietaer (1984) argued persuasively that in considering the concept of unconditionality, one must distinguish the client's inner experience from his or her external behavior. Unconditionality refers to acceptance of the client's experience (feelings, fantasies, thoughts, desires). Lietaer stated, "My client ought to experience the freedom to feel *anything* [emphasis added] with me; he should sense that I am open to his experience and will not judge it" (p. 46). Further, as Bozarth (1997) noted, if the counselor truly climbs into the client's world empathically, that counselor will indeed fully accept the person. Lietaer, however, noted that his receptiveness to the inner experiential world of the client does not mean that all behavior is equally welcome: "Both within and without the therapeutic relationship there can be specific behaviors of which I disapprove, would like to change, or simply cannot accept" (Lietaer, 1984, p. 48). At the same time, it is important that the counselor attempt to look beyond the behavior of which he or she disapproves and try to understand the behavior from the perspective of everything the client has experienced in his or her life.

Given the complexity of the concept of unconditional positive regard, it is not surprising that studies have shown it to be multidimensional. For example, Barrett-Lennard (1986) differentiated two dimensions: *level of regard* and *unconditionality of regard*. He defined level of regard as the overall level or tendency of one person's affective acceptance of or positive regard for another. Positive regard entails warmth, liking, caring, "being drawn toward," and valuing the client in a nonpossessive way. Examples of positive items from Barrett-Lennard's aforementioned Relationship Inventory are

> She respects me as a person.
> I feel appreciated by her.
> She cares for me.

Unconditionality of regard refers to the degree of constancy in accepting the client, or, as Lietaer stated, the extent to which the client is accepted without ifs. *Unconditionality of acceptance* implies that the therapist's basic attitude toward the client does not fluctuate according to the client's emotions or behavior, and it implies that one can have positive regard for a person despite that person's flaws. Positively worded unconditionality items from BarrettLennard's Relationship Inventory are

> How much he likes or dislikes me is not altered by anything that
> I tell him about myself.
> Whether the ideas and feelings I express are "good" or "bad"
> seems to make no difference to his feelings toward me.

The most recent review of research indicates that the therapist's degree of positive regard is an important factor in the success of the treatment (Farber & Doolin, 2011). At a minimum, it set the stage for other change-inducing interventions and in some cases has a profound effect in itself. According to Farber and Doolin, "To many, if not most clients, the conviction that 'my therapist really cares about me' likely serves as a critical function, especially during times of stress" (p. 184).

CONGRUENCE

Congruence, or *genuineness*, as it is often termed, has been considered a foundation variable since Rogers's initial statement. This means, as Barrett-Lennard (1986) noted, that empathy, positive regard, and unconditionality cannot have their desired effects if the therapist is not congruent or genuine. In fact, theoreticians such as Barrett-Lennard question whether one can really be empathic or unconditionally positively regarding in the absence of congruence. In this sense, congruence sets an upper limit on the degree to which the other conditions can exist and have their expected effects.

What do we mean by the words *congruence* and *genuineness?* The concept of genuineness was discussed earlier in this chapter as part of the "real relationship" in counseling. We now examine this condition further. Rogers (1957) believed that *congruence* meant the following:

> Within the relationship he [the counselor] is freely and deeply himself, with his actual experience accurately represented by his awareness of himself. It is the opposite of presenting a facade, either knowingly or unknowingly. . . . It should be clear that this [being congruent] includes being himself even in ways which are not regarded as ideal for psychotherapy. (p. 98)

Then, regarding whether the counselor must be congruent at all times, Rogers told us,

> It is not necessary (nor is it possible) that the therapist be a paragon who exhibits this degree of integration, of wholeness, in every aspect of his life. It is sufficient that he is accurately himself in this hour of this relationship, that in this basic sense he is what he actually is, in this moment of time. (p. 98)

When one studies Rogers's observations, a number of questions about congruence arise. Why does Rogers refer to congruence as implying integration or wholeness? Is the congruence between one's underlying experience and awareness of that experience, between that underlying experience and one's overt communication with the client? Between awareness and communication? Or among all of these levels? How does congruence relate to therapist spontaneity and to acting out of one's impulses in counseling? In an effort to be congruent, to what extent should the therapist focus on expressing his or her own feelings to the client?

These complex questions have been addressed over the years by Rogers and other theoreticians who have studied the facilitative conditions. As we shall see, the answers must be interrelated. For example, in response to why Rogers seems to equate congruence with integration and wholeness, from its inception, the concept of congruence has implied a consistency among the different levels of experience. One's underlying experience, awareness, and communication are all consistent. In this sense, the person is integrated. When theorists who write about the facilitative conditions discuss wholeness and integration, they clearly do not mean that the therapist has all positive feelings or has no problems of his or her own. In Rogers's first statement above he made that clear. The counselor may have negative feelings in the relationship and be whole, integrated, and congruent if he or she is able to be non-defensively aware of these feelings and share them when appropriate. But, again, integration and wholeness refer to a consistency among the various levels of experiencing and communication.

If the counselor is not open to his or her experience, what is experienced at an underlying level will not be in awareness. In effect, the counselor is not conscious or aware of this experience, and to that extent there is incongruence between experience and awareness. This state will also create incongruence between experience and overt communication with the client, because experience tends to be expressed indirectly to the client—verbally and nonverbally—and this may contradict what the therapist communicates overtly.

We noted in our earlier discussion of the real relationship in counseling that the concept of counselor genuineness is controversial. Although no theoretical approach advocates therapist phoniness or disingenuousness, approaches differ in the extent to which they advocate the counselor's sharing his or her feelings about the client, the counseling, and the relationship directly with the client. In general, psychoanalytic approaches promote less direct sharing of counselor feelings, and humanistic approaches promote greater sharing. Virtually no legitimate approach, though, would advocate the counselor's acting out his or her impulses with the client, discussing his or her personal problems with the client except in some unusual circumstances, or telling the client whatever is on the counselor's mind. In terms of direct communication of negative feelings about the client or the relationship, the humanistic perspective would generally support such expressions and in fact view them as extremely important, especially if the counselor's experienced feelings were interfering with his or her counseling effectively and experiencing empathy and regard.

Finally, as for the other facilitative conditions, items from Barrett-Lennard's Relationship Inventory provide operational examples of the concept of congruence. Two items are

> I feel that she is real and genuine with me.
> At times I sense that she is not aware of what she is really feeling with me. (negatively stated)

A PERSPECTIVE ON FACILITATIVE CONDITIONS

As noted at the beginning of this discussion of the facilitative conditions, research over the years strongly supports the contention that these conditions are generally not sufficient and probably not even necessary in some cases. Yet, the research also just as clearly suggests that the conditions are indeed facilitative.

A number of reviews over the year have clearly indicated that the facilitative conditions are much more strongly related to a range of counseling outcomes when these conditions are based on the client's perception rather than on the ratings made by outside judges (who, for example, base ratings on taped segments of sessions). In other words, when the client rates his or her therapist in terms of the facilitative conditions (on, e.g., Barrett-Lennard's Relationship Inventory), these ratings will be far more related to how the counseling turns out than will ratings of the facilitative conditions as viewed by outside raters. Although some observers believe this indicates that the facilitative conditions are not that important, in our view this finding is entirely consistent with Rogers's initial theory. Rogers's focus was on the client's perception of the relationship as the most important indicator of the effects of the conditions, not on "objective" ratings made by nonparticipants in the relationship.

Relationship Components, Facilitative Conditions, and the Therapeutic Process

Do the facilitative conditions, as discussed above, and the relationship components, as explored earlier in this chapter, interrelate during counseling? If so, how would this occur? Although some research supports such interrelation (Gelso, 2011, 2014), most of what can be offered is theoretical speculation. Research is needed to help inform this speculation.

We suggest that the facilitative conditions are probably central in the development of the working alliance. Thus, the working alliance on real relationships will be more positive and stronger to the extent that the therapist is empathic, positively regarding, and congruent.

The facilitative conditions may also have their effect through the alliance they foster. In fact, the therapist-offered facilitative conditions may have their effect on the client through their effects on the transference and real relationship, as well as on the working alliance. For example, the therapist who is high on empathy, unconditionality, positive regard, and congruence will probably foster positive transference. At least as important, though, is that the counselor who is facilitative, and experienced as such by the client, will create the kind of safe climate that allows the client to explore negative transference reactions when they occur. If one feels deeply understood, cared about, and accepted personally with few if any conditions by a therapist who is experienced as genuine, the exploration and expression of negative feelings when they boil up are more possible. Of course, given a sound alliance (which is also affected by therapist facilitativeness), the client is better able to stand back, observe, and ultimately understand these feelings for what they are; that is, transference.

The counselor's facilitativeness both affects and is a part of the real relationship. It will be recalled that genuineness is one of the defining features of the real relationship, and of course counselor genuineness is one of the facilitative conditions. In this sense, facilitativeness is part of the real relationship. Also, the facilitative therapist will promote realistic and genuinely positive feelings on the part of the client toward that therapist. We would then expect a reciprocal effect. To the extent that the client experiences and expresses positive feelings toward the therapist, in the context of the real relationship, the therapist will do likewise.

The above discussion would appear to imply that therapist facilitativeness is a basic causal factor, having desirable effects on the counseling outcomes and a favorable impact on the relationship components. Yet, clinically we know that some clients are easier to be facilitative with than others. Thus, the client affects how facilitative the therapist can and will be. An important research direction is the study of both the client factors and relationship factors that promote or retard therapist facilitativeness. The reader is referred to Gelso and Hayes (1998) for an extensive discussion of how therapist facilitativeness is related to each of the components of the therapeutic relationship.

Summary

Although there have been ongoing debates about whether the therapeutic relationship or the techniques used by the therapists are most important, it has become increasingly clear that, in general, both are vital to successful therapy. Indeed, the therapeutic relationship and therapist techniques operate interactively, with each influencing the other, and the quality and effectiveness of the other. In this chapter, we have focused on the relationship, defined as the feelings and attitudes the counseling participants have toward one another and the manner in which these are expressed.

The therapeutic relationship may be seen as consisting of three interrelated components: a working alliance, a transference configuration, and a real relationship. All three components are an important part of therapy, regardless of the theoretical orientation of the therapist. The *working alliance* is defined as the alignment of the client's reasonable and observing side with the counselor's working or therapizing side for the purpose of facilitating the work of counseling. A large amount of research supports the importance of the working alliance to therapy. The transference configuration consists of client transference and therapist countertransference. Both have received research attention in recent years and have been shown to be important in therapies of all persuasions, even though these constructs were originally rooted in psychoanalysis. *Transference* is defined as the client's perceptions and experience of the therapist based on the client's psychological structures and past rather than the actual person of the therapist. *Countertransference* is the therapist's reaction to the client based on the therapist's unresolved conflicts and issues. It is important that the therapist understand and manage countertransference reactions so that they do not hinder the therapy. The *real relationship* may be seen as the personal relationship between the therapist and client marked by the extent to which each is genuine with the other and experiences and perceives the other in ways that befit him or her. Of the components, the real relationship is the most recent to be studied empirically.

Any writing about the therapeutic relationship must include Carl Rogers's highly influential statement about the necessary and sufficient conditions for successful counseling. Over the years, research and theory have focused on three of these conditions: *therapist-offered empathic understanding, unconditional positive regard,* and *congruence.* It now seems clear that Rogers was onto something. The three conditions have been empirically supported as important to successful counseling, although they may not be sufficient, as Rogers asserted.

Science and Practice of Assessment | 10

The psychological test was the invention that revolution-
ized psychological science, comparable in its impact to the
telescope in physics and the microscope in biology. . . .
In terms of practical application, the psychological test is
the technological innovation from psychology that has
had the greatest effect on society. (Dawis, 1992, p. 10)

Critics argue that psychological assessment is time-
consuming, expensive, and not useful in the context
of current patterns of care. . . . The profession's lack of
advocacy in encouraging, collecting, and disseminating
research that demonstrates the efficacy and utility of
psychological assessment has compounded the problem.
(Eisman et al., 2000, pp. 131–132)

The contrasting messages in the preceding quotes make clear
that psychology's attitude toward psychological testing and
assessment may be best characterized as ambivalent. The
ambivalence applies to counseling psychology, as well, and it
has persisted for several decades. In this chapter, we explain
the ambivalence and clarify why assessment is so important
to psychological treatment and a range of decisions made
about people. We describe the concepts, tests, and skills that
counseling psychologists need in order to be competent in

http://dx.doi.org/10.1037/14378-010
Counseling Psychology, Third Edition, by C. J. Gelso, E. N. Williams, and
B. R. Fretz

psychological assessment in an age of industrialized health care with an increasingly diverse society.

The Pros and Cons of Testing and Assessment

In today's world, the primary cognitive association most of the public has with a psychologist is that of "a shrink"; that is, a mental health practitioner (who may well be analyzing you at this very moment). Even other health practitioners will typically view psychologists primarily as therapists for mental problems. Given these perspectives, it may be difficult to comprehend that until the 1960s psychologists were viewed primarily (if not exclusively) as professionals who developed, administered, and interpreted psychological tests in hospitals, clinics, counseling centers, and employment bureaus.

That our professional roles in those years were so focused on psychological assessment was a direct outgrowth of successful development, in the first half of the 20th century, of ability, then personality, and then interest measures. There was strong governmental support for the development and use of such tests, first in World War I and then in the Great Depression. These advances were so highly regarded that they led to the development of the U.S. Employment Service, the precursor to the agency that today produces such documents as the *Dictionary of Occupational Titles* and the General Aptitude Test Battery.

During the same time period, the development of both objective and projective personality tests (a distinction that is explained later in this chapter) became the foundation for psychologists having a unique role in what were then called mental hospitals. All states had one or more hospitals that focused on severe and chronically mentally ill patients; psychologists were called on to use their testing skills to differentiate organic from nonorganic mental illness, schizophrenia from depression, psychosis from neurosis, and so forth. The psychological test information was typically combined with information from psychiatric interviews (psychologists were almost always supervised by psychiatrists in these hospitals) and observations from nurses and attendants in order to make a final diagnosis, treatment plan, prognosis, and posthospitalization treatment plan. At the end of World War II, the Veterans Administration developed training programs for psychologists primarily for these assessment functions. At that time, psychologists were rarely involved in providing psychotherapy for the veterans.

Moreover, during the post–World War II era and continuing until the 1960s, counseling psychologists in most university and college counseling centers were also heavily involved in psychological testing. Indeed, in those times, students were expected to complete at least one or more personality and interest measures, possibly ability measures as well, before seeing a counselor. The counselor would then be expected to study all that information, along with any intake interview information, before beginning counseling.

The definitions of the specialties of counseling, school, and clinical psychology that were developed in the 1940s explicitly emphasized psychologists' roles in assessment; the revisions of these definitions over the years, through to those definitions archived in 2013 by the American Psychological Association, continue to emphasize the role of assessment. Yet, in surveys conducted in recent decades, counseling psychologists typically spent only about 10% of their time on testing, plus or minus 5% depending on their work setting. Fewer counseling psychologists do psychological testing now than in past years (Goodyear et al., 2008). Psychological testing had changed from a primary role to a distant, subsidiary role.

What happened? Two major developments of the 1960s brought about the decline of psychological testing in many settings. The first was the increasing role of psychologists in providing psychotherapy and counseling. The development of client-centered therapy most especially affected counseling psychology. Rogers's (1951) emphasis on facilitative conditions, regardless of the presenting problem (see Chapter 11), arguably eliminated the need for formal diagnosis. How could one justify the routine practice of testing all individuals before counseling if the intervention strategy to be used was the same whatever the result of the testing? Also, from the client-centered perspective, testing placed the locus of evaluation outside the client, whereas client-centered counselors believed that the locus needed to be in the client. The absence of any empirical data showing that diagnostic information yielded by psychological testing related in any way to which kind of therapy was provided or what outcome could be expected led to increasing criticism of routine testing of clients. The best way to know what kind of treatment a client would be provided in the middle of the 20th century was not to know what his or her problem or diagnosis was but rather to know the theoretical predilection of the counselor.

A second factor in the decline of psychological testing was the emergence of evidence, beginning in the 1960s, of the adverse impact of many psychological test results on the employment opportunities and educational placements of women and members of racial and ethnic minorities. Walsh and Betz (2001) provided a concise summary of some of the issues of race and gender bias that appeared in test content and in test usage prior to the 1980s. Some members of the U.S. Congress, as well as some psychologists, called for a moratorium on the use of psychological test results in admitting students to educational programs or in selecting employees. In that era of strident critiques of psychological testing, many universities reduced required courses in psychological assessment.

Yet, there were at least two positive developments from these critical challenges to psychological assessment. The first was the shift from what was referred to as a shotgun approach to a laser approach. This analogy refers to a shift from giving a battery of tests to every patient or student who was referred for assessment to a more focused selection of tests, specifically designed to provide the kind of information needed for the diagnosis or placement decision to be made. In the former tradition, a comprehensive picture of the patient or student was developed by integrating the results of the battery of tests. That picture may or may not have specifically answered the question in the referral. In the more focused model of assessment, less time is needed and extraneous material is eliminated. Forensic psychology today still relies heavily on focused test results in determining psychological functioning for legal cases involving disability, discrimination, custody, and emotional injury (Gregory, 2011).

The other positive development was the creation of psychological tests that were less culturally biased in content, norms, and usage. Although the search for "culture free" tests proved to be an impossible goal, the construction of somewhat more culturally fair tests proved attainable. A culturally competent counseling psychologist uses psychological testing in ways that will be truly helpful to culturally diverse clients (Fuertes, Spokane, & Holloway, 2013). Almost all of the major tests reviewed later in this chapter have been revised to be more useful with a wide range of clientele.

Although the criticisms discussed in the foregoing threatened to make assessment irrelevant, the positive developments, along with the earlier successful history of assessment in psychology, limited the damage. Assessment was in some ways limping along and in others strengthening until the 1990s. At that time, managed care organizations took a very restrictive position regarding assessment. In their survey of more than 400 psychologists in managed care, for example, Eisman et al. (2000) found that managed care companies placed extreme restrictions on what assessments could be covered by insurance. In this way, the field of psychological assessment was hit right in the breadbasket!

Perhaps somewhat ironically, the highly conservative position of managed care on assessment may have been just the impetus the profession of psychology needed to attend to issues that should have been addressed much earlier. What is needed is hard empirical evidence that assessment results in improved performance and that it is also cost effective. In many ways, the past decade has seen an effort within psychology to clarify the value, including the financial value, of psychological and educational assessment. If the current and next generation of counseling psychologists can meet these challenges from managed care, psychological assessment may once again be "the technological innovation from psychology that has had the greatest effect on society" (Dawis, 1992, p. 10).

Assessment: More Than Psychological Tests

In the opening section of this chapter, the terms *assessment* and *psychological test* have been used interchangeably. Until the 1960s, with the emergence of the critiques of the substance and use of psychological tests, such interchangeability was both conceptually and practically sound. In those times, use of assessment in practice and research—whether for diagnosis and treatment or for evaluation of the results of counseling—relied primarily on published psychological tests rather than specially designed measures. However, in more recent decades, the public's criticisms and misunderstandings about psychological tests have led many psychologists to desire that a distinction be made between *assessment* and *testing*. For example, psychologists concerned with how managed care looks at assessment take the position that in assessment, in contrast to psychological testing,

> The focus is on taking a variety of test-derived pieces of information, obtained from multiple methods of assessment, and placing the data in the context of historical information, referral information, and behavioral observations made during the testing and interview process, in order to generate a cohesive and comprehensive understanding of the person being evaluated. (Meyer et al., 1998, p. 8)

There is no clear consensus in the profession of psychology about what constitutes psychological tests compared with assessment. Some psychologists narrowly limit the use of the word *tests* to those achievement and ability measures that have right and wrong answers. They use the word *inventories* for those measures of interest and personality that have no right or wrong answers but rather compare an individual's answers to those of a norm group. They use the word *scales* (or *checklists*) for lists of behaviors, symptoms, problems, and so forth that are frequently used in diagnostic and therapeutic progress research.

The critical issue for whatever is called "assessment" is the degree to which the assessment process meets acceptable standards (described in the next section). However, before moving on to a discussion of standards, we may find it useful to ask seemingly obvious questions: Why are assessment measures even necessary? Why does a person need to be psychologically measured? At a fundamental level, assessment is the psychologist's way of communicating. Although each person is unique in some ways, each is similar in many ways to other persons. Without ways to identify and communicate similarities and differences within and among individuals, psychologists cannot make accurate predictions beyond a chance level of accuracy. Means must exist to determine, for example, what kind of persons will be most satisfied in people-oriented compared with data-oriented occupations. As another example, knowing that counseling strategies should differ for a client whose problem is depression compared to dependency is useless information unless there is some way of assessing whether the client is depressed or dependent (or possibly both). Thus, assessment is central to both the science and practice of counseling psychology.

Why not just ask persons in which ways they are unique or whether their problem is depression or dependence? After all, one often hears, "No one can know us better than ourselves." But how well does each of us know ourself? Most of us do not know ourselves very well with regard to the normative aspects of our feelings and behaviors. How often do other persons feel depressed compared with how often I feel depressed, and am I depressed enough that I should seek help? If I feel that my verbal skills are relatively poor, should I try to avoid all jobs requiring verbal skills? It is certainly just as important in making career decisions to have an understanding of one's abilities and interests compared with others' as it is to realize their place within one's own range of strengths, weaknesses, preferences, and dislikes. Therefore, psychologists can proceed in practice or research only when they have some way of making assessments.

Standards for All Assessment Techniques

For readers who have not had prior coursework in the basics of psychological assessment, we recommend a reading of Green's (1981) classic "A Primer of Testing" before proceeding. His 11-page article, written for the general public, concisely described the constructs and considerations that underlie much of the material and recommendations in this section. Ethical use of assessment by counseling psychologists fundamentally requires an understanding of the topics covered by Green.

Decisions about just how extensive standards for assessment should be and how rigorously they should be applied have been major sources of controversy for psychologists for more than six decades. When the 1999 version of the Standards for Educational and Psychological Testing (American Educational Research Association, American Psychological Association, and National Council of Measurement in Education, 1999 [hereafter cited as AAN]) was being prepared, a draft was sent to all members of the participating organizations. More than 8,000 pages of comments were received! Most of these comments reflected two over-arching concerns: First, when is it acceptable to use a psychological assessment compared with some other form of assessment; for example, a high school diploma as the only requirement for acceptance into a training program for nursing compared with some measure of the applicant's emotional stability and/or attention to detail? Second, should the level of rigor of application of the standards vary according to how the measure will be used? For example, does one have to observe established assessment standards as fully and rigorously when developing a scale for evaluation of a teacher as when developing a scale for selecting security employees for a nuclear energy facility? If it were possible to easily meet all assessment standards, this issue would not exist. However, meeting high levels of assessment standards is costly in terms of time and of dollars. Let us now look more closely at both of these issues.

With rare exceptions, all psychological assessments have limited effectiveness in making predictions; the critical issue is whether there is anything else, such as past school or job performance, recommendations, and so forth, that can result in more effective predictions than psychological assessments. Consider, for example, a test that most readers have taken or will soon be taking: the Graduate Record Examination (GRE). There is a wide range of limitations to the GRE, and yet it is a reasonably sound predictor of graduate school performance and predicts performance above and beyond other variables (Burton & Wang, 2005). The limitations of the GRE call to mind the saying that "yes, democracy is a flawed political system, it's just that we've never found any better system of government." Yes, psychological assessments are flawed, but for many situations in which we are trying to make diagnoses and interventions to help people improve their mental and physical health and/or their options in life, we have not found, all things considered, any fairer or better predictor of performance.

Arguments about how rigorously to apply the standards are no less easily resolved than the issue of when to use psychological assessment as compared to other data about persons. An ideal exercise in a course on psychological assessment is to have each student evaluate a published assessment measure according to the Standards for Educational and Psychological Testing (AAN, 1999). When one makes such an evaluation, the introduction to the current standards is most important to consider:

> Evaluating the acceptability of a test or a test application does not rest on the literal satisfaction of every standard in this document, and acceptability cannot be determined by using a checklist. Specific circumstances affect the importance of individual standards. Individual standards should not be considered in isolation. Therefore, evaluating acceptability involves (a) professional judgment that is based on a knowledge of behavioral science, psychometrics, and the professional field to which the tests apply; (b) the degree to which the intent of the standard has been satisfied by the test developer and user; (c) the alternatives that are readily available; and (d) research and experiential evidence regarding feasibility of meeting the standard. (AAN, 1999, p. 1)

The next three sections are based on the three major sections of these standards; we identify some key problem areas for counseling psychologists as both scientists and practitioners and make recommendations for how to proceed when using assessments in both practice and research.

EVALUATING AND CONSTRUCTING ASSESSMENTS

The words in the heading of this section may seem reversed—*evaluating* before *constructing?* Our choice of order is deliberate. As noted, if an existing assessment instrument can be evaluated as appropriate, that instrument is what should be used in either practice or research settings. However, for some problems for which counseling psychologists wish to make assessments, there may be few if any measures that have adequate psychometric support or evidence of fairness and usefulness. We encourage counseling psychologists to develop appropriate assessment instruments in these situations. Before computers became readily available, development of assessment measures of any sophistication was beyond most psychologists' capabilities. What were once considered complex analyses, such as measures of internal consistency, factor analyses, or discriminant analyses, now can be executed on personal computers. Thus, the scientist–practitioner counseling psychologist is now able to obtain basic psychometric data quite easily on any newly developed measure or, for existing tests, psychometric data for unique samples (e.g., a culturally diverse population).

Of the major concerns in evaluating assessments, *reliability* and *validity* are the linchpins of adequate assessment. Reliability refers to the consistency with which one measures something. Without consistency, one cannot develop validity; that is, predictable and useful relationships with other variables that are important to us, such as clients' mental health, employees' career adjustment, or adolescents' self-esteem. Our one recommendation regarding reliability is that measures should be evaluated for both *temporal consistency* and *internal consistency*. The former is most easily illustrated by considering test–retest reliability. One asks, "If a test is given this week and the same test is given 2 weeks later, how well does the second set of scores for examinees correlate with their first scores?" The higher the correlation, the more reliable, or consistent, the results are said to be.

Internal consistency refers to the homogeneity of the items on a test. Whereas there are a number of theoretical arguments about the importance of homogeneity in a test, both Green (1981) and Nunnally (1978) have argued persuasively, "A test gains its reliability and its power by adding up a large number of homogeneous items" (Green, 1981, p. 1005). Homogeneous items are found by inspecting the intercorrelations of all items in a measure with each other. Computer software statistical packages exist that determine coefficient alpha, the key measure of internal consistency. If alpha coefficients are low, Nunnally noted, it is almost fruitless to try to demonstrate validity of measures. He described ways for improving internal consistency, thereby permitting a new measure to become more useful in predicting and understanding human behavior.

With regard to the issue of *validity* of assessment measures, there are at least two basic questions to consider. Among the many kinds of validity (see Green, 1981), the validity question that should take precedence is "What evidence is there that the use of this test in the past has been useful in answering questions like the one I'm asking now?" For example, if one is trying to assess depression in a deaf client, is there any evidence that the measure of depression being considered produces useful results with deaf clients? If no such evidence exists, one has to consider whether to (a) find another measure that has established usefulness for deaf persons, or, if no such measure exists, (b) consider the development of a scale that might become useful for such assessments. Although the second option seems almost overwhelming to students, counseling psychologist practitioners who work extensively with a specific population, such as deaf clients, may well begin the development of more useful assessment tools. For researchers, development of unique scales has become widely practiced; simply consult any recent issue of the *Journal of Counseling Psychology* to see how researchers have developed unique measures, assessing both reliability and validity.

Whenever new measures are developed, a second major validity question pertains to the extent to which measures possess convergent and discriminant validity (Campbell & Fiske, 1959). *Convergent validity* refers to finding significant relationships with other indices of the trait or behavior being measured. For example, we would expect persons who score high on a measure of extroversion to prefer being with people to being alone. *Discriminant validity* is the opposite; that is, finding only minimal relationships between variables we think are very different (e.g., extroversion and anxiety). Unless a test has discriminant validity, it can add little to what is already known from other measures. Additionally, if tests measure similar constructs but have different names, both the public and users can become confused. Researchers in the areas of self-efficacy and competence face this problem: Are these two different constructs with different relationships or simply two different names for essentially the same human characteristic? Reaching a conclusive answer to such questions is difficult, but it is an essential step in meeting high standards of assessment.

FAIRNESS IN ASSESSMENTS AND TESTING

As discussed earlier, a major positive development from the extensive criticisms of psychological tests in the 1960s was a greatly increased sensitivity to bias in the construction and use of tests. Over the past several decades there has been a great deal of attention to reducing bias in the substance and norming of tests. There is agreement that all assessment instruments should have evidence of fairness with respect to absence of bias in content and provision of equitable treatment of all examinees in the testing process. For counseling psychologists, Fouad and Chan (1999) provided a concise review of the psychometric issues in using psychological assessments with women and ethnic minorities as well as a review of how cultural status affects both counselor and client use of assessment results.

More controversial are those issues that relate to equality of testing outcomes of examinee subgroups (e.g., ethnicity, gender). Is the issue one of unfair tests or of unequal opportunities to learn pertinent knowledge and skills? This issue is especially critical for educational and industrial/organizational psychologists, who use tests for placement in various programs. Although there is a ready consensus among psychologists that all persons should have equal opportunity to learn the material covered in selection and placement tests, providing that opportunity is the ethical responsibility of all educators and psychologists alike, not the primary responsibility of those who develop tests. Moreover, in current assessment standards, the idea that fairness requires all subgroups to have comparable passing rates is not supported as a standard for the assessment instrument itself. However, once again, because there is consensus among psychologists that persons who are equivalent, except for cultural group membership, should have equal opportunity for being chosen for competitive programs, assessment strategies should attend carefully to situations where lack of equivalence on a test seems determined primarily by cultural status. Various assessment methods and complex statistical techniques have been developed over the years to better understanding of how to achieve fairness in the use of psychological assessments (Hambleton, Merenda, & Spielberger, 2005; Suzuki, Onoue, Fukui, & Ezrapour, 2012). In keeping with counseling psychology's deep involvement in social justice, the study of culture, and the incorporation of cultural considerations into psychological theory and practice, greater attention is currently being paid to cultural factors in testing and assessment than ever before (see, e.g., Pieterse & Miller, 2010; Suzuki et al., 2012).

APPLICATIONS OF ASSESSMENTS

For counseling psychologists, standards for applications of assessment relate primarily to using tests with an increasingly diverse clientele. Fortunately, several comprehensive books have been published that address the issues that counseling psychologists need to attend to in meeting acceptable standards in the application of psychological assessments (Dana, 2000, 2005; Paniagua, 2005; Suzuki, Ponterotto, & Meller, 2008). Care must be taken by counseling psychologists that they not make either of two frequent errors, errors that may be just as harmful as using psychological tests without consideration of clients' culture. The first of these errors is simply to eliminate the use of any psychological assessments because they have all been developed largely with Anglo, middle-class Americans. As Dana (2005) pointed out, when test results are appropriately interpreted with consideration for culture, the results can be every bit as valuable for culturally diverse clients as for Anglo, middle-class Americans.

The second error to avoid is assuming that all persons of a given subgroup (e.g., Native Americans or African Americans) are similar in their ways of looking at the world and in cultural background and immediately "adjusting" assessment results for a member of a given group. Such adjustments lead to over- or underdiagnosing of critical psychological phenomena. Ridley, Li, and Hill (1998) provided all counseling psychologists with an excellent conceptualization of how to improve attention to cultural concerns in all parts of the assessment process, from a choice of measures to interpretations of results. Space constraints here do not permit a full description of their Multicultural Assessment Procedure, but training in assessment for all counseling psychologists should now include training in the use of such a model. As Spengler (1998) noted, their recommended procedures are built on established principles derived from psychologists' knowledge of behavior, decision making, and information processing.

Psychological Tests

Although there has been a gradual decline in the use of psychological tests in counseling psychology (Goodyear et al., 2008; Watkins, Campbell, & McGregor, 1988), testing continues to be an important part of the specialty. Competency in testing and assessment is also one of the major areas of expected competency in doctoral training in the field (Fuertes et al., 2013).

There are now hundreds of published psychological tests, many of which have been revised and updated to comply with the standards we have reviewed. In addition, new tests often appear with the aim of helping practitioners make more effective assessments. In this section we describe the major categories of tests most used by counseling psychologists and, within each category, give brief descriptions of particular tests that are most used. Many texts now offer much more detail on each of these texts, as well as on categories of tests that we do not cover (e.g., Watkins & Campbell, 2000; Whiston, 2009).

INTEREST MEASURES

Counseling psychologists have been more visibly involved with the development of interest measures than of any other type of psychological assessment. Because counseling psychology has been the specialty most centrally involved in career development and career counseling, almost every key person in the history of interest measurement has also been a key figure in the leadership and scholarship in counseling psychology. A bit of history: By the 1920s, early psychologists began to see major limits to the usefulness of considering only abilities as predictors of occupational success. Increasing attention was therefore given to the role of interests in understanding occupational success and adjustment. The work of E. K. Strong (1943), started in the late 1920s, laid the foundation for the development of the Strong Interest Inventory (SII; Donnay, Morris, Schaubhut, & Thompson, 2005), the most widely used measure of interests throughout much of the 20th century and now the 21st century.

The reasonable skeptic may ask, "Why does one need a measure of interests? Why not simply ask the person to state his or her interests?" The SII manual concisely reviews the decades of data showing how *expressed interests* and *measured interests* often disagree and examines the various hypotheses that have been put forward to explain why. These data, along with the extensive literature on the significant contributions of measured interests in predicting who will stay in a position and find success in it, have led not only to several revisions of the SII but also to the development of several other well-developed measures of interests, especially the Kuder Occupational Interest Survey (Kuder & Zytowski, 1991) and the Self-Directed Search (SDS; Holland, 1998; Reardon & Lenz, 1998). Although the two latter measures have somewhat different formats and conceptual histories than the SII, all have entered the counseling psychology mainstream as useful and adequately validated instruments in assisting clients in exploring and choosing satisfying and successful careers (see Whiston, 2009).

Of the three measures, the SII provides the widest range of information and has the most extensive empirical history. Beginning in 1974, the SII included the six occupational themes of Holland's SDS (see next paragraph) as well as 25 basic interest areas (e.g., sales, teaching, medical sciences) and 207 occupational scales (e.g., audiologist, forester, police officer, psychologist), all grouped within Holland's six occupational themes. Norms for both males and females in each of these areas are provided except in those few occupations where there are either too few females or too few males to develop a separate norm. The manual for the newest 2004 version of the SII (Donnay et al., 2005) provides evidence of the validity and usefulness of the current SII for the major racial and ethnic groups in the United States.

All three interest measures noted above are used in schools and universities to assist students in extensive exploration of career options both for those who have no idea which career they want to enter as well as for those who seek to confirm their interests. Moreover, counseling psychologists in independent practice whose clients' problems are related to career concerns also find the measures immensely valuable in opening new horizons for these clients. The research uses of the interest inventories are also extensive. Almost every issue of *Career Development Quarterly*, *Journal of Vocational Behavior*, and *Journal of Career Assessment* contains one or more research reports in which an interest inventory has been a major assessment technique.

PERSONALITY MEASURES

Although the history of the development of psychometrically based personality tests coincides chronologically with the development of interest measures, the diversity of personality measures far exceeds that of interest measures. The multiplicity of personality theories in the first half of the 20th century resulted in very different kinds of tests (e.g., some tests asked written questions, others showed inkblots or pictures, others asked for drawings), yet all were called "personality" tests. Although the Minnesota Multiphasic Personality Inventory (MMPI) is currently far and away the most widely used personality test, nearly a dozen other personality measures are used frequently by counseling psychologists.

These include the Sixteen Personality Factor Questionnaire, the California Psychological Inventory, the Edwards Personal Preference Schedule, the Myers–Briggs Type Indicator, the Thematic Apperception Test, and the Rorschach. Descriptions of each of these tests and their uses in practice and research may be found in any of the major textbooks on psychological tests (e.g., Walsh & Betz, 2001; Watkins & Campbell, 2000).

All but the last two of the measures just listed could be described as objective personality tests, whereas the last two are what are called projective personality tests. Objective personality tests typically include lists of questions or statements to which one responds with true or false, agree or disagree, like or dislike. (As we explain later in this section, these objective tests have also been most useful to counseling psychologists whenever the focus is on identifying strengths rather than psychopathology.) Projective tests involve the presentation of an ambiguous stimulus such as a vague picture or an inkblot; subjects "project" themselves into their open-ended responses to the presented stimulus. Projective tests were developed by adherents of the psychoanalytic approach as a way of assessing the unconscious experience. By definition, one cannot get direct access to unconscious experience through client self-report because the client is not aware of what is in the unconscious. For many years, the only way of interpreting projective techniques was through a clinician's judgment regarding dominant themes apparent in the client's responses. There were significant problems both in reliability of scoring and in establishing validity of test results for making diagnoses or prognoses. In the past few decades, Exner (2003) developed a comprehensive scoring system for the Rorschach that has addressed many of these problems of reliability and validity. The key variables, clusters, and constellations derived from Exner's system are now becoming more widely used in both diagnostic and treatment aspects of practice and in a variety of research projects. Counseling psychologists have traditionally not been trained in the use of projective techniques, for both theoretical and practical reasons (Watkins, Campbell, Hollifield, & Duckworth, 1989). The situation appears to have changed, as counseling psychologists now more often work with very distressed clients in counseling centers in industrialized health care settings and in independent practice. Projective testing now seems to be part of the discussion of assessment in counseling psychology (e.g., Suzuki et al., 2012).

By far the most exhaustively researched personality assessment instrument of any type is the MMPI, which is specifically designed to identify different types of psychopathology. Over the better part of a century, literally thousands of studies have been completed on its clinical and validity scales. The MMPI is now in its second edition, and, with a separate edition for adolescents, its use in practice and research is unparalleled. From true–false responses to more than 500 items, scores are provided on 10 clinical scales (e.g., Depression, Paranoia, Social Introversion), four validity scales (e.g., Lie, Defensiveness), and 15 content scales (e.g., Anxiety, Obsessiveness, Bizarre Mentation, Low Self-Esteem). The MMPI–2 was published in 1989 and has been updated several times (e.g., 2003, 2008) since then. There is now a shortened version, taking only about 45 minutes to complete, rather than the hour to hour and a half required to complete the full-length version.

Even the earliest research with the MMPI indicated that a high score on any one scale meant very little; it is the configuration of scores that has been most valuable. Over the years many codebooks have been produced for various types of clientele. Valuable books for counseling psychologists working with the MMPI–2 continue to be those by Duckworth and Anderson (1995), as well as Butcher's *MMPI–2: A Practitioner's Guide* (2005) and *A Beginner's Guide to the MMPI–2* (3rd ed., 2011) to using and interpreting the MMPI. These books help counseling psychologists identify patterns of MMPI responses that are useful both in making diagnoses and in exploring personal and career concerns. Even with the help of such resources, however, the strong psychopathological focus of the MMPI makes it a difficult personality assessment measure to use beyond diagnosis (i.e., in interpreting results to clients and having them use personality assessment information as part of the process of counseling). For such uses, counseling psychologists have long preferred other personality measures that focus more on strengths and assets.

Prior to the 1980s, the personality tests most often used by counseling psychologists were the California Psychological Inventory, the Edwards Personal Preference Schedule, and the Sixteen Personality Factor Questionnaire. Although these tests are still used by some counselors and updated reliability and validity data are available, counseling psychologists who wish to incorporate personality assessment as part of counseling now more often use the Myers–Briggs Type Indicator. This measure was originally developed primarily to assess four key dimensions of Jung's personality theory (Quenk, 2009), but it has proved to be very useful in personal and career counseling, as well as in industrial consulting. The measure has what is called high "face validity"; that is, persons who complete the 126 two-choice items find both the questions and their results meaningful and logical. Four preference scores (extroverted vs. introverted, sensing vs. intuitive, thinking vs. feeling, and judging vs. perceiving) are combined into one of 16 personality types. Each type has been related to compatibility in various careers. Moreover, because descriptions of these types explain how persons differ in their information-processing and decision-making styles, learning about their own type has often proved useful to clients in understanding conflicts with management styles and in interpersonal and marital relationships. Still, there are scientific questions about aspects of the measure's validity (Murphy, 2005). Quenk (2009) provided both a critical review and a practical guide to the range of uses of the Myers–Briggs Type Indicator.

APTITUDE AND INTELLIGENCE TESTS

Of all the categories of tests reviewed in this chapter, it is in this category of aptitude and intelligence tests that the role of counseling psychologists has changed most drastically. A few sentences of history about the development and use of aptitude and intelligence tests are essential for understanding that change. Intelligence tests date back to the beginning of the 20th century with the work of Binet. His carefully developed, individually administered battery of subtests was increasingly used in schools as a way both of assessing potential and of understanding students' learning difficulties. Later, the desire of military leaders to assess both intellectual potential and specific aptitudes in World War I and World War II had a major impact on the development of group-administered tests, so that large numbers of persons could be quickly tested. The development of group-administered intelligence tests for the military was the forerunner of tests now known to every college student, such as the SAT and the American College Test. Less well known are group tests such as the Differential Aptitude Tests and the General Aptitude Test Battery, which had as their impetus work conducted during and between the two world wars to address aptitudes beyond the kinds of intelligence measured by Binet. It was assumed that an identification of specific aptitudes could help select those who were most apt to be successful in skilled jobs like airplane mechanic or radio operator.

Recall that counseling psychology, along with the other applied specialties, emerged immediately after World War II. Given the relatively successful development and use of intelligence and aptitude tests in World War II, it is not surprising that counseling psychologists made extensive use of such tests in their work with the millions of returning veterans who were making a delayed entry into the labor force or going on to higher education with financial assistance from the GI Bill. Counseling psychology texts of the 1950s discussed the most effective ways to use a variety of intelligence and aptitude tests in counseling.

However, with the two exceptions discussed below, counseling psychologists are currently much less involved in the development and use of intelligence and aptitude tests than they were during previous times. What happened? It eventually became clear to counseling psychologists working in college settings that intelligence tests did not add much to counseling beyond the information provided by general aptitude tests, such as the SAT, that were a standard part of college admissions. In addition, the number of white-collar workers increased after World War II into the 1960s because there was a boom in the percentage of the population pursuing higher education. Specialized intelligence or aptitude measures (that assess, for example, manual dexterity, coding speed, and mechanical reasoning) became far less relevant to career counseling for this workforce. Thus, the routine administration of an intelligence or specialized aptitude measure as part of counseling died out by the 1960s.

Having noted these decreases in use of aptitude and intelligence testing in general, we identify two areas in which some counseling psychologists continue to have significant involvement with such tests. The area most clearly related to the profession's history is that of the use of specialized aptitude tests. Counseling psychologists working with the military, with Job Corps type programs, or with corrections facilities will still find the use of specialized aptitude tests quite useful. Clients in those settings will typically be beginning their work careers at the very lowest of entry-level jobs. Such clients also typically know very little about their own aptitudes and can benefit immensely from any counseling that will direct them into training or positions in which they are likely to find success. For clients such as enrollees in Job Corps programs, having an early successful job experience is perhaps the most critical factor in their developing a sense of competence and becoming integrated into the workforce and into society. Counseling psychologists working with such populations need to develop a full awareness of the range of available aptitude tests and how the results of such tests can become an integral part of the counseling.

The second area of continued involvement of counseling psychologists with respect to this category of tests concerns the use of individually administered intelligence tests. Although school and clinical psychologists have been the primary users of such tests, counseling psychologists who work in either general or psychiatric hospitals will find that individual intelligence tests are widely used as part of the diagnostic evaluation of patients who have a wide range of medical and/or psychiatric problems. Why are individually administered intelligence tests particularly useful in such settings? Does one really need to know the patient's IQ? No, not really. If only an IQ were desired, a group-administered intelligence test would be far more efficient. There are two factors that make individually administered intelligence tests particularly useful in hospital settings. Such tests allow for determining whether there are specific areas of perceptual and/or cognitive dysfunctions, both of which may be related to brain injuries, substance abuse, or psychiatric problems such as depression. We further explain how intelligence tests may be used in this connection after providing a brief description of the most widely used family of individualized intelligence tests.

Since the early 1950s, Wechsler and colleagues have developed and revised individually administered intelligence tests for all ages, from preschool through adulthood. All of the tests have essentially the same structure: a verbal scale containing five or six subtests and a performance scale containing five or six subtests. Three areas of IQ are computed: a Verbal IQ, a Performance IQ, and a Full Scale IQ. Because counseling psychologists are generally most likely to be working with an adult-age population, we describe here the most recent edition of the Wechsler Adult Intelligence Scale, the WAIS–IV (Wechsler, 1998).

The WAIS–IV Verbal subtests include vocabulary, similarities, arithmetic, digit span, information, and comprehension. Performance subtests include picture completion, digit symbol coding, block design, picture arrangement, and object assembly. This most recent version of the WAIS now provides, in addition to IQs, indexes on verbal comprehension, perceptual organization, working memory, and processing speed—all valuable assessment indexes in assessing cognitive functioning among the elderly.

Simply reviewing the diversity in the names of the subtests listed above should give some hint of the diagnostic value of the WAIS–IV for determining types of perceptual and/or cognitive dysfunctions. In normal intellectual functioning, the examinee earns approximately the same level of score for each subtest of the WAIS. Therefore, whenever there are significant deviations (e.g., a very poor performance on digit span compared to other verbal tests), the psychologist would certainly want to check for the cause of that interference in concentration. Although the intelligence test result cannot say what is causing the problem, it does indicate an area of dysfunction that needs further assessment, probably neurological (see the next section on neuropsychological tests) as well as psychological.

A second diagnostic value of an individually administered intelligence test derives from the extensive observations made on how the examinee approaches each test. For example, when the client encounters difficulties in one of the subtests, is it a lack of perseverance? Slowness? Carelessness? Is the examinee too depressed to respond to many items or made particularly anxious by some of the subtests? All of these observations can be highly useful in making diagnostic formulations about any cognitive problems the patient is having as a result either of psychiatric problems, such as depression or alcoholism, or of medical problems, such as cardiovascular dysfunction, chronic diabetes, or head injuries. Whereas training in individually administered intelligence testing has more typically been part of clinical than of counseling psychology training programs, in recent decades, more and more counseling psychology training programs have arranged for doctoral-level students to obtain training and supervised experience in administering at least the adult version of the Wechsler scales. Once training in administering such tests is completed, guidance in how to use individualized intelligence tests in making diagnoses and planning treatment may be found in Lichtenberger and Kaufman (2013) and, for the children's form, Flanagan and Kaufman (2009).

NEUROPSYCHOLOGICAL TESTS

When discussing individually administered intelligence tests, we pointed out that observations of behavior during the testing and/or significant variations in levels of scores obtained on the subtests could indicate the need for neuropsychological testing. Since the 1960s, psychologists have developed greatly improved neuropsychological tests. These tests remain essential even today because although computed tomography scans and magnetic resonance imaging can indicate the location and extent of brain damage they cannot provide information on how the patient can perform. Learning to administer and make careful use of the results of these batteries has proved to require both extensive and intensive training. A less than fully trained person using these measures can make serious diagnostic errors; therefore, training in these techniques is usually now undertaken primarily in internships and postdoctoral residencies. Although the number of counseling psychologists who are involved in formal assessment has decreased over the decades, the amount of neuropsychological assessment being done by counseling psychologists has increased (Goodyear et al., 2008). Counseling psychologists who have an interest in neuropsychology do need to choose both internships and postdoctoral residencies that focus on neuropsychology.

BEHAVIORAL AND SYMPTOM CHECKLISTS

Beginning in the 1970s, numerous inventories and checklists that are designed to be sensitive to small changes in behaviors, affect, and symptoms have been developed (Derogatis, 1977). Such measures, in contrast to global personality inventories, are especially useful for demonstrating significant relationships among diagnoses, therapeutic progress, and eventual outcomes. As noted earlier, establishing such empirical relationships is the key to having industrialized health care provide more authorization for the use of assessment in behavioral health care.

The emergence of behavioral approaches to counseling (see Chapter 12) greatly enhanced development of such measures. That theoretical emphasis requires therapists, external observers, and clients themselves to learn how to record behaviors in reliable ways (Drummond, 1996). Such measures are often initially administered as part of the diagnostic stage to establish what behaviorists call *baseline* behaviors (or *levels of affect* or *symptoms*). These measures can then be readministered periodically throughout therapy because many of them are relatively brief (as few as 15–30 items) and can be completed in just a few minutes.

Lambert and his collaborators, longtime contributors to the counseling outcome literature in psychotherapy, have developed measures suitable for assessing small changes in ongoing therapy (see Lambert & Vermeersch, 2008). By employing such measures, with just a few minutes of the client's and therapist's time after each session, or at least every few sessions, the counselor can immediately obtain information on whether the client is experiencing any changes in behavior, affect, beliefs, or symptoms. Just as important, the counselor obtains information on the normative aspects of the client's level in each of these areas. The client may be making some measurable gains in psychotherapy but still be substantially below what one would call adjusted; such information establishes the need for continued counseling. It also can help determine when a shift in the counseling approach may be called for.

CAREER DEVELOPMENT AND DECISION-MAKING MEASURES

As we have noted, the earliest forms of career counseling relied heavily on the use of interest and aptitude measures. Next most frequently used were personality inventories. For many or even most clients, these assessments, appropriately integrated into the counseling process, provided the assistance they needed in reaching a satisfactory resolution to their career-related issues. However, there have always been a notable number of clients for whom such assessments, even with extensive counseling, have not led to satisfactory outcomes. Over the past few decades, a number of kinds of measures have been developed to help those in the field better understand and counsel such clients. In this section we identify four kinds of such measures and briefly refer to their theoretical and empirical origins.

From careful study of those clients for whom traditional counseling proved unsatisfactory, Holland, Johnston, and Asama (1993) and Osipow, Carney, Winer, Yanico, and Koschier (1976), from quite different theoretical perspectives (see Chapter 15), developed measures of *indecisiveness*. Over the years these measures have proved very useful in diagnosing those for whom traditional or self-directed career interventions would likely be insufficient for obtaining satisfactory counseling outcomes. Those with low scores on Holland et al.'s 18-item Vocational Identity Scale (1993) or high scores on Osipow et al.'s 18-item Career Decision Scale (1976) are most likely those who will need at least several sessions of counseling, along with appropriate interest and/or personality assessments, in order to make progress on career decision making. These measures are also quite useful in indicating areas where clients feel blocked or conflicted; for example, conflicts with parents or significant others about career choice, value conflicts, and so forth.

The theoretical and empirical work of Super and colleagues focuses on determining when and how effective career decisions are made (see Chapter 15). This work led to the development of measures of *career development* (Super, Thompson, Lindeman, Jordaan, & Myers, 1981) and *career maturity* (Crites, 1981). These measures focus on whether individuals have mastered the tasks essential for effective career decision making (e.g., self-appraisal, occupational information, goal selection, planning, problem solving). Having scaled scores in these several domains can make clear to counselors where and how to focus the counseling process for clients who have difficulty reaching career decisions.

Krumboltz and others, working from a social learning perspective, have shown that career indecision and career problems are often related to clients' irrational beliefs about the world of work: for example, women never become successful architects; one can't become a software programmer without passing calculus. Krumboltz developed the Career Beliefs Inventory (1988) to assess the types and pervasiveness of such beliefs. Sampson, Peterson, Lenz, Reardon, and Saunders (1996) have further developed this concept of beliefs into both a diagnostic and a treatment modality. Through factor analyses they found that dysfunctional beliefs derive primarily from (a) confusion about how to make effective decisions, (b) commitment anxiety, and (c) external conflicts (e.g., parental vs. own choices, perceived discrimination). Sampson et al.'s Career Beliefs Inventory is accompanied by a workbook designed to assist individuals in identifying, challenging, and altering their negative career thoughts and following up with appropriate action.

The fourth and final type of career assessment measure to be reviewed here is that of values. Although there has long been some attention to the assessment of values as part of career counseling (Weiss et al., 1975), attempts to help both indecisive and culturally diverse clients have resulted in increased attention to the role values play in making career decisions. Some clients experience strong value conflicts between, for example, need to achieve and need for security or between need for social service and need for high compensation (conflicting needs in the U.S. culture). Measures such as the Minnesota Importance Questionnaire (Weiss et al., 1975) and Super's (1973) Work Values Inventory and Super and Nevill's (1986) Values Scale may help identify conflicts clients are experiencing that lead to avoidance of the career decision-making process.

The development of all of these measures in recent decades has clearly helped in the development of more cost-effective services for career counseling clients; by using these kinds of measures as screening assessments, the counselor can identify many clients who can use self-administered measures such as the Self-Directed Search and Career Beliefs Inventory to work through their career concerns largely on their own or with only minimal assistance from the counselor. For those who need individualized counseling, use of the kinds of measures described in this section will help the counselor quickly and effectively focus on the client's most troublesome areas. Despite these very real practical gains, many theoretical and empirical questions remain about the independence of the four types of measures described. They have different labels primarily because they were developed within different theoretical frameworks. Are they separate and complementary measures or actually competing ones, such that it would be redundant to use more than one of them? What may be needed are more integrative theories that would guide measure development. For example, on the basis of their review and analysis of existing measures of problems people have in career decision making, Brown and Rector (2008) have theorized four fundamental reasons for indecision: chronic indecisiveness, lack of readiness to make a decision, insufficient information upon which to base wise decisions, and interpersonal problems and barriers. Subsequent tests of this empirically driven theoretical model could produce measures that are highly useful in counseling.

Using Assessment: Meeting the Challenges of Industrialized Health Care

It is no wonder that psychological testing went through a period of disfavor in the 1960s and 1970s. Psychologists felt that testing was an antiquated enterprise that had little bearing on the real work of modern clinical psychology. The empirical foundations of testing were questioned by behaviorists and others trained in the experimental traditions of academic psychology, whereas analytic psychologists felt this attitude reflected the bankruptcy of the entire diagnostic enterprise. There was little agreement about the meaning of diagnostic terminology or the relationship between diagnosis and treatment. (B. L. Smith, 1998, p. 229)

In this section, we describe some of the factors that made diagnosis almost a "dirty word" for some years and the changes that have occurred both within and outside the profession that now bring renewed attention to the diagnostic process. In subsequent parts of this section we review the emerging use of assessment, not only for diagnosis but also for treatment planning, for treatment (using tests as part of the counseling process), and for evaluating the effectiveness of counseling.

MAKING DIAGNOSES: A NECESSARY, BUT INSUFFICIENT, STEP

In the earliest years of the profession of counseling psychology, every counseling text had major sections on making diagnoses (e.g., Pepinsky & Pepinsky, 1954). Some of the first studies published in the *Journal of Counseling Psychology* focused on the diagnostic process. Part of the reasons for those studies was the fact that making agreed-upon psychological diagnoses was far more difficult than making medical diagnoses. Cases of pneumonia share far more symptoms than do cases of depression. Moreover, psychological symptoms are displayed less consistently than are symptoms of physical illness. Compounding these problems were notable variations in what factors psychologists attended to when making diagnoses. Analytically oriented psychologists tended to emphasize underlying dynamics, whereas behaviorists emphasized overt behaviors. Given all of the above, it is not surprising that there were often alarming differences in diagnoses made on the same patient but by different psychologists.

Concerns about diagnoses in psychology quickly accelerated throughout the 1950s for two more reasons beyond the lack of consistency just described. First was the growing evidence of the lack of significant relationships between diagnosis and treatment activity, as reviewed in the beginning of this chapter. Second was the growing concern of the stigma of diagnoses, both for how the counselor viewed the client and how clients viewed themselves if they became aware of the diagnosis assigned to them. Rogers (1951), in fact, came to believe that traditional diagnoses were in many ways inimical to facilitating client growth and development. In his view, because diagnosis in the medical tradition is very focused on deficits and problems, the very act of diagnosis served to reduce the attention paid to possibilities for growth and development. This tendency is of particular concern to counseling psychologists. Rogers also believed that making diagnoses forces psychologists to focus on similarities rather than unique differences and individuality. Finally, the labeling of persons was of concern to Rogers in how it would affect not only clients' views of their own potential but also how significant others would treat them. He quite properly anticipated later disturbing empirical evidence: Rosenhan (1973) took a group of people who were functioning quite normally in their everyday lives, then had them, as part of an experiment, hospitalized on the basis of psychiatric diagnoses. He found the participants were treated like "crazy" people by hospital staff even though the subjects ("patients") did not behave any differently than they did in everyday life. Given all these concerns about making diagnoses, it should not be too surprising to learn that diagnosis practically disappeared as a major topic in many counseling psychology texts in the last half of the 20th century, at least until the 1990s.

Then why was there renewed interest in diagnosis in the 1990s (Barron, 1998)? The simplest and most concise answer is the industrialization of health care, through its authorization of treatment only after a diagnosis is provided. The increasing use of practice guidelines, specifying the kind of therapy that should be used with particular kinds of problems, obviously also requires that a diagnosis be made. How can one know what treatment guidelines apply if there is no differential diagnosis? Thus, the industrialization of health care has actually helped psychology focus on the need for diagnoses and the need to relate these diagnoses to treatment plans. By the late 1990s, new texts focused on the use of psychological assessment both in making diagnoses and treatment planning were emerging (e.g., Beutler & Berren, 1995; Maruish, 1999; Quirk, Strosahl, Kreilkamp, & Erdberg, 1995).

What is now involved in making a diagnosis, and what kinds of assessment need to be made? The next section focuses on what most psychologists associate with diagnosis: that is, the *DSM–5*, the current diagnostic manual of the American Psychiatric Association (2013).

DSM–5

Attempts to provide a manual that would assist mental health practitioners in making reliable and useful diagnoses, even in the face of the problems with diagnoses outlined above, go back to 1952 when the first edition of the *Diagnostic and Statistical Manual of Mental Disorders* was published by the American Psychiatric Association. Nathan (1998), one of many psychologists involved in the preparation of the fourth edition (no psychologists were involved in preparing the first edition, and only one psychologist was involved in preparing the second edition), provided an excellent and concise history of the development of the first four editions of the manual. He described the criticisms of earlier editions that were addressed as much as possible in each subsequent edition. The fifth edition has continued the trend in prior editions of becoming more user-friendly. Some diagnoses have been deleted, and some have been added to or modified. The classifications of the latest *DSM* are more reliable and valid, as research on psychopathology has continued at an accelerated pace during recent decades. However, the *DSM–5* is still very medically oriented in its terminology. For counseling psychologists, the focus on illness and deficit rather than wellness and strength presents major philosophical problems. In addition, the categorical division of disorders flies in the face of evidence that people do not fit easily into simple categories but rather are composed of many qualities. Notwithstanding these criticisms, the *DSM–5* is, without question, the foundation for decision making by managed care companies as to what behavioral health care will be covered for their subscribers. If a problem cannot be given a *DSM–5* diagnosis, it is likely that no treatment will be authorized by a managed care company. Clients will then have to pay, entirely from their own resources, if they wish to have counseling for their problems.

The *DSM–5* evidences an increased sensitivity to the fact that human dysfunction occurs not simply in categories but in terms of dimensions. Thus, although the *DSM–5* maintains categorical classification of disorders, dimensional ratings have been added; for example, severity ratings of states that cut across disorders (e.g., anxiety, depression, suicide risk). There are also dimensional ratings that are specific to given disorders (e.g., frequency of flashbacks in posttraumatic stress disorder). As for the classification of disorders, some disorders have been added, some deleted, and a few radically redefined. A key aspect of the revision is that it is steeped in the latest scientific evidence about disorders.

There is no question that five editions of the *DSM* have continuously improved in their scientific basis and ease of use in diagnosis. However, it must be remembered that people do not readily fit into categories, no matter how valid and reliable the categories. A personal example may help clarify this phenomenon. Some years ago, the first author sought to make a *DSM* diagnosis of all of the 12 clients he was seeing in his private practice. Although he had taught abnormal psychology for many years and was highly versed in the *DSM–IV* (American Psychiatric Association, 1994) he was able to make a clear, single diagnosis for only one of these 12 clients. The others appeared to have dual or triple diagnoses or no diagnosable disorder, despite the fact that all 12 clients were experiencing serious psychological difficulties and problems in living. This problem in diagnosing these 12 clients with the *DSM* may have been a difficulty specific to the first author. However, given his experience level and familiarity with the *DSM* and psychological assessment, this seemed unlikely.

Despite the many positive features of the *DSM–5* and the advances it has made over previous editions, it is and always will be, by definition, an assessment of disorder. What is missing for counseling psychologists is a sound system for assessment strengths and assets (Suzuki et al., 2008). As regards assessing strengths when doing treatment planning, some key questions to be asked are "What psychological resources and strengths does this client have?" "What is this client's level of psychological development or maturity?" and "How will this client's strengths manifest themselves in the forthcoming therapy?"

USING ASSESSMENT AS A TREATMENT MODALITY

Counseling psychologists have, since the formal beginnings of the profession in the 1940s, incorporated the use of test results in to the process of counseling (Goldman, 1961; Zunker, 1990). Counseling psychologists in those earlier times, in contrast to clinical psychologists, typically worked with college students rather than hospitalized psychiatric patients. Consequently, the counselors could consider sharing directly with the client the results of the extensive psychological assessments that were often, as described earlier in this chapter, a routine part of being seen at a clinic or counseling center. Ever since the 1940s there has been a steady flow of research examining how best to have clients involved in the selection and interpretation of psychological assessments so that they, the clients, obtain the maximum benefits of psychological assessment. Goodyear (1990), who summarized much of the first 40 years of such research, found that "clients who receive test interpretations—regardless of format or of the particular outcome criteria employed—do experience greater gains than do those in control conditions" (p. 242).

The earliest research on the effects of using tests as part of the counseling process focused on whether clients who were actively involved in selecting the tests they would take would then make more effective use of the results in dealing with their personal problems (Bordin & Bixler, 1946). Brammer and Shostrom (1977) reviewed the positive effects of such client participation if (a) the counselor and client discussed the kinds of data that were needed to help solve the client's problem, and (b) the counselor described the tests that could provide such information. On the basis of the findings of Gustad and Tuma (1957), some counselors also ask clients to make predictions after taking the tests of what the results will be. This strategy allows the counselor to assess whether the client understands the kinds of data a given test can provide and increases the client's commitment to finding out what the test can tell him or her.

An even larger research literature concerns ways in which test interpretation might be varied to improve clients' learning from test results. As Goodyear (1990) noted, variation in individual versus group interpretation, computer-provided versus counselor-provided interpretation, or using versus not using actual test profiles as part of the interpretations does not seem to matter substantially. Much more potent is simply the comparison of using test results versus not using them: Using test results as part of counseling yields significant gains for clients. Of importance, S. D. Brown et al. (2003) found that individualized feedback and interpretation of test results are critical elements of career counseling, especially when clients had interest test profiles that were complicated or difficult to interpret. Thus, the importance of individualized test interpretations is a strongly replicated finding, although, unsurprisingly, not every study that has been done supports this assertion (Whiston & Rahardja, 2008)

Hanson, Claiborn, and Kerr (1997) again focused on differential styles of test interpretation and found that when the counselor used a more collaborative (compared to "expert") style of interpretation, there were no differences in cognitive gains for students; however, students who participated in the more collaborative process felt their sessions had more depth and that their counselors were more expert, trustworthy, and attractive. Counseling psychologists have long been more comfortable with the collaborative than the expert style; the research of Hanson et al. is nicely reassuring that playing the expert is actually perceived as less expert than being a collaborative participant with the client in conducting the feedback. It is important that such research now be replicated with more clinical populations, compared with college students, to see if similar effects can be found to result from collaborative interpretations when the outcome criteria include changes in affect and behavior as well as changes in cognitions.

Both Healy (1990) and Tinsley and Bradley (1986) described strategies allowing for greater integration of test interpretation in the process of counseling, with the counselor more as a collaborator than an expert. Tinsley and Bradley articulated two fundamental principles underlying all their recommendations for test interpretation:

> First, test interpretation must not be viewed as a discrete activity but conceptualized as part of the ongoing counseling process. . . . Counselors who take "time out" from being sensitive, warm, empathic, and caring individuals while conducting test interpretations engage in a practice detrimental to the overall counseling process. . . . Second, it seems useful to think of tests as structured interviews designed to provide information about clients in an efficient manner. They should not be deified or thought of as magically providing answers. (p. 462)

Tinsley and Bradley's (1986) recommendations are just as relevant today as when they were originally offered. Some of the recommendations, however, are often overlooked by counselors. We strongly urge any counseling psychologists who provide test interpretations to be thoroughly familiar with all their recommendations before engaging in the use of psychological tests as a treatment modality. Current texts on assessment provide in-depth coverage of assessment as treatment (Hood & Johnson, 2007; Whiston, 2009).

Clinical Judgment in Psychological Assessment

With the many years of experience psychologists now have in using psychological assessments, how accurate are they in making predictions and judgments about clients? Are some psychologists better than others in making more accurate assessments? From the very beginnings of the specialties of applied psychology such as counseling, clinical, and school, there have been studies of both processes and outcomes of psychological assessment. In the next section we review some of these results; in the subsequent section, we describe the significant progress that has been made in determining how to improve judgment accuracy. This progress has been made primarily by counseling psychologists and is widely recognized by a broad range of authorities in assessment: "These [judgment] processes help refine the final conclusions and treatment recommendations and ultimately increase the accuracy and clinical utility of the assessment" (Meyer et al., 1998, p. 48).

IS THE COMPUTER THE WINNER?

In those times before there were computers in psychologists' offices, the heading for this section would have been "Clinical Versus Statistical Prediction" (Holt, 1970; Meehl, 1954). *Statistical prediction* refers to using actuarial tables to make predictions of behavior and relying on test scores alone to make diagnostic and prognostic decisions. (Today, many major tests are packaged with software that when downloaded to a computer once a client's test results are entered will generate a number of diagnoses and predictions; e.g., *DSM–5* diagnosis, client probability of being a substance abuser or committing suicide.) In contrast to statistical prediction, *clinical prediction* refers to the process of the psychologist making diagnoses and predictions based on interviews with a client or a combination of interview data with his or her interpretations of results from tests such as the Rorschach or MMPI–2. From an outcome perspective, the question has always been Are statistical or computer-generated classifications and predictions as good as those made by psychologists who incorporate a wide variety of data in making their assessments? The controversy is not one of idle curiosity. If diagnoses and prognoses generated by computerized testing can be as accurate as those made by psychologists (who require several interview and assessment sessions to generate their diagnoses), managed care companies will certainly be willing to authorize only computerized assessments!

In 1954, Meehl published the first large set of such comparisons. He found that although there were often no significant differences in accuracy of straightforward, test-based statistical predictions compared to clinical judgments, whenever one was better than the other, it was almost always the statistical-based procedure that was superior. These results have generated decades of controversy (Aegisdottir et al., 2006). Fortunately, there have been three quite useful outcomes of this controversy. Those who felt that psychologists' judgments had been unfairly impugned devoted significant empirical effort into determining (a) whether there were some psychologists who were more accurate than others in making assessment judgments, and if so, what their strategies were (see next section for useful outcomes of these investigations); and (b) whether there were some situations, especially quite unique ones, in which the judgment of a psychologist would almost always be better than statistical prediction. The short answer to this second question is "yes"; see Chwalisz (2006) for some of the key factors that determine when clinical judgment will generally be more accurate than statistical prediction. The third positive outcome of the comparisons of clinical versus statistical prediction was psychologists' increased respect for the comparative power of psychological tests. Contemporary psychologists who are called on to testify in court when dealing with custody cases, prerelease assessments, discrimination cases, and so forth, will almost always include formal psychological assessments and be aware of the predictions made by statistical prediction rules and automated assessment reports generated by a published test's software. Any predictions or recommendations a psychologist makes that disagree with test-based predictions must be extraordinarily well justified. Garb (1994) provided an excellent set of basic assessment considerations that should be consulted by any psychologist who is called upon to give testimony in court.

IMPROVING JUDGMENT ACCURACY

Concern with understanding and improving the accuracy of psychologists' judgment began even before Meehl's (1954) controversial results. At the same time Meehl's work was published, the very first volume of the *Journal of Counseling Psychology* included McArthur's (1954) article "Analyzing the Clinical Process." In that year the Pepinskys published their text on counseling (Pepinsky & Pepinsky, 1954), which outlined a model of the counselor judgment process. This model even today serves as the foundation for the contemporary work of Strohmer and his collaborators (see, e.g., Strohmer & Arm, 2006).

Spengler, Strohmer, Dixon, and Shivy (1995) found many studies indicating that there is substantial variability in the accuracy of psychologists' judgments on a range of tasks. Some psychologists are not very accurate at all; others are quite expert, even though they may not have many years of experience or recognition as national leaders in the profession. The processes used in making judgments turn out to be far more critical than demographics (e.g., experience, age, gender) or theoretical orientation (e.g., behavioral, analytic). From years of study of how accurate assessment judgments are made and synthesis of these findings with research in social cognition, Spengler et al. (1995) generated a model they described as a self-correcting "reciprocal interaction between assessment and intervention decisions or judgments" (p. 517). In other words, accuracy improves when a psychologist (a) carefully checks the outcome of each assessment-based prediction in terms of actual outcomes and then, (b) using such data, adjusts for subsequent clients his or her assessment interpretations and predictions.

Although the brief description of this model may seem simply a statement of the way scientist–practitioner psychologists should operate, Spengler et al. (1995) found numerous impediments to such functioning. It is beyond the scope of this chapter to describe the four types of common judgment errors they found, all supported by extensive research. What needs to be noted most critically is that the assessment training of all psychologists should include explicit exposure to the types of errors and strategies for how to reduce their impact on judgment accuracy. As Spengler et al. (1995) noted, their work is relevant not only to assessment procedure per se but also to the entire process of effective counseling and psychotherapy. They lamented that supervisors all too rarely require students to engage in the reciprocal process of building, then testing, and then reformulating hypotheses about their clients. For counseling psychologists to attain increased accuracy and effectiveness, as Belar and Perry (1992) noted, "The process of critical thinking, hypothesis-testing, and other elements of the scientific method should be engendered and integrated into *all* [emphasis added] experiential activities throughout the training process" (p. 72), whether the topic is assessment, counseling, or research.

For a review of the most recent meta-analysis of the findings regarding clinical versus statistical prediction in psychological assessment, including suggestions for practice, the reader is referred to Aegisdottir et al. (2006). Although it is clear that statistical predictions have many advantages in a range of situations, it is important to keep in mind Chwalisz's (2006) caution:

> In real-world settings [in contrast to settings in which the research has typically been conducted] clients' lives are much more complicated . . . and many clients present with comorbidity and other issues that interact with their presenting concerns. I would need to be assured that statistical procedures would not miss the important diagnostic data that a skilled clinician often uncovers on interview by constantly adjusting the interview

with each new data point. Consider, for example, a client seen by a former colleague of mine in a hospital session. An older man presented with symptoms and behaviors suggestive of delirium and dementia, but his presentation was atypical. During the interview, my colleague, who is an expert neuropsychologist, discovered that the patient had lead shrapnel still embedded in his shoulder since World War II. His symptoms reflected lead poisoning rather than dementia, and removal of the shrapnel resulted in alleviation of the symptoms. A statistical prediction model would have misclassified the patient's symptoms because the prediction would have occurred without that critical piece of information, and the patient would not have received the successful treatment. Thus, for expert clinicians, statistical prediction results might serve as one source of data when making decisions, especially . . . when false negative decisions are potentially costly. Statistical procedures might also be used in settings where the available clinicians have less experience and expertise or where the volume of clients is too high to allow for thorough assessment. (p. 394)

Communicating Assessment Results

There are a number of factors to consider when writing reports. Here we focus on two of them: what is the purpose and who is the audience.

PREPARING WRITTEN REPORTS

Thus far in this chapter, when we have discussed communicating assessment results, we have focused primarily on communicating results to clients or to health care managers in order to justify requests for services for clients. Yet, traditionally in applied psychology, especially school and clinical psychology, assessments were completed most frequently in response to a referral for a "psychological evaluation." The referral request might come from a general practice physician (Is the client's sexual dysfunction psychologically based?), a teacher (Does the student have a learning disability?), an attorney (Has the client been harmed psychologically by forced early retirement?), a court (Is the client a danger to himself or others?), and so forth. In hospitals and clinics, referrals may be made by other mental health professionals, none of whom have the specialized training in assessment that psychologists have. These latter types of referrals are usually made in order to obtain information that can be used in diagnosing and planning the treatment for a patient. Or if the referral is made near the end of treatment, the request is usually for an assessment of the patient's prognosis without further inpatient treatment. If the patient is not ready for independent functioning, what outpatient services should be provided?

For each of the referrals just described, the expectation has always been that the psychologist would provide a written report that provides an answer to the referral question, with clear specification of the assessment results that underlie that answer. Almost every text on assessment includes major points to consider in writing such reports, as well as examples of various kinds of reports. In the next sections, we highlight just two of the major points that should be considered when writing assessment reports.

What Is the Purpose?

This question actually should pervade every aspect of a psychologist's response to a referral from another professional, from establishing a clear understanding with the referring professional as to why the request for psychological assessment is being made, to the selection of assessments to use, to the psychologist's own interpretation of the results obtained, and, finally, to considerations of how to frame the written report. Does the referring professional want as straightforward an answer as possible, or would a more comprehensive description of functioning be most helpful? Consider two examples from the kinds of possible referrals listed above: Is the client's sexual dysfunction psychologically based? and Does the student have a learning disability? For the first example, the physician probably wants a concise, straightforward answer, yes or no; in the second example, especially if there is no evidence of a learning disorder, the teacher will want as much assistance as possible in understanding the academic performance problems of the student. Obviously, very different reports would be written in the first as compared to the second example. In either case, the report should contain clear and precise information as to what kinds of assessment were completed and how results support the response to the referral question.

Who Is the Audience?

The second major question to consider when writing a psychological report is to whom it is addressed. Consider the examples of referrals given above, made by those outside the mental health professions. Such persons may have little understanding about the kinds of tests available and the tests' various strengths and weaknesses. Yet, for counseling psychologists, our primary training in writing reports may have been in writing for other psychologists, whether writing research reports or case presentations to our peers and supervisors in practice settings. We learn to write in very technical terms, with assumptions that we do not need to explain such terms as ego, strength, self-efficacy, narcissistic injury, construct validity, predictive validity, and so forth. Obviously, such language will leave many professionals who make referrals to psychologists frustrated at not having received a comprehensible answer to the question asked. Before writing any report, counseling psychologists need to think carefully about the professional persons who will be reading their report and attend to minimizing professional jargon, yet clearly and comprehensibly explaining the strengths and weaknesses of the assessment procedures and results. In addition, those writing reports need to attend to the fundamental guidelines in effective writing that can make for more easily understood reports. As noted by Harvey (1997), too often, reports are written using highly technical language, very long sentences, and complicated prose. Just as in good writing in general, simplicity and clarity of thought and writing are very important aspects of high-quality reports.

Summary

In the first half of the 20th century, the development of psychological tests and assessment techniques was regarded as psychology's major contribution to society. Yet by the second half of that century, two major challenges emerged to the use of psychological tests. In the first third of this chapter, we reviewed how those challenges resulted in a significant decline in use of tests as psychologists shifted from assessment/testing roles to more therapeutic roles as evidence accumulated showing the adverse impact of some tests on women and racial/ethnic minorities. We described how, fortunately, some counseling psychologists have been among the leaders in attending constructively to these issues, rather than simply abandoning psychological tests and using what are often even more biased and inaccurate strategies. Their contributions to standards for psychological assessments were reviewed in sections on evaluating and constructing assessments, fairness in multicultural assessment, and standards in applying assessments.

The middle third of this chapter was devoted to an exploration of seven types of psychological tests frequently used by counseling psychologists. For each type we described the best known tests of that type and how counseling psychologists use them in both practice and research. The training of counseling psychologists ideally includes coursework and supervised practice in the use of each of these types of tests.

The last third of this chapter focused on issues in and strategies for more effective use of psychological assessment. The emergence of industrialized health care has clearly provided new challenges to psychologists' use of assessment. Fortunately, these challenges have helped psychologists develop new strategies for using assessment in diagnosis, in treatment planning, as a treatment modality (using tests in counseling), and in evaluation of the outcomes of psychotherapy. In addition to identifying these strategies, we described how counseling psychologists have conducted the most useful research on improving the accuracy of clinical judgment when using psychological assessment. The final sections of the chapter identified two key points in effective communication of test results to other professionals.

The Psychodynamic Approach

11

There are virtually dozens of theories of counseling and psychotherapy today, and indeed each practitioner may be seen as developing his or her own unique theory. At the same time, it is possible to combine the most prominent theories into four main clusters. In this chapter and the following three, we examine the four theory clusters that have been dominant in counseling psychology and in the counseling and therapy that is practiced by counseling psychologists. These clusters may be labeled *psychodynamic* (including Freudian approaches, their derivatives, and departures), *learning* (including the behavioral, cognitive, and cognitive–behavioral approaches), *humanistic* (including experiential and existential), and *feminist multicultural*.

Many excellent presentations of theories of counseling are available. Our goal in the following four chapters is not to duplicate these. Rather, we aim to delineate the major ingredients of each of the three theory clusters, exemplify treatment approaches and procedures within each, and

http://dx.doi.org/10.1037/14378-011
Counseling Psychology, Third Edition, by C. J. Gelso, E. N. Williams, and B. R. Fretz

clarify the place of each perspective in counseling psychology. Key references will enable the student to pursue each individual theory in greater depth.

Will the real psychodynamic practitioner please stand up? If this question was asked of a large group of therapists, those who stood would probably represent a dizzying array of viewpoints about personality development, health and psychopathology, and psychological interventions. It is not surprising that the beginning student often feels overwhelmed by the enormous diversity of views and approaches within the general psychoanalytic or psychodynamic perspective. This diversity, along with the awesome complexity inherent in psychoanalytic theories, makes it difficult for the beginner to decipher just what is and is not psychoanalytic. With experience, practice, and much reading, things do become clearer, although the seasoned practitioner and scholar does not have an easy time with this question either.

One of the principal goals of this chapter is to provide the reader with a framework for understanding common ingredients of the multifold approaches found under the psychoanalytic–psychodynamic umbrella. We use the terms *psychodynamic* and *psychoanalytic* interchangeably, while acknowledging that there are some subtle differences between the two (Prochaska & Norcross, 2007). We also explain how psychoanalysis fits with counseling psychology.

We begin by taking a glimpse at the life and personality of Sigmund Freud, the originator of psychoanalysis. Subsequently, we (a) examine some distinctions that are too often not addressed and are frequent sources of confusion for the beginning student of psychoanalysis; (b) clarify the main theory clusters within psychoanalysis; (c) discuss ingredients that are common to all psychoanalytic approaches; (d) present an integrative theoretical approach to psychoanalytic therapy that seems well suited to counseling psychology; and (e) conclude with a discussion of the relationship of psychoanalysis to counseling psychology, the ways in which these two endeavors have not meshed, and how their "fit" has become much better in recent years. Research issues and findings related to psychoanalytic interventions are presented in the final section of the chapter.

It should be noted that the material in this chapter assumes the reader has a beginning understanding of basic psychoanalytic concepts, such as Freud's psychosexual stages (e.g., oral, anal, phallic stages), the Oedipus complex, structures of the psyche (id, ego, superego), defense mechanisms, and levels of consciousness (unconscious, preconscious, conscious). Excellent discussions of these concepts are provided by Prochaska and Norcross (2007) and Murdock (2013). The advanced student can consult Brenner's (1973) classic work.

The First Freudian and the Beginnings of Psychoanalysis

All fields of psychology in which counseling interventions are involved must be indebted to psychoanalysis and especially to Sigmund Freud for the beginning development of therapeutic treatment. It was Freud, after all, who discovered and developed the "talking cure," the treatment upon which the entire field of verbal counseling has been built. Because of the profound impact of Freud and his early work on all approaches to psychological intervention, examining his life and the early psychoanalytic movement in some depth is worthwhile.

Sigmund Freud was born in 1856 in Freiberg, Moravia (formerly Austria). His father, Jakob, was a wool merchant in Vienna, where Freud lived from the age of 4. Jakob was married twice; Sigmund was the first child of Jakob's second marriage, to Amalie, a 20-year-old woman who was 20 years Jakob's junior. Jakob and Amalie bore seven other children, so Sigmund was the eldest child of a large family. Freud's childhood seems to have been a relatively happy one. Jakob was a liberal-minded Jew with progressive views. He was apparently a loving father with a good sense of humor, although he seemed to represent discipline and authority to Sigmund. Freud's relationship with his father seemed somewhat distant. Freud's mother is described as having a lively personality, and she gave Sigmund considerable affection and attention. She was proud of her firstborn, and Sigmund remained fond of her until her death at age 95.

A deep scholarly orientation pervaded Freud's life from very early on. His great intellectual capacity was recognized early by his family, and it was established that he would be a scholar. His destiny was incontestable: Freud's study-bedroom was the only one in his house equipped with an oil lamp; the other family members' rooms had candles. Freud was a precocious reader who studied a great deal. He began to enjoy Shakespeare at the age of 8 and, as a teenager, ate his evening meals in his room so he would lose no time from his studies. Freud's passion for learning and understanding never faded. In fact, although Freud was steeped in psychoanalytic practice throughout most of his adult life, his most passionate interests revolved around understanding what makes people tick—the workings of the human psyche—rather than providing psychological help.

Freud received his MD from the University of Vienna in 1881, after which he took a position at the city's well-known general hospital. His practice flourished, and he wrote books on aphasia and infantile cerebral paralysis. It looked as though the young Freud was destined for a smooth and lucrative career. Things were not to be easy, though, for Freud's restless and creative genius goaded him to new and deeper understandings of the human psyche. These understandings were to be the source of much professional ferment and emotional pain in his life. In 1886 he presented his first paper on hysteria. It was badly received by his medical colleagues, probably the first in what became a long series of rejections for one of the great minds of history.

While a medical student, Freud met Joseph Breuer, a prominent general practitioner 14 years his senior. They became friends, and their friendship continued over the years. Breuer discussed with Freud a case he treated from 1880 to 1882, the now-famous case of Anna O, in which a variety of symptoms, including conversion reactions, were cured by means of hypnosis and the free discharge of emotions, called *catharsis*. Freud was fascinated by this case and by what he felt to be a remarkable discovery. Following his return in 1889 from the Nancy School, where he studied hypnotic suggestion with Bernheim and Liebault, Freud further tested the new method of catharsis, or abreaction, along with hypnosis.

Breuer and Freud eventually published the case of Anna O in *Studies in Hysteria* (1895/1955), but the book did not receive the acceptance they had hoped for. The medical profession of that time explained all symptoms on the basis of some organic lesion or brain abnormality. As Freud continued to develop his views about the sexual basis of the neuroses, things heated up further. When Freud theorized that hysterical and other symptoms were, at their core, the results of sexual repression, Breuer withdrew from the work. Freud essentially worked alone and was the object of professional ridicule by fellow physicians. He was seen as a crackpot, and his private practice nearly dried up. In early 1900 Freud reported that he had had no new cases for months, and his financial outlook was again bleak. Having a wife, six children, and a mother to support (Freud's father had died) surely added stress.

The final years of the 19th century were crucial for Freud and psychoanalysis. Working essentially alone, he began his self-analysis as a way of understanding the psyche and resolving some personal neuroses, and he further developed his theories about sex and the meaning of dreams (Freud, 1900/1938). He soon was to discontinue the use of hypnosis. Too many patients could not be hypnotized, and too many of the "cures" were short-lived. Instead, Freud began to use a procedure he called *free association* to get his patients to remember repressed experiences and feelings from their past. Thus began the revolutionary new method, psychoanalysis.

Freud's work began to receive positive recognition in the early 1900s. Although he continued to work largely alone, during this time

Freud met a number of men who were to form the inner sanctum of psychoanalysis. For example, in 1902 he initiated weekly discussions in his home with a small group of budding analysts, the famed Vienna Psychoanalytic Society. Given the great struggles and isolation that Freud endured during his initial years of developing psychoanalysis, as well as some aspects of his character structure, it was perhaps inevitable that psychoanalysis would become a system revolving around the beliefs of one man. As the first decade of the 20th century was drawing to a close, Freud's views were becoming increasingly influential both in Europe and the United States.

Although his genius is now widely recognized, Freud often complained of not having been born with a better brain. He believed that his main virtues were his courage and his self-criticalness. These qualities— courage and self-criticalness—constantly pushed Freud to further his and the field's understanding of the deepest aspects of the human psyche in the face of professional rejection and even humiliation.

Freud often changed his views. Yet, he had difficulty with others deviating from his position, especially if they used the word *psychoanalysis* as a label for their theorizing. Psychoanalysis was Freud's creation, and he alone could decide what rightfully belonged in its province. Once Freud was convinced that a theory was valid, he maintained it with complete conviction. He could not admit contradiction. As Ellenberger (1970) noted, his opponents viewed this as intolerance, whereas Freud's followers saw this trait as a passion for truth.

Whatever the case may be, Freud inarguably was deeply passionate about his intellectual pursuits and had an enormous capacity for work. A look at his daily schedule gives a picture of how devoted he was to it. On a typical day, Freud saw his first patient at 8 a.m. and continued his clinical practice until 1 p.m., with a 5-minute break between sessions. At 1 p.m. he ate lunch and took a walk with his family. He then saw more patients from 3 until 9 or 10 p.m., followed by dinner and another walk with his wife. He then returned to his study and wrote from 11 until 1 or 2 a.m. This amounted to about an 18-hour workday. In commenting on this, Prochaska and Norcross (1999) noted the irony that a man whose professional life was so devoted to understanding sex appeared to have left so little time in his life for his own sexuality.

Freud was a man of compassion who cared deeply about his patients and people in general. His courage and passion for knowledge, though, truly stand out. These qualities were evidenced clearly in how he dealt with his terribly painful cancer of the jaw and palate. In 1923 he was operated on for this cancer, the first of 33 such operations. For 16 years Freud suffered agonizing pain. His speech, hearing, and eating were seriously affected. Despite the worsening cancer, Freud worked on, usually without medication (which he felt clouded his thinking), until his death in 1939. Some of his most profound works were produced during these years, including *An Outline of Psychoanalysis* (1940), his final statement about revised psychoanalytic theory.

For in-depth reading on Freud's life and the background of the psychoanalytic movement, the reader is referred to the three-volume biography by one of Freud's most trusted colleagues, Ernest Jones (1953, 1955, 1957).

Psychodynamic Interventions: Some Key Distinctions

To understand modern psychoanalytic thought, it is helpful to make some key distinctions that are often ignored in the psychoanalytic literature. Three such distinctions are discussed in the following.

THEORIES OF THE PERSON VERSUS THEORIES OF THE TREATMENT PROCESS

Psychoanalysis includes a diverse and complex set of assumptions, theories, and laws about how human beings develop as they do. There are psychoanalytic personality and development theories and psychoanalytic theories of health and psychopathology. We call these viewpoints about human personality development, health, and pathology *theories of the person*. Later in this section, we present four theories of the persons that are prominent in psychoanalysis.

In addition to developing theories of the person, psychoanalysis formulates theories of the treatment process. Such theories examine, for example, what goes on during analysis or therapy between the therapist and client and how the client's issues are expected to unfold within the hour and during the course of treatment. Psychoanalytic theories of treatment specify the techniques that the analyst or therapist is to use with the client and, more generally, how the therapist is to behave during the sessions.

Most psychoanalytic practitioners would agree that the therapist should strive for a deep understanding of both psychoanalytic theories of the person and psychoanalytic theories of intervention. At the same time, it is important to keep in mind that these two theories are by no means the same. One can conceptualize the individual client in psychodynamic terms (using any psychoanalytic theory) but provide treatment that is decidedly nonanalytic. On the other hand, if the therapist conceptualizes the treatment process in dynamic terms (e.g., focus on interpretation and insight, transference and countertransference), she or he has probably also relied on psychoanalytic/psychodynamic formulations of the person.

The central point is that when we talk about psychoanalysis, we need to be clear on whether we refer to formulations about the person (his or her personality, development, degree of health, and degree or kind of psychopathology) or about the treatment being offered.

PSYCHOANALYTIC THEORY VERSUS PSYCHODYNAMIC THEORY

Although the words *psychoanalytic* and *psychodynamic* are often used interchangeably, as they are in this chapter, it is useful to note the subtle differences. The word *psychodynamic* is the broader of the two. This word has different meanings to different people, but even differing definitions share the assumptions that underlying processes (feelings, ideas, impulses, drives, etc.) influence much of overt behavior; that these underlying processes are often not at the conscious level; and that humans frequently use defense mechanisms to keep anxiety-provoking feelings, ideas, and impulses out of conscious awareness.

What then makes a theory *psychoanalytic?* In addition to incorporating unconscious processes and defense mechanisms (as do psychodynamic theories), virtually all modern psychoanalytic theories (a) are developmental in that they posit a sequence to learning and development, often in the form of stages that may be psychosexual (e.g., Freud, 1923/1961), psychosocial (e.g., Erikson, 1950), or relational (e.g., Mahler, Bergman, & Pine, 1975); (b) attend to the interplay of instinctual, social, interpersonal, and biological determinants (although theories vary in their emphasis on these four classes); and (c) subscribe to the primacy of mental functions or structures, which are constitutionally determined or learned early in life.

Once these structures (e.g., the ego) are in place, they have a great impact on the person's life, including what environments and relationships are consciously or unconsciously sought out (Gelso & Hayes, 1998; Robbins, 1989). These ingredients are discussed further in the section Common Elements Among Psychoanalytic Approaches.

The distinction between psychodynamic and psychoanalytic theories largely pertains to theories of the person. When we refer to theories of the treatment process, the distinction largely disappears. This is especially so when we move beyond psychoanalysis proper, as discussed in the next section.

LEVELS OF PSYCHODYNAMIC INTERVENTION

When psychodynamic interventions are examined, it is useful to differentiate among three levels of treatment: psychoanalysis proper,

TABLE 11.1

Levels of Psychoanalytic Interventions

Treatment	Session frequency (per week)	Duration	Major techniques	Practitioner
Psychoanalysis proper	3–5	3–7 years	Interpretation Free association	Psychoanalyst
Psychoanalytically oriented therapy	1–2	A few months to years	Interpretation and others	Mental health professional
Analytically informed counseling	1	Varied	Technically eclectic	Mental health professional

Note. Mental health practitioners may be psychoanalysts or nonpsychoanalyst psychologists, psychiatrists, social workers, or counselors.

psychodynamically oriented therapy, and analytically informed therapy. These three levels are summarized in Table 11.1. In the following, we describe each level in greater detail.

Psychoanalysis Proper

Psychoanalysis is the most intensive and depth-oriented form of therapeutic intervention. Sessions occur usually three to five times a week, and analysis is virtually always long term. Length of treatment is typically from 3 to 7 years. Analysis is carried out by a certified psychoanalyst, who ordinarily has received an MD degree with a specialization in psychiatry or a PhD degree in psychology. After receiving the MD or PhD, the psychoanalyst receives several years of additional training in psychoanalysis from one of the many psychoanalytic training institutes. For several decades, these training institutes admitted only practitioners with MD degrees, but during the 1980s (Slavin, 1989), training in psychoanalysis became widely available to psychologists.

Psychoanalysis proper is ordinarily carried out with the analyst sitting behind the analysand while the analysand in turn reclines on a couch. The analysand's main task is to free-associate; that is, to say whatever comes to his or her mind without editing or trying to formulate intellectually the meaning of his or her associations. Another task of the analysand is to report dreams to the analyst. From the time of Freud's seminal work on the meaning of dreams (Freud, 1900/1938), dreams and their interpretation have held a special place in psychoanalysis. Analysts believe that dreams provide a powerful way of accessing the analysand's subconscious. On reporting dreams during the analysis, the analysand is asked to free-associate to parts of the dream. The analyst subsequently offers interpretations as to the meanings of these dreams in terms of the analysand's dynamic issues.

The analyst's task throughout the analysis is to be noninterfering, to offer what Freud called "even-hovering attention," and to make interpretations as the emerging material from the analysand makes sense to him or her. These interpretations should be close to the analysand's level of awareness and experience; if they become too removed from what the analysand is feeling, the treatment can become a sterile intellectual exercise.

Three interrelated features of the analyst's interactions with the analysand deserve special note because they are fundamental to psychoanalysis. First, throughout the work the analyst seeks to maintain what is called the *analytic attitude*. This attitude is one in which the analyst's most basic mission is to engage the analysand in an exploration—an investigation—of the analysand's internal world. Virtually all of the work is aimed at fostering this in-depth exploration and the resulting insights.

The second feature of the analyst's interaction with the analysand is the analyst's stance toward gratifying the analysand's wishes or demands to be loved and taken care of in the analysis. Given that all therapeutic interactions involve a strong press toward giving and receiving help, it is inevitable that the analysand experiences these wishes or demands. Yet, the analyst follows Freud's *rule of abstinence* and in so doing avoids direct expressions of affection and advice. There are two good reasons for this. First, directly gratifying affectional and dependency needs runs the risk of fueling these needs and thus increases the likelihood that the analysand will become too attached to the treatment rather than to the goal of resolving his or her problems. Second, when such needs are gratified in the analysis itself, it is less likely that the underlying issues will become conscious. Thus, gratification works against the analyst's mission of fostering insight.

The third element of the analyst's interaction that deserves special note is highly related to the first two. This element involves the analyst's stance of *neutrality* and *ambiguity*. This stance is often misunderstood to be a kind of coldness, aloofness, or impersonality. This is far from the case in good analytic work. The analyst is deeply involved in the analysand's inner experience, and the analyst certainly cares about the analysand (see Greenson, 1967; Langs, 1976). Neutrality, however, implies that the analyst does not take sides in the analysand's struggles. Although the analyst is on the side of the analysand's healthy ego, he or she does not, for example, agree or disagree with the analysand's feelings toward significant others in his or her life and generally does not take a position on what the analysand should do in his or her life.

Again, the analyst's job is to help the analysand understand himself or herself as deeply as possible; taking a position on what the analysand should do or who is right or wrong in the analysand's struggles interferes with the analyst's main task.

The concept of ambiguity, similarly, implies that analysts should refrain from displaying too much of their own issues, lives, and viewpoints. Such restraint provides an atmosphere in which the analysand's issues may unfold without these being confounded by those of the analyst. The analyst's ambiguity also permits the analysand to project feelings and thoughts onto him or her, and in this way the all-important transferences are allowed to develop more purely than would be the case if the analyst's person intruded on the work. In recent years, psychoanalysts have moved toward greater self-disclosure, although psychoanalysts as a group are still very careful about what and when to self-disclose.

During the course of analysis, as the analysand continues to free-associate and the analyst carries out the tasks discussed above, the analysand naturally regresses in his or her associations. That is, the analysand's associations and memories continually move backward in time (although not in a straight line). As this happens, the analysand gets more and more into the childhood conflicts and issues that form the fabric from which the present problems derive. Also, as this occurs, transference reactions (discussed in Chapter 9) continue to develop and build.

If there is a pivotal point around which psychoanalysis revolves, it is this unfolding transference. Indeed, many analysts (e.g., Gill, 1994; Kernberg, 1975) have defined psychoanalysis itself as the *systematic analysis of the transferences*. As these transferences develop, they become increasingly intense, until what is called a *transference neurosis* emerges. During this transference neurosis, it is as if great amounts of energy are invested in the analyst, and the core of the analysand's neurosis gets funneled into and fuels the analysis. At this stage the analyst becomes central to the analysand.

As defined in Chapter 9, transference is a repetition of past conflicts with significant others, in which feelings, behaviors, and attitudes belonging rightfully in those earlier relationships are displaced onto the analyst or therapist. In psychoanalysis, the key to helping the analysand resolve neurotic conflicts resides in providing insight into the distortions involved in the transferences. As the transference intensifies, the analyst maintains his or her ambiguity and neutrality, and this permits the continuing unfolding of these projections. The cure in analysis occurs as the transferences are repeatedly interpreted, worked through, and resolved. The analyst's timing in offering interpretations is crucial.

As the transferences are worked through, the analysand develops deep insight into how his or her early conflicts cause him or her to distort and misperceive the self and others. The analysand's defenses become reduced so that he or she can lead a better life. Again, the aim of analysis is this depth insight, most centrally of the analysand's hidden needs and issues, as manifested in the transferences. There is an assumption that the amount and type of transference that develops in analysis reflect in a deep and significant way the analysand's inter- and intrapersonal conflicts outside of the analytic setting. Thus, working through the transferences in analysis deeply and positively affects the analysand's relations with others as well as the self. It results in deep-seated changes in personality structure.

Psychoanalytically Oriented Therapy

Much of what is called psychoanalysis in beginning texts is really psychotherapy with an analytic orientation rather than analysis proper, as described in the preceding section. In psychoanalytic therapy, the client and therapist usually sit face-to-face. Sessions are usually once or twice a week, and the duration of the work may be anywhere from a few sessions to several years. Although practitioners of psychoanalytic therapy may be certified psychoanalysts, they may also be psychologists, psychiatrists, counselors, and psychiatric social workers who are not analysts but who have training in psychoanalytic treatment.

Differences between analysis proper and analytic therapy are generally differences of degree rather than kind, and many believe these two treatments represent the same underlying processes (Fosshage, 1997). Because of the less frequent meetings, analytic therapy is not considered as intensive a treatment as analysis. Although transference reactions are central in this therapy, the therapist does not seek to cultivate the transference neurosis. Free association may be used at times during analytic therapy, but it is not the modus operandi as in analysis. The focus tends to be on the problems the client is experiencing in his or her life and what is going on inside—the intrapsychic factors—that are the root of the problem. Just as there is somewhat less focus on transference in this therapy, there is greater emphasis on helping the client cope with and solve real-life problems (as opposed to purely intrapsychic issues).

The therapist's stance in analytic therapy is very similar to the analyst's stance, and again the differences are matters of degree. Interpretation is still an important technique, but deviations from this interpretive stance are more frequent in therapy. The analytic therapist still subscribes to the analytic attitude, follows Freud's rule of abstinence, and maintains neutrality and ambiguity. But the therapist is more willing to depart from these positions, to be involved in a give-and-take interaction with the client, and to guide the session more actively. The goals of psychoanalytic therapy are similar to those of analysis, although psychoanalysts make the arguable point that the changes occurring in this treatment are not as pervasive and deep as in analysis.

The dynamic treatment described above is often referred to as insight oriented. However, psychoanalytic therapy may also be supportive rather than insight oriented. Long-term supportive therapy from a psychodynamic perspective is most often indicated for clients with severe emotional problems but in need of support rather than insight, although as these clients become stronger emotionally, the therapy may shift to being more insight oriented. Briefer supportive therapy may be best suited to clients who are in crises. In supportive dynamic therapy the therapist makes the decision that the client needs support and, at least at present, the client will not respond well to an approach that seeks to uncover underlying conflicts (i.e., insight-oriented treatment). As part of the supportive stance, more often than in insight therapy, the therapist may provide suggestions, reassurance, and reinforcement to facilitate the client's positive steps in resolving life problems and to boost self-esteem. The therapist may at times take an educational posture, providing information and even teaching when necessary.

Analytically Informed Therapy or Counseling

Analytically informed counseling may be the psychoanalytically related intervention that is most often used by counseling psychologists and other nonpsychoanalyst psychologists. In this treatment, psychoanalytic theories of the person are used to inform the work; that is, to gain an understanding of the client and his or her dynamics as well as of how these dynamics are expected to play out in counseling or therapy. But the techniques and procedures used by the counselor are many and varied. In essence, the therapist uses an analytic theory of the person but does not necessarily use an analytic approach to the treatment. Rather, the therapist is technically eclectic in the sense that she or he uses whichever techniques and procedures seem to best fit the client.

An example of analytically informed therapy might be that of a therapist working in a university counseling center who conceptualizes student–clients in terms of dynamics and defenses and even formulates these defenses as id–ego conflicts, just as a classical psychoanalytic theorist would. This therapist, however, uses a range of techniques that take into account the fact that treatment at the center is brief and time limited, having, for example, a 12-session duration limit. With a given student–client, for example, the therapist might use primarily gestalt therapy techniques (see Chapter 13) along with verbal reinforcement of behavior changes in the desired direction (see Chapter 12). Reflective techniques (Chapter 13) are also used to help the client explore feelings. All these techniques together might help shorten the treatment time from what it would be if strictly analytic techniques, procedures, and attitudes (e.g., analysis of transference, interpretation, analytic attitude, abstinence) were used. The therapist also has greater latitude in terms of technique than is the case with supportive–analytic therapy, and unlike that treatment, this analytically informed counseling may or may not be supportive.

As the reader would suspect, analytically informed therapy may be practiced by counselors from several disciplines. It may occur once, twice, or even three times a week, and the duration of treatment depends more on the treatment setting than anything inherent in the treatment itself. In fact, techniques of treatment are often selected to fit the setting. For example, different techniques might be used in a university mental health clinic specializing in brief therapy than in a private clinic specializing in longer term treatment.

Perspective on Levels of Psychoanalytic Intervention

The main factor that differentiates psychoanalytically oriented practitioners is their theory of the person. Thus, for example, a psychoanalytic self psychologist following the theories of Heinz Kohut (1971, 1977, 1984) would attend to somewhat different aspects of the personality than would an analytic practitioner using orthodox Freudian drive theory. These practitioners would attend to different issues because theories they espouse make different, often divergent, statements about how personality develops, how intrapsychic problems occur, and which forces or factors serve to foster health and psychopathology. At the same time, however, and with some notable exceptions, the levels of analytic intervention discussed above cut across the differing psychoanalytic theories of the person. Thus, our discussion of psychoanalysis proper applies largely without regard to the analyst's perspective: Freudian drive theory, ego psychology, object relations theory, or psychoanalytic self psychology. These different theoretical perspectives guide the practitioner's understanding of the person and suggest content on which the therapist can focus, but the different theories generally say little about the process of treatment or how the therapist should work with the client. Below we explore each of the four main theory clusters that dominate psychoanalytic thought.

The Four Psychologies of Psychoanalysis

A common misconception is that psychoanalysis as a theory of the person and the treatment process is restricted to Freud's basic theories. Departures from Freudian conceptions are seen as something other than psychoanalysis, often given the term *psychodynamic*. In fact, many theories have developed within psychoanalysis, some being significant departures from Freudian ideas. These departures began to develop even as Freud was framing his basic theories, and they have continued to this day. During the past several decades in particular, major changes have occurred, changes that to many appear revolutionary in nature (Eagle, 2011; S. A. Mitchell, 1993). As a way of organizing this growing diversity, several authors (e.g., Gelso & Hayes, 1998; McWilliams, 2011; Mishne, 1993; Pine, 1990) have divided the psychoanalytic pie into theory clusters, or what are referred to as "psychologies." Below we describe four such clusters. The first two of these are Freud's *drive psychology* and *ego psychology*. Historically, these two clusters were the earliest to develop. They are often referred to as classical psychoanalytic theory. The next two, *object relations theory* and *psychoanalytic self psychology*, have emerged into prominence in more recent times and may now be seen as ruling the theoretical roost in psychoanalysis (Eagle, 2011; Gelso, 1995). Although there is significant overlap among the four psychologies of psychoanalysis, there are also substantial differences in their visions of human development, functioning, and therapy. Because of these differences, it is important for the student to understand the major features of the four psychologies. The four major theory clusters within psychoanalysis are summarized in Table 11.2. The key concepts for each cluster, given on the right side of the table, pertain to theories of the person rather than to treatment. This is because the key concepts about treatment are highly overlapping across the four clusters.

TABLE 11.2

Summary of the Four Psychologies of Psychoanalysis

Theory	Originator(s)	Key concepts
Drive psychology	Sigmund Freud	Basic drives (sex and aggression) Psychosexual stages Unconscious processes
Ego psychology	Heinz Hartmann Anna Freud	Adaptation Ego defenses Ego strength and weakness
Object relations	Ronald Fairbairn Melanie Klein H. S. Sullivan	Human relatedness and relationships Internal representations
Self psychology	Heinz Kohut	Healthy and pathological narcissism Lines of development (grandiose self and omnipotent object) Empathy

FREUD'S DRIVE PSYCHOLOGY

In Freud's writing, *drive* and *instinct* are the same. They are part of our biology and a source of energy that produces psychic excitation. This excitation (or tension) stirs the individual toward action. The person does not of course feel a drive; rather, drives are experienced as urges, which themselves lead to wishes and fantasies. The key point is that the urges, wishes, and fantasies experienced by human beings are rooted in their biology in the form of basic drives. The specific urges that are experienced vary with the psychosexual stages the growing child is in (for example, oral, anal, phallic, latency, genital). Early experiences, especially with parents, are deeply important in Freud's drive psychology, but these experiences always occur in the context of basic drives and affect the individual through the basic drives.

Freud's drive psychology posits two basic drives: sexuality and aggression. Not only does drive psychology seek to understand these two general drives, it also focuses on the urges that spring from them, on the conflicts such urges create, and on the defenses that humans use to keep potentially dangerous urges out of awareness. Many urges stir anxiety, guilt, or shame, and the individual responds by subconsciously repressing such urges through the use of defense mechanisms (e.g., repression, sublimation, projection, denial). Dangerous and conflictual urges thus become hidden, channeled, and transformed. As a result, the individual's actual behavior may appear very different from the underlying urges that the behavior expresses. For example, the client who seems perpetually "nice" may be unconsciously expressing his or her anxiety-provoking yearning to be loved or perhaps his or her frightening aggressive urges. Or the excessively moralistic person may be defending against threatening sexual feelings. Innumerable examples may be generated of how outward behavior differs vastly from underlying urges, and the student is encouraged to reflect on such examples.

We can see in this summary of drive psychology basic Freudian concepts of sexual and aggressive instincts, psychosexual stages (e.g., oral, anal, phallic), and consciousness (e.g., conscious, unconscious). Drive psychology is often referred to as an *id* psychology, in the sense that the drives or instincts are seen as residing in the id (rather than in other agencies of the mind, such as ego or superego).

With regard to treatment, much of what we have described under psychoanalysis proper fits well with drive psychology. Perhaps the key feature of psychoanalytic treatment from a drive perspective is the attempt to understand the client's urges and wishes and the defenses and conflicts surrounding them. Concepts such as therapist neutrality, ambiguity, and abstinence, as described in the Psychoanalysis Proper section, are deeply rooted in drive psychology. So is the concept of transference as being almost purely the client's projection onto a neutral, ambiguous analyst. The unique person of the analyst matters little, as the analysand would transfer the same material unto any well-functioning analyst. The analyst's role is then to help the analysand understand these transference projections and resolve the conflicts underlying them.

EGO PSYCHOLOGY

Although Freud's early theorizing represented an id psychology, he eventually grew much more concerned with the role of ego (Freud, 1923/1953). This concern became apparent when he created his famous structural model, where ego was given a key role, as it was in all of his later theorizing. At the same time, in Freud's thinking the ego grew out of and derived its energy from the id; the ego's role was to erect defenses against the urges emanating from the id when those urges threatened the individual. The id was still the fundamental agency of the mind.

It remained for key figures such as Anna Freud (the daughter of Sigmund) and, in particular, Heinz Hartmann to craft an ego psychology in which the ego played a more fundamental role in psychic life (A. Freud, 1936/1966; Hartmann, 1939/1958). Hartmann, for example, viewed ego as the agency within the individual that enabled adaptation to the world outside the individual. Whereas drive psychology focuses on the taming, socialization, and gratification of drives, ego psychology "emphasizes the development of defenses with respect to the internal world, adaptation with respect to the external world, and reality testing with respect to both" (Pine, 1990, p. 50). Thus, to the ego analytic therapist, the ego does much more than erect defenses against threatening inner urges or the dictates of a harsh superego. It is also the part of the mind that helps us adapt to our outer world, including the world of relationships, and, through the process of perception, it helps us perceive relationships and other aspects of life realistically (referred to as reality testing).

Just as a strong, healthy ego is part of emotionally healthy development, a weak or defective ego is seen as forming the seeds from which psychopathology grows. The ego's strength is determined by both constitutional factors and early family relationships. Once ego defects occur in early life, they have major implications for subsequent development. Such defects may result in the individual having weaknesses in reality testing, difficulties in regulating feelings, and a lack of firm boundaries between the self and others. Also, a weak ego is part of why people cannot control impulses effectively, why they have difficulty handling strong feelings, and why they may have panic reactions in certain situations (Mishne, 1993). Because early ego development is crucial, psychoanalytic ego psychologists focus much of their theory on very early life; for example, prior to the oedipal period at ages 4 to 6.

Psychoanalytic treatment from an ego psychology perspective is similar to therapy from a drive perspective. The concepts we have noted under psychoanalysis proper would apply readily to psychoanalysis within an ego analytic framework. The most distinctive feature of ego analytically oriented treatment is its content: a greater focus on the client's conscious experience and adaptation to the world outside, on reality testing in the world, and on the effectiveness of his or her defense mechanisms. Also, in psychoanalytically oriented therapy (as opposed to psychoanalysis proper), the therapist is likely to be more active and to engage in more give-and-take as part of the focus on the client's adaptation to the outer world. When the client has a weak ego, the ego analytic therapist is more likely to take a supportive, reality-oriented, guiding approach to treatment.

OBJECT RELATIONS THEORY

Object relations theory developed out of a belief by many that something fundamental was missing from drive and ego psychology: a central emphasis on human relationships and the human need for relatedness. This cluster emerged into center stage after the development of ego psychology, around the middle of the 20th century. Actually, several theories fall under the object relations umbrella; for example, those referred to as interpersonal theory, the relational perspective, and attachment theory (Eagle, 2011; J. R. Greenberg & Mitchell, 1983; Mishne, 1993; Osofsky, 1995; Silverman, 1998; Sullivan, 1954). Harry Stack Sullivan is generally considered to be the founder of the interpersonal approach, one of the key departures from Freudian psychoanalysis.

Although viewpoints within the general object relations camp often seem to clash, the tie that binds them all and differentiates object relations theory from the other psychoanalytic theories is the proposition that people are fundamentally object or relationship seeking rather than drive or pleasure seeking. (Note that the word *object* in psychoanalysis is generally used as a substitute for the word *person*.) In this sense, all object relations theories posit an inherent tendency toward relatedness and relationships. This need is hardwired into us as a basic part of human nature (Eagle, 2011).

Although object relations theories are deeply concerned with human attachments and relationships, that is not their sole concern. Also crucial is the concept of internal representations. These representations are usually formed early in life and are of significant others (e.g., parents, siblings). Representations are far from exact replicas. They are based on how the other is experienced by the person, which is itself determined by many factors. Pine (1990) captured the essential role of such representations:

> The individual is seen in terms of an internal drama, derived from early childhood, that is carried around within memory (conscious or unconscious) and in which the individual enacts one or more or all of the roles. . . . These internal images, loosely based on

childhood experiences, also put their stamp on new experience, so that these in turn are assimilated to the old dramas rather than being experienced fully in their contemporary form. These internal dramas are understood to be formed out of experiences with the primary objects of childhood, but are not seen as veridical representations of those relationships. The object relation *as experienced* by the child is what is laid down in memory and repeated, and this experience is a function of the affect and wishes active in the child at the moment of the experience. . . . The same quietly pensive and inactive mother will be experienced as a depriver by the hungry child, but perhaps as comfortingly in tune by the child who is contentedly playing alone. Significant for the clinical relevance of the object relations psychology is the tendency to repeat these old dramas, a repetition propelled by the efforts after attachment or after mastery or both. (pp. 34–35)

The psychologically healthier person has greater ability to take current relations for what he or she is, rather than to experience and perceive the present to a great extent as a repetition of internal representations. Also, for the healthier person, the representations are more positive, nurturant, and supportive. With regard to the internal drama referred to by Pine (1990), stated simply, some dramas are healthier (more positive) than others (Gelso & Hayes, 1998).

What is psychoanalytic treatment like from an object relations perspective? How might such treatment differ from therapy derived from the other psychoanalytic clusters? As we have noted, the single most distinctive feature of object relations oriented treatment is the central focus on relationships in the client's life and on the client–therapist relationship. Although drive psychology is more oriented toward relationships than it is often given credit for (see Frank, 1998), to the object relations therapist, interpersonal relationships, internal representations of earlier relationships, and the therapeutic relationship are the pivotal points around which everything else revolves. Because the client is inherently object and relationship seeking, even when defending against this basic need, the therapist becomes a key person to be related to; and the person of the therapist matters a great deal. Everything the therapist does contributes to the relationship (including the transference), and in fact, the therapist along with the client shape that relationship. Even the therapist's neutrality contributes. In other words, the person of the therapist is seen as more important in object relations therapies than in other analytic approaches.

Among current object relations theorists, the client–therapist relationship is seen as having curative elements in itself (Eagle, 2011). The good therapeutic relationship allows the client to "rework internal object representations so that the images carried with the person are more constructive and more responsive to realities of current relationships, rather than distortions of them" (Gelso & Hayes, 1998, p. 176).

Although transference and countertransference are quite central, there is also a deep person-to-person relationship that coexists with transference that helps heal the client's emotional wounds.

PSYCHOANALYTIC SELF PSYCHOLOGY

This fourth and most recent of the four theory clusters developed out of the writings of Heinz Kohut (1971, 1977, 1984). Although this cluster is often considered an object relations approach, there is good reason to keep it in a separate but related category (see Eagle, 2011). As the term implies, *psychoanalytic self psychology* is concerned with development of the self; the word *narcissism* is often used liberally as a synonym for self. Rather than reflecting psychopathology as in other theories, narcissism is seen as a fundamental characteristic of all persons, a characteristic that may develop in healthy or unhealthy ways, depending on how the growing child is responded to by parents and other significant persons in his or her life.

In his original work, Kohut (1971) posited two lines of self or narcissistic development: that of the grandiose self and that of the omnipotent object. The first of these pertains to the young child's sense of greatness and need to show off his or her accomplishments. The proper mirroring of these needs by parents (e.g., genuinely appreciating the child's accomplishments) results in healthy maturation of the grandiose exhibitionistic self.

The second line of self development (the omnipotent object) reflects the child's need for all-powerful parent figures. This connection between the self and the all-powerful self–object provides the child with strength and protection. As the child gradually sees that the parent is imperfect, the child is able to internalize the strength that the parents had provided. Problems of the self occur if parents fail to provide sufficient empathic mirroring and all-powerful self–object experiences. As examples of self or narcissistic problems, the child may grow to feel empty inside, constantly crave attention, continually seek all-powerful figures to align and merge with, lack sustained emotional energy, or be unable to love others as others (rather than as extensions of the self).

Analytic therapy from a self psychology perspective follows from the developmental issues noted above. Growth occurs through the client's connection with an empathic therapist who mirrors the client's needs and who allows himself or herself to be idealized by the client. The client's experiences of the therapist as a good mirror and an all-powerful parent figure are referred to, respectively, as mirror transferences and idealizing transferences. Through understanding and interpretation, the therapist helps the client work through these transferences and the profound self-issues they reflect.

In comparison with therapists who use the other three approaches, the self psychologist is more likely to focus on empathically understanding the client or analysand. Empathy aids therapy because it allows the therapist to deeply understand the client's inner world and thus form more effective interpretations. It is also seen by self psychologists as curative in itself through its direct effects on the client (e.g., Wolf, 1991).

Psychoanalytic self psychologists are deeply concerned with being responsive to the client and seek to develop—more than the other analytic approaches—a climate of interested and attuned responsiveness (Doctors, 1996; MacIsaac, 1996; Wolf, 1991). The therapist aims to provide as much empathy, support, and guidance as is necessary to facilitate the process of "uncovering, illuminating, and transforming" the client's needs (Eagle, 2011; Lindon, 1994).

Common Elements Among Psychoanalytic Approaches

Now that we have reviewed the four basic theory clusters within psychoanalysis, we may ask the question "What elements are common among all psychoanalytic theories?" We briefly referred to such common elements when differentiating the words *psychoanalysis* and *psychodynamics*. Now we elaborate the eight ingredients that are characteristic of all psychoanalytic theories of the person and the treatment process. See Table 11.3 for a summary of these ingredients.

PSYCHIC DETERMINISM

Generally speaking, scientific theories in psychology are deterministic, which implies that behavior is caused or determined and may thus be explained in terms of those causes or determinants. Psychoanalytic theories are no different from other scientific theories in this sense. Where psychoanalytic theories do tend to differ, however, is in their emphasis on *intrapsychic* factors as determinants. Such an approach may be most readily contrasted to behavioristic theories (see Chapter 12), which are also deterministic but do not look inside the person's mind or psyche for causes. For the behaviorist, causes are to be found outside the person, in terms of the outside reinforcers and punishers of behavior. In psychoanalytic theories, in contrast, various factors (biological, social, familial) are seen as shaping the person's intrapsychic world early in life. Once this intrapsychic world or psyche is formed, it becomes a crucial determinant of behavior. The psyche contains the basic structures

TABLE 11.3

Common Elements of All Psychoanalytic Theories

Concept	Basic proposition
Psychic determinism	Human reactions are caused by intrapsychic factors.
Genetic–developmental hypothesis	Early childhood crucially determines personality, psychological health, and psychopathology.
	Development occurs in stages (psychosexual or psychosocial).
Unconscious processes	Unconscious processes are crucial determinants of behavior.
Defense mechanisms	Threatening internal impulses are repressed by unconscious defenses.
Repetition and transference	Humans tend to repeat in the present unresolved issues from the past.
	Insight into transference can greatly benefit the client.
Therapy relationship	The client–therapist relationship is of central importance, especially the working alliance and transference components of the relationship.
Treatment techniques	Interpretation is the key technique of insight-oriented therapy.
Client insight	Insight is the key internal mechanism that instigates and represents change in behavior.

in the form of id, ego, superego; basic drives, wishes, beliefs, conflicts, and needs; and differing levels of consciousness.

One derivative of the principle of psychic determinism that has great implications for psychoanalytic treatments is that because virtually all of the client's behaviors are caused by the interplay of these intrapsychic forces, all behavior in treatment is seen as meaningful. Everything the client does and says has purpose, meaning, and relevance to the therapist's understanding of and working with that client, and psychoanalytic practitioners place a premium on understanding their clients in terms of these intrapsychic determinants.

THE GENETIC–DEVELOPMENTAL HYPOTHESIS

A fundamental assumption of all psychoanalytic theories is that the past crucially determines the present and that, in order to understand the present inter- and intrapersonal functioning of the client as fully as possible, the therapist needs to examine the person's past. What is meant by the past is usually the person's childhood years, and the more classical analytic theories tend to focus on the earliest years as the key in personality development. For example, in analytic theories such as orthodox Freudian, object relations, and self psychological theories, the first 6–7 years of life are seen as crucial to the development of one's basic personality.

The genetic–developmental hypothesis not only implies that the client's childhood is crucial in personality formation and in health/ psychopathology but also incorporates the idea of developmental stages. Thus, Robbins (1989) noted that all contemporary psychoanalytic theories subscribe to stages of development. Just what defines these stages, however, may differ across the various analytic theories. Freudian theory, for example, posits what are called *psychosexual* stages: oral, anal, phallic, latency, and so forth. For a clear discussion of these stages, with implications for counseling interventions, the reader is referred to Patton and Meara's (1992) work. Erikson's theory, on the other hand, conceptualizes personality development in terms of a series of *psychosocial* stages (see Erikson, 1950, 1968).

The psychoanalytic implications of stage theory become clearer when we consider two additional concepts: *fixation* and *regression*. For example, as children pass through the various stages of development, whether psychosexual or psychosocial stages, their healthy development is facilitated by parents who gratify their psychological needs to an optimum extent. Too much gratification or, as is more often the case, too much deprivation of needs that become most pressing during given stages will result in fixation, regression, or both. Part of the child's psyche becomes stuck (fixated) at the stage in which he or she experienced too much frustration, or the psyche regresses to an earlier stage at which there was neither too much nor too little frustration. Once fixation or regression occurs during development, the remnants of this tend to show themselves in the individual's personality throughout development. The seeds of the neuroses and other psychological difficulties are to be found in the person's childhood experiences of frustration or overgratification of needs and in the resulting tendency to become fixated or to regress. (See Fenichel's 1945 psychoanalytic classic for a full discussion of fixation and regression.)

What are the implications of the genetic–developmental hypothesis for intervention? Just as the past determines the present and just as the seeds of human emotional problems are contained in childhood, so the most powerful and far-reaching treatments facilitate the in-depth exploration of childhood issues. Even more, the most powerful treatments, from the analytic perspective, aid the client in emotionally reliving and working through of the early experiences that form the core of his or her neurosis. (Note that we are not talking about a sterile intellectual inspection of the past but rather an emotional reliving of it in the present.) It is not that all psychoanalytically based treatments do, in fact, require this exploration and reliving. Many do not, especially for practical reasons (e.g., time constraints). And analytic practitioners generally would agree that effective treatment can be carried out in the absence of an in-depth examination of the past. Yet, psychoanalytic theories believe that such examination makes for the most effective intervention.

THE CENTRALITY OF THE UNCONSCIOUS

In essentially all psychoanalytic theories of the person, primacy is placed on forces outside of the person's conscious awareness that motivate behavior. In Freud's earlier theorizing, the conscious mind had only a relatively minor role in determining behavior. As we have noted, early Freudian psychology was an id psychology. With the development of ego psychology by Freud and others (e.g., Anna Freud, Heinz Hartmann), significantly more attention was given to conscious experience, because much of the ego involved the conscious mind. Consciousness continues to play a more important role in contemporary psychoanalytic thought than in early Freudian theory.

Be that as it may, unconscious factors are still seen as extremely important in personality development within all analytic theories, and the most effective interventions work, at least to an extent, to make the unconscious conscious. Underlying and unconscious beliefs, wishes, and needs are seen as being implicated in almost all pathological symptoms and behaviors. And from an analytic perspective, the most effective treatments must go beyond work on those symptoms or overt and maladaptive behavior. Interventions need to work with and through the unconscious, core conflicts underlying the symptoms. This value on making the unconscious conscious can be seen in Freud's famous dictum regarding the goals of analytic treatment: "Where there was id there shall be ego."

Most analytic practitioners, it should be stressed, would agree that treatment may still be effective without making the unconscious conscious or resolving core unconscious conflicts. Indeed, research conducted at the Menninger Clinic on several types of psychoanalytic interventions clearly supports the view that durable change can occur in the absence of such resolutions (Wallerstein, 1989). The general view, though, is that (a) unconscious processes are tremendously important in personality development and (b) the most effective treatments help clients, at least to some extent, become conscious of previously unconscious conflicts, beliefs, and so forth.

THE ROLE OF DEFENSES

The concept of defense is a key one in contemporary psychoanalytic theories (Eagle, 2011). As discussed by Brenner (1973) and further clarified in Patton and Meara (1992), a *defense* is any operation of the mind that aims to ward off anxiety or depression. Defenses are usually thought about in terms of the now well-known defense mechanisms; for example, repression, denial, rationalization, intellectualization, isolation, projection, displacement, and reaction formation. In essence, one may experience wishes, impulses, thoughts, beliefs, or affects that are seen as bad or potentially harmful to oneself. For example, they threaten loss of love from parental figures; abandonment; or punishment, either from one's conscience or external figures. These wishes (for example) are prevented from becoming conscious, and thus from causing anxiety or depression, by the use of defenses. The wishes are usually seen as coming from the id, and it is the ego that erects defenses against them to protect the individual from internal punishment (from the superego) or external harm.

Although defense mechanisms are often seen as operations of the ego, one can view them more broadly as any intrapsychic operations that reduce anxiety or other painful states. Thus, personality traits, attitudes, and perceptions could serve as defenses. For example, the character trait of extreme orderliness may serve as a defense against anxiety caused by the individual's impulses or wishes to be messy and out of control. Why such wishes would cause anxiety in the first place may be explained in terms of the specifics of the individual's interactions with parents, often during the anal stage, the psychosexual stage during which issues of control are primary.

In terms of treatment, psychoanalytic interventions seek to affect defenses. The aim may be to reduce or eliminate defenses or to help the client institute healthier defenses. Through working with and on the client's defenses, the treatment helps previously unconscious or subconscious reactions to become conscious and thus to be under the client's rational control. Working through defenses also frees up energy that had been expended unconsciously in maintaining these defenses, so that it may be used for healthier purposes. In effective therapy, the therapist is highly sensitive to the issue of the client's need for his or her defenses. Therapeutic interventions are paced such that defenses are worked on and through as the client is emotionally ready to give them up.

REPETITION AND TRANSFERENCE

From the time of Freud's early theorizing, psychoanalytic theorists have noted how the individual's past unresolved problems get repeated and lived out in present life and, in turn, how the individual's emotional problems in the present are tied to unresolved conflicts in the past. Freud's in-depth analysis of the compulsion to repeat, the repetition compulsion, was his attempt to struggle with and understand why the conflictual past is so often repeated in the present and why in fact people distort the present so that it becomes consistent with the past (see Gelso and Carter's 1985 discussion, pp. 169–173). This concept of repetition has become a deep and inherent part of contemporary as well as earlier psychoanalytic theory, and the repetition of unresolved conflicts tends to be viewed as a universal aspect of the human experience.

Examples of the kind of repetition we are referring to abound in clinical practice and in everyday life. The client who has experienced too much or too early loss (emotional or physical) in his or her early years with parents tends to carry a fear of being abandoned by others. He or she responds to friends and lovers as if they were similar to his or her parents, clinging to them for fear of being again abandoned and thus pushing others away. The client who constantly oscillates between defiance and excessive obedience with authority figures (bosses) at work is repeating in the present the early and unresolved issues with a dominant father, toward whom the person felt fearful when defiant and angry when obedient. The client who needs to attract and conquer women but loses interest after doing so is acting out the unresolved conflict originating in his relationship with mother and father much earlier in his life.

Psychoanalytically based interventions seek to help the client understand repetitions such as those above, and through this understanding the client is able to perceive the present more accurately or at least to better control the repetitions. It should be noted that analytic treatment would not seek to help the client understand and work through all such repetitions. Rather, the therapist or analyst will tend to focus on certain core issues and the repetitions stemming from them. Usually, the focus would be on the issue or issues that were causing the greatest suffering in the client's life.

A key point regarding analytic treatment and repetition is that the unresolved issues going back to earlier times in the client's life tend to get played out in the treatment hour itself, especially through the transferences that are developed toward the therapist/analyst. This fact gives the therapist a powerful tool for dealing with neurotic repetitions. That is, as sufficient material unfolds to allow for convincing interpretations, the therapist is able to point out to the client how he or she is distorting in the present real-life situation of the therapy and how these distortions (i.e., transferences) represent repetitions. Therapist and client can thus work together to seek understanding of the client's issues underlying the distortions.

THE ROLE OF THE CLIENT–THERAPIST RELATIONSHIP

In an early large-scale investigation of psychotherapy (Sloane, Staples, Cristol, Yorkston, & Whipple, 1975), the researchers noted that for the psychoanalytic therapists they studied, the client–therapist relationship and psychoanalytic treatment were almost synonymous. The client–therapist relationship is central to the process and outcome of treatment in virtually all contemporary psychoanalytic interventions (Eagle, 2011; Gelso & Hayes, 1998, McWilliams, 2011). In trying to understand the particular ways in which the relationship is central, the reader may find it useful to think back to Chapter 9, where components of the therapeutic relationship were discussed: the working alliance, the transference configuration, and the real relationship. Although all contemporary psychoanalytic approaches to treatment would agree that a sound working alliance is essential if analytic work is to be effective, the real hallmark of psychoanalytic interventions is attention to the transference relationship, including therapist countertransference. For what we have labeled "psychoanalysis proper," cultivation, interpretation, and working through of the transferences are the heart of treatment. For analytic interventions other than analysis proper, transference is still central in terms of its unfolding and interpretation in the work and/or its use as a vehicle to aid the therapist in understanding the client's dynamics. The real relationship, on the other hand, has not been an important part of psychoanalytic thinking, although because of conceptualizations such as Greenson's (1967), greater emphasis on the real relationship has appeared in recent years (Gelso, 2011).

INTERPRETATION AND OTHER TECHNIQUES

In the sense of verbal response modes as discussed in Chapter 8, the single technique that distinguishes psychoanalytic treatments from other therapies is *interpretation*. In his classic treatise on psychoanalysis, Greenson (1967) noted that interpretation is the ultimate and decisive instrument. Other techniques are seen as deviations from this baseline and are to be used only in exceptional circumstances. For example, when conducting psychoanalysis the analyst may on rare occasions offer direct guidance, but for him or her to do so, there would have to be a clear and pressing need (e.g., an indication that the analysand will do something that would have long-term and very negative consequences).

The aim of interpretations is to provide insight; that is, to help make conscious what was heretofore unconscious. The analyst allows the analysand's material to unfold during the hour or a series of hours and, when the time is right, offers an interpretation. Such interpretations seek to illuminate the hidden connections between aspects of the analysand's communications and/or uncover hidden causes. In fact, as Greenson (1967) clarified, rather than making a single interpretation, the analyst usually offers a series of partial interpretations over a period of sessions, each aimed at shedding light on particular dynamics. Great emphasis is placed on offering interpretations that are well timed, that constitute an effective dosage, and that are tactfully presented. Timing is perhaps the most complex of these issues. Interpretations are well timed if the client is ready to hear and work with them, and for this to be the case, sufficient material pertinent to that interpretation must have already come to light. Only then will there be enough emotional evidence to make the interpretation convincing to the client.

In psychoanalytic treatments other than psychoanalysis proper, interpretation is still a key technique, although greater latitude is permitted to the therapist. As one moves from analysis proper to analytically oriented therapy there is an increasing flexibility in technique. More active techniques, even those in the category of directives (see Chapter 8), may be used very carefully and with a well-thought-out rationale. (These comments would not apply so clearly to what we have termed "analytically informed" therapy because this form of therapy is eclectic regarding techniques.) An especially helpful discussion of the interpretive process within the context of psychological counseling was presented by Patton and Meara (1992). We should note that although interpretation continues to be seen as the most powerful and appropriate technique in psychoanalysis, there has been a trend in recent years toward permitting a broader range of techniques and seeing other techniques as useful (Eagle, 2011; Fosshage, 1997; Holinger, 1999; McWilliams, 2011).

THE IDEAL OF INSIGHT

Baker (1985) stated that broadly speaking, all forms of psychoanalytic treatment tend to share five basic psychotherapeutic goals. They include (a) a reduction in the intensity of irrational impulses and a corresponding increase in the mature management of instinctual striving; (b) an enhancement of the repertoire, maturity, effectiveness, and flexibility of defenses used by the individual; (c) the development and support of values, attitudes, and expectations that are based on an accurate assessment of reality and that facilitate effective adaption; (d) the development of capacity for mature intimacy and productive self-expression; and (e) a lessening of punitiveness of superego and perfectionism rooted in the demands and prohibitions of the conscience.

What is the mechanism or vehicle for the attainment of these goals? The central internal mechanism in psychoanalysis traditionally is called *insight* (Gelso & Hayes, 1998). Thus, it is through insight, attained during the treatment hour and beyond, that the client is enabled to move forward and attain the healthy goals noted by Baker (1985). Such insight fosters healthy goal attainment through essentially two means. First and foremost, through the self-awareness that comes with insight, the client experiences increased conscious control (Baker, 1985). When needs, impulses, and strivings are brought under conscious control, the client is better able to make logical choices and is less driven by self-destructive and nonproductive patterns of behavior. The second means through which insight facilitates attainment of healthy goals is called "objectification of the self." In essence, through insight, the client is better able to stand back and observe himself or herself and thus gain a clearer and more accurate perspective.

What precisely do we mean by insight? Patton and Meara (1992) defined *insight* as client and therapist production and understanding of factors within the client that contribute to his or her emotional difficulties. Within the treatment itself, client insight may pertain to any of a number of arenas: how present conflicts are related to past issues; the defenses being employed; the feelings and needs being hidden from awareness; how one's conflicts are being played out in current life; how these conflicts are being acted out in the transference relationship with the therapist, and so forth.

In psychoanalytic writing, two kinds of insight are often differentiated. *Intellectual insight* reflects an understanding of cause–effect relationships in one's life but lacks depth because it does not connect this understanding to one's feelings. It is more like observing the self from a distance, without the feelings that go along with what is being observed. *Emotional insight*, on the other hand, connects affect to intellect; the client is emotionally connected to his or her understanding. As the client comes to understand his or her issues, strong feelings are likely to surface. The simultaneous experience of self-understanding with these feelings is insight in the most powerful and curative sense. Because that kind of insight integrates intellectual understanding with emotional feelings, Gelso and Harbin (2007) suggested the term *integrative insight*.

We must note that not all treatments of a psychoanalytic nature strive for depth insight. The shorter, more focused treatments (e.g., less than 6 months), although often insight oriented, tend to promote more limited insight into one or a few central problem areas. In addition, even long-term work of an analytic nature may not strive for depth insight when the therapist believes that support is the client's crucial need. This may be especially the case with the more troubled client, whose fragile ego and/or degree of dysfunction dictates supportive strategies.

It should be noted that in recent years, the importance of insight has been vigorously challenged by some psychodynamic theorists, especially those within the relational perspective and those aligning with a postmodern philosophical stance. An examination of this perspective is beyond the scope of this book, but the interested reader is referred to Morris Eagle's thoughtful and thorough analysis (Eagle, 2011).

Brief Psychodynamic Therapy: An Approach for Counseling Psychologists

Of the many different psychoanalytic approaches to treatment, the ones that seem most relevant to the counseling psychologist are those that shorten the usually very long-term nature of psychoanalytic treatment. Such approaches gained popularity during the 1980s and 1990s for many reasons (Johnson & Gelso, 1980; Messer & Warren, 1995), and they have maintained and even deepened their appeal in recent years (Levenson, 2010). There is now a wide range of brief psychoanalytic and psychodynamic therapies (see comprehensive reviews by Crits-Christoph and Barber, 1991, and Messer and Warren, 1995). All of these approaches share some assumptions about brief analytic interventions: (a) clients who have long-standing psychological problems could be treated with dynamically based therapy in a much shorter time than had been previously thought, (b) basic principles of psychodynamic treatment could be applied to time-limited treatments, and (c) time-abbreviated therapies could effect lasting changes in the client's basic personality.

In past editions, we presented the time-limited psychotherapy of James Mann as a psychoanalytic model of brief treatment that was well suited to counseling psychologists. However, because there are now so many demonstrably effective psychodynamic approaches to brief psychotherapy, we have decided to provide the reader with key references to such approaches in this edition while also exploring the primary common ingredients of brief psychodynamic psychotherapy (BDT).

In her overview of the history of BDT, Levenson (2010) described four generations of such treatments. The first generation was involved in breaking the taboos against shortening lengthy psychoanalysis and developing more active interventions, with leaders such as Otto Rank, Sandor Ferenczi, and Franz Alexander and Thomas French. The second generation of BDT, roughly from 1960 to 1980, was led by clinicians such as James Mann, Peter Sifneos, David Malan, and Habib Davanloo. This generation sought to use psychoanalytic techniques such as interpretation in a way that would abbreviate treatment. The therapist actively interpreted defenses and how the past was being reenacted in the present. The approaches created by these theorists are still very relevant today. The third generation of BDTs, beginning in the mid-1980s, was the first group to empirically assess brief therapy, and this cluster of therapies moved from a focus on strictly intrapsychic events to interpersonal or relational models in which the basic importance of relationships, both in causing and in treating problems, was stressed. Examples are Strupp and Binder's (1984) time-limited dynamic psychotherapy and Luborsky's (1984) supportive–expressive psychotherapy. Finally, the fourth and current generation of BDTs have, according to Levenson, three distinguishing features: (a) they are integrative in the sense that they incorporate techniques and concepts from outside of psychoanalysis (e.g., cognitive–behavior therapy, research in developmental psychology); (b) they focus on the client's in-session affective experience as a crucial element of treatment; and (c) like most of their predecessors, they are strongly affected by powerful socioeconomic and political forces toward efficiency and pragmatism. Because this fourth-generation cluster of therapies is so integrative, thus breaking the taboo against theoretical and clinical purity, Levenson said that "they have become the mutts of the psychodynamic kennel" (p. 28). Examples of such treatments are McCullough Vaillant's (1997) short-term anxiety-regulating psychotherapy, Safran and Muran's (2000) brief relational therapy, Fosha's (2000) accelerated experiential dynamic therapy, and Levenson's version of Strupp and Binder's time-limited dynamic psychotherapy.

KEY INGREDIENTS OF BRIEF DYNAMIC THERAPIES

Are there fundamental ingredients that cut across most or all BDTs? A review of the large body of writing on BDTs suggests five key elements found in most or all treatments.

Treatment Abbreviation

Inherent to BDT is the abbreviation of what might otherwise be lengthy psychoanalytic therapy. The durations of the different BDT approaches vary, as does whether or not a strict limit is established. In addition, it is important to appreciate that one person's brief treatment is another person's long-term treatment. For example, although many BDTs seem to have around 25 sessions as an outer limit, at most university counseling centers, 25 sessions is long-term work! When looking at all major current approaches to BDT, it appears that the large majority of BDTs vary from about eight or 10 sessions to around 25 sessions, or 2 to 6 months of treatment. As implied, some treatments establish a hard and fast duration limit (e.g., the 12-session limit set by Mann, 1973), whereas others formulate a range, communicating to patients that treatment will likely last for 3 to 6 months. In these latter approaches, treatment is abbreviated by delimiting goals rather than strictly limiting duration of treatment. It is crucial that the duration limits, whether strict or flexible, be discussed with the client very early in therapy, in most cases in the first session.

Delineation of a Central Issue

Whether or not a duration limit is specified in advance, virtually all BDTs require that the therapist delineate very early in treatment a central issue to work on and then maintain the focus on that issue rather than any of the myriad other issues that may emerge in psychotherapy. This concept of a central, delimited problem to work on goes by many terms: *core conflictual relational theme* (Luborsky, 1984), *cyclical maladaptive pat-*

tern (Strupp & Binder, 1984), and *the central issue* (Mann, 1973). The fundamental point, though, is that the therapist delimits what appears to be the key dynamic problem and maintains focus on that.

It is also important that the client be brought into the process of delimiting a central issue. Thus, after exploration of the client's reasons for seeking treatment and the history as it informs those reasons, the therapist commonly tells the client what he or she sees as the central issue, asks the client if that sounds right, or asks the client what he or she sees as the central problem. The first author, for example, had conducted 12-session time-limited therapy at the University of Maryland's counseling center for a number of years. After holding an intake/assessment session (or more than one, in some cases), he customarily stated that

> we are all complex enough to be in therapy for many years, but we only have 12 sessions. Twelve sessions can help quite a bit, but if it is to be helpful, it will be important that we focus on a key issue rather than try to solve all your problems. Given what we have talked about today, can you tell me what you think your central issue is?

The author then worked with the client to further refine the statement. Overall, it was both surprising and heartening to hear how effectively clients were able to delineate their central issue!

Just what do we mean by a central issue? There are many ways to frame this, but we have found James Mann's (1991) views compelling. Mann suggested that therapists formulate the central issue as the client's present and chronically endured pain. Thus, the central issue is not the same as the presenting problem, or the immediate difficulty, but instead gets at that strand of the inner life and behavior that has been the source of pain for a long time. These are deep, underlying self-issues that have plagued the client's existence from early in his or her life. Furthermore, it is crucial that the central issue be framed in feeling terms and never in technical jargon. Witness the following examples, adapted from Mann (1991, pp. 32–33):

- To a 30-year-old Asian American woman who struggles with basic self-esteem issues: "You have always felt like you were not good enough and just not enough, and this feeling is with you all the time today. It seems to affect who you choose as friends and how you act with them."
- To a 36-year-old African American man who found himself in a conflictual situation in his field of work and became physically ill followed by depression: "You are a man of ability in your field and have done very well in it. Yet you feel and have always felt that there is something about you that makes you feel unwanted, even irrelevant."

▪ To a 55-year-old White female organizational consultant suffering from anxiety and depression: "Despite your achievements, you feel unsuccessful and empty inside unless others boost you up. This feeling has been with you from as long as you remember."

Again, once the central issue has been delineated, the BDT therapist continues to focus primarily on that and to avoids being pulled into other areas in the patient's life that will usually emerge. Therapist trainees often find it very difficult to learn to delineate a central issue and stick with it in brief work, and considerable clinical supervision is needed to help develop this advanced skill in both assessment and stating the central issue directly, in experience-near words rather than professional jargon.

Therapist Activity Level and Directiveness

Both research and theory in BDT indicate that therapists are more active when conducting these dynamically oriented brief treatments than in longer term therapy. What this translates into is a more active, focused exploration around the central issue, as well as more active interpretation of the links of the client's present issues to the past and to the therapeutic relationship, as well. Of course, the therapist cannot be too active, and activity should be balanced with patient listening. Still, given the time constraints, the therapist will often need to point to conflicts and issues more directly rather than wait for the client to arrive at understandings that may take many months or years. In addition, the therapist is more directive in, first, directing the sessions and, second, occasionally making suggestions both in the session and out of the session in the form of recommending homework.

As Levenson (2010) has clarified, fourth-generation BDTs tend to be less bound to strict psychoanalytic technique and are more likely to conduct what we term a psychoanalytically informed therapy (see earlier chapter discussion). This integration of psychoanalytic technique with techniques from other theories is aimed at moving the therapy along. Still, the BDT therapist must walk a fine line between being too passive, on the one hand, and moving too quickly, before the client is ready, on the other.

Termination

In comparison with longer term dynamic approaches, BDTs end quickly. It is important that they also end effectively. An important part of this effectiveness is the therapist's paying attention to ending and what it means for the client. Some BDTs focus on the feelings of loss that clients inevitably experience when brief treatments end and advocate an attention to this loss throughout the treatment. On the basis of both research and theory presented by Gelso and Woodhouse (2002), we suggest that when therapy is brief, time during at least one sixth of the sessions be devoted to termination issues. For example, if BDT has a 12-session duration limit, time during at least two sessions ought to be used to discuss the ending. Of course, this will vary greatly from client to client. A client who has many conflicts around separations and loss may need much more time spent on the ending of treatment, what it means, and what his or her feelings about the ending are about.

What occurs during the termination phase of BDTs? Gelso and Woodhouse (2002) recommended that as in all therapies, the therapist help the client look back on what they have explored and accomplished, look forward to the client's future and what he or she may need to work on, and say goodbye to one another. Evidence indicates that effective endings can help further the client's growth, whereas poorly handled endings can undo some of the accomplishments of the therapy.

Positive Expectancies and Attention to Strengths

The therapist who does BDT needs to believe in the power of brief interventions; that is, that important changes can be made in the brief period of time allotted to the treatment (Levenson, 2010; Messer & Warren, 1995). The empirical evidence certainly supports the attitude of optimism (Levenson, 2010). At the same time, it is equally important that the BDT therapist appreciate that one cannot usually make obviously far-reaching changes in personality and dynamics in brief work and accept the value that a brief piece of work that helps the client take a step or two forward in his or her growth can be tremendously valuable. If needed, more work in therapy can be done at a later time. Clients who have had BDT can and often do return for another stint in therapy at a later time. A number of years ago, Gelso and Johnson (1983) referred to this return to therapy as *time-interrupted therapy*. Finally, Levenson (2010) pointed out that BDTs pay closer attention to clients' psychological strengths than do other psychodynamic approaches. BDTs more likely assess for strengths and seek to build on them during the work than do psychoanalytic therapists in general. This attention to strengths in such approaches is very appealing to counseling psychologists.

The Psychodynamic Approach in Perspective

For many years, the influence of psychoanalysis on counseling psychology was marginal at most. However, during the past decade or so an increased amount of research and theory from the psychodynamic perspective has been produced by counseling psychologists. This research pertains especially to the therapeutic relationship (e.g., Gelso & Samstag, 2008; Mallinckrodt, 2010; Markin & Kivlighan, 2007). Within a psychoanalytic theory of the person, John Bowlby's attachment theory has probably garnered more attention than any other theory of development, and research has been done on how client and therapist attachment patterns affect and play out in the therapeutic relationship (Mallinckrodt, 2010; Mohr, Gelso, & Hill, 2005).

FROM STRANGE BEDFELLOWS TO COMPATIBLE PARTNERS

Historically, psychoanalysis and counseling psychology could be seen as strange bedfellows for several reasons. For one, the focus in psychoanalysis on lengthy treatment, often lasting many years, ran counter to counseling psychology's emphasis on brevity. Whereas counselors were interested in abbreviating interventions often to a few sessions, within psychoanalysis there appeared to be an ethos suggesting that only very extended treatments were valuable. A second source of incompatibility (historically) pertains to the tendency within psychoanalysis to focus on psychopathology, or underlying lack of health, in contrast to counseling psychology's focus on individuals' assets and strengths. In this area, the two fields actually seemed to move in opposite directions: Psychoanalysis paid attention to the deficits or pathology of even relatively healthy people, whereas counseling psychology focused its energies on the strengths of even very disturbed clients. Third, over the years psychoanalysis singled out internal, or intrapsychic, factors to explain human behavior, whereas counseling psychology placed its focus at once on the person (intrapsychic), the environment (external), and the person–environment interaction as the root causes of behavior.

Over the past 2 decades, however, this has changed, and the two fields have become more compatible. The differences noted above are still present, but they are much less extreme than in the past. In the early chapters of this book we have discussed changes in counseling psychology. Let us now look at some of the changes in psychoanalysis that have made it more compatible with the work of the counseling psychologist.

Perhaps most fundamental, drive psychology has diminished in popularity, and ego psychology, certain versions of object relations theory, and psychoanalytic self psychology have gained ascendency. This basic shift has resulted in several major changes in emphases. First, a greater stress has been placed on the environmental, cultural, and interpersonal factors that contribute to psychological health and maladaptive behavior. A literature has begun to develop within psychoanalysis on multicultural concerns in development and treatment. In addition, in current thinking Freud's psychosexual states (e.g., oral, anal, phallic) are often translated into psychosocial stages during which the maturing individual's experiences with significant others (rather than hidden sexual impulses) are seen as the key determinants of development. These interpersonal experiences are seen as influencing behavior throughout life, rather than only during childhood. Thus, in current analytic theories, psychological development is viewed as a lifelong process, although early childhood is still seen as highly significant in establishing a psychological blueprint for later development.

Ego analytic, self psychology, and object relations approaches pay significant attention to psychological health and the processes of normal development. In addition, they pay much attention to positive human strivings for creativity, mastery, and the capacity for love. The ego analysts, for example, view the ego's functions as going well beyond creating defenses against anxiety. The ego also serves to help people adapt to stress, to life situations, to interpersonal relations, and so forth. The emphasis is on coping and even mastery rather than simply defense.

One of the difficulties with orthodox Freudian theory that limited its relationship with counseling psychology was its inattention to female sexual development and portrayal of women as psychologically inferior (Gelso & Fassinger, 1992). Classical analytic concepts such as penis envy seem archaic and sexist and have been unsupportable scientifically. The more recent "psychologies," however, have been much less likely to conceptualize female development in such a manner and have demonstrated willingness to seriously study female sexual development. At the roots of this change has been the reformulation of the dynamics of the Oedipus complex, which they are more likely to see in psychosocial, rather than sexual, terms.

Finally, the movement during the past few decades toward abbreviating the length of analytic interventions has taken a huge step in making analytically based treatments more suited to counseling psychology, at least as practiced in places like university counseling centers and other community mental health agencies. Especially pertinent in this respect are the brief or time-limited therapies noted in the last section.

SCIENCE, RESEARCH, AND PSYCHOANALYSIS

One major area of incompatibility historically between psychoanalysis and counseling psychology has been their divergent viewpoints about scientific research. Psychology (including counseling psychology) has deeply invested in its self-definition as a science (as well as a field of practice), seeing controlled empirical research as a major way in which science is to be practiced.

Psychoanalysis has also viewed itself as a science (as well as a field of practice), but from Freud on it has taken a pessimistic stance toward the value of controlled empirical research. Stated in the extreme (which was all too frequently also the norm), the view has been that controlled research could not possibly help the field understand the great complexities of human personality and the psychoanalytic treatment situation. In fact, the only kind of research that could be revealing is that done by a psychoanalyst *during* psychoanalysis. In this view, the psychoanalyst's observations and inferences during the psychoanalytic treatment process constitute science and, further, are the only kind of research that can help us understand the human psyche and the psychoanalytic treatment situation.

Unfortunately, there are enormous scientific problems with such research: the psychoanalyst's biases, which are free to invade the process; the nearly total lack of controls and control groups; extremely global observations; and so forth. Such problems, however, either seemed to be unrecognized within psychoanalysis or were seen as problems that simply had to be lived with. Moreover, undergirding this viewpoint of science was belief that truth could be revealed through the expert psychoanalyst's observations of the analysand. These serve both as a sufficient vehicle for theory construction and as an adequate method for testing theory.

Historically, psychology was not without its contribution to the problem. Stated in the extreme (which was all too frequently the norm), the only road to truth and only viable form of good science in psychology was the controlled experiment, preferably done under laboratory conditions, whereby very specific forms of overt behavior could be studied with great precision. Anything else was seen as subjective and thus unscientific. Theory development counseling psychologists in the psychotherapy area was infrequent.

Fortunately, things have changed in recent years to bring psychoanalysis and psychology closer together in their views of science and research. Psychoanalysts and psychoanalytic psychologists have clearly become more accepting of controlled empirical research. Such research is evident in publication outlets such as *Psychoanalytic Psychology*, published by Division 39 (Psychoanalysis) of the American Psychological Association. Although it appears that psychoanalytic treatment as research is still the most prominent approach, there is growing recognition of the need for scientific controls and, in fact, the quantity of controlled research has been growing, especially in psychoanalysis within psychology (in contrast to psychoanalysis within medicine). At the same time that these changes in psychoanalysis have occurred, views of acceptable scientific methods in psychology in general have broadened. This is most clearly seen within counseling psychology in increased use of qualitative methods (see

Chapter 4). Counseling psychologists are becoming much more embracing of research that is qualitative in nature, focuses on the individual, is done in a field setting, and seeks to examine broad patterns of behavior and subjective meaning.

What has controlled research revealed about psychoanalytic interventions? In regard to psychoanalysis proper, it is extremely difficult to conduct controlled outcome research on this treatment, given its long-term nature. Thus, little research exists; the findings that do exist, however, are favorable. Psychoanalysis, from a variety of perspectives (e.g., object relations), does appear to have positive effects on analysands on a variety of dimensions, effecting, for example, deeper personality change (Shedler, 2010). The picture is equally positive for psychoanalytically oriented counseling or therapy. Controlled outcome studies indicate that clients who receive such treatments improve, on the whole, in a range of ways, including when the interventions are relatively brief and/or time limited (Town et al., 2012). Even more encouraging is the finding that the positive outcomes of dynamically based theories not only may be maintained after treatment but may continue to increase (Shedler, 2010). Undemonstrated is psychoanalytically oriented interventions' superiority to any other theoretical approach. All major approaches appear to be effective. Yet to be clarified is which approach is most effective for which clients under what conditions.

During the past decade, in addition, there has been a substantial increase in research on the process of such treatments. This process research examines how treatment unfolds from session to session, which factors within the client and the therapist relate to this unfolding, and which factors relate to client improvement during treatment. Although this research is too extensive to summarize here, it is worth noting that much of it has focused on aspects of the therapeutic relationship (e.g., working alliance, transference, countertransference) and analytic techniques such as interpretation (see reviews by Levy & Scala, 2012; Marmarosh, 2012).

Summary

The originator of psychoanalysis and all talking cures was Sigmund Freud. His genius, courage, and thoughtfulness were evident throughout his career and are part of his legacy to psychoanalysis as a science and as an approach to psychological treatment.

In getting a grasp on psychoanalysis, one may usefully distinguish between psychoanalysis as a *theory of the person* and as a *theory of the treatment situation*. In addition, there are different levels of psychoanalytic treatment; namely, psychoanalysis proper, psychoanalytic psycho-therapy, and psychoanalytically informed therapy. Psychoanalysis proper is the most long term and intensive of these. Psychoanalytically informed therapy makes use of psychoanalytic theories of the person to understand the client but uses whichever treatment techniques best fit the client and his or her situation.

It is a common error to view the theories of Freud and his follow-ers as the only psychoanalysis. Actually, at least four major clusters of theories, often referred to as "psychologies," may be placed under the broad umbrella of psychoanalysis: Freud's drive psychology, ego psy-chology, object relations theory, and psychoanalytic self psychology. Eight common ingredients of psychoanalysis as theory of the person and of the treatment situation are (a) psychic determinism, (b) the genetic–dynamic hypothesis, (c) the centrality of the unconscious, (d) the role of defenses, (e) repetition and transference, (f) the therapeutic relation-ship, (g) techniques in psychoanalysis, and (h) insight as the ideal out-come of psychoanalysis.

Of the many psychoanalytic approaches to therapy, those that may be most relevant to counseling psychology seek to abbreviate the often long-term nature of psychodynamic treatments. These briefer treat-ments, here termed BDTs, have certain features in common. They seek to abbreviate what may have been long-term treatments, either setting a strict duration limit or having a more flexible but still brief duration; focus on a central issue that is dynamically based; involve greater thera-pist activity and directiveness than do longer dynamic treatments; pay special attention to termination; and are practiced by therapists who are optimistic about the potential for change in a brief period, value the kind of delimited change that is possible in brief treatment, and pay close attention to clients' strengths and building on those strengths in therapy.

Over the years, psychoanalysis and counseling psychology, once strange bedfellows, have become potentially compatible partners. Research on psychoanalytic interventions strongly supports the efficacy of such treatments, although there is no evidence that psychoanalytic treatments are more or less effective than others. Research on the pro-cess of psychoanalytic treatments has increased substantially, and it has tended to focus on the main components of the therapeutic relationship and their effects, as well as on key treatment techniques.

The Cognitive–Behavioral Approach

12

T he theory cluster discussed in this chapter is actually a combination of two overlapping approaches to counseling: behavioral and cognitive. As will be seen, each approach relies heavily on the other in the modern practice of counseling, and the two perspectives are theoretically compatible. The cognitive and behavioral approaches, along with the currently popular combination of the two, called *cognitive–behavioral therapy*, have become a major force in the practice of counseling psychology. For example, studies of counseling psychologists (Bechtoldt, Norcross, Wyckoff, Pokrywa, & Campbell, 2001; J. A. Hayes, personal communication, February 8, 2013; Zook & Walton, 1989) indicate that well over half of the large samples of faculty and practitioners who were surveyed were heavily influenced by cognitive and behavioral approaches to counseling, as either their primary or secondary theoretical orientation. Although some of these studies were done several years ago, all indications are that the cognitive and behavioral approaches are just as influential in current practice.

http://dx.doi.org/10.1037/14378-012
Counseling Psychology, Third Edition, by C. J. Gelso, E. N. Williams, and B. R. Fretz

We begin this chapter by giving a brief historical review of the development of behavioral and cognitive approaches. This is followed by an examination of nine basic assumptions common to both. As these assumptions are reviewed, it will become clear that just as with the other major theory clusters, there is no single behavioral or cognitive approach that dominates the current counseling scene. Rather, the present-day practice of behavior therapy and its cognitive cousin is marked by diversity and heterogeneity, which many believe to be a sign of health and growth.

The third section of the chapter delves into specific methods and techniques of the two approaches, exploring their common ground as well as their distinctiveness. After behavioral procedures are reviewed, two primarily cognitive therapies are singled out and summarized. The chapter concludes with a perspective on behavioral and cognitive therapy in today's practice of counseling psychology.

A Historical Sketch

Of the two approaches reviewed in this chapter, the behavioral developed much earlier. Wilson (2011) noted that two historical events overshadow all others in the development of behavior therapy. The first is the rise of behaviorism—the theoretical and philosophical foundation of at least early behavioral treatments—at the beginning of the 20th century. In the United States, this movement's leading figure was John B. Watson. Watson's viewpoints were a reaction to the then-prevalent introspectionist theories, which proposed that to understand human behavior one must look inside. In contrast, Watson posited that such "mentalistic" approaches were unscientific and not very fruitful. Instead, psychology ought to be the study of overt behavior. Watson saw human behavior as fully caused by environmental factors (those outside the person) and believed that behavior could be fully understood as a result of learning. This extremist position implied that humans could learn to be anything, could learn and unlearn any and all behaviors: Virtually any human could be conditioned to become a doctor, a lawyer, a criminal, and so forth.

Watson's position, popular in the earlier part of the 20th century, has been widely rejected in recent years. The call of behaviorism has been taken up by more sophisticated versions, the primary example being B. F. Skinner's radical behaviorism. Although Skinner saw internal events, as well as one's biological makeup, as important, he promoted the view that human behavior is best understood and modified through the study of overt stimuli and behavior. Operant conditioning principles (i.e., principles of reinforcement and punishment), in the Skinnerian view, are the most powerful influences determining behavior. Skinner's views have had a deep impact on both behavior therapy and psychology in general.

The second historical event crucial to the development of behavior therapy was experimental research on the psychology of learning and the consequent discovery of principles of classical and instrumental conditioning. The most seminal event took place near the turn of the century: Russian physiologist Ivan Pavlov's experiments demonstrating classical conditioning principles, as revealed in the salivation responses of dogs. Around the same time in this country, E. L. Thorndike was developing his famous law of effect, in which he detailed how behavior was learned according to principles of reward and punishment. Similarly, in the late 1930s, Skinner elaborated the principles of instrumental learning with his work on operant conditioning.

These two interrelated events, the rise of behaviorism and the development of the experimental study of learning, however, did not quickly pave the way toward behavioral therapy. Applications of conditioning principles to clinical problems had in fact occurred early in the century; for example, in the 1920s, Mary Cover Jones demonstrated the use of conditioning in overcoming certain fears in children. Likewise, in the 1930s, O. Hobart Mowrer and E. Mowrer used conditioning procedures (which remain effective today) to treat bed-wetting problems in children. Yet, such behavioral treatments did not take hold in applied psychology, for, as Wilson (2011) noted, they were seen as simplistic by practicing psychologists. In the schism that developed, behavioral treatments were seen as part of academic–experimental psychology, whereas practitioners were most often psychodynamically oriented and concerned themselves with clients' unconscious issues and motivations.

ENTER BEHAVIOR THERAPY

It remained for Joseph Wolpe (1958) to present what may have been the single most important book in the development of behavior therapy, *Psychotherapy by Reciprocal Inhibition*. Until that time, counselors and therapists lacked a set of techniques that would allow them to apply conditioning principles to their work with clients. For several years, Wolpe, working in his clinic in South Africa, devised and applied behavioral techniques to his work with clients. Like psychoanalysts, Wolpe theorized that all neurotic problems were caused by anxiety. But here the similarity to psychoanalysis ended. Wolpe used a combination of classical conditioning theory and Clark Hull's then-popular learning theory as the basis for his work. Anxiety was learned through conditioned autonomic reactions, and Wolpe devised several techniques to extinguish this anxiety. The most widely cited and used of these was Wolpe's systematic desensitization, which continues to be a powerful behavioral treatment today (Murdock, 2013; Wilson, 2011). Moreover, Wolpe maintained that fully 90% of the adult neurotic patients he treated with his behavioral approaches improved markedly.

By the time Wolpe presented his groundbreaking work, another behavioral therapist, Hans J. Eysenck (1952), had published one of the most controversial papers in the history of counseling and therapy (see Chapter 8). Eysenck reviewed existing studies on the outcomes of psychoanalytic and eclectic psychotherapy with neurotic clients and found that their improvement rates were no better than those for neurotics receiving no formal therapy. About two thirds of both groups improved significantly. Although their validity was debated for years and was decisively refuted only after many years of research (Lambert & Bergin, 1994), the findings had a profound effect on the professionals training to be counselors and therapists in the 1950s and 1960s. When Eysenck's findings were viewed in light of Wolpe's claim of very high cure rates in behavioral therapies (and that of other behavior therapists, including Eysenck himself in the early 1960s), the popularity of these approaches increased dramatically.

After its healthy birth in the late 1950s and christening in 1959 by a parent figure (see Eysenck's 1959 statement), behavior therapy grew quickly in the 1960s. As Rimm and Cunningham (1985) noted, psychologists seeking an alternative to psychodynamic approaches found a convincing one in an amalgamation of Skinner's operant conditioning and Wolpe's classical conditioning. The 1960s began with the appearance of the first textbook in behavior therapy, Eysenck's (1960) *Behavior Therapy and the Neuroses*. In the mid-1960s, Ullmann and Krasner (1965) produced their famous *Case Studies in Behavior Modification*, which demonstrated the use of Skinnerian operant conditioning principles with a wide range of psychological problems. Within counseling psychology, the behavioral banner was carried most effectively by John D. Krumboltz and Carl E. Thoresen, and behavioral treatments developed so quickly that Krumboltz wrote about the "revolution in counseling" (Krumboltz, 1966).

The 1960s ended as significantly as they had begun. Albert Bandura (1969) published the tremendously influential *Principles of Behavior Modification*. Among the many important aspects of this book was the concept of *modeling*, or *imitation learning*. Bandura reasoned that classical and operant conditioning were insufficient to explain how people learn. (In trying to learn to fish or hunt, using the principles of operant conditioning, you would receive reinforcement only after appropriate responses—a highly inefficient way to learn.) People also learn by observing others, models so to speak, and then by being reinforced for performing whatever was modeled.

THE COGNITIVE REVOLUTION

As the behavior therapies mushroomed in the 1960s, another therapeutic approach was just beginning to take shape. The seeds of the cognitive approach were planted with the 1962 publication of Albert Ellis's famous *Reason and Emotion in Psychotherapy.* In it, Ellis argued that our feelings and behavior are caused by our cognitions; that is, what we think and say to ourselves. Ellis's rational-emotive therapy gained in popularity during the 1960s, but it was not until the 1970s, when it was joined by the cognitive revolution in psychology in general, that it flourished.

Behaviorism was the ruling force within psychology in general from the time of Watson through the 1960s. In the 1970s, however, theories about how cognitive processes determined behavior not only caught on but appeared to become the ruling force among theories of behavior. Within applied psychology, including cognitive psychology, this movement was evidenced in the increased popularity of Ellis's approach and, perhaps even more significant, in the incorporation of cognitive concepts within behavioral counseling approaches. Bandura (1969) was one of the original forces promoting such an integration of cognitive and behavioral theories. Behavior therapists continued to be concerned with overt behavior, but they also began to pay close attention to the interaction of thoughts, beliefs, values, and other internal and cognitive mechanisms and how these affect behavior. For example, one of the most important investigated concepts in recent years is Bandura's (1977, 1997) concept of self-efficacy (people's beliefs about what they are able to do). Self-efficacy has been found to influence a wide range of behaviors; for example, sports performance, social skills development, educational achievement, and career development (see Bandura, 1997; Lent, Brown, & Hackett, 1994).

As part of this cognitive revolution, a number of treatment theories were developed. Although some of these cognitively oriented theories were developed within and some outside the behavioral tradition, all are compatible with behavior therapy in that they make use of behavior therapy techniques and can be conceptualized in learning terms. Beck (1976), for example, developed a cognitive therapy that is best known for its treatment of depression but has much wider applications. His approach is basically cognitive but employs many behavioral methods. Meichenbaum (1977), on the other hand, developed a form of counseling that from the beginning sought to integrate cognitive and behavioral notions. These cognitive–behavioral approaches were each updated and further developed during the 1990s (e.g., Goldfried & Davison, 1994). To be sure, by the beginning of the 21st century, the integration of cognitive and behavioral approaches was remarkable (Beck & Weishaar, 2011). There are now few pure behavior or cognitive therapists.

Whereas behavior therapy discovered "mind" (cognition) in the 1970s, according to Wilson (2011), the 1980s and 1990s witnessed growth in the interest in feelings and emotions and how these states interact with cognitions and overt behavior. Also, within behavior therapy much greater attention was given to the biological bases of behavior, including "biobehavioral" interactions (O'Leary & Wilson, 1987). Throughout the 1990s the diversity of cognitive and behavioral approaches further expanded, so that at times it is difficult to distinguish these approaches from other theories (Wilson, 2011). There is no unifying theory behind these approaches (Prochaska & Norcross, 2010). Still, there currently are a number of distinguishing features, and these shall now be addressed.

Basic Approaches and Assumptions of Behavioral and Cognitive Treatments

Although counseling encompasses a wide range of cognitive and behavioral treatments, Wilson (2011) provided a useful framework in identifying three basic approaches. These three differ in the extent to which each focuses on overt behavior or cognitive processes. Before discussing the nine common assumptions of the behavioral and cognitive perspectives, we briefly summarize these three approaches.

THE THREE BASIC APPROACHES

First, *applied behavior analysis*, or radical behaviorism, focuses exclusively on overt behavior, with cognition seen as excess baggage unnecessary to the understanding and modification of behavior. Its leading spokesperson has been B. F. Skinner, and operant conditioning (see discussion later in this chapter) has been its main procedure.

Second, the *neobehavioristic mediational stimulus–response model* makes use of the learning theories of such eminent psychologists as Clark Hull, Neil Miller, and Kenneth Spence. Mediational models pay attention to what goes on inside the organism. Wolpe's systematic desensitization is a prime example of such a model. Systematic desensitization seeks to extinguish anxiety (an internal response). As part of this process, the client uses imagery (another internal event) to visualize scenes that arouse anxiety. Internal processes are considered to follow the same laws of learning as do overt behaviors.

The third approach within the behavioral and cognitive perspective, the *social cognitive model*, derives from the work of Albert Bandura (1977, 1986, 1997). Behavior is seen as dependent on the interaction of three systems: (a) external stimulus events, (b) external reinforcement, and (c) cognitive mediational processes.

According to the social–cognitive model, just how the environment affects behavior depends on how the person *perceives* and *interprets* these environmental events and stimuli, rather than on the environmental events themselves. These perceptions and interpretations are fundamentally cognitive. Also, reciprocity is a key concept in social–cognitive theory. For example, one's behavior itself affects how the environment (e.g., other persons) responds and the reinforcements that are received. These environmental reinforcements, in a reciprocal fashion, have a marked effect on behavior. The experiences that we have based on our behavior partly affect what and how we think, expect, and can do; these cognitive processes, in turn, alter behavior. Thus, there is a constant interaction among behavior, cognitive processes, and the environment.

In terms of counseling, the social–cognitive model has fueled the integration of cognitive and behavioral approaches. Behavior therapy, for example, has increasingly used the methods of cognitive therapy (see, e.g., discussions of Aaron T. Beck and Albert Ellis later in this chapter) and thus focuses on the internal cognitions that underlie human problems and conflicts. When cognitive and behavioral approaches are combined based on the social-cognitive model, the person is seen more as the fundamental agent of change, rather than as a passive recipient of stimuli, as in earlier models of behavioral treatment.

NINE BASIC ASSUMPTIONS

In discussing the nine basic assumptions of the behavioral and cognitive perspectives, we do not mean to imply that all these assumptions are uniformly held by all counselors. Indeed, there is so much diversity, even among the strictly behavioral approaches, that many critics have wondered if behavior therapy really exists. At the same time, there are many more differences between the cognitive–behavioral and psychoanalytic or humanistic clusters than there are within the cognitive and behavioral cluster. In discussing the nine assumptions, we shall try to make clear what differences exist within the behavioral and cognitive approaches as well as between them and the psychoanalytic and humanistic perspectives. For the reader's convenience, these nine assumptions are summarized in Exhibit 12.1. In the following sections, we discuss these in greater detail.

Attention to Overt Behavior and Processes Close to Overt Behavior

Virtually all behavioral and cognitive therapies pay close attention to overt behavior, although the radical behaviorists (applied behavior analysts) are

---

EXHIBIT 12.1

Nine Assumptions of Cognitive–Behavioral Approaches to Counseling

---

1. When intervening, it is best to attend to overt behavior or at least processes close to the overt level.
2. Behavior is learned and can thus be unlearned and relearned.
3. The most effective treatment integrates cognitive and behavioral approaches.
4. Although the past is important in shaping behavior, it is most effective to focus on the present when attempting to change behavior.
5. The client's presenting problem and symptoms should be the focus of treatment.
6. Counseling proceeds most effectively when clear and specific goals have been established for the treatment.
7. The cognitive–behavioral counselor most frequently and effectively works in an active, directive, and prescriptive manner.
8. The client–counselor relationship is important in cognitive–behavioral counseling, but it is not sufficient for constructive change.
9. The cognitive–behavioral counselor is an applied behavioral scientist who stays abreast of and applies research findings to practice.

---

the only ones who focus exclusively on such overt process (Spiegler & Guevremont, 2010). As one moves more toward the cognitive side of the continuum (with cognitive modification at the end point), the counselor's attention shifts toward more internal processes, such as cognitions. At the same time, the amount of attention given to the modification of overt behavior is high in all of these approaches, even the explicitly cognitive ones, and is greater than that for the other theory clusters, for example, psychoanalysis.

Even when behavior therapists' attention shifts away from overt behavior, they will be inclined to address processes nearer the surface (nearer overt behavior) than will, for example, psychoanalytic therapists. Thus, in Wolpe's systematic desensitization, counselors seek to work directly on conditioned anxiety (an internal state), and cognitive therapists may go even further and work with the cognitions presumed to cause that anxiety. Psychoanalysts, on the other hand, tend to posit a number of forces even further removed from overt processes. A phobia may be seen by the analyst as a defensive maneuver stemming from the unconscious need to restrict anxiety to one situation rather than a range of them. This anxiety, in turn, may be conceptualized as stemming from unconscious childhood fears of punishment, tied to the wish to do away with father and the accompanying wish to win over mother. Here we have an unconscious defense (the phobia itself) caused by even more deeply unconscious fears, in turn, caused by equally deep unconscious wishes! Contrast this to Wolpe's view, in which the phobic avoidance and internal anxiety are seen as conditioned reactions to the feared object or situation.

The Belief That Behavior, Including Cognitive Behavior, Is Learned and Can Be Unlearned and Relearned

Although nearly all theories of personality and therapy now assume that human functioning is a result of the interaction of biological predispositions and environmental factors, the behavioral and cognitive approaches focus more on how humans go about learning behavioral, emotional, and cognition reactions and patterns. Despite biologically based predispositions, behavior still tends to be learned, the three basic models of learning being instrumental learning, classical conditioning, and modeling. Further, it is not assumed that maladaptive behavior is acquired through processes that differ from those for adaptive (healthy) behavior. The two behavior types are acquired according to the same fundamental principles of learning. Just as behavior is learned according to certain principles, it can be unlearned and relearned. The same principles may be used to explain this unlearning and relearning process. Let us look briefly at each of the three forms or models of learning and the principles they include.

Instrumental Learning

In this form of learning, often referred to as *operant conditioning*, behavior is seen as controlled by its consequences. The consequence, *positive reinforcement*, is anything that increases the probability of a response. If a counselor, for example, responds favorably ("Great idea!") when her career-counseling client says he plans to gather more information, and if such a favorable response is followed by increased information seeking, we would call the counselor's response a positive reinforcer. Positive reinforcement is seen as the most powerful procedure through which behavior is learned.

In like fashion, *negative reinforcement* is anything that increases the probability of a response as a result of avoiding something negative that would have occurred had the escape behavior not been emitted. An example of this would be a client whose avoidance of public speaking is strengthened by the relief that comes from avoiding such activity. A similar concept, *punishment*, refers to the aversive consequences of a response and is often followed by a decrease in that response. For example, a student whose question is ridiculed by a professor would likely reduce his or her questioning. However, the use of an aversive stimulus often has undesirable side effects, so behavior therapists usually prefer a second kind of punishment: the removal of a positive reinforcement. An often-used example of this form of punishment is called *time out* (see Sundel & Sundel, 1999). Typically, the individual is taken to a place lacking the usual reinforcers (e.g., the misbehaving child is placed in a room holding no rewarding stimuli such as toys or TV).

The final concept to be mentioned under operant conditioning is *shaping* or *approximation*, whereby a person is rewarded for successively closer approximations of the desired behavior or end state. For example, a young child utters "mmmm" in the presence of his mother and is reinforced by her pleasurable response. Then the child is similarly reinforced for uttering "ma" and then only for the gold-star response "Ma, ma!"

Classical Conditioning

This form of learning was discovered by Pavlov in his experiments with dogs. When a stimulus that is neutral is paired with a stimulus that has an effect—the *unconditioned stimulus* (UCS); for example, food in the presence of hungry dogs—the associated *neutral stimulus* begins to elicit the same effects as the UCS. In other words, the bell becomes a *conditioned stimulus* (CS) in that, just like the food, it elicits salivation in the dog. The dog's response to the food, or UCS, is called an *unconditioned response* (UCR); its response to the bell, once the bell becomes a CS, is called a *conditioned response* (CR). Even after the dog is conditioned, its CR will *extinguish* if the CS is presented repeatedly without at least an occasional occurrence of the UCS. (This is similar to extinction of an operant response when reinforcement does not occur.)

In both classical and operant conditioning, two additional principles are crucial to the learning process. The first is *stimulus generalization*, the process through which a person generalizes to others from a specific conditioned or reinforced stimulus. For example, the male client who has learned to trust his mother may also tend to trust other women unless there is reason not to trust. The child who has learned to stay away from fast-moving cars also stays away from other fast-moving objects. However, both accurate and inaccurate generalizations are possible. Thus, a principle called *discrimination*—the learning of proper differentiations among stimuli—must work in tandem with stimulus generalization. The client who grew up with an emotionally destructive father needs to learn not to generalize her reactions to all males but to discriminate among males regarding their capacity for kindness versus destructiveness.

There are innumerable examples of how classical conditioning may operate in the learning and unlearning of complex behaviors, and the student is invited to suggest such examples as they may apply to the counseling situation. One point we add here is that classical conditioning is no longer seen as the simple pairing of a single US with a single CS. Rather, as Wilson (2011) noted, the correlations between entire classes of stimulus events can be learned. The examples above of generalizing from mother or father to other women or men demonstrate such global conditioning.

Modeling

The third form of learning, modeling, is also referred to as *imitative learning* and *vicarious learning*. Much human behavior is learned by observing others (the models), doing what they do, and emotionally experiencing and imitating what they are seen experiencing. Much of what we learn could not at all be learned or could be learned only very inefficiently without modeling.

Of the three forms of learning, modeling is the newest to be theorized about, and some psychologists continue to believe that modeling is only a subset of classical and operant conditioning. It is true that aspects of operant and classical conditioning are part of the modeling process. For example, to an important extent, modeling occurs because the behaviors exhibited by the model are reinforced, in the model, the learner, or both. Yet, modeling seems distinctive enough to warrant its separate discussion. Think about learning any complex skill (flying an airplane, driving a car, becoming an effective counselor) through only operant and classical conditioning (i.e., without modeling). It is hard to imagine learning with any degree of efficiency or, in some cases, even safety. At the same time, one can readily see how the other two forms of learning may be added to modeling. In learning to be a counselor, you observe others both directly (on film, in practice sessions) and through reading. But you also receive reinforcement of appropriate counseling reactions and approximations of them. Further, you may observe others as they experience emotional responses to certain client behaviors, and, through vicarious classical conditioning, you may experience the same reactions to such behaviors when you begin counseling.

Before concluding this discussion of the three forms of learning (instrumental learning, classical conditioning, and modeling), we should emphasize that even therapists who lean toward the cognitive side of the cognitive–behavioral continuum are also inclined to conceptualize their clients' problems, at least partly, in learning terms. Ellis (1995), for example, talked about how individuals are socially conditioned to perceive and cognize in certain ways. In like fashion, Beck and Weishaar (2011) endorsed social learning theory and the importance of reinforcement in an attempt to understand how cognitive processes develop, go awry, and can be changed.

The Melding of Behavioral and Cognitive Approaches in Practice

Although the primarily cognitive approaches to counseling (such as Ellis's rational–emotive therapy and Beck's cognitive therapy) were developed outside the mainstream of behavior therapy, behavioral and cognitive approaches tend to be melded in the present-day practice of counseling psychology, as we have noted, so that practitioners usually consider themselves cognitive–behavioral counselors rather than one or the other (e.g., Persons, 2008). This melding has occurred because (a) the cognitive theories have stated explicitly their use of behavioral techniques and their conceptualization of human behavior in learning terms and (b) the most popular behavior therapy theories consider internal constructs (e.g., cognition) crucial to development and change.

As implied in (b) in the preceding paragraph, the behavior therapy scene has encountered dramatic changes in recent years. Applied behavior analysis, a form of radical behaviorism focusing on only overt behavior, was a dominant force in American psychology (including applied psychology) in the not-so-distant past. In the 21st century, however, few radical behaviorists still practice. Social-cognitive theory, as represented by the work of Albert Bandura, its leading spokesman, now prevails. Internal constructs, such as expectancies, values, thoughts, and self-efficacy, are key concepts in this approach. Overt behavior still receives much attention in social-cognitive theory, but internal cognitive concepts are now studied in addition to external behavioral concepts. Thus, the modern behavioral counselor is almost always a cognitive–behavioral counselor (Persons, 2008).

The Predominance of the Present

All cognitive and behavioral approaches place a premium on the here and now. Problems reside in the present, and thus it is the present that requires attention in counseling. To be sure, virtually all agree that the past is important in shaping present cognitive and behavioral patterns. Thus, behavioral and cognitive therapists are interested in the client's learning history, and many gather careful assessment data about it. A counselor may, for example, solicit detailed information about the development of a client's social phobia because the sheer duration of this phobia over time is relevant to the methods of treatment. In the same way, the counselor examines past performance because this reveals important information about the client's assets.

Although the assessment of the client's learning or reinforcement history is seen as valuable, even crucial by some, treatment focuses on the present problem. Few, if any, behavioral-cognitive counselors seek in-depth insight into material buried in the client's past; such insight is not seen as especially helpful in resolving current problems. The past may be very interesting, but its revelations alone change nothing. Nevertheless, behavioral and cognitive counselors may indeed search for other kinds of insight; for example, insight into what clients are telling themselves or insight into the conditions under which certain fears occur. But these kinds of insight are very different from that sought in psychoanalytic or even humanistic treatments.

The emphasis on the here and now clearly separates the cognitive–behavioral counselor from the more classical psychoanalytic therapist. On the other hand, centeredness on the present in cognitive and behavioral approaches is similar to the orientation of humanistic counselors.

Taking the Presenting Problem Seriously

A client seeks counseling because of anxiety about speaking in class. The problem has become more pressing because this client has just been admitted to a graduate program in counseling where the class sizes are very small and emphasis is placed on class discussion. The behavioral counselor would make a careful assessment of this problem—its frequency, intensity, and duration—but would likely view the speaking problem as the key intervention issue. The cognitive therapist may go a step beyond and work on the cognitive beliefs that contribute to the speech anxiety, but this counselor will also stay very close to the presenting problem.

The psychoanalytic or humanistic counselor, on the other hand, may view the speaking problem as a symptom of other issues. These issues are generally seen as unconscious (by the analytic therapist) or outside awareness (by the humanist). What needs treatment is not the symptom but the "real" cause that underlies it. The primarily behavioral counselor, however (differing somewhat from the cognitive), will treat the symptom itself. In fact, behavioral counselors have traditionally adhered to the expression "The problem is the symptom, and the symptom is the problem."

The Importance of Specific, Clearly Defined Goals

Behavioral and cognitive counselors have a particular aversion to counseling goals that are stated in global—or what they consider "fuzzy"—terms. Thus, goals such as "self-actualization," "personality reorganization," and "resolution of core unconscious conflicts" have always been eschewed by such counselors. Even when clients seek counseling for such reasons and express their goals in these terms, the behavioral–cognitive counselor works hard to help them be clear and specific. In fact, the counselor usually tries to *operationalize* what constitutes client improvement; that is, he or she tries to state goals so that they are readily measurable and subject to public scrutiny.

An example of this might be seen in a female university student who seeks counseling because she vaguely senses that she does not think highly enough of herself. Careful assessment reveals that this client holds unattainable standards and harshly criticizes herself when she fails to meet these. The counselor also observes that she tends to denigrate herself verbally. The counselor and client enunciate three goals: The client is to make fewer self-deprecating remarks, reduce her self-critical cognitions, and develop more attainable standards. Such specific problems and goals can be worked on through a variety of behavioral and cognitive interventions. They can also be readily measured.

Similarly, with a client who seeks counseling for specific problems, goals are likewise stated as far as possible in terms of specific behavioral and emotional changes. For example, a male agoraphobic client who fears both enclosed spaces and the outdoors may have counseling goals expressed in terms of increasing the frequency of his visits to a local food store and lowering his anxiety level during such visits. The client suffering from depression might seek to smile more, make fewer self-blaming comments, engage in a greater number of positive activities, and achieve a more favorable score on an inventory of depression.

A Value on the Active, Directive, and Prescriptive Counselor Role

Behavioral and cognitive counselors work actively with their clients to develop the goals of counseling. As counseling proceeds, the counselor's stance (much more than for humanistic and psychoanalytic counselors) is active, directive, and prescriptive.

Thus, the counselor will actively guide the client during the interview; make suggestions about what the problem is and how it can best be resolved; suggest activities to be engaged in within the interview (e.g., role-playing, imagery, desensitization); and prescribe client behaviors outside the interview. Such outside activities, called homework, are a hallmark of the behavioral and cognitive approaches. Much in treatment is accomplished between sessions through what the client finds out about himself or herself, practices, and attempts as the result of homework assignments.

Cognitive and behavioral counselors are thus far from the stereotype of the silent analytic counselor. They do not hesitate to talk during the session. In return, the counselor expects parallel client activity. Wilson (2011) made clear that, more than any other form of treatment, behavior therapy involves asking a client to do something (e.g., practice relaxation, self-monitor daily caloric intake, confront anxiety-eliciting situations, refrain from carrying out compulsive rituals).

The Counselor–Client Relationship as Important but Not Sufficient

When behavior therapy first hit the applied psychology scene in the late 1950s and early 1960s, it presented itself as the superscientific alternative to treatment approaches such as client-centered therapy and, especially, psychoanalysis, both of which were portrayed as something less than scientific. In the behavior therapy literature, the apparent need for rigor was expressed in the use of impersonal language, such as "experimenter and subject" for "therapist and client." Given the premium placed on scientific objectivity, the role of the client–counselor relationship was downplayed as a "soft" factor. It was not a readily observable overt behavior and did not lend itself to rigorous scientific measurement.

As behavior therapy has matured and become more open to the study and treatment of internal processes and as notions of science and what is scientific have expanded and liberalized (see Chapter 4), the role of the counselor–client relationship has received much greater attention. Virtually all cognitive and behavioral counselors now express the belief that effective treatment is more than the application of a set of techniques and that the counselor–client relationship is highly important to the change process. At the same time, unlike Carl Rogers and devotees of the person-centered approach (see Chapter 13), cognitive and behavior therapists do not believe that a good relationship is in itself sufficient to bring about durable change. The relationship is important, rather, inasmuch as it sets the stage for the effective use of techniques.

As Persons (2008) explained, a good relationship in cognitive–behavioral therapy is necessary but not sufficient. The key word in a good relationship is *collaboration*, and the therapist's main job is to build collaboration so the client and therapist can work as an effective team to carry out the technical interventions of the therapy.

> The idea is that a warm, trusting, respectful, and collaborative relationship will help the patient accept the therapist's input, agree with the therapist on the goals and tasks of therapy, work hard to comply with the technical interventions of the treatment, and discuss with the therapist any problems that arise in the therapy. (Persons, 2008, p. 167)

The therapeutic relationship to the modern cognitive–behavioral therapist, according to Persons (2008) and others (e.g., Goldfried & Davila, 2005), is also useful as an assessment and intervention tool. Here, the therapist views the client's behaviors in the session as samples of behaviors that also occur outside the session. The occurrence of these behaviors in the session provides the therapist with a firsthand example of the client's difficulties and, thus, presents an opportunity to modify such behaviors right as they occur in the therapeutic relationship. The role of the relationship in behavior therapy as portrayed by Brady (1980) more than 3 decades ago is still fitting.

> The feelings of the therapist toward the patient are also important. If the therapist feels that the patient is not a desirable person or a decent human being or simply does not like the patient for whatever reasons, he may not succeed in concealing these attitudes toward the patient, and in general they will have a deleterious effect. (pp. 285–286)

The relationship in behavioral therapies is important but is not an end in itself. It provides leverage for the counselor to have the client follow the treatment regimen, and it makes the therapist a more effective reinforcer. Thus, the role of the relationship is very different from either psychoanalytic or humanistic interventions. (See Chapter 9 on the therapeutic relationship and Chapters 11 and 13 on psychoanalytic and humanistic counseling, respectively.)

The Value of Empirical Data and Scientific Methods

There have been so many changes in behavior therapy over the years that even its definition is no longer clear. This confusion has become especially salient as behavior therapy has incorporated cognitive theory and as cognitive therapy has adopted both behavioral techniques and learning theory as basic explanatory tools. At the same time, it is possible that the only assumption or element common to all so-called behavioral and cognitive approaches is the great value placed on careful empirical study of treatment techniques. Probably more than counselors of any other theoretical persuasion, the behavioral counselor sees himself or herself as an applied behavioral scientist who gathers scientific data and uses research findings about specific treatments in his or her counseling (Goldfried & Davison, 1994; Murdock, 2013).

Given the great emphasis on specificity in behavioral counseling, it is not surprising that practitioners value careful and precise investigations of specific treatment techniques for use with particular client populations. The aim is to build an armamentarium of specific techniques of scientifically demonstrated effectiveness for use with certain client problems in particular situations. It is also not surprising that the impetus for the "empirically validated treatments" and "empirically supported treatments" movement, as described in Chapter 8, has emerged from researchers aligned with cognitive–behavioral therapy. The value on rigorous scientific study of treatment techniques is a deep and inherent part of the cognitive–behavioral approach.

Methods and Procedures of Behavioral and Cognitive Approaches

In this section we summarize a variety of selected assessment and treatment procedures and methods often used by cognitive–behavioral therapists. We follow with presentation of two primarily cognitive theories of counseling, Ellis's behavior therapy and Beck's cognitive therapy. This section constitutes, however, only a skeletal summary of some frequently used methods and procedures. For a fuller presentation, the reader is referred to book-length discussions by Butler, Fennell, and Hackmann (2008); Dattilio and Freeman (2007); Goldfried and Davison (1994); Hofmann (2011); and Persons (2008). Excellent chapters on specific behavioral and cognitive approaches can be found in Murdock (2013) and Prochaska and Norcross (2010).

ASSESSMENT PROCEDURES

The first task of the cognitive–behavioral counselor is to develop a sense of rapport and trust with the client. The counselor listens sensitively and empathically as the client discusses the presenting problem. The emerging relationship allows the counselor to seek information from the client that might be too upsetting to divulge in the absence of such a bond. In the initial meeting or meetings, the therapist seeks full understanding of the client's presenting problem. Using his or her theory of behavior and counseling as a guide, the counselor elicits detailed information about the client's problem: how and when it developed; its duration, frequency, intensity, and severity; and the situations in which it occurs. The client's thoughts and feelings about the problem and how the client has tried to cope with it (including past attempts at counseling) are explored. The counselor looks carefully for the environmental and cognitive influences that may be maintaining the problem and that may be expressed through the client's thoughts, feelings, or behavior. (See, e.g., Persons' 2008 case formulation approach.)

As Wilson (2011) indicated, cognitive and behavioral counselors rarely ask "why" questions (e.g., "Why do you get anxious before exams?" or "Why do you feel stressed out at work?"). Such questions may be central to the assessment work of the psychoanalytic therapist, but cognitive and behavioral therapists strongly prefer *how, when, where,* and *what* questions as they seek to understand the factors maintaining the problem behavior and situation. The counselor relies heavily on the client's self-reports but does not necessarily take them at face value. Instead, the therapist looks for ways in which the client's reports seem inconsistent or otherwise inaccurate. Such inconsistencies are gently probed or silently noted for later use. In an effort to develop a picture of the problem and its context, the counselor helps the client to be as specific as possible, particularly in terms of how, when, and where the problem is manifested.

The counselor uses a variety of techniques in addition to verbal interaction as aids in assessment. Among the most prominent are role-playing, guided imagery, self-monitoring, behavioral observation, and psychological testing. In using *role-playing*, the counselor may ask the client to role-play a particular interpersonal situation that seems to be troubling. The counselor can take the role of the person with whom the client is having difficulty or may engage in role reversal, whereby the client plays the other person while the therapist plays the client, or both of these activities. Such role-playing provides the counselor with some preliminary behavioral observations of the client and also helps the client see more clearly what motivates the interaction with the person with whom he or she has a problem.

In *guided imagery* the counselor asks the client to create a visual image of the problem situation and then verbalize this image to the counselor. This enables both counselor and client to get a step closer (more than simple verbal explanation) to what actually goes on in the problem situation and to what the client thinks and feels in that situation. Self-monitoring entails the client's keeping a careful daily record of events or reactions that indicate the main problem. For example, the client with anxiety problems may keep a record of situations in which she or he feels anxious, the amount of anxiety experienced, and what triggered the anxiety. As a result, both client and counselor should develop a clearer, more detailed picture of the problem and what is maintaining it.

Unlike the other techniques, *behavioral observations* are ordinarily used by people other than the client (e.g., parents, teachers, hospital personnel) and are created in the client's natural environment (school, home, hospital), where the problem is occurring. The behavioral counselor shows these people how to observe and record the client's behavior objectively. Most often, this procedure is used from an operant conditioning perspective. The observer learns to observe the client's behavior—for example, in the classroom or at home—and note the reinforcers and punishers that may influence the behavior. The observers can then be taught how to modify their own behavior so as to help change the client's behavior. For example, parents often learn about reinforcement procedures and how their own behavior may reinforce the problematic behaviors of their child. The parents can then be taught how to use reinforcements to produce the desired behaviors.

Psychological tests, questionnaires, and *checklists* are used by behavioral and cognitive counselors but only when these measure specific qualities directly relevant to the client's problem situation or behavior. General psychodiagnostic tests, such as the Minnesota Multiphasic Personality Inventory or the varieties of projective devices, are clearly not favored. Instead, checklists and questionnaires that assess, for example, fears, anxiety, depression, or assertiveness may be quite useful in obtaining a preliminary picture of the level of severity of the client's problem and determining how the degree of this severity changes across the course of treatment.

As a final note, it must be added that assessment does not cease after the presenting problem has been fully studied. The behavioral–cognitive counselor continues assessment throughout treatment. In such counseling, in fact, assessment is an integral part of the ongoing treatment.

BEHAVIORAL AND COGNITIVE TREATMENT PROCEDURES

More than counselors of any other theoretical orientation, the behavioral-cognitive counselor attempts to match specific treatment techniques to particular client problems. Techniques are selected on the basis of all aspects of the client's problem, the research literature on the effectiveness of the techniques, and the counselor's own clinical judgment about what will work best with the client. The following text presents a sample of behavior therapy techniques (also see Exhibit 12.2). As we present these, it is important to keep in mind that in actual treatment, various methods are usually combined and that both cognitive and behavioral procedures are frequently used with the same case.

Operant Conditioning

Operant conditioning is both a set of principles that explain how behavior is learned and a technique for modifying behavior. The use of operant conditioning techniques may occur in the counselor's office as well as in the environment in which the client's problems occur. Let us look at within-session operant conditioning first.

EXHIBIT 12.2

Some of the Many Techniques of Cognitive–Behavioral Therapy

1. Operant conditioning
2. Positive reinforcement
3. Shaping
4. Desensitization
5. Systematic desensitization
6. In vivo desensitization
7. Cognitive restructuring
8. Assertiveness and social skills training
9. Behavior rehearsal
10. Flooding
11. Participant modeling
12. Self-control procedures
13. Aversive conditioning

If the client feels a sense of positive connection to the counselor or at least values the counselor's expertise, he or she will be receptive to the counselor's views and reactions. The counselor in this instance can be a potent reinforcer of behavior change. The behavioral counselor decides which behaviors are to be changed and, if within-office reinforcement techniques seem to fit the situation, the counselor will apply them, usually verbally. For example, in working with a client trying to resolve some career problems and move in a more suitable career direction, the counselor may believe that it is highly important for the client to seek occupational information. If the counselor senses that the client will tend to resist such activity, he or she will verbally reinforce (e.g., "Great idea!" or "That sounds like a real step in the right direction") any hints on the client's part that such information would be helpful. Then, as the work proceeds, the counselor positively reinforces the client's expressed willingness to seek information. Positive reinforcement is thus combined with a shaping procedure. Such methods have been found to be highly effective in promoting occupational information seeking.

In this example, positive reinforcement is used to increase a response. What about operant conditioning procedures to extinguish a behavior? Using an out-of-session example, suppose a mother, Ms. Weary, seeks counseling because her 3-year-old child, Jimmy, has recently been having frightful, disruptive temper tantrums in which he holds his breath and throws his toys. The counselor carefully interviews Ms. Weary about the conditions under which the problem occurs and finds that they only occur in the presence of the mother, who has just begun a new job that reduces her time at home with Jimmy. The counselor decides to visit the Weary household to directly observe the situation. It becomes apparent that Ms. Weary picks up her son warmly and verbally expresses affection whenever he grows angry. Jimmy is thus getting reinforced for angry behavior. Further discussion reveals that Ms. Weary feels guilty about being away from home, although her new job is stimulating and a clear step forward for her vocationally. The counselor works with Ms. Weary to help her to stop reinforcing Jimmy's angry behavior and ignore it instead. Ms. Weary is to leave the room whenever the tantrums begin. The counselor also suggests that she provide Jimmy with lots of physical and verbal affection when he behaves well. The father, too, who often would get preoccupied with work issues while spending time with the child, is shown how to be more reinforcing when the child is well behaved. In a short time, Ms. Weary, who has been keeping careful records as part of the counseling, reports that Jimmy has essentially stopped his tantrums, is getting lots of loving from both parents, and seems happier generally.

Desensitization

Systematic desensitization (SD) is one of the most thoroughly studied behavioral interventions for extinguishing anxiety and other fear-based responses; it has been found effective for a wide range of anxiety-related problems (Goldfried & Davison, 1994). Growing out of studies that sought to remove conditioned fears in animals, it was adapted for use with humans by Joseph Wolpe (1958). The idea is that when anxiety is systematically paired with an incompatible state, the anxiety will disappear as a result of counterconditioning or will be inhibited, according to the principle of *reciprocal inhibition.* The response used most frequently to inhibit anxiety is relaxation—specifically, deep-muscle relaxation.

SD comprises four steps (Deffenbacher & Suinn, 1988). The first step is to give the client a rationale for the procedure. This should be stated in a nontechnical manner and should impart the concept that fears are learned and thus can be unlearned through desensitization. The second step is relaxation training. The client is usually taught progressive deep-muscle relaxation, a technique Wolpe adapted from Jacobson (1938). The client is also asked to remember a specific experience in which she or he felt deeply relaxed, and the counselor helps the client construct a scene around this. In the third step, the counselor and client work together to construct a visual hierarchy of anxiety-arousing scenes, ranging from non-anxiety-arousing to extremely upsetting, all related to the specific problem. For example, if the client is seeking counseling because of exam anxiety, the most upsetting scene may picture that student sitting in a classroom about to receive the final exam from the teacher. Visual hierarchies typically include eight to 15 scenes, none of which should elicit more anxiety than those next to it. The counselor usually tries to space scenes evenly according to their anxiety-arousing potential.

The final step in SD is desensitization proper, in which the scenes in the hierarchy are, step by step, paired with relaxation. Typically, after the client is deeply relaxed, the counselor asks him or her to visualize the least anxiety-arousing scene in the hierarchy. If the client feels any significant anxiety when visualizing this scene, he or she is to raise a finger. If this happens, the client is instructed to visualize the highly relaxing experience on which they initially worked. If no anxiety is felt after two more trials of the first scene, the counselor asks the client to visualize the next one in the hierarchy. If anxiety is experienced, the counselor drops back to the scene and repeats the visualization of that scene two more times. This process continues until the client is able to visualize all scenes in the hierarchy without experiencing anxiety. Termination of counseling occurs when the client is able to experience success dealing with the actual feared situation. For example, the test-anxious client is able to take exams with relative ease; the person with a phobia is able to perform activities that he or she was phobic about earlier.

One variant of SD is *in vivo desensitization*. The procedure is the same except that the hierarchy is presented in real life. The housebound agoraphobic client may have a hierarchy that begins with stepping outside the house and ends with shopping at the local grocery store. The counselor usually accompanies the client in moving through the hierarchy. If the client becomes anxious, she or he is assisted in relaxation behavior. In vivo desensitization can be a powerful procedure and is recommended whenever it is viable (see Beidel & Turner, 1998; Goldfried & Davison, 1994). To be effective, however, the counselor must have full control over the implementation of the hierarchy. This is not always feasible, for example, when anxiety is tied to public speaking, social interaction, or sexual situations.

It should be noted that the progressive relaxation component of SD is often used as a treatment in itself and can be an effective procedure for coping with anxiety and stress. Another variant of SD, called *covert sensitization*, is used to extinguish undesirable behaviors such as alcoholism and certain sexual disorders (e.g., exhibitionism). Here, the client is asked to imagine aversive consequences in response to the undesired acts. An alcoholic might be asked to imagine nausea at the thought of a drink, an exhibitionist to imagine being handcuffed in public by the police. A hierarchy of scenes that depict the unwanted behaviors is developed, and each scene is presented in a step-by-step fashion until the client is able to control the problem behavior.

Exposure

In certain ways, exposure therapies are the opposite of SD. SD seeks to *minimize* anxiety by pairing small doses of it with a contradictory state (e.g., deep relaxation). Exposure *maximizes* anxiety. The agoraphobic client might be asked to imagine being away from home, in a crowded supermarket, without having first gone through a hierarchy of scenes. The anxiety here will be quite high, but it usually dissipates if the client stays with the scene long enough. Thus, through repeated exposure to high-anxiety scenes, in the absence of any actual harm, anxiety becomes extinguished.

A form of exposure that is frequently used is *in vivo exposure*, which has been found to be effective with agoraphobics. Again, using a trip to the supermarket as our example, the client might first approach the task in a graduated fashion (as in vivo desensitization). Then, once the client is able to approach the supermarket, the counselor may go with the client to the market, urging him or her to stay there regardless of the anxiety, until the anxiety subsides. The principle, again, is that anxiety will disappear if not reinforced. The client sees that he or she is not endangered, that nothing bad happens, so the anxiety eventually dissipates.

Exposure therapy has been especially studied for treating anxiety and trauma disorder. Several extensive research reviews have strongly supported its effectiveness for a range of anxiety-based problems (Prochaska & Norcross, 2010).

Assertiveness and Social Skills Training

Counselors often work with clients who are inhibited in expressing their emotions and who do not stand up for themselves. Such people lack assertiveness, a skill that behavioral and cognitive counselors have worked with considerably over the years. The major strategy used within assertiveness training is called *behavior rehearsal*. Here the counselor helps the client specify situations in which he or she is unassertive. The counselor then plays the role of the person toward whom the client wants to be more assertive while the client role-plays assertiveness. The client pays attention to his or her feelings during and after the role-playing; the counselor observes specific strengths and weaknesses, positively reinforcing positive behavior and nonjudgmentally noting the negative. In addition, the therapist often models effective assertive behaviors for the client. Therapist modeling is especially effective if the client lacks knowledge about effective assertiveness; it also gets the client in touch with what it feels like to be the target of the modeled response.

Following counselor modeling, the client imitates the modeled responses, and the counselor verbally reinforces improvements (*shaping*), attending to both verbal and nonverbal client behavior. If the client is working on expressing negative emotion, it is best to have the client begin with a mild response. Doing so aims at reducing the chances that the target person will be "backed into a corner" and forced to respond defensively (Rimm & Cunningham, 1985). In case the minimal responses are not effective, assertiveness training helps the client learn how to escalate assertions. Also, it may be best for the counselor to fade out both modeling and reinforcement during treatment because modeling does not occur in the real world and the client must learn to be *self-reinforcing*. This fading out is thought to lead the client to greater self-directed mastery and persistence in his or her natural environment (Rimm & Masters, 1979).

Participant Modeling

In discussing assertiveness training, and at other points, we have commented on the use of modeling in counseling. The term *participant modeling* (or equivalents such as *contact desensitization* or *demonstration plus participation*) is often used to describe a specific set of procedures that involve the counselor's modeling through demonstration, followed by the client's imitation of the modeled responses. These procedures are carried out in a graduated fashion. Participant modeling has been found to be effective for a wide range of specific fears and anxieties and is currently being used a great deal to treat social phobias (e.g., agoraphobia).

Consider the steps that might be taken with participant modeling in treating the client suffering from agoraphobia. The goal of treatment might be for the client to be able to walk comfortably to the local food market. The first step would be to teach the person relaxation techniques, with a focus on deep breathing. The step would be for the counselor to walk out onto the client's sidewalk, in the client's full view, and then do some deep breathing. Then the counselor and client would walk together out onto the sidewalk, with the counselor offering instruction and support. Finally, the client would perform this task alone, using the skills she or has just learned. The same procedure (counselor first, the client and counselor together, and finally client alone), is used for each step, with the final step being the goal: the client's comfortably walking to the local market. At each step, the counselor should positively reinforce the client's behavior with verbal praise.

Self-Control Procedures

Self-control methods grew out of behavior therapists' desire to help clients control their own destiny rather than be passive recipients of conditioning procedures. Self-control methods emphasize the client as an active agent who can cope and exert effective control in problem situations. These methods are most appropriate in situations where natural reinforcements are long term and no short-term reinforcements are available for the desired behavior. An example is academic performance, wherein effective study behavior is usually not reinforced soon after it occurs. Rather, the student must wait until the next exam or even the end of a semester for reinforcement. Such delays make it extremely difficult to learn new desired behaviors or extinguish old, undesirable ones. Self-control methods provide short-term reinforcements until the longer term reinforcers become available.

Clients who use self-control methods serve as their own therapists in administering their own rewards and punishments. Because of this, therapists often give such clients instruction in behavior modification, with particular emphasis on operant conditioning principles. Thus, clients are taught basic learning principles, the importance of reinforcement being contingent on given behaviors, and the idea of stimulus control.

Behavior therapists now use a range of self-control procedures (Persons, 2008; Wilson, 2011). Kanfer (1977) devised a multistage procedure for helping clients enhance their self-control, a procedure that has been particularly effective in the treatment of obesity (Rimm & Cunningham, 1985). The first stage entails the client's carefully monitoring his or her behavior; for example, the frequency of eating (how much, how fast, how often) and the surrounding situations (when watching TV, late at night). This gives the counselor and client a baseline for the problem behavior. The second stage entails establishing goals. It is essential that these be specific, reinforceable, and short term. Thus, the counselor might work with the client to specify daily caloric intake. When goals are short term, the client is able to experience more reinforcements; when goals are specific, the client has a clearer sense of what is needed.

The third step is the actual treatment in which the self-control methods are applied. Rimm and Masters (1979) detailed the following procedures for the treatment of obesity: (a) removing undesirable foods from the house, particularly high-calorie foods that do not require preparation; (b) changing eating behavior, for example, returning eating utensils to the table between bites, taking short breaks during the meal; (c) restricting eating to certain places, called *stimulus narrowing*; (d) having the client eat in situations where he or she does not typically overeat; (e) reinforcing improvements in eating behavior; and (f) encouraging competing responses, for example, taking a walk while delaying eating.

Contingency Contracting

Contingency contracting, which relies on operant conditioning principles, is a form of behavioral management in which the rewards and punishments for desired and undesired behaviors are established in advance, frequently by a *written contract* with the client (Rimm & Masters, 1979). The first step is assessment. The counselor and client work together to specify the behaviors that need to be modified. They may work toward increasing the frequency of desired behaviors that occur too seldom or decreasing undesirable behaviors undertaken too often. During assessment, counselor and client decide on who will dispense the rewards and punishments (e.g., client, parent, teacher) and what these will be. Rewards might be money, praise, being allowed to attend movies—anything that the client enjoys. Punishments usually entail withholding the preferred rewards. During the assessment, it is helpful to get a baseline for the target behaviors. Note that such monitoring and recording of the behaviors is also useful during treatment, to get a clear picture of change. Also, seeing change is in itself reinforcing.

Treatment involves simply enforcing the contingencies. Again, this can be done by the client (a self-control method) or by someone else. The reinforcers should be applied each time the target behavior is manifested. If this is not possible, "points" can be given for each performance of the target behavior. After reaching a specified amount, the points would convert into a reward or punishment. A good example of contingency contracting as a self-control procedure might be a college student who seeks help because of poor study behaviors. The counselor and client would work together to specify the desired study behaviors to be rewarded and the undesirable ones to be punished. Care would be taken to allow for rewards for effective short-term steps (shaping); for example, if the student typically studies only a half hour per day, points or rewards could be given for studying 1 hour per day at first, with study time gradually increasing. With the counselor's guidance, the student would decide on the reinforcers. These could include self-praise, often an effective reinforcer. Note that the treatment occurs between sessions. During the sessions themselves, the counselor and client review progress and adjust the contract if necessary. The counselor could also provide verbal reinforcement for desired behavior.

Cognitive Restructuring

On a cognitive–behavioral spectrum, the methods and procedures discussed so far would be found on the behavioral end. Cognitive restructuring, on the other hand, is the one overarching method that would be found on the cognitive end. The assumption underlying this method is that, in one way or another, what clients say to themselves and how they say it (their self-talk or cognitions) determine or shape their problems. Thus, cognitive restructuring entails helping clients change their cognitions.

Cognitive restructuring is a broad term that includes identifying and changing anxiety-causing cognitions. As detailed by Meichenbaum and Deffenbacher (1988) these cognitions may be in the form of cognitive *events*, cognitive *processes*, cognitive *structures*, or all these. Cognitive events are what people say to themselves and the images they have that they are aware of and can report. Cognitive processes operate at an automatic and "unconscious" level and include the way people process information: how they appraise events, selectively attend to and remember events, and incorporate information consistent with their beliefs. Cognitive structures are even broader, constituting the individual's assumptions and beliefs about the self and the world in relation to the self. There is clearly much overlap in the three concepts, and it may be useful to think of them as existing on a continuum ranging from specific thoughts to global assumptions. The latter have a pervasive and general effect on how people behave and feel.

A wide variety of cognitive approaches now exists (Murdock, 2013), but as Meichenbaum and Deffenbacher (1988) noted, all cognitive restructuring procedures include the following: (a) evaluating how valid and viable are the client's thoughts and beliefs; (b) assessing what clients expect, what they tend to predict about their behavior and others' responses to them; (c) exploring what might be a range of causes for clients' behavior and others' reactions; (d) training clients to make more effective attributions about these causes; and (e) altering absolutistic, catastrophic thinking styles (discussed below under rational–emotive therapy).

Two Primarily Cognitive Approaches to Counseling

In the following, we summarize the two most prominent cognitive approaches to therapy, Ellis's rational emotive behavior therapy and Beck's cognitive therapy. We single out these because each is a theory of therapy in and of itself, is well known, and has substantial research support. Both are cognitive–behavioral therapies, which rely on principles of learning and use behavioral methods in addition to focusing on cognitive change. But, at the core, the two approaches are more cognitive than behavioral because they posit that cognitions are the primary motivators of behavior and emotions, and that changing cognitions provides the most effective treatment.

In addition to consulting the two approaches discussed below, the interested student may consult Goldfried's (1988) rational restructuring, a method that provides more structure than Ellis's rational emotive behavior therapy and a greater focus on personal coping skills. Also, Meichenbaum's stress inoculation training (see Meichenbaum & Deffenbacher, 1988) is substantially cognitive and has proved effective for many anxiety-related problems (Prochaska & Norcross, 2010). In Table 12.1 we summarize the key concepts of these two therapies as well as the therapist's approach to the client. Below we describe the theories of Ellis and Beck in greater detail.

THE RATIONAL EMOTIVE BEHAVIOR THERAPY OF ALBERT ELLIS

Albert Ellis began his clinical practice by conducting psychoanalytic psychotherapy but found that such treatment did not yield the degree of change that he sought, particularly given the long duration of analysis. As a consequence, he developed his own system of therapy, labeled *rational-emotive therapy*. The work that provided the basis for

| TABLE 12.1 | | | |

Key Concepts of Ellis's Rational Emotive Behavior Therapy and Beck's Cognitive Therapy

Theory	Originator	Key concepts	Therapist approach
Rational emotive behavior therapy	Albert Ellis	ABC theory Irrational beliefs Catastrophizing Musturbating Absolutistic thinking	Active–directive–persuasive
Cognitive therapy	Aaron T. Beck	Cognitive distortions Arbitrary inference Selective abstraction Overgeneralization Magnification and minimization Personalization	Collaborative Empiricism Socratic dialogue

this treatment and for all Ellis's subsequent and prolific writing was his *Reason and Emotion in Psychotherapy* (Ellis, 1962). Eventually, Ellis changed the name of his therapy from rational emotive therapy to rational emotive *behavior* therapy (REBT; Ellis, 2011). Although his theory continues to be fundamentally cognitive, the name change was due to that fact that Ellis has always considered behavior change an important element of treatment. He has pointed out how behavior and cognitions reciprocally influence each other and has paid close attention to his clients' behaviors as he seeks to affect their cognitions (Ellis, 2011).

The most fundamental aspect of REBT is what Ellis calls his *ABC theory*. In this theory, A is the activating event, B is the client's beliefs or cognitions, and C is the client's resulting emotional reactions and behavior (the outcome). In most conceptions the activating event (A) is seen as causing the client's feelings and behavior (C). This is not so in Ellis's theory. Instead, it is point B, the client's beliefs or cognitions, that cause the resulting behavior and feelings. In other words, it is how we cognitively interpret activating events that most basically determines our resulting emotional reactions and behavior. These cognitions include what the client tells himself or herself about A and about the self in relation to A; they are so to speak internalized sentences the person utters. The cognitions of B may also be broader, representing the client's belief system. Emotional difficulties are caused when the person's cognitions are irrational and self-defeating. The job of REBT is to correct these irrational beliefs and replace them with rational and emotionally healthy beliefs.

Ellis (2011) used as an example of irrational beliefs at point B a woman with severe emotional problems who is rejected by her lover.

This troubled woman does not simply feel that it is undesirable to be rejected. Rather, she is inclined to also believe that "(a) it is *awful*; (b) she *cannot stand it*; (c) she *should not*, must not be rejected; (d) she will *never* be accepted by any desirable partner; (e) she is a *worthless* person because one lover has rejected her; and (f) she *deserves to be damned* for being so worthless" (p. 164).

In his earliest work, Ellis listed 11 basic irrational, "senseless" ideas that are common in our culture and lead to neurosis. Perhaps the two most common (Goldfried, 1988) involve approval from others and perfection. An example of the former is "I am not liked and approved of by others, that is terrible and I am no good." An example of the latter is "If I don't do a perfect job at everything I try, then I am no good." The common element of such beliefs is "catastrophizing" (if this or that happens or does not happen, it would be terrible and a catastrophe), "musturbating" (such and such happen or must not happen), and "absolutistic" thinking (this or that is always so).

Where do such irrational beliefs and schemas come from, and how are they to be treated? Although human beings have vast resources for growth, they also have powerful inborn tendencies to think irrationally and harm themselves. They are born with a very strong tendency to want and to need and to condemn themselves, others, and the world when they do not immediately get what they believe they "need" (Ellis, 2011). These tendencies are then deeply influenced by one's family upbringing and by social conditioning; early conditioning is the most durable. The irrational beliefs, once conditioned, are maintained by the person's continual reindoctrination of himself or herself. By the time a client seeks counseling, his or her cognitive beliefs and assumptions are deeply ingrained.

Counseling is most effective if the counselor actively exposes and corrects the client's irrational, self-defeating thinking. Because irrational thinking is deeply ingrained, it requires active and powerful treatment methods to change. The more passive approaches, for example, psychoanalysis, are less effective than active and directive therapy. On the other hand, Ellis (1995), who does not mince words, told us that irrational beliefs, such as those of the woman rejected by her lover, "can be elicited and demolished by any scientist worth his or her salt, and the rational–emotive therapist is partly that: an exposing and skeptical scientist" (p. 164). The rational–emotive therapist uses a wide range of techniques: role-playing, assertion training, operant conditioning, desensitization, humor, suggestion, support, and so forth. But above all, REBT entails active, vigorous, logical persuasion to help the client see and change irrational thinking and behavior.

REBT does not place value on insight into the unconscious or childhood causes. Rather, REBT therapists help their clients develop insights into how their own beliefs and assumptions, once learned, are the root causes of their problems because clients keep reindoctrinating themselves. Once the client understands this, REBT strives to give the client insight that only through *hard work and practice* will these irrational self-defeating beliefs be corrected and remain corrected. Only repeated rethinking and actions will extinguish the irrational beliefs. Ellis's view of REBT is nicely summarized in the following quote:

> REBT practitioners often employ a fairly rapid-fire active-directive-persuasive, philosophic methodology. In most instances, they quickly pin clients down to a few basic dysfunctional beliefs. They challenge them to try to defend these ideas; show that they contain illogical premises that cannot be substantiated logically; analyze these ideas and actively dispute them; vigorously show how they cannot work and why they will almost inevitably lead to more disturbance; reduce these ideas to absurdity, sometimes in a humorous manner; explain how they can be replaced with more rational philosophies; and teach clients how to think scientifically, so they can observe, logically parse, and minimize any subsequent irrational ideas and illogical deductions that lead to self-defeating feelings and behaviors. (Ellis, 1995, p. 178)

THE COGNITIVE THERAPY OF AARON T. BECK

Aaron T. Beck, like Albert Ellis, was originally trained in psychoanalysis. In the early 1960s he investigated Freud's theory of depression as "anger turned on the self" but found that the data he gathered did not support the theory. Instead, Beck found that the basic problem in depression was how patients processed information; that is, their cognitive processing. On the basis of this research, Beck (1967) developed a cognitive theory of depression and subsequently a cognitive therapy for depression as well as other disorders (Beck, 1976). A recent overview of this cognitive therapy was provided by Beck and Weishaar (2011).

Cognitive therapy is a brief (typically 12–16 sessions), present-centered, active, directive, and problem-oriented approach to counseling. In these ways it resembles REBT. Beck noted these similarities as well as Ellis's influence on the development of cognitive and behavioral therapies in general (Beck & Weishaar, 2011). Cognitive therapy differs from REBT, however, in aspects of its theory of personality and maladaptive behavior and in the manner in which the therapist works with the client. Unlike REBT, cognitive therapy does not assume that the troubled person has "irrational beliefs" and that the disorder will be corrected by modifying these beliefs through persuasion. Rather, the therapist and client work collaboratively to find and understand the "dysfunctional" cognitive thoughts and underlying assumptions that contribute to the client's problems. Beck theorized, also in contrast to REBT, that each psychological disorder has its own unique cognitive content. For example, people suffering from panic disorders show different cognitive content from those experiencing depression, obsessive–compulsive disorders, and paranoid problems. Each disorder requires a different approach to treatment.

Cognitive therapy uses a learning model to conceptualize how personality develops and how dysfunctional cognitive thoughts and assumptions form. Beck has delineated several kinds of systematic errors in reasoning (cognitive distortions) that appear when people are in distress. *Arbitrary inference* entails drawing conclusions in the absence of supporting evidence. An example of this might be the counselor who concludes, after an especially difficult day with her clients, "I am an ineffectual counselor." *Selective abstraction* involves conceptualizing a situation on the basis of a detail taken out of context; for example, a man becomes jealous on seeing his fiancée lean toward another man to hear him at a noisy gathering. *Overgeneralization* means abstracting a general rule from a few instances and applying it too broadly. For example, on the basis of the indifferent response of students in one undergraduate class to a few of his lectures, a college professor concludes, "All students are alike; my lectures will never be well received." *Magnification* and *minimization* involve perceiving something as far more or less significant than it is; for example, "If I don't do well on this date, that will be a disaster"; "This will be a piece of cake for me" (think of the situations in which this form of minimization occurs). *Personalization* entails attributing blame for some event to self without any evidence; for example, when an acquaintance does not return a woman's hello from across a crowded room, the woman concludes, "I have offended him." Finally, *dichotomous thinking* is rigid either/or thinking; for example, a man has the cognitive assumption that "either women will reject and hate you or they will love you and give you everything you want."

Cognitive therapists, according to Beck and Weishaar (2011), are warm, empathic, and genuine as they try to understand how their clients experience the world and cognize their experiences. Unlike REBT therapists, cognitive therapists do not persuasively confront their clients' irrational beliefs. Rather, they work together with their clients in what Beck calls collaborative empiricism. Therapists often help their clients frame their thoughts and assumptions into hypotheses. When these hypotheses represent cognitive distortions, therapists will seek to help clients see the faulty logic. At other times, counselors devise "behavioral experiments" that require clients to test their hypotheses outside of the counseling session. Beck conceptualized the therapeutic process as one of guided discovery, rather than the therapist exhorting and cajoling the client to adopt a new set of beliefs. A major therapeutic technique used by cognitive therapists is Socratic dialogue. Thus, therapists carefully develop a series of questions that they ask clients to promote learning. The purpose of this questioning is to help the client arrive at logical conclusions. Cognitive therapists do more than raise questions, though. They actively point out cognitive themes and underlying assumptions that appear to be working against their clients; they devise homework assignments aimed at helping clients see and correct dysfunctional thoughts, assumptions, and behavior; and they use a wide range of both cognitive and behavioral procedures to correct faulty cognitions and behavior.

Four common specific cognitive techniques are decatastrophizing, reattribution, redefining, and decentering. *Decatastrophizing*, or "what if" hypothesizing, helps clients think through the outcomes they most fear and to make plans to cope with them. *Reattribution* moves clients toward considering alternative causes for events and reactions. This technique is especially helpful to clients who erroneously take responsibility for events and others' reactions. *Redefining* the problem seeks to make it more concrete and specific and to state it in terms of the client's behavior. For example, the client who feels "nobody cares about me" may be led to redefine the problem to "I need to reach out to people and show that I care about them." *Decentering* is a technique for treating anxious people who believe they are the constant focus of others' attention. After exploring in detail the logic of this belief, the cognitive therapist designs behavioral experiments that test it. Beck and Weishaar (2011) used the example of an anxious student who believed everyone was focusing on him. This student was instructed to observe others carefully, and he became aware that some were taking notes, some daydreaming, some watching the professor, and so forth. He concluded that his classmates had other concerns.

The Behavioral and Cognitive Approaches in Perspective

How effective are the behavioral and cognitive approaches to therapy? How do they stack up against the other major approaches to treatment? And what is the degree of compatibility between the cognitive and behavioral approaches, on the one hand, and the field of counseling psychology on the other? We now explore these questions.

THE EFFICACY OF BEHAVIORAL AND COGNITIVE THERAPIES

Abundant research has been carried out on the effects of behavior therapy, cognitive therapy, and cognitive–behavioral therapy, on these therapies in general as well as on specific behavioral techniques and procedures. From their beginnings in the 1950s, the behavior therapies have been shown to have positive effects on clients, as have the cognitive therapies and cognitive–behavioral amalgamations in more recent times. In the overwhelming majority of studies, behavioral and cognitive procedures have demonstrated effectiveness well beyond what would be expected when using a control or subjects (see summaries in Prochaska & Norcross, 2010). Also, in comparison with the psychoanalytic and humanistic therapies (see Chapter 8), behavioral and cognitive approaches appear to fare at least as well. The typical finding is that all of the major approaches to counseling perform equally well. When differences have been found, however, between behavioral or cognitive therapies on the one hand and psychoanalytic or humanistic therapies on the other, outcomes have usually slightly favored the cognitive and behavioral therapies. However, even this slight superiority seems to disappear when certain methodological problems (e.g., type of outcome measures used) are controlled.

The main, overarching question to which behavior therapy has addressed itself from its beginnings goes something like "What techniques offered by which therapists work best when used with which clients possessing what kinds of problems?" (see Krumboltz, 1966; Paul, 1967). Referred to as the *"who, what, when,* and *where"* question of counseling research, this formulation contains the numerous specific questions that counseling psychology researchers need to address. Behavioral and cognitive counselors have probably done more to address these multifaceted issues than anyone else in the applied psychology fields. Answers are elusive, however, and the overwhelming majority of studies comparing, for example, one cognitive or behavioral technique to another tend to show no differences. Although some answers are now emerging, just how to match clients to treatments remains one of the most challenging research questions in behavioral and cognitive therapy.

As we conclude this section, one further issue in behavior therapy presents itself. One early and potentially devastating criticism of behavior therapy by, for example, psychoanalysts was that when one treats a symptom, even if the treatment is successful, the underlying problem will just appear in another form. Unless the underlying problem is treated, the resolution of one will be followed by the emergence of yet another symptom. Because this *symptom substitution* could be so damning to behavior therapy, the early behavior therapy researchers were sure to examine carefully whether empirical evidence existed to suggest such a phenomenon. In fact, of the numerous studies on this topic, none supports symptom substitution in behavior therapy. If anything, the hard data seem to suggest that successful treatment of a specific symptom or behavior in behavior therapy is likely to positively affect the person in other ways. For example, if a client with speech anxiety is successfully treated with systematic desensitization (see Paul's classic study and follow-up in Paul, 1966, 1967), the client is also likely to experience overall reduced anxiety and improved self-concept.

COUNSELING PSYCHOLOGY AND THE BEHAVIORAL AND COGNITIVE APPROACHES

Most likely, behavioral and cognitive approaches are a major force in counseling psychology today because of their basic compatibility. In terms of counseling psychology's defining features, it can be seen that the cognitive and behavioral approaches also focus very clearly on clients' strengths or assets. In contrast to classical psychoanalysis, where it seems as if everything is a defense against something and pathology is latent in every behavior (we exaggerate to make the point), behavior therapy, since its inception, has been adroit in uncovering the client's strengths and building on those. In fact, in a recent study it was found that practicing therapists' attention to their clients' strengths was related to their identification with a cognitive–behavioral perspective (Harbin, Gelso, & Pérez Rojas, 2013).

A second defining feature of counseling psychology that has made for an excellent fit with the cognitive and behavioral approaches is its emphasis on brevity in treatments. Although both counseling psychology and these learning-based approaches can permit and are not opposed to long-term treatments, the norm is brief treatment. Translated into duration of individual counseling or therapy, the behavioral and cognitive approaches are typically completed well within 6 months; the usual number of sessions is probably 10 to 12.

Finally, one of the principal defining features of counseling psychology has been attention to both the person and the environment (the person–environment interaction) in determining behavior. Yet, it has seemed that in counseling psychology research and practice, the environmental part of the equation has often been left out. Of all the approaches to counseling, though, the learning-based ones do pay very close attention to the environment, in terms of what originally caused behavior, what currently serves to control it, and how to modify it. Emphasis on environment or external factors has been especially strong in the behavior therapies.

Despite these ways in which counseling psychology and the learning-based approaches are highly compatible, the behavior therapies did not become a major force in counseling psychology until cognitive processes began to be addressed. In the earlier days of behavior therapy, when only external events and limited aspects of the person's internal life (e.g., autonomically based conditioned anxiety) were considered and treated, it seemed as though the center of the person was being left out of the equation. To many counseling psychologists, behavior therapy, true to its behaviorist roots, placed too little value on the worth and dignity of humans, viewing them instead as no more than conditioned reactions, albeit complex ones. With the advent of social–cognitive theory and the cognitive–behavioral approaches, however, this has changed. The human's interior is amply attended to in the dominant forms of learning-based approaches, and the individual is seen as an active agent in the learning process of living, rather than as a passive recipient of stimuli.

Summary

In present-day counseling psychology, the behavioral and the cognitive perspectives rely heavily on each other, and nearly all practitioners who lean toward cognitive and behavioral theories mix the two. Such theoretical orientation is called *cognitive–behavioral counseling.*

Of the two approaches to counseling, the behavioral developed first, growing out of the behaviorism movement that began in the early part of the 20th century as well as out of the experimental research on the psychology of learning that had begun around the turn of that century. Principles of classical conditioning (as in Pavlov's experiments) and operant conditioning (as in the work of B. F. Skinner) were formulated. Behavior therapy itself was born in the 1950s; its most important early book, Joseph Wolpe's *Psychotherapy by Reciprocal Inhibition,* appeared in 1958. In the 1960s, behavior therapy began to pay attention to internal cognitive processes such as expectancies, values, and beliefs. Albert Ellis, Albert Bandura, and Aaron T. Beck, each of whom stressed cognition in one way or another, contributed significantly to the cognitive revolution that deeply affected behavioral and cognitive counseling.

Nine basic assumptions of the cognitive and behavioral perspectives were discussed: (a) attention to overt processes; (b) the belief that behavior is learned, with a focus on classical, operant, and imitative learning; (c) the melding of cognitive and behavioral approaches in today's practice of counseling psychology; (d) the prepotency of the present in the conduct of counseling; (e) the fact that the client's presenting problem is taken very seriously by these approaches; (f) the great importance of specific and clearly defined goals in treatment; (g) the value placed on an active, directive, and prescriptive approach during counseling; (h) the view of the counselor–client relationship as important but not sufficient; and (i) the central value of controlled, scientific research in the practice of counseling.

A wide range of behavioral and cognitive procedures was described, from operant conditioning as it may be used in counseling, to desensitization, to the more cognitive procedure of cognitive restructuring. The two most prominent cognitively oriented therapies are Ellis's rational emotive behavior therapy and Beck's cognitive therapy. The research on the effectiveness of behavioral and cognitive therapies and their combination shows them to be at least as effective as other therapies. Further supporting the efficacy of cognitive–behavioral counseling, the available evidence clearly refutes the criticism that symptom substitution diminishes the effectiveness of these therapies.

The cognitive and behavioral approaches are a major force in counseling psychology today because they are highly compatible with counseling psychology's emphasis on human beings' assets, on treatment brevity, and on the person–environment interaction. The behavioral and cognitive approaches have become even more attractive to counseling psychologists in recent times because of the attention given to the internal life of the person.

The Third Force
The Humanistic–Experiential Approach

13

The humanistic–experiential approach includes an array of therapies, such as client-centered, or person-centered; existential; gestalt; and experiential. These approaches are often combined under the rubric *third force* because they reached prominence later than the two earlier dominant forces in American psychology during the first half of the 20th century, psychoanalysis and behaviorism.

The humanistic–experiential approach (referred to hereafter as *humanistic*) not only followed psychoanalysis and behaviorism chronologically in both the United States and Europe; as Belkin (1980) pointed out, humanistic psychotherapy evolved as a reaction to the determinism of Freudian psychoanalysis and to the mechanism of the behavioristic approaches to studying and treating disordered behavior. To many humanistic thinkers, the Freudian approach, which views all behavior as determined by intrapsychic forces outside the control and consciousness of the individual, does worse than miss the mark in terms of the creative, intangible, and unpredictable aspects of the human personality and

http://dx.doi.org/10.1037/14378-013
Counseling Psychology, Third Edition, by C. J. Gelso, E. N. Williams, and B. R. Fretz

spirit. Rollo May (1967; in Belkin, 1980), one of the leading theoreticians within the third-force approach, offered this trenchant critique of Freudian determinism:

> The danger of the Freudian system of analysis arises when it is carried over into a deterministic interpretation of personality as a whole. The system can become simply a scheme of cause and effect: blocked instinctual urge equals repression equals psychic complex equals neurosis. . . . The danger lies in the influence of Freudian theory in setting up a mechanistic, deterministic view of personality in the minds of the partially informed public . . . *to imagine that the whole of the creative, oftentimes unpredictable, certainly intangible aspects of the human mind can be reduced to cause-and-effect mechanistic principles is sheer folly. . . . If such determinism is accepted, human responsibility is destroyed* [emphasis added]. (pp. 48–49)

Indeed, attacks on behaviorism by humanistic theorists and therapists are at least as strong as May's critique of psychoanalysis. What is found objectionable is not only the strict determinism of the behavioristic approach but also the focus only on observable behavior (and nothing more) that had been so typical of American behaviorism in the past (see Chapter 12).

Because of these concerns about psychoanalysis and behaviorism, humanism flourished as a social movement within counseling and psychotherapy in the 1960s, synchronizing with the expansiveness and hopefulness of that decade and the early 1970s. Names often associated with the humanistic movement in this country include Gordon Allport, Sidney Jourard, Abraham Maslow, Rollo May, and Carl Rogers. American humanism was closely linked to the existential psychotherapy movement in Europe, and in fact the two are often seen as being highly similar if not the same, at least in terms of the practice of counseling and therapy. In Europe, the existential therapy movement aimed to integrate the insights of existentialism as a philosophy of human existence with the practice of psychiatry and psychotherapy. The major contributors to the European movement were Medford Boss, Ludwig Binswanger, Viktor Frankl, R. D. Laing, and Frederick Perls. Belkin (1980) noted that Rollo May was for many years the leading American spokesperson for existential psychotherapy.

Although the humanistic movement reached full bloom in the 1960s and 1970s in the United States, its seeds had been planted much earlier. Its most prominent proponent in counseling and psychotherapy probably was Carl Rogers, who completed his first major book on counseling in the early 1940s (Rogers, 1942) and published his seminal *Client-Centered Therapy* a decade later (Rogers, 1951). Also in the early 1950s, Fritz Perls produced his fundamental theoretical statement about gestalt therapy (Perls, Hefferline, & Goodman, 1951), an approach that fits clearly within the humanistic realm.

The humanistic perspective grew up with, or at least alongside, counseling psychology (see Chapter 2). The formal beginnings of counseling psychology can be traced to the Northwestern Conference of 1951, the same year as the publication of the seminal books by Rogers and Perls. More important than chronology, though, is the deep influence that the humanistic approach has always had on counseling psychology. As will be seen, the humanistic approach to studying and working with human beings is extremely compatible with some of the central defining features of counseling psychology as delineated in Chapter 1.

Today, in fact, the humanistic influence remains quite strong among practicing psychologists in general and counseling psychologists in particular. When one pieces together data on theoretical orientation (Goodyear et al., 2008; Hayes, personal communication, February 8, 2013; Prochaska & Norcross, 2010), it appears that humanistic theories have guided the practices of a very high percentage of counseling psychologists. For example, although only about 10% of a sizable sample of counseling psychologists view one or another of the humanistic orientations as their primary theoretical orientation, in data provided by Jeffrey A. Hayes and collected through the Center for Collegiate Mental Health, nearly 80% of a large sample of 613 counseling psychologists reported that their current practice was moderately to very greatly guided by humanistic theories. In fact, over 50% indicated that their practice was greatly or very greatly influenced by humanistic therapy. Many or perhaps most of these therapists would likely view themselves as theoretically integrative or eclectic but as having been heavily influenced by humanistic principles. Thus, humanistic theories may well have their main impact through how they influence those aligned with other, nonhumanistic orientations more than through being a primary orientation.

Humanistic Assumptions About Human Beings, Counseling, and Science

Wide differences in technique separate practitioners adhering to theories within the humanistic perspective (Elliott, Greenberg, Watson, Timulak, & Freire, 2013). For example, in the two approaches examined later in this chapter, person-centered and gestalt therapy, major differences exist in what might be called *therapist activity*, or *directiveness*. The gestalt therapist is, in a word, much more *active–directive* than the traditional person-centered therapist. At the same time, common assumptions about human beings, treatment, and science cut across all of the differing approaches under the humanistic–experiential umbrella. Six of these are especially applicable.

THE DEMOCRATIC IDEAL

In Grummon's (1965) early and still highly apt description of client-centered counseling, "belief in the democratic ideal," is noted as a major assumption underlying Carl Rogers's theories. In fact, this belief is inherent in virtually all humanistic approaches. Although the democratic ideal is difficult to define, it can be summed up in terms of one of its most central tenets: *belief in the worth and dignity of each individual.* Another basic tenet is belief in the individual's right to his or her own opinions, thoughts, and interests. Further, each individual has the right and responsibility to control his or her own destiny. The democratic ideal is best served by a society and social institutions that encourage the individual to be independent and self-directing (Grummon, 1965).

The value placed on the individual and individual choice has been a key element of the philosophy of humanism from its beginnings. Although this value does not negate concern for others or for broader social institutions, it does bespeak a kind of individualism peculiar to the humanistic tradition (Lowe, 1969). This individualism is strikingly evident in Fritz Perls's (1969a) "Gestalt Prayer."

> I do my thing and you do your thing.
> I am not in this world to live up to your expectations.
> And you are not in this world to live up to mine.
> You are you, and I am I.
> And if by chance, we find each other, it's beautiful.
> If not, it can't be helped.

THE FUNDAMENTAL PREDOMINANCE OF THE SUBJECTIVE

Since the Renaissance, humanistic philosophers have placed a premium on ability to reason. Within the counseling and psychotherapy community of humanists, however, equal value is placed on the subjective side of life. In fact, the humanistic therapist tends to see the subjective side of life as dominant in healthy functioning (e.g., Schneider & Krug, 2010). Rogers elucidated this position thusly: "Man lives essentially in his own personal and subjective world, and even his most objective functioning, in science, mathematics, and the like, is the result of subjective purpose and subjective choice" (Rogers, 1959, p. 191). Gestalt therapists' investment in subjective experiencing and the awareness and living of one's inner subjective experiencing is unmistakable. On the other side of the ledger, equally clear is their view that to deny one's subjective experience by living in one's intellect is an indication of dysfunctioning.

The humanist's belief in the predominance of the subjective side is most powerfully stated by Rogers (1961; as cited in Grummon, 1965) in the following passage:

> No matter how completely man comes to understand himself as a determined phenomenon, the products of past elements and forces, and the determined cause of future events and behaviors, he can never live as an object. He can only live subjectively. . . . The person who is developing his full potential is able to accept the subjective aspect of himself, and to *live* subjectively. When he is angry he is *angry*, not merely an exhibition of the effects of adrenalin. When he loves he is loving, not merely "cathected towards a love object." He moves in self-selected directions, he chooses responsibly, he is a person who thinks and feels and experiences; he is not merely an object in whom these events occur. He plays a part in a universe which may be determined, but he lives himself subjectively, thus fulfilling his own need to be a person. (pp. 20–21)

Grummon (1965) noted that one of Rogers's major conceptions of humans is that they are "wiser than their intellects." Effective functioning is brought about by living one's full experiencing, of which our conscious thinking is only a fraction.

THE TENDENCY TOWARD GROWTH AND ACTUALIZATION

"A musician must make music, an artist must paint, a poet must write if he is to be ultimately at peace with himself." Abraham Maslow (1954, p. 91) wrote this in his first major theoretical statement about the human tendency toward actualizing of one's basic nature. For Maslow and essentially all humanists, human motivation is guided by much more than the need for drive reduction, freedom from tension, and the elimination of undesirable states. Humans are active, initiating organisms possessing an inherent tendency toward and capacity for growth and self-actualization. The capacity may be latent because of negative upbringing or any of the myriad factors that suppress an individual's potential, but it exists nonetheless and can be released under the right conditions (e.g., through effective education or therapy). Rogers defined this actualizing tendency as the "inherent tendency of the organism to develop all its capacities in ways which serve to maintain or enhance the organism" (1959, p. 196). He viewed the actualizing tendency as the fundamental characteristic of all life, applying not only to human beings but also to one-celled protozoans, flowers, wild animals, and everything that lives.

What constitutes this process of self-actualization? The answer to this question is best seen in the work of Abraham Maslow. Over a period of several years, Maslow studied self-actualized people and developed theories about human motivation and self-actualization. His writings continue to be a touchstone for humanistic counselors in this area.

Maslow defined the process as the

> ongoing actualization of potentials, capacities and talents, as fulfillment of mission (or call, fate, destiny, or vocation), as a fuller knowledge of and acceptance of, the person's own intrinsic nature, as an unceasing trend toward unity, integration, or synergy with the person. (1968, p. 25)

Maslow theorized the existence of a "hierarchy of basic needs" common to all humans. One's more basic needs—the physiological requirements for air, water, food, shelter, sleep, and sex—are at the bottom of the hierarchy. These are followed in ascending order by the needs for safety and security, for belongingness and love, and for self-esteem and respect. At the top of the hierarchy are the growth needs, such as those for self-actualization. As needs at one level of the hierarchy are taken care of, people then strive to satisfy those at a higher level. Thus, one continually strives to move up the hierarchy toward self-actualization. Maslow believed all needs must be met if good mental health is to ensue. If they are not, a "deficiency condition" results, referred to as neurosis, personality disturbance, psychosis, and the like.

Humanistic counselors may be viewed as *growth psychologists* because they tend to view mental health in terms of growth, personal maturity, and actualization, rather than the absence of psychopathological symptoms (Elliott, Bohart, Watson, & Greenberg, 2011). Formulations of the mature, actualizing individual (Maslow, 1970) or the fully functioning person (Raskin, Rogers, & Witty, 2011) are used by the humanistic counselor as a gauge of mental health.

THE ESSENTIAL TRUSTWORTHINESS OF PERSONS

If we were to baldly categorize the humanistic, psychodynamic, and learning perspectives on the basic goodness or trustworthiness of human beings, the psychodynamic perspective would lean toward the bad or untrustworthy view. To exaggerate the point, humans in the psychodynamic model are at the core a bundle of instincts (the id) that must be tamed by later development (ego, superego) if society is to survive. We are essentially irrational and driven by irrational impulses. From the learning (e.g., behavioristic) perspective, humans are at the core tabulae rasae, or clean slates. We have no basic nature but rather learn to be what we are through conditioning and imitating.

In contrast to the psychodynamic and learning perspectives, the humanistic perspective has always taken a positive stance, believing the basic rationality of human beings is an aspect of their trustworthiness. As Lowe (1969) stated, "The first humanistic value is that man is a rational being. If man is valued as a creature who above all else is good, then the rationality which sets him apart from the animal is his crowning glory" (p. 99).

Words such as *trustworthy, good, reliable,* and *constructive* are seen over and over in the writings of Rogers and other humanists. These humanists are by no means naive about the evil and untrustworthiness of many human acts but tend to see them as a function of defensiveness that people learn as an unhappy consequence of their environmental backgrounds. This essentially positive view of human nature was stated eloquently by Rogers (1961):

> I have little sympathy with the rather prevalent concept that man is basically irrational, and that his impulses, if not controlled, will lead to destruction of others and self. Man's behavior is exquisitely rational, moving with subtle and ordered complexity toward the goals his organism is endeavoring to achieve. The tragedy for most of us is that our defenses keep us from being aware of this rationality, so that consciously we are moving in one direction, while organismically we are moving in another. But in the person who is living the process of the good life, there would be a decreasing number of such barriers, and he would be increasingly a participant in the rationality of his organism. The only control of impulses which would exist, or which would prove necessary, is the natural and internal balancing of one need against another, and the discovery of behaviors which follow the vector most closely approximating the satisfaction of all needs. (pp. 299–300)

We should add that not all third-force counselors advocate this positive view of human nature. To the gestalt therapist, human nature is more a mixture of the good with the bad, and humans have equivalent potentialities for both. Even some person-centered theorists (e.g., Levant & Shlien, 1984) have promoted this mixed view. Yet, there is no doubt that the legacy left to us by the humanist perspective over the years is one of optimism about human nature and its possibilities.

THE VALUE OF AN AUTHENTIC HUMAN ENCOUNTER IN THE PRESENT

Each and every humanistic approach promotes the counselor's being "real," being involved in a person-to-person encounter, and focusing on the here and now in that encounter. Although early client-centered therapy tended to inhibit the role of the counselor and limit his or her responses to paraphrasing, significant changes have occurred over the years. A major aspect of these changes has been the increased implied permission granted to counselors to be genuine in the therapeutic encounter.

Whereas this focus on authenticity developed in the later person-centered approach, it has always been a basic feature of other humanistic approaches. For example, in gestalt therapy, therapist authenticity occurs through an I–thou relationship between counselor and client (Greenberg, 1985), in which the therapist is fully present in the moment and both participants are open to each other. The therapist cannot force the client to be open but can be open himself or herself while maintaining the belief that the client will eventually enter the I–thou relationship.

Humanistic therapists do not suggest that the counseling relationship be fully reciprocal. After all, the client is the one seeking help and exploring his or her feelings, thoughts, and experiences. However active, the therapist attempts to put himself or herself aside and enter the world of the client, albeit in a partial and temporary fashion. The I–thou relationship advocated by gestalt therapists and virtually all others within the humanistic perspective is not a strictly mutual one wherein the therapist is equally acknowledged and confirmed by the client (Greenberg, 1985). The therapist participates in the relationship with an I–thou attitude but does not seek confirmation from the client. Thus, the therapist's full presence in the moment, unreserved communication, and abiding involvement with another human being are what define his or her contribution to the "I–thouness" of the relationship.

Greenberg (1983) gave some good examples from the gestalt perspective of the kinds of responses the therapist makes that reflect this authentic and open I–thou encounter. These examples are broadly applicable to all humanistic approaches.

> To engage at the level of I–thou, without the demand that the other confirm one, is the essence of the therapist's attitude when he or she enters into an I–thou dialogue. The therapist might share with the client what he or she feels in the first moment of their contact, "I feel eager to meet you and find out what it is you want," or later in the encounter might say, "When I hear you say that, I feel sad and I wonder how you feel." As the encounter intensifies, the therapist might give the client some feedback by saying, "My heart is pounding as I say this to you but I want to tell you that I find myself pulling away from you when you are like that" or "I am aware that I am not listening to you and I'm wondering if you're feeling involved in what you're saying." The therapist must also accept and share his or her own sense of self in the encounter: "I felt defensive when you didn't want to do what I asked and I found myself trying to force you to do it" or "I feel frustrated with your deadness and I realize I'm expecting you to be lively so I'll feel good about myself." Another important moment for the therapist to share is when he or she is feeling lost and doesn't know where to go with the client. An essential feature of all encountering is that the therapist must express his or her feelings in an undemanding way and be willing to explore with the client what these feelings are about. In addition, the therapist must express all his or her feelings by saying not only "I am angry" but also "I am afraid that I may alienate you when I say this." In this way, the therapist shares his or her total humanness. (p. 141)

Obviously, these responses and the vision they reveal of the therapeutic encounter differ highly from those promoted by the psychoanalytic and learning perspectives.

THE NECESSITY OF SCIENTIFIC METHODS ACCOMMODATING THE HUMAN EXPERIENCE

The humanistic movement in psychology has not focused on counseling and therapy alone. Of almost equal concern has been the scientific study of human behavior and the methods used for such study. Humanistic theoreticians and researchers over the years have been critical, though, of a scientific orthodoxy that equated science with a specific method and restricted its subject matter. Thus, the humanistic psychologist strongly advocated methods beyond the traditional psychological experiment, usually conducted in an antiseptic laboratory environment. Relatedly, the humanist has been critical of the belief that behavior could be dissected into minuscule parts and then studied in terms of those parts. Likewise, the humanist has always deeply opposed the behaviorist notion that only overt behavior is the proper subject matter of psychological science.

In contrast, humanistic psychologists have promoted scientific heterodoxy (Maslow, 1970). They believe that scientific methods should fit the subject matter being studied, ranging from rigorous experiments to less controlled qualitative methods. The wholeness of human behavior needs to be addressed scientifically, rather than the study of human nature being reduced to a narrow obsession with microscopic parts. In the same vein, the proper subject matter of psychology must be the complex human experience, including all of those internal processes and experiences so difficult to study neatly and simply. In research, humans are seen as active agents, capable of choice and of shaping their own destiny.

It will be recalled that in Chapter 4 we discussed qualitative methodologies in scientific research in counseling psychology. Much of the attack on the "received view" and what is being called for by way of alternative methods has a clear connection to the humanistic tradition in psychology. The roots of scientific heterodoxy are deeply embedded in counseling psychology because of the humanistic influence. Exhibit 13.1 summarizes the six humanistic–experiential assumptions we have been describing.

We shall now look at the two humanistic approaches to counseling that have been the most prominent in counseling psychology: Carl Rogers's person-centered approach and gestalt therapy, which was originated by Fritz Perls but modified in significant ways over the years. Throughout the discussion we shall be mindful of the relationship of the two theories to counseling psychology and its practice.

EXHIBIT 13.1

Fundamental Assumptions and Propositions of Humanistic–Experiential Theories

1. Each individual possesses worth and dignity.
2. Life should be lived subjectively.
3. All humans have an inherent tendency toward self-actualization.
4. People are fundamentally rational and trustworthy.
5. Effective counseling involves an authentic, I–thou encounter.
6. Science needs to study subjective meaning of whole persons construed as active agents.

The Person-Centered Therapy of Carl Rogers

Theories of counseling and therapy are to an important extent a reflection of the lives, needs, and personalities of their creators (Dolliver, 1981a; Prochaska & Norcross, 2010). Nowhere is this clearer than in the two humanistic approaches that we shall discuss. In this section, we offer a glimpse of the life and professional accomplishments of Carl Rogers, the founder and intellectual leader of person-centered therapy. We shall look at Rogers's background in some detail because, in our view, he is probably the most influential scientist–practitioner in the history of counseling. Rogers's effect on counseling psychology has been so pervasive that many of his ideas now seem like self-evident truths. They have become so ingrained in counseling that many counselors forget they ever came from Rogers!

Carl R. Rogers (1902–1987) was one of six children raised in a fundamentalist religious atmosphere. He attended grade school in a wealthy Chicago suburb before the family moved to a Wisconsin farm, where his engineer father applied scientific techniques to farming. Rogers (1973) had this to say about his family and early years:

> I knew my parents loved me, but it would never have occurred to me to share with them any of my personal or private thoughts or feelings because I knew these would have been judged and found wanting. . . . I could sum up these boyhood years by saying that anything I would today regard as a close and communicative interpersonal relationship with another was completely lacking during that period. My attitude toward others outside the home was characterized by the distance and the aloofness which I had taken over from my parents. I attended the same elementary school for seven years. From this point on, until I finished graduate work, I never attended any school for longer than two

years, a fact which undoubtedly had its effects on me. Beginning with high school, I believe my hunger for companionship came a little more into my awareness. But any satisfaction of that hunger was blocked first by the already mentioned attitudes of my parents, and second by circumstances. (pp. 3–4)

It is easy to see how the counseling theory Rogers developed, focusing on a close, accepting, nonjudgmental relationship between counselor and client, reflects the unmet needs of Rogers's childhood. The flexibility in Rogers's theory, as well as its ability to embrace new concepts, is also a reflection of his style and personality. Note, for example, these observations about Rogers, presented as a preface to Prochaska and Norcross's (1999) extensive discussion of person-centered therapy.

The air and aura about him were warm and gentle though his words were strong and poignant. He was willing to field any question and respond to even the most critical comments. When asked how he as a therapist could be both genuine and non-disclosing, he surprised us with his candor. He said that over the past several years of working first with psychiatric clients and then with growth-oriented groups, he had come to see that his model of a therapist as reflective and nondirective had been very comfortable for a person like him. For most of his life he had been rather shy and therefore non-disclosing. In the sunny climate of California with its emphasis on openness in groups, he had come to recognize that too much of his former style was a convenient role that had protected him from having to reveal much of himself. Right until his death, Rogers was realizing more fully in psychotherapy, as in his life, the genuineness he had always valued but never fully realized. (p. 136)

After his years on the farm, Rogers majored in agriculture and then history at the University of Wisconsin. (Rogers is one on a long list of prominent psychologists whose undergraduate major was not psychology.) Breaking with his fundamentalist background, he then entered the very liberal Union Seminary in Manhattan to prepare for the ministry. After 2 years, Rogers again changed, this time to his lasting vocation, psychology.

Rogers completed his PhD in clinical and educational psychology at Columbia University in 1931. Significantly, the theoretical emphasis during his graduate training was Freudian; Rogers's subsequent theory was in many ways a reaction to the orthodox psychoanalytic perspective.

ROGERS'S PATH TO THE PERSON-CENTERED APPROACH

After receiving his doctorate, Rogers spent 12 years as an intern and then psychologist at a child guidance clinic in Rochester, New York. There he developed theories of intervention based on his own personal experience. During this time, Rogers was influenced by the work of Otto Rank, a prominent psychoanalyst who had developed views about personality and therapy markedly different from those of orthodox psychoanalysis. Rogers was especially affected by Rank's views on human will and the prime importance of the relationship in therapy (as opposed to techniques).

In 1939 Rogers published his first book, *The Clinical Treatment of the Problem Child.* In it one can see the seeds of what eventually became his person-centered approach. In 1940, Rogers moved to Ohio State University so that he could be more involved in training psychologists to do counseling. In this stimulating environment, with a coterie of graduate students to help further his thinking, Rogers published the controversial *Counseling and Psychotherapy* (1942). In this book, Rogers stressed the importance of the counselor's being warmly receptive to the client and establishing a permissive atmosphere. Counseling was seen as essentially nondirective, with the client taking the lead in its progress. Thus, the basic nondirectiveness of therapy was established. Rogers also emphasized his antidiagnostic views, which were almost heretical for that time. Diagnosing the client, Rogers argued, was nontherapeutic at best, taking the counselor away from his or her primary focus, that of understanding the client's internal frame of reference and helping the client move in the direction that was best for that individual.

At Ohio State, Rogers also began what became a lifelong pursuit: scientific study of the counseling process. He and his students conducted a series of studies of nondirective counseling. Rogers and Francis P. Robinson organized separate but related research programs that made use of newly developed tape recorders to study counseling sessions. Audiotapes allowed researchers to witness for the first time what went on in counseling. The use of such tapes brought about major scientific breakthroughs in the study of counseling.

In 1945 Rogers moved to the University of Chicago to head that university's counseling center. He continued his vigorous research program and published what many consider his most significant book, *Client-Centered Therapy* (Rogers, 1951). The change in the name of his theory, from *nondirective* to *client-centered* therapy, reflected key modifications in Rogers's approach. Whereas the use of techniques had still been emphasized in *Counseling and Psychotherapy,* in the new book the therapist's attitudes toward the client became the focus—one that has remained and even been strengthened over the years. Also new in *Client-Centered Therapy* was the stress on counselor attention to the client's unstated and underlying feelings, rather than his or her words and explicit feelings.

The 1950s was a period of great productivity for Rogers and his colleagues and students. In fact, nearly all of the fundamental ideas about therapy formulated by this group were published or written during that decade. The book *Psychotherapy and Personality Change,* based on research on client-centered therapy, was published in 1954 (Rogers & Dymond, 1954). In 1957 Rogers presented his famous paper on "necessary and sufficient conditions" (Rogers, 1957), discussed in Chapter 9 in this volume. Few if any articles in the history of counseling and psychotherapy have promoted so much research. At the end of the 1950s, Rogers presented his full view of the process of client-centered therapy, along with his theory of personality and interpersonal relationships (Rogers, 1959). His next book, *On Becoming a Person* (Rogers, 1961), presented a wonderful array of articles on therapy, science, education, and life. It is lucidly and interestingly written for the lay audience as well as the professional, and it remains as relevant today as when it was first published in 1961.

In 1957 Rogers moved back to his home state. There, at the University of Wisconsin, he continued research on the "necessary and sufficient conditions" and sought to test his theories with one of the most difficult populations possible: hospitalized schizophrenics. The 5-year study he organized may be the largest therapy study ever done, even to this day. The results provided only partial support for the effectiveness of client-centered therapy and the necessary and sufficient conditions, when applied to hospitalized schizophrenics (Rogers, 1967). Rogers and his collaborators had set themselves an extremely difficult task: They compared subjects of client-centered therapy not to an equivalent group of nontreated patients but to patients receiving the hospital's regular treatment program (including, for example, group therapy).

In any event, this work with schizophrenic patients brought about more changes in client-centered theory. The movement toward greater therapist openness and authenticity, already under way for several years, was further energized by the individual therapy experience with these difficult patients. Eugene Gendlin, one the principal researchers in this project, was moved to comment,

> It is already certain that the patients did a great deal to us. I might say that our improvement has been remarkable. . . . Thus, for example, genuineness has changed for us from the mere absence of a false front, to a very active, self-expressive mode of making an interaction. (Gendlin, 1970, p. 284)

In 1964 Rogers left the university environment, moving to the Western Behavioral Sciences Institute in La Jolla, California, to work with normal individuals and groups. In 1968, he helped to found the Center for the Study of the Person in La Jolla. There he worked to apply his theories to a wide range of situations, especially in relation to education, groups, and couples. The move away from therapy techniques and toward relationship attitudes reached fulfillment in 1974, with the change from *client*-centered to *person*-centered therapy. This second change was again not simply in name but reflected what, over the years, had become an attitude toward life and being. Rogers noted in 1980,

> The old concept of "client-centered therapy" has been transformed into the "person-centered approach." In other words, I am no longer talking simply about psychotherapy, but about a point of view, a philosophy, an approach to life, a way of being, which fits any situation in which *growth*—of a person, a group, or a community—is part of the goal. (Rogers, 1980, p. ix)

THEORY OF PERSONALITY: GROWTH AND MALADJUSTMENT

Rogers was always more concerned with the conditions for change and growth than with the roots of personality development. Because of this interest, his ideas about intervention came *before* his statements on personality. Yet, he did offer formal conceptions of personality, its development and unfolding. Rogers's key formulations on this topic were published in his *Client-Centered Therapy* (Rogers, 1951, pp. 481–533) and later in a major chapter (Rogers, 1959). In his 1951 work he presented 19 propositions about personality development. Seven of these propositions seem to capture a major part of the theory and are presented in Exhibit 13.2.

Inspection of Exhibit 13.2 suggests the key elements of Rogers's personality theory. First, the theory is based on *phenomenology*. That is, it is the person's subjective perceptions of self and environment, his or her subjective experience and reality that guide behavior. Second and relatedly, each individual has his or her own private world, and to

---

EXHIBIT 13.2

Rogers's Major Propositions About Personality Development

---

1. Each individual exists in a continually changing world of experience of which he or she is the center.
2. The organism reacts to the field as it is experienced and perceived. This perceptual field is, for the individual, "reality."
3. Behavior is basically the goal-directed attempt of the organism to satisfy its need as experienced, in the field as perceived.
4. The organism reacts as an organized whole to this phenomenal field.
5. The best vantage point for understanding behavior is from the internal frame of reference of the individual himself or herself.
6. A portion of the total perceptual field gradually becomes differentiated as the self.
7. Most of the ways of behaving that are adopted by the organism are those that are consistent with the concept of *self*.

---

understand this individual we must enter this private world and seek to comprehend the individual from his or her internal frame of reference. "External" understanding—the kind that involves, for example, diagnosis by an expert—often leads us away from the internal frame of reference. Third, all persons develop a self-concept or self-structure. For Rogers, this self-concept contains the person's perceptions of himself or herself alone and interactively with his or her environment as well as the values attached to those perceptions. This self-structure is fluid and changing but, once formed, serves to guide one's behavior and perceptions. Finally, persons' reactions are based on the whole of their self-structures and perceptions of themselves and their world, rather than on specific portions of their perceptions, as other theories might maintain.

INCONGRUENCE, CONGRUENCE, AND THE FULLY FUNCTIONING PERSON

If all individuals are basically trustworthy and have a tendency toward self-actualization, why is there so much unhappiness in the world? What goes wrong so as to interfere with and often cripple people's actualizing tendencies? In several of his early papers, Rogers developed the client-centered (now person-centered) theory of maladjustment, in which *incongruence* is the key concept.

Maladjustment occurs when an incongruence or rift exists between the person's self-concept and his or her organismic experiencing; that is, between the person's image of self and his or her inner experiencing. Why and how does this happen? As children develop, so does their inherent need for *positive regard* and *positive self-regard*. As experiences with the world (mostly family and primary caretakers) unfold, children also develop a self-concept. If children experience enough love, especially love without conditions, they develop a positive self-concept and, just as important, do not develop *conditions of worth* (conditions under which they feel worthwhile). If, on the other hand, parents are too restrictive or conditional (e.g., telling the child "We love you if you're a good boy or girl in the ways we define it"), the child develops these conditions of worth.

If our self-concept includes too many conditions of worth, it becomes rigid or "frozen," so that we lack a sense of positive self-regard. Thus, too many of our inwardly felt experiences (called "organismic experiencing") must be distorted or blocked from awareness, and we experience a sense of incongruence. Individuals in this situation are at odds with themselves because their self-concept and experiencing are not unified; they are in conflict.

When such incongruence occurs—and Rogers would add that it occurs ever so frequently in modern Western civilization—individuals are at cross-purposes with themselves and are vulnerable to psychological maladjustment. They can no longer live as integrated whole persons. If such individuals were to perceive accurately what is being experienced at the feeling level, their self-concept would be threatened. Threat causes anxiety, which the individual defends against by either denying inner experience or misperceiving experience.

If, however, the child develops in an environment in which there are no or minimal conditions of worth, the self-concept is more flexible, and the person may acknowledge his or her organismic experiencing without feeling a threat to the concept. This congruence permits the actualizing tendency to do its work and the individual to become what Rogers called a *fully functioning person*. The qualities of the fully functioning person reflect the humanistic assumptions discussed as well as those of the person-centered theory of development as examined above. Fully functioning persons are increasingly (a) open to their experience, (b) accepting of their feelings, (c) capable of living in the present without preoccupation with past or future, (d) free to make choices that are best for them and to act on those choices spontaneously, (e) trusting of self and of human nature, (f) capable of balanced and realistic expressions of both aggression and affection, and (g) creative and nonconforming (see Burke, 1989; Prochaska & Norcross, 1999).

COUNSELING AND THERAPY USING A PERSON-CENTERED APPROACH

The person-centered view of counseling flows directly and logically from the humanistic assumptions discussed earlier and from the above-mentioned formulations about personality development, incongruence, and full functioning. The counselor seeks to gently enter the client's subjective world, to understand this client from his or her internal frame of reference, and to provide an experience in which the person is accepted and cared about without conditions of worth. As Prochaska and Norcross (2010) noted, whether the client seeks counseling because of inadequate functioning tied to perceptual distortion, because defensive symptoms are causing too much emotional pain, or because of a wish for greater self-actualization, the goals of therapy are the same: to increase the congruence between self-concept and organismic experience. The therapeutic relationship, especially its personal and emotional components, is the primary vehicle for this reintegration of self and experience. In fact, it is this relationship, in and of itself, that produces growth in the client. Rogers (1951) made this point decisively: "The process of therapy is seen as being synonymous with the experiential relationship between client and therapist" (p. 172).

Lest the reader get the impression that any kind of positive relationship will promote change, we hasten to add that, according to person-centered theory, it is only when certain relationship conditions predominate that constructive change occurs. To begin with, Rogers said, "I launch myself into the therapeutic relationship having a hypothesis, or a faith, that my liking, my confidence, and my understanding of the other person's inner world, will lead to a significant process of becoming" (Rogers, 1951, p. 267). This statement effectively summarizes relationship conditions that Rogers believed "necessary and sufficient" for constructive change to occur. Briefly, they are as follows:

1. Two persons, the client and counselor, are in psychological contact.
2. The client is in a state of incongruence, being vulnerable or anxious.
3. The counselor is congruent or integrated in the relationship.
4. The counselor experiences unconditional positive regard for the client.
5. The counselor experiences empathic understanding of the client's internal frame of reference.
6. The counselor succeeds in communicating Conditions 4 and 5 to the client; the client perceives these conditions.

As discussed in Chapter 9, the conditions that have been given the greatest attention in person-centered therapy are Items 3, 4, and 5 on the preceding list, which are the counselor's contributions to the relationship: congruence, unconditional positive regard, and empathy. It is crucial that the counselor enter the therapeutic relationship with these attitudes, and counseling techniques are simply the way of implementing these attitudes. Without these attitudes, all the polished techniques in the world will not produce effective therapy.

Rogers (1980) described empathy as a way of being that is powerfully curative because (a) the nonevaluative and accepting quality of the empathic climate facilitates clients taking a prizing, caring attitude toward themselves; (b) being listened to by an understanding other allows clients to listen more accurately to themselves, with greater empathy for their own organismic experiencing, their own vaguely felt experiences; and (c) clients' greater understanding and prizing of themselves opens them up to inner experiences that, in turn, become part of a more accurately based self-concept.

In discussing the profound impact of the therapist's empathic way of being with clients, Rogers noted a paradox: As clients change during counseling due to the therapist's empathy, positive regard, and congruence, these clients become more empathic, positively regarding, and congruent toward and with themselves. Thus, as one experiences the empathic way of being from another (e.g., a counselor), one develops attitudes toward oneself that enable one to become an effective therapist, for one's self. (For an in-depth examination of this process, see

Barrett-Lennard, 1997.) Although Rogers (1980) focused mostly on the empathic way of being, he also reiterated the person-centered view of the primacy of all three facilitative conditions. In comparing the influence of the three conditions, he noted that in ordinary life interactions (between members of a couple, teacher and student, colleagues, friends) congruence is probably the most important element. Because congruence or genuineness involves your letting the other person know your emotional state, Rogers believed it was the basis for living together in a climate of realness. In other situations, though, caring or prizing (i.e., unconditional positive regard) may be most important. For example, such positive regard may be of great importance in nonverbal relationships, such as those between therapist and profoundly disturbed client, between parent and infant, and between physician and very ill patient. Finally, Rogers believed that empathy may be the most important of the three conditions when "the other person is hurting, fused, troubled, anxious, alienated, terrified, or when he or she is doubtful of self-worth, uncertain as to identity" (1980, p. 160). For Rogers, the gentle and sensitive companionship provided by an empathic person helps to clarify and heal. As Rogers talked about this sensitively empathic person, it appears that empathy merges with the other conditions, and we are back to the trio operating in a creatively interactive way.

We have focused mostly on what the person-centered therapist is and does with clients. As a final comment, we add that there are as many "do not's" as "do's" in this approach. Thus, person-centered therapists avoid with the client any expression that has an evaluative connotation. Nonevaluativeness is essential to their approach. Person-centered counselors also do not interpret meanings to clients, do not question them in a probing manner, and do not diagnose, reassure, criticize, judge, praise, or describe them. These "do not's" are crucial. A common misunderstanding is that the person-centered therapist provides a great deal of praise and reassurance. Not so. The therapist prizes the client as a person, but his or her regard and empathy do not translate into continual positive evaluation or reassurance (see Raskin et al., 2011).

THE PERSON-CENTERED APPROACH IN PERSPECTIVE

Just what does the person-centered therapist do in a session? Despite the emphasis on attitudes and relationship rather than techniques, are there techniques that are favored by the person-centered approach? What differentiates the person-centered therapist from therapists of other persuasions?

In fact, everything we have seen (case presentations, examples of client–counselor interactions) indicates that the person-centered counselor responds to clients in a distinctive manner. His or her responses are, for example, "following" rather than "leading" responses. That is, the client's expressions are followed by the therapist, and paraphrasing responses are the most commonly used. Reflection of feeling is a predominant technique, as can be seen in virtually all of the cases Rogers himself presented in the literature. At the same time, it would be inaccurate to equate the person-centered approach and the empathic way of being with one or a few techniques (e.g., reflection of feeling). Reflection is used because it fits well with person-centered theory and philosophy. Over the years an increasingly broad range of techniques has been permitted. The bottom line theoretically is that the techniques be in sync with person-centered theory and philosophy (Bozarth, 1997).

Person-centered therapy, from its beginnings, has always been a non-directive approach, even though the term *nondirective therapy* has now fallen into disfavor. Advocates of the person-centered approach believe that the term has come to connote a much narrower range of responses to clients than is desirable and seems to put the emphasis in the wrong place (i.e., on techniques). At the same time, it is clear that a very deep non-directiveness is a fundamental part of person-centered therapy (Bozarth, 1990, 1997; Raskin & Rogers, 1995). Bozarth (1990) stated that the implications of this nondirective attitude "are staggering" and that the therapist must have no other intentions than the following:

> The therapist goes with the client—goes at the client's pace—goes with the client in his/her own ways of thinking, of experiencing, of processing. The therapist cannot be up to other things, have other intentions without violating the essence of CC/PC [client-centered/person-centered] therapy. To be up to other things—whatever they may be—is a "yes but" reaction to the essence of the approach. (p. 63)

We have noted that from early in his career Rogers was deeply invested in the empirical study of his theories. What can in fact be said about the empirically demonstrated efficacy of the person-centered approach? Put simply, does it work? The person-centered approach has been studied extensively over the years, and the results of controlled studies have been largely positive, particularly when the facilitative conditions are present to a high degree. There is now ample research support for the importance of the three facilitative conditions in a wide range of treatments, not just in person-centered therapy. The findings are especially positive when the conditions are assessed from the vantage point of the client, which Rogers believed was the most valid perspective (see reviews on empathic understanding by Elliott et al., 2011; on positive regard by Farber & Doolin, 2011; and on congruence/genuineness by Kolden, Klein, Wang, & Austin, 2011). In addition, the evidence on the effectiveness of person-centered therapy itself is positive, although, as is the case with virtually all treatments, the evidence does not indicate that person-centered therapy is superior to other legitimate therapies (Elliott et al., 2013; Murdock, 2013)

The person-centered approach and the field of counseling psychology have always been highly compatible. The person-centered therapist's belief in human beings' inherent potential for growth and self-actualization is deeply ingrained within counseling psychology and is in keeping with the core values of the specialty as discussed in Chapter 1; specifically, that of the focus on optimal functioning and on assets or strengths. Also, because of belief in the inherent human tendency toward actualization, the person-centered approach has favored briefer treatments (a central value of counseling psychology discussed in Chapter 1) over extended treatment. Overall, throughout its development from nondirective counseling to client-centered therapy to person-centered therapy, this approach to life and intervention has had a profound impact on counseling psychology and its practitioners.

For more extensive and highly readable discussions, including case materials, the reader is referred to chapters by Bozarth (1997), Murdock (2013), Prochaska and Norcross (2010), and Raskin et al. (2011). The edited book by Cooper, O'Hara, Schmid, and Wyatt (2007) provides an extensive, up-to-date look at the person-centered approach and its applicability to a wide range of treatments. Finally, Rogers's (1980) *A Way of Being* is a wonderfully rich, interesting, and still very relevant statement of issues and directions in person-centered therapy.

Fritz Perls and Gestalt Therapy

Just as the development of person-centered therapy is inextricably tied to the personhood and writings of Carl Rogers, the beginnings and early advancement of gestalt therapy are a consequence of the personality and work of Fritz Perls. Although Rogers and Perls belong to the same camp—the humanistic, third-force, growth-oriented therapies—and share several basic assumptions about personality and therapy, it would be hard to find two people whose outward personalities differed more. If Carl Rogers, for example, was the prototypical warm, kindly, gentle minister (or grandfather in his advanced years), Fritz Perls can be seen as a sort of flamboyant, creative, and somewhat eccentric movie director.

Prochaska and Norcross (2010) noted that as a person Fritz was much like his writings—both vital and perplexing. In his writings and especially in his gestalt therapy workshops, Perls was keenly perceptive, provocative, manipulative, evocative, hostile, and inspiring. His great charisma, as well as his effectiveness, created an almost cult-like following, particularly among professionals who participated in his workshops and spread the gestalt therapy gospel. Consider how Rogers's gentle and modest presentation of himself contrasts with Perls's statement:

> I believe that I am the best therapist for any type of neurosis in the States, maybe in the world. How is that for megalomania. At the same time I have to admit that I cannot work successfully with everybody. (Perls, 1969b, unnumbered page)

If it was a gentle, soft-spoken grandfatherliness that people were looking for from Perls, they came away from encounters with him disappointed and frustrated; if a stimulating, lively, spontaneous, and genuine encounter his workshop participants was wanted, they came away feeling enriched and enlightened (see Prochaska & Norcross, 2010).

Frederich S. Perls (1893–1970) began his therapy career as a psychoanalyst. After obtaining his MD degree in 1920 from Frederich Wilhelm University, he studied at the Berlin and Vienna Institutes of Psychoanalysis. Within the psychoanalytic framework, he was strongly influenced by Karen Horney, Otto Rank, and especially Wilhelm Reich, who was Perls's psychoanalyst in the early 1930s. Although Perls practiced analysis throughout much of the first half of his career, it is hard to see him using an analytic approach or attitude. His irrepressible, spontaneous, outgoing, and aggressive character seems to us to run counter to the restraint and control required in effective analysis.

Along with his training in analysis, Perls knew and was heavily influenced by the leading gestalt psychologists of the time (e.g., Kohler, Wertheimer, Lewin). In 1926 he became an assistant to the eminent gestalt psychologist Kurt Goldstein at Goldstein's Institute for Brain-Damaged Soldiers. While at Goldstein's institute, Perls met his wife to be, Laura Posner. Many (e.g., Simkin & Yontef, 1984) view Laura Perls as the cofounder of the gestalt movement. She received her DSc in 1932 from the University of Frankfurt. She was well versed in general and gestalt psychology. Although Laura wrote little, within the gestalt movement she is considered a leader.

By the time of his first book (*Ego, Hunger, and Aggression*, 1947), Perls had moved away from Freudian theory, but it was not until 1951 that he took his dramatic departure from psychoanalysis. At that time, he published (with Ralph Hefferline and Paul Goodman) *Gestalt Therapy: Excitement and Growth in Personality*.

Fritz and Laura had fled Hitler's Germany for South Africa in 1934; soon afterward he organized the South African Institute for Psychoanalysis. Then, with apartheid on the rise, the Perlses moved to New York in 1946. In 1952 they, along with the American psychologist Paul Goodman, formed the New York Institute for Gestalt Therapy. Run in the Perlses' apartment, the institute became the prototype for many gestalt therapy centers that sprang up around the country in the 1950s and 1960s. In 1960 Perls moved to California and in 1964 accepted an appointment at the Esalen Institute, where he held many of his training workshops and seminars along with gestalt leaders James Simkin, Walter Kempler, Irma Shepherd, and John Enright. It was during this time that Perls wrote two of his most interesting books. *Gestalt Therapy Verbatim* (1969a) is an engaging firsthand account of gestalt therapy and is generally considered Perls's best presentation of his approach. *In and Out of the Garbage Pail* (1969b) is a fascinating autobiography of one of the most creative and unusual personalities psychology has known. Perls spent the final year of his life, 1970, on Vancouver Island, where he was in the process of building a gestalt commune at the time of his death.

The gestalt therapy movement grew slowly at first and did not reach full force until the 1960s. The emotional climate of the 1960s, with its emphasis on self-expression in the here and now, seemed the ideal setting for gestalt therapy to take hold. And take hold it did. Belkin (1980) noted that no approach to therapy received more rapid popularity in a short period than did gestalt therapy in the late 1960s and 1970s. It is hard to convey in writing the climate and the excitement of the gestalt therapy movement. Burke (1989) got close with the following characterization:

> It is the late 1960s, and you are one of the lucky ones to attend a "human potential" seminar at the Esalen Institute, a center for workshops and training programs nestled between the mountains and the Pacific Ocean at Big Sur, California. You walk into a large room jammed with people, some seated on chairs, some sitting cross-legged on the floor, some standing along the sides. Every type of person imaginable appears to be here. There are young people, denim-clad, some a bit seedy. There are professional types, casually dressed, engaging in lively debate. There is even a psychoanalyst in the group, bearded, smoking a pipe, and looking more than a trifle uncomfortable in these environs. As a grandfatherly man walks into the room, the hum of conversations becomes a hush punctuated by cries of "Fritz, Fritz." Fritz is wearing a dashiki, and his round, smiling face peers out from an abundant white beard. What follows is a miracle to behold. One by one, like children before a Santa, members of the group volunteer to join Fritz at one end of the room on a "stage" set with three chairs, one for Fritz, one for the volunteer, and one empty. Fritz seems to know each person's soul, if not their names. One by one, he cajoles them, picks on them, intimidates them, surprises them. In response, they cry, laugh, scream, hug, and, from most reports, heal. (p. 252)

Burke (1989) pointed out that although the setting he has tried to capture seemed, 20 years later, to be an unlikely one for training in therapy (and it seems even more unlikely as we write this chapter), it indeed was one in which many bright, young practitioners learned to become gestalt therapists. Scenes like the above were repeated over and over in the 1960s, and to many at the time (professional therapists as well as laypersons) Fritz Perls was a sort of guru, a one-man liberator of human potential (Burke, 1989).

THEORY OF PERSONALITY: GROWTH AND MALADJUSTMENT

Neither Fritz Perls nor other gestalt therapists have developed a systematic theory of personality or psychopathology. Also, although many principles and procedures of counseling have been enunciated over the years, no comprehensive or definitive work is available. Perhaps this deficiency is related to Perls's view (a view endorsed in the gestalt arena) that gestalt therapy needs to be lived. Writing about it misses its essence. The creation of comprehensive theories and definitive positions ignores the reality that the gestalt approach to therapy, like any living organism, is in a continual process of change and evolution.

The theory of personality that does exist is more a cluster of loosely connected ideas that have evolved from the clinical experience of gestalt practitioners, rather than an overall theory of personality. Careful examination of the gestalt literature, though, does suggest several themes related to personality development and to healthy versus unhealthy functioning. It must be underscored that gestalt therapy is not synonymous with gestalt psychology. Although Perls and other gestalt therapists drew some ideas from gestalt psychology, the personality theory of gestalt therapy is really a loose and unique mixture of psychoanalysis, phenomenology, existentialism, gestalt psychology, Eastern religions, humanistic philosophy, and even behavioral psychology. Below we list and briefly discuss what appear to be central themes.

1. Humans are unified organisms and always function as *wholes*. Behavior is guided by the whole person; the whole determines the part.
2. The individual is continually faced with factors that disturb his or her balance and is continually seeking to restore balance or achieve equilibrium by satisfying his or her physical and organismic needs. The unmet need is the *incomplete gestalt* that demands completion.
3. Personality consists of many *polarities*, or opposites (e.g., strength and weakness, activity and passivity); in healthy functioning these polarities are integrated such that they work in harmony: the person is *centered*. In unhealthy functioning the polarities develop into splits, or dichotomies, throwing the person into a state of conflict.
4. The principle of *ecological interdependence* suggests that persons exist by differentiating self and other as well as by connecting

self and other. The boundary between self and environment or other must be kept permeable to allow exchanges (*contact*); at the same time, the boundary must be firm enough for organismic autonomy.

5. Human regulation is, to varying degrees, based on acknowledgment of *what is* (organismic) or on arbitrary imposition of what the person believes *should be* ("shouldistic"). The former reflects and leads to healthy functioning, the latter to neurosis.

6. *Awareness*—of what one is feeling, sensing, experiencing in the present, the *here and now*—is the key to healthy development and change and is the immediate goal of gestalt therapy.

What ties these diverse propositions together? Perls and other leading gestalt therapists are more concerned about healthy and unhealthy development than personality development per se. The healthy individual is responsible for himself or herself and seeks to be that self. As Perls (1969a) asserted, "Responsibility means simply to be willing to say 'I am I' and 'I am what I am'" (p. 70). If the individual seeks to be aware of his or her organismic needs, rather than living by "shoulds" or by some image of what is good, emotional health results. When this self-acceptance occurs, the polarities referred to above are accepted (for example, we accept our aggressive side as well as our gentle side); thus, the sides are integrated rather than being at war with each other.

As implied, the mature person lives in the present, in the so-called here and now. This does not mean that the individual is a hedonist who is concerned only with his or her own ego needs. It does mean that preoccupation with the past and the future is largely given up, so that one lives one's experience in the now. Values and standards are part of the immediate experience. The gestalt therapist understands the need for values; what is unhealthy is the all-too-frequent tendency to be driven by internalized "shoulds" at the expense of who one basically is and what one needs. When taking the responsibility to be oneself and to live in the present, one follows Perl's suggestion to live and review every second afresh. As people do this, the joy, excitement, and creative potential in their lives may be actualized.

GROWTH GONE AWRY: THE LAYERS OF NEUROSIS

What happens to interfere with the process of growth and with the actualizing tendency in all of us? Why is it that so many people become stuck in the deadness of living out social roles, in childish dependency, and in functioning more like computers than humans? Although Perls did not develop a formal theory of the causes of what he called growth disorders, he did point to some childhood factors (Perls, 1969a, 1970). To address the question of what goes wrong, we first have to look at Perls's concept of maturation. For Perls, "maturing is the transcendence from environmental support to self-support" (Perls, 1969a, p. 30). Parents can impede this process by undersupporting the child, so that needed support is pulled away before the developing child is ready for independence. More common is the critical, imposing parent who knows what is best for the child. The child either follows these unemphatic parents' dictates or runs the risk of losing love and approval. The child thus becomes fearful of independent behavior and becomes what he or she is "supposed" to become. The third and most common impediment to maturity is the spoiling of the child. Parents, out of their own unmet needs, all too often give the developing child everything they did not have. The parents are afraid to frustrate the child's wishes, and yet such frustration is needed if the child is to move and develop his or her own self-support. If the home environment is so secure and gratifying that the child's every need is met, that child will not move forward and will become stuck.

Whichever of these impediments occurs, the result is the same. Instead of learning to stand on his or her own two feet, "the child—or the childish neurotic—will use his or her potential not for self-support but to act out phony roles. These roles are meant to mobilize the environment for support instead of mobilizing one's own potential. We manipulate the environment by being helpless, by playing stupid, asking questions, wheedling, flattering" (Perls, 1970, pp. 17–18).

Perls and other gestalt therapists never developed a systematic or formal theory of neurosis (or *growth disorders*, as Perls liked to call them), but Perls did formulate an interesting concept of what he called the "layers of neurosis." These layers seen as the defensive shields that the person must work through to grow from neurosis to health. Because Perls placed no premium on consistency, the actual layers are somewhat different in two works published only a year apart (Perls, 1969a, 1970).

There are five layers of neurosis that form what Perls views as the structure of neurosis. In combining Perls's publications on these layers, the first layer can be seen as the *phony*, or *synthetic*, level. The neurotic spends most of his or her time at this level, a level in which one plays roles and games and tries to act out an ideal self-concept rather than being authentic. Perls (1970) described this layer colorfully as follows:

> We behave as if we are big shots, as if we are nincompoops, as if we are pupils, as if we are ladies, as if we are bitches, etc. [Thus the neurotic has] . . . given up living for his self in a way that would actualize himself. He wants to live instead for a concept . . . like an elephant who had rather be a rose bush, and a rose bush that tries to be a kangaroo. We don't want to be ourselves; we don't want to be what we are. We want to be something else, and the existential basis for being something else is the experience of dissatisfaction. We are dissatisfied with what we do, or parents are dissatisfied with what their child is doing. He should be different, he shouldn't be what he is; he should be something else. (p. 20)

Once the person gets through the phony layer, she or he must then pass through the *phobic, impasse,* and *implosive* layers. Although the distinctions between these layers are very murky in Perls's writing, the key issue is that as persons become more real, they encounter the internal objections to being authentic—all of the "should nots" in their psyche. Beyond this is a sense of being stuck and of deadness. At this implosive layer, persons contract and compress themselves. To move beyond this they must get into contact with the deadness involved in their imploding. When they do that, the next layer is entered. Implosion becomes explosion, as the *explosive layer* is experienced. The person comes to life, as this explosion is "the link-up with the authentic person who is capable of experiencing and expressing his emotions" (Perls, 1969a, p. 60).

The emerging healthy individual may explode into *grief* if he or she needs to work through loss experiences that had not been assimilated; *orgasm* if he or she is sexually blocked; *anger* if this feeling has been denied; and/or *joy* when there previously had been none. In fact, to be truly well functioning, the individual must be capable of all four of these explosions or experiences. In response to questions about the dangers involved in the explosion layer, Perls noted that the one way the danger is diminished is through the process of "melting." When in therapy the client becomes moved, he or she begins to melt, to feel soft, or to cry, which is a kind of melting that buffers against a dangerous explosion. Yet, at the same time, "basically one has to be willing to take risks" (Perls, 1970, p. 23).

THE PRACTICES AND PROCEDURES OF GESTALT THERAPY: EXERCISES AND EXPERIMENTS

What do gestalt therapists actually do? No other major theory of counseling presents as wide an array of interesting and evocative techniques and procedures as does gestalt therapy. To begin with, in the response modes sense (see Chapter 8), the main verbal technique is confrontation. The gestalt therapist vigorously confronts discrepancies in the client's presentation of himself or herself and challenges the client to express what he or she truly is and feels in the moment.

> "You are telling me you're sad, but you are smiling."
> "You say you're relaxed, but I see your feet are fidgeting."
> "You say you'd like to be strong but that's hard to believe right now because my fantasy is that you're a little baby."

These are the kinds of confrontations gestalt therapists often make. Discrepancies in the moment are noted, highlighting contradictions in what the client says, in what the client does, and between what the client says or does and what the counselor fantasizes about him or her.

Another response mode that typifies the gestalt therapist is *direct guidance*. The gestalt therapist often instructs the client about exercises (see below) and other behaviors that are desired in the moment. In addition, the gestalt therapist is probably more self-disclosing than any other kind of therapist, and *self-involving disclosures* about what is being experienced in the here and now with the client are the preferred kinds. On the negative side, the one response type that is clearly taboo in gestalt therapy is *interpretation*. This response mode seeks to get at the "whys" of behavior, whereas the gestaltists are more interested in "hows" and "whats." Interpretations more often than not lead to intellectualized responses that do not reflect immediate experiencing. To Perls, the search for underlying causes is useless at best. It takes the client away from where she or he needs to be.

Before discussing gestalt exercises and experiments, we must talk about how material from the client's past is to be dealt with in the gestalt approach. The focus on here-and-now experiencing, with the aim of developing awareness, does not preclude the exploration of past experiences. The critical thing is that those past experiences be explored in a way that is alive in the present. Thus, the client isn't to simply talk about the past; she or he is to experience the past in the now. Gestalt therapists will often encourage this process by asking clients to be themselves during the past time being examined: for example, "Be the 7-year-old of memories right now, and tell me what is going on for you."

Although Perls and other gestalt therapists have repeatedly cautioned against overreliance on techniques in the form of exercises, gestaltists do use a range of these strategies. We discuss some of these exercises and experiments here, both because they are valuable procedures in gestalt work and because this is a way of clarifying some of the major elements of gestalt counseling. It should be noted that the therapist is not to preplan the use of techniques. Following the rule of working with the experience (the therapist's as well as the client's), the gestalt counselor uses exercises as they are felt to fit the moment.

The basic purpose of exercises and experiments in gestalt therapy is to enhance the client's *awareness*, especially awareness of inner experiencing and feelings in here and now. *Exercises* are techniques that are used in individual or group counseling. *Experiments* are innovations that therapists use when client awareness and progress are blocked. These terms are often used simultaneously; the term *game* is also often used by gestaltists. Below we give a sampling of some key gestalt techniques. The reader is referred to Levitsky and Perls (1970), Passons (1975), and more currently Murdock (2013) for a thorough exploration of gestalt exercises and experiments. The major exercises and techniques are summarized in Table 13.1.

TABLE 13.1

Examples of Some Gestalt Therapy Exercises and Experiments

Exercise	How it's done and why
Two-chair technique	When the therapist sees conflict in client, he or she has the client enact both sides by engaging in a dialogue where one side is enacted when the client sits in one chair; then the other side is enacted when the client sits in the second chair. This helps the client resolve internal splits or polarities.
Empty-chair technique	The therapist asks the client to place into an empty chair the visual image of a person with whom the client has present conflicts. This is an excellent technique for resolving unfinished business.
"I take responsibility"	The client is asked to say, for example, "I won't" or "I don't want to," rather than "I can't."
Playing the projection	The client is invited to be the person he or she is projecting feelings or reactions onto. This helps clients realize that they are projecting and accept that the projections are actually their own feelings.
Reversals	The therapist asks the client to play the *opposite* of what the client is expressing. This helps to get at hidden reactions.
Exaggeration	The client is instructed to exaggerate gestures or body movements that reflect and help the client get in touch with his or her hidden feelings.
Repetition	The therapist asks the client to repeat—over and over and louder and louder—statements that reflect hidden feelings. This helps the client really see what was being glossed over.
"I see"	Members of a couple share perceptions of how they perceive each other. This helps them to understand and communicate what each sees in the other.

Games of Dialogue

As discussed earlier, gestalt therapy views personality as consisting of many polarities or opposites; for example, passive and aggressive, weak and strong, masculine and feminine, controlled and impulsive. In healthy functioning, these opposites are integrated: They coexist in a harmonious way and in fact support each other. For example, the dominant and submissive poles in us can each be given expression, and each helps the other become less extreme. The individual is *centered* when these polarities have been integrated. Often, however, there exists a split between the polarities, causing a state of conflict.

Games of dialogue are especially suited to situations in which such splits occur, and the aim of these games is to create full awareness of the split in the client. Awareness leads to resolution, so that the person may become centered. In games of dialogue, the client is asked to stage a dialogue between the two parts of himself or herself. With the counselor's guidance, each part is acted out and the dialogue goes on until it feels appropriate to stop. Often this dialogue is carried out with a "two-chair technique," whereby the client sits in one chair representing one side of the split and talks to the other side. Then, when he or she feels it is time to respond as the other side, the client switches chairs, and the dialogue continues.

Although, as we have noted, a wide range of polarities exists in all of us, the one that has been given the greatest attention by gestaltists is called the *top-dog* and *under-dog split*. The top-dog is that side of personality that moralizes and lives in a world of "shoulds." Top-dog tends to be bossy and condemning. On the other side, under-dog tends to be childlike, impulsive, and irresponsible; this side makes excuses and resists responsibility passively. You can see how easy it would be for a split to exist between these two sides (note their similarity to the superego and id in psychoanalytic theory; see Chapter 11), and in fact it may help clarify the concept to consider how this polarity might exist in yourself. In any event, given the prevalence of the topdog versus under-dog split, many gestalt dialogue games focus on it.

Unfinished Business

"Unfinished business" is a form of "incomplete gestalt" in gestalt psychology. Whenever unfinished business is detected in gestalt therapy (usually in the form of unresolved feelings), the client is asked to finish it. Clearly, any person will have a wide array of unfinished business in the interpersonal arena; for example, with parents, siblings, and spouses. In Perls's opinion, resentments are the most common and significant type of unfinished business.

"I Take Responsibility"

In gestalt therapy a premium is placed on the person's taking responsibility for his or her feelings and actions. The client is asked to say "I won't" rather than "I can't" and is also asked to say "and I take responsibility for it" as an addendum to his or her perceptions, feelings, and actions. Thus, "I am aware that I am smiling when I talk about this painful feeling—and I take responsibility for it." Or, "I don't know what to say—and I take responsibility for it." Although this may seem like a foolish and mechanical game, it does eventually drive home the point that responsibility resides in the person for all behaviors and that we constantly make choices about what we do and feel.

Playing the Projection

Probably the major defense mechanism according to gestalt therapists is projection. Whenever the gestalt therapist sees signs of projections, the client is asked to play the projection, as a way of becoming aware of the parts of himself or herself that are being projected onto others. Thus, for example, if the client feels the therapist is being critical, the client is asked to play the critical therapist. Often, a two-chair dialogue may be used to highlight the split occurring along with this projection.

Nowhere is playing the projection seen more vividly in gestalt therapy than in work on dreams. Such dream analysis is vastly different than in psychoanalysis. Whereas in psychoanalysis, the client is to free-associate to segments of the dream, in gestalt therapy the client is asked to actually *be* each and every object in the dream. Imagine, for example, a dream as follows (one actually reported by a client of one of the authors): "I was in the attic and a monster was looking at me hatefully. A little baby was sitting near the monster and was very frightened. The attic door slammed shut; I ran out and tripped over a cinder block."

In a gestalt analysis, the client was asked to play the roles of the monster, the baby, the cinder block, and the door that slammed shut. Each was eventually experienced as a warring part of herself, and the awareness that resulted took this client a step toward resolving these splits.

Reversals

As an example of a particular kind of split, the client's behavior is often seen as a reversal of underlying impulses. To bring about awareness of the hidden side, the gestaltist asks the client to play the opposite of what is being expressed. For example, the client who is expressing excessive timidity is asked to play an exhibitionist; the client who is hostile and critical is asked to be receptive and nonjudgmental; the client who is overly sweet is asked to play one who is unreceptive and attacking.

Exaggeration and Repetition

Exaggeration is aimed at helping clients understand body language. When unwitting gestures or movements seem to be significant communications (e.g., a wave of the arm, tapping of the foot), clients are asked to exaggerate the movement repeatedly so as to become more aware of its meaning. This attention to nonverbal behavior forms a significant part of gestalt treatment.

In fact, probably no other theoretical persuasion is as attentive to nonverbal behavior. Gestaltists believe that the body is used as a crucial vehicle for communicating messages of which the client is unaware.

Thus, attention to nonverbals aids greatly in the effort to enhance awareness. Earlier we noted confrontation as the major response mode used in gestalt therapy. Many such confrontations attend to discrepancies between verbal and nonverbal expressions.

The verbal counterpart of the exaggeration game is called *repetition*. Here, the gestalt therapist asks the client to repeat a statement over and over, often in a louder and louder voice. This is done when the therapist suspects that the client is not hearing himself or herself or is emotionally glossing over verbalizations that are significant. The repetition and the increased loudness help the client really hear rather than just form words.

Marriage Counseling Games

Gestaltists use several exercises when working with couples. For example, the therapist may have partners face each other and take turns beginning sentences with "I resent you for. . . ." This work may be followed by beginning sentences with "I appreciate you for. . . ." Other games reflective of important relationship themes are "I spite you by . . . "; "I am compliant by. . . ."; and "I see." This last preface, "I see," aims at helping discover what members of a couple see in each other. Perls felt that a major problem in marriages is that partners are in love with a concept rather than an individual. The "I see" game seeks to help the partners see each other as they really are.

When involved in the exercises we have just described, the gestalt therapist seeks to have the client follow some "rules." The most common rules are to (a) stay in the here and now; (b) communicate with the other person, the "thou," rather than an "it"; (c) use "I" language rather than "it" language (e.g., "*I* feel bad" rather than "*It* is a bad feeling"). Throughout all of the exercises and in fact throughout all of gestalt therapy there is one overriding goal, rule, and exercise: to make use of the awareness continuum. That is, the therapist seeks to facilitate the client's awareness of bodily sensations, perceptions, and emotions. The therapist often asks the client to "stay with this feeling" as a way of heightening awareness. As noted earlier, if there is a key to health in gestalt therapy, it resides in being aware. As Fritz Perls urged, "Lose your mind and come to your senses."

THE GESTALT APPROACH IN PERSPECTIVE

Just as there is a lack of clarity in person-centered therapy as to the role of therapist techniques, in gestalt therapy the role of the counselor–client relationship has been inconsistently and unclearly articulated, at least until recent times. Although Fritz Perls was fond of the expression "here and now, I and thou," in his own counseling it never seemed that

Perls developed "I–thou" relationships. Dolliver (1981b), for example, pointed out how the interpersonal quality that is necessary for an I–thou encounter was missing in Perls's work with clients and workshop participants. His exclusive focus seemed to be on the client and on exercises to promote awareness, and the "I" was missing from his interactions. In fact, Laura Perls commented that "what was problematic in Fritz's approach was that he was not interested in the person as such but in what he could do with her" (quoted in Friedman, 1983, p. 89).

Other gestalt therapists have noted this deficiency and have sought to strengthen the relationship component of gestalt therapy (e.g., Jacobs & Hycner, 2009; Polster & Polster, 1973; Simkin & Yontef, 1984). For example, whereas Perls seemed never to examine or reveal his own feelings and biases in his work, Shepherd (1970) asserted that "the therapist needs to listen carefully and admit, what you say is true of me if it fits, rather than dealing with this as the patient's fantasy and implying inaccuracy or distortion of perception [as Perls so often did]" (p. 237)

In fact, the apparent inconsistency and lack of clarity that mark the role of relationship in gestalt therapy appear to stem from its two distinct lines of thought about the role and importance of the relationship. Greenberg (1983) highlighted this role when he noted that some gestalt therapists, in the Perls tradition, focus on the role of "therapist as teacher of the method," whereas others key in on the relationship. Those who take the role of teacher use techniques and exercises to help clients focus attention on experiencing in the moment. For these counselors, I–thou relating is engaged in only as a means of teaching clients the significance of I–thou relationships. For the relationship-oriented gestalt therapists, however, the role of the authentic human encounter in the present is the key to change. These therapists seek to share themselves as part of the work and deemphasize the role of techniques and exercises.

It is clear that gestalt therapy as it is currently practiced is far more relationship-oriented than during Perls's time. Gestalt therapists now tend to use techniques as an extension of the kind of relationship that has been developed with the client (Gelso & Hayes, 1998). Jacobs and Hycner (2009) reflected this trend when they noted that emotional *contact* between therapist and client (the relationship part) is essential for full *awareness*. They proposed that therapy that makes use only of awareness techniques, without contact engagement of the therapist/person with the patient/person, will actually limit the awareness possibilities for the client and interrupt the becoming of both people.

GESTALT THERAPY NOW

What is the current status of gestalt therapy in counseling psychology? As a system of intervention, its creativity and confrontiveness (often aggressiveness when practiced by some gestaltists) fit beautifully with the turbulence of the late 1960s and early 1970s. The focus on the self, on "doing your own thing," seemed to capture the Zeitgeist. However, as the 1960s and 1970s have long faded from the field's consciousness, the immense popularity of gestalt therapy has clearly waned. By the 1980s, few counseling psychologists claimed gestalt therapy as either their primary or secondary theoretical orientation (Watkins et al., 1986; Zook & Walton, 1989).

In part, the decline in popularity of gestalt therapy was due to its lack of a research base. Few outcome studies had been conducted to support its effectiveness, partly because of the indifference among gestaltists to scientific study. Perhaps the deemphasis of intellect in gestalt therapy was inappropriately applied to research. If we should "lose our minds and come to our senses," perhaps scientific study is unnecessary. It should be noted that during the past two decades there has been a gradual accretion of research on the efficacy of gestalt therapy and of humanistic–experiential therapies in general. The evidence is quite favorable. It seems clear that humanistic–experiential therapies in general produce client change above and beyond changes in no-treatment control groups (Elliott et al., 2013) and that in seven studies of gestalt therapy, the treatment effects were equivalent to those of other humanistic–experiential treatments.

Although few counseling psychologists are now gestalt therapists, the gestalt approach has had an enormous influence on the practice of counseling psychology. Many of the techniques and exercises created by Perls and others are often used by therapists in their day-to-day practice (e.g., requesting first-person pronouns, staying in the here and now, bringing out internal dialogues). As Burke (1989) noted, a technique such as the two-chair technique and its variations is immensely versatile in its applications. This technique is exceptional in the gestalt therapy literature in that a solid line of research does exist supporting its positive effects on clients' awareness and behavior change (Elliott et al., 2013). Similarly, there is sound evidence of the effectiveness of the empty-chair technique (Elliott et al., 2013).

Not only have the techniques been influential, the concept of an authentic "I–thou" relationship has become a central part of the work of many counseling psychologists. No other theory has so powerfully articulated the importance of an I–thou relationship in counseling. The belief in its value in therapy is even stronger today than when Perls was alive (see Elliott et al., 2013; Gelso & Hayes, 1998; Jacobs & Hycner, 2009).

Finally, the influence of gestalt therapy is also evidenced in approaches that seek to integrate gestalt principles and techniques with other theories. Such integrative efforts are perhaps more notable in what is called process–experiential and, more currently, emotion-focused therapy (Greenberg, 2002) than in any other writings. This approach successfully blends the empathic emphasis of person-centered therapy with the more active techniques of gestalt therapy. Integrations such as this lead us to believe that gestalt and person-centered therapies are indeed alive and well in the practice of counseling psychology, although not in pure form. And research evidence strongly supports the effectiveness of the process–experiential or emotion-focused integration (see Elliott et al., 2013).

We have offered only a glimpse of the main ingredients of gestalt therapy. For more in-depth discussions, we suggest chapters by Murdock (2013) and Prochaska and Norcross (2010). Perls's (1969a) *Gestalt Therapy Verbatim*, in tandem with Polster and Polster's (1973) engaging book and Fagan and Shepherd's (1970) *Gestalt Therapy Now*, remain the classics. Jacobs and Hycner (2009) and Joyce and Sills (2010) have provided book-length treatments of gestalt therapy as it currently stands, with a particular focus of the gentler relationship orientation that has expanded so that gestalt therapy has become very similar to the process–experiential approach noted in the above paragraph.

Summary

Although the philosophy of humanism is rooted in much earlier times, humanistic approaches to counseling are a product of the mid-20th century. These approaches developed as a reaction to both psychoanalysis and behaviorism. As a group, they are aptly labeled the "third force" in psychology and counseling.

The different humanistic approaches vary in their specifics, but they share several assumptions about human beings, counseling, and science, regarding the democratic ideal as an essential value, the fundamental predominance of subjective experience, the inherent tendency of humans toward growth and self-actualization, the essential trustworthiness of people, the value of authentic human encounters in the present as a powerful way of helping clients grow and develop, and the necessity for scientific methods to fit the human experience if they are to enlighten us.

The two humanistic approaches that have had the greatest impact on counseling psychologists are Carl Rogers's person-centered therapy and Fritz Perls's therapy. Although Rogers's approach to counseling came before any theory of personality, Rogers did develop a set of clear and consistent theoretical statements about personality development. His emphasis was phenomenological, emphasizing the need to understand the private world of the individual and the whole person, rather than isolated parts. The self and self-concept are key components in Rogers's personality theory. In his effort to delineate healthy and unhealthy development, he focused on the actualizing tendency, how it goes awry, and how it may be facilitated. Difficulties caused by the formation of *conditions of worth* are pivotal in humans' estrangement from themselves, whereas in healthy functioning congruence exists between inner experiencing and behavior.

To Rogers, the key to successful counseling lies not in techniques or in accurate diagnosis but in the therapeutic relationship. In fact, the kind of relationship that is both necessary and sufficient for client change is marked, on the person-centered counselor's side, by empathic understanding, unconditional positive regard, and congruence.

Although techniques are deemphasized in person-centered therapy, counselors of this persuasion mainly use paraphrasing techniques, especially reflection of feeling. The person-centered approach to life and therapy is clearly one of nondirectiveness.

Largely because of Rogers's own self-actualization as a scientist as well as a practitioner, his ideas have been subjected to careful and thorough scientific scrutiny. Many ideas have been supported, some not; but in the main, client-centered therapy and now person-centered therapy have received empirical support for their effectiveness, at least with clients who are not severely disturbed. Rogers and his approach to treatment have had a profound effect on counseling psychology.

The gestalt approach of Fritz Perls also emphasized intervention more than personality development. Perls's theoretical statements about personality were unsystematic, although they were related to gestalt therapy formulations about treatment. Regarding neurosis, or growth disorders, Perls speculated that there are five layers to the neurosis—the synthetic, phobic, impasse, implosive, and explosive layers—each of which must be worked through if a person is to become mature.

In terms of verbal techniques or response modes, the gestalt therapist uses primarily confrontation, direct guidance, and self-involving disclosures. A hallmark of the gestalt approach is the use of exercises or games during counseling. Revealing key issues, these exercises include dialogues, "unfinished business," "I take responsibility," "playing the projection," role-playing reversals, exaggeration and repetition, and marriage counseling games. The overriding goal in gestalt therapy, whether approached through exercises or the counselor–client relationship, is the creation of awareness in the here and now of one's subjective experiencing.

Regarding the counselor–client relationship, there has long been a division in gestalt therapy between those who emphasize their roles as teacher of the method and those who focus on the I–thou relationship. Current gestalt theory emphasizes the importance of the I–thou relationship as a precondition for the development of client awareness.

Although the popularity of gestalt therapy has clearly declined since its heyday in the late 1960s and early 1970s, many of its techniques and ideas continue to appeal and have been incorporated by practitioners. The process–experiential approach of Greenberg represents an empirically supported integration of person-centered and gestalt therapies.

Feminist Multicultural Counseling

Integration and Cultural Competence in a Changing World

14

T he first line in the 2001 Mental Health Report of the U.S. Department of Health and Human Services reads, "America draws its strength from its cultural diversity" (p. 3). Yet, the 1999 Surgeon General's report on mental health in the United States documented striking disparities in access and quality of mental health services for ethnic minorities. It has long been acknowledged that not all people have equal access to counseling; nor do they have equally successful experiences when in counseling (see Lopez, Barrio, Kopelowicz, & Vega, 2012; Snowden, 2012; S. Sue, Cheng, Saad, & Chu, 2012). This has been particularly true for ethnic minority populations in the United States, who have tended to underutilize mental health services and often drop out of counseling prematurely (Brinson & Kottler, 1995; Carter & Forsyth, 2010; Cheung & Snowden, 1990; Sanders Thompson, Bazile, & Akbar, 2004). In addition, there has been a history of societal discrimination and oppression experienced by women; by ethnic minorities; by lesbian, gay, bisexual, and transgendered

http://dx.doi.org/10.1037/14378-014
Counseling Psychology, Third Edition, by C. J. Gelso, E. N. Williams, and B. R. Fretz

individuals; by those living in poverty; by individuals with disabilities; and by individuals immigrating to the United States, among others (e.g., Koss et al., 1994; Palombi, 2012; Root, 1995; L. Smith, Appio, & Chang, 2012; Speight, Isom, & Thomas, 2012; Szymanski & Hilton, 2012; Tolin & Foa, 2006), that has not always been appropriately addressed by traditional models of counseling.

As a response to the need to better serve people of different cultural backgrounds and various demographic variables (e.g., sex, race–ethnicity, sexual orientation, social class), two philosophical and counseling approaches were developed during the second half of the 20th century: *feminist therapy* (see Enns, 2004; Remer & Oh, 2012) and *multicultural counseling* (Fuertes, 2012; Ponterotto, Casas, Suzuki, & Alexander, 2001). We review below the historical developments of these two models of counseling, their counseling assumptions and strategies, and the ways in which current approaches to cultural competence attempt to blend and integrate these models.

Historical Overview

Feminist therapy has its roots in the consciousness-raising groups of the 1960s. In the 1960s, women began forming consciousness-raising groups that offered them the opportunity to see their personal problems as problems shared by other women (Kaschak, 1981). This idea, that one's individual experiences might in fact be shared social experiences, led to the phrase most often associated with feminist therapy: *the personal is political* (Enns, 2004). Although consciousness-raising groups were not initially designed as therapy groups, many women found them to be therapeutic (Kravetz, 1978) and to be a viable alternative to traditional psychotherapy (Kirsh, 1974).

By the 1970s, feminist therapists had begun to infuse aspects of consciousness-raising groups into traditional modes of therapy by including an analysis of gender roles and oppression and by endorsing group therapy as a safe place where women could practice new skills (Enns, 1993). The 1970s also brought changes within the American Psychological Association (APA). In 1970, the APA created a Task Force on the Status of Women in Psychology, which led to the establishment of Division 35 (Psychology of Women) in 1973. Because women of color participated in and contributed to Division 35, it became an instrument for bringing the concerns of ethnic minority women to light (Mednick & Urbanski, 1991). Division 35 began to publish the *Psychology of Women Quarterly*, which has been noted as publishing on both gender and multicultural issues (Davenport & Yurich, 1991). In addition, Division 35 organized a task force on Black Women's Priorities in 1976, shortly followed by a Task Force on the Concerns of Hispanic Women in 1977 (Mednick & Urbanski, 1991).

However, the feminist research of the 1980s did not focus much on minority women's issues. For example, the *Handbook of Feminist Therapy* (Rosewater & Walker, 1985) did not mention the concerns of ethnic minority women (Enns, 1993). The 1980s were more focused on developing an overall psychology of women and defining the needs of women in therapy. For example, new theories were offered (e.g., Chodorow, 1978; Gilligan, 1982) as replacements for previous, more androcentric theories of personality and development.

In the 1990s, feminist therapists and researchers called for changes within the profession, particularly in addressing broader diversity issues (Brown, 1994; Comas-Diaz & Greene, 1994). Enns (1993) called on feminist therapists to "recognize the diversity of women and men that is conveyed by their various problems, racial/ethnic identifications, economic statuses, personality styles, and exposure to 'isms' such as racism, sexism, ageism, and heterosexism" (p. 64). Thus, the history of feminist thought in counseling has demonstrated a growing commitment toward emphasizing multiple aspects of identity, a concept that in the 21 century has been referred to as *intersectionality* (Cole, 2009; Shields, 2008). Theory and research have shifted over time from focusing on male–female differences to masculine–feminine intersections (e.g., androgyny) to the intersection of various aspects of our diverse selves (e.g., gender, race/ethnicity, class, age, sexual orientation).

Similarly, multicultural counseling has experienced multiple stages of growth and development over the past half century. Although literature on counseling ethnic minorities during the 1950s was minimal, Jackson (1995) considered the 1950s to be the birth of the multicultural counseling movement, with the 1960s as its infancy period. During the early 1950s, counseling for ethnic minorities was primarily focused on issues of integration into the majority society by assimilating into the dominant culture (Copeland, 1983). However, there was a noticeable shift in approach as counselors were cautioned not to impose their belief systems onto their clients (Wrenn, 1962). With the new emphasis on respecting clients' beliefs and cultural backgrounds, the groundwork for the multicultural movement was laid (Jackson, 1995).

In the 1960s the multicultural counseling movement began to gain momentum. The Civil Rights Act of 1964 brought attention to racial and ethnic minority members of society. The goal of counseling ethnic minorities was no longer assimilation in the name of integration but appreciation of diversity (Copeland, 1983). During the 1960s, "minority counseling" referred to a White counselor paired with a non-White client. In the 1970s, the focus shifted with a change in the language to "cross-cultural" and "multicultural" counseling, which included any racial, ethnic, or culturally different therapist–client pair (Robinson & Morris, 2000).

With the 1970s came research focused on minority and multicultural issues. The *Journal of Non-White Concerns* played a major role in the multicultural movement. Because most counseling journals at the time were not publishing articles on minority concerns, many minority authors found the *Journal of Non-White Concerns* to be a channel for discussing research and ideas (Harper, 2003). Sundberg (1981) studied several mainstream APA journals (*Journal of Abnormal Psychology*, *Journal of Consulting and Clinical Psychology*, *Journal of Counseling Psychology*, and *Professional Psychology*) from 1975 to 1979 and found only 1% to 3% of the articles had any indication of cultural or ethnic material. Furthermore, Sundberg found that in the journals devoted to cultural and ethnic concerns, such as the *International Journal of Psychology* and *Journal of Cross-Cultural Psychology*, the articles almost never included studies on therapy or counseling.

The 1980s and 1990s brought about a plethora of research on multicultural counseling. D. W. Sue et al. (1982) published a seminal paper on the need for cross-cultural counseling competencies. The Association for Non-White Concerns in Personnel and Guidance changed its name to the Association for Multicultural Counseling and Development in 1985; along with this name change came a new outlook on inclusiveness that encouraged all racial and ethnic groups, including Whites, to join (Harper, 2003). The 1990s recognized the need for all counselors to have an understanding of cultural, racial, and ethnic issues (Davenport & Yurich, 1991). In 1992, D. W. Sue, Arredondo, and McDavis published the widely cited "Multicultural Counseling Competencies and Standards: A Call to the Profession." Their article included three primary areas of competencies, in which the culturally competent counselor is one who is (a) aware of his or her own cultural values and biases; (b) knowledgeable about different worldviews (and the cultural backgrounds of his or her clients); and (c) able to skillfully apply appropriate techniques and interventions. It has now been over 30 years since D. W. Sue et al.'s (1982) model of multicultural competencies was published (see Worthington, Soth-McNett, & Moreno, 2007, for an analysis of the field from 1986 to 2005), and the model has been updated several times (Arredondo et al., 1996; Sue, 2001; D. W. Sue et al., 1992, 1998). As of more than a decade ago, most counseling psychology training programs had incorporated multicultural competencies training into their graduate programs (Constantine & Ladany, 2001).

Despite different foci in their histories, both feminist and multicultural theory and counseling stand poised at this time to engage in a broader dialogue about inclusiveness (Enns, Williams, & Fassinger,

2012). To what extent can counseling theory and practice truly integrate various aspects of personal identity, including but not limited to gender, race, ethnicity, sexual orientation, social class, age, religion/spirituality, and ability? Indeed, counseling psychologists have begun to focus on these multiple identities and intersections of identities in recent years (Enns, 2010; Yakushko, Davidson, & Williams, 2009). Although there have long been calls for integration of these varying identities (Brown, 1994; Comas-Diaz & Greene, 1994), the integration has proven challenging and often elusive (Williams & Barber, 2004).

Enns et al. (2012) pointed out several similarities in the feminist and multicultural approaches that make integration possible. For example, they noted that an emphasis in both feminist and multicultural counseling is the sociocultural environment of the individual. Pope-Davis, Liu, Toporek, and Brittan-Powell (2001) noted that "one of the significant hallmarks of multicultural counseling is the recognition that context (sociopolitical, historical, and cultural) is an influential factor that affects clients' behaviors, attitudes, experiences, worldviews, and perceptions" (p. 131). Likewise, feminist therapy is based on the premise that personal and social identities are interdependent (Remer & Oh, 2012). Just as the importance of context and environment is critical to both multicultural and feminist therapies, it is also one of the central values in counseling psychology (see Chapter 1).

A second way that feminist and multicultural approaches are similar is the attention both give to issues of power, privilege, and oppression (Enns et al., 2012). Morrow and Hawxhurst (2012) noted the importance of examining power in feminist multicultural approaches to counseling, including sources of power and disempowerment in the individual client's life, the client's cultural views of expertness and authority, and power dynamics within the client–counselor relationship. In addition, Crethar, Rivera, and Nash (2008) expressed the importance within feminist and multicultural counseling of examining privilege, which they defined as

> the systematic and unearned benefits select groups of persons in society are bestowed based on specific variables. These variables are consistent with various characteristics manifested among persons in the dominant group in society. This includes but is not limited to one's racial/ethnic/cultural background, gender, socioeconomic class standing, age, sexual orientation, and physical/mental ableness, to name a few. (p. 269)

A third way the two counseling approaches are similar is that both emphasize the importance of awareness and critical consciousness in facilitating empowerment and equity (Enns et al., 2012). This similarity stems from the historical developments of the two movements, in which consciousness-raising groups were essential to the development of feminist therapy and awareness of bias has been noted as a critical ingredient in culturally competent therapy. Finally, feminist and multicultural counseling approaches value both individual and societal change, making the personal political. Like feminism (Brown, 1994; Enns & Williams, 2012), multiculturalism is "infused with political meaning" (Pope-Davis et al., 2001, p. 128). The politics of social change in both philosophies and approaches requires a focus on discrimination and oppression. In the early years of development of feminist therapy and multicultural counseling, some acts of discrimination were quite blatant (e.g., hate crimes, unequal pay for equal work). However, due to changing societal norms and legislative actions that have made some acts of discrimination illegal (as well as immoral), there has been a decline in overt expressions of prejudice over the last half century (Dovidio & Gaertner, 1998; Dovidio, Gaertner, Kawakami, & Hodson, 2002). Dovidio et al. (2002) contended that modern racism is more "subtle, often unintentional, and unconscious" (p. 88). This more unconscious and less overt bias has been called *aversive racism* (Kovel, 1970) and is something of which both feminist and multicultural practitioners should be aware.

Aversive racism occurs when *unintentional bias* is enacted by those who espouse nonracist values and attitudes. For example, a White counselor trainee who publically claims nonracist values reacts with noticeable negativity, adopting a superior and condescending tone, when meeting an African American client for the first time. Such actions are typically implicit in nature (Greenwald & Banaji, 1995), meaning they are automatically (or unconsciously) activated. People exhibiting aversive bias may deny bias in self-report questionnaires; however, social psychologists have found ways of measuring the experience of aversive bias nonverbally, such as by measuring amount of eye contact and rates of blinking (Dovidio, Kawakami, Johnson, Johnson, & Howard, 1997), which are interpreted as signs of discomfort or anxiety. Of course one cannot assume the aversive racism has caused the anxiety, but these nonverbal indicators of subtle bias could potentially create miscommunication and distrust in interpersonal relationships. In fact, these types of unconscious acts of bias have also been referred to as *microaggressions*, in which those with power and privilege subtly convey superiority over others (Fouad & Arredondo, 2007; Vasquez, 2007). Both feminist and multicultural therapy approaches help clients explore their own experiences with bias (both overt and implicit expressions) and empower them to advocate for social change.

Although feminist and multicultural counseling approaches "grew up" in separate ways beginning in the second half of the 20th century, they share many fundamental principles. Thus, in the 21st century, the emphasis has become the integration of these philosophical and applied approaches (Enns & Williams, 2012). The rest of this chapter explores the ways in which counseling psychologists can apply feminist and multicultural counseling approaches to their practice with clients, first by examining the approaches separately and then by highlighting their integration through culturally competent practice.

Feminist Therapy

There are many different forms of feminism, thus creating a number of different approaches to feminist therapy (Enns, 2004). Enns (2010) commented that older forms of feminism "tended to underscore single causes of gender inequality such as gender socialization (liberal feminism), the patriarchal foundations of society (radical feminism), and the devaluation of women's 'different voice' and relational strengths (cultural feminism)" (p. 333). Contemporary theories of feminism (or locational feminisms; Enns, 2010) are more integrative, focusing on the individual's diverse social identities and the importance of multiculturalism. Locational feminisms (e.g., postmodern feminism, women of color feminism, lesbian feminism, transnational feminism, and third-wave feminism), more explicitly than earlier forms of feminism, invite an analysis of privilege, oppression, and power, rejecting the notion that gender can be analyzed without considering other aspects of social identity. Yet, even the most modern approaches to feminist therapy still rely on several basic principles.

In 1980, Gilbert identified two primary elements of feminist therapy: (a) the personal is political and (b) the therapy relationship strives to be egalitarian. As previously discussed, the concept that the personal is political rests on the importance of environmental context and personal empowerment of individuals (see Chapter 1). Contrary to more traditional forms of therapy in which intrapsychic factors hold a primary role (such as in examining the individual's cognitions, personality structure, and emotional states), feminist therapy has always emphasized the context, structures, and social forces that impact individuals' mental health needs and experiences. For example, clients' symptoms are often seen as ways of coping with environmental stressors, such as in the case where a client learned to dissociate during traumatic early life events as a way to live through the experience and survive. Enns (1993) noted that

> rather than viewing symptoms such as depression, anxiety or passivity as problems to be eliminated, the feminist therapist views these patterns as indirect forms of expression that can be refocused in more direct and productive forms of communication as the client gains a stronger sense of self. (p. 11)

Thus, the client who used dissociation as a coping strategy in childhood can learn that, though they served a protective function early in life, the dissociative strategies may have lost their helpfulness in adulthood and are instead getting in the way of productive relationships. The therapist might help the client learn new ways to cope with anxiety. This approach lets the client know that it was functional for him or her to have adopted a protective strategy as a child (so emphasizing that the client used the strategies as a survival tactic) and empowers the client to seek out new, more functional ways to cope in the present.

The second primary element of feminist therapy, that the therapy relationship should be egalitarian, stems from the contention that therapists should model genuineness, empathy, and unconditional positive regard, as in traditional Rogerian approaches to counseling (see Chapter 13), while attempting to share power with the client and help the client learn to negotiate within relationships. Clients are seen as the experts on their own lives and are encouraged to become active agents of change for themselves and advocates for social changes that go beyond simply their own personal concerns (such as by becoming aware of the ways in which societal norms have shaped their perceptions and often their lived experiences). Essentially, feminist therapists take on a perspective of strength and coping, where women are considered capable, pain is considered adaptive not pathological, and strength and resilience can be enhanced even in the face of challenge. The approach emphasizes the need to grapple with power and the ideal of personal empowerment. Enns (2012a) noted that the emphasis in the model is on "power within," not "power over."

Modern feminist therapy also emphasizes the importance of diversity, social activism, and attention to the interdependence of personal and social identities (Enns, 2010; Morrow & Hawxhurst, 2012). Worell and Remer (2003) described the use of social identity analysis in therapy where clients identify and label each of their social locations (with regard to, e.g., gender, race, ethnicity, sexual orientation, class, age, ability status). The activity is used to help clients understand which elements of their identities are most salient and most useful for focus in the therapy. Other types of analysis are also typically used in feminist therapy, such as gender-role analysis (see Worell & Remer, 2003) and political analysis (see Morrow & Hawxhurst, 1998). In addition, reframing and relabeling distress as located within the society rather than the individual (Brown, 2000) allows clients to adopt a different perspective on their pain and coping. This perceptual shift allows new feelings and interpretations to surface (Remer & Oh, 2012), empowering clients to take action. For example, a teenage girl struggling with anorexia can acknowledge that her anxieties about her body image are related to the media's typical focus on thinness as an ideal. Although psychological issues are quite complex and so typically cannot be reduced to a simple description of their etiology, the feminist approach would be to help clients see the connection between their internal distress and the environment around them. With that new understanding, clients can often start to "give themselves a break," allowing more personal energy to be directed into the healing process.

As a specific example of this counseling approach, Morrow and Hawxhurst (2012) provided seven steps to address a particular problem or concern in therapy. First, they suggested that a person assess the situation (what happened, how did you feel, who held the power?) and then affirm him- or herself (asking what do you value about yourself, what are your limitations and vulnerabilities?). The next steps are to acknowledge one's power and areas of powerlessness at the personal (what can you do for yourself?), the interpersonal (who are your allies?), and the social levels (what are other areas of support or barriers, such as lack of information or permission?). Then the client analyzes his or her possibilities, weighs the risks involved, and makes a choice. Morrow and Hawxhurst also encouraged the use of questions, such as *Where did you learn that?* to *Who benefits?* and *What happens when you break the rules?*

Although feminist therapy did not initially give enough attention to the diversity of women (Enns, 2004), the past 2 decades in particular have produced a paradigm shift in the field. In 1995, Laura Brown called on feminist therapists to infuse antiracist approaches into their work. In 1998, the Section for the Advancement of Women (SAW) of Division 17 (Society of Counseling Psychology) of the APA held a conference on integrating feminism and multiculturalism (Fassinger, 2004). Contemporary feminist therapy now very clearly emphasizes sociocultural context, multicultural issues, and social justice.

Multicultural Counseling

Fuertes (2012) suggested that a good definition of multicultural counseling would be when counselors integrate, into both their theoretical and technical counseling approaches, relevant "human diversity factors" (i.e., factors that may stem from the client, the counselor, or the therapeutic relationship; see Chapter 9) and thus work toward good counseling process and successful outcomes. Fuertes and Ponterotto (2003) noted that

> human diversity refers to salient group-reference factors that are meaningful to the individual; these may include gender, socioeconomic background, religion, race, ethnicity, and/or regional/national origin, sexual orientation, all or any of which may inform or shape individual identity, behavior, values, attitudes, and/or beliefs. (p. 52)

Fuertes (2012) went on to point out the assumptions inherent in multicultural counseling contained in the definition. First, the definition highlights the importance of integration of human diversity information with decisions about assessment and interventions in counseling. Second, the definition makes clear that multicultural counseling should be concerned with affecting positive change in both the process (e.g., relationship building) and the outcome (e.g., symptom relief) of the therapeutic work. Third, the definition acknowledges that culture permeates all levels of the counseling experience, from the individual (client, counselor) to the interaction (relationship of client and counselor). Thus, the definition also highlights what Fuertes called the "layered complexity" (p. 572) of understanding the sources of diversity in the room and the ways in which that information can impact the success of the counseling.

Many different forms of multicultural counseling have been developed (for reviews, see Fuertes & Gretchen, 2001; Ponterotto, Fuertes, & Chen, 2000). Yet, D. W. Sue et al.'s (1992) classic work still informs the different models, focusing on counselors' awareness, knowledge, and skill (Fuertes & Ponterotto, 2003). First, a multicultural counselor is aware of his or her own cultural background, salient cultural beliefs and values, and biases. One way to begin this journey of self-awareness is by hauling out the crayons and taking a few minutes to draw the symbols of those aspects of your identity that are most important to you. How aware are you of those many dimensions of your identity? Are some more salient than others? Were you surprised by any of the dimensions you came up with? The second author has participated in this exercise multiple times (and can admit that, yes, she does still like playing with crayons!) and is always intrigued by which aspects of her self become salient at different times. She usually identifies her basic demographic attributes (e.g., a White woman) and her ethnic heritage (e.g., Irish American), but she also includes roles (e.g., mother) and experiences (e.g., obtaining a doctorate) that are salient in her life. In graduate school, she began a lifelong approach to learning about herself as a racial being and feels that without a commitment to becoming aware of herself, her beliefs and values, and her biases and blind spots she would not be able to engage fully and appropriately in multicultural counseling.

Becoming aware of yourself as a racial, gendered, ethnic, sexual being (among other salient characteristics) is important, but so is gaining knowledge about other cultures and about multicultural issues in general. Thus, a multicultural counselor stays current with multicultural theories, research, and applications. Fuertes (2012) insisted that

> a competent practitioner with a high percentage of racial/ethnic minority clients must know the literature in multicultural counseling, and have thought consciously about how multiculturalism fits with him or her as a person, with his or her approach to assessment and intervention, and how it can inform his or her approach to maximize effectiveness. (p. 580)

This search for knowledge is not something that can ever be completed. One must continually seek new knowledge as cultural diversity factors are both ever present and ever changing. And one must learn to integrate this new knowledge with existing knowledge and skills. The important common factors or core conditions of good counseling in general are important in all multicultural counseling as well: safety, support, rapport, and the therapeutic relationship (Fuertes & Ponterotto, 2003). It is about using multicultural knowledge to connect deeply with a client, support that client, and help him or her achieve goals. Fuertes (2012) said it well:

> Multicultural competence is not so much about having knowledge about various cultures of the world, although this can help in therapy and be personally valuable to counselors. The real, crucial knowledge is how racism, marginalization, or poverty can affect the individual. (p. 581)

Having an understanding of these issues and staying current with recent research findings (see Chapter 6) can help the counselor both relate to the client and seek appropriate ways to intervene in counseling.

The third aspect of multicultural counseling is the skills that the counselor brings to therapy. Although there is less research on particular skills (Constantine, Fuertes, Roysircar, & Kindaichi, 2008), certain skills have been identified as important in multicultural counseling. For example, multicultural counselors establish a strong personal and working bond with their clients, providing a safe environment conducive to building a strong working alliance and real relationship (Pope-Davis et al., 2001; see also Chapter 9). Multicultural counselors should also be willing and able to engage in difficult dialogues about gender, race, ethnicity, sexual orientation, or other cultural variables that are salient to the client, as well as about issues of discrimination, privilege, power, and empowerment (Brown, 2013). Multicultural counselors also use intervention strategies and techniques that are appropriate to and consistent with the cultural values and life experiences of the client (D. W. Sue & Sue, 2003). D. W. Sue and Sue (2003) suggested that "because groups and individuals differ from one another, the blind application of techniques to all situations and all populations seems ludicrous" (p. 20). In other words, multicultural counseling requires that therapists be culturally competent.

Integration of Theories and Cultural Competence

What does it mean to be culturally competent? D. W. Sue and Sue (2003) described cultural competence as "the counselor's acquisition of awareness, knowledge, and skills needed to function effectively in a pluralistic democratic society (ability to communicate, interact, negotiate, and intervene on behalf of clients from diverse background)" (p. 21). Whaley's (2008) linguistic analysis examining the use of varying terms (*cultural competence, cultural sensitivity, multicultural counseling*) suggests that there are two important dimensions to attend to: *sensitivity* (much like the knowledge and awareness highlighted by D. W. Sue et al., 1992) and *competence* (or skills, again mirroring the work of D. W. Sue et al., 1992). Whaley suggested that training should follow a two-stage process whereby a counselor works on enhancing his or her cultural sensitivity and then addresses his or her abilities to provide culturally competent interventions (see also Ridley, Mendoza, Kanitz, Angermeier, & Zenk, 1994b). Because some have suggested that all counseling is multicultural (Fukuyama, 1990) and because counseling can never be culturally neutral (Coleman, 1998), becoming culturally competent is critical for *all* counseling psychologists, integrating both feminist and multicultural perspectives (Enns et al., 2012). Hall (1997) even suggested that psychologists must become more culturally competent in today's multicultural society or face obsolescence.

Laura Brown (2008) has suggested that a contemporary approach to cultural competence is less about acquiring specific knowledge of specific groups (though that is useful information) and more about adopting an attitude of curiosity about others and a willingness to not ignore or pretend not to notice difference. It requires an understanding that identities are not always apparent from direct observation (of, e.g., a person's phenotypes); rather, coming to know a person requires an understanding of their multiple social contexts. Brown likes to use examples from *Star Trek* (e.g., Borg, Klingon, Romulan, and Vulcan) to highlight ways to understand what it means to work with others from different ethnicities (see Brown, 2009). To use her approach, imagine being in counseling with a Romulan. What is the person like? How salient is the client's Romulan status to him or her at this time? What are you curious about? How can you be aware of Romulan experiences and also be willing to set them aside when they are not relevant to the issue at hand? If you are a Borg, what types of complexities enter the counseling relationship? What questions would you ask if you were simply being curious about another person and not trying to establish "expert knowledge" about his or her cultural background?

Cultural competence also requires a curiosity not just about and an understanding of the cultural background of the client but about the ways in which privilege and oppression work (in both personal and societal ways). In her presidential address for the Society of Counseling Psychology, Israel (2012) noted the importance of understanding privilege in counseling psychology. We mentioned earlier that Crethar et al. (2008) defined privilege as the unearned benefits members of society's dominant group enjoy. Similarly, McIntosh (1989) likened privilege to an "invisible knapsack" that members of the dominant group in society carry with them. In the United States, privilege has historically been provided to "White, middle- and upper-class, heterosexual, English-speaking, and able-bodied males" (Crethar et al., 2008, p. 270). An analysis of power (privilege) and responsibility is a critical element of feminist multicultural counseling practice (Williams & Barber, 2004). Yet, such awareness is often difficult to achieve without training, and there is evidence that appropriate training can facilitate counselors' development of more sophisticated and sensitive awareness (Neville et al., 1996).

Ridley (1995), Kiselica (1998), Leong and Santiago-Rivera (1999), and Neville, Worthington, and Spanierman (2001), among others, have all contributed to understanding some of the challenges and resistances encountered in developing the self-awareness needed for multicultural competence. Often, despite counselors not having any overt prejudicial attitudes, actions and behaviors occur in counseling sessions that are indeed biased and stereotypical and that therefore significantly impede the development of trusting relationships. Kiselica's (1998) description of discomforts he encountered in exploring highly charged areas of diversity is quite helpful. Ridley's (1995) identification of particular defenses is also very helpful. He clearly explained that these defenses, like psychological defenses in general, are typically used quite unconsciously. His eight racially related defenses are especially helpful in understanding what he called "unintentional racism," as compared to overt or covert intentional racism. The eight defenses are color blindness, color consciousness, cultural transference, cultural countertransference, cultural ambivalence, pseudotransference, overidentification, and identification with the oppressor. We have space to describe just one of these defenses, so readers may want to consult Ridley for his very useful and understandable explanations and illustrations of the other seven. As one example, Ridley (1995) described the defense of color consciousness as

> the opposite of color blindness . . . based on the premise that the client's problems stem essentially from being a minority. . . . The color-conscious counselor places too much on the color of the client, while overlooking the client's contribution to the presenting problem. (p. 68)

Leong and Santiago-Rivera (1999) provided other examples of challenges to self-awareness that arise from quite normal and typical socialization processes. Of the six challenges they described, perhaps most unexpected are their explications of the pitfalls in multicultural understanding presented by the social psychological forces of false consensus and the workings of the attraction–selection–attrition framework. False consensus is the well-documented process of seeing one's own behavior as most typical and assuming that, under the same circumstances, others would react in the same way. What has often been called Eurocentric thinking is not necessarily an overt philosophical position but often just false consensus operating (e.g., "the way I think is how most people think"). Regarding attraction–selection–attrition frameworks, organizational psychologists have shown that one of the reasons organizations often find it extremely difficult to institute change is that members keep being selected who are like those present and those who are not quickly leave (Schneider & Smith, 2004). Thus, getting new perspectives on how people think or how to do things differently is greatly impeded.

Finally, Neville et al. (2001) overviewed the complexities of racism, White privilege, and color-blind racial attitudes (see also Chapter 6). A color-blind approach means that a counselor denies the existence of racism and does not believe that race plays an important role in people's life experiences. Neville et al. suggested that color-blind racial attitudes ("I just don't pay attention to race at all. A person's race shouldn't matter") are a form of racial prejudice deeply embedded in our worldview and cognitive schema. They suggested we need to work against this ideology, its resulting forms of racism, and the miscommunication that arises when one interprets others' behaviors from this perspective. To work against this ideology involves a revisioning of the literature and textbooks in the field to include an analysis of racism and inclusion of these concepts in counselor training. Because of the many ways that we may be unaware of our own biases, as several authors have pointed out (e.g., Dovidio, Neville, Ridley), training is a critical aspect of becoming a culturally competent counselor.

MULTICULTURAL TRAINING

Hills and Strozier (1992), in their review of the status of multicultural training in the 1980s, reported that "although most respondents agreed in principle with the need for expanded training and clinical experience in multicultural issues, their actual course and practical offerings did not mirror this attitude" (p. 43). Ponterotto (1997) compared his survey results with those of the prior 10 years, and he concluded that there had been notable progress in at least the development of curriculum related to multicultural training and in inclusion of research training opportunities, but far less progress in incorporating multicultural training in counseling practice and supervision. Pope-Davis, Reynolds, Dings, and Nielson (1995) found that counseling psychology students received greater amounts of coursework, training, and multicultural supervision than did clinical psychology students; however, the differences were significant mostly because there was so little training in clinical programs, not because of extensive amounts in counseling psychology. D. W. Sue,

Rivera, Capodilupo, Lin, and Torino (2010) noted that although "acquiring the awareness, knowledge, and skills to facilitate difficult dialogues on race should be a top priority in the training of educators, helping professionals, supervisors, and trainers" (p. 212), White trainees in particular express a number of negative emotions (e.g., anxiety, helplessness) and problematic perspectives on race (e.g., denial of Whiteness or White privilege, color blindness) that make it difficult to have productive dialogues in the classroom and in supervision (Constantine & Sue, 2007; D. W. Sue, Lin, Torino, Capodilupo, & Rivera, 2009; Utsey, Gernat, & Hammar, 2005).

The deficits in multicultural supervision found by Ponterotto (1997) are also reflected in the findings of Mintz, Bartels, and Rideout (1995), who found that the psychology interns they surveyed "reported mediocre preparation for counseling ethnic minority clients" (p. 316). Incorporation of a multicultural focus in practica and internships has no doubt been slowed by the fact that 70% of the current generation of supervisors has had no formal training in dealing with multicultural issues (Constantine, 1997). Almost every survey has found that directors of training programs believe that these are transitional times in which they are continuously engaged in improving available multicultural training and supervised experience (Quintana & Bernal, 1995; Speight, Thomas, Kennel, & Anderson, 1995). Although evidence of multicultural training effectiveness has been well established (see T. B. Smith, Constantine, Dunn, Dinehart, & Montoya, 2006, for a meta-analytic review of the training literature), some mixed results remain, with some researchers finding training benefits (particularly to White counselors) on levels of multicultural awareness (Chao, Wei, Good, & Flores, 2011) and on knowledge (Chao, 2012), and others finding little systemic differences posttraining (Lee, Sheridan, Rosen, & Jones, 2013).

CONCEPTUAL MODELS OF TRAINING

It has been much easier to agree on the need for training in multicultural competence than on what the content of such training should be. Until the beginnings of integrative developments of the 1990s (described in the next few paragraphs), both the content and processes of training varied immensely from program to program and even within programs from one year to another. For many students, relationships were unclear; for example, between development of self-awareness about culture and how that awareness could affect counseling practice. Or, once students have learned about Native American culture, how should their counseling strategies be modified, if at all? Students might learn a long series of "do's" and "don'ts" for each different culture (for example, "be fairly direct with Native American clients, pay increased attention to extended family with African American clients," and so forth). Such lists increase the risks of counselors engaging in the kinds of overgeneralizations of culture described above; moreover, how many separate lists of "do's" and "don'ts" can a counselor be expected to remember?

Fortunately, in the 1990s two kinds of integrative conceptualizations began to appear that hold promise for a more comprehensive multicultural counseling in the years to come. The first of these integrative movements to be described relates primarily to the development of skills in incorporating attention to universal (etic), culture specific (emic), and individual (idiosyncratic) factors. We have already reviewed the problems of overgeneralization of culture that emerged from the first developments in multicultural counseling, with their emphasis on cultural awareness and cultural knowledge. Yet, to simply shift back to traditional universal factors would be just as erroneous; in fact, the errors of the past led to development of multicultural counseling. Leong (1996), in building the case for his integrative model, highlighted the problem of focusing too narrowly on any one of the three perspectives reflected in the classic saying that 'every person is in certain respects: (a) like all other persons, (b) like some other persons, and (c) like no other person' (p. 190). While noting the progress that had been made on identifying intragroup differences within a given culture (see discussion of racial identity and acculturation in Chapter 6), Leong pointed out that these models have failed to account for "the existence and constant interplay of all three levels of human personality in a complex and dynamic fashion" (Leong, 1996, p. 201). Carter and Qureshi (1995) also emphasized the need for understanding the interplay of these factors, not just their simultaneous existence.

The second kind of integration is an outstanding exemplar of the scientist–practitioner model of counseling psychology. Several multicultural leaders, also dissatisfied with the fragmentary nature of much multicultural training and its lack of established relationships to either theoretical or empirical bases, have focused on integrations that bring together some long-established theoretical perspectives in psychology with what we have learned from the early developments of multiculturalism. Two major examples of such integrations appeared in *The Counseling Psychologist* (Fischer, Jome, & Atkinson, 1998; Ridley, Mendoza, & Kanitz, 1994).

Ridley et al. (1994), in their reexamination, operationalization, and integration of multicultural training, called on the well-established literature on the principles of effective instruction in order to provide a framework for multicultural training. They generated a matrix of 10 learning objectives by 10 instructional strategies. Each learning objective (e.g., cultural empathy, ability to critique existing counseling theories for cultural relevance, knowledge of within-group differences) was accompanied by relevant literature demonstrating the need for including this learning objective in multicultural training. Their 10 instructional strategies (e.g., participatory learning, modeling–observational learning, introspection) were all illustrated by examples from multicultural counseling training programs. Their model provided the best "map" of multicultural training that had ever been presented. Although it did not provide a great deal of information and strategies on "how" all the learning objectives can be achieved, it did show "all the places one needs to go to [or] touch base with" in the process of becoming multiculturally competent.

Whereas Ridley et al.'s (1994) integration called on the psychological literature on effective instruction, Fischer et al. (1998), for their integrative model, called on the psychological literature on common factors of effective psychotherapy and healing. They also addressed (a) concerns noted in the first part of this section regarding tensions between etic and emic considerations in working with culturally diverse clientele, (b) the "somewhat fragmented and sometimes particularist literature" (Fischer et al., 1998, p. 540) of multicultural counseling and (c) how five prior models of multicultural counseling (e.g., Helms, 1995; Leong, 1996) might become more unified through their common factors approach.

From their review of the literature on common factors of effective psychotherapy, considered from both Western and transcultural approaches, Fischer et al. (1998) identified four essential components of effective multicultural counseling: the therapeutic relationship, shared worldview, client expectations, and ritual or intervention. After building their case for how each of these four rest upon significant results obtained from the study of both traditional and multicultural counseling, they concluded,

> The counselor needs (continually) to hypothesize what he or she can do, within the context of the client's unique culture, to enhance the therapeutic relationship, to facilitate convergence in worldview, raise the client's expectations, and implement culturally relevant interventions. We believe that psychologists can best serve culturally different clients by applying their knowledge of common factors in a cultural context. (p. 566)

Fischer et al. (1998) also spelled out specific research implications for each of four common factors; the results of such research will be quite helpful in identifying the strengths and weaknesses of the model. The very positive conclusion is that there are now several fairly comprehensive integrative models one can utilize for multicultural training, all of which represent significant advances over accumulating fragmentary and unintegrated experiences of and knowledge about diverse cultures.

Beyond the notion that there are essential multicultural counseling skills to be learned, there are also questions about how and when to incorporate training in these skills. There has been a healthy ongoing dialogue (e.g., Ancis & Ali, 2005; Reynolds, 1995) about whether multicultural content should be covered in a single course or by modules in several courses, at beginning or advanced levels, and so forth. Perhaps the clearest consensus that has been reached is that both a course (or courses) on multicultural counseling and infusion of multicultural concerns into most of the curriculum of a counseling psychology training program are essential. Experience has shown that a single course often left participants not only with inadequate exposure to all of the essential components of competent multicultural counseling but also with the perspective that cultural diversity was a separate, specialized interest. Similarly, consensus has emerged that counselor awareness about one's own culture is clearly fundamental to being able to make effective use of whatever knowledge and skills are taught regarding other cultures. A natural corollary position to this observation is that self-awareness training should begin very early in the program, so that the knowledge and skills infused in other parts of the curriculum can be meaningfully understood and applied by students as they proceed through their programs. Finally, far more attention is now being given to ensure that there is follow-through in practica and internships so that all students have well-supervised experiences (Brown & Landrum-Brown, 1995) in applying multicultural knowledge and skills with a broadly diverse range of clientele.

ASSESSING MULTICULTURAL COMPETENCE OF COUNSELORS

Although training in multicultural competence is critical, it is equally essential to have some way to establish whether training has been successful. Thus, a number of counseling psychologists have developed measures to assess multicultural competence. Early in the development of the initial (and most widely used) measures, LaFromboise, Coleman, and Hernandez (1991) diplomatically confronted counseling psychologists with a "notable" deficiency in research regarding the effectiveness of training in multicultural counseling. Their review of investigations of the effectiveness of such training indicated that almost every such study included only traditional global measures of counseling effectiveness; the studies lacked measures assessing the cultural sensitivity and competence of the counselors. Such a lack was at least understandable, given that measures of multicultural competence had not been developed; however, investigations of effectiveness of multicultural training could hardly be conclusive without such measures. For example, if the measure of effectiveness of training in a multicultural program is the same as the measure of effectiveness for a generic or traditional program, how does one know that the multicultural component had any effect? Or, in a study with clients, if client ratings are obtained only on measures of satisfaction and perceptions of counselors, how can it be known whether clients were helped by culturally sensitive interventions?

Since that time, a number of multicultural competence measures have been established. The earliest of the self-report measures was the Multicultural Awareness–Knowledge–Skills Survey (MAKSS; D'Andrea, Daniels, & Heck, 1991). Note from its title that this survey has three scales based on the tripartite model of the Sue et al. (1982) reported on multicultural competence. The MAKSS consists of 60 items, with 20 items each for the awareness, knowledge, and skills areas. Counselors respond to each item on varying 4-point scales; for example, *Very Limited* to *Very Aware* for an item like "At this point in your life, how would you rate your understanding of the impact of the way you think and act when interacting with persons of different cultural backgrounds?"; or *Strongly Disagree* to *Strongly Agree* for an item like "In the early grades of schooling in the United States, the academic achievement of such ethnic minorities as African Americans, Hispanics, and Native Americans is close to parity with the achievement of Anglo mainstream students." These two sample items indicate not only the varying response format but also the fact that some items are self-descriptions, whereas others are items that could be scored right or wrong. Pope-Davis and Dings (1995) reviewed some of the assets and limitations of this mixture of items. In 2003, Kim, Cartwright, Asay, and D'Andrea created the 33-item Multicultural Awareness, Knowledge, and Skills Survey–Counselor Edition—Revised (MAKSS-CE–R), which allowed the comparison of self-ratings of cultural competence with observer ratings, highlighting an exaggeration effect in self-report when compared with observer-rated skills.

Using a slightly different approach, Sodowsky, Taffe, Gutkin, and Wise (1994) developed the Multicultural Counseling Inventory (MCI) as a comprehensive measure of the various domains within multicultural competence. Their factor analysis of responses from hundreds of graduate students yielded four factors with varying number of items: multicultural counseling skills (11 items), multicultural awareness (10 items), multicultural counseling knowledge (11 items), and multicultural counseling relationship (8 items). The relationship subscale (to differentiate it from the multicultural counseling skills scale) refers specifically to "the counselor's interactional process with the minority client such as the counselor's trustworthiness, comfort level, stereotypes of the minority client, and world view" (Sodowsky et al., 1994, p. 142). Counselors are asked to indicate how accurately each of the 40 items describes them using a 4-point scale ranging from *Very Inaccurate* to *Very Accurate*.

Also using factor analysis but focusing primarily on the first two aspects of D. W. Sue et al.'s (1982) model (knowledge and awareness), the Multicultural Counseling Knowledge and Awareness Scale (MCKAS; Ponterotto, Gretchen, Utsey, Rieger, & Austin, 2002) was developed as an extension of the Multicultural Counseling Awareness Scale (MCAS; Ponterotto, Rieger, Barrett, & Sparks, 1994). The MCKAS is a 32-item measure general knowledge related to multicultural counseling and worldview biases, consisting of two factors: Knowledge (20 items) and Awareness (12 items). Responses are made on a 7-point Likert scale from *Not at all True* to *Totally True*. D'Andrea (2004) also developed the updated Multicultural Counseling Awareness Scale—Form B (MCAS:B). Designed specifically for self-assessment, this 45-item measure uses a 7-point Likert-type format (as cited in Cartwright, Daniels, & Zhang, 2008). Higher scores on the MCAS:B indicate greater amounts of perceived multicultural competence. Ponterotto and Potere (2003) found that users of this assessment who had participated in multicultural education or received supervised clinical training reported significantly higher scores on the subscales for knowledge and skills.

Constantine and Ladany (2001) suggested that all three of the early self-report measures developed in the 1990s (MAKSS, MCI, and MCKAS) have established strong evidence of reliability and validity but that later revisions clearly have added a new layer of sophistication to the assessments. A major limitation of the early scales was that they are all based on a counselor's self-report (i.e., a counselor's perceptions of his or her own multicultural awareness, knowledge, and skills). Self-report scales notoriously struggle with the limitation of social desirability (Pope-Davis & Dings, 1995). Although they provide important information, they do not provide an analysis of the client's or an observer's perspective. Later revisions, such as with the MAKSS-CE-R (Kim et al., 2003), have allowed for observer ratings.

The earliest measure to be designed for observer ratings of multicultural competence, however, was the Cross-Cultural Counseling Inventory—Revised (CCCI–R; LaFromboise et al., 1991). The measure was developed to assess a counselor's effectiveness with culturally diverse clients, awareness of sociopolitical issues, and cultural sensitivity. The CCCI–R includes 20 items that are organized with 11 competencies with three general areas including cultural awareness and beliefs, cultural knowledge, and flexibility in counseling skills. The supervisor rates a counselor's demonstration of a particular competency on a 6-point scale ranging from *Strongly Disagree* to *Strongly Agree*. The CCCI–R has had less extensive use in evaluating multicultural training programs primarily because it requires that a supervisor observe and rate students, which is obviously not nearly as efficient as the use of self-report measures. On the other hand, the CCCI–R does have the distinct advantage of being closer to a measure of behavioral competence because a supervisor has to observe a manifestation of cultural competence rather than the counselor simply self-reporting that he or she feels competent regarding a particular scale item.

There have been constant updates to the assessment measures in the field, but more research is still needed to improve assessment of both outcomes of multicultural training programs and outcomes of culturally sensitive counseling. Although multicultural counseling outcome research has been steadily increasing in quantity and sophistication in the past 45 years, D'Andrea and Heckman (2008), in extending the earlier work of Atkinson and Lowe (1995), referred to the state of empirical outcome research in the field as a "serious dearth" (p. 360). Fuertes (2012) has suggested the need for more outcome research that not only examines the effectiveness of therapy and particular methods with ethnic minority clients but also addresses issues of unique interest to counseling psychologists, such as multicultural connections with positive psychology, vocational development, and psychological well-being.

Development of Practice Guidelines for the Profession

Perhaps some of the most useful pieces to include in training on becoming culturally competent are the number of practice guidelines that have been developed and published in the last 30 years. Counseling psychologists have been foremost among all psychologists in developing principles and guidelines for counseling and therapy with culturally diverse populations. The earliest such developments were by the Committee of Women (now Section for the Advancement of Women) in the Society of Counseling Psychology. This committee developed a consensus document ("Principles Concerning the Counseling and Therapy of Women," in 1979), which was adopted as Division 17 policy (Fitzgerald & Nutt, 1986) and received, throughout the 1980s, a large number of adoptions and endorsements from divisions within the APA and other mental health organizations. In 2007, an interdivisional task force between Divisions 17 and 35 updated the principles as formal APA policy in the *Guidelines for Psychological Practice With Girls and Women* (see APA, 2007b). The purpose of these practice guidelines was to "enhance gender- and culture-sensitive psychological practice with women and girls from all social classes, ethnic and racial groups, sexual orientations, and ability/disability statuses in the United States" (APA, 2007b, p. 950).

The 2007 guidelines reviewed the literature related to problems women have experienced when treatment includes problematic ethnic and gender biases (such as bias in diagnosis and sexual misconduct by therapists) and contemporary social forces that differentially impact women's lives (such as media influences and reproductive issues).

Although the guidelines were not overtly organized according to D. W. Sue et al.'s (1982) tripartite model of cultural competence, the authors did explicitly acknowledge that the guidelines were designed to help psychologists "increase their awareness, knowledge and skills in psychological practice with women and girls" (APA, 2007b, p. 950).

In 1990, APA published the *Guidelines for Providers of Psychological Services to Ethnic, Linguistic, and Culturally Diverse Populations*. In 2002, Divisions 17 and 45 led the important process for revised guidelines and the adoption of the *Guidelines for Multicultural Education, Training, Practice, and Organizational Change for Psychologists* (see APA, 2003a). When the guidelines were formally adopted by the APA in 2002, following the earlier guidelines in 1990, the authors noted that the guidelines had been in the process of development for 22 years. The guidelines were set to expire as APA policy in 2009 but were granted an extension. Revised guidelines are due out around the time of publication of this text. The original guidelines (APA, 2003a) established the changing demographics and increasing diversity of the United States as well as the historical and sociopolitical issues that impact the psychological treatment of a diverse group of clients (e.g., civil rights abuses and health care disparities). The guidelines also noted the external societal forces marking worldwide changes in psychology (from cloning to migration to climate change). Demographic and perceptual shifts in the population are rapid and significant and call for increased sensitivity to multicultural issues.

The APA also officially established the *Guidelines for Psychological Practice With Lesbian, Gay, and Bisexual Clients* in 2000 (APA, 2000). The guidelines were set as documents that would be in place for a decade, consistent with APA policy. Thus, the 2000 *Guidelines for Psychological Practice With Lesbian, Gay, and Bisexual Clients* expired at the end of 2010. The updated guidelines were adopted in 2011 (see APA, 2012b). They noted the important stance of the APA in 1975 when it adopted a resolution stating that "homosexuality per se implies no impairment in judgment, stability, reliability, or general social or vocational capabilities" as well as the 2009 affirmation that "same-sex sexual and romantic attractions, feelings, and behaviors are normal and positive variations of human sexuality regardless of sexual orientation identity" (APA, 2012b, p. 10).

In 2004, Division 17 members also participated in the development of the *Guidelines for Psychological Practice With Older Adults*, although the guidelines were developed primarily by an interdivisional task force between Divisions 12 (Clinical) and 20 (Adult Development and Aging; see APA, 2004a). The changing and aging demographics of the United States were detailed, with issues of Medicare reimbursement, psychological services in nursing homes, and the lack of geriatric training typically obtained by psychologists noted. Most recently, as of the writing of this book, *Guidelines for Assessment of and Intervention With Persons With Disabilities* passed the APA Council in 2011 (see APA, 2012a). As approximately 50 million Americans live with a disability (U.S. Department of Education, 2007), these guidelines are both important and timely. As the authors of the guidelines noted, "To work effectively with people who have disabilities, psychologists need to become familiar with how disability influences a client's psychological well-being and functioning" (APA, 2012a, p. 43), including understanding the unique meaning each client assigns to his or her disability. They also pointed out that psychologists "rarely receive adequate education or training in disability issues" (p. 43). The purpose of these guidelines is to provide psychologists with necessary information to be better prepared to serve people with disabilities and to seek ways to make their practices more accessible.

The idea that all of the practice guidelines introduced in this chapter are aspirational and intended to enhance psychologists' awareness, knowledge, and skills about a variety of diversity issues is so important. All counseling psychologists and students of counseling psychology should be familiar with these documents and should seek further dialogues on these topics. Such a process will help develop a more culturally competent profession and ensure the best practices available for the vast diversity of clients who seek counseling.

Summary

Striking disparities remain in quality of and access to mental health services for ethnic minorities in the United States. Feminist therapy and multicultural counseling developed as a response to this problem; as a way to address issues of discrimination, oppression, and aversive bias in counseling; and to acknowledge the growing awareness of the importance of diversity in our society. Both feminism and multiculturalism grew up in the 1960s and have now reached a point where true integration seems not just possible but already in motion.

We reviewed the basic tenets of both feminist therapy and multicultural counseling (though both approaches have a range of specific applications and models). Feminist therapy is grounded in two basic concepts: the personal is political, and the therapy relationship should strive to be egalitarian. The concept that "the personal is political" rests on the importance of context in a person's lived experience. Although our thoughts, feelings, and actions may feel unique, in many ways we experience common reactions based on societal and cultural forces.

Rather than looking inward alone for an answer or solution, feminist therapists empower clients to see the ways in which their environment, including the ways they have or do not have power and privilege, impacts their own personal experiences. Feminist therapists also believe, though there is an inherent power difference when a client in distress comes to seek help from a trained professional, that power differences should be minimized as much as possible.

Multicultural counseling relies on three basic tenets: awareness, knowledge, and skills. Introduced by D. W. Sue et al. (1982), this tripartite model still forms the foundation of all multicultural counseling approaches. Multicultural counselors must be aware of their own cultural backgrounds, values, and beliefs and be aware of why diversity and difference are so important in our relationships. Multicultural counselors must also seek to constantly update their knowledge, sometimes about particular cultures but, more important, about the broader issues of power, privilege, bias, oppression, and the personal meaning and salience clients apply to their various diverse aspects of self. Finally, multicultural counselors must skillfully apply appropriate techniques, never using a "one size fits all" approach to counseling theories and strategies.

Cultural competence requires sensitivity and skills, both of which can be enhanced in multicultural training. There is good evidence now that multicultural education is effective (Smith et al., 2006). Our ability to establish the efficacy of training models relies heavily on the advancements we have seen in multicultural assessment. Finally, we must underscore the importance of the practice guidelines developed in the last 30 years, which help psychologists understand the best practices for working with clients of diverse backgrounds and experiences. The extensive work of counseling psychologists in this domain has earned the profession recognition by other specialties in psychology as a national leader in the development of effective standards and strategies for multicultural counseling.

Career Psychology
Theories and Interventions

15

T hroughout the history of counseling psychology, there has been ongoing attention to both the "normal" developmental and the "dysfunctional" aspects of vocational behavior. How and why do people follow particular vocational paths? The focus of this chapter is on the foundational theories that attempt to answer this question and on the interventions used in career counseling to address these issues with individuals. We wish to make clear that theories of career choice and development are not per se theories of career counseling and interventions. The study of the "what, how, when, and why" of career choice and development is as much a part of the basic psychological study of personality and development as it is a foundation for the development of intervention strategies. However, the theoretical and the applied are very clearly linked.

The first half of this chapter is devoted to an overview of developments in three foundational approaches to the study of vocational choice and development. As will be evident in that exploration, theorists and researchers have called on various traditions within psychology—for example, personality,

http://dx.doi.org/10.1037/14378-015
Counseling Psychology, Third Edition, by C. J. Gelso, E. N. Williams, and B. R. Fretz

development, cognitive processes—to explain the what, how, when, and why of people's patterns of vocational behavior. Our grouping of theories into three approaches is just one of many possible groupings. Some textbooks list nearly a dozen approaches, others as few as two. Within the three approaches we have chosen, we review just one specific, foundational theory each. For each theory, we briefly describe its historical roots, key concepts, key measures, and theoretical and practical strengths and limitations. Our purpose is to acquaint readers with the basic theories before moving on, in the second half of the chapter, to discuss specific intervention strategies. More extensive presentations of theory and career counseling interventions can be found in texts such as those by Amundson, Harris-Bowlsbey, and Niles (2009); Brown and Lent (2005); Gysbers, Heppner, and Johnston (2009); Niles and Harris-Bowlsbey (2005); Savickas (2011); Sharf (2006); and Swanson and Fouad (1999).

Definitions

Before proceeding any further, we must clarify the use of the many terms related to vocational behavior. Over the years, changing terms reflect changing perspectives about what needs to be studied. Although there is much overlap and interchangeability among the terms we explore, there are good reasons why variations have emerged. In the next few paragraphs, we describe the origins and unique meaning of the terms *vocational choice, vocational guidance, vocational psychology, career development, career psychology, career counseling, educational development,* and *educational counseling.*

Vocational choice is, in one sense, a behavioral term. In our society, there is a clear expectation that everyone will seek gainful employment. To the extent that someone chooses to find something more than just a paying job—that is, some kind of work that is appealing and satisfying—we speak of making a vocational choice. Studies of the antecedents, correlates, and consequences of such choices constitute the major portion of the literature in the study of vocational behavior. (*Vocational choice* and *occupational choice* are essentially interchangeable terms. Sociologists and economists tend to prefer the word *occupational,* whereas psychologists tend to prefer the word *vocational.*) *Vocational guidance* is the term applied to the processes developed to help individuals with the assessments and reasoning needed to make wise career choices. Perhaps the most encompassing term is *vocational psychology,* defined by Crites (1969) as the study of vocational behavior and development. *Vocational behavior* can be defined as the responses the individual makes in choosing and adjusting to an occupation, and *vocational development* can be defined as that the systematic changes that can be observed in vocational behavior over time.

The terms *career development, career counseling*, and *career psychology* all evolved from theoretical and research developments in vocational psychology in the 1950s and 1960s. Much of the research in those decades turned to developmental psychology to understand the processes of vocational choice and development. Noting that most persons engage in several related vocations during their lives, Super (1957) promoted use of the word *career* to cover the sequence of major positions held by a person throughout his or her preoccupational (student) years, working years, and retirement years. *Career*, compared with *vocational*, became the preferred word to use when theorizing and researching vocational behaviors and development. However, as Blustein (2006) noted, our use of the term *career* is "deeply embedded in a sociocultural framework that is relevant to only a minority of individuals around the globe" (p. 3) because not all people have the luxury of making career "choices." We focus in this chapter on career psychology; the growing emphasis on *work* (as a more encompassing term) was highlighted in Chapter 5 on the current research in vocational psychology.

In addition, we want to mention the terms *educational development* and *educational counseling*, which may, at first, seem out of place for commentary in this chapter. However, if one considers education as part of career development (and in contemporary technological society, education becomes more and more a critical factor in setting the range of career possibilities), then it can be seen that choices of degree programs and performance in those programs are inextricably involved with career psychology. Consequently, since the earliest days of the profession, there have been counseling psychologists who focused on issues related to selecting, adjusting to, and performing satisfactorily in college settings. Lapan, Turner, and Pierce (2012) provided one of the more recent reviews of the research contributions to and issues in the study of academic adjustment and success.

Foundations in Career Theory

Before reviewing the evolution in career choice and development theories, we need to ask how it is that we can account for more than 100 years of almost uninterrupted attention to career-related behaviors and why there are currently at least three professional journals (*Journal of Vocational Behavior, Career Development Quarterly, Journal of Career Assessment*) devoted exclusively to theoretical and practical issues related to vocational behavior. From one perspective, career choices are simply a few of the many choices made in everyone's life—whether to marry, to buy a house, to take a vacation, and so forth. On the other hand, according to Erikson (1950), Freud wrote explicitly about the positive relationship of one's mental health to the ability to love *and to work*. The second half of the 20th century yielded an impressive accumulation of empirical evidence in support of Freud's observation. Lofquist and Dawis (1984) cited some of the classic studies of the impact of work on both life satisfaction and mental health. Perhaps most intriguing is the study by Palmore (1969), who found that work satisfaction was a better predictor of how long one lives than physicians' ratings, use of tobacco, or genetic factors.

Socially and economically, there are yet other driving forces for a focus on career psychology. Recall from earlier chapters the role of both world wars in advancing the vocational guidance movement and development of assessment techniques. Using human resources effectively was and continues to be the major impetus for governmental support of the development of occupational classification, selection, and promotion procedures. Some jobs demand specific talents; placing employees in positions who do not possess these talents is at best economically wasteful and in wartime potentially catastrophic. On a less dramatic basis, everyday issues such as absenteeism and job turnover are two of the highest, most preventable costs businesses incur. Each year, millions of dollars are invested in research to find out what steps can be taken to increase workers' satisfaction, a factor directly linked to absenteeism, job turnover, and overall mental health (Dawis, 2005; Swanson, 2012).

From the societal compared with the economic viewpoint, a well-functioning society is one in which there are low levels of social alienation; that is, one in which few persons are found who are not contributing to (or possibly are even acting against) society as a community. Worker dissatisfaction has long been a major component of social alienation when it occurs. There is a great deal of social unrest in times of high unemployment and/or when groups of individuals are systematically denied the opportunity to enter and succeed in valued careers. Continued issues of unemployment, underemployment, and inequalities in pay and advancement opportunities, all as related to gender, ethnicity, and culture, are major factors in paradigmatic shifts in what and how to study vocational behavior and development.

During the first half of the 20th century, psychologists working in areas of vocational behavior were focused primarily on the development and use of assessment techniques. It was not until the 1950s that theories began to address just how persons go about implementing the "true reasoning" of Parsons's (1909) pioneering model. Parsons postulated that wise vocational choices were a matter of true reasoning about the relationships between knowledge of self and knowledge of the world of work. In the first half of the 20th century, assessments were created to develop the two types of knowledge, but how was true reasoning to be ensured?

The three approaches reviewed in this chapter reflect historical developments not only from Parsons's fundamental concepts but also from research emphases in the discipline of psychology at large. The first approach we review is most commonly referred to as "trait oriented," building on the measurement accomplishments of the first half of the 20th century. The second approach, referred to as developmental, was built upon the growing literature in developmental psychology during the middle of the 20th century. The third approach, social learning and cognition, is distinctively a product of psychology of the 1960s and subsequent decades, when cognitive–behavioral viewpoints became the preeminent explanatory concepts in developmental and personality psychology. Although we focus here on the foundational theories in career psychology, we also reviewed the most recent work and emerging theories in Chapter 5.

TRAIT-ORIENTED THEORIES: HOLLAND'S THEORY OF VOCATIONAL PERSONALITIES AND WORK ENVIRONMENTS

Historical Roots

In their earliest form, trait-oriented approaches were known as trait and factor approaches. The essence of this approach is that the counselor measures the traits of the person, finds out the requirements of a job, and then counsels the person into a job that provides a match between person traits and job factors. During the first half of the 20th century, several studies indicated that as much as one third of the information needed to predict occupational success could be obtained simply by knowing the measured ability of workers (D. Brown, Brooks, & Associates, 1990). Yet, what about the remaining two thirds of the variance? Many persons have the required abilities for particular jobs (e.g., teaching or engineering) but for personal reasons do not wish to enter those professions. External factors such as discrimination, low income potential, undesirable job environment, and peer and parental influences all keep many persons from selecting a profession that is a good match between their measured abilities and job requirements. Additionally, internal factors such as interests and personality style may lead to persons not choosing jobs for which they have all the requisite abilities.

On the job side of the coin, there are an equally large number of reasons for inadequacies in a simple matching approach. A primary reason is the immense variety of activities subsumed under any one job title, even though there are over 20,000 different job titles listed in the United States. Consider what seems to be a relatively narrow occupation, that of oceanographer. Some oceanographers focus their work on alternative energy resources; others are involved in movements of the ocean that affect weather; still others are concerned largely with the biology of life in the oceans. Even within each of these categories, some oceanographers may be involved in research, others in applied design technology, others in sales of an innovative process for using ocean resources.

John Holland, on the basis of experiences early in his career in military and educational settings, became astutely aware of the limitations of a simple matching of persons' traits and job requirements. In perhaps one of the finest manifestations of the value of the scientist–practitioner model, he drew upon these experiences as a counselor and researcher to develop a theoretical model that addresses some of the limitations of the basic trait and factor matching approach.

Key Concepts

The basic premise Holland derived from his early experiences as a counselor was that people choose occupations as an expression of their personalities. Nearly 50 years after Holland began his work on this premise, it is impossible to overstate the impact he has had on the theory and research in career development and the practice of career counseling. In one sense, his premise created a major new way of looking at career choice and development. Instead of focusing on a match of abilities and possibly other traits to job requirements, Holland's work shifted attention to persons' *perceptions of themselves.* Such perceptions could be assessed by examining persons' perceptions of various jobs (Holland, 1997).

Persons who find work environments that are congruent with their personalities will tend to flourish in their work. "Lack of congruence between personality and environment leads to dissatisfaction, unstable career paths, and lowered performance" (Holland, 1996, p. 397). To study such congruence, Holland needed a way to assess both personality and environment related to vocational behavior. Although a few of the measures he and his colleagues developed are outlined in the next section, what must be noted here is the resulting structure that evolved from those assessments, the now well-known RIASEC model. Each letter in the acronym RIASEC stands for one of six types of personality, each with a corresponding type of environment. To illustrate as well as to identify each of the six different types, we list typical occupations here for each.

1. _R_ealistic: mechanic and air traffic controller
2. _I_nvestigative: economist and biologist
3. _A_rtistic: editor and photographer
4. _S_ocial: athletic coach and minister

5. *E*nterprising: real estate sales agent and radio/TV announcer
6. *C*onventional: receptionist and accountant

The key concepts to be used in conjunction with this model are *congruence, consistency, differentiation,* and *identity. Congruence* is the fit between an individual's type and the environment in which he or she works. For a person whose primary type is artistic and who works in an artistic environment, a fully congruent match has been made. The match of an artistic person to a conventional environment is totally incongruent (Conventional is opposite Artistic on the RIASEC hexagon, as shown in Figure 15.1), and one would predict that such a person is unlikely to remain in such a position, at least with any degree of satisfaction. *Consistency* for an individual can be determined by looking at his or her highest two or three scores on the six different types and examining the positions of these types on the RIASEC model. A person who has primarily realistic interests but also strong social interests is less consistent (opposing types in Figure 15.1) than one whose strongest interests are realistic and investigative (adjacent types in Figure 15.1). For Holland,

FIGURE 15.1

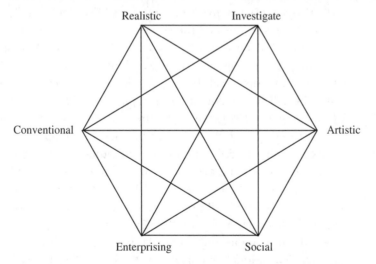

The RIASEC model. A hexagonal model for defining the psychological resemblances among types and environments and their interactions. Reproduced by special permission of the Publisher, Psychological Assessment Resources, Inc., 16204 North Florida Avenue, Lutz, FL 33549, from *Making Vocational Choices*, Third Edition, Copyright 1973, 1985, 1992, 1997 by Psychological Assessment Resources, Inc. All rights reserved.

the principle of consistency is that the more consistent persons are in their types, the more predictable they are as to the occupation in which they will find success and satisfaction. The concept of *differentiation* is assessed by looking at the size of the differences in the highest versus lowest of the six type scores. The greater the magnitude of the difference, the more likely one can make an accurate prediction of what career choice a person will find satisfactory. Conversely, the person who has a "flat profile"—that is, relatively similar scores for all types—is one for whom no serious gambler would bet a lot of money in predicting that person's eventual career choice. Persons with flat profiles might find satisfaction in a very wide range of careers (e.g., when all scores are about equally high) or just as likely might not find satisfaction in any career (e.g., when scores are about equally low).

Identity refers to the clarity of one's goals, interests, and talents and is measured by a separate scale on either the Vocational Preference Inventory or the Self-Directed Search; both measures are described in the next section. The concept of identity can also be assessed with Holland's Vocational Identity Scale (Holland, Johnston, & Asama, 1993).

Key Measures

The earliest measure developed by Holland was the Vocational Preference Inventory (VPI), currently available in its seventh revision (Holland, 1985). Extensive analyses of thousands of students' and adults' scores on this measure yielded the six personality types that form the foundation of Holland's RIASEC model. Although the VPI is still useful to researchers studying the structure and interrelationships of the six types to other psychological dimensions, in the practice of career counseling, the VPI has essentially been replaced by the Self-Directed Search (SDS; Holland, 1994). This measure, now in its fourth edition (though more recently an online version has been developed and marketed), is extensively used by millions of individuals from the early teens to retirement years. It is designed to be self-administered and self-scoring. The measure includes a variety of questions about self-assessments of abilities, interests, and preferences. From these responses, scores are obtained on each of the six RIASEC types. These scores, when examined in connection with auxiliary materials such as an Occupations Finder, Educational Opportunities Finder, or Leisure Activities Finder, help the examinee determine where the best fits occur between himself or herself and the environment (occupation, education, or leisure) being searched for. Similarly, Holland's RIASEC code formed the foundation for the Strong Interest Inventory, one of the most widely used measures of interests (Donnay, Morris, Schaubhut, & Thompson, 2005; see details on the Strong Interest Inventory in Chapter 10).

Theoretical and Practical Strengths

Holland's theory with its broad array of practice applications is now regarded as the strongest of all theories of career choice and development. That statement does not mean to imply that all the research is fully supportive of all the key concepts (see next section). What cannot be challenged, however, is the value of the theory in generating important research and new kinds of career interventions. Borgen (1991) found that citations and publication of studies related to Holland's theory were more than six times greater than for any other career choice and development theory. The strongest research support is for the six RIASEC types of persons and environments (Betz, Borgen, & Harmon, 2006; Spokane & Cruza-Guet, 2005).

From the practice perspective, there is no real competitor in terms of numbers of persons who use the SDS compared with any other measure of interests. It has been incorporated into self-help books such as *What Color Is Your Parachute?* (Bolles, 2013), thousands of high school guidance programs, and countless other career intervention programs. "Consumer satisfaction" in use of the measure has always been high compared with that of other measures. The SDS has truly become, with all the revisions made over the years, a "user friendly" measure that is cost effective in terms both of the time of the person taking the SDS and of counselor or administrative staff time. In fact, there may be essentially no staff time required if the person taking the measure has no questions during the self-administered and self-interpretation phases.

Theoretical and Practical Limitations

Holland was the first to admit that the research evidence supporting the key concepts of congruence, consistency, differentiation, and identity has been less impressive than he would have wished. In his last book publication before his death in 2008, Holland (1997) had begun to look at persons' attitudes and strategies regarding careers as one way of possibly improving predictions about who would be satisfied and stable in careers.

In addition, Holland's RIASEC model has been tested with individuals from widely diverse ethnic, socioeconomic, and international backgrounds. The fact that the SDS has now been translated to many languages speaks in part to the practical usefulness that has been found for it around the world. More rigorous research investigations on the structure of interests have yielded interesting data. For example, differences based on race and ethnicity have been small (Fouad, 2002), but gender differences remain clear (Betz & Gwilliam, 2002; Tracey & Robbins, 2005). As described in Chapter 10, although care must be taken when using assessments with culturally diverse populations, there is at least a reasonable amount of empirical support to use of Holland's theory and assessments with culturally diverse populations.

DEVELOPMENTAL THEORIES: SUPER'S LIFE SPAN, LIFE SPACE PERSPECTIVE

Historical Roots

During the early years of his career, while working as an employment counselor in the 1930s, Super became acutely aware of some of the deficiencies of the trait and factor model as it was then practiced; that is, assessing clients' abilities and finding a job for clients that matched their abilities. The concept of making a "once and for all," supposedly satisfactory career choice struck Super as missing much of importance. Even by 1942, Super was proposing to theorists and practitioners that vocational adjustment was more a matter of dynamic unfolding than a one-time-choice event with static consequences. To put it concisely, he regarded career development as a process, one that occurs throughout the life span.

Key Concepts

In Super's career of more than 50 years of seminal, innovative (Borgen, 1991) thinking and writing, there were at least three key conceptual developments, each leading to new kinds of assessment measures and researchable hypotheses. By 1953, Super had incorporated several developmental concepts from both psychologists and sociologists who were increasingly, in the 1930s and 1940s, focusing on development in the adult years compared with earlier emphases that were pretty much restricted to the years of childhood and adolescence. Super (1953) outlined five stages of growth that had great implications for career development: childhood, exploration during adolescence, establishment during young adulthood, maintenance during middle adulthood, and decline during old age. Within each of these age periods, the critical question, according to Super, was, "What are the appropriate vocational behaviors that should be occurring for someone in this age group in order eventually to attain career adjustment?" For each age, there are then developmentally appropriate tasks that a person needs to negotiate to achieve career maturity. As each age is successfully handled, the person moves on to the tasks of the next age (see Figure 15.2).

Perhaps the most critical research finding to emerge from all of Super's decades of theorizing and research was the key result of his 30-year longitudinal study of career success. Before examining that result, keep in mind that during the first 60 years of the 20th century, the prevailing view was that the sooner persons made realistic career decisions, the more likely they were to become successful. They would have more streamlined

FIGURE 15.2

Age

Life Stage	Adolescence 14–25	Early Adulthood 25–45	Middle Adulthood 45–65	Late Adulthood 65 and over
Decline Developmental tasks at each age	Giving less time to hobbies	Reducing sports participation	Focusing on essentials	Reducing working hours
Maintenance Tasks at each age	Verifying current occupational choice	Making occupational position secure	Holding one's own against competition	Keeping what one enjoys
Establishment Tasks at each age	Getting started in a chosen field	Settling down in a suitable position	Developing new skills	Doing things one has wanted to do
Exploration Tasks at each age	Learning more about opportunities	Finding desired opportunity	Identifying new tasks to work on	Finding a good retirement place
Growth Tasks at each age	Developing a realistic self-concept	Learning to relate to others	Accepting one's own limitations	Developing and valuing non-occupational roles

Cycling and recycling of developmental tasks throughout the life span.

preparation, earlier career entry, and opportunities for success. When Super and colleagues assessed students longitudinally from ninth grade through their mid-20s, collecting a wide variety of biosocial, environmental, vocational, personality, and achievement-related data, they found that ninth graders who had already decided what they wanted to become had often made poorly grounded, unstable choices. The best predictor of later vocational adjustment was not having reached a decision by ninth grade but rather simply being actively oriented toward gathering career-relevant information. The tremendous effects of this finding on subsequent educational policy were summarized by Osipow (1983):

> Super suggested, based on such data, that the school curriculum should "foster planfulness" aimed at helping youngsters become aware of their level of occupational aspirations and the general

amount of education required to achieve that level. This self-knowledge could be developed without specifically deciding on an occupational goal, which would be premature in the ninth grade. In fact, rather than restrict occupational choice possibilities at that age, the school should exert its efforts to broaden occupational perspectives and to teach the student to use available resources for exploration effectively. In this statement lie the roots of the Career Education movement. (p. 163)

By 1963, Super had incorporated much of Rogers's thinking about self-concept (see Chapter 12) as a way of explaining the process aspects of how career development unfolds. Briefly, Super postulated that we make career choices and, possibly, career changes in accordance with developments and changes in our self-concepts. Like Holland, Super used the idea of congruence; however, the congruence was not between personality traits and environment but rather between how persons perceive a job, or occupation, career, fitting their self-concepts.

Super's focus on self-concept led him to look at the many different roles individuals have in their lives; career is just one of many roles a person might have, and each role has an impact on self-concept. The more he studied multiple roles among people in our culture as well as in international cultures (Šverko, 2001), the more he saw shifting emphases and recycling developmental phenomena in roles such as worker, student, housewife, leisurite, and so forth, throughout the life span.

A concise overview of how these studies led Super to develop first a Life-Career Rainbow (see Figure 15.3) and then an Archway of Career Determinants may be found in one of Super's last major papers (Super, 1994), published in the year of his death. Although it is beyond the scope of this overview to delineate all the details of these developments, his writings continue to keep career psychologists attending to both multiple roles and issues of vocational behavior throughout the life span. In fact, though Super's work was first identified as a developmental stage theory, then as a self-concept implementation theory, in the final years Super preferred the label a "life-span, life space perspective."

Key Measures

Super's theoretical propositions led to the development of two kinds of new measures. The Career Development Inventory (Super, Thompson, Lindeman, Jordaan, & Myers, 1981) is just one of several measures that Super's work engendered to assess what kinds of career planning and career explorations people were engaged in at different developmental stages. This measure and others like it have come to be called *career maturity* or *adaptability* measures (Juntunen & Even, 2012) because individuals' scores on these measures indicate whether or not these individuals are engaging or have engaged in those age-appropriate career-related

FIGURE 15.3

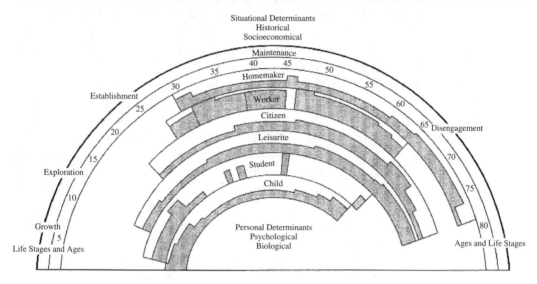

The Life-Career Rainbow: Six life roles in schematic life span.

tasks. Perhaps the greatest contribution of these measures is that, in identifying "immature" attitudes and competencies, counselors have been better able to focus intervention programs to address these "developmental deficiencies," whether they are in 7-year-old girls' socially induced restrictive career stereotypes or in 70-year-olds' abandonment of hope for fulfillment in life.

The other key measure stimulated by Super's work was that of work salience (Nevill & Super, 1986). As Super worked with colleagues around the world, he found that individuals, in various roles and life stages, differed greatly in the importance they assigned to work/career as part of their lives. Super was one of first to see the need to assess this variable if one is ever to be able to make reasonably accurate predictions about career choice and development. Although the measures of salience have not yet been widely used outside of those working specifically with Super's concepts, they should receive increased attention as career psychologists attend to some of the issues described in the last half of this chapter regarding expanding and shifting paradigms for vocational behavior research.

Theoretical and Practical Strengths

The impact of Super's 50 years of theory and research has been tremendous for both the scientific and practical components of counseling psychology. By being among the first to bring a developmental emphasis to the study of vocational behavior, he provided the foundation for looking at *how* people make career choices, rather than just the content of the choice and its consequences. His delineation of stages and later expansion to life span considerations have affected the content and timing of career education and career interventions for all ages. Super's work proved especially adaptable to the computer technology that emerged in the past few decades; although no longer available as of 2012, the extremely successful computerized career guidance system DISCOVER was developed specifically within his developmental task framework. His increasing attention to the multiple roles we all hold, in what he called "life space," foreshadowed the need for more attention to constructivism (an emerging approach described in Chapter 5).

Super often described himself as an eclectic, even when eclecticism was a "dirty word" in psychology (Borgen, 1991), and his theory, in later years, was clearly a segmental one. The different parts hang together only loosely. The positive side of that eclecticism and looseness is its breadth of attractiveness to theorists and practitioners. Without doubt, Super's theorizing has been more comprehensive than many others'; at least some parts of his theory can be readily integrated with any other theory of vocational behavior, making it an attractive framework for many researchers to consider.

Theoretical and Practical Limitations

Comprehensive theory often has the loosest connections between parts and the least specifiable hypotheses. Thus, the same factor that makes Super's theory very attractive to many theorists and practitioners limits the possibilities for clear testing by researchers. Although there are ample data to support many parts of Super's theory, it would be extremely difficult to lay out a set of specific propositions that have been sufficiently confirmed to allow a confident level of prediction for anyone individual. Moreover, Super's work lends itself more readily toward understanding broad concepts of career choice and development and their educational implications for any age, less so toward understanding how to intervene with an individual's work adjustment issues.

Super began his work in an era when the workforce being examined consisted of mainly White males; much of the research regarding his theory reflects that population. Somewhat ironically, although Super's later theoretical "segments" give much attention to the social context of career development, there are very few studies (with studies of career maturity being an exception) within the United States that have looked at how ethnicity might affect his proposed developmental relationships. His work, however, has laid the foundation for newer models (see Savickas, 2005; Vondracek, 2001; Young, Valach, & Collin,

2002), supporting the continued emphasis on development and life span perspectives in career psychology.

SOCIAL LEARNING AND COGNITION THEORIES: KRUMBOLTZ'S SOCIAL LEARNING THEORY

Historical Roots

By the early 1960s, the principles of Skinner's (1938) behaviorism and other learning models were increasingly being applied to a broad range of human behaviors. Krumboltz and colleagues were the first counseling psychologists to incorporate principles of social learning (Bandura, 1986) into a comprehensive approach to understanding the factors that influence people to pursue various lines of work, as well as the impediments to their making and implementing choices (Krumboltz, 1979; Krumboltz, Mitchell, & Jones, 1976).

Key Concepts

Four categories of factors are postulated as influencing career decisions: (a) genetic endowment and special abilities; (b) environmental conditions and events, such as number and nature of job opportunities; (c) learning experiences; and (d) task-approach skills. In this social learning approach, three major types of learning are described as they apply to career decisions. The first two are similar to the instrumental (operant) and associative (classical) conditioning models taught in introductory psychology (see also Chapter 12). *Instrumental* learning experiences are identified as those that occur when one experiences a positive outcome for a behavior. For example, if one successfully completes a science project that receives an award or receives compliments for writing an essay, these behaviors are far more likely to be repeated. *Associative* learning is used to describe the associations developed between a neutral event or stimulus with an emotionally laden one, such as the classical conditioning of salivation to a bell in Pavlov's dogs. For a career-related example, if a young person's only experience with plush furnishings comes from waiting in a dentist's office, he or she may decide that being a dentist is the best way to achieve a comfortable lifestyle. This example may seem like an oversimplification; however, Krumboltz et al. (1976) documented numerous examples of pervasive generalizations that resulted from the effect of a single stimulus or event. It is a well-established fact that enrollments in particular kinds of career or skill training programs are temporarily affected by the appearance of any new "hero" in the media; for example, lawyers, figure skaters, fighter pilots. The third kind of learning that is critical to career development is *vicarious* learning. New behaviors and skills can be learned merely by observing the behaviors of others via the media or direct observation. Think of how one dance style after another spread throughout the country in the last half of the 20th century because of its display on television. Krumboltz et al. showed, more specific to career development, that students can learn how to obtain useful occupational information simply by observing someone (ideally, a role model of the students) go through the process.

By incorporating social learning theory into these basic types of learning, this approach specifies three components of successful career development (Mitchell & Krumboltz, 1996). The first component, *self-observation generalizations*, is statements persons make to themselves based on their own experiences. The experiences each person has lead to generalizations about whether or not he or she can do something (task efficacy); these generalizations are then extended to what the person thinks are his or her interests and values. Someone unskilled at fixing a bike, compared with a friend who is adept at it, might well conclude that he or she has neither mechanical skills nor interests.

Moreover, on the basis of the various kinds of learning outlined above, each person forms views about the world around him or her and its characteristics. These views are referred to as *worldview generalizations*. Television shows have had a tremendous impact, for example, in determining which stereotypes the public holds about what gender and ethnicity occupations "are"; for example, until relatively recently, TV shows portrayed all nurses as females, most cleaning personnel as African American, and so forth. The fact that such stereotypes on television have become widely discussed and reported as social issues speaks to their importance as a source of vicarious learning in the shaping of young people's worldviews about careers.

To shape these various kinds of learning and resultant self and worldview generalizations into career decisions and actions, individuals must learn and engage in *task approach skills*. The most important of these skills for career decision making are clarifying values, setting goals, predicting future events, generating alternatives, seeking information, and planning and generalizing (Krumboltz & Baker, 1973). "People will be more likely to learn these task approach skills if they (1) have been positively reinforced for demonstrating or attempting these skills or (2) have observed models being positively reinforced for demonstrating these skills" (Mitchell & Krumboltz, 1996, p. 267). In their 1984 presentation of the theory, Mitchell and Krumboltz (1984) provided six excellent examples of how distortions in these processes lead to inappropriate career choices or, even more often, to avoidance of making a decision that could lead to more satisfying results:

> (1) drawing faulty generalizations ("I'm the only person in my class who is afraid of public speaking"), (2) making self-

comparisons with a single standard ("I'm not as warm as Carl Rogers, so I could never be a counselor"), (3) exaggerating the estimates of the emotional impact of an outcome ("If I don't succeed in business school I just couldn't stand it"), (4) drawing false causal relationships ("To get ahead, you just have to be in the right place at the right time"), (5) being ignorant of relevant facts ("High school English teachers spend their day helping eager students to appreciate the finer points of literature"), and (6) giving undue weight to low probability events ("I wouldn't accept a job in California because it's going to fall into the ocean during the next earthquake"). (p. 266)

These distortions underlie the development of the major assessment device related to this theory and described in the next section: the Career Beliefs Inventory (Krumboltz, 1991). In the latest iteration of this theory, Mitchell and Krumboltz (1996) took the interesting position that we should be attending less to indecision and congruence (a key factor in Holland's and Super's theories) and attending more to the following three questions:

1. How successful have my interventions been in stimulating new learning on the part of my clients?
2. How well have my interventions helped my clients to cope with a constantly changing work world?
3. How much progress are my clients making in creating a satisfying life for themselves? (Mitchell & Krumboltz, 1996, p. 264)

Key Measures

The Career Beliefs Inventory (Krumboltz, 1991) was developed to help clients understand some of their beliefs that could be blocking them from achieving their career goals. The measure has five major scales and 25 subscales, providing counselors and clients with examples of irrational beliefs and overgeneralizations that impede the decision-making process. There is also a workbook (Levin, Krumboltz, & Krumboltz, 1995) that facilitates clients' examination of their responses in conjunction with their results on the Strong Interest Inventory and Myers–Briggs Type Indicator.

Theoretical and Practical Strengths

By bringing together new psychological principles and knowledge from learning and cognition with what is known and what needed to be known about career behavior, Krumboltz has provided a model of the kind of disciplinary collaboration that can best advance the science and profession. His thoughtful integrations of social learning models and vocational behavior directly stimulated the development of the next two approaches reviewed in this chapter, both of which have moved on to higher levels of specificity in addressing important issues in vocational behavior. This model has also stimulated the development of some novel approaches to encouraging information seeking and career planning. In fact, the most supportive research regarding the social learning theory of career decision making is found in the results of studies showing that either direct reinforcement of career-seeking behavior (instrumental learning) or presentations by models (vicarious learning) can lead to students making more informed and rational career decisions. Moreover, the theory's articulation of problematic career beliefs and the development of relevant cognitive interventions provide important new strategies for career counselors.

Theoretical and Practical Limitations

Although Krumboltz's initial theoretical presentation included many testable propositions, only those related to clients' seeking occupational information have received much attention. Without research on most of the other propositions, no significant refinement of the theory has been accomplished. Also, while the theory could easily be extended to vocational behavior issues throughout the life span and to culturally diverse groups, no research programs have been developed for these populations. Krumboltz has more recently (2009) turned his attention to the role of happenstance or serendipity (Williams et al., 1998) in career development. Krumbotz's work, however, was an early precursor to later cognitive approaches to career counseling, such as the widely used social-cognitive theory (Lent, Brown, & Hackett, 1996, 2000; see also Chapter 5).

Career Counseling Interventions

Now that we have reviewed the major and foundational models of career development, we turn our attention to the practical applications of these models. How does one translate the theories into career counseling, with specific interventions to help individuals with a vast complexity of issues related to vocational behavior? We hope to provide in this section a model for integrating career intervention decisions into a counseling context.

For much of the public and even the profession of psychology, career counseling connotes an individual counselor administering some tests to a client who has not decided which job/career to pursue, then telling the client what choices are best. As early as 1991, Spokane (1991) described that particular perception of career counseling as already

30 years out of date. Since the 1960s, there has been a steady increase in development of new interventions, built upon the theories just described, that address both individual problems with and social concerns about the world of work. These interventions range from highly structured classroom activities, to computer-assisted interventions, to job clubs, to individualized relationships that are essentially indistinguishable from personal counseling. Because all but the last type of these interventions are quite different from most people's conceptions of career counseling, we use *career interventions* as the encompassing term. Like Spokane, we define career interventions as "any activity (treatment or effort) designed to enhance a person's career development or to enable that person to make more effective career decisions" (p. 22). The primary goal of this section of the chapter is to acquaint the reader with the broad range of career interventions that have been and continue to be developed by counseling psychologists.

The world of work at the beginning of the 21st century is indeed a quite different place from the world of work in the middle of the 20th century. As Herr (1996) spelled out quite clearly, the globalization of the world economy, a world oversupply of labor (except for highly computer-literate positions), and the establishment of "contingent"— that is, temporary—workforces have all affected earlier patterns of career stability. Today's clients may have grandparents who worked for the same employer for most of their adult working years, but it is unlikely that their parents did so. Even if their parents kept working in the same position, the chances are that mergers or acquisitions meant a change in employer, even if the job did not change. Others were "downsized" out of their positions after 20 or 30 years of highly rated work performance. Although experts differ on the exact number of positions an adult can now be expected to hold during the 30 to 40 working years, the number seven is frequently cited. Not the one, two, or three positions of past generations but now five to 10 or more, not counting the odd jobs of adolescence or part-time work during college years. Herr raised questions about whether we need new theories to take these kinds of changes into account in our career counseling; Meara (1996) argued that we at least need to make our assumptions explicit to our clients and ourselves. That is, we, as counseling psychologists, still believe being future-oriented and rationally planful is the best way to cope with the vicissitudes of the contemporary world of work.

The concept of "career" as Super used the word (described earlier), referring to a pattern of related employment and activities throughout the life span, may certainly appear challenged by current world-of-work trends (Blustein, 2006). Yet, in one sense, his underlying concept becomes even more critical as a worker is forced to seek multiple jobs. Every approach reviewed in this chapter confirmed the need for

individuals to understand that job satisfaction and satisfactory performance were related to some fit between person characteristics and the
work environment. No longer will it be a one-time fit; now a career will
truly span a variety of "fits." The remainder of this chapter should be
read with the perspective that career interventions must help individuals perceive that there is always a wide range of possible fits that can be
discovered with extended effort and that one can indeed learn useful
strategies for finding satisfactory fits. Krumboltz (1996) astutely stated
that the goal of career counseling in today's world should be

> to facilitate the learning of skills, interests, beliefs, values, work
> habits, and personal qualities that enable each client to create a
> satisfying life within a constantly changing work environment. The
> task of career counselors is to promote client learning. Thus, career
> counselors can be seen as coaches, educators and mentors—not
> simply matchmakers. (p. 61)

INTERVENTION DIVERSITY

The incredible array of career interventions now being offered by counseling psychologists can perhaps best be comprehended by looking at
how interventions vary along at least five different dimensions: questions asked, social identities, strategic goals, theoretical orientation, and
techniques. Our choice of these five dimensions has been determined
by our review of the growing literature on types of career interventions.
Although the dimensions are certainly not mutually exclusive, nor are
the components within each dimension, each dimension does lead to a
somewhat different emphasis and format for career interventions.

Questions Asked by Clients

In 1996, Savickas articulated a framework for career interventions
that we find very useful as we consider the changing worldviews, economic conditions, and career paths of those who seek career counseling.
Savickas identified six questions that career clients ask. Each of these
questions calls for different kinds of interventions, often offered by different kinds of agencies. The six questions are (a) How do I get a job?
(b) What shall I choose? (c) Who am I? (d) How do I shape my career?
(e) How can work help me grow as a person? and (f) How can I do
better? Well-trained counseling psychologists might be prepared to offer
services to address each of these career-related questions, but it is usually true that, depending on the question they have, students, workers,
or clients will go to different agencies. For example, to get help with the
first question, one might go to a job placement service; whereas for the
third question one would most likely seek personal counseling; for

the last question a worker might well go to the human resources services of his or her present employer.

Social Identities

There are at least four important social identities to consider when contemplating which career interventions to offer: age, gender, race/ethnicity, and sexual orientation. Counseling psychologists are continuing to learn about needed variations in career interventions when the population of participants is very different from the middle-class White males who were the initial focus of most of the early theory and research on career interventions.

Looking first at age, we note that career interventions now truly cover the life span. Even though the primary focus of career counseling theory and research has often been the adolescent and young adult years, considerable work is being done in K–12 schools (Lapan et al., 2012). One example of a younger age group for whom career interventions have been used effectively is preschool children (Barak, Shiloh, & Haushner, 1992). The positive results they obtained with cognitive restructuring exercises in order to expand the children's interests suggest that much of the stereotyping and narrowing of interests found in children of young ages can be overcome by interventions at the preschool level. At the other end of the age span, career counseling has been modified to suit the needs of retirees, all of whom are facing new life role decisions that will impact both their psychological and physical health (Harper & Shoffner, 2004; Tinsley & Schwendener-Holt, 1992; see Chapter 5 for more information). Considering a client's age will help guide the counselor in asking questions about what stage of career development the individual finds himself or herself in and what issues are most relevant to the counseling.

Similarly, counselors should consider a client's gender when attempting to frame the client's needs in a social context. We think that counselors must be well versed in the literature on gender and career development. There is an accumulation of over four decades of literature on special issues in interventions designed to enhance women's career development. For career counselors, a great resource regarding the critical components in a broad range of effective career interventions for women may be found in the diverse articles in *The Handbook of Career Counseling for Women* (2nd ed.) edited by Walsh and Heppner (2006). Chapter 5 also details much of the current research in this area, including issues related to the work–family balance.

It was not until the 1990s that significant numbers of published studies began to appear regarding issues in and strategies for career counseling with racial ethnic minorities (Bingham & Ward, 1996; Fouad

& Bingham, 1995; Leong, 1993). More recent work emphasizes the importance of multiculturalism and social justice in career counseling (Byars-Winston & Fouad, 2006; Ratts & Santos, 2012; Vespia, Fitzpatrick, Fouad, Kantamneni, & Chen, 2010). Because the research in this area is growing, we again emphasize that counselors need to stay current with issues related to ethnicity in career development and to assess the salience of ethnicity in the client's career concerns.

Finally, sexual minorities constitute another cultural group for which specific guidelines regarding career counseling have emerged. Whereas the 1970s through the 1990s saw a tremendous growth in the attention in the literature to women's development (Fitzgerald, Fassinger, & Betz, 1995), the 1990s saw significant advances in the theory and empirical study of the vocational development of gay, lesbian, bisexual, and transgendered persons (Chung, 2003). Chung (2003) suggested that the first decade in the 21st century should focus on issues of assessment, counselor training, and specifically on underrepresented groups (lesbians, bisexual and transgendered individuals). Certainly, the past decade has seen advances in understanding the career development issues of sexual minorities (Bieschke & Toepfer-Hendey, 2006; Datti, 2009; Pope et al., 2004; Schmidt & Nilsson, 2006). Unlike a few decades ago, there is now pertinent literature to guide career counselors working with culturally diverse populations.

Strategic Objectives

Although career counseling is stereotypically regarded as a "remedial" intervention to address some career-related decision making or work dysfunction, the actual objective of an increasing array of career interventions is to fulfill the developmental and/or preventive roles of counseling psychologists outlined in Chapter 1 of this text. It may be useful to repeat Jordaan, Myers, Layton, and Morgan's (1968) brief definitions of the developmental, preventive, and remedial roles; illustrations of career interventions matching those descriptions are then provided for each.

The developmental role is to "help individuals to plan, obtain, and derive maximum benefits from the kinds of experiences which will enable them to discover and develop their potentialities" (Jordaan et al., 1968, p. 1). Much of the research in career psychology by counseling psychologists has become the basis for career education programs for junior and senior high school students (Lapan et al., 2012). Moreover, in large industries and governmental agencies there may now be career development centers. One of the key functions of such centers is to help employees learn more about ways in which they can advance their careers. Employers know that many employees see such centers as a valuable benefit, thereby enhancing employees' morale and perceptions of their employer. Employers also know that some of their most talented and motivated employees will become better prepared for advancement within the company if they take part in the various programs offered in a career development center. Cooper and Shullman (2012) provided useful information regarding the nature of consulting, and Hesketh (2000) provided a helpful overview of career development interventions in organizations and the workplace.

The preventive role is to "anticipate, circumvent, and, if possible, forestall difficulties that may arise in the future" (Jordaan et al., 1968, p. 1). Recall the example of the work of Barak et al. (1992), cited in the section above on age, regarding an intervention with preschool children to overcome narrow perspectives on interests. Such an intervention is indeed designed to forestall difficulties that may arise because of overly circumscribed interests. High school and college students are typically a population in which the preventive role is key. As a significant portion of first-year college students never make it to graduation (Solberg Nes, Evans, & Segerstrom, 2009), establishing students' college and career readiness is critical (Lapan et al., 2012). In order to minimize dropout rates, counselors need to help students develop meaningful and coherent work and career plans (Flum & Blustein, 2000). Similarly, outplacement counseling, a concept that has grown rapidly as many companies "downsize"—that is, dismiss many satisfactory employees—is most often seen by the dismissed employees as a way of helping them get another job. In one sense that is the purpose of outplacement, but the more important reason for having the "dismissing" company provide the outplacement counseling is to prevent the significant personal and family dysfunction that comes with unemployment (Mallinckrodt & Fretz, 1988).

The remedial role is used when something is awry, needs to be "fixed." This role is, of course, the role most people assume is being served by career counseling: A client can't seem to find a satisfactory choice or has a work adjustment problem that needs to be addressed. To help make the distinction of remedial career counseling from other kinds of career interventions, Lowman (1993) used the phrase "counseling of work dysfunction" to refer to issues of work-related anxiety and depression, overcommitment to work, and so forth. More recently, Swanson (2012) clearly stated that "job loss and unemployment causes mental health problems" (p. 20) and that interventions can help individuals recover their sense of well-being and satisfaction.

Theoretical Orientations

Almost every career intervention—no matter which question is being addressed, for whatever population, with whichever strategic objective—will typically be framed primarily within one of the theoretical orientations reviewed earlier in this chapter. For example, developmental theory leads quite naturally to interventions with a developmental strategic objective, perhaps addressed to the question "How can work help me grow as a person?" A social learning theory approach is a most natural fit for remedial interventions for a client "stuck" on the question of "What shall I choose?" Trait-oriented approaches play a key role in outplacement counseling, helping the person see a new and larger array of opportunities than were considered while satisfactorily employed, thereby preventing some of the stress and despair of just throwing oneself on the job market looking for any paying job. Sharf (2006) is an excellent resource for seeing how each of the major theories of career development can be "translated" into career counseling practice.

Techniques

The dimension of techniques differs qualitatively from the first four dimensions reviewed. A career intervention may focus primarily on one question, one salient aspect of social identity, one particular strategic goal, within one general theoretical framework, but when it comes to techniques, the choices are typically eclectic and multiple for each intervention. The techniques of career counseling fall into two large categories: (a) assessment strategies for learning about oneself, the world of work, and putting the two together and (b) job-finding, job-getting, and job-holding skills. Many of the strategies in this first group were reviewed in the Key Measures section for each theory summarized earlier in the chapter. Although traditional assessment continues to be popular in career counseling, there has also been a growing emphasis on the use of technology. In particular, with the pervasive use of the Internet, a number of computer-assisted career guidance systems have become available (Bobek et al., 2005). Sometimes such assessments are used within the context of career counseling or via a college career development center, but they are also used by individuals searching on their own. There are some well-established measures out there (though we have found that the field is in constant flux). We suggest that counselors become familiar with the particular benefits and challenges of using the Internet in their practice (Osborn, Dikel, & Sampson, 2011).

For an understanding of the range and good illustrations of techniques for job finding and getting, the *Job Club Counselor's Manual* (Azrin & Basalel, 1980) is still a widely used resource. The Job Club concept has been used effectively both in assisting welfare recipients to find satisfactory employment, as well as in "outplacement" services set up to help soon-to-be-terminated employees (due to mergers, downsizing, etc.)

find compatible new positions. Another similar club is Kate Wendleton's series on the Five O'Clock Club (e.g., the *Job Search Workbook*; Wendleton, 2007). Again, the use of Internet for information, blogs, career search engines, and social networking (Osborn et al., 2011) is becoming a vital part of today's career counselor's repertoire.

Indecisiveness: The Ultimate Career Counseling Challenge

Although most participants in career counseling and career interventions experience measurable positive gains, it has long been evident that there is a small group of career counseling clients who never reach any satisfactory decisions and remain unhappy with their counseling experience. In most cases, the counselors of these clients have been as unhappy, or even more unhappy, than their clients with the experience and outcomes of working with these indecisive clients. In this section, we provide an overview of the conceptual and empirical results of the work of counseling psychologists as scientist–practitioners, addressing the problems presented by this most challenging group of clients. Three questions have been addressed, each question having emerged based on developments regarding the prior question. First, Are there reliable and meaningfully different types of indecisive clients? Second, If such types exist, are there different treatments that should be employed when providing career counseling for them? Third, If a different treatment is needed, should it be some variation of career interventions, some version of psychotherapy, or some kind of combination?

THE RETURN OF DIAGNOSIS

Crites (1981) has concisely reviewed some of the issues and problems with career-related diagnostic systems developed in the early years of the profession of counseling psychology. One of the major problems with such systems was that they were never closely tied to providing different kinds of career interventions. Career counseling strategies were based more on the theoretical predilections of the counselor than on any differential diagnosis of the client. Yet, even within a given theoretical framework such as trait-oriented ones, Holland and Holland (1977) noted, there were clearly some career counseling clients who had concerns about being undecided but simply did not respond favorably to traditional interventions that emphasized learning information about oneself and the world of work and then how to find and choose satisfactory options.

Over the past few decades numerous theoretical and empirical studies have been undertaken to understand more about these clients. In the earliest phases of that research, the focus was on how to separate those clients who were simply undecided from those who were called indecisive and the different treatments needed for each client type (Fuqua & Hartman, 1983; Holland & Holland, 1977; Salomone, 1982). Undecided clients were those individuals who had not made career decisions but generally responded quickly and well to a variety of career interventions, even self-administered ones like the SDS; their undecided state may have been simply a normal developmental phase or a temporary reaction to the need to consider other career options, either because of dissatisfaction with a current career or because of involuntary dismissal from previous employment. On the other hand, studies of those labeled indecisive—that is, those who did not respond well to many career interventions and were not able to make career or vocational decisions—showed that such clients typically had high levels of anxiety and often inadequate decision-making and coping skills. Over the years it also became evident that "indecisive" clients were themselves not a homogeneous group (Brown & Rector, 2008). Some indecisive clients seemed immobilized by anxiety, others perceived what they considered insurmountable barriers, others were simply poor and ineffectual decision makers. In some cases, clients possessed all three types of problems.

Various measures have been developed to help make differential diagnoses related to these types of indecisiveness. The two most widely used clearly have been the Career Decision Scale (CDS; Osipow, Carney, Winer, Yanico, & Koschier, 1980) and My Vocational Situation (MVS; Holland, Daiger, & Power, 1980; Holland et al., 1993), though others have also been developed, such as the Coping with Career Indecision scale (Larson, Heppner, Ham, & Dugan, 1988). These measures have been used with many age groups and studied for their factor structure, reliability, and validity. These measures have yielded the clearest distinctions between "undecided" and "indecisiveness." There is much less clarity about whether indecisiveness is a unidimensional or multidimensional construct (Lee, 2005; Lucas, 1993).

Recent research on indecisiveness has looked at issues of anxiety and attachment (Braunstein-Bercovitz, Benjamin, Asor, & Lev, 2012; Tokar, Withrow, Hall, & Moradi, 2003) and a variety of cognitive factors (Bullock-Yowell, Peterson, Reardon, Leierer, & Reed, 2011; Creed, Patton, & Bartrum, 2004; Guay, Senécal, Gauthier, & Fernet, 2003). Just how to make the most effective diagnoses about these hard-to-help career counseling clients is not yet conclusively evident; there will no doubt continue to be further developments of assessment techniques in the coming years. If counseling psychologists continue to follow the good advice of Phillips (1992), there will also be increased attention to tying the results of assessments to differential treatments in order to determine what works best with different types of indecisive clients. Such differential treatment planning is the focus of the next section.

TREATMENT PLANNING

Even as early as the late 1970s, Holland could conclude from his research (Holland & Holland, 1977) that compared with those labeled "indecisive," those who were identified simply as "undecided" could be provided much less intensive, even self-administered career interventions like the SDS (Holland, 1994). The tremendous cost savings in professional time that arise from simply knowing who can benefit from essentially self-help treatments, like the SDS or computer-assisted counseling, makes the use of even present forms of diagnostic instruments such as the CDS or MVS extremely useful as treatment-planning devices.

Heppner and Hendricks (1995) provided one of the first process and outcome studies comparing treatment of an undecided client to an indecisive client. Their findings were quite illuminating regarding the complexities in treating indecisiveness. They found that the undecided client made the most and fastest progress and had the greatest satisfaction at the completion of the brief career counseling sessions. Moreover, they found that the undecided client rated the counseling relationship (not just a rating of the counselor) even more highly than did the indecisive client who had been working with the counselor on more personal issues. The limited outcomes and poor ratings of counseling from their indecisive client no doubt elicited responses of "I told you so" from those counseling psychologists who have consistently stated that some "career clients" really need to be referred for "personal counseling," as those career issues are embedded in a larger life context (e.g., Juntunen, 2006; Swanson, 2002). The provocative and ongoing discussions about the relationships of career counseling and personal counseling are the basis for the final section on meeting the challenge of the indecisive client.

Career Counseling and Psychotherapy: Fusion, Diffusion, and Confusion

Given the kinds of difficulties just described for counseling indecisive clients, it is not surprising that almost all counseling psychologists agree that, for some clients, some *fusion* of personal and career counseling is necessary. Just what the nature of that fusion should be was the subject of numerous articles in the 1990s; a special 1993 issue of the *Career Development Quarterly* (Vol. 42, pp. 129–173) included a variety of views about and examples of the need for more fusion of career counseling and personal counseling/psychotherapy. Hackett (1993) spelled out what she believes to be numerous false dichotomies between career and personal counseling that are perpetuated by graduate programs offering separate courses and practica in the two areas as well as many counseling centers offering separately labeled services in career counseling and personal counseling.

Just as it is clear that for some clients, some fusion of career counseling and psychotherapy is necessary, it is also clear that for some career interventions, no fusion is necessary or reasonably possible. Some career interventions involve almost no personal interactions with counselors; for example, a computer-assisted guidance program or self-administration of the SDS. Some career education classes, development workshops, and preretirement programs are offered to groups of 30 to 100 persons. With these types of interventions, many conducted outside of any personal relationship with a counselor, there is clearly a *diffusion* of activities with little or no relationship to psychotherapy. This is not to say that a person who completes one of these kinds of interventions may not at a later time request a counseling relationship to deal with concerns raised by the intervention; however, there would still be, at least initially, separate phases of the career- and personal-focused counseling activities.

When it comes to looking at those individual or small group counseling situations where career concerns are taken up in the context of a relationship with a counselor, there is an immense array of opinions (Swanson, 1995, 2002), one could even say confusion, about the nature of any fusion between career counseling and personal counseling–psychotherapy. Are career counseling and psychotherapy basically separate "sets" that have limited intersections or overlap only in times of stress? Or is career counseling just one of many subsets of psychotherapy?

To illustrate the separate sets notion, there are some counselors who feel that a person with pervasive anxiety, depression, and so forth cannot benefit from consideration of career concerns until those symptoms are treated. This position is often taken by those counselors who work primarily with trait-oriented approaches and expect the client to be able to engage in active exploration of self and environmental assessment and then engage in a rational decision-making process—all steps that may prove extremely difficult for a highly anxious or depressed client to undertake.

The "subset" position is illustrated by person-centered counselors, who see a client with career concerns as really no different from one with sexual dysfunction concerns or substance abuse concerns. Krumboltz and Coon (1995), from their social learning perspective, viewed career concerns as simply just one of many possible unique sets of concerns, like deciding whether to enter into a long-term relationship or dealing with a phobia. Thus, a growing number of counseling psychologists (Blustein & Spengler, 1995; Juntunen, 2006; Swanson, 2002) have argued for the fusing career counseling and psychotherapy in ways in which career problems simply become one of many sets of concerns a client might bring to counseling, shifting the focus from "helping people develop careers to helping people construct lives through work and relationship" (Richardson, 2012, p. 191). Richardson (1996) has even argued that we should retire the label "career counseling." DeBell (2006) suggested that all counselors and therapists should be aware of world-of-work issues (such as increased globalization and the increasing economic disparities between the wealthy and the poor). Whether you engage in "career counseling," in "domain-sensitive counseling" (Blustein & Spengler, 1995), or in integrative career/personal counseling that defies labeling (Richardson, 2012), the important point is that you understand the significance and reciprocal impacts of career issues on a person's self-concept, developmental choices, and mental health.

Summary

Career psychology is one of the oldest and most central components of counseling psychology. The robustness of career psychology as a field of research and practice, for over 100 years, is no doubt related to the importance counseling psychologists place on career psychology for both individual and societal well-being. The major part of this chapter was devoted to the presentation of three diverse approaches to the study of career psychology.

Trait-oriented theories began to develop in the early part of the 19th century, when much psychological research was focused on measurement. Early theories were known as trait and factor and emphasized matching individual abilities to job requirements. The foundational theory of this type that we explored was Holland's theory of vocational personalities. Holland's RIASEC model has proved extraordinarily valuable in generating new research and innovative career counseling interventions that attend more to a congruence of persons' assessment of themselves and job environments than to a matching of persons' abilities and job requirements.

Developmental theories of career psychology emerged largely in the middle of the 20th century, just as psychology as a discipline was attending much more to developmental processes. These theories focus highly on "how" career choices are made compared with "what" choices are made. Super's lifetime of work in developing a life span stage theory of career development has stimulated a great deal of innovative research and new psychological assessments (e.g., work salience). His research findings radically altered the nature of career guidance for young adolescents.

Social learning and cognitive theories of career choice and development have been the most recent to develop, reflecting again the emphases in psychology at large; cognitive learning theories emerged largely after 1960. Krumboltz and colleagues were the first to incorporate basic principles of learning to help us understand what goes on in the minds of individuals as they make career choices. How do individuals come to believe what they do about both themselves and the world of work? This model has been especially useful in examining how various mistaken beliefs lead to unsatisfactory vocational choices. The specificity of the model has been particularly helpful in devising new kinds of career assessments and interventions to rectify individuals' inappropriate beliefs about themselves and the world of work.

Concomitant with changing meanings of the word *career* in recent decades, an extraordinarily broad array of career interventions has emerged. These interventions range from classroom activities to self-administered computerized programs to individualized career counseling. We described five dimensions on which this diversity of interventions can be compared: clients' questions, social identities, strategic objectives, theoretical orientation, and techniques used.

The persisting difficulties presented to career counselors by a small group of clients known as "indecisive" clients provided an opportunity to explore the values of diagnosis and treatment planning in individualized career counseling. When one works with such clients, there is great overlap between traditional psychotherapy and career counseling. There are indeed many important shared change processes in psychotherapy and career counseling that are beneficial for counseling psychologists to explore.

Beyond the Individual

Group, Couple, and Family Therapy

16

U p to this point, our focus in the chapters on interventions has primarily been on one-to-one individual counseling and psychotherapy. Counseling psychologists, however, are involved in many interventions beyond individual work. They work with groups as well, including group, couple, and family therapy. These treatments have slowly but surely gained wide acceptance in the psychological community because they are both efficient and effective, as shall be discussed in this chapter. The chapter is divided into two parts. Because group therapy is very different in many ways from couple and family therapy, we explore it separately. Then we look at couple and family treatments.

http://dx.doi.org/10.1037/14378-016
Counseling Psychology, Third Edition, by C. J. Gelso, E. N. Williams, and B. R. Fretz

Group Counseling and Therapy

Research has now clearly demonstrated that individual counseling or therapy is effective for a variety of client concerns (see Chapter 8). Also, clients who seek counseling typically have individual help in mind. Why then should counseling psychologists bother with group treatments such as group counseling and psychotherapy? Why not simply assign all clients to individual counseling? Doing so would certainly simplify the training of counseling psychologists, for then they could be trained only in individual interventions. Assigning all clients to individual treatments would also simplify agency practices because counseling agencies would no longer need to worry about whom to assign to which interventions. Neither would agencies need to grapple with logistical problems such as how to arrange for group meeting times.

To begin with, group procedures allow for an efficient use of the counseling psychologist's time, as a number of individuals may be worked with simultaneously in a group format. More important than this efficiency, however, is the fact that group interventions such as group therapy, just like individual counseling, have been shown to be especially helpful for a wide range of concerns (Burlingame, Strauss, & Joyce, 2013).

Advantages and Limitations

Are there unique advantages to group interventions such as group counseling or therapy? Although the research evidence is as yet unclear about this, the major advantages of group treatment are generally seen as *interpersonal*. Thus, the client in group therapy learns by observing other group members, receiving feedback from others, giving feedback and being helpful to other group members, becoming part of a cohesive group, and, moreover, participating in the sharing and the give and take of this very personal form of interpersonal interaction.

It follows that clients who will profit most from group interventions are those whose difficulties are in the interpersonal arena. For example, clients who suffer from interpersonal anxiety, who are unsure of their relationship skills, and who desire close relationships but for one reason or another shy away from them are all prime candidates for group therapy. Group therapy also can be particularly effective in less obvious cases. For example, the client whose family dynamics breed secrecy and shame may experience enormous growth from a group experience in which his or her inner feelings are shared and accepted by other members. Likewise, the client whose major problem itself breeds secrecy and shame may find group therapy strikingly helpful. An example of this latter type might be the female incest survivor who participates in group therapy as a way of coming to grips with her sense of shame and self-blame about her incestuous experiences. Recent literature on women who have experienced the trauma of incest supports the idea that group treatments can be highly effective for these clients (Burlingame et al., 2013; Ford, Fallot, & Harris, 2009). Similarly, for members of oppressed groups, group counseling–therapy can be a source of support and solidarity. It can help people know they are not alone as well as reduce isolation.

The major advantages of therapeutic groups, as discussed by Corey, Corey, and Corey (2010), are as follows.

1. Participants can explore their style of relating to others and learn more effective social skills.
2. The group situation offers support for new behaviors and encourages experimentation. Members can try out new behaviors and decide whether they want to incorporate these behaviors into their repertoire outside the group.
3. More than in individual counseling, there is a re-creation of the everyday world in many groups, especially if the membership is diverse with respect to interest, age, background, culture, socioeconomic status, and problem type. When groups are heterogeneous in this way, members are able to contact a wide range of personalities and receive rich and diverse feedback.
4. Members are able to learn about themselves through the experience of others; to experience emotional closeness and caring, which encourages meaningful self-disclosure; and to identify with the struggles of others.
5. The group setting optimally helps participants discover how they affect others. Members can effectively learn what they may be doing interpersonally to create some of their problems (e.g., loneliness, isolation). And members also learn to change unhelpful patterns.

Despite the many advantages of group interventions and the consistent evidence of the overall effectiveness of therapeutic groups, groups are certainly not cure-alls. Just as certainly, groups are not for everyone. In fact, some clients can be emotionally damaged by participating in certain groups. For example, in virtually all forms of group work, there is often a subtle pressure to conform to the group's norms and expectations. Some members may be especially vulnerable to such pressures, taking in these expectations without questioning. As Corey et al. (2010) noted, some clients are too suspicious, too hostile, or too fragile to benefit from group treatment. Persons suffering from certain personality disorders (e.g., borderline personality, narcissistic personality, sociopathy) may also be ill suited for group therapy (Yalom & Leszcz, 2005). Before a person is accepted into a group, both counselor and client should weigh the advantages and limitations of whatever type of group is being considered for that person. The counseling psychologist needs to assess how likely the client is to profit from the group, as well as how the client's presence will impact on that group.

Therapeutic Group Work: Definition and Basic Features

A *group* may be defined as any aggregate of individuals among which some degree of interdependence exists. A *therapeutic group* may be defined as an aggregate of interdependent individuals whose interaction is in pursuit of some shared goal or goals. The therapeutic group is always more than the sum of its individual parts because the group itself takes on its own life; its own psyche, so to speak; and its own personality.

Therapeutic groups can include a wide range of interventions, such as group psychotherapy, group counseling, encounter and growth groups, training or T groups, structured groups, and self-help groups. Our focus in this chapter, however, is group counseling and psychotherapy, probably the two major therapeutic group interventions used by counseling psychologists. As will be seen, the terms *group counseling* and *group psychotherapy* are often used interchangeably, but they do have some differences.

Group counseling tends to be more oriented toward prevention (vs. remediation) than is group psychotherapy. Also, group counseling is more likely to focus on the conscious concerns of the client, to include attention to educational and vocational issues as well as personal issues, to occur in educational settings (in contrast to medical or clinical settings), and to be used with clients within the normal range rather than with severely troubled persons. Group counseling is, on the whole, briefer than group therapy, with generally an upper limit of about 20 to 25 sessions. Group therapy, on the other hand, may continue for several years and is more likely than counseling to seek deep personality change in clients.

It should be emphasized that these differences are more of degree than kind. There is considerable overlap between the two, just as there is much overlap between the words *counseling* and *therapy* (see definitions in Chapter 1). In fact, except at the extreme ends of the continuum, the differences become blurred or eliminated with most groups in counseling practice, and we shall use the terms interchangeably throughout this chapter. Corey et al.'s (2010) description of group counseling applies to both group counseling and therapy. According to these authors, participants in group counseling or therapy often have problems of an interpersonal nature, which are well suited to the group format. Clients are able to see a reenactment of their everyday struggles and problems unfold before them in the group. In the group, however, the client is able to work on and through these problems, with the feedback and help of group members. In this way the group provides a slice of reality to the client as well as a vehicle for change. Members are encouraged to get feedback from others about how they are seen, as well as to give such feedback. They also have the chance to reexperience early conflicts with significant others and, in the process of reliving, to work through old issues. The empathy and support of the group also allow members to identify what and how they want to change and to try out new behaviors. Clients can learn to respect individual and cultural differences and, at the same time, discover that on a deep level they are more alike than different. Life situations differ, but their pain and struggles are universal.

Group Leadership: Approaches, Tasks, and Qualities

Leading counseling and therapy groups is both highly complex and exciting. As you will see in this section, there are a number of approaches to leading therapeutic groups, each with its own particular focus. In addition, the therapist needs to perform certain tasks skillfully if the group is to be successful. Finally, there appear to be certain therapist qualities that make for effectiveness in leading groups. Each of these features of group work is explored in this section.

THE LEADER'S FOCUS

Over the years, there has been considerable controversy over whether the group leader ought to focus his or her observations on the group as a whole or on the individuals within the group. A third possibility is to focus on the interactions between and among members.

The *group-centered approach*, which received its strongest voice at the Tavistock Clinic in England (e.g., Bion, 1961), is based on the idea that the group is an entity in itself and that individuals learn most by understanding this entity, how they fit into it, and how they contribute to it. In the extreme, the therapist's comments are rarely aimed at individuals but rather seek to clarify the underlying meanings and processes in the group as a whole. By contrast, in the *individual-centered approach*, the focus is on each individual group member. Examples of the individual-centered approach are gestalt groups, in which the individual participant is placed in the "hot seat" and the counselor devotes his or her therapeutic energies for a period of time to that client and the issues he or she is experiencing at the moment. Other participants presumably learn through observing and identifying, although their comments are sought at times. Individual members take turns in the hot seat. In the third approach, the *interpersonally centered approach*, the main attention of the leader is given to the interactions between and among members. The focus tends to be on how the members affect and experience one another.

As a way of clarifying the three approaches, imagine a group therapy client, Jane, entering her group for a given session, expressing that "I feel angry today. I've had this sense of irritation since yesterday, and today it has just gotten bigger and bigger. I feel so abusive toward this group but don't know why." Consider the three therapist responses given below, and decide which of the three approaches they fit.

1. "I notice the group has responded with silence, like last week when Jim expressed irritation. Actually, it feels more like silent irritation. I wonder what is happening in the group right now."
2. "Jane, could you share with us what these feelings are like [about] for you right now?"
3. "Jane, you looked at Jim when you said that, and now he's looking very responsive. Jim, what are you feeling right now about Jane's experience?"

Perhaps most group leaders attempt to integrate the group and individual approaches (the interpersonal approach fits well with both) because for several years now, theory and research have suggested that neither extreme is very helpful (Horwitz, 1986).

THE LEADER'S TASKS

In virtually all types of therapeutic groups but especially in the less structured, more interactional ones, such as group counseling–therapy and growth groups, there are common tasks in which the leader must engage. Although one could think of numerous leader tasks in therapeutic group work, Yalom and Leszcz (2005) have convincingly proposed that there are three fundamental tasks: (a) the creation and maintenance of the group, (b) group culture building, and (c) activation and illumination of the here and now.

Creation and Maintenance of the Group

The therapist's first crucial task is to create and convene the group. The importance of selecting and preparing members cannot be over-emphasized. Research and clinical experience generally support the observation that certain types of individuals tend to do poorly in therapeutic groups. It is probably wise not to include persons who are paranoid, hypochondriacal, sociopathic, brain damaged, acutely psychotic, or addicted to drugs or alcohol (unless the group is explicitly aimed at the drug-dependent person). Also, Yalom (1995) suggested that persons who have extreme difficulties with intimacy are not good group candidates (with the emphasis on *extreme*), and those in an acute life crisis may need more individual attention than can be given in the group format. Finally, Yalom and Leszcz (2005) discussed at length the group "deviant," who should not be placed into an interactional group. What is meant by *deviant* is someone who cannot or will not examine himself or herself and his or her relationship with others in the group.

On the positive side, it is wise to select members who fit well with the group and to form groups with a reasonable balance of interpersonal styles. Try for a "reasonable diversity," while avoiding potential scapegoats and "misfits" (Dies, 1987). Considerable clinical skill is required to "screen in" suitable members and "screen out" those who will not do well in the group. Often, more than one individual interview is required to perform this selection.

During the process of selection and during the early phase of the group's life, it is important that members be well informed about what groups are like, what can be expected of them, and what they can expect from others. Indeed, people have many misconceptions about what group therapy is like, and much of this misinformation is negative: For example, groups are unpredictable and will force individuals to reveal what they do not want to (Corey, Corey, & Corey, 2010). Correcting these misconceptions is a valuable beginning.

Once the group begins, the therapist's job is to deter anything that threatens the group's cohesiveness. Thus, the therapist works to prevent dropouts because these, more than perhaps anything else, will threaten the group's existence. Continued tardiness, absences, the formation of cliques within the group, certain kinds of socializing between members outside the group, and scapegoating all threaten the integrity of the group and require the therapist's intervention. The creation and maintenance of the group is so important in the early stages that at times the pressing needs of the individual must be put aside. Yalom (1995) used the example of a group that contained four core members who were male and that had trouble keeping female members. During their first group meeting, two new female members were ignored. One of the male members entered the group late and immediately began discussing a problem he was having without acknowledging the new members' presence or existence. After a half hour, Yalom interrupted the client with the question, "Mike, I wonder what hunches you have about how our two new members are feeling in the group today?" This question turned the members' attention to how they had ignored the two new members and helped Mike begin to work on his tendency to ignore the needs of others.

Group Culture Building

Once the group becomes a physical reality, the counselor's main job is to develop it into a therapeutic social system. In seeking to do this, the counselor works to establish a code of behavioral rules (often unstated), or norms, that guides the interactions of the group members. This norm building is more complicated in group than in individual counseling. In individual counseling, the counselor is the only agent of change, but in group therapy other group members serve as perhaps the most potent agents of change. The therapist's task is to create a group culture that facilitates therapeutic interaction among members.

This therapeutic culture, as we said, contains the norms that guide client behavior. Just which norms are we talking about? Active involvement, self-disclosure of immediate feelings, nonjudgmental acceptance of other members, spontaneity of expression, desire for self-understanding, dissatisfaction with at least some of one's present behavioral patterns, and the desire for change—these are the main norms (or values) that the group leader works toward establishing. Both group theory and research support the notion that the therapist facilitates the building of therapeutic norms through two roles: that of a technical expert and that of a *model-setting participant* (Dies, 1987; Yalom & Leszcz, 2005). The therapist functions as a technical expert when instructing the client about the rules of the group prior to the group's beginning and during the early stages. Such instruction is reinforced by the weight of the therapist's authority and experience and by the fact that the rationale presented by the therapist for these rules makes good, clear sense to the client.

During the early stages of the group, the counselor as technical expert can use a variety of means to help shape norms. Yalom (1995) and Yalom and Leszcz (2005) provided examples of the methods available. If therapists want to create an interactional network in which the members freely interact rather than directing all comments to the therapist, then therapists may implicitly instruct members in their pregroup interviews or in the first group sessions; they may, repeatedly ask for all members' reactions to another member or toward a group issue; they may wonder why conversation is always directed toward the therapist; they may refuse to answer questions; they may ask the group to engage in exercises that teach clients to interact (e.g., asking each member of the group to give his or her first impressions of every other member); or therapists may shape behavior by rewarding members who address one another (e.g., address them warmly, or shift their posture into a more receptive position). The same approaches may be applied to the many other norms the therapist wants to promote: self-disclosure, open expression of emotions, promptness, self-exploration.

The therapist also shapes norms through serving as a model-setting participant. For example, by offering a model of nonjudgmental acceptance and appreciation of members' strengths along with their problem areas, the leader helps shape a group that is health oriented. The therapist also models honesty, spontaneity, and human fallibility. This does not imply, however, that the counselor freely expresses all feelings. Clients' needs must take preeminence, as in any form of therapy, and the effective therapist models responsibility and restraint, as well as honesty and openness. Integrating such qualities as restraint and openness is no easy task, even for the seasoned counselor.

Activation and Illumination of the Here and Now

Some group counselors will focus on material in the client's past, whereas others will attend only to the present. Whether the counselor's focus is primarily on the past or present, however, group members live their group lives in the present, in the here and now. Thus, even when past material is being explored, it may be done so in a way that is fresh and alive in the present. To this extent, we agree with Yalom and Leszcz's (2005) suggestion that the activation and illumination of the here and now is one of the three primary tasks of group therapy.

According to Yalom (1995), if the here-and-now focus is to be effective, it must consist of two interrelated tiers. The first tier is the "experiencing" one. The members must live with each other in the present. They develop strong feelings toward each other, toward the therapist, and toward the group. These here-and-now feelings need to be expressed and indeed form the main interactions in the group. As vital as this experiencing (called "activation of the here and now") is, it is not enough. If group members express only immediate feelings, they would have a powerful experience that would be soon forgotten, without behavior change taking place.

If clients are to change, the counselor must also illuminate the here-and-now process. Thus, the effective counselor helps members to observe and think about what is happening in their interactions and what the meanings are of those interactions. This is the cognitive component, the observing and thinking about one's experience, and, just as in individual therapy, it is critical to effective change in groups. Whereas the group members, with the aid of the counselor, are responsible for activation of the here and now, only the therapist is responsible for commenting on the process, for directing the client's attention to the meaning of what is happening in the group. We should also note that if only this second tier is actualized in the group, that too would not be effective. The interactions would be emotionally sterile.

The counselor has many techniques at his or her disposal in the effort to activate and illuminate the here and now. The bottom line, however, was noted nicely by Yalom (1995), when he suggested that counselors "think here-and-now." He further stated,

> When you grow accustomed to thinking of the here-and-now, you automatically steer the group into the here-and-now. Sometimes I feel like a shepherd herding a flock into an ever-tightening circle. I head off errant strays—forays into personal historical material, discussions of current life situations, intellectualisms—and guide them back into the circle. Whenever an issue is raised in the group, I think, "how can I relate this to the group's primary task? How can I make it come to life in the here-and-now? *I am relentless in this effort, and I begin it in the very first meeting of the group."* (p. 143)

THE LEADER'S PERSONAL QUALITIES

Just as in individual counseling, the personal qualities of the group leader are of utmost importance, and the ability to offer a good relationship may be the most important of these. Thus, the group counselor's ability to experience and communicate (a) empathic understanding; (b) positive regard, warmth, and respect; and (c) genuineness or congruence forms the groundwork of effective therapeutic group work. In group interventions, however, the relationship task is more complicated than it is in individual work. The leader not only must be effective in developing therapeutic relationships with his or her clients but must also facilitate therapeutic relationships among the members of his or her groups.

In line with these relationship qualities, Corey et al. (2010) discussed 15 personal characteristics of effective group leaders: courage, willingness to model, presence, goodwill and caring, belief in group process, openness, becoming aware of your own culture, nondefensiveness in coping with attacks, personal power, stamina, willingness to seek new experiences, self-awareness, sense of humor, inventiveness, and personal dedication and commitment. This list should be studied and integrated by the beginning group counselor. Let us elaborate on a few of these qualities.

Courage

Courage is a personal quality that is all too infrequently addressed in both the individual and group intervention literature. It is probably an important trait for both counselors and clients. It may take courage as well as other ingredients for clients to take the risks involved in opening up in counseling and making the changes that need to be made. For group leaders, courage may be reflected in, among other things, their willingness to (a) be vulnerable, admitting to mistakes and taking the same risks that are expected of group members; (b) confront members even when they are not sure that they are right; (c) be emotionally touched by their group members; and (d) continually examine themselves and strive for a depth of awareness.

Becoming Aware of Your Own Culture

The self-insight of leaders into how their own culture influences decisions and behavior provides a frame of reference for understanding the worldview of others who may differ from them. The most effective group leader, in our view, embraces diversity in its many forms, ranging from cultural to individual (and their interaction). Cultural and individual self-awareness is a fundamentally important starting point.

Belief in Group Process

As a scientist–practitioner, the counseling psychologist who leads therapeutic groups must balance an appropriate scientific skepticism and thoughtful clinical judgment with a belief in the value of group treatment and the therapeutic forces in groups. The leader need not accept group efficacy on faith, for there is plenty of research evidence (as well as clinical evidence) that group treatment is effective (Burlingame et al., 2013). The counselor who believes in the effectiveness of group process will likely behave in a way that actualizes that belief. On the other side of the ledger, Corey, Williams, and Moline (2005) noted that some therapists lead groups despite the belief that group work does not effect significant client change.

Inventiveness

Inventiveness is another leader quality that is underemphasized. The capacity to approach each group with fresh ideas, spontaneity, and creativity is a key part of effectiveness (Corey et al., 2010). The ability to think up new techniques and new ways of approaching a group prevents group-leader burnout. Many group experts recommend co-leadership as a way of staying fresh and reducing burnout. Having a co-leader takes some of the strain off the leader; it also provides fresh interpersonal and technical input. One may also reduce the number of groups one leads when energy and enthusiasm are diminished.

Nondefensiveness

Criticism and other negative reactions toward the group leader occur in virtually all groups of any duration. The group counselor will be seen as structuring too much, structuring too little, not caring enough or caring too selectively, being too critical or demanding, and so forth. One reason for this is that the leader cannot be what everyone wants at all times. Second, many of the members will have issues related to authority, parenting, and helping; often, when helping and authority are combined, as in the role of the group leader, reactions are inevitable. At the same time, the spirit of openness and sharing that must exist in groups encourages members to express and reflect upon whatever negative reactions they have. The counselor must not only expect some reactions but must also facilitate their expression and examination.

THE LEADER'S THEORETICAL ORIENTATION AND THE "TYPICAL GROUP"

There are as many theoretical orientations and approaches to therapeutic group work as there are to individual counseling and therapy. The leader's ways of implementing his or her theoretical orientation map closely to the orientations presented in Chapters 11 to 14 in this volume. Corey (2008) provided a full coverage of how differing theoretical orientations are applied to group counseling. Apart from these specific theoretical orientations, the typical group in practice tends to be relatively unstructured and has about six to 10 members, is held once a week for 1.5 to 2 hours, continues for anywhere from 6 months to several years, and is closed in the sense that new members are added only on occasion. The focal points of the typical therapy group tend to be at all three levels: the individual, the group, and interaction among members. Immediate experiencing is of fundamental importance but so is the need to cognitively understand this experiencing of the group and its individuals. The leader is not highly directive, but neither is she or he nearly as nondirective as the person-centered therapist. This leader uses his or her role of expert to maintain the group, develop the group culture, and help the group focus on the present. She or he is not nearly as dominant or knowing as, for example, the rational–emotive group leader. It is safe to say that the leader of group therapy as typically practiced is a combination of theoretical orientations, especially the humanistic and psychodynamic approaches.

Stages of Therapeutic Groups

An extensive literature has accumulated on group development, and there is general agreement within this research and clinical literature that therapeutic groups progress through different stages or phases of development (Burlingame & McClendon, 2008; Dies, 2003). Tuckman (1965) appears to have been the first to summarize the literature on stages, labeling them as "forming," "storming," "norming," and "performing" (to which others later added "adjourning"). Although different authors propose differing numbers of stages, considerable similarities exist in the way these stages are described and their sequencing. Below we describe a sequence of four stages: exploratory, transition, working, and termination.

First, it should be pointed out that all formulations of stages apply in a clear way only to groups in which membership is more or less closed. The closed group maintains the same or nearly the same membership throughout the life of the group, adding new members only on occasion. Just as there is general agreement that therapeutic groups progress in stages or phases, group therapy authors are unanimous in their agreement that these stages do not unfold in a discrete and orderly way.

EXPLORATORY STAGE

During this beginning stage, members introduce themselves, tell why they are in the group, and explain what they hope to get out of it. Some ground rules of the group are established early on. The interaction of group members tends to be on the superficial side. Issues of inclusion and influence are primary in this first stage. Members wonder if they will fit in and be liked and listened to and, as a result, try to present themselves in a way that is acceptable to others. There is also the question in each member's mind, however framed, of how much influence he or she will have in the group. In fact, as Bonney (1969) long ago noted, the group does consciously and unconsciously assign varying degrees of power and influence to each member.

There are often periods of silence and awkwardness in the early meetings, as members seek to find direction and wonder what the group really will be about, *really*. In the exploratory stage, members also wonder if the group is a safe place in which to share their inner feelings. Beginning efforts at self-disclosure are made, partly as a way of testing the waters. If members are able to express themselves, a beginning sense of group cohesion emerges. It is essential that a sense of trust be built up during this stage.

During this crucial and delicate stage, as discussed in the section on leadership, the group counselor helps to establish therapeutic norms through a sensitive use of instruction and through his or her behavior. Thus, he or she functions both as the technical expert and as the participant model. The primary mission of this stage is simply to maintain the group and to build a solid foundation.

TRANSITION STAGE

As the group moves beyond the exploratory stage, members will seek to disclose a bit more deeply. They go beyond talking about their background and presenting their beginning stories. This movement is not without ambivalence, however, as anxiety and defense also become heightened during the transition stage. Thus, there is the urge to move forward into deeper explorations and also the counterpoint, the flight away from more personal (and thus dangerous) ways of being.

As members move beyond superficial expressions, aggression seems to enter the scene. (Note that the word *storming* has been used for this stage.) Members will often alternate between "fight and flight," between aggressiveness and avoidance of emotions. Power and influence become even more central in the transition stage than they were during the exploratory stage. The leader is frequently the object of aggressive reactions, and at this stage such aggressiveness is often related to the leader's structuring and controlling too much or too little. Some members will seek to wrestle power from the leader, and others will be sure to find the leader's shortcomings.

The major challenge to the leader in the transition stage is to intervene in a sensitive and timely way. The leader must offer both encouragement and challenge in helping clients face their resistances, which are tied to anxiety. These same leader ingredients must be used to help the group work with the conflict and negative feelings that are emerging in this stage. It is particularly important that the leader not be defensive or hostile in response to challenges or downright attacks from group members. The leader must at once be open about his or her feelings and maintain a therapeutic stance of helping the group explore itself. During this period, the leader also has to reinforce growth-enhancing behaviors such as acceptance and respect, constructively expressed feedback, nondestructive expression of disagreements, and deeper self-explorations and self-disclosures.

WORKING STAGE

During the next stage, the group has already worked through many of its doubts and anxieties. Those who were not able to commit to the group or who should not have been there to begin with have already left. The group has a deeper sense of trust and cohesion, and members are able to express themselves deeply as well as give and receive feedback without great defensiveness. When confrontation occurs, it is done in a way that does not attack or judge the person being confronted. The leader is seen more realistically, and the individual is more ready to explore the transferences and other distortions that do occur. Leadership functions are more readily shared by members, without the power struggles characteristic of the transition stage. Members during the working stage feel accepted and supported in a deeper way than earlier and are consequently willing to risk new behavior. This support–risk sequence forms a spiral such that support leads to greater risks and more openness, which leads to greater support and acceptance.

The working stage may be the most exciting one for the leader. The initial resistances and defensiveness have been worked through, therapeutic norms have been established, and members are able to live in the here and now. The leader can focus energies on facilitating continued and deepened exploration of the interpersonal and intrapersonal issues in the group. A crucial leader function during the working stage is to help members translate their understandings into constructive action, certainly within the group but also outside the group. The leader of course continues to function as the participant model, who confronts in a caring way and appropriately discloses ongoing reactions to the group.

TERMINATION STAGE

In the final stage of group development, ending, or termination, becomes the central issue. The duration of this stage will depend on the length of time it has been a group, with longer term groups having longer termination stages. The major tasks of the group during this stage are looking back at what has been accomplished, looking forward in terms of members' plans and hopes for the future, and saying good-bye. It is fairly common for clients to initiate a "going around" procedure in which feedback is solicited from all other members. The group experience itself is usually evaluated as part of ending. Members naturally tend to experience some sadness and anxiety about ending the group and the relationships that have been developed, although this is usually overshadowed by the sense of growth and accomplishment that has been evidenced during the life of the group. Self-disclosures tend to taper off in the final stage, as members are reluctant to open up new issues with the end of the group in close sight.

The group leader's main task during the ending phase is to help members face termination and deal directly with termination issues, such as separation and loss, and with positive feelings as well. The leader provides a structure in which members can clarify the meaning of the group experience to them and think actively about how their learning may be generalized and continued after the experience ends. Positive development and behavior of clients are reinforced by the leader. In structured groups, the leader often helps members formulate specific contracts and homework assignments aimed at fortifying changes.

Now it is time to take a look at what makes for positive change in group interventions. This is discussed in the following section.

Therapeutic Factors in Group Work

At the beginning of this chapter, we noted that research evidence clearly indicates that group interventions, on the whole, do foster change and growth in participants. What is it about these groups that helps people? Are there certain ingredients that allow for such change? One of the masters of group therapy, Irving Yalom (1995), proposed that there are 11 therapeutic factors that are either mechanisms of change or conditions for change to take place in group therapy and other therapy-like interventions. Yalom derived these factors both from his experience leading groups and from research findings, and his formulation has been a potent guide to theory and research on group work. As we describe the 11 therapeutic factors, the reader should keep in mind that during group therapy, the factors work together interdependently. Additionally, they operate in different ways for differing types of groups. The 11 factors are as follows.

1. *Instillation of hope.* Clients often begin therapy feeling demoralized. If therapy is to be effective, clients need to begin feeling a sense of hopefulness that they can change as a result of the treatment. Observing others in the group change is a major impetus to hope.

2. *Universality.* Many people enter counseling feeling isolated and alone in their problems, as if they are different from the rest of the human race in the conflicts that they experience. Universality, experienced early in the group, is the sense that we all have problems, that we are all alike in this way, and that others can understand and share our concerns.

3. *Imparting information.* Included here is instruction, given by therapists about mental health and illness and general psychodynamics, along with advice, suggestions, and direct guidance offered by the counselor and other group members. Instruction is especially pertinent in certain kinds of groups (e.g., structured groups) and therapies (e.g., rational–emotive therapy). Although direct advice may not itself help, the interest and caring it implies may do so.

4. *Altruism.* The desire experienced by group members to help others is a key factor because clients receive through giving. Not only does giving stimulate others to return the giving, but giving in itself often enhances one's sense of effectiveness and self-esteem. Clients can be enormously helpful to one another—for example, through support, suggestions, shared insights, and experiences.

5. *The corrective recapitulation of the primary family group.* The ongoing group comes to resemble the client's original family, and the client tends to interact with the group in the way he or she did with the family. As early family experiences are relived with the help of the therapist and other members, the client comes to resolve many central issues and change fixed patterns tied to unresolved issues.

6. *Development of socializing techniques.* Social learning or the development of social/interpersonal skills is fostered in all therapeutic groups, although the types of skills taught and how directly they are taught vary tremendously from group to group. Some groups train social interpersonal skills directly, and others do so implicitly, mainly through feedback from members and leaders.

7. *Imitative behavior.* Clients learn in groups by identifying with leaders and other members. Although blind imitation may reflect unresolved problems, there is a healthy kind of learning through observing and identifying that occurs in therapeutic groups. Such learning may occur at a conscious level but is more often than not unconscious.

8. *Interpersonal learning.* This is a particularly powerful factor. As a group unfolds (particularly a less structured one), it evolves into a social microcosm: a miniature representative of the individuals' social worlds. At the same time, the client becomes more open about the self and is able to display his or her interpersonal issues and problems. As this occurs and with the help of feedback and self-observation, the client gains insight into his or her impact on others, maladaptive behavior with others, distortions in interpersonal relationships (e.g., transference), and his or her responsibility for relationships and the responses he or she gets from others.

9. *Group cohesiveness.* This is the parallel of the client–therapist working alliance in individual counseling. In groups, it includes the client's relationship to the therapist, other group members, and the group as a whole. This has been an extremely elusive factor to define over the years, although it is seen as crucial by virtually all theoreticians of therapeutic groups, especially in less structured groups, and has been the subject of numerous studies. One may simply define it as the attractiveness of a group for its members, keeping in mind that there is a difference between group cohesiveness and individual member cohesiveness (the individual's attraction to the group). Groups with a greater sense of solidarity, bonding, or "we-ness" are high on cohesion. In cohesive groups, members are accepted,

approved of, and have a sense of being "taken in." Group cohesiveness is not in itself a mechanism of change but is rather a precondition for group therapy to be effective in helping clients.

10. *Catharsis.* The release of emotions, the open expression of affect, is a necessary factor in group work but by itself is not sufficient. For change to occur, the feelings that are released need to be understood, processed, and dealt with. Catharsis also helps through its interaction with other therapeutic factors. For example, members' catharsis enhances group cohesiveness, allows for interpersonal learning, and deepens members' sense of universality.

11. *Existential factors.* This factor is actually a constellation of factors revolving around one's basic and ultimate responsibility for one's life and actions, one's basic aloneness, the recognition of one's mortality, and the inevitability of some human problems and pain. Although this factor was included by Yalom almost as an afterthought, some of the items within it have been rated by group therapy clients as extremely important in what they got out of their group experience.

We noted at the beginning of this section that the 11 therapeutic factors would be expected to operate differently for different types of groups. Research findings suggest that in personal growth groups and outpatient groups, for example, interpersonal learning (including self-understanding) and catharsis are seen as most important by clients, whereas in inpatient groups, clients place more importance on instillation of hope, universality, and existential factors ("assumption of ultimate responsibility for my own life"; Kivlighan, Coleman, & Anderson, 2000; Yalom & Leszcz, 2005). Yalom proposed that, in addition to being affected by type of group or setting, the factors operate differently according to the stage of group development. For instance, early in the group life, instillation of hope, universality, and imparting of information are seen as relatively more important. Factors such as altruism and cohesion are important throughout the life of the group, but their nature changes as the group matures. Early in therapy, altruism often takes the form of offering suggestions and asking help-oriented questions, whereas later on it may appear as a deeper caring and "being with." Cohesiveness first operates as a therapeutic factor through support, acceptance, and facilitation of attendance. It has its later effect, however, through the kinds of deeper self-disclosure, confrontation, and conflict that are an inherent part of the interpersonal learning factor. A review of the most current research on these therapeutic factors may be found in Kivlighan, Miles, and Paquin (2010).

Ethical Issues in Therapeutic Group Work

Professional ethics have been discussed in depth in Chapter 3. Ethical codes do exist that are focused specifically on group work, and these codes should be studied carefully by anyone who plans to work with groups. For counseling psychologists, the most relevant documents are the *Ethical Guidelines of the Association for Specialists in Group Work* (Association for Specialists in Group Work, 2007) and the *Guidelines for Ethics of the American Group Psychotherapy Association* (American Group Psychotherapy Association, 2002).

For our purposes, four issues deserve special note. The first is *informed consent*. Potential group members or clients have a right to know what they are getting in to. Clearly informing potential members about the group should begin as soon as the leader decides to recruit. Recruitment of members should include statements of the purpose, time length, and size of the group; the leader's qualifications; and the financial cost. Claims should not be made without scientific evidence. Those who join the group have the right to expect at least (a) a statement of the purpose of the group and the leader's policies and ground rules, (b) respect for member privacy, (c) a notice any observations or recording of the group, and (d) full discussion of the limitations of confidentiality.

The second issue deserving special note is *confidentiality*. Confidentiality becomes more complicated in groups than in individual therapy because the leader needs to be concerned about members as well as him- or herself maintaining confidentiality. This is no easy task because group members naturally want to talk about their group experiences with significant others. The therapist needs to underscore the importance of confidentiality from the first contact with potential clients. It is wise to let members know that it is better to talk about what they learned in the group rather than how they learned it or what they did in the group (Corey et al., 2010). For example, the man who learns how he protects himself by withdrawing from others can share that he learned this in the group without violating confidentiality. Groups simply cannot function as they must without the trust that their expressions will stay within the group.

The third noteworthy issue pertains to *involuntary membership*. Much of the theory and practice of therapeutic group work as discussed throughout this chapter hinges on voluntary membership. At times, though, group work is required. This may occur in psychiatric hospitals or prison settings or in outpatient clinics as a court-mandated procedure (e.g., for someone charged with spouse abuse, delinquency, or substance abuse).

Requiring groups for sex offenders is a fairly common practice in many inpatient settings. In other settings, potential clients are pressured into joining groups. One of the authors, for example, worked at a university agency in which, because of a very long waiting list, students seeking counseling had to wait for several weeks before being seen. To provide some service while students waited for individual counseling, the agency offered "transitional groups." This was a fine idea, except that students were often pushed to join these groups rather than remain on the waiting lists. A study of this procedure (A. Collins, Gelso, Kimball, & Sedlacek, 1973) revealed that the dropout rates from such groups were exceedingly high, significantly higher than when students simply waited for the treatment they preferred. Unless there are legal or moral issues that dictate requiring group experiences, it is at best unwise to make such requirements; at worst, it is unethical.

The fourth issue around the ethics of group work pertains to *training*. Therapeutic group work has had a shaky history in counseling psychology and other psychological specialties. On the one hand, there is much empirical evidence to suggest that group experiences tend to be effective. On the other hand, unfortunate abuses have occurred in this area of psychological intervention. Some of these abuses are tied to the extreme practices in which some leaders engaged during the 1960s and early 1970s as part of the encounter group movement. Highly confrontational and aggressive leaders at times sought to push participants of encounter and marathon groups to do more and more emoting, seemingly for its own sake, and some clients were psychologically harmed by such aggressive pushing (Lieberman, Yalom, & Miles, 1973).

What is the proper training for individuals who wish to lead therapeutic groups? Unfortunately, there is no clear-cut answer to this question because different types of groups require different types of training. Yet, some general guidelines are possible. In terms of academic training, in addition to basic coursework in individual counseling and assessment received in a counseling psychology program, potential group leaders should take a minimum of one course in the theory and practice of therapeutic groups. Also, the Association for Specialists in Group Work (2007) has long recommended the following types of experience in group work:

- critiquing of group tapes;
- observing group counseling sessions;
- participating as a member in a group;
- co-leading groups with supervision;
- gaining practicum experience—leading groups alone with critical self-analysis of performance along with a supervisor's feedback; and
- interning—doing further work in leading groups under supervision.

Family and Couple Interventions

Consider the following case example and in doing so also think about these questions: Who is the client to be counseled? Which treatment format would be used? How would the causes of the client's problems be conceptualized?

> Parents seek psychological help for their 18-year-old son. In recent months he has been increasingly angry and belligerent at home and has been unwilling to help out around the house. His grades in school have dropped, and the parents are worried that he has been drinking and possibly involved in drugs. Because of his behavior, the boy has been upsetting his younger brother and sister. The parents say that they can no longer reach the boy, although they have tried everything.

Based on what you have read in the preceding chapters, your answers to the three questions we have posed would be relatively straightforward. Traditionally, the adolescent boy, who is seen as the "identified patient" in family therapy terms, would be the client. He would probably be seen in individual counseling, with the aim of facilitating greater responsibility, self-control, and adjustment and of controlling and eliminating, respectively, alcohol and drug involvement. The causes of the client's problems would be seen as residing in the client's psyche and as relating to underlying conflicts and complexes by the psychoanalytically or humanistically oriented counselor. Alternatively, the cognitive–behavioral or feminist multicultural counselor might conceptualize the client's problems as being tied to environmental contingencies that serve to promote his behavior.

Here, we present a different way of thinking about and treating human problems. The approach is called the *family therapy perspective*. From such a perspective, the answers to the three questions we have raised are very different from those presented by the traditional, individual counseling perspective. For one, the troubled adolescent would probably not be seen as the client who is to receive treatment. The client to be treated would be the entire family and/or subunits within the family. Second, the treatment mode would probably not be individual counseling for the adolescent but rather family counseling for the entire family or subunits, including, for example, the parents. Finally, as to the causes of the adolescent's problems, they would be seen as residing in the family *system;* that is, the system of interactions that have been established in the nuclear family and possibly the extended family.

To continue with our example, the family therapist might hypothesize that the boy's problems are a symptom of distress in the family (rather than simply a cause of such distress). A closer look at this family might reveal that the father behaves in a critical, dominating manner with the boy. The mother, who seems to passively submit to the father's authority, actually undermines his authority in numerous, often non-verbal, ways. She might send the boy to the father for discipline but then passively disagree with the rules he establishes. The parents themselves may have many conflicts with each other, but these have gone underground, and attention to the teenager's rebelliousness helps the parents to avoid their own problems. The other children unconsciously seek to maintain their roles as the "good kids" and thus have some investment in their brother's being the "bad kid." In such a situation, individual treatment of the adolescent would probably not be very effective because the family system itself is the problem. Much of this chapter will serve to elaborate and clarify the observations just made and in doing so will seek to give the reader the fundamentals of the family therapy perspective.

The treatment of families and couples (married or unmarried) and conceptualization of problems in terms of systems rather than individuals are among the more recent phenomena in professional psychology. This way of conceptualizing and helping originated in the 1950s, and only in the 1980s did this approach really become prominent in counseling psychology (Gelso & Fassinger, 1990). In this part of the chapter, we present key assumptions and concepts that appear to undergird most approaches to family interventions. We review major theoretical approaches to family interventions and changes in the couple/family counseling scene.

In presenting the key assumptions and concepts that underlie family interventions, we shall underscore the main features of what is called general systems theory, a theoretical stance that cuts across most of the different approaches to treatment. Finally, the major approaches to working with family problems are reviewed.

The Beginnings of Family Interventions

Throughout the history of professional psychology, the importance of the family in shaping the psyche and behavior of the individual has been recognized. Sigmund Freud, for example, was acutely aware of the role of the client's family background in this respect. Freud, and virtually all other therapists in the first half of the 20th century, however, sought to isolate the family from the individual client's treatment. The aim was to free the client from the unhealthy influence of the family. In contrast, the aim of family therapists is to assist the family and the individual through work on and with the family.

According to Foster and Gurman (1985), the earliest forerunners of family therapy interventions were the child-guidance and marriage counseling movements in the United States and England during the first half of the 20th century. Child guidance and marital counselors developed treatment models that involved concurrent treatment of two or more family members, despite the prevailing view that dictated that the individual be understood and treated.

The family therapy movement, which began in the 1950s, originated from two directions. One of these was the study of families in which one or more of the offspring became severely disturbed psychologically. The second source of family therapy was the independent work of several creative clinicians who began in the 1950s to experiment with family-based treatment. An excellent review of the rich and colorful history of the couple and family therapy movement is provided by Nichols (2010).

Key Assumptions and Concepts of Family and Couples Therapy: Systems Theory

Although the field of couple and family therapy (CFT) has moved beyond what at times seemed like rigid adherence to systems theory, the systems' way of conceptualizing and treating couples and families has had a profound and enduring effect on CFT. This perspective contains several key concepts that most therapists who do CFT at least partly share (see Lebow, 2008).

Systems theory in family work draws heavily from what is called *general systems theory.* Systems theory has been applied widely to physical systems and also extended to social and biological systems. Von Bertalanffy's (1968, 1974) writing on general systems theory is generally credited with having a profound effect on the family therapy movement, although family therapists have drawn at least as heavily from theoreticians in the field who have applied basic principles of systems theory to living systems such as families. Members of the Palo Alto group, as shall subsequently be described, had been leaders in the application of general systems principles (e.g., Bateson, 1972, 1979; Watzlawick, Beavin, & Jackson, 1967).

What are some of the basic assumptions and concepts of systems theory as applied to families? Following Patricia Minuchin's (1985) discussion, we describe the five most basic concepts below. This description is summarized in Table 16.1.

TABLE 16.1

Basic Assumptions and Concepts of Systems Theory Applied to Families

Concept	Definition
Wholeness and interdependence	Systems organized as wholes; all interdependence elements are interdependent
Circular causality	Members of system mutually influence one another
Equafinality	One does not need to go to origins in order to solve problems; start anywhere to solve problem
Homeostasis and change	Families seek equilibrium and they also strive to meet new challenges effectively
Systems, subsystems, and triangles	Family systems consist of subsystems and interlocking triangles
Boundaries	Subsystems within families separated by boundaries; unspoken rules for interactions across boundaries

WHOLENESS AND INTERDEPENDENCE

Perhaps the most fundamental assumption of systems theory is that systems are organized wholes, and elements within a system are necessarily interdependent (P. Minuchin, 1985). When we talk about a system being an organized whole, we imply that this whole is greater than the sum of its parts. Thus, a family is more than the sum of the individuals in it. It also includes all of the interactions between and among these individuals and the unique ways in which these individuals interrelate. The concept of interdependence implies that the behavior of each partner (e.g., each member of a family) is dependent to some extent on the behavior of every other part.

Family therapists are interested in the interactional patterns developed over time among family members and how these patterns regulate the behavior of members within this system. From the systems perspective, with the concepts of wholeness and interdependence in mind, it is most effective to study or treat a member of a family as part of an organized system because that member can best be understood in context.

CIRCULAR CAUSALITY AND EQUIFINALITY

Psychologists typically conceptualize behavior in terms of linear causality. Thus, A (e.g., mother's rejection) is assumed to cause B (e.g., child's low self-esteem). According to systems theory, thinking in terms of linear causality does not yield a valid picture of reality. The problem goes beyond the simplistic nature of our example. Point A may be extended so that it includes many causes (e.g., the father's behavior, the mother and father's interaction), but this is still linear causality, with A and its subparts causing B.

A more valid way of thinking about causality, say the systems theorists, is what is called *circular causality*. Here, A may cause B, which in turn causes A1, which in turn causes B1, and so forth. In other words, A and B mutually influence each other. Consider, for example, the domineering father, who stimulates dependency in his son, and when the son behaves dependently, the father increases his dominance. This in turn further robs the son of his self-confidence, and he becomes more passive. The father reacts by taking over. Here, father and son are involved in a causal pattern, with each affecting and reinforcing the behaviors of the other.

When the counselor is working with a family system or subsystem, this circular causality shows itself consistently and powerfully. It takes only minimal experience with couples, for example, to see that neither individual is the cause of the other's behavior but rather that each influences the other in a circular way.

A central concept that stems from the assumption of circular causality is that of *equifinality*. This concept implies that any family problem—regardless of its original causes—may be solved if modifications are made at any point in time in the system. Open systems are not governed by their initial conditions, and systems have no memories. Because of these features, the concept of equifinality suggests that the family therapist need not explore the past. The therapist may focus on the present and get the job done just as effectively (and certainly more efficiently) as when original causes are explored. Most CFT therapists, even those who are psychoanalytically oriented, focus much of their energies on the present interactions within the family and believe that it is the current interaction within the system that perpetuates, if not causes, the problem.

HOMEOSTASIS AND CHANGE

Since Jackson (1957) of the Palo Alto group first theorized about family homeostasis, this concept has been crucial for family therapists. Just as a thermostat serves to maintain room temperature, family mechanisms serve to regulate the patterns of interaction within the family unit. Homeostasis maintains a constancy of functioning within the family. This does not mean that the family is rigid. As discussed by Nichols (2010), family homeostasis is seen as a nonstatic, dynamic state, a state of equilibrium in which the family may be at Point A on one day and Point B on another day. Although families seek to maintain the status quo, the result is not rigid invariance in behavior. Rather, the result may be stable variance; the family may vary from one day to the next, but the pattern of variability is stable.

Homeostatic processes in the family, on the whole, are adaptive. They allow the family to maintain a state of equilibrium. In disturbed families, however, the processes that serve to maintain homeostasis may also incorporate symptoms and maladaptive behavior as necessary parts of the system. As P. Minuchin (1985) noted, the need to maintain established patterns makes the family rigid and inhibits needed changes. Resistance to change in therapy, for example, is seen as a homeostatic process.

An example of how psychological symptoms may serve a "positive" function (e.g., to maintain the family balance) would be the case of a teenage boy who has a history of low self-esteem and indecisiveness. Through therapy and life experiences, this teenager gradually becomes more confident and decisive. His parents, who have been deeply concerned about him for several years, then become depressed and feel lost. The mother begins drinking in secret, and the father has trouble becoming sexually aroused. As long as the parents could focus on the son, they could avoid facing their own problems and homeostasis in the family could be maintained (of course at a great cost to everyone).

The literature of family therapy is virtually filled with examples of how symptoms serve a function in families and thus also serve to maintain balance. In fact, the concept of family homeostasis has been so powerful in CFT that it took a long time to develop the companion concept of morphogenesis, or change (P. Minuchin, 1985). Just as systems seek to maintain homeostasis, they also strive to meet new challenges and circumstances in effective ways (Lebow, 2005). As families develop they go through several stages, and each stage seems to have its own crises and challenges (Carter & McGoldrick, 2005). The family must meet these demands and periodically reorganize if it is to continue to function in a healthy way. In this sense, homeostasis must be balanced by morphogenesis.

SYSTEMS, SUBSYSTEMS, AND TRIANGLES

Another assumption of systems theory is that complex systems are made up of subsystems. Although the individual may be considered a subsystem, family therapists pay attention to larger subsystems within the family— for example, the parent subsystem (more complex than just the spouses in divorced or blended families), the sibling subsystem, the parent(s)– child(ren) subsystem, the grandparent subsystem, and so forth.

A kind of subsystem that has particular importance for family therapists is called the *triangle*. As theorized by Bowen (1976), triangles are viewed as the building blocks of all interpersonal systems, including families. Families may be seen as consisting of a series of interlocking triangles. Such triangles occur when tension arises in two-person subsystems. Thus, a third person or thing is triangulated into the relationship. For example, two lovers may have a stable relationship as long as the tension between them is low. When stress occurs, however, one of the lovers may feel the need to triangulate in a third person or thing, such as alcohol, a friend, or a psychotherapist. Unfortunately, common examples of triangulation are husbands in a troubled marriage resorting to drinking heavily or having affairs, and wives in such situations becoming overinvolved with the children, clubs, the family, and so forth. The classic example of triangulation in families exists when husband and wife are experiencing tension in their relationship and, as a means of avoiding it, focus on the children. Instead of fighting with each other, the parents concentrate on the kids. If the unresolved issues between parents are too great, one of the parents is likely to become over attached to one or more of the children, with the regrettable consequence that the child may develop emotional problems.

Family therapists typically pay close attention to the triangles that exist in the family system. One of the major tasks in most family interventions is to work with triangles so that unhealthy triangulations are modified. In the classic example above, the therapist would work with the couple, with the aim of helping them resolve their issues and reducing their triangulation with the children.

BOUNDARIES, RULES, AND PATTERNS

Most family therapists would subscribe to the systems theory concept that subsystems within the family are separated by psychological boundaries. Further, a systems view suggests that family interactions across these boundaries are governed by unspoken rules and patterns (P. Minuchin, Colapinto, & Minuchin, 2007).

The concept of emotional boundaries between subsystems of a family, one of the major theoretical advances in family interventions, was proposed by Salvador Minuchin (S. Minuchin, 1974). More will be said about the concept of boundaries and rules when we discuss S. Minuchin's structural family therapy in the next section. For now, suffice it to say that boundaries are seen by S. Minuchin as invisible barriers surrounding individuals and subsystems. These boundaries regulate the amount and kind of contact with others and serve to protect the separateness and independence of the family and its subsystems. When young children can interrupt their parents' conversation whenever they wish, the boundary between the parent and child subsystems in the family is seen as too "soft," or diffuse. Likewise, if parents rush in to protect their children whenever they experience some threat, the boundaries are diffuse. Diffuse boundaries tend to inhibit healthy development, especially in the area of autonomy. They lead to enmeshment between members of different subsystems.

On the other hand, boundaries may be rigid and allow for little emotional contact between subsystems, resulting in disengagement. If we use the example of parent and child subsystems, rigid boundaries and lack of emotional contact between these two subsystems allow for plenty of independence but also lead to emotional isolation.

Classic Theoretical Approaches to Couple and Family Therapy

As noted at the beginning of this chapter, apart from the assumptions and concepts of general systems theory as just described, there are few general principles or techniques of CFT that cut across the different theoretical perspectives. Rather, there are clusters of theories that differ from one another in terms of the conceptual framework used to understand families (Lebow, 2008; M. P. Nicholas, 2010).

The six classic approaches to CFT, as well as two more recent ones, are briefly described in the following and in Table 16.2. Although space considerations permit us only to present the essential ingredients of each perspective, it must be kept in mind that there is often much variability in viewpoints within a given perspective, as well as overlap

TABLE 16.2

Major Theories of Couple and Family Therapy

Theory	Originator(s)	Key concepts
Psychoanalytic object relations	Ronald Fairbairn Melanie Klein John Bowlby	Internal representation, projective identification (see Chapter 11)
Experiential	Carl Whitaker Virginia Satir	Emotional experience, awareness, genuine expression
Family systems	Murray Bowen	Triangles, differentiation of self, family projection, multigenerational transmission
Strategic	Jay Haley Chloe Madanes	Circular sequences, triangles, first- and second-order change, directives, and paradoxical techniques
Structural	Salvador Minuchin	Family structure, subsystems, boundaries
Cognitive–behavioral	Gerald Patterson Robert Liberman Neil Jacobson	Parent and couple training, behavioral techniques, cognitive restructuring
Narrative	Michael White David Epson	Organizing stories, empathy and questioning, externalizing the problem
Solution focused	Michael de Shazer Insoo Berg	Solutions and goals, exception questions, language

between perspectives. For a thoughtful and clear review of these systems and others, the reader is referred to Nichols (2010).

THE PSYCHOANALYTIC APPROACH

The psychoanalytic approach most relevant to CFT is object relations theory (see Chapter 11). Object relations theorists posit an innate human need for relationships. From birth on, the human being seeks sustaining relationships with significant others, especially with mother and father in early life. Like all psychoanalytic theories, object relations theory posits developmental stages, but these are quite different in many ways from the psychosexual stages posited by Freud (oral, anal, phallic, etc.). Rather, the stages generally revolve around the child's relationship with primary caretakers. The earliest stage, for example, involves profound dependency on the primary caretaker, usually mother. Subsequent stages focus on the differentiation of a separate self from caretakers and individuation of that self while maintaining connection to others. Parents should respond to the growing child's needs during each of these stages. All parents will of course make mistakes, and most of us make many of them. What is needed is not perfection but rather "good enough parenting" (i.e., parents who are able to respond appropriately, on the whole, to the child's needs). As supposed in all analytic theories, if the child's needs are too frustrated during the early stages, they will go underground but then show up later. What is of greatest interest to couples–family therapists is that these needs show themselves in the choice of and behavior toward love objects and in terms of one's strengths and weaknesses as a parent. The heart of object relations theory is how early relationships are "taken in" (internalized) by the person and carried with him or her in subsequent relationships. See Chapter 11 for a description of this internalizing process and its effects.

Although object relations therapists do work with entire families and various family subsystems, it is safe to say that most analytic work involves the couple subsystem. The concept of *projective identification* is used by most object relations therapists as a key to the troubled interactions of members of a couple and of a family. When using this defense, the person unconsciously projects hidden feelings and ideas (which in turn reflect hidden object representations from childhood) onto the spouse or other significant objects. The person not only projects hidden parts of the self onto others but then identifies with those parts because these are, after all, parts of the self. The object (e.g., spouse) takes on these projections and then acts them out. For example, in his earliest years a husband has internalized the bad mother, represented as a hostile rejecting object who will not provide him nurturance. He then sees rejection and hostility in his wife, even when it is not present in reality. Significantly, the wife "takes in" this projection and acts out the role of the hostile rejecting object. To carry this example further, the wife, too, has her internal object representations—for example, the cool, distancing father introject. She may project these into her husband, and he may in turn act them out. Thus, in the systems theory sense, we have a true system in operation, with definite circular causality. The cure, from an object relations perspective, is for each to learn to acknowledge and accept his and her own repressed parts (object representations) and, just as significantly, not to accept the projections of the other (Scarf, 1987).

The psychoanalytic family therapist assesses his or her cases in terms of both the dynamics of the individuals in the family and the dynamics of the family system and subsystems (Nichols, 2010). During the initial assessment, most analytic therapists would meet with the family as a whole. Following this initial phase, a decision is made as to which members of the family should be worked with. The couple dyad is typically what is worked with. As in virtually all psychoanalytic approaches, great emphasis is placed on the client's transference, although in CFT this transference gets even more complicated than in individual treatment. Thus, in evidence are transferences to the therapist from each of the family members as well as transferences between and among family members themselves.

The psychoanalytic family therapist usually does longer term work than do therapists of other persuasions. The main goals are (a) deep changes within individual members of the family and (b) differentiation of individual members (from other family members) and at the same time improvement of the quality of relationships with the family. As Nichols (2010) said, the overarching goal is for members to work through unconscious conflicts so that they can interact with one another in a healthy way rather than on the basis of unconscious issues from the past.

THE EXPERIENTIAL APPROACH

Experiential family therapy grew out of the humanistic psychology movement of the 1960s, and because of this it bears a close resemblance to the humanistic counseling perspective described in Chapter 13. The essential problem with families, just as with individuals, is that they are emotionally frozen and stuck; the job of therapists is to help the family and its members to become unstuck. This process entails learning to experience one's underlying feelings and to express what is experienced. Through such experiencing and expressing, members of the family both get in touch with themselves and are enabled to touch each other emotionally.

Experiential family therapy differs from most systems-oriented family work in its focus on expanding immediate personal experience, and in the early days of this approach, attention was directed far more to the individuals than to the family system. To be sure, there was great stress on sharing among individuals in the family, but the individual emphasis was unmistakable. Also, unlike the systems therapists to be discussed later but similar to psychoanalytic family therapists, experiential therapists work to help members of the family get in touch with feelings that are hidden from awareness, the awareness of the individual as well as the awareness of other family members. In more recent years, experiential therapists have focused to a greater extent on the family as a system, on the interconnectedness of the family. As Nichols (2010) pointed out, experientialists now see the family as a team in which none of the players can perform effectively without the unity and wholeness of the group. Individual problems are broadened to include the involvement of other family members, and members are invited to consider their own part in maintaining the behavior of other members with which they are unhappy.

As Nichols (2010) indicated, the experiential focus on unblocking honest emotional expression in families is important and is a useful counterweight to the cognitive emphasis of currently popular approaches (see discussion of solution-focused therapy). Modern experientialists use and teach expressive techniques that any family or couples therapist will find useful. Also, the area of experiential CFT has been revitalized by the research-based approach developed by Johnson and her collaborators (e.g., Johnson, 2004; Palmer & Efron, 2007).

THE FAMILY SYSTEMS APPROACH

A school of CFT that strongly adheres to the main tenets of general systems theory is the family systems approach. Although a number of creative therapists have refined this approach, the creator and prime mover over many years was Murray Bowen. He not only originated family systems therapy but was responsible for the training of many of its leaders.

Bowen was always more interested in developing theories of how families operate than in creating techniques of treatment because effective theories will guide the treatment of family systems (Bowen, 1966, 1976). Bowen was originally trained as a psychoanalyst, and his family systems theory is decidedly psychodynamic, with many psychoanalytic elements. It is one of the most powerful, comprehensive, and widely used theories of families and family interventions.

Bowen began theorizing about families in the 1950s, and although his theory has evolved, the most fundamental constructs have revolved around two sets of opposing forces: One set pulls the person into the family and makes for family togetherness; the other set pushes the person toward individuality. The key assumption of the theory is that excessive and conflictual emotional attachments to one's family need to be resolved, rather than accepted passively or reacted against, if one is to differentiate into a mature personality and become a well-functioning parent (Becvar & Becvar, 1993; Bowen, 1976, 1978).

Five interrelated concepts serve as the nucleus of Bowen's rich and far-reaching theory. First, the notion of *triangulation* is a significant part of Bowen's theory. As discussed previously, family systems therapists pay close attention to triangles in troubled families and work actively at helping their clients detriangulate. Couples, for example, are helped to work directly with their issues and to avoid triangulating a third person or object into their situation. Second, perhaps the most fundamental construct in family systems theory is *differentiation*, as it occurs both within a person and between persons. Undifferentiation, or fusion, occurs when people do not separate feelings from intellect but instead are flooded by their feelings. At an interpersonal level, the undifferentiated person tends to either absorb others' feelings or react against others. Such intra- and interpersonal undifferentiation is passed from one generation to the next in families, and a central aim of family systems therapy is to help clients learn to become differentiated within themselves and from other members of their nuclear and extended families. Helping an individual or couple become differentiated has a healthy effect on the entire family system.

The third key concept, that of the *nuclear family emotional system*, refers to emotional entanglements that become transmitted from one generation to the next in families and that form unhealthy patterns. When lack of differentiation exists in the family of origin, the person is either emotionally fused with his or her parents or cut off emotionally from them. The consequence, though, is lack of differentiation within the person. Persons then unconsciously seek out mates with about an equal level of undifferentiation, and the two people form a new fused relationship. This will produce any of the following: (a) a defensive distancing between spouses, (b) overt conflict in the relationship, (c) psychological or even physical dysfunction in one of the spouses, or (d) projection of the problem onto one or more of the children.

The *family projection process* is the fourth concept. Parents transmit their own lack of differentiation to their children through a kind of projection. As noted, undifferentiation causes stress in the marriage. Consequently, one or more of the children often get unconsciously triangulated into the process. A common scenario is for the husband to withdraw from his wife and for the wife to project her needs into the children, such that she becomes fused with one of them. The husband unconsciously supports this entanglement because it relieves him of the stress of the relationship. The wife is also enabled to avoid the marital situation. The child, however, does not develop healthy differentiation and often becomes emotionally crippled. The parents then invest even more concern in the child, and the family pattern becomes deeply embedded.

Multigenerational transmission process is the fifth key concept. Not only do parents transmit their lack of differentiation to their children, but this transmission process goes on for generations. Thus, in family systems theory the constructs of differentiation and fusion are applied to individuals, nuclear family systems, and the extended family system. In each family, the children who are most affected by the family's fusion will go on to create families, there is lack of differentiation, and the cycle continues. Along the way, some spouses and some children develop symptoms of emotional disorder, for which treatment is sought. These individuals become the "identified patient," but the problem of undifferentiation is a deep part of the system.

Although problems reside in the family system, Bowenians aim to help individuals differentiate, which in turn affects the system. Family systems therapists work with all combinations of family members, including individuals (Kerr, 1981), but it is the marital dyad they most often treat. In striking contrast to some of the family therapists described earlier (e.g., Ackerman, 1958; Whitaker, 1976), Bowenians believe it is crucial for the therapist to maintain an unemotional and rational stance with patients. If the therapist gets too emotionally involved, she or he will become triangulated and be less effective.

In working with couples, family systems therapists do not encourage interaction between the members. These therapists invite each member to take turns interacting with the therapist, while the other member observes and tries to empathize. Clients are discouraged from becoming too emotional because it is through the use of reason and intellect that one learns to be differentiated. This "de-emotionalizing" is a distinctive feature of family systems therapy.

A major shortcoming of the family systems approach is that it tends to neglect the power of working directly with the family (Nichols, 2010). Also, constructs such as differentiation are culturally embedded, and it is unclear how this concept would work in collectivist cultures. Despite its limitations, along with little research to test its efficacy, the family systems approach has maintained its great appeal to practitioners over the years, and it continues to be revised and refined by many clinicians trained in the Bowenian tradition (e.g., Carter & McGoldrick, 2005).

THE STRATEGIC FAMILY THERAPY (SFT) APPROACH

Strategic family therapy (SFT) is actually a cluster of approaches with a common systems orientation to family problems and some shared conceptions of how treatment is best performed. Also called *problem-solving therapy* and *systemic therapy*, SFT is typically a short-term treatment in which the therapist is highly active and directive. The treatment is aimed at modifying overt behavior in the form of family members' communications with one another. SFT represents a controversial approach to treatment because the therapist takes control of the interactions with his or her clients and actively manipulates clients into behaving more constructively. Virtually all strategic therapists agree on one point: Insight is of no help and may in fact serve to deepen clients' resistance to change. What helps is behavior change, actively instigated by the therapist's directives.

There are many leading figures in SFT, although several leaders have recently moved on to other approaches (Nichols, 2010). Probably the most towering figures within this approach are Jay Haley and Chloe Madanes, each having made creative contributions to theory and practice (e.g., J. Haley, 1976; Madanes, 1981). The Brief Therapy Center of the Mental Research Institute in Palo Alto, California, has also been the home of many creative insights (e.g., Fisch, Weakland, & Segal, 1982). The Milan (Italy) Group, led by Mara Selvini Palazzoli (Selvini Palazzoli, Boscolo, Cecchin, & Prata, 1978), was a major force in the SFT movement during the 1970s and 1980s, but therapists from this group have now essentially sought to develop other treatments.

On the whole, strategic therapists, like their behavioral cousins, focus treatment on the primary symptom presented by the family, usually in the form of maladaptive behaviors exhibited by the identified patient. These symptoms, however, are seen as originating in the family system and are treated within that system. Thus, the identified patient (often a misbehaving child in the family) is usually not isolated for treatment. He or she may be treated as part of family treatment, or the marital dyad may be worked with in an effort to resolve the child's symptom.

True to its systems theory roots, SFT conceptualizes the symptom in terms of circular sequences in the family. In addition, strategic therapists, borrowing Bowen's concept of triangles, view these circular sequences as usually involving three persons. A common sequence, noted by J. Haley (1976), is as follows: (a) Father becomes unhappy and withdraws; (b) child misbehaves; (c) mother deals with the misbehavior ineffectively; (d) father moves toward involvement with mother and child; (e) child behaves more appropriately; (f) mother becomes more effective and expects more from the father and the child; (g) father becomes unhappy and withdraws.

Selvini Palazzoli and colleagues (Selvini Palazzoli et al., 1978) view troubled families as playing games that serve to maintain homeostasis in the family. Healthy systems balance homeostasis and change, and they do change when transitions in the family require it (e.g., when a first child enters the family, a child leaves the family, or a parent's vocational situation changes). Pathological families, however, seem to maintain the status quo at all costs.

A key distinction in SFT is that between first-order change and second-order change (Watzlawick et al., 1967). First-order change involves "more of the same," as the family seeks change without changing the system. Such change is ineffective. Second-order change alters the system itself and is more likely to be effective. Troubled families only employ first-order change. Nichols (1984) noted, for example, that parents of a clinging, dependent child might change from telling the child to stay home to telling the child to go out and play as a way of facilitating independence. This does not work, however, because it does not alter the basic system pattern—dominant parents dictating to a dependent child.

In terms of interventions, strategic therapists work with any combination of family members, and some even include the entire family and the extended family. Most common, however, is work with either the marital dyad or the parents along with one of the children, usually the identified patient. Unlike the experiential and family systems approaches, SFT usually does not involve co-therapists, although strategic therapists do typically use consultation in a unique way. For example, consultants may observe the therapy through a one-way mirror and even enter the therapy session to make active suggestions. As noted, SFT is symptom oriented and tends to be brief because of this. Strategic therapists at Palo Alto's Mental Research Institute, for example, typically implement a treatment that continues for only 10 sessions.

The most frequent technique used by strategic therapists is the directive. Clients are given directives for in-session behavior, but most often directives are given in the form of homework assignments. These directives may entail straightforward suggestions, or they may be in the form of paradoxical interventions, as described below.

Perhaps the most distinctive feature of SFT is the use of active therapist manipulations aimed at dramatically changing behavioral sequences in the family system. The most frequently used manipulations are those called paradoxical interventions. A number of years ago, Dowd and Milne (1986) offered an extensive discussion of how such interventions work. One of the most common forms of paradox is symptom prescription. Here, the therapist instructs the client to actually engage in the behavior that the client seeks to eliminate. An example given by Watzlawick, Weakland, and Fisch (1974) took place in a family in which the mother rationalized her son's frequent misbehavior by stating, "It's all the result of psychological problems." Her strategic therapist directed the child to misbehave even more during the coming week, and the mother was to forgive him with even greater amounts of understanding. Here, the mother can comply with the therapist's directive and come to see the problem as controllable. Alternatively, she could rebel against the directive, in which case a big step is taken toward solving the problem. The dynamics of such paradoxical interventions involve the client being placed in a therapeutic double-bind, in which a positive outcome is accomplished, regardless of what the client does. Strategic therapists view this as a "no-lose" situation.

Although current SFT is still technique oriented, it is less "gimmicky" than in the past. More attention is being paid to the development of a respectful, caring relationship between therapists and clients (Cade & O'Hanlon, 1993). Also, more attention is now paid to collaboration between therapist and clients, rather than the therapist pulling all the strings. Thus, although its initial glitter has worn off, SFT continues to develop, and it ought to maintain its status as one of the main approaches to treating family and couple problems.

THE STRUCTURAL APPROACH

The structural approach entered the family therapy scene in full force in the 1970s and has remained one of the most popular and influential approaches to family intervention (Lebow, 2008; Nichols, 2010). Structural theory is deeply embedded in systems theory, holding similar conceptions of how families operate and how to intervene with troubled families. It is an appealing theory in several ways. Structural theory offers ideas about the structure or underlying organization of families that make a great deal of sense to the practicing counselor. The theory of how families operate and go emotionally awry also has clear implications for assessment and treatment. Finally, a number of clear therapy techniques are suggested by the theory.

The founder and leader of the structural approach is Salvador Minuchin, whose ideas about family intervention took shape when he worked with multiproblem, economically impoverished families of delinquent children in the 1960s. Some of the most important and useful works on the structural approach are as follows: S. Minuchin's definitive work (1974), S. Minuchin, Lee, and Simon (1996), S. Minuchin and Nichols (1993), and P. Minuchin et al. (2007). Three concepts form the nucleus of the structural theory of family functioning: structure, subsystems, and boundaries. The concept of *family structure* may be defined as the organized pattern in which family members interact. All families have predictable patterns of interaction, and such patterns reveal the who, when, and how of family interactions. Patterns that are repeated develop into psychological structures. For example, a father may play the role of distant disciplinarian, whereas the mother may be affectionate but be unable to set limits. This pattern may be enacted in numerous interactions between the spouses and their children when affection and discipline are at issue. These parental roles are a clear, if implicit, part of the family's structure.

Part of the family's structure involves a number of unspoken rules about how members are to interact within and outside the family.

Examples of such rules are that mother spends time with the children while father works, the children act up whenever the parents seem to have a conflict, father plans and orchestrates the family trips, family members do not share their feelings directly. Rules, patterns, and structure in families, once established, are highly resistant to change. The second concept is that of *subsystems.* All complex systems are divided into subsystems. Such subsystems may contain any number of people within the family, and subsystem groupings may be determined by age, generation, gender, interests, and so forth. Thus, there is usually a parent subsystem and a children subsystem, as well as less obvious ones; for example, the mother aligned with the male children, and the father forming another subsystem with the female child. Subsystems may be fluid in the sense that any individual within the family may belong to more than one subsystem. The mother in a particular family may be part of the spousal subsystem in certain ways, of the female subsystem in other ways, and of the athletic subsystem in still other ways.

The third major concept in the structural approach is that of *boundaries.* In all families there are invisible barriers that surround and to an extent insulate all individuals and subsystems, and S. Minuchin's notions about the characteristics of these boundaries are among the most interesting and significant concepts within structural theory.

Boundaries serve to control the amount of contact with those outside the boundary. As noted earlier, these boundaries range from being rigid to diffuse, with the boundary labeled "clear" being at the midpoint on the continuum. Neither of the extremes (rigid or diffuse) is healthy. Rigid boundaries permit little emotional contact with individuals or systems outside of the boundary, which results in what S. Minuchin has called *disengagement.* Diffuse boundaries, on the other hand, are not solid enough, and foster too much emotional connection with outside individuals or systems. This results in *enmeshment.*

Disengaged individuals or subsystems tend to be isolated. Although this isolation permits independence and at times mastery, there is a cost. Disengagement also limits warmth, affection, and a sense of support. On the other side of the continuum, enmeshment allows for plenty of support and affection across subsystems. Enmeshed parents provide an abundance of love and affection, but, at the same time, their children are not given room to develop themselves as independent, effective individuals.

Structural therapists pay close attention to boundaries in families. If enmeshment exists (e.g., between any of the combinations of parent and child subsystems), structural therapists seek to solidify boundaries. If individuals or subsystems are disengaged, on the other hand, the therapist works to soften boundaries and open communication.

As regards interventions, structural therapists, like strategic therapists described in the previous section, are very active, directive, and at times manipulative. Unlike the strategic group, however, structuralists do not work directly on presenting symptoms. Instead, they seek to modify structure because the best and longest lasting way to change problem behavior is to change the family patterns (structure) that maintain it. Structuralists typically work with families in which a child or adolescent is the identified patient, and they may work with any combination of family members, at times dealing with individuals and at times with different subsystems within the family. The therapist, for example, may meet with the entire family for a while. Then, feeling that the parent subsystem needs clearer boundaries from the child subsystem, the therapist may meet with the parents alone. In the same family, it may be clear that the father and son need their boundaries softened, and the therapist may also meet with this pair.

In the 2nd decade of the 21st century, the structural approach is as popular with family therapists as ever. The appeal of this approach rests on its simplicity, inclusiveness, and practicality. Its basic concepts are easy for practitioners to grasp and apply. They pay attention to the individual, the family, and culture, and they provide a cohesive framework for understanding and counseling families. The appeal of structural family therapy is further enhanced by the sound empirical support for its effectiveness garnered over the years (Lebow, 2008; Nichols, 2010).

COGNITIVE–BEHAVIORAL APPROACHES

Of all the approaches to family intervention discussed in this chapter, the cognitive–behavioral approach most often incorporates the results of empirical research into the development of treatment guidelines. Although there is more evidence on the effectiveness of behavioral interventions than of other family therapies, this approach is often not even included in discussions of family therapy. This is so because the behavioral approach is generally not considered to be family therapy treatment, in the sense that there is little attention to systems theory or the family as a system. The focus in behavioral treatment has tended, for example, to be on two-person situations. The marital couple and parent–child dyads have been given almost exclusive attention. The triad and the entire family system, so often the focus of family therapists, have tended to be ignored.

The behavioral approach is also unlike the other, more systems-oriented family therapies in that it most often conceptualizes family problems in terms of linear causality rather than circular causality. The behavioral family counselor seeks to isolate specific and concrete problem behaviors, identify what in the (usually) interpersonal environment is controlling them, and use behavioral techniques to reduce the problem behaviors while increasing positive behaviors. In recent years, cognitive concepts have been added to behavior therapy. Today, just as is the case for individual counseling, most family counselors who are behaviorally oriented are actually cognitive–behavioral family counselors. As part of the cognitive element, heavy emphasis is placed on the clients' schema (or core beliefs) of their families and how these family schemata influence and are influenced by family members' interactions (Dattillio, 1993, 1997).

Like most family therapists, cognitive–behavioral counselors tend to be active and directive, and they emphasize their clients' active involvement in the treatment, as well. These counselors often serve as educators, teaching their family clients to apply learning and cognitive principles and techniques to develop and reinforce desired behaviors in their clients. Cognitive–behavioral family counselors have worked primarily in two general areas: couples counseling (which may itself focus on a range of issues; e.g., communication, sexual problems) and parent training. In both these areas, treatment is preceded by a careful assessment to determine which behaviors and cognitions are to be modified. A range of assessment techniques is used (discussed in Chapter 12). The goal is to pinpoint target behaviors and cognitions (those to be changed) and get a baseline on these.

Numerous behavioral and cognitive techniques and programs have been presented in the literature, in both the couples counseling and parent training areas. In couples counseling, the therapist helps each member of the couple identify behaviors in the other that are desirable and to communicate what is wanted. The therapist also develops a behaviorally oriented treatment plan aimed at increasing the desired behaviors. Focus is more on increasing the positive than decreasing the negative. Various types of contingency contracting are frequently used. Here, positive behavior of one member is made dependent on positive behavior of another. For example, Charlie agrees to spend a half hour with the children each night before bedtime if Jane does the dishes. Such a contingency is usually also balanced; for example, Jane goes on weekly hiking trips with Charlie if Charlie vacuums twice a week. In such contracting, it is important that none of the behaviors be objectionable to either member. Also, for problems that are too conflictual to be dealt with by simple contingency contracting methods, the behavioral counselor uses structured problem-solving techniques. The couple is taught to clearly define problems, discuss one problem at a time, listen to and paraphrase what the other has said, avoid verbal abuse, and state what they want in positive terms rather than deficiencies (for example, "I like the way you do . . . " and "I would like it if you did . . . ").

In behavioral parent training, behavioral and cognitive principles are used to modify the behavior and cognitions of the parent(s) and child and the parent–child interactions. But if the child is brought for help as the identified patient, the cognitive–behavioral counselor tends to accept that. At times, though, the problem the family seeks help with may not be the one the therapist judges to be appropriate for the first phase of treatment. For example, a family seeks help because the children seem to be fighting all the time. On observation, the therapist notices that the children fight with each other especially when the parents argue, which is often. The therapist is likely to judge that marital counseling is the best first step; that is, before working directly on modifying the children's behavior.

As a first step in parent training, the parent(s) is (are) taught to specify the problem behavior in the child or adolescent, record its frequency, and note the events that accompanied the problem behavior. The last step is aimed at determining what events might be the stimuli or reinforcers for the problem behavior. The parents are then taught to intervene systematically, using behavioral techniques. The most common techniques involve operant conditioning, whereby desirable behaviors are positively reinforced and undesirable ones are either ignored or punished. Care is taken in selecting effective reinforcers, as children vary greatly in what is reinforcing to them. The Premack principle is a long-standing one followed in parent training. Thus, a high-frequency behavior is used as a reinforcer for a low-frequency but highly desired (by the parents) behavior. For example, let us say that the parents of Johnny, a 5-year-old boy, are driven to distraction by his constant refusal to eat reasonably balanced meals (rather than just sweets). We find that Johnny's favorite activities are riding his tricycle and playing with his buddy, Stan, in the backyard. The Premack principle would involve making Johnny's favored (high-frequency) behaviors contingent on his eating properly while reducing complaining behavior. This program might be implemented in steps, so that reinforcers would be given as desired behaviors approximate the end goals.

In sum, cognitive–behavioral therapists have devised an arsenal of techniques that appear to modify behavior and cognitions in couple and parent–child interactions. Although cognitive–behavioral counselors have historically ignored systems, this has begun to change in recent times because treatment programs have been developed that take the family system into account (e.g., Christensen & Jacobson, 2000; Sexton & Alexander, 2005). For example, in Sexton and Alexander's (2005) functional family therapy, the therapist analyzes the function of particular family members' troubling behaviors within the family matrix and then helps the family satisfy that function in more constructive ways.

Couple and Family Therapy in a Postmodern World

The 1970s and 1980s have been described as the golden age of couple and family therapy (Nichols, 2010). Enormous growth occurred as "training centers sprouted up all over the country, workshops were packed, and leaders of the young movement took on the aura of rock stars" (Nichols

& Schwartz, 1998, p. 59). However, eventually a reaction began to set in. Rather than being brilliant and creative, some of the approaches seemed manipulative and overbearing. Too often, the systems orientation seemed to forget that the system was composed of individuals. For example, S. Minuchin and his collaborators (S. Minuchin, Rosman, & Baker, 1978, p. 91) worried about the dangers of "denying the individual while enthroning the family." Some of the successes of family therapy began to appear tied to the charisma of the movement's leaders (e.g., Haley, Madanes, Whitaker, Minuchin) rather than the theories. In addition, the family that was studied and treated by classical theories was largely a two-parent nuclear, heterosexual family, and next to no attention was given to other variations (e.g., blended families, single-parent families). Little attention was paid to race, ethnicity, culture, sexual orientation, and power imbalances between men and women. To boot, the impact of larger systems, such as schools, social agencies, institutions and, more broadly, culture, was also essentially ignored.

During the past decade or so, changes have occurred in CFT and the theories and philosophies upon which it was based. As implied above, human problems were seen as residing within the individual as well as the family. This was particularly true in the case of severe psychological problems. For example, whereas schizophrenia was seen in the early days of CFT as residing in the family, it became clearer that this was not so, and educationally based treatments were developed to help families learn to cope better with troubled individual members (Lebow, 2008; Nichols, 2010). In addition to greater attention to the individual, the field of CFT is now paying much more attention to the role of ethnicity and, more broadly, culture in family development and treatment (see, e.g., McGoldrick, Giordano, & Garcia-Preto, 2005).

The changes that were building throughout the 1990s in family and couples therapy actually were part and parcel of a broader philosophical movement that reflected changes in how we think about knowledge, reality, and truth. Such philosophical shifts were themselves part of broader cultural changes during the decade. A profound change in how scholars and counselors considered truth, reality, and knowledge has been termed *postmodernism*. Unlike the modernism that came before it (and began. around the turn of the 20th century), postmodernism reflects the assumption that absolute truth cannot be known and that reality is a construction of the observer (or a co-construction of counselor and client). Whereas modernism reflected the belief that truth and, in fact, universal principles could be uncovered by science—which itself was seen as objective—postmodernism suggested that neither truth nor universal principles were there to be uncovered. Science can only produce useful information about differing viewpoints. The postmodernist does not try to determine which family therapy theory has the greatest truth value. Theories are but different perspectives, useful guides.

The philosophies underpinning postmodern thought are *constructivism* and *social constructionism*. Although there are subtle differences between these philosophies, they share the basic view that reality is a construction of the observer. As a constructivist, the family counselor does not ask "What are the actual interaction patterns in this family?" Instead, the key question is "What assumptions do the family members have about the problem?" Rather than seeking truth, the constructivist therapist seeks to find what meaning the problem has for each family member.

A constructivist society entertains a plurality of views. As part and parcel of this pluralism, attention to issues of race, ethnicity, gender, sexual orientation, and, more broadly, culture has permeated the family therapy movement and is a key part of it in the 21st century. Lack of attention to cultural factors can render a treatment useless.

The present-day family therapist does not presume to have all the answers, as his or her predecessors seemed all too often to have. Nichols (2010) discussed how constructivism has fostered greater therapist humility in dealing with families. The family therapist is more often seen as a collaborator with the family rather than as an expert who can brilliantly undo family dysfunction. Just as the therapist does not have the answers, no theory represents the truth. Because of this belief, the present-day family therapist is far more likely to seek an integration of the different theories in his or her practice (see Prochaska & Norcross, 2010).

Much of the CFT that occurs today is within the framework of existing classical theories and seeks to modify those theories to take into account the factors we have been discussing. However, two approaches have emerged in recent times that deserve note: narrative therapy and solution-focused therapy. Although very appealing to therapists, the approaches do not as of yet have a body of research supporting their effectiveness.

NARRATIVE THERAPY

This approach is decisively postmodern and constructivist in its orientation. Narrative therapists are antirealists, in that for them no reality exists beyond the stories we create to understand our lives (Held, 1996). The two names most often associated with narrative family therapy are the Australian Michael White, and David Epston, a family therapist in New Zealand.

Narrative therapy is concerned most basically with how human experiences create expectations that become organizing stories, which in turn deeply shape experience. Unlike the systems approaches, narrative therapy seeks to help individuals reexamine themselves rather than discuss family issues. This reexamination occurs almost exclusively via questioning. That is, the narrative therapist becomes an expert question asker, one who seeks a nonimposing and respectful approach to whatever the client or family's story is (Freedman & Combs, 1996; White, 1995). The counselor also places a premium on *narrative empathy* (Omer, 1997), which sounds to us essentially the same as empathy from the perspective of person-centered therapists.

To an unusual extent, this approach seeks to keep clients blameless, and the major way to do this is to externalize the problem. The problem thus becomes something outside the individual and the family; an external source of pain and grief, so to speak. As clients tell their "problem-saturated story," the narrative therapist separates the problem from the person. The problem becomes the "it" outside of the person or family that has ill effects. The therapist fosters this externalization by asking questions about how this "it" does its demonic work (for example, "How does the *anger* affect you?" "What does *anger* tell you?" "What does *anger* do to your relationship?"). The problem is not possessed by the client but rather is possessing the client.

A key to change in this therapy is the therapist's listening for "unique outcomes" or "sparkling events" in the client's life. Stated simply, these events and outcomes represent situations in which the client or family won a victory over the problem, and as such they are viewed as heroic episodes. By highlighting these with further questions, the narrative therapist helps the client bring success and ways of succeeding into the foreground. People can come to view themselves as courageous protagonists rather than powerless victims. In keeping with its constructivist roots, narrative therapy is also highly sensitive to cultural issues.

SOLUTION-FOCUSED THERAPY

A second family therapy approach that is embedded in social constructionism hit the scene in the 1990s: solution-focused therapy (SFT). The primary developers of this approach are Michael de Shazer and Insoo Berg (Berg & de Shazer, 1993; de Shazer, 1988, 1994). SFT actually grew out of strategic therapy (described earlier) and maintained the emphasis on very brief work (usually 2–5 sessions). However, SFT represents a significant departure from the strategic approach in that the almost exclusive focus is on solutions rather than the client's problems. Like their strategic cousins, practitioners of SFT rank high on cleverness. They have devised several ingenious strategies for helping clients solve problems in a short time.

Consistent with a counseling psychology orientation, SFT emphasizes clients' strengths and seeks to capitalize on them. Although SFT practitioners certainly listen to clients' problems and histories, they seek most fundamentally to address goals and solutions. For example, rather than delving into a client's tendency toward depression and the roots of that depression, the SFT counselor asks, "When are the times you don't feel depressed?" The therapist uses the answers to devise strategies that avert depression. If the answer is "When I am with friends, and when I am at prayer services," the SFT practitioner helps the client consider how to develop and expand these situations. The therapist is highly reinforcing of steps clients take in the right direction.

The focus on solutions and goals begins in the first session. In what is referred to as the *formula first task*, clients are asked to observe what happens in their life or relationships that they want to continue. Like the narrative therapist, the SFT counselor becomes an expert in asking the right questions (i.e., questions focusing on goals and solutions). For example, the miracle question is "Suppose one night, while you were asleep, there was a miracle and this problem was solved. How would you know? What would be different?" The *exception question* circumvents attention to the problem and asks about times when the client didn't experience the problem, when he or she otherwise would have. The couple is asked, "When did you manage to not blame each other?" or "When did you feel good with each other?" The couple's answers are used to build solutions.

Another class of questions are called *scaling questions:* "On a scale of 0 to 10, with 0 being how you felt in your marriage when you called me for couples work, and 10 being how you felt the day after the 'miracle,' how do you feel in your relationship right now?" If the client says "3," the SFT counselor asks, "How did you achieve this improvement?" Or, in order to encourage and reinforce small steps, the therapist might ask, "What do you need to do to get to 4?" Alternatively, a client might be asked, "On a scale of 1 to 10, how sure are you that you won't blame your wife for something this week?" Then, "What can you do to increase the chances that you won't blame her?" As Nichols and Schwartz (1998) noted, scaling questions are clever ways of "anticipating and disarming resistance, and of encouraging commitment to change" (p. 387).

During SFT, counselor and client co-construct solutions through their conversations. Language is itself what needs to change because language to the SF counselor is reality and nothing exists outside of language. Change problem-talk to solution-talk, says the SFT counselor, and you are most of the way to solving the problem.

Group, Couple, and Family Counseling in Perspective

For somewhat differing reasons, the treatments covered in this chapter were slow to be accepted as central interventions in counseling psychology. For many years, group therapy was seen as a fill-in of sorts, to be used primarily when waiting lists got too long or individual therapy openings were not available. The group field was slow to develop a research base, and some of the excesses of the 1960s and 1970s, often occurring in group settings, did not help. However, as it became increasingly clear that group counseling and therapy had many advantages, as both an adjunct to individual counseling and a treatment in itself, it became more and more central to counseling psychology. By the 21st century, Kivlighan et al. (2000) observed, group treatment was a fundamental element of the work of counseling psychologists.

For CFT, the slow acceptance also was partly due to the lack of a research base. Also, because so many counseling psychologists worked with college students whose developmental tasks seemed to involve individuation and healthy independence from their families, CFT did not seem highly relevant. However, as both counseling psychology and the CFT field expanded, they grew close together, such that, in their review, Gelso and Fassinger (1990) suggested that "in the 1980s, counseling psychology finally discovered the family" (p. 361).

As implied, the embracing of group therapy and CFT by counseling psychology was also partly due to the increasing research support for these approaches. Individual research studies have accumulated to the point that several meta-analyses have been possible on these treatments. Especially for group counseling and therapy, it has become clear that the treatment effects are, on the whole, highly positive and equivalent to the effects for individual therapy (Burlingame et al., 2013). These reviewers not only described the wide range of client problems and diagnoses for which group therapy is of benefit but also pointed to the effectiveness of group counseling and therapy for groups with many mixtures of diagnoses. One highly noteworthy development has been the study of the role of clients' attachment styles in group therapy (e.g., Markin & Marmarosh, 2010; Marmarosh, Markin, & Spiegel, 2013). Here, attachment theory as developed by the psychoanalyst John Bowlby is examined as it relates to important variables like group cohesion, client self-disclosure, interpersonal perceptions, and the outcome of group therapy.

Regarding CFT, the findings are also quite positive. Sexton, Datchi, Evans, LaFollette, and Wright (2013) have done the most recent review of the existing literature on the effectiveness of CFT. Although the findings are highly diverse and cover hundreds of studies, it does appear that, on the whole, CFT is effective when compared with nontreated controls. Studies have been done in a wide range of settings, examining a wide array of treatments and studying a wide variety of factors. However, just as in individual therapy, the key question at this time is just what treatments are most effective for what for what problems when offered by which therapists and which outcomes. Although it seems clear that CFT is effective on the whole, some of the theories covered in this chapter have not been sufficiently studied (e.g., the family systems approach, the strategic approach). In many cases the overall effects of treatment, although statistically significant and superior to no-treatment control groups, are not very strong. So, although the research findings are highly promising, there is much more to be done.

As of the 2nd decade of the 21st century, group, couple, and family counseling and therapy are, on the whole, empirically supported treatments. They work. They, along with individual counseling and psychotherapy, have become central treatments with a growing research base, and they are now a standard part of doctoral training in counseling psychology.

Summary

This chapter has been divided into two main parts. The first part pertained to group counseling and therapy, and the second part focused on couple and family counseling and therapy (CFT). With regard to group counseling or therapy, groups may be seen as especially helpful for clients with interpersonal or relational difficulties, and the effects of groups are greatest with interpersonal issues. Groups, however, are not helpful to everyone, and we noted some of the characteristics that do not bode well for effective group treatment. The leader's focal point in groups may be the group as a whole, the individuals within the group, the interactions between and among individuals within the group, or, preferably, an integration of these approaches. Whatever the focal point, the leader has the main tasks of (a) creating and maintaining the group, (b) facilitating the building of a group culture, and (c) activating and illuminating the here and now. The leader must actively shape the desired norms for the group, and in doing so his or her role is that of technical expert and a model. Personal qualities of the leader may be especially important, even more so than the techniques that are used.

Although the terms may differ, there is general agreement that in the development of closed groups there is an unfolding process marked by stages. We described the exploratory, transition, working, and termination stages. A landmark contribution to group treatments is Irving Yalom's therapeutic factors that contribute to group effectiveness. Most of these factors have been studied extensively and should be internalized by anyone planning to lead groups. Ethical issues in group work were described, and the slow acceptance of group interventions in counseling psychology was clarified. Research has clearly supported the general effectiveness of group counseling and therapy, as well as its effectiveness for a range of problems.

The family therapy movement began in the 1950s, and CFT was described as a diverse set of perspectives having in common a systems perspective on behavior. Several basic assumptions of systems theory as applied to families and couples were noted, and both classic and post-modern approaches to CFT were briefly described.

The 1970s and 1980s were the golden age of CFT, with the field showing phenomenal growth during that time. By the 1990s, many questions and concerns about what were by then the classic CFTs emerged, and newer models emerged. Fitting both postmodern thinking and the economically driven mandate for brief treatment, approaches such as narrative therapy and solution-focused therapy gained increasing ascendancy. These approaches are gentler and more focused on clients' strengths, and they seem more client centered than therapist centered, like the classic approaches. Still, more research is needed to determine the efficacy of these approaches.

Research supports the overall effectiveness of CFT for a range of individual, childhood, and family/couple difficulties. The leading edge of research revolves around what family/couple problems are best treated by which approaches, techniques, and therapists.

CAREERS IN COUNSELING PSYCHOLOGY | IV

Training and Professional Issues in Counseling Psychology

17

T This chapter is quite different from the previous chapters, all of which provide an introduction to the foundational concepts, research, and practice issues in the profession of counseling psychology. This chapter is intended to assist readers who are at least contemplating if not already on their way to becoming counseling psychologists. It is designed to be advisory as well as informative. Our selection of perspectives and topics has been derived, for the most part, from several decades of personal observations and discussions about which factors facilitate the career development of young counseling psychologists. We offer many suggestions that we hope not only will facilitate the career development of each reader but also provide readers with an increased sense of self-efficacy as a result of becoming acquainted with the "normality" of the sometimes trying experiences of pursuing graduate education, choosing internships and postdegree career options, and becoming a fully credentialed counseling psychologist.

http://dx.doi.org/10.1037/14378-017
Counseling Psychology, Third Edition, by C. J. Gelso, E. N. Williams, and B. R. Fretz

Training, Job Settings, and Activities

In this section, we review the kind of graduate training required to be a counseling psychologist, where counseling psychologists work, and the typical job activities in which they are involved.

HOW AND WHERE ARE COUNSELING PSYCHOLOGISTS TRAINED?

Unlike numerous psychological and educational–vocational counselors who work with a master's degree, the counseling psychologist is trained at the doctoral level. It is strongly recommended that the doctorate be earned from a university training program accredited by the American Psychological Association (APA). Such accreditation influences several factors that are typically quite important to the professional life of the counseling psychologist: how readily he or she can become licensed as a psychologist in the state in which he or she practices, the range of psychologist positions in which he or she is employable, whether he or she can become a member of several important organizations (e.g., the National Register of Health Service Providers in Psychology), and how likely his or her clients are to obtain insurance payments when being treated on a private basis. Although in the past many counseling psychologists received their doctoral degrees in nonaccredited programs, it has become increasingly important and now the standard practice for graduates to be trained in APA-accredited programs.

As of this writing, there are 71 counseling psychology doctoral training programs that are APA accredited (66 of which are PhD programs and five of which are PsyD programs). The APA Center for Workforce Studies (2012) reported that there were more than 5,000 applications for counseling psychology doctoral programs in 2009 competing for approximately 350 slots. The exact numbers vary year to year, but between 350 and 400 doctoral degrees in counseling psychology are awarded annually. Although the number of accredited programs increased dramatically during the 1980s, the number of programs seeking accreditation in the past decade has leveled off. Some programs have become accredited, and others have lost accreditation. For information on the most up-to-date listing of APA-accredited doctoral programs, see the APA website (http://www.apa.org/ed/accreditation/programs/index.aspx).

CHARACTERISTICS OF TRAINING IN COUNSELING PSYCHOLOGY

What are the main features of counseling psychology doctoral programs? And what is the nature of training in counseling psychology?

To begin with, most doctoral programs are organized so that students will need about 5 to 6 years to complete graduate study. Also, in most programs, students either earn a master's degree on the way to the doctorate or have already earned the master's prior to admission to the doctoral program.

Doctoral training programs in counseling psychology are typically located either in colleges of education or in departments of psychology, and these two settings often differ with respect to whether or not the master's degree is required or expected before admission to the doctoral program. In departments of psychology, students are typically admitted to the doctoral program regardless of whether they have earned a master's. If they do not already have that degree, they usually earn it on the way to the doctorate. In many programs located in colleges of education, on the other hand, students must first get a master's degree and then apply for admission to the doctoral program. Some of these programs also consider it desirable for the student to gain work experience in the counseling field before being admitted to a doctoral program. Counseling psychology programs in colleges of education and those in departments of psychology are extremely similar in nearly all other important respects. However, students contemplating a career in counseling psychology should think through the pros and cons of these issues (experience, master's before admission) in deciding to which programs they should apply.

Another main feature of training in counseling psychology is that the scientist–practitioner or scientist–professional model is seen as the basic training model in the field. (Note that the terms *practitioner* and *professional* are used interchangeably here.) Thus, counseling psychology training at the doctoral level seeks to prepare students both to practice psychology (e.g., conduct counseling) and to conduct and utilize research. Three or 4 years of coursework are followed by the completion of a doctoral dissertation. The dissertation is a major piece of scientific research aimed at advancing knowledge in the field. The student works closely with a research advisor, typically a faculty member in his or her counseling psychology program, in developing the project. During the last phase of training and what for many is the end point of their program, students complete a predoctoral internship (ordinarily a full-time, 1-year experience in which the student receives in-depth supervised training in a service setting such as a university counseling center, community mental health center, or medical hospital). We describe the dissertation and internship in more detail later in the chapter.

WHERE DO COUNSELING PSYCHOLOGISTS WORK?

Over the years, a number of surveys have been conducted on counseling psychologists, examining where they work and what they do. Most of these surveys have sampled members of Division 17 (Society of

Counseling Psychology) of the APA. The largest samples are derived from the surveys done by the APA's Center for Workforce Studies. Table 17.1 presents data on job settings from a recent APA directory survey (APA Center for Workforce Studies, 2012).

The numbers have changed dramatically in the past 20 years. As you can see, more than a third of the participants are in the job-setting category of independent practice. This percentage has nearly doubled since in the mid-1990s. In fact, if one combines all the practice settings (independent practice, other human service, hospital, and clinic), two thirds of all counseling psychologists are in some kind of counseling practice. In contrast, only 19.4% of the counseling psychologists surveyed reported working in college, university, or other academic setting (a number nearly cut in half since the mid-1990s). However, of those who had just received their doctorates in 2009, more than half, 52.9%, went to work in an academic setting. These numbers, although vastly different from the APA Directory results prior to the turn of the century, are entirely consistent with the findings of Munley, Pate, and Duncan (2008), who surveyed both counseling psychologists who were members of APA's Division 17 and those who were not.

Thus, the percentage of counseling psychologists who are employed primarily as independent practitioners has increased markedly in the recent past. For many years, the percentage of counseling psychologists who chose private practice as their primary career hovered around 5%. In the late 1970s and early 1980s this began to change, so that by the mid-1980s greater numbers of counseling psychologists had as their

TABLE 17.1

Percentage of Counseling Psychologists in Various Job Settings

Setting	APA (2012) %	Munley et al. (2008) %
Independent practice	41.9	38.7
University	15.0	17.0
Other human service	11.9	14.8
Hospital	7.3	6.2
Clinic	4.3	5.0
Government	3.7	3.5
Other academic setting	2.7	2.2
Medical school	2.7	1.4
Schools and other educational settings	1.9	2.2
Four-year college	1.7	2.1
Business and industry	0.9	0.9
Other	6.0	4.6

Note. Data are from APA Center for Workforce Studies (2012) and Munley et al. (2008), excluding the unspecified category. APA = American Psychological Association.

primary job setting private practice rather than counseling centers, the traditional practice setting for their specialty (Fitzgerald & Osipow, 1986; Watkins, Lopez, Campbell, & Himmell, 1986). At that time, the fact that younger counseling psychologists who were sampled were even more likely to seek private practice careers suggested that the trend would continue. And in fact, during the 1990s, there was a further increase in the numbers of counseling psychologists in private practice (Gaddy, Charlot-Swilley, Nelson, & Reich, 1995; Holahan & Yesenosky, 1992). That trend clearly has continued and increased (APA, 2012; Goodyear et al., 2008; Munley et al., 2008).

It is important that beginning students and professionals alike recognize the trends and data we have just discussed and understand that doctoral training programs incorporate these data into their planning. Division 17, which was once considered a home for academics only, has made serious efforts in recent years to increase its relevance to counseling psychologists in practice settings while maintaining its long-standing relevance to college- and university-based counseling psychologists.

WHAT DO COUNSELING PSYCHOLOGISTS ACTUALLY DO?

Probably the most fundamental and clear finding from job analyses is that counseling psychologists are involved in performing an extensive range of jobs (APA, 2012; Goodyear et al., 2008; Munley et al., 2008). That has been our own experience in our careers because we, collectively, have been educators, counselors, writers, researchers, supervisors, editors, professional leaders, and administrators (among other roles). So, just as the job settings of counseling psychologists are highly diverse, so are their actual job activities. For example, sizable numbers of counseling psychologists devote at least a portion of their work time to each of the following: counseling and psychotherapy (individual, group, couples–family); consultation; psychological testing, assessment, and evaluation; research and writing; teaching, training, and supervision; and administration. When one considers the specific activities incorporated under each of these general job categories, as well as the various job settings in which the activities are carried out, one can appreciate the rich diversity of activities within counseling psychology. (See Table 17.2.)

Within the context of this diversity, the activity performed by the greatest number of counseling psychologists for the greatest amount of time is counseling in general and individual counseling in particular. When we piece together findings from earlier studies (Fitzgerald & Osipow, 1986; Watkins et al., 1986) with surveys conducted in the 1990s (Holahan & Yesenosky, 1992) and those conducted in the 21st century (APA, 2012; Goodyear et al., 2008; Munley et al., 2008), the primacy of

TABLE 17.2

Primary Work Activities of Counseling Psychologists

Work activity	APA (2012) %	Munley et al. (2008) %
Health and mental health services	63.9	59.1
Education	13.0	14.2
Management/administration	9.8	9.6
Research	5.2	3.5
Other applied psychology	3.5	1.9
Educational services	2.9	2.9
Other activities	1.7	0.9

Note. Data are from APA Center for Workforce Studies (2012) and Munley et al. (2008), excluding the unspecified category. APA = American Psychological Association.

counseling is clear and consistent. We do not, however, interpret these changes as indicating that the specialty is becoming increasingly service oriented and decreasingly research oriented. To begin with, it is inevitable that as the specialty graduates more and more counseling psychologists, the percentage holding service positions will increase. After all, we cannot simply train counseling psychologists to be academicians because of the finite number of academic posts available and because the training, by definition, focuses on teaching students to practice counseling psychology, not merely to study it.

When earlier studies are compared with more recent studies, there does appear to be a substantial increase in the numbers of counseling psychologists who call what they do "psychotherapy." In earlier times, that activity appeared to be the sole province of clinical psychologists (within psychology). In more recent times, counseling psychologists have joined the large number of professionals from several fields (psychiatry, psychiatric social work, clinical psychology, etc.) who perform therapy as a part of their clinical practice. Although this trend is not fully documented, it does appear to us that, given the specialty's historical and current emphasis on brevity, the psychotherapy performed by counseling psychologists has tended to be more short term, even before brief treatments were required by managed-care companies for insurance reimbursement (see Gelso & Johnson, 1983; Tyler, 1961).

As increased numbers of counseling psychologists have become focused on personal counseling and psychotherapy, some observers have suggested that participation in vocational practice (e.g., career counseling) has been eroding simultaneously (Goodyear et al., 2008). However, career counseling remains a vital activity for counseling psychologists (Chope, 2012). As our identity as counseling psychologists becomes more varied (Heppner, Carter, Casas, & Stone, 2000), it is important to remember our central values (see Chapter 1). The central values that are important to counseling psychology (e.g., vocational psychology, social justice and multiculturalism, wellness and positive psychology, counseling process and outcomes) are still vibrant and developing. Our profession can enhance its historical roots as well as infuse "cutting-edge" information from other areas such as globalization, technology, translational research, neuroscience, and genetics (Hansen, 2012).

Thus, rather than seeing the specialty as becoming less oriented toward research and science, we see the research emphasis being a major thread of continuity in the specialty from its beginnings to the current time. From our review of the research over the past decade, it appears that the research role of the counseling psychologist is as strong as ever (see Chapters 4–8) and that there is an increased commitment to making the scientist–practitioner model work (Hansen, 2012; Vespia & Sauer, 2006).

Now That You Know About Counseling Psychology, How Do You Become a Counseling Psychologist?

SELECTING A GRADUATE PROGRAM

This section provides information and advice for readers who are not yet in graduate programs in counseling psychology and yet have liked what they learned about the profession and have decided to learn more about the various kinds and levels of graduate training programs. The first difficult decision to make is whether to consider master's degree programs, typically requiring 2 years of full-time study (or several more years of part-time study), or doctoral degree programs, typically requiring 5 to 6 years of full-time study, including the internship. (Only a few doctoral programs allow much part-time study; part-time doctoral degrees often require 10 or more years.) Psychology has, since the 1940s, viewed the doctoral degree as the only degree appropriate for fully independent practice. Completion of only a master's degree in psychology will impose significant limits to career opportunities in psychology. On the other hand, there are more practice opportunities for one with a master's degree in counseling compared with a master's degree in psychology. Readers interested primarily in a practitioner's master's degree in counseling should consider the variety of counseling programs, such as mental health counseling, marriage and family counseling, rehabilitation counseling, and community counseling.

For those considering pursuing the doctoral degree in counseling psychology, there may be a number of reasons to complete a master's degree. First, the shorter period required allows a more reasonable test of whether one is really interested in and likes making the kinds of academic and professional commitments needed for the several years it takes to become a counseling psychologist. Some students decide that the opportunities available as a professional counselor at the master's-degree level are sufficient, especially because the doctoral degree would require another 3 (minimally) and possibly 4 to 5 years of study and internship.

Second, there are times when students interested in doctoral degree programs do not have the academic credentials needed to gain acceptance directly into psychology doctoral programs (often a 3.5 grade point average in extensive psychology coursework and Graduate Record Exam scores of 1100 or more), yet do have the 3.0 grade point average in general undergraduate coursework typically needed for entering a master's degree program. The choice to pursue a master's degree as a way to improve one's credentials for getting accepted into a doctoral program typically adds a year or two to the time needed to eventually earn a doctoral degree; however, this option does have the distinct advantage of increasing chances for entry into a doctoral program. There are, of course, no guarantees; however, each year a number of master's graduates are able to achieve their goal of going on to doctoral studies when initially they were ineligible for such programs.

For those considering doctoral programs in psychology, there are several major resource books that are important to consult. The first and most basic is *Graduate Study in Psychology*, which is updated annually by the APA (see the most recent version to date: APA, 2013). This book lists all programs that offer degrees of all types of psychology in regionally accredited universities. Doctoral-level counseling, clinical, and school programs accredited by the APA are clearly indicated. Each program is briefly described in terms of the kinds of degrees it offers, the grade point averages and various kinds of exams required for admission to the program (e.g., Graduate Record Examination), the number of applicants versus the number accepted, the amount of financial support available, and so forth. In short, the book provides a great deal of statistical information about almost every program in psychology.

A second major resource includes several how-to books on the process of applying to graduate school: *Getting In: A Step-by-Step Plan for Gaining Admission to Graduate School in Psychology* (APA, 2007a); *Insider's Guide to Graduate Programs in Clinical and Counseling Psychology* (Norcross & Sayette, 2011); and *The Complete Guide to Graduate School Admission: Psychology, Counseling, and Related Professions* (Keith-Spiegel & Wiederman, 2000). These books not only describe timelines and procedures for applications but also describe how to prepare oneself both academically and experientially to become a competitive applicant for doctoral-level programs. For example, they describe how the kinds of courses one takes as an undergraduate may be even more important than simply obtaining high grades. Other sections describe the steps that may be taken to increase the possibilities of attending graduate programs in psychology for those who lack outstanding grades or high Graduate Record Exam scores.

It is important for applicants to counseling psychology programs to understand that these programs vary greatly in how many credit hours and what specific psychology courses must be taken before becoming an applicant. Even though typical guidelines for many graduate psychology programs suggest that applicants have the equivalent of an undergraduate major in psychology, many programs—especially in counseling psychology—will consider applicants from very diverse undergraduate backgrounds, particularly if they have completed courses in statistics and research design, either as part of their own majors or as electives before or after completing their bachelor's degree.

TYPES OF DOCTORAL DEGREES

For students who are now in or expecting to be in a master's degree program and will subsequently be considering various doctoral degree programs, it is important to become aware of some actual differences and, more important, some perceptions about differences in types of doctoral degrees in terms of the opportunities they provide for both short- and long-range professional developmental goals. Doctoral programs in counseling psychology most frequently offer the PhD (Doctor of Philosophy) degree; a few offer an EdD (Doctor of Education) degree; some programs offer a choice of either degree. Because the PhD degree has long been the primary recognized research degree from universities, it is not surprising that counseling psychology, with a scientist–practitioner emphasis, has most often offered the PhD degree. However, because many APA-approved counseling psychology programs have long been housed in colleges and schools of education, some of those programs offer primarily the EdD degree. In earlier times, that degree choice may have indicated less stringent research training and dissertation requirements than in other parts of a university, but that is rarely true in today's colleges of education.

The PsyD (Doctor of Psychology) degree is less common in counseling psychology than in clinical psychology. These more practice-oriented degree programs are often very attractive to students who are less interested in research and have a clear and primary interest in professional practice. Because they face fewer research requirements, students in PsyD degree programs typically take about 5 years to complete their degrees compared with approximately 6 years for those in PhD degree programs (Gaddy et al., 1995). With less attention to participation in research as part of PsyD programs, graduates from these programs are less likely to hold positions in psychology departments or medical schools that award appointments and promotions on the basis of research productivity. Graham and Kim (2011) found that graduates of PsyD programs were significantly less likely to obtain an APA-accredited internship and scored lower on the Examination for Professional Practice in Psychology licensure exam (discussed later in this chapter), highlighting the importance of research training at the doctoral level. In short, they noted that their findings "point towards the fact that programs that incorporate research as a central component outperform those that do not" (p. 350). On the other hand, the extensive practicum training provided in PsyD programs makes graduates attractive to service settings that want to immediately involve new psychologists in extensive practice.

THE CHALLENGES OF GRADUATE SCHOOL

Graduate school in counseling psychology is ideally a time of significant professional and personal growth as well as attainment of knowledge. We have noted throughout this book the emphasis of counseling psychology on person–environment interactions. In the next sections of this chapter we look at the interactions of graduate students (persons) and graduate schools (environments) that are essential to attaining the ideal. Graduate school environments, like most environments, tend to elicit certain feelings and behaviors. Many of these feelings and behaviors help students achieve their goals. However, others may also frequently be elicited that limit the range of goals and/or make attainment of goals more difficult and frustrating than necessary. The next section identifies six perspectives that greatly facilitate satisfaction and productivity during the graduate school years in terms of both professional and personal development. Unfortunately, many of these perspectives are poorly cultivated in the graduate school environment. In fact, there are a variety of factors in our educational system that press toward the antithesis of these perspectives. Understanding both the needs of persons developing as counseling psychologists and the environmental presses of graduate school is therefore an essential part of the next section.

Changing the Means-to-an-End Attitude Into Professional Development

We find many graduate students enter graduate school with what we call a means-to-an-end perspective, one that served them well in high school and college. In high school, one tries to do well to have the opportunity to go to a good college; in college, one tries to do well to get into graduate school; then one focuses on surviving graduate school in order to earn the doctoral degree. Then life begins! We would like to interrupt this means-to-an-end course of study. *The end is here! You are now part of counseling psychology.* (We shift here to the second-person "you" for the remainder of the chapter, feeling the need for a more personal frame of reference for this largely advisory material.)

We recommend that you look at graduate school as the beginning of your professional development. Such a change will require you to adopt an activist position as you encounter a variety of challenges. Essentially, you must ask how you can get the most out of each experience instead of doing just enough to get by or "over the hurdle." Taking a professional development view rather than a means-to-an-end perspective is best accomplished by understanding the five other challenging perspectives in this section: (a) changing self-preservation into self-actualization, (b) balancing dependence and independence, (c) finding a mentor, (d) actively coping with disappointments, and (e) finding personal development in professional development. For these five perspectives we examine some typical problem areas and frustrations you may encounter as a graduate student and then suggest ways of mastering the challenge of growing professionally and personally.

Changing Self-Preservation Into Self-Actualization

For students just beginning graduate study, turning self-preservation into self-actualization may be the most salient challenge. The quantity and quality of the requirements of graduate courses will probably exceed those you had in undergraduate courses. Moreover, other students in the class are usually as academically talented as you (or perhaps seemingly more so). Seeing "first clients," even if only role-playing, may leave you tongue-tied. The thought of completing a dissertation ("Did you hear her dissertation was 210 pages long?") may simply be beyond your expectations of what you could do. In the absence of some of the psychological supports we talk about later in this chapter, any student facing all these threats might well consider a different career.

The major concern we need to address is the possibility that these challenges will lead to self-doubts and avoidant behaviors, the latter in the service of a felt need for self-preservation. We are not concerned that you experience some self-doubts; you will probably not be stretched enough to reach your full potential without them. We want to "certify" that it is all right to have such doubts. How you react to them is the critical factor to be discussed here. All too often, the way any of us copes is to minimize or avoid contact with the difficult situation. At the extreme, such avoidance may mean withdrawal from graduate school and termination of a long-planned career objective. At a lesser extreme, it results in students minimizing their work in the threatening area and considering the requirement as simply a hurdle to get over. "Get by with as little as possible and get out as soon as possible" is the creed of the self-preservation specialist.

Such a strategy, however, may lead to many unfortunate disappointments both for students and for program faculty. If course demands are the threat and one responds by avoiding much material related to that course, one is engaging in a self-defeating behavior that leads to the self-fulfilling prophecy of not doing well. Graduate students sometimes deal with the threat of research by avoiding any research activities until absolutely compelled to confront them—that is, until they must start their dissertation.

What should you do when confronted by these challenges? First, as we have said, simply recognize what is happening to you. Initial feelings of acute anxiety, dread, or the need to get away from it all may simply be the result of these challenges. They are not necessarily indications of more serious psychological problems and/or unsuitability for the profession of counseling psychology. Second, at the risk of oversimplifying, we urge you to think of reframing the challenges as a problem to be solved. The literature on personal problem solving and counseling (Heppner, Witty, & Dixon, 2004) describes many of the strategies for appraisal of problems, goal setting, and problem-solving actions. There are many steps you can take on your own; also, as we discuss later, if your doubts seem overwhelming, they may be a good catalyst for considering the benefits of personal counseling for yourself. In response to demands from academic courses, you may want to consider new methods of reading, studying, or time management. For threats from initial counseling experiences, you may want to consult additional skill-building workbooks (e.g., Egan, 2009), study casebook materials, observe peers counsel, and so forth. For research, you might seek out a research team project where you would have much smaller and more defined activities than you would in personally planning and conducting a full study.

In summary, we suggest that you ask yourself what you need to do to make the source of the challenge an area in which you grow and develop; that is, actualize your potential. Easier said than done, we agree. (One advisee said, "I'd like to self-actualize, but I have this horrible exam next week.") If you find yourself at any time in the future looking at your own avoidant tendencies generated by self-doubts, say, "Stop! I need to look at what I can *do* rather than what I can *avoid*." If you do this, we will have accomplished our goal for this brief section of the chapter.

We do recognize that striving for self-actualization in the face of the many demands of graduate work will test your ability to set limits. There are indeed only 24 hours in a day, and we all need sleep. If you are being challenged in many areas simultaneously, it may be important to sort out your priorities. Which challenges will you work on at this time versus some future time? If you entered graduate school directly from undergraduate school, you may still be working on the assumption that you will be able to reach a reasonable level of mastery on most of the tasks and demands that come with each semester. Part of the process of becoming a professional and dealing with often vague and extensive tasks is learning to live with the feeling that one is never truly completely "on top" and "caught up." Feelings of completeness and mastery that sometimes come at the end of semesters may be ones you have to file in long-term memory. Being a professional is not defined in terms of number of tasks for a given semester. Part of self-management as a professional is deciding throughout your entire career which tasks can be accomplished in the near future and which will have to wait for coming months or even later. The bottom line for this kind of setting of limits is to remember that you are *deferring* rather than *avoiding* work that you cannot manage at the present time.

Some of those tasks that we suggest are important to consider adding into your graduate school experiences as a way to better prepare for your future career path are those of teaching and externships. Many graduate students have obtained a teaching assistantship to help cover the cost of their graduate training. As such, they are typically assigned as teaching assistants (TAs) to various courses. If you are considering an academic career (as a professor in a graduate or undergraduate program), we strongly urge you to seek out additional teaching experience. Many programs have opportunities for graduate students to teach a course as the instructor (not the TA), particularly during summer sessions. Teaching a course not only gives you valuable experience but helps you learn whether a career in teaching will fit with your personality, interests, needs, and values.

Similarly, we encourage graduate students to seek out additional experience through "externships." The term *externship* refers to practical experiences in agencies outside of program practica but prior to the internship year. Externship experiences may range from relatively formal training programs involving the student in 20 hours a week of training and service to more informally arranged training experiences for as little as a half day a week for one semester. Externships have several very specific values for subsequent internship and career opportunities for many graduate students. First, most internship programs are looking for persons who have had at least some prior significant experience in that particular kind of setting. For example, a university counseling center may be slightly reluctant to consider an intern whose total experience in practica and employment has been in inpatient psychiatric facilities. Second, students in traditional scientist–practitioner programs may often have fairly intensive but not very extensive practicum experience in terms of number of hours of practical experience. On the other hand, graduate students in PsyD doctoral programs and other, more practice-oriented programs may be assigned to work 20 hours a week in an agency throughout their doctoral training and therefore have literally thousands of hours of accumulated experience prior to the internship. Consequently, you may want to consider an externship as a way of increasing your number of hours of experience. In addition, although externship choices may be a way of preparing yourself for specific internships or careers, they may also be chosen simply because you want breadth of exposure to different populations or modalities of counseling. Whether you add in teaching or externship experiences to your graduate training, again, it will be important to do so strategically without becoming overwhelmed by additional activities.

Our final point related to changing self-preservation into self-actualization concerns the role of competition in our society, sometimes most blatantly evident in our system of higher education (e.g., curving exam scores). Such procedures obviously foster individual competitiveness, meaning that students may almost studiously avoid any collaborative work and mutual assistance. Much has been written about how such procedures are inimical to higher level thinking and creativity. Because students in graduate programs in counseling psychology are already a very select group, there is little if any need for students to feel in competition with each other. We genuinely believe that a well-functioning graduate program will include some aspects in which students work together; for example, studying in groups for the most demanding courses, assisting each other in research projects, and providing constructive peer supervision in counseling practica.

Balancing Dependence and Independence

Balancing dependence and independence and the next two perspectives—finding a mentor and actively coping with disappointments—are, in our view, inextricably bound together. Indeed, they also are, in a sense, integral to the challenge just discussed regarding self-actualization. However, we believe that some points are best made by considering the perspectives separately. Both graduate and undergraduate studies exert some strong environmental press toward dependence; that is, they elicit dependent behaviors from students. Relatively clear requirements are laid out; students then perceive hurdles they must get over to obtain the coveted degree. Moreover, students may feel they should rely on available experts (e.g., faculty and supervisors) to tell them explicitly and specifically what to do.

Although it is true that much effective learning can take place by depending on available program structures and resources, the challenge is to be sure that you do not limit your professional development to a passive dependence on what is routinely given to you. Thus, the challenge is *balancing* dependence and independence. What steps do you need to take to ensure some independent action for your professional development?

The antidote begins with recognition that the push toward dependency in graduate school must be met by some counteraction on your part. First, you must ask what you want from your graduate program, compared with asking, "What will my graduate program provide for me?" We advise students to continually think about both long-term (e.g., 5-year) goals and short-term (e.g., coming year) goals. What specific kinds of practice and research experiences would you like to have during the coming year? What roles would you like to be prepared to fill in 5 years? Do you have any styles of personal interaction that you want to try to modify in the near future?

Students should ask themselves what arrangements they have made to have some balance, so that graduate school does not fill their entire life. The demands of graduate school can be totally absorbing. Professors are skilled in making demands on both themselves and students that will fill all available waking hours. If one is to have any kind of avocational or recreational interests, the somewhat clichéd saying is all too appropriate: One doesn't *find* time, one *makes* time.

Finding a Mentor

Since the 1970s, the concept of mentoring as a significant contributor to career development in all professions has been increasingly explored (Levinson, 1980). Although the definition has varied widely, the one most useful for our purposes was presented by Bova and Phillips (1982):

> Mentors are those who practice most of the following principles: 1. Try to understand, shape, and encourage the dreams of the protégés, 2. Often give their blessing on the dreams and goals of their protégés, 3. Provide opportunities for their protégés to observe and participate in their work by inviting their protégés to work with them, 4. Teach protégés the politics of "getting ahead" in the organization. A mentor is usually a person of high organizational or specific career status who by mutual consent takes an active interest in the career development of another person. (p. 7)

Bogat and Redner (1985) were among the first to call attention to the role of the mentor graduate school as it subsequently affects one's professional development in psychology. H. D. Ellis (1992) stated,

> I believe that quality graduate programs have some sort of a faculty mentor system, in which students can obtain advice, counseling, and helpful direction in their training. This must be a relationship of trust, in which ideas can be freely shared and confidences held. (p. 575)

The values and characteristics of effective mentors have been explored by counseling psychologists, particularly in the realm of multicultural feminist mentoring (Benishek, Bieschke, Park, & Slattery, 2004; Fassinger & Hensler-McGinnis, 2005; Gormley, 2012). To the extent that students have a means-to-an-end perspective, they may not view faculty as people with whom they will continue to have relationships in subsequent years and therefore do not look for mentors among the faculty. Moreover, faculty and student roles in courses might sometimes seem almost adversarial. For example, faculty seem to hold all the power and may be making course and/or program demands that students find neither valuable nor interesting: obviously not the conditions to promote mentoring. Yet, Schlosser and Gelso (2001) suggested that rapport between a student and his or her advisor is an important factor in a positive mentor working alliance, where the advisor "facilitates the advisee's development and teaches the advisee how to function within the profession" (p. 165).

Thus, it is important think carefully about how to initiate finding a mentor among the faculty and supervisors in your graduate program. This statement reveals one of our assumptions; that is, that career development of counseling psychologists is indeed facilitated by having a mentor or several close mentors (also referred to as composite mentoring; B. Packard, 2003). Although we clearly know of many outstanding counseling psychologists who have developed rewarding and significant careers without having mentors, it is our own view that progress in the early stages of one's career—from the internship through first positions—is greatly accelerated by their assistance. We urge you to go back and reread the definition provided by Bova and Phillips (1982) and begin thinking about your current or possible future advisors as suitable to this kind of role. In short, we urge you to think about advisors as more than a signature on your course requests at the beginning of each semester!

Actively Coping With Disappointments

No matter how carefully you have researched your choice of programs, you are likely to find, at some point, a course or professor, a practicum or requirement, that does not meet your own view of what you expected from graduate school.

> Any system imposes limitations on you. The challenge is to learn how to work creatively within that system to obtain your key goals without sacrificing your integrity by "selling out." We often hear both students in college and professionals in a human services system argue that the "system" won't allow them to be themselves, that they feel stifled, and that they could be creative and productive "if it weren't for . . . so much reading and so many papers to write, leaving me with no time to be concerned with what I am learning . . . the silly requirements and the

grading game . . . the unrealistic pressures placed on me by the professors. (M. S. Corey & Corey, 1989, p. 19)

Again, a means-to-an-end perspective leads to a passive accommodation to such disappointments. We encourage you to think about a more activist self-management response. First, explore any of your disappointments with your fellow students, both at your own beginning level and those at more advanced levels in the program. In this way, you may (a) gain some perspective on whether the concern is widely shared or one unique to you and (b) discover ways in which other students have actively dealt with that disappointment. Then, if your concern is widely shared, those of you who share it may want to bring it to the attention of the faculty or program director through student representatives, grievance procedures, or other mechanisms. In a sense, such procedures are a way of learning to cope with some inevitable disappointments in one's professional career.

When the problem is one that is not shared by others, the courses of action may seem less evident. Just as we discussed in the earlier section on changing self-preservation into self-actualization, the primary need is to reframe the concern as a problem to be solved. What, in more behavioral concrete terms, is the problem? What kinds of possible solutions can you envision? What kinds of alternatives are available? What are the costs and benefits of some of the various solutions in terms of how much they involve changes in you and changes from others? In short, consider how to take an activist role in reaching alternative solutions through changing something about "the system" and/or yourself. This is the focus of the final perspective we discuss.

Finding Personal Development in Professional Development

Graduate study in counseling psychology is qualitatively different from that in, for example, history, physics, or music. Becoming an effective counselor happens only by learning a great deal about yourself. It is not simply a matter of applying a set of techniques. *You* are the major tool— one that must be highly adaptable to be effective with a wide range of clients and interventions. To become that adaptable, you will have to examine many of your values, assumptions, and personal styles. As a counselor you might experience value conflicts with clients, for example, in matters of religion, abortion, gender roles, perceived responsibilities for family members, and so forth. Clients may be part of a culture that has a value system very different than your own, leading them to close out options that you consider viable and effective choices for them. Even less obvious to most counselors are the assumptions we all make about various cultures (see Chapter 14). Understanding how your own cultural background, personality, and style of interacting affect clients is a critical part of your learning.

Some areas of your own personal struggle may be the source of significant countertransference issues (see Chapter 9) that block progress in a counseling relationship. All of these areas can often be addressed by personal counseling for yourself, a topic that has long been debated as to whether or not it should be a required part of training in counseling psychology (Kaslow & Friedman, 1984; McEwan & Duncan, 1993; Pope & Tabachnick, 1994). Holzman, Searight, and Hughes (1996) found that the overwhelming majority of students have very favorable responses to participating in therapy while in graduate school. They felt that their counseling skills had been helped primarily through their being able to make more effective use of their feelings in their own counseling. For those who are experiencing personal distress during the graduate school years, counseling offers a way of dealing with that stress and of improving one's sense of skills and techniques for relating to clients. From a professional developmental point of view, then, engaging in personal counseling while in graduate school may be a highly valuable option to consider.

We have described six perspectives that we believe will help you become an effective manager of your own professional development. We turn now to some special opportunities for you to consider in planning your professional development during graduate school years.

GRADUATE SCHOOL YEARS: PROFESSIONAL DEVELOPMENT

We describe four topics we believe merit some special consideration in your plans for the graduate school years.

Professional Readings

You may feel almost overwhelmed with the amount of reading already required in your graduate courses and cannot imagine taking on any more reading. Yet, if you are to become an effective manager of your own professional development, the time to start some elective professional reading is right now. Courses, by design, have limited breadth; moreover, professors or instructors teaching these courses do not know everything (at least the ones we know!). As a way to stay abreast of current developments in psychology in general, we highly recommend a regular perusal of the *APA Monitor*, the monthly publication of the American Psychological Association, and the *American Psychologist*, the primary journal of the association.

For counseling psychology specifically, we recommend a similar perusal of the table of contents of each issue of the *Journal of Counseling Psychology*, the primary empirical research journal of the field, and of

The Counseling Psychologist, the primary conceptual journal of the field. Other journals to consider are *Psychotherapy* (the primary publication of Division 29, the Division of Psychotherapy, of the APA) and *Professional Psychology: Research and Practice*, the major APA journal about professional practice issues. Granted, few if any of us read any of the journals from cover to cover, yet by taking time to read the abstracts of the articles in these journals, we get a feel for the current issues and topics of greatest concern and can take note of articles that we do specifically want to read or consult when time permits.

We also urge you to think about some elective reading in your own area of special interest. That may be a topic such as vocational psychology, multicultural counseling, health and wellness, or particular approaches to psychotherapy. Almost every different population of clients, treatment technique, theoretical orientation, and/or scientific research problem has a specialized journal that is probably worth consulting with some frequency, again if only to review the table of contents, read the abstracts, and identify articles of specific interest. A handy way to keep up to date on recent books in your specialized area of interest is to order them directly from a publisher if you notice that several are published by the same house. The publisher will put your name on a mailing list; you will then receive catalogues listing many current publications in your particular area of interest.

As we close this section, we recognize that we have devoted all of our space to telling you what to read, not when to read it. As we noted in one of the earlier sections of this chapter, a continual task of professional life is learning how to make time for what we think is valuable; if you wait to find time to read, your accumulation of newsletters and books will soon be overwhelming. Another value of regularly reading these journals is that you will soon realize that some of your own work in classes and research may be of the same caliber as that being published. Thus, you can begin to visualize yourself as a contributor to journals, not merely a reader of them. If you incorporate some editorial suggestions from an advisor or faculty member, many research projects or conceptual papers of graduate students may become suitable for publication in these journals.

Professional Conventions

We could not have written wisely about professional conventions ourselves until we had been in the profession many years and slowly began to realize the many unexpected ways in which these conventions can affect graduate students' professional development. If you were to stop reading at this point and rush off to a professional convention, you might well be overwhelmingly disappointed. Regional and national psychology conventions are large and complex affairs, often with thousands of participants and many paper sessions and symposia scheduled for almost every hour. Simply attending some of these sessions and then returning to your home or hotel room is *not* how a convention contributes to your professional development.

The greatest benefits of professional conventions for graduate students, as we have observed them, are derived from their presenting a paper or participating in a symposium at a convention. How can you have such an opportunity? You might expect conventions to be primarily for well-established professionals with active research programs. On the contrary, it is much easier to present a paper at a professional convention than to have a paper published. Most master's thesis research projects completed in counseling psychology programs have a good chance of acceptance for presentation at a regional or national convention poster session. *Poster sessions* refer to times when a large number of papers are posted on bulletin boards with accompanying illustrative tables. The authors stand by for the selected time period so that interested persons can come and discuss the papers with them. In contrast to poster sessions, symposia are often made up of several brief research presentations from various research team members followed by comments from a few knowledgeable discussants. Having the opportunity to present at a symposium is most often related to being part of a research team or having a mentor. At every convention, there are symposia that include several graduate students from the same program or from different universities but working on similar projects known to the symposium organizer (typically, an established researcher from a practice setting or from a faculty).

We have gradually become aware of the immense benefits of such participation by both undergraduate and graduate students. Those who do take part in such presentations, although initially frightened about the prospects, typically come away with a greatly increased sense of self-efficacy and feeling connected to the field of counseling psychology. Suddenly, they have found a number of people (in addition to their advisor) quite interested in the details of their work and have indeed found themselves to be the expert in that particular area. It is also important to note that presenting at a convention is something that is listed on your résumé. Such a listing strongly marks your professional commitment. Most employers in both practitioner and academic settings want to be sure that they are considering someone not only competently skilled in psychological services but also involved in the broader profession. Such involvement not only is a promise of remaining a vitalized professional but can also bring credit to an agency when staff participate in national conventions.

There are other aspects of convention participation that are very important for professional development. All conventions run a number of social hours—that is, occasions when the participants meet very informally. These times are especially significant for the networking experience of graduate students. This is a time to meet many other counseling psychologists with widely varying levels of experience but all with strong commitments to professional development. You can meet the best-known practitioners and researchers as well as those who, like yourself, may just be beginning a career. Making such contacts may well lead to further correspondence that will help you with your own research and career opportunities. Most important, those social activities can greatly enhance your sense of being part of a profession by establishing your personal professional identity as a counseling psychologist.

In a related way, these activities at conventions can help you identify your professional "home." Because conventions can be overwhelming, finding smaller groups within the larger group with whom to network and connect is vital. Within APA Division 17 (Society of Counseling Psychology), for example, numerous sections of the division have socials, roundtable discussions, or specialized programming at convention (see http://www.div17.org for a full list of the Society of Counseling Psychology's sections and special interest groups). Attending these events is a great way to meet other professionals and students interested in the issues in which you are interested (e.g., independent practice; lesbian, gay, bisexual, and transgender issues; health psychology). As a graduate student, you can become a member of the Student Affiliates of Seventeen to learn more about participating in the sections and in regional and national conventions.

The Internship

In the past 3 decades, the number of doctoral students in counseling and clinical psychology has doubled (Norcross, Kohut, & Wicherski, 2005; Peterson, 2003). Although this increase has been driven primarily by new PsyD programs in clinical psychology (Graham & Kim, 2011), all of these psychologists will end up competing for internship slots and postdoctoral positions. Thus, preparing counseling psychology doctoral students for the highly competitive internship application process is important. As Mary Casey Jacob said in 1987, "Having gone through it, I now believe preparation should begin in the first year of graduate school" (p. 146). Several helpful books have been developed to help with the application process, such as *A Guide to Obtaining a Psychology Internship* (Megargee, 2001) and *Internships in Psychology: The APAGS Workbook for Writing Successful Applications and Finding the Right Fit* (Williams-Nickelson, Prinstein, & Keilin, 2012). We strongly suggest that student use these books, among other sources, to help prepare themselves for the process early in their graduate training.

Choosing from the many recognized internship sites may seem a daunting process; moreover, because internship application, like entry into graduate school, is a competitive process, students have considerable anxiety about it. The combination of these two features no doubt accounts for the plethora of articles on this topic. Unfortunately, most of the literature is focused on the application process and managing potential difficulties in the transition to the internship rather than looking at the longer term professional development aspects regarding the choice of internships. Our primary focus will therefore be on those aspects, and we will leave to you, the reader, the task of reviewing the literature for the many useful pieces of advice regarding the application process itself.

Each internship provides a somewhat different set of intensive training experiences. The primary question for you, when considering the choice of internships, is which kinds of experiences you would want to have enhance and complement your current doctoral training. Students readily think about some of the choices regarding settings, such as hospitals, counseling centers, and community mental health centers, but are less likely to think about what the internship will offer them in terms of experience with other theoretical orientations, such as behavioral, psychodynamic, and opportunities with various client populations, whether by diagnostic category (e.g., eating disorders, career dissatisfaction, posttraumatic stress syndrome) or demographic characteristics (e.g., gender, age, ethnicity).

Your choice of an internship has both direct and indirect career implications. The direct implications come from the more obvious connection between your gaining experience with a particular kind of setting or service and your marketability for that kind of career for your first job. Obviously, persons with internships completed in hospital settings will be in a stronger position when applying for psychology positions in hospitals; similarly, someone completing an internship in a university counseling center will be more competitive for a career position in a counseling center than will a candidate who has completed only one practicum in a counseling center.

The more indirect career implications from choice of internship relate to the concept of networking. Typically, the persons with whom you work in your internship setting most likely know other professionals in that kind of setting and will therefore be able to tell you more about job opportunities in that setting than any other. Thus, your informal network for potential jobs will be shaped in part by your choice of internship setting.

There are also some important aspects to consider about internships and their effect on your qualifications for licensure, other professional credentials, and employment. Several hundred internships are listed in the directory of the Association of Psychology Postdoctoral and

Internship Centers (APPIC), issued each fall, providing brief descriptions of the kinds of training available in each internship, the prerequisite qualifications for candidates, and application procedures (see http://www.appic.org). APPIC also has developed guidelines for internship offers and acceptances and monitors compliance with these guidelines to provide assurance of compliance by both agencies and intern applicants. Several authors have provided recent overviews of the kinds of problems applicants experience and how their concerns may be addressed (Huang, Lin, & Chang, 2010; Miville, Adams, & Juntunen, 2007; Parent & Williamson, 2010).

For licensing and other credentials as professional psychologists, internships that are APA approved are typically fully accepted, without further question or documentation, as meeting requirements for internship-level training. Other internships listed in the APPIC directory may also be acceptable, after provision of some documentation from the agency, to many licensing boards and some employers (e.g., the Veterans Administration and some states require that the internship be completed in an APA-approved program).

It is possible to complete a specially arranged internship in an agency that does not officially list its program in the APPIC directory to gain some specialized experience (e.g., working with AIDS patients in a hospital without an internship program). Although a graduate from an APA-approved doctoral training program is permitted to complete an internship that is not APA approved but that does provide appropriate supervised experience and training, the lack of formal recognition as an internship has significant licensing and career implications. Some students who know that the state in which they want to practice will admit them for licensure without having a formally recognized internship sometimes choose this route. However, we feel that this is such a high-risk choice, in case there is ever a decision to change one's employer or the state in which one practices, that we require the occasional student who chooses this route to sign a statement indicating that he or she realizes the potential limits of such an internship choice to licensing eligibility and career opportunities.

It is preferable that you give primary attention to the above considerations in your choice of internships before looking at the other factors that seem so tempting to graduate students, such as location, cost of living, and distance from significant others. Although all of these personal factors may be very useful secondary considerations, when used as primary considerations, they may lead to choices of internships that are gratifying in the short range but result in significant missed opportunities in terms of long-range career development. You might best serve your long-term career development when you are able to adopt the attitude "I can live anyplace for just 1 year." In summary, the choice of internship is a major component in long-range professional development and provides an opportunity for both depth and breadth that will complement training experiences gained in your program and any previous employment experiences as you make the transition to your first career.

The Dissertation

The final section of considerations for program development during graduate school applies to the dissertation, one of the final requirements for obtaining a doctoral degree. The primary purpose of this section is to help you plan your dissertation in the context of your professional development. This purpose may be challenging to fulfill.

The history of students' views toward and work on dissertations is replete with means-to-an-end perspectives. Ironically, in such a view the dissertation then gains more importance in the life of the student than it ever should. Whatever ambivalence about your program is still keeping you only partially engaged in the program and whatever threats to self-esteem have been leading you toward avoidance may all become fixated on this final hurdle. Thus, it is not surprising that Garcia, Malott, and Brethower (1988) reported that nearly a quarter of those students who drop out of graduate school did so after they had completed all the course work save the dissertation (a status often called "ABD": all but dissertation). Current numbers from *Graduate Study in Psychology* (APA, 2013) suggest that only 1% of students in counseling psychology doctoral programs actually withdrew or were dismissed. Thus, most students gather their resources and complete the dissertation.

You may rightfully say the preceding paragraph sounds like blaming the victim because the failure to complete the dissertation is explained in terms of the students' perspectives or neuroses. However, ever since the 1960s, there has been an increasing amount of literature indicating that part of this failure to complete theses is related to a lack of supervision and effective incentives (see Garcia et al., 1988). More recently, other environmental aspects have been suggested by the work of Mallinckrodt, Gelso, and Royalty (1990), who found that Holland personality types (see Chapter 15) were significantly related not only to research interests in counseling psychology but also to delays in the completion of research requirements. "Investigative and investigative-artistic students have the highest interest in research. Enterprising interests were related to lower levels of research interest and a delay in completing training" (Mallinckrodt et al., 1990, p. 26). Thus, both individual and environmental factors can work against the dissertation being a positive professional developmental experience.

We first attempt to address the environmental factors. One of the logical interventions that is increasingly promoted is the development of structured courses or supervisory systems that provide for a higher level of supervision of the dissertation. Garcia et al. (1988) found that students who participated in a system including weekly meetings, task specification, feedback, and incentives completed significantly more tasks than those in a control group. Of note, though, there was no judged difference in the quality of the projects that were completed in either of the two groups.

If you encounter significant problems in making progress on the dissertation, you may indeed want to look into more structured opportunities for supervision and support available in your own university. If there is no structured program in your area, you may be able to find similar kinds of help from a writing center that is part of campus services. Although such centers are geared primarily for undergraduates, the writing counselors often look forward to working with the higher level challenges that graduate students provide.

In picking your dissertation advisor, you may want to be sure that you select not only for expertise in a topical area but also for fit with your own style of functioning. The advisor can assist you with relatively undefined tasks, such as deciding on a topic for a dissertation and then executing it. Although there may seldom be more than one faculty member with expertise in your area of interest, whenever there can be congruence between your style and the advisor's, your progress will be facilitated. If you have difficulty choosing an advisor who seems to naturally fit your style, it is not unreasonable to explore the possibility of asking your advisor to work with you in a way that might differ from his or her usual style.

Two other bits of useful advice come from the Mallinckrodt et al. (1990) study of supportive environments for research. They noted that positive change in research interests is related to a program's conveying

> to students that all experiments are flawed and that a particular study need not make a great contribution to knowledge to be worth doing and . . . "wedding science to practice"—that is, teaching students to use their clinical experience as a source of research ideas. (p. 30)

From the professional developmental perspective, you can also look at the dissertation in its environmental context as one of the transitions, along with the internship, between your graduate school years and the beginnings of your establishment in a career as a counseling psychologist. Your choice of topic for the dissertation could well be the beginning of a program of research that you plan to continue in either a service setting or an academic position. Your dissertation topic may also be one with special implications for your subsequent practice—for example, conducting research with abused spouses attending a community clinic or with "plateaued" employees served by an employee assistance plan. In short, rather than simply looking for a dissertation topic that is feasible, you should think about the topics that will have practical use for you as well. Obviously, this is a major way to provide yourself with both intrinsic and extrinsic incentives for working on the dissertation. Topics that are supposedly feasible but are unrewarding sometimes make for the least feasible dissertations!

I Have My Doctorate, Now What? Postdoctoral Training, Licensure, and Beginning Your Career

The moment for which you have worked so hard finally comes. You receive the doctoral degree in counseling psychology. The first post-doctoral requirement is that you celebrate appropriately—whatever that means for you. Then, we need to discuss what happens next, in the early postdoc years, as you begin the work of being a counseling psychologist.

WHY A DOCTORAL DEGREE MAY NOT BE ENOUGH

The heading for this section may be distressing because just completing the doctoral degree may seem like an arduous and long process to most readers. The good news is that each of the three reasons why a doctoral degree is not enough can now be more easily addressed than in past years. The three reasons relate to (a) past deficiencies in the monitoring of quality of postdoctoral supervised experience, (b) the emergence of specialization within psychology, and (c) the rapidly changing world in which we live. Although the problems in these areas affect all psychologists, we have focused our discussions on the specific aspects most pertinent for counseling psychologists.

A long-standing problem in professional psychology has been the very uneven quality of supervision that new psychologists have received as part of their qualifications for licensure as psychologists. This variation in quality is most directly related to large variations in state licensing laws regarding required postdoctoral supervised experience. Some states, for example, allow individuals to take the licensure exam after receipt of the doctoral degree (including internship), but others have more specific requirements of particular hours (e.g., 1,500 hours of supervised experience in Louisiana) or years (e.g., 1 year postdoctoral experience in Connecticut; see http://www.asppb.net for details). Some states specify how many hours of service and supervision are required; some only require a licensed psychologist to report that he or she supervised the new professional without providing any evidence of how much, if any, actual face-to-face interaction the supervisor had with the supervisee. Obviously, such latitude has resulted in some new professionals never really receiving any actual supervision during their 1st year of postdoctoral work experience.

At the other extreme, some new psychologists have received intensive additional training in postdoctoral residencies where they may have had as much as 8 hours a week of formal training and 5 hours a week of individual supervision of their caseload. Despite these variations, new professional psychologists of both types could meet some states' requirements for postdoctoral supervised experience. State licensing boards have been reluctant to enter into the long and contentious processes that would make experiential requirements more uniform; many psychologists feel that the quality cannot be legislated because boards do not have the personnel or time to monitor the quality of supervision. As we explore in the next section, accredited postdoctoral residencies are one way to address this issue without getting into changes of state licensing laws and regulations.

A second major reason for the emergence of more attention to postdoctoral education relates to the emergence of specialization within psychology. Until the late 1970s, specialization within psychology usually referred only to the four "specialties" that had emerged at the end of World War II: counseling, clinical, school, and industrial (later called industrial/organizational, or I/O). As the profession continued to mature, more specialized areas, such as neuropsychology, behavioral psychology, health psychology, and forensic psychology (see Chapter 2), began to emerge and sought recognition for their training programs and in credentialing. Yet, until the 1990s the APA had accreditation procedures only for the original four. Although some ongoing discussion remains about the extent to which training in these various specialties can and should be taught at the doctoral degree level compared with the postdoctoral level, there has been no debate about the appropriateness of having postdoctoral training and supervision in these new specialty areas. In fact, by the 1980s a number of postdoctoral residencies focused on areas such as neuropsychology and health psychology were already well established in a number of hospitals (Wiens, 1993).

The third reason for increased attention to postdoctoral education is found in the socioeconomic changes affecting the profession as a whole. The rapidly changing economics and technology of the 21st century will continue to result in changes in how and where services are provided. No matter how up to date a training program may be today, it is unlikely that its graduates will be practicing in much the same way 25 years from now. Consider, for example, that the Internet, which provides so much of our information now and new possibilities for managing our lives (e.g., purchasing, banking), did not even exist when the first edition of this book was written! A mature profession will ensure that there are ample opportunities for its maturing members to develop the knowledge and skills needed to remain valued and contributing professionals in a changing world.

> Changing demands and economic stress evident in all aspects of our workplace underscore the importance for all psychologists to remain vigorous players, able to adjust readily to new questions and ways of answering them. It has become abundantly clear that it is no longer feasible to think of educating a workforce able to meet the demands of the discipline within the boundaries of a doctoral degree program. Moreover, this lifelong learning we have so long espoused must now be more visible, formal and systematic to ourselves and others because of the demands it must meet and the rapidity with which these demands are expected to change. (APA, 1995, p. 4)

EMERGENCE OF ACCREDITED POSTDOCTORAL RESIDENCIES

According to the 2009 *Doctorate Employment Survey* (APA Center for Workforce Studies, 2009), approximately two thirds of counseling psychologists report participating in a postdoctoral fellowship or traineeship. According to the APA website (http://www.apa.org), there are 79 accredited post docs, 42 of which are "traditional," with the others being in specialties such as child clinical (7), clinical health (7), clinical neurospsychology (19), forensics (1), and rehabilitation psychology (3). Raney, Hwang, and Douce (2008) provided additional information on finding postdoctoral training, particularly for international students.

Although a significant number of the oldest postdoctoral programs were oriented toward the development of research skills, an increasing number of them, during the final decades of the 20th century, were designed to provide advanced training in professional psychology, sometimes fairly generalized training, other times very specialized training in focused areas like neuropsychology, health psychology, or psychoanalysis. Concerns about quality control in these practice-oriented postdoctoral programs, combined with a desire for the profession of psychology to have a way of ensuring more quality control in postdoctoral experiences used to qualify for licensure in psychology, led to the development of formal standards and procedures for accreditation of postdoctoral programs. In the 1990s, representatives from most of the long-standing credentialing and accrediting organizations in psychology, along with representatives of developing organizations of postdoctoral specialty groups such as neuropsychology, behavioral, family, and health psychology, worked with the APA Committee on Accreditation to formulate postdoctoral accreditation standards and procedures. When the APA formally adopted these standards, the programs to which they were applied were identified as APA-accredited postdoctoral residencies (APA, 1996). Postdoctoral training programs can seek to become accredited postdoctoral residencies either in advanced general professional psychology or in specialty practice areas within professional psychology (e.g., neuropsychology and psychoanalysis). In the initial year that accreditation of postdoctoral residencies was offered, two were approved. Many others seeking accreditation were too small to meet the accreditation criteria; ongoing developments in such programs, as well as in the formulation of the accreditation procedures, make it difficult to predict how quickly there will be a significant number of accredited postdoctoral residencies.

It is important to note—especially for counseling psychologists—that completion of a postdoctoral residency is not now, or expected to become in the near future, a requirement for beginning a career in counseling psychology. For psychologists who wish to specialize beyond a more traditional area such as counseling or clinical psychology, the expectation may well develop that one will complete a postdoctoral residency in a specialized area like health psychology or neuropsychology. It should also be noted that there may be some distinct advantages (even though not required or even expected) for counseling and clinical psychologists to complete one of the postdoctoral residencies in general (as compared to a specialty residency) professional psychology. As the number of accredited postdoctoral residencies increases, it is likely that some states will change their licensing regulations to recognize an accredited postdoctoral residency as automatically fulfilling postdoctoral experience requirement. Therefore, any counseling psychologist who completes such a residency will not need to seek further documentation regarding the kinds of services provided and amount and kinds of supervision received during the first years of his or her career in order to meet a state's postdoctoral experience eligibility requirements for licensing. There may also be developments such as most selective employers giving preference to those who have completed an accredited postdoctoral residency, just as happened in the 1980s when several major employers of psychologists, such as the Veterans Administration, began requiring that applicants for psychology positions must have completed an APA-accredited predoctoral internship. Although the postdoctoral residency will add 1 to 2 years to the "formal" training period in professional psychology, such residencies do not often add any time needed to obtain licensure as a psychologist because a postdoctoral residency more than fulfills the postdoctoral experience requirements required by most states.

Tangentially related to the emergence of accredited postdoctoral residences is the ongoing debate about whether the predoctoral internship should remain at that level or be moved to the postdoctoral level (Boggs & Douce, 2000). APA-accreditation criteria currently require that the internship be completed prior to the granting of the doctoral degree. Some psychologists have been arguing for moving the internship to the postdoctoral level. Interns could then, like intern physicians, be identified as doctors. Reimbursement for professional services in hospitals and health care companies would then be easier to achieve. Another argument in favor of the move is that an intern who has already completed all the doctoral degree requirements could then dedicate all of his or her time and energy to the internship rather than also trying to complete a dissertation and/or other predoctoral requirements. Arguments against are concerns about a training program's loss of control over the selection and completion of an internship appropriate to the prior training of the student. Also, what controls would there be against exploitation of a new professional psychologist who has to have supervised training to obtain licensure yet no longer has advocates from a training program? Much of this discussion about the placement of internship began and evolved in the same period as the development of accredited postdoctoral programs. Counseling psychology program directors have taken the position that the internship should remain at the predoctoral level. Now that accreditation of postdoctoral residencies is in place, it seems unlikely that the internship status will be moved to postdoctoral status as well. Whatever develops regarding such placement, it is very important to note that whether the internship is predoctoral or postdoctoral does not change the length of time needed for completing training as a professional psychologist; the impact of a change, in most cases, would be limited simply to the order in which doctoral requirements were completed.

LICENSURE: NECESSARY BUT NOT SUFFICIENT

Psychologists, like lawyers, medical doctors, and many other professionals, are subject to some form of licensure in every state. Because professions, by definition, include high levels of training in a specific kind of expertise, it is a reasonable assumption that the public cannot readily make informed decisions about whether the services being offered are of adequate quality. Licensure enables a state to regulate the use of the title of the profession and legally define the activities that constitute its practice. Psychology licensure laws typically include definitions of the training and supervised experience necessary to be eligible for licensure, required examination procedures, definitions of the scope of practice, and the sanctions that apply to people who violate specifics of the licensing regulations. In many state psychology licensing laws, the ethical standards of the APA are included as part of the legal responsibilities of the psychologist.

Fretz and Mills (1980) provided a review of the early decades of controversy surrounding the need for and development of psychology licensing laws, primarily in the 1960s. Although a few psychologists were in independent practice from the beginnings of clinical and counseling psychology in the 1940s, the vast majority of such psychologists in earlier decades were employed in hospitals, clinics, and university settings where licensure was not viewed as necessary. With the emergence in the late 1960s of health insurance policy reimbursements for some counseling and psychotherapy, the number of psychologists seeking licensure increased rapidly. This increase occurred because such reimbursements were often limited to licensed professionals, as in medicine.

The psychology license laws that were developed in the 1950s and 1960s had very broad definitions about who could be eligible for licensing as a psychologist. Many persons who had become licensed as psychologists had completed degrees in graduate programs other than those in psychology (e.g., law, divinity, public health, guidance, family studies). In those early years there were no differences in the licensing procedures for someone who had completed a research doctorate, in sensation and perception, for example, and someone who had completed a doctorate in counseling, school, or clinical psychology. In order to address the great variations in states' requirements for licensure, the APA and the National Register of Health Service Providers in Psychology held two credentialing conferences in the 1970s that resulted in recommendations that have continued to affect significantly requirements both for accreditation of training programs and for licensing of psychologists.

These recommendations included a far more restrictive definition of the educational backgrounds that could be submitted to licensing boards for eligibility for licensure. However, if appropriate educational requirements were included, there was flexibility about the location of the training. Of major importance for counseling psychology was the recommendation that "the program, wherever it may be administratively housed, must be clearly identified and labeled as a psychology program. Such a program must specify in pertinent institutional catalogs and brochures its intent to educate and train professional psychologists" (Wellner, 1978, p. 33). It then became possible for many programs in counseling and guidance that wished to train counseling psychologists as well to make the curricular changes necessary for a formal transition to psychology training programs. In fact, the more than 100% increase in the number of APA-accredited programs in counseling psychology from the early 1970s to the late 1980s was directly related to this change. The majority of the newly approved programs were formerly counselor education or counseling and guidance programs in colleges of education.

Another issue in psychology licensing has been the desire for more unified examination procedures. Despite the existence of numerous licensing laws in psychology since the 1960s, it was not until the 1990s that all U.S. states and Canadian provinces required license-eligible psychologists to achieve a specified minimum score on the Examination for Professional Practice in Psychology (or what is often referred to as the "E, Triple P"), a standardized exam that been developed and administered by the Association of State and Provincial Psychology Boards (ASPPB; see http://www.asppb.net for details). There remains variation in the required passing score (e.g., some states require a particular score, such as 500, and others note a percentage correct, such as 70% or 75%), though there appears to be movement toward acceptance of the passing score recommended by the ASPPB as the standard for most states.

In recent years, efforts have been made to ease mobility between U.S. states and Canadian provinces with regard to licensure. The ASPPB has developed a certificate of professional qualification in psychology (CPQ) to aid psychologists in the process of obtaining licensure in states and provinces to which they move. The ASPPB website (http://www.asppb.net) notes that the purpose of the CPQ is "to document that the individual holding the certificate has met specific requirements in licensure, education, examination and training and has never had disciplinary actions taken against his or her license." Although each state retains autonomy as to whether it will recognize the CPQ (which in and of itself does not constitute a license to practice), at the time of this writing 33 states, 10 Canadian provinces, and the District of Columbia accept the CPQ for licensure; two additional states were "in process" toward acceptance; and 11 states "recognize" the CPQ (meaning they will waive at least one licensure requirement based on the provision of the CPQ).

SPECIALTY CREDENTIALS

Over the years a number of credentials have been developed to provide professional psychologists with attainment of advanced levels of training, experience, and competence. The credential most widely held by professional psychologists (after licensing as a psychologist, which is a prerequisite for every credential discussed here) is listing in the National Register of Health Service Providers of Psychology (NR), or its Canadian equivalent, the Canadian Register of Health Service Providers in Psychology. These registers were developed to identify which generically licensed psychologists have had appropriate training and supervised experience to qualify as health service providers. The NR is now used in designating health service providers in many states and is also used by managed care companies.

The oldest form of specialty recognition in psychology is the American Board of Professional Psychology (ABPP). Founded in 1947, congruent with the establishment of the first applied specialties—that is, counseling, clinical, and industrial (later I/O) psychology—the ABPP was established to recognize the highest levels of attainment in the specialty. It required a rigorous examination process that, when successfully completed, resulted in the award of a diplomate in the specialty. For a variety of reasons, very few psychologists in the first 40 years of ABPP completed the diplomate requirements. In the late 1980s all the application and examination issues that psychologists had raised over the years were carefully addressed by the ABPP. Also, recognizing the emergence of new specialties within psychology, the ABPP created procedures for becoming board certified in behavioral, neuropsychology, family, forensic, health, and psychoanalysis as well as the specialties of counseling, school, clinical, and I/O psychology (Fuertes, Spokane, & Holloway, 2013). For each of the specialties there are now standardized examination procedures that a psychologist may take at the completion of 2 years of supervised practice in the specialty (see www.apbb.org). Awarding of the diplomate entitles the psychologist to be identified as "board certified," a term that is widely used and recognized in medicine and therefore a valuable credential for recognition by hospitals other health care organizations.

There are ongoing issues in the field of psychology as to which credentials should be developed and recognized by the profession. The Council of Credentialing Organizations in Professional Psychology (CCOPP) was created in 1996 in order to ensure that the development of any new procedures for accreditation or credentialing of psychologists meets the quality of standards of existing procedures. The CCOPP coordinates with the participating groups in order to facilitate the career progress of professional psychologists and to provide the public with clear information about the meaning of each credential.

THE TRANSITION FROM GRADUATE SCHOOL TO FIRST POSITION

"Graduate programs in psychology typically do not provide their students with anticipatory socialization concerning entry into a professional setting, the role demands of professional life, and the personal adjustments needed for professional development" (Olson, Downing, Heppner, & Pinkney, 1986, p. 415). No matter what your career choice, your preparation for this critical transition should begin with a reading of Olson et al.'s (1986) article. Their analysis remains as accurate today as it was in the 1980s. We list their six myths, or what might alternatively be called "Six Irrational Beliefs of New Professionals," in Exhibit 17.1. In the article Olson et al. described the realities that render these statements myths and suggested what new professionals need to do to cope with the realities. They suggested, and we concur, that being prepared to deal with these transitions is the greatest service you can do for yourself. In addition to some of the factors that they pointed out in dealing with the realities behind these myths, we believe there are other key surprises. As you read these, they will probably strike you as just common sense; however, again and again we find new professionals feeling unprepared for what, with hindsight, seems obvious. Let us provide a few examples.

In a new setting you will have to learn the norms of that setting: What are the behaviors that are rewarded? Who interacts with whom? What are the taboos (e.g., topics of discussion, behaviors, theoretical positions, research areas, or political activities that are deemed unacceptable or at least second class)? How can you establish your own role and identity within that local culture? You will be expected, in most positions, to be able to handle the multiple roles of being a subordinate, a peer, and a superior (supervisor). Each of these positions has implications for how you will interact with others, ranging from how you address each other to what kinds of information, concerns, and issues you share with one another. Just as for some of the avoidant behaviors we discussed that went with self-preservation in graduate school, you may experience similar avoidant tendencies in your professional position if you find some aspects of your position disappointing. Most especially, if you believe little can be done about those disappointments, you will find yourself increasingly cynical, possibly withdrawing and even undermining others.

Schlossberg (2011), a counseling psychologist, has written extensively in the past few decades about the factors that determine how

EXHIBIT 17.1

Six Irrational Beliefs of New Professionals

1. As soon as I unpack my bags, I will be settled.
2. My new associates will welcome me enthusiastically and accept me as one of them.
3. I will never be an apprentice again.
4. I will easily perform the varied demands of my job.
5. I must perform perfectly, lest someone discover that I am a fraud.
6. Because I worked so hard to get here, I will love my job.

Note. From "Is There Life After Graduate School? Coping With the Transition to Postdoctoral Employment," by S. K. Olson, N. E. Downing, P. P. Heppner, and J. Pinkney, 1986, *Professional Psychology: Research and Practice, 17*, pp. 416–418. Copyright 1986 by the American Psychological Association.

stressful a transition can be. Anderson, Goodman, and Schlossberg (2012) used Schlossberg's original transition theory to describe practical strategies for coping with change. The skills of any counseling psychologist in assessing the strengths and limitations of both persons and environments are the fundamentals needed for implementing her recommended steps of taking stock of your situation, taking stock of yourself and supports, and taking stock of your strategies as a prerequisite for taking charge of your transitions so that they become part of, rather than an impediment to, your professional development.

ESTABLISHING YOUR CAREER

After you have chosen your first position and begun managing the transitional phase described above, you will need to take a few more specific planning steps to guide you into a lifelong pattern of satisfying positions as a counseling psychologist. By this point in your "career" you will very likely feel over the worst hurdles and more in control of your own life, even if, as described in the previous section, your first position is not quite everything you hoped it would be.

If your first position is in a group practice of psychologists or a multi-disciplinary practice, you may well find yourself a bit overwhelmed by how much you do *not* know about the nitty-gritty, day-to-day duties you will have in addition to delivering the services you have been so well prepared to provide (Stone, Dew, & Sackett, 1998). Training programs in psychology have long held negative or at least ambivalent attitudes about including in their curriculum anything about the "business of doing psychology." Until recent years, it was often difficult for new professionals to obtain good advice on how to cope with some of the business aspects. Fortunately, in the past few years, a number of books have been dedicated to the new professional in psychology, giving tips about careers in academic, counseling centers, and independent practice (Lanci & Spreng, 2008; E. Morgan & Landrum, 2012; R. Morgan, Kuther, & Habben, 2005).

Although a very large majority of psychologists consistently report satisfaction with their positions and careers, almost everyone has times when a current position or status leaves much to be desired. Two counseling psychologists, Rønnestad and Skovholt (2013), have written about the stages and themes in therapist and counselor development based on their research on master therapists and novice therapists. In their book *The Developing Practitioner*, they identified the developmental tasks of therapists at different career phases, as well as issues related to work style and satisfaction. In particular, we like the process they identified as continuous professional reflection, whereby we regularly and actively monitor our own development.

We close this chapter on professional development with what we believe to be the most cost-effective use of time and energy of counseling psychologists who wish to be actively engaged in continuous professional reflection. APA Division 17 (Society of Counseling Psychology) provides extensive networks for counseling psychologists to maintain active colleagueship. In particular, the division has numerous sections and special interest groups, providing opportunities for groups of colleagues to share materials and concerns through their newsletters and websites, as well as to meet together regularly at conventions. As counseling psychologists, we strongly urge you to join the division and at least one of the sections. We have always found that the colleagueship, networking, and friendship gained from participating in the division and its sections have been deeply rewarding.

Closing Thoughts

Throughout this book, we hope that you, the reader, have gained an understanding of what it means to be counseling psychologist, what the critical points in the history of the profession have been, and how to incorporate ethical values and principles into your daily work. We also hope you have gained an appreciation for the scientific foundations of the field (in vocational psychology, diversity and social justice, health and positive psychology, and psychotherapy research) and the nuances of practice vis-à-vis the importance of the therapeutic relationship, assessment, and foundational theories of counseling and psychotherapy (e.g., psychodynamic, cognitive–behavioral, humanistic–experiential, and feminist multicultural). We also hope we have provided you with both the knowledge and the strategies you need to become a counseling psychologist. We have found counseling psychology to be a profession that provides for a rare combination of extraordinary levels of fulfillment and meaningfulness in our work and an ever-expanding network of long-lasting, deeply caring interpersonal relationships for us and our families. We enthusiastically invite you to join us!

Summary

Our primary purpose in this chapter has been to help the reader develop a perspective on graduate education and early career experiences that marks it as the beginning of lifelong professional development in counseling psychology. We began with an overview of how counseling psychologists are trained, where they work, and what they actually do. We noted that although counseling psychologists participate in a very diverse set of work-related activities, the job settings they find themselves in have been changing over time. More counseling psychologists now note independent practice as their primary job setting. However, the importance and vibrancy of research in counseling psychology (and the scientist–practitioner model) are still an important part of the identity of counseling psychologists.

Once a student has made the decision to become a counseling psychologist, different types of programs and graduate degrees (e.g., PhD or PsyD) must be considered. Then, six challenging perspectives help to explore the ramifications of a professional development view of graduate school: (a) changing the means-to-an-end attitude into professional development, (b) changing self-preservation into self-actualization, (c) balancing dependence and independence, (d) finding a mentor, (e) actively coping with disappointments, and (f) finding personal development in professional development.

The next section reviewed a variety of opportunities for professional development and enrichment available in most counseling psychology doctoral programs. These opportunities are often not made explicit and therefore are overlooked. Opportunities for professional development can be obtained through professional readings, professional conventions, the internship, and the dissertation. In the final parts of the chapter, we focused on the initial postdoctoral years, licensure and credentials, and establishing your career as a counseling psychologist. The chapter concluded with a brief description of the ways in which the Society of Counseling Psychology provides new professionals many more opportunities to become actively involved with the vigor and vitality of all members of the profession.

References

Abeles, N. (2010). Ethics and the interrogation of prisoners: An update. *Ethics & Behavior, 20*, 243–249. doi:10.1080/10508421003798976

Ackerman, N. (1958). *The psychodynamics of family life.* New York, NY: Basic Books.

Aegisdottir, S., White, M. J., Spengler, P. M., Maugherman, A. S., Anderson, L. A., Cook, R. S., & Rush, J. D. (2006). The meta-analysis of clinical judgment project: Fifty-six years of accumulated research on clinical versus statistical prediction. *The Counseling Psychologist, 34*, 341–382. doi:10.1177/0011000005285875

Ali, S. R., McWhirter, E. H., & Chronister, K. M. (2005). Self-efficacy and vocational outcome expectations for adolescents of lower socioeconomic status: A pilot study. *Journal of Career Assessment, 13*, 40–58. doi:10.1177/1069072704270273

Allen, T. D., Herst, D. E. L., Bruck, C. S., & Sutton, M. (2000). Consequences associated with work-to-family conflict: A review and agenda for future research. *Journal of Occupational Health Psychology, 5*, 278–308. doi:10.1037/1076-8998.5.2.278

Allport, G. W. (1963). *Pattern and growth in personality.* New York, NY: Holt, Rinehart & Winston.

Altmaier, E. M., & Hansen, J. C. (2012). *The Oxford handbook of counseling psychology.* New York, NY: Oxford University Press.

American Educational Research Association, American Psychological Association, and National Council of Measurement in Education. (1999). *Standards for educational and psychological testing.* Washington, DC: American Psychological Association.

American Group Psychotherapy Association. (2002). *AGPA and IBCGP guidelines for ethics.* New York, NY: Author.

American Psychiatric Association. (1994). *Diagnostic and statistical manual of mental disorders* (4th ed.). Washington, DC: Author.

American Psychiatric Association. (2000). *Diagnostic and statistical manual of mental disorders* (4th ed., text revision). Washington, DC: Author.

American Psychiatric Association. (2013). *Diagnostic and statistical manual of mental disorders* (5th ed.). Arlington, VA: American Psychiatric Publishing.

American Psychological Association. (1952). Recommended standards for training counseling psychologists at the doctorate level. *American Psychologist, 7,* 175–181. doi:10.1037/h0056299

American Psychological Association. (1990). *Guidelines for providers of psychological services to ethnic, linguistic, and culturally diverse populations.* Washington, DC: Author.

American Psychological Association. (1995). *Education and training beyond the doctoral degree.* Madison, CT: International Universities Press.

American Psychological Association. (1996). *Guidelines and principles for accreditation of programs in professional psychology.* Washington, DC: Author.

American Psychological Association. (1999). Archival description of counseling psychology. *The Counseling Psychologist, 27,* 589–592. doi:10.1177/0011000099274006

American Psychological Association. (2000). Guidelines for psychotherapy with lesbian, gay, and bisexual clients. *American Psychologist, 55,* 1440–1451. doi:10.1037/0003-066X.55.12.1440

American Psychological Association. (2002). Ethical principles of psychologists and code of conduct. *American Psychologist, 57,* 1060–1073. doi:10.1037/0003-066X.57.12.1060

American Psychological Association. (2003a). Guidelines on multicultural education, training, research, practice, and organizational change for psychologists. *American Psychologist, 58,* 377–402. doi:10.1037/0003-066X.58.5.377

American Psychological Association. (2003b). Report of the Ethics Committee, 2002. *American Psychologist, 58,* 650–657. doi:10.1037/0003-066X.58.8.650

American Psychological Association. (2004a). Guidelines for psychological practice with older adults. *American Psychologist, 59,* 236–260. doi:10.1037/0003-066X.59.4.236

American Psychological Association. (2004b). *Resolution on same-sex families.* Washington, DC: Author.

American Psychological Association. (2005). *Report of the American Psychological Association Presidential Task Force on Psychological Ethics and National Security.* Retrieved from http://apa.org/pubs/info/reports/pens.pdf

American Psychological Association. (2006). *Resolution against torture and other cruel, inhuman, and degrading treatment or punishment.* Retrieved from http://www.apa.org/about/policy/chapter-3.aspx

American Psychological Association. (2007a). *Getting in: A step-by-step plan for gaining admission to graduate school in psychology.* Washington, DC: Author.

American Psychological Association. (2007b). Guidelines for psychological practice with girls and women. *American Psychologist, 62,* 949–979. doi:10.1037/0003-066X.62.9.949

American Psychological Association. (2007c). Report of the Ethics Committee, 2006. *American Psychologist, 62,* 504–511. doi:10.1037/0003-066X.62.5.504

American Psychological Association. (2010). 2010 amendments to the 2002 "Ethical Principles of Psychologists and Code of Conduct." *American Psychologist, 65,* 493. doi:10.1037/a0020168

American Psychological Association. (2012a). Guidelines for assessment of and intervention with persons with disabilities. *American Psychologist, 67,* 43–62. doi:10.1037/a0025892

American Psychological Association. (2012b). Guidelines for psychological practice with lesbian, gay, and bisexual clients. *American Psychologist, 67,* 10–42. doi:10.1037/a0024659

American Psychological Association. (2012c). Report of the Ethics Committee, 2011. *American Psychologist, 67,* 398–408. doi:10.1037/a0028356

American Psychological Association. (2013). *Graduate study in psychology.* Washington, DC: Author.

American Psychological Association (2013, November 4). Guidelines for Prevention in Psychology. *American Psychologist.* Advance online publication. doi:10.1037/a0034569

American Psychological Association, Education Directorate. (1995). *Education and training beyond the doctoral degree.* Madison, CT: International Universities Press.

Amundson, N. E., Harris-Bowlsbey, J., & Niles, S. G. (2009). *Essential elements of career counseling: Processes and techniques.* Upper Saddle River, NJ: Pearson.

Ancis, J. R., & Ali, S. R. (2005). Multicultural counseling training approaches: Implications for pedagogy. In C. Z. Enns & A. L. Sinacore (Eds.), *Teaching and social justice: Integrating multicultural and feminist theories in the classroom* (pp. 85–97). Washington, DC: American Psychological Association. doi:10.1037/10929-005

Andersen, S. M., & Przybylinski, E. (2012). Experiments on transference in interpersonal relations: Implications for treatment. *Psychotherapy, 49,* 370–383. doi:10.1037/a0029116

Anderson, M. L., Goodman, J., & Schlossberg, N. K. (2012). *Counseling adults in transition: Linking Schlossberg's theory with practice in a diverse world* (4th ed.). New York, NY: Springer.

Anderson, S. E., Coffey, B. S., & Byerly, R. T. (2002). Formal organizational initiatives and informal workplace practices: Links related to work–family conflict and job-related outcomes. *Journal of Management, 28*, 787–810.

Andrews, W., Twig, E., Minami, T., & Johnson, G. (2011). Piloting a practice research network: A 12-month evaluation of the Human Givens approach in primary care at a general medical practice. *Psychology and Psychotherapy: Theory, Research and Practice, 84*, 389–405. doi:10.1111/j.2044-8341.2010.02004.x

APA Center for Workforce Studies. (2009). *Doctorate employment survey.* Washington, DC: American Psychological Association.

APA Center for Workforce Studies. (2012). *2011 APA directory survey and employment update.* Washington, DC: American Psychological Association.

Arbona, C., & Coleman, N. (2008). Risk and resilience. In S. Brown & R. Lent (Eds.), *Handbook of counseling psychology* (4th ed., pp. 483–499). New York, NY: Wiley.

Arredondo, P., Toporek, R., Brown, S. P., Jones, J., Locke, D. C., Sanchez, J., & Stadler, H. (1996). Operationalization of the multicultural counseling competencies. *Journal of Multicultural Counseling and Development, 24*, 42–78. doi:10.1002/j.2161-1912.1996.tb00288.x

Arulmani, G. (2009). The internationalization of career counselling: Bridging cultural processes and labour market demands in India. *Asian Journal of Counselling, 16*, 149–170.

Association for Specialists in Group Work. (2007). *Best practice guidelines, 2007 revisions.* Alexandria, VA: Author.

Astin, H. S. (1984). The meaning of work in women's lives: A sociopsychological model of career choice and work behavior. *The Counseling Psychologist, 12*, 117–126. doi:10.1177/0011000084124002

Atkinson, D. R., & Lowe, S. (1995). The role of ethnicity, cultural knowledge, and conventional techniques in counseling and psychotherapy. In J. G. Ponterotto, J. M. Casas, L. A. Suzuki, & C. M. Alexander (Eds.), *Handbook of multicultural counseling* (pp. 387–414). Thousand Oaks, CA: Sage.

Audet, C., & Everall, R. D. (2003). Counsellor self-disclosure: Client-informed implications for practice. *Counselling and Psychotherapy Research, 3*, 223–231. doi:10.1080/14733140312331384392

Auletta, A. F., Salvatore, S., Metrangolo, R., Monteforte, G., Pace, V., & Puglisi, M. (2012). The grid of the models of interpretation (GMI): A trans-theoretical method to study therapist interpretive activity. *Journal of Psychotherapy Integration, 22*, 61–84. doi:10.1037/a0028009

Azrin, N. H., & Basalel, V. A. (1980). *Job Club counselor's manual: A behavioral approach to vocational counseling.* Baltimore, MD: University Park Press.

Baker, E. (1985). Psychoanalysis and psychoanalytic psychotherapy. In S. J. Lynn & J. P. Garske (Eds.), *Contemporary psychotherapy: Methods and models* (pp. 19–68). Columbus, OH: Merrill.

Bandura, A. (1969). *Principles of behavior modification.* New York, NY: Holt, Rinehart & Winston.

Bandura, A. (1977). *Social learning theory.* Englewood Cliffs, NJ: Prentice-Hall.

Bandura, A. (1986). *Social foundations of thought and action: A social cognitive theory.* Englewood Cliffs, NJ: Prentice-Hall.

Bandura, A. (1997). *Self-efficacy: The exercise of control.* New York, NY: Freeman.

Barak, A. (2003). Ethical and professional issues in career assessment on the Internet. *Journal of Career Assessment, 11*, 3–21. doi:10.1177/106907202237457

Barak, A., Shiloh, S., & Haushner, O. (1992). Modification of interests through cognitive restructuring: Test of a theoretical model in preschool children. *Journal of Counseling Psychology, 39*, 490–497. doi:10.1037/0022-0167.39.4.490

Barlett, D. L., & Steele, J. B. (2012). *The betrayal of the American dream.* New York, NY: Public Affairs.

Barlow, D. H. (2010). Negative effects from psychological treatments: A perspective. *American Psychologist, 65*, 13–20. doi:10.1037/a0015643

Barnett, J. E. (2008). The ethical practice of psychotherapy: Easily within our reach. *Journal of Clinical Psychology, 64*, 569–575. doi:10.1002/jclp.20473

Barnett, J. E., & Lorenc, S. (2003). APA's new ethics code: An update for psychologists. *The Maryland Psychologist, 48*(3), 1, 26.

Barnett, J. E., & O'Leary, M. (1997). Caveat emptor: Cautions for Internet use. *The Maryland Psychologist, 42*(7), 16–18.

Barnett, J. E., & Scheetz, K. (2003). Technological advances and telehealth: Ethics, law, and the practice of psychotherapy. *Psychotherapy: Theory, Research, Practice, Training, 40*, 86–93. doi:10.1037/0033-3204.40.1-2.86

Barnett, R. C., & Hyde, J. S. (2001). Women, men, work, and family. *American Psychologist, 56*, 781–796. doi:10.1037/0003-066X.56.10.781

Barrett-Lennard, G. T. (1962). Dimensions of therapist response as causal factors in therapeutic personality change. *Psychological Monographs, 76* (43, Whole No. 562).

Barrett-Lennard, G. T. (1986). The Relationship Inventory now: Issues and advances in theory, method, and uses. In L. Greenberg & W. Pinsoff (Eds.), *The psychotherapeutic process: A research handbook* (pp. 439–475). New York, NY: Guilford Press.

Barrett-Lennard, G. T. (1997). The recovery of empathy toward others and self. In A. C. Bohart & L. S. Greenberg (Eds.), *Empathy reconsidered: New directions in psychotherapy* (pp. 103–121). Washington, DC: American Psychological Association. doi:10.1037/10226-004

Barrick, M. R., Mount, M. K., & Gupta, R. (2003). Meta-analysis of the relationship between the five-factor model of personality and Holland's occupational types. *Personnel Psychology, 56*, 45–74. doi:10.1111/j.1744-6570.2003.tb00143.x

Barron, J. W. (1998). *Making diagnosis meaningful*. Washington, DC: American Psychological Association.

Bateman, A., & Fonagy, P. (2007). The use of transference in dynamic psychotherapy. *American Journal of Psychiatry, 164*, 680. doi:10.1176/appi.ajp.164.4.680

Bateson, G. (1972). *Steps in an ecology of mind*. New York, NY: Ballantine.

Bateson, G. (1979). *Mind and nature*. New York, NY: Dutton.

Beauchamp, T. L., & Childress, J. F. (1994). *Principles of biomedical ethics* (4th ed.). New York, NY: Oxford University Press.

Beauregard, T. A., Ozbilgin, M., & Belle, M. P. (2009). Revisiting the social construction of family in the context of work. *Journal of Managerial Psychology, 24*, 46–65. doi:10.1108/02683940910922537

Bechtoldt, H., Norcross, J. C., Wyckoff, L. A., Pokrywa, M. L., & Campbell, L. F. (2001). Theoretical orientations and employment settings of clinical and counseling psychologists: A comparative study. *The Clinical Psychologist, 54*(1), 3–6.

Beck, A. T. (1967). *Depression: Clinical, experimental, and theoretical aspects*. New York, NY: Hoeber.

Beck, A. T. (1976). *Cognitive therapy and the emotional disorders*. New York, NY: International Universities Press.

Beck, A. T., & Weishaar, M. E. (2011). Cognitive therapy. In R. J. Corsini & D. Wedding (Eds.), *Current psychotherapies* (9th ed., pp. 276–309). Belmont, CA: Brooks/Cole.

Becvar, D. S., & Becvar, R. S. (1993). *Family therapy: A systemic integration* (3rd ed.). Boston, MA: Allyn & Bacon.

Beers, C. W. (1908). *A mind that found itself*. Garden City, NY: Longman, Green.

Beidel, D. C., & Turner, S. M. (1998). *Shy children, phobic adults*. Washington, DC: American Psychological Association.

Belar, C. D., & Perry, N. W. (1992). National conference on scientist–practitioner education and training for the professional practice of psychology. *American Psychologist, 47*, 71–75. doi:10.1037/0003-066X.47.1.71

Belkin, G. S. (1980). *Contemporary psychotherapies*. Chicago, IL: Rand McNally.

Bell, M. E., & Goodman, L. A. (2006). Seeking social justice for victims of intimate partner violence: Real-world struggles in pursuit of systemic change. In R. L. Toporek, L. H. Gerstein, N. A. Fouad, G. Roysircar, & T. Israel (Eds.), *Handbook for social justice in counseling psychology: Leadership, vision, and action* (pp. 155–169). Thousand Oaks, CA: Sage. doi:10.4135/9781412976220.n12

Benishek, L. A., Bieschke, K. J., Park, J., & Slattery, S. M. (2004). A multicultural feminist model of mentoring. *Journal of Multicultural Counseling and Development, 32*, 428–442.

Benjamin, A. (1987). *The helping interview.* Boston, MA: Houghton Mifflin.

Bennett, V. C. (1985). School psychology. In E. M. Altmaier & M. E. Meyer (Eds.), *Applied specialties in psychology* (pp. 129–144). New York, NY: Random House.

Bennett-Levy, J. (2003). Mechanisms of change in cognitive therapy: The case of automatic thought records and behavioural experiments. *Behavioural and Cognitive Psychotherapy, 31*, 261–277. doi:10.1017/ S1352465803003035

Berg, I. A., Pepinsky, H. B., & Shoben, E. J. (1980). The status of counseling psychology: 1960. In J. Whiteley (Ed.), *The history of counseling psychology* (pp. 105–113). Monterey, CA: Brooks/Cole.

Berg, L. K., & de Shazer, S. (1993). Making numbers talk: Language in therapy. In S. Friedman (Ed.), *The new language of change* (pp. 5–25). New York, NY: Guilford Press.

Bergin, A. E., & Garfield, S. L. (1971). *Handbook of psychotherapy and behavior change.* New York, NY: Wiley.

Bernstein, B. L., & Kerr, B. (1993). Counseling psychology and the scientist-practitioner model: Implementation and implications. *Counseling Psychologist, 21*, 136–151.

Bersoff, D. N. (2008). *Ethical conflicts in psychology* (4th ed.). Washington, DC: American Psychological Association.

Betz, N. E. (2006). Basic issues and concepts in the career development and counseling of women. In W. B. Walsh & M. J. Heppner (Eds.), *Handbook of career counseling for women* (2nd ed., pp. 45–74). Mahwah, NJ: Erlbaum.

Betz, N. E. (2008). Advances in vocational theories. In S. D. Brown & R. W. Lent (Eds.), *Handbook of counseling psychology* (4th ed., pp. 357–374). Hoboken, NJ: Wiley.

Betz, N. E., Borgen, F. H., & Harmon, L. W. (2006). Vocational confidence and personality in the prediction of occupational group membership. *Journal of Career Assessment, 14*, 36–55. doi:10.1177/ 1069072705282434

Betz, N. E., Borgen, F. H., Rottinghaus, P., Paulsen, A., Halper, C. R., & Harmon, L. W. (2003). The expanded Skills Confidence Inventory: Measuring basic dimensions of vocational activity. *Journal of Vocational Behavior, 62*, 76–100. doi:10.1016/S0001-8791(02)00034-9

Betz, N. E., & Fitzgerald, L. F. (1987). *The career psychology of women*. New York, NY: Academic Press.

Betz, N. E., & Gwilliam, L. R. (2002). The utility of measures of self-efficacy for the Holland themes for African American and European American college students. *Journal of Career Assessment, 10*, 283–300. doi:10.1177/10672702010003001

Beutler, L. E., & Berren, M. (Eds.). (1995). *Integrative assessment of adult personality*. New York, NY: Guilford Press.

Beutler, L. E., Harwood, T. M., Michelson, A., Song, X., & Holman, J. (2011). Resistance/reactance level. *Journal of Clinical Psychology, 67*, 133–142. doi:10.1002/jclp.20753

Beutler, L. E., Rocco, F., Moleiro, C. M., & Talebi, H. (2001). Resistance. *Psychotherapy: Theory, Practice, Research, Training, 38*, 431–436. doi:10.1037/0033-3204.38.4.431

Bieschke, K. J., & Toepfer-Hendey, E. (2006). Career counseling with lesbian clients. In W. B. Walsh & M. J. Heppner (Eds.), *Handbook of career counseling for women* (2nd ed., pp. 351–385). Mahwah, NJ: Erlbaum.

Biggs, P., & Blocher, D. (1987). *Foundations of ethical counseling*. New York, NY: Springer.

Bingham, R. P., & Ward, C. M. (1996). Practical applications of career counseling with ethnic minority women. In M. L. Savickas & W. B. Walsh (Eds.), *Handbook of counseling theory and practice* (pp. 291–314). Palo Alto, CA: Davies-Black.

Bion, W. R. (1961). *Experiences in groups*. New York, NY: Basic Books. doi:10.4324/9780203359075

Bischoff, M. M., & Tracey, T. J. G. (1995). Client resistance as predicted by therapist behavior: A study of sequential dependence. *Journal of Counseling Psychology, 42*, 487–495. doi:10.1037/0022-0167.42.4.487

Blaine, B., & McElroy, J. (2002). Selling stereotypes: Weight loss infomercials, sexism, and weightism. *Sex Roles, 46*, 351–357. doi:10.1023/A:1020284731543

Blair, L. (2010). A critical review of the scientist-practitioner model for counselling psychology. *Counselling Psychology Review, 25*, 19–30.

Blais, M. A., Malone, J. C., Stein, M. B., Slavin-Mulford, J., O'Keefe, S., Renna, M., & Sinclair, S. J. (2013). Treatment as usual (TAU) for depression: A comparison of psychotherapy, pharmacotherapy, and combined treatment at a large academic medical center. *Psychotherapy, 50*, 110–118. doi:10.1037/a0031385

Blatt, S. (1995). Why the gap between psychotherapy research and clinical practice: A response to Barry Wolfe. *Journal of Psychotherapy Integration, 5*, 73–76.

Blocher, D. H. (1966). *Developmental counseling*. New York, NY: Ronald Press.

Blocher, D. H. (1974). *Developmental counseling* (2nd ed.). New York, NY: Ronald Press.

Blustein, D. L. (2001). Extending the reach of vocational psychology: Toward an integrative and inclusive psychology of work. *Journal of Vocational Behavior, 59*, 171–182. doi:10.1006/jvbe.2001.1823

Blustein, D. L. (2006). *The psychology of working: A new perspective for career development, counseling, and public policy.* Mahwah, NJ: Erlbaum.

Blustein, D. L., Chaves, A. P., Diemer, M. A., Gallagher, L. A., Marshall, K. G., Sirin, S., & Bhati, K. S. (2002). Voices of the forgotten half: The role of social class in the school-to-work transition. *Journal of Counseling Psychology, 49*, 311–323. doi:10.1037/0022-0167.49.3.311

Blustein, D. L., Murphy, K. A., Kenny, M. E., Jernigan, M., Perez-Gualdron, L., Castaneda, T., . . . Davis, O. (2010). Exploring urban students' constructions about school, work, race, and ethnicity. *Journal of Counseling Psychology, 57*, 248–254. doi:10.1037/a0018939

Blustein, D. L., & Spengler, P. M. (1995). Personal adjustment: Career counseling and psychotherapy. In W. B. Walsh & S. H. Osipow (Eds.), *Handbook of vocational psychology* (2nd ed., pp. 295–329). Hillsdale, NJ: Erlbaum.

Bobek, B. L., Robbins, S. B., Gore, P. A., Harris-Bowlsbey, J., Lapan, R. T., Dahir, C. A., & Jepsen, P. A. (2005). Training counselors to use computer-assisted career guidance systems more effectively: A model curriculum. *Career Development Quarterly, 53*, 363–371. doi:10.1002/j.2161-0045.2005.tb00667.x

Bogat, G. A., & Redner, R. L. (1985). How mentoring affects the professional development of women in psychology. *Professional Psychology: Research and Practice, 16*, 851–859. doi:10.1037/0735-7028.16.6.851

Boggs, K. R., & Douce, L. A. (2000). Current status and anticipated changes in psychology internships: Effects on counseling psychology training. *Counseling Psychologist, 28*, 672–686. doi:10.1177/0011000000285005

Bohart, A. C. (2000). Paradigm clash: Empirically supported treatments versus empirically supported psychotherapy practice. *Psychotherapy Research, 10*, 488–493. doi:10.1080/713663783

Bohart, A. C., & Tallman, K. (2010). Clients: The neglected common factor in psychotherapy. In B. L. Duncan, S. D. Miller, B. E. Wampold, & M. A. Hubble (Eds.), *The heart and soul of change: Delivering what works in therapy* (2nd ed., pp. 83–111). Washington, DC: American Psychological Association. doi:10.1037/12075-003

Bolles, R. N. (2013). *What color is your parachute?* Berkeley, CA: Ten Speed Press.

Bonitz, V. (2008). The use of physical touch in the "talking cure": A journey to the outskirts of psychotherapy. *Psychotherapy: Theory, Research, Practice, Training, 45*, 391–404. doi:10.1037/a0013311

Bonney, W. C. (1969). Group counseling and developmental processes. In G. M. Gazda (Ed.), *Theories and methods of group counseling in the schools* (pp. 157–180). Springfield, IL: Thomas.

Borders, L. D., Fong-Beyette, M. L., & Cron, E. A. (1988). In-session cognitions of a counseling student: A case study. *Counselor Education and Supervision, 28,* 59–70. doi:10.1002/j.1556-6978.1988.tb00788.x

Bordin, E. S. (1979). The generalizability of the psychoanalytic concept of the working alliance. *Psychotherapy: Theory, Research and Practice, 16,* 252–260. doi:10.1037/h0085885

Bordin, E. S., & Bixler, R. S. (1946). Test selection: A process of counseling. *Educational and Psychological Measurement, 6,* 361–373. doi:10.1177/001316444600600306

Borgen, F. H. (1984). Counseling psychology. *Annual Review of Psychology, 35,* 579–604. doi:10.1146/annurev.ps.35.020184.003051

Borgen, F. H. (1991). Megatrends and milestones in vocational behavior: A 20-year counseling psychology retrospective. *Journal of Vocational Behavior, 39,* 263–290. doi:10.1016/0001-8791(91)90037-M

Borgen, F. H. (1992). Expanding scientific paradigms in counseling psychology. In S. D. Brown & R. W. Lent (Eds.), *Handbook of counseling psychology* (pp. 111–130). New York, NY: Wiley.

Borkovec, T. D., Echemendia, R. J., Ragusea, S. A., & Ruiz, M. (2001). The Pennsylvania Practice Research Network and future possibilities for clinically meaningful and scientifically rigorous psychotherapy effectiveness research. *Clinical Psychology: Science and Practice, 8,* 155–167. doi:10.1093/clipsy.8.2.155

Borkovec, T. D., & Sibrava, N. J. (2005). Problems with the use of placebo conditions in psychotherapy research, suggested alternatives, and some strategies for the pursuit of the placebo phenomenon. *Journal of Clinical Psychology, 61,* 805–818. doi:10.1002/jclp.20127

Boswell, J. F., Nelson, D. L., Nordberg, S. S., McAleavey, A. A., & Castonguay, L. G. (2010). Competency in integrative psychotherapy: Perspectives on training and supervision. *Psychotherapy: Theory, Practice, Research, Training, 47,* 3–11. doi:10.1037/a0018848

Botta, R. A. (2003). For your health? The relationship between magazine reading and adolescents' body image and eating disturbances. *Sex Roles, 48,* 389–399. doi:10.1023/A:1023570326812

Bova, B. M., & Phillips, R. R. (1982, November). *The mentoring relationship as an educational experience.* Paper presented at the national conference of the Adult Education Association of the United States of America, San Antonio, TX. (ERIC Document Reproduction Service, No. ED224 944)

Bowen, M. (1966). The use of family theory in clinical practice. *Comprehensive Psychiatry, 7,* 345–374. doi:10.1016/S0010-440X(66)80065-2

Bowen, M. (1976). Theory in the practice of psychotherapy. In P. Guerin (Ed.), *Family therapy* (pp. 42–89). New York, NY: Gardner Press.

Bowen, M. (1978). *Family therapy in clinical practice.* New York, NY: Aronson.

Bowlby, J. (1973). *Attachment and loss: Vol. 2. Separation.* London, England: Hogarth Press.

Bowman, G. D., & Stern, M. (1995). Adjustment to occupational stress: The relationship of perceived control to effectiveness of coping strategies. *Journal of Counseling Psychology, 42,* 294–303. doi:10.1037/0022-0167.42.3.294

Bozarth, J. D. (1984). Beyond reflection: Emergent modes of empathy. In R. F. Levant & J. M. Shlien (Eds.), *Client-centered therapy and the person-centered approach* (pp. 59–75). New York, NY: Praeger.

Bozarth, J. D. (1990). The essence of client-centered therapy. In G. Lietaer, J. Rombouts, & R. Van Balen (Eds.), *Client-centered and experiential psychotherapy in the nineties* (pp. 59–64). Leuven, Belgium: Leuven University Press.

Bozarth, J. D. (1997). Empathy from the framework of client-centered theory and the Rogerian hypothesis. In A. C. Bohart & L. S. Greenberg (Eds.), *Empathy reconsidered: New directions in psychotherapy* (pp. 81–102). Washington, DC: American Psychological Association. doi:10.1037/10226-003

Brabeck, M., Walsh, M. E., Kenny, M., & Comilang, K. (1997). Interprofessional collaboration for children and families: Opportunities for counseling psychology in the 21st century. *Counseling Psychologist, 25,* 615–636. doi:10.1177/0011000097254006

Brady, J. P. (1980). Some views on effective principles of psychotherapy. *Cognitive Therapy and Research, 4,* 271–306.

Brammer, L., & Shostrom, E. (1977). *Therapeutic psychology: Fundamentals of counseling and psychotherapy* (3rd ed.). Englewood Cliffs, NJ: Prentice-Hall.

Brammer, L. M., & Abrego, P. J. (1981). Intervention strategy for coping with transitions. *Counseling Psychologist, 9*(2), 19–36. doi:10.1177/001100008100900203

Brammer, L. M., Abrego, P. J., & Shostrom, E. L. (1993). *Therapeutic counseling and psychotherapy* (6th ed.). Englewood Cliffs, NJ: Prentice-Hall.

Brammer, L. M., & MacDonald, G. (1996). *The helping relationship: Process and skills* (6th ed.). Boston, MA: Allyn & Bacon.

Braunstein-Bercovitz, H., Benjamin, B. A., Asor, S., & Lev, M. (2012). Insecure attachment and career indecision: Mediating effects of anxiety and pessimism. *Journal of Vocational Behavior, 81,* 236–244. doi:10.1016/j.jvb.2012.07.009

Brenner, C. (1973). *An elementary textbook of psychoanalysis.* New York, NY: International Universities Press.

Breuer, J., & Freud, S. (1955). *Studies on hysteria. The standard edition of the complete works of Sigmund Freud* (Vol. 2, pp. 1–305). London, England: Hogarth Press. (Original work published 1895)

Brinson, J. A., & Kottler, J. A. (1995). Minorities' underutilization of counseling centers' mental health services: A case for outreach and consultation. *Journal of Mental Health Counseling, 17,* 371–385.

Brown, D., Brooks, L., & Associates. (1990). *Career choice and development* (2nd ed.). San Francisco, CA: Jossey-Bass.

Brown, D., Brooks, L., & Associates. (1996). *Career choice and development* (3rd ed.). San Francisco, CA: Jossey-Bass.

Brown, L. S. (1994). *Subversive dialogues: Theory in feminist therapy.* New York, NY: Basic Books.

Brown, L. S. (1995). Cultural diversity in feminist therapy: Theory and practice. In H. Landrine (Ed.), *Bringing cultural diversity to feminist psychology: Theory, research, and practice* (pp. 143–161). Washington, DC: American Psychological Association. doi:10.1037/10501-007

Brown, L. S. (2000). Discomforts of the powerless: Feminist constructions of distress. In R. A. Neimeyer & J. D. Raskin (Eds.), *Constructions of disorder: Meaning-making frameworks for psychotherapy* (pp. 287–308). Washington, DC: American Psychological Association. doi:10.1037/10368-012

Brown, L. S. (2008). *Cultural competence in trauma therapy: Beyond the flashback.* Washington, DC: American Psychological Association. doi:10.1037/11752-000

Brown, L. S. (2009). Cultural competence: A new way of thinking about integration in therapy. *Journal of Psychotherapy Integration, 19,* 340–353. doi:10.1037/a0017967

Brown, L. S. (2013). Compassion amidst oppression: Increasing cultural competence for managing difficult dialogues in psychotherapy. In A. W. Wolf, M. R. Goldfried, & J. C. Muran (Eds.), *Transforming negative reactions to clients: From frustration to compassion* (pp. 139–158). Washington, DC: American Psychological Association. doi:10.1037/13940-006

Brown, M. T., & Landrum-Brown, J. (1995). Counselor supervision: Cross-cultural perspectives. In J. G. Ponterotto, J. M. Casas, L. A. Suzuki, & C. M. Alexander (Eds.), *Handbook of multicultural counseling* (pp. 263–286). Thousand Oaks, CA: Sage.

Brown, S. D., & Lent, R. W. (1984). *Handbook of counseling psychology.* New York, NY: Wiley.

Brown, S. D., & Lent, R. W. (Eds.). (2005). *Career development and counseling: Putting theory and research to work.* Hoboken, NJ: Wiley.

Brown, S. D., & Rector, C. C. (2008). Conceptualizing and diagnosing problems in vocational decision making. In S. D. Brown & R. W. Lent (Eds.), *Handbook of counseling psychology* (4th ed., pp. 392–407). Hoboken, NJ: Wiley.

Brown, S. D., Ryan Krane, N. E., Brecheisen, J., Castelino, P., Budisin, I., Miller, M., & Edens, L. (2003). Critical ingredients of career choice interventions: More analyses and new hypotheses. *Journal of Vocational Behavior, 62,* 411–428. doi:10.1016/S0001-8791(02)00052-0

Brown, T. (2002). A proposed model of bisexual identity development that elaborates on experiential differences of women and men. *Journal of Bisexuality, 2,* 67–91. doi:10.1300/J159v02n04_05

Browne, A. (1993). Violence against women by male partners: Prevalence, outcomes, and policy implications. *American Psychologist, 48,* 1077–1087. doi:10.1037/0003-066X.48.10.1077

Bruce, N., Shapiro, S. L., Constantino, M. J., & Manber, R. (2010). Psychotherapist mindfulness and the psychotherapist process. *Psychotherapy: Theory, Research, Practice, Training, 47,* 83–97. doi:10.1037/a0018842

Buki, L. P., & Selem, M. (2012). Health disparities: Issues and opportunities for counseling psychologists. In N. A. Fouad, J. A. Carter, & L. M. Subich (Eds.), *APA handbook of counseling psychology: Vol. 2. Practice, interventions, and applications* (pp. 235–251). Washington, DC: American Psychological Association. doi:10.1037/13755-010

Bullock-Yowell, E., Peterson, G. W., Reardon, R. C., Leierer, S. J., & Reed, C. A. (2011). Relationships among career and life stress, negative career thoughts, and career decision state: A cognitive information processing perspective. *Career Development Quarterly, 59,* 302–314. doi:10.1002/j.2161-0045.2011.tb00071.x

Bureau of Labor Statistics, U. S. Department of Labor. (2010). Earnings and employment by occupation, race, ethnicity, and sex. Retrieved from http://www.bls.gov/opub/ted/2011/ted_20110914.htm

Burkard, A. W., Ponterotto, J. G., Reynolds, A. L., & Alfonso, V. C. (1999). White counselor trainees' racial identity and working alliance perceptions. *Journal of Counseling & Development, 77,* 324–329. doi:10.1002/j.1556-6676.1999.tb02455.x

Burke, J. F. (1989). *Contemporary approaches to psychotherapy and counseling: The self-regulation and maturity model.* Pacific Grove, CA: Brooks/Cole.

Burlingame, G. M., & McClendon, D. T. (2008). Group therapy. In J. Lebow (Ed.), *Twenty-first century psychotherapies: Contemporary approaches to theory and practice* (pp. 347–388). New York, NY: Wiley.

Burlingame, G. M., Strauss, B., & Joyce, A. S. (2013). Change mechanisms and effectiveness in small group treatments. In M. J. Lambert (Ed.), *Bergin and Garfield's handbook of psychotherapy and behavior change* (6th ed., pp. 640–689). New York, NY: Wiley.

Burton, N. E., & Wang, M. (2005). *Predicting long-term success in graduate school: A collaborative validity study* (GRE Board Research Report No. 99-14R). Princeton, NJ: Educational Testing Service.

Butcher, J. (Ed.). (2005). *MMPI–2: A practitioner's guide.* Washington, DC: American Psychological Association.

Butcher, J. N. (2011). *A beginner's guide to the MMPI–2* (3rd ed.). Washington, DC: American Psychological Association.

Butler, G., Fennell, M., & Hackmann, A. (2008). *Cognitive-behavioral therapy for anxiety disorders.* New York, NY: Guilford Press.

Byars-Winston, A. M., & Fouad, N. A. (2006). Metacognition and multicultural competence: Expanding the culturally appropriate career counseling model. *Career Development Quarterly, 54*, 187–201. doi:10.1002/j.2161-0045.2006.tb00151.x

Byron, K. (2005). A meta-analytic review of work–family conflict and its antecedents. *Journal of Vocational Behavior, 67*, 169–198. doi:10.1016/j.jvb.2004.08.009

Cade, B., & O'Hanlon, W. (1993). *A brief guide to brief therapy.* New York, NY: Norton.

Caldwell, J. C., & Vera, E. (2010). Critical incidents in counseling psychology: Professionals and trainees' social justice development. *Training and Education in Professional Psychology, 4*, 163–176. doi:10.1037/a0019093

Campbell, D. T., & Fiske, D. W. (1959). Convergent and discriminant validation by the multitrait–multimethod matrix. *Psychological Bulletin, 56*, 81–105. doi:10.1037/h0046016

Campbell, T. C., & Durrah, D. (2012). Homelessness: An unnatural disaster. In N. A. Fouad, J. C. Carter, & L. M. Subich (Eds.), *APA handbook of counseling psychology: Vol. 2. Practice, interventions, and applications* (pp. 285–303). Washington, DC: American Psychological Association.

Carlson, D. S. (1999). Personality and role variables as predictors of three forms of work–family conflict. *Journal of Vocational Behavior, 55*, 236–253. doi:10.1006/jvbe.1999.1680

Carmichael, S., & Hamilton, C. (1967). *Black power: The politics of liberation.* New York, NY: Vintage.

Carroll, L. (2001). *Alice's adventures in wonderland.* London, England: Macmillan. (Original work published 1865)

Carroll, L., Gilroy, P. J., & Ryan, J. (2002). Counseling transgendered, transsexual, and gender-variant clients. *Journal of Counseling & Development, 80*, 131–139. doi:10.1002/j.1556-6678.2002.tb00175.x

Carter, B., & McGoldrick, M. (Eds.). (2005). *The expanded family life cycle: Individual, family, and social perspectives.* Boston, MA: Allyn & Bacon.

Carter, J. A. (2006). Theoretical pluralism and technical eclecticism. In C. D. Goodheart, A. E. Kazdin, & R. J. Sternberg (Eds.), *Evidence-based psychotherapy: Where practice and research meet* (pp. 63–79). Washington, DC: American Psychological Association. doi:10.1037/11423-003

Carter, J. A., & Goodheart, C. D. (2012). Interventions and evidence in counseling and psychology: A view on evidence-based practice. In N. A. Fouad, J. A. Carter, & L. M. Subich (Eds.), *APA handbook of counseling psychology: Vol. 1. Theories, research, and methods* (pp. 155–166). Washington, DC: American Psychological Association. doi:10.1037/13754-006

Carter, R. T., & Forsyth, J. (2010). Reactions to racial discrimination: Emotional stress and help-seeking behaviors. *Psychological Trauma: Theory, Research, Practice, and Policy, 2*, 183–191. doi:10.1037/a0020102

Carter, R. T., & Qureshi, A. (1995). A typology of philosophical assumptions in multicultural counseling and training. In J. G. Ponterotto, J. M. Casas, L. A. Suzuki, & C. M. Alexander (Eds.), *Handbook of multicultural counseling* (pp. 239–262). Thousand Oaks, CA: Sage.

Cartwright, B. Y., Daniels, J., & Zhang, S. (2008). Assessing multicultural competence: Perceived versus demonstrated performance. *Journal of Counseling & Development, 86*, 318–322. doi:10.1002/j.1556-6678.2008.tb00515.x

Cass, V. C. (1979). Homosexuality identity formation: A theoretical model. *Journal of Homosexuality, 4*, 219–235. doi:10.1300/J082v04n03_01

Castonguay, L. G. (2011). Psychotherapy, psychopathology, research and practice: Pathways of connections and integration. *Psychotherapy Research, 21*, 125–140. doi:10.1080/10503307.2011.563250

Castonguay, L. G., Boswell, J. F., Constantino, M. J., Goldfried, M. R., & Hill, C. E. (2010). Training implications of harmful effects of psychological treatments. *American Psychologist, 65*, 34–49. doi:10.1037/a0017330

Castonguay, L. G., Boswell, J. F., Zack, S. E., Baker, S., Boutselis, M. A., Chiswick, N. R., . . . Holtforth, M. G. (2010). Helpful and hindering events in psychotherapy: A practice research network study. *Psychotherapy: Theory, Research, Practice, Training, 47*, 327–344. doi:10.1037/a0021164

Castonguay, L. G., Locke, B. D., & Hayes, J. A. (2011). The Center for Collegiate Mental Health: An example of a practice-research network in university counseling centers. *Journal of College Student Psychotherapy, 25*, 105–119. doi:10.1080/87568225.2011.556929

Cattell, R. B. (1973). The measurement of the healthy personality and the healthy society. *Counseling Psychologist, 4*(2), 13–18. doi:10.1177/001100007300400205

Chambless, D. L. (1996). In defense of dissemination of empirically supported psychological interventions. *Clinical Psychology: Science and Practice, 3*, 230–235.

Chambless, D. L., & Ollendick, T. H. (2001). Empirically supported psychological interventions: Controversies and evidence. *Annual Review of Psychology, 52*, 685–716. doi:10.1146/annurev.psych.52.1.685

Chao, R. C. (2012). Racial/ethnic identity, gender-role attitudes, and multicultural counseling competence: The role of multicultural counseling training. *Journal of Counseling & Development, 90*, 35–44. doi:10.1111/j.1556-6676.2012.00006.x

Chao, R. C.-L., Wei, M., Good, G. E., & Flores, L. Y. (2011). Race/ethnicity, color-blind racial attitudes, and multicultural counseling competence: The moderating effects of multicultural counseling training. *Journal of Counseling Psychology, 58*, 72–82. doi:10.1037/a0022091

Charles, S. T., & Carstensen, L. L. (2010). Social emotional aging. *Annual Review of Psychology, 61*, 383–409. doi:10.1146/annurev.psych.093008.100448

Chesir-Teran, D. (2003). Conceptualizing and assessing heterosexism in high schools: A setting-level approach. *American Journal of Community Psychology, 31*, 267–279. doi:10.1023/A:1023910820994

Cheung, F. K., & Snowden, L. R. (1990). Community mental health and ethnic minority populations. *Community Mental Health Journal, 26*, 277–291. doi:10.1007/BF00752778

Chien, J.-C., Fischer, J. M., & Biller, E. (2006). Evaluating a metacognitive and planned happenstance career training course for Taiwanese college students. *Journal of Employment Counseling, 43*, 146–153. doi:10.1002/j.2161-1920.2006.tb00014.x

Chin, J. L. (Ed.). (2004). *The psychology of prejudice and discrimination: Vol. 3. Bias based on gender and sexual orientation.* Westport, CT: Praeger.

Chodorow, N. J. (1978). *The reproduction of mothering.* Berkeley: University of California Press.

Chope, R. C. (2012). Career counseling. In E. M. Altmaier & J. C. Hansen (Eds.), *The Oxford handbook of counseling psychology* (pp. 545–569). New York, NY: Oxford University Press.

Christensen, A., & Alexander, J. F. (2000). *Reconcilable differences.* New York, NY: Wiley.

Chronister, K. M., & Aldarondo, E. (2012). Partner violence victimization and perpetration: Developmental and contextual implications for effective practice. In N. A. Fouad, J. C. Carter, & L. M. Subich (Eds.), *APA handbook of counseling psychology: Vol. 2. Practice, interventions, and applications* (pp. 125–151). Washington, DC: American Psychological Association. doi:10.1037/13755-006

Chung, R. C., Bemak, F., Ortiz, D. P., & Sandoval-Perez, P. A. (2008). Promoting the mental health of immigrants: A multicultural/social justice perspective. *Journal of Counseling & Development, 86*, 310–317. doi:10.1002/j.1556-6678.2008.tb00514.x

Chung, Y. B. (2003). Career counseling with lesbian, gay, bisexual, and transgendered persons: The next decade. *Career Development Quarterly, 52*, 78–86. doi:10.1002/j.2161-0045.2003.tb00630.x

Chung, Y. B., & Singh, A. A. (2009). Lesbian, gay, bisexual, and transgender Asian Americans. In N. Tewari & A. N. Alvarez (Eds.), *Asian American psychology: Current perspectives* (pp. 233–246). New York, NY: Psychology Press.

Chung, Y. B., Szymanski, D. M., & Markle, E. (2012). Sexual orientation and sexual identity: Theory, research, and practice. In N. A. Fouad, J. C. Carter, & L. M. Subich (Eds.), *APA handbook of counseling psychology: Vol. 1. Theories, research, and methods* (pp. 423–451). Washington, DC: American Psychological Association. doi:10.1037/13754-016

Chwalisz, K. (2006). Statistical versus clinical prediction: From assessment to psychotherapy process and outcome. *The Counseling Psychologist, 34*, 391–399. doi:10.1177/0011000005285878

Chwalisz, K. (2012). Counseling health psychology: Applications. In N. A. Fouad, J. C. Carter, & L. M. Subich (Eds.), *APA handbook of counseling psychology: Vol. 2. Practice, interventions, and applications* (pp. 205–234). Washington, DC: American Psychological Association.

Chwalisz, K., & Obasi, E. (2008). Promoting health and preventing and reducing disease. In S. Brown & R. Lent (Eds.), *Handbook of counseling psychology* (4th ed., pp. 517–534). New York, NY: Wiley.

Claiborn, C. D., & Lichtenberg, J. W. (1989). Interactional counseling. *Counseling Psychologist, 17*, 355–453. doi:10.1177/0011000089173001

Coalition for an Ethical Psychology. (2010). *A call for annulment of the APA's PENS report.* Retrieved from http://ethicalpsychology.org/pens/

Cohen, L. H., Sargent, M. M., & Sechrest, L. B. (1986). Use of psychotherapy research by professional psychologists. *American Psychologist, 41*, 198–206. doi:10.1037/0003-066X.41.2.198

Cokley, K. O. (2002). Testing Cross's revised racial identity model: An examination of the relationship between racial identity and internalized racism. *Journal of Counseling Psychology, 49*, 476–483. doi:10.1037/0022-0167.49.4.476

Cokley, K. O. (2003). What do we know about the motivation of African American students? Challenging the "anti-intellectual" myth. *Harvard Educational Review, 73*, 524–558.

Cole, E. R. (2009). Intersectionality and research in psychology. *American Psychologist, 64*, 170–180. doi:10.1037/a0014564

Coleman, E. (1982). Developmental stages of the coming out process. *Journal of Homosexuality, 7*, 31–43. doi:10.1300/J082v07n02_06

Coleman, H. L. K. (1995). Strategies for coping with cultural diversity. *The Counseling Psychologist, 23*, 722–740. doi:10.1177/0011000095234011

Coleman, H. L. K. (1998). General and multicultural counseling competency: Apples and oranges? *Journal of Multicultural Counseling and Development, 26*, 147–156. doi:10.1002/j.2161-1912.1998.tb00194.x

Collins, A., Gelso, C. J., Kimball, R., & Sedlacek, W. E. (1973). Evaluation of a counseling center innovation. *Journal of College Student Personnel, 14*, 144–148.

Collins, L. H. (2007). Practicing safer listserv use: Ethical use of an invaluable resource. *Professional Psychology: Research and Practice, 38*, 690–698. doi:10.1037/0735-7028.38.6.690

Comas-Díaz, L., & Greene, B. (Eds.). (1994). *Women of color: Integrating ethnic and gender identities in psychotherapy.* New York, NY: Guilford Press.

Connolly Gibbons, M. B., Thompson, S. M., Scott, K., Schauble, L. A., Mooney, T., Thompson, D., . . . Crits-Christoph, P. (2012). Supportive-expressive dynamic psychotherapy in the community mental health system: A pilot effectiveness trial for the treatment of depression. *Psychotherapy, 49*, 303–316. doi:10.1037/a0027694

Constantine, M. G. (1997). Facilitating multicultural competency in counseling supervision. In D. B. Pope-Davis & H. L. K. Coleman (Eds.), *Multicultural counseling competencies* (pp. 310–324). Thousand Oaks, CA: Sage.

Constantine, M. G., Fuertes, J. N., Roysircar, G., & Kindaichi, M. M. (2008). Multicultural competence: Clinical practice, training and supervision, and research. In W. B. Walsh (Ed.), *Biennial review of counseling psychology* (Vol. 1, pp. 97–127). New York, NY: Routledge.

Constantine, M. G., & Ladany, N. (2001). New visions for defining and assessing multicultural counseling competence. In J. G. Ponterotto, J. M. Casas, L. A. Suzuki, & C. M. Alexander (Eds.), *Handbook of multicultural counseling* (2nd ed., pp. 482–498). Thousand Oaks, CA: Sage.

Constantine, M. G., & Sue, D. W. (2006). Factors contributing to optimal human functioning in people of color in the United States. *Counseling Psychologist, 34*, 228–244. doi:10.1177/0011000005281318

Constantine, M. G., & Sue, D. W. (2007). Perceptions of racial microaggressions among Black supervisees in cross-racial dyads. *Journal of Counseling Psychology, 54*, 142–153. doi:10.1037/0022-0167.54.2.142

Coogan, P. A., & Chen, C. P. (2007). Career development and counselling for women: Connecting theories to practice. *Counselling Psychology Quarterly, 20*, 191–204. doi:10.1080/09515070701391171

Cook, D. A., & Helms, J. E. (1988). Relationship dimensions as predictors of visible racial/ethnic group students' perceptions of cross-racial supervision. *Journal of Counseling Psychology, 35*, 268–274. doi:10.1037/0022-0167.35.3.268

Cook, T. D., & Campbell, D. T. (1979). *Quasi-experimentation: Design and analysis for field settings.* Chicago, IL: Rand-McNally.

Cooper, M. (2008). *Essential research findings in counselling and psychotherapy: The facts are friendly.* Thousand Oaks, CA: Sage.

Cooper, M., O'Hara, M., Schmid, P. F., & Wyatt, G. (Eds.). (2007). *The handbook of person-centered psychotherapy and counseling.* New York, NY: Palgrave Macmillan.

Cooper, S. E., & Shullman, S. L. (2012). Counseling psychologists as consultants. In E. M. Altmaier & J. C. Hansen (Eds.), *The Oxford handbook of counseling psychology* (pp. 837–855). New York, NY: Oxford University Press.

Copeland, E. J. (1983). Cross-cultural counseling and psychotherapy: A historical perspective, implications for research and training. *Personnel and Guidance Journal, 62*, 10–15. doi:10.1111/j.2164-4918.1983.tb00108.x

Corazzini, J. G. (1997). Using research to determine the efficacy and modes of treatment in university counseling centers. *Journal of Counseling Psychology, 44*, 378–380. doi:10.1037/0022-0167.44.4.378

Corey, G. (2008). *Theory and practice of group counseling* (7th ed.). Pacific Grove, CA: Brooks/Cole.

Corey, G., Corey, M. S., & Callanan, P. (1979). *Professional and ethical issues in counseling and psychotherapy.* Monterey, CA: Brooks/Cole.

Corey, G., Williams, G. T., & Moline, M. E. (1995). Ethical and legal issues in group counseling. *Ethics and Behavior, 5,* 161–183.

Corey, M., Corey, G., & Corey, C. (2010). *Groups: Process and practice* (8th ed.). Pacific Grove, CA: Brooks/Cole.

Corey, M. S., & Corey, G. (1989). *Becoming a helper.* Belmont, CA: Wadsworth.

Coster, J. S., & Schwebel, M. (1997). Well-functioning in professional psychologists. *Professional Psychology: Research and Practice, 28,* 5–13. doi:10.1037/0735-7028.28.1.5

Costigan, C. L., Koryzma, C., Hua, J. M., & Chance, L. J. (2010). Ethnic identity, achievement, and psychological adjustment: Examining risk and resilience among youth from immigrant Chinese families in Canada. *Cultural Diversity and Ethnic Minority Psychology, 16,* 264–273. doi:10.1037/a0017275

Cottone, R. R., & Clause, R. E. (2000). Ethical decision-making models: A review of the literature. *Journal of Counseling & Development, 78,* 275–283. doi:10.1002/j.1556-6676.2000.tb01908.x

Courtois, C. A. (1988). *Healing the incest wound: Adult survivors in therapy.* New York, NY: Norton.

Courtois, C. A. (2000). *Recollections of sexual abuse: Treatment principles and guidelines.* New York, NY: Norton.

Courtois, C. A. (2011). Retraumatization and complex traumatic stress: A treatment overview. In M. P. Duckworth & V. M. Follette (Eds.), *Retraumatization: Assessment, treatment, and prevention* (pp. 163–190). New York, NY: Routledge.

Courtois, C. A. (2012). Feminist multicultural counseling with traumatized individuals. In C. Z. Enns & E. N. Williams (Eds.), *The Oxford handbook of feminist multicultural counseling psychology* (pp. 373–391). New York, NY: Oxford University Press. doi:10.1093/oxfordhb/9780199744220.013.0020

Crawford, M., & Unger, R. (2004). *Women and gender: A feminist psychology* (4th ed.). New York, NY: McGraw-Hill.

Creed, P. A., Patton, W., & Bartrum, D. (2004). Internal and external barriers, cognitive style, and the career development variables of focus and indecision. *Journal of Career Development, 30,* 277–294. doi:10.1023/B:JOCD.0000025116.17855.ea

Crethar, H. C., Rivera, E. T., & Nash, S. (2008). In search of common threads: Linking multicultural, feminist, and social justice counseling paradigms. *Journal of Counseling & Development, 86,* 269–278. doi:10.1002/j.1556-6678.2008.tb00509.x

Crites, J. O. (1969). *Vocational psychology.* New York, NY: McGraw-Hill.

Crites, J. O. (1981). *Career counseling: Models, methods, and materials.* New York, NY: McGraw-Hill.

Crits-Christoph, P., & Barber, J. P. (Eds.). (1991). *Handbook of short-term dynamic psychotherapy*. New York, NY: Basic Books.

Crits-Christoph, P., Barber, J. P., & Kurcius, J. S. (1993). The accuracy of therapists' interpretations and the development of the therapeutic alliance. *Psychotherapy Research, 3*, 25–35. doi:10.1080/10503309312 331333639

Crits-Christoph, P., & Connolly Gibbons, M. B. (2001). Relational interpretations. *Psychotherapy: Theory, Practice, Research, Training, 38*, 423–428. doi:10.1037/0033-3204.38.4.423

Cross, W. E., Jr. (1971, July). The Negro-to-Black conversion experience: Toward a psychology of Black liberation. *Black World, 20*, 13–27.

Croteau, J. M., Bieschke, K. J., Fassinger, R. E., & Manning, J. L. (2008). Counseling psychology and sexual orientation: History, selective trends, and future directions. In S. D. Brown & R. W. Lent (Eds.), *Handbook of counseling psychology* (4th ed., pp. 194–211). Hoboken, NJ: Wiley.

Dana, R. H. (2000). *Handbook of cross-cultural and multicultural personality assessment*. Mahwah, NJ: Erlbaum.

Dana, R. H. (2005). *Multicultural assessment: Principles, applications, and examples*. New York, NY: Taylor & Francis.

D'Andrea, M. (2004). *Development of the Multicultural Counseling Assessment Survey Form I*. Honolulu: University of Hawaii at Manoa, Department of Counselor Education.

D'Andrea, M., Daniels, J., & Heck, R. (1991). Evaluating the impact of multicultural counseling training. *Journal of Counseling & Development, 70*, 143–150. doi:10.1002/j.1556-6676.1991.tb01576.x

D'Andrea, M., & Heckman, E. F. (2008). A 40-year review of multicultural outcome research: Outlining a future research agenda for the multicultural counseling movement. *Journal of Counseling & Development, 86*, 356–363. doi:10.1002/j.1556-6678.2008.tb00520.x

Datti, P. A. (2009). Applying social learning theory to career decision making in gay, lesbian, bisexual, transgender, and questioning young adults. *Career Development Quarterly, 58*, 54–64. doi:10.1002/j.2161-0045.2009.tb00173.x

Dattilio, F. M. (1993). Cognitive techniques with couples and families. *The Family Journal, 1*, 51–65. doi:10.1177/106648079300100108

Dattilio, F. M. (1997). *Integrative cases in couples and family therapy: A cognitive-behavioral perspective*. New York, NY: Guilford Press.

Dattilio, F. M., & Freeman, A. (Eds.). (2007). *Cognitive-behavioral strategies in crisis intervention* (3rd ed.). New York, NY: Guilford Press.

Davenport, D. S., & Yurich, J. M. (1991). Multicultural gender issues. *Journal of Counseling & Development, 70*, 64–71. doi:10.1002/j.1556-6676.1991.tb01562.x

Dawis, R. V. (1992). The individual difference tradition in counseling psychology. *Journal of Counseling Psychology, 39*, 7–19. doi:10.1037/0022-0167.39.1.7

Dawis, R. V. (1996). The theory of work adjustment and person–environment correspondence counseling. In D. Brown, L. Brooks, & Associates (Eds.), *Career choice and development* (3rd ed., pp. 75–120). San Francisco, CA: Jossey-Bass.

Dawis, R. V. (2005). The Minnesota theory of work adjustment. In S. D. Brown & R. W. Lent (Eds.), *Career development counseling: Putting theory and research to work* (pp. 3–23). Hoboken, NJ: Wiley.

Dawis, R. V., Dohm, T. E., Lofquist, L. H., Chartrand, J. M., & Due, A. M. (1987). *Minnesota Occupational Classification System III.* Minneapolis: Vocational Psychology Research, Department of Psychology, University of Minnesota.

Dawis, R. V., England, G. W., & Lofquist, L. H. (1964). A theory of work adjustment. *Minnesota Studies in Vocational Rehabilitation, 15,* 1–27.

Dawis, R. V., & Lofquist, L. H. (1978). A note on the dynamics of work adjustment. *Journal of Vocational Behavior, 12,* 76–79. doi:10.1016/0001-8791(78)90008-8

Dawis, R. V., & Lofquist, L. H. (1984). *A psychological theory of work adjustment.* Minneapolis: University of Minnesota Press.

DeBell, C. (2006). What all applied psychologists should know about work. *Professional Psychology: Research and Practice, 37,* 325–333. doi:10.1037/0735-7028.37.4.325

Defense of Marriage Act, Public Law 104-199, 110 Stat. 2419 (1996). Retrieved http://www.gpo.gov/fdsys/pkg/BILLS-104hr3396enr/pdf/

Deffenbacher, J. L., & Suinn, R. M. (1988). Systematic desensitization and the reduction of anxiety. *Counseling Psychologist, 16,* 9–30. doi:10.1177/0011000088161002

Delgado-Romero, E. A., Lau, M. Y., & Shullman, S. L. (2012). The Society of Counseling Psychology: Historical values, themes, and patterns viewed from the American Psychological Association presidential podium. In N. A. Fouad, J. C. Carter, & L. M. Subich (Eds.), *APA handbook of counseling psychology: Vol. 1. Theories, research, and methods* (pp. 3–29). Washington, DC: American Psychological Association. doi:10.1037/13754-001

Dermer, S. B., Smith, S. D., & Barto, K. K. (2010). Identifying and correctly labeling sexual prejudice, discrimination, and oppression. *Journal of Counseling & Development, 88,* 325–331. doi:10.1002/j.1556-6678.2010.tb00029.x

Derogatis, L. (1977). *SCL-90: Administration, scoring and procedures manual for the revised version.* Baltimore, MD: Clinical Psychometric Research.

de Shazer, S. (1988). *Clues: Investigating solutions in brief therapy.* New York, NY: Norton.

de Shazer, S. (1994). *Words were originally magic.* New York, NY: Norton.

Diamond, L. M. (2008). *Sexual fluidity: Understanding women's love and desire.* Cambridge, MA: Harvard University Press.

Dies, R. R. (1987). Clinical implications of research on leadership in short-term group psychotherapy. In R. R. Dies & K. R. MacKenzie

(Eds.), *Advances in group psychotherapy: Integrating research and practice* (pp. 27–78). New York, NY: International Universities Press.

Dies, R. R. (2003). Group psychotherapies. In A. Gurman & S. Messer (Eds.), *Essential psychotherapies* (2nd ed., pp. 515–550). New York, NY: Guilford Press.

DigitalBuzzBlog. (2011). *Facebook stats.* Retrieved from http://digitalbuzzblog.com/facebook-statistics-stats-facts-2011/

Doctors, S. R. (1996). Notes on the contribution of the analyst's self-awareness to optimal responsiveness. In A. Goldberg (Ed.), *Progress in self psychology: Vol. 12. Basic ideas reconsidered* (pp. 55–66). Hillsdale, NJ: Analytic Press.

Dolliver, R. H. (1981a). Personal sources for theories of psychotherapy. *Journal of Contemporary Psychotherapy, 12,* 53–59. doi:10.1007/BF00946234

Dolliver, R. H. (1981b). Some limitations in Perls' Gestalt therapy. *Psychotherapy: Theory, Research & Practice, 18,* 38–45. doi:10.1037/h0085959

Donnay, D., Morris, M., Schaubhut, N., & Thompson, R. (2005). *Strong Interest Inventory manual: Research, development, and strategies for interpretation.* Mountain View, CA: Consulting Psychologists Press.

Dovidio, J. F., & Gaertner, S. L. (1998). On the nature of contemporary prejudice: The causes, consequences, and challenges of aversive racism. In J. Eberhardt & S. T. Fiske (Eds.), *Confronting racism: The problem and the response* (pp. 3–32). Newbury Park, CA: Sage.

Dovidio, J. F., Gaertner, S. L., Kawakami, K., & Hodson, G. (2002). Why can't we just get along? Interpersonal biases and interracial distrust. *Cultural Diversity and Ethnic Minority Psychology, 8,* 88–102. doi:10.1037/1099-9809.8.2.88

Dovidio, J., Kawakami, K., Johnson, C., Johnson, B., & Howard, A. (1997). The nature of prejudice: Automatic and controlled processes. *Journal of Experimental Social Psychology, 33,* 510–540. doi:10.1006/jesp.1997.1331

Dowd, E., & Milne, C. (1986). Paradoxical interventions in counseling psychology. *Counseling Psychologist, 14,* 237–282.

Drummond, R. J. (1996). *Appraisal procedures for counselors and helping professionals* (3rd ed.). Englewood Cliffs, NJ: Merrill.

Duckworth, J. C., & Anderson, W P. (1995). *MMPI & MMPI–2: Interpretation manual for counselors and clinicians* (4th ed.). Odessa, FL: Psychological Assessment Resources.

Duncan, B. L., Miller, S. D., Wampold, B. E., & Hubble, M. A. (Eds.). (2010). *The heart and soul of change, second edition: Delivering what works in therapy.* Washington, DC: American Psychological Association.

Dunkle, J. H., & Friedlander, M. L. (1996). Contribution of therapist experience and personal characteristics to the working alliance. *Journal of Counseling Psychology, 43,* 456–460.

Eagle, M. N. (2011). *From classical to contemporary psychoanalysis: A critique and integration.* New York, NY: Routledge.

Eagle, M. N., & Wolitzky, D: L. (1997). Empathy: A psychoanalytic perspective. In A. Bozart & L. Greenberg (Eds.), *Empathy reconsidered: New directions in psychotherapy* (pp. 217–244). Washington, DC: American Psychological Association.

Eby, L. T., Maher, C. P., & Butts, M. M. (2010). The intersection of work and family life: The role of affect. *Annual Review of Psychology, 61,* 599–622. doi:10.1146/annurev.psych.093008.100422

Egan, G. (1986). *The skilled helper* (3rd ed.). Monterey, CA: Brooks/Cole.

Egan, G. (1998). *The skilled helper: A problem-management approach to helping* (6th ed.). Pacific Grove, CA: Brooks/Cole.

Egan, G. (2009). *The skilled helper.* Belmont, CA: Brooks/Cole.

Eisenman, R. (1995). Why psychologists should study race. *American Psychologist, 50,* 42–43. doi:10.1037/0003-066X.50.1.42

Eisman, E. J., Dies, R. R., Finn, S. E., Eyde, L. D., Kay, G. G., Kubiszyn, T. W., . . . Moreland, K. (2000). Problems and limitations in the use of psychological assessment in the contemporary health care delivery system. *Professional Psychology: Research and Practice, 31,*131–140. doi:10.1037/0735-7028.31.2.131

Ekman, P., & Friesen, W. V. (1969). The repertoire of non-verbal behavior. *Semiotica, 1,* 49–98.

Ellenberger, H. (1970). *The discovery of the unconscious.* New York, NY: Basic Books.

Elliott, R. (1998). Editor's introduction: A guide to the empirically supported treatments controversy. *Psychotherapy Research, 8,* 115–125.

Elliott, R., Bohart, A. C., Watson, J. C., & Greenberg, L. S. (2011). Empathy. In J. C. Norcross (Ed.), *Psychotherapy relationships that work* (2nd ed., pp. 132–152). New York, NY: Oxford University Press.

Elliott, R., Greenberg, L. S., Watson, J. C., Timulak, L., & Freire, E. (2013). Research on humanistic-experiential psychotherapies. In M. J. Lambert (Ed.), *Bergin and Garfield's handbook of psychotherapy and behavior change* (6th ed., pp. 495–538). New York, NY: Wiley.

Ellis, A. (1962). *Reason and emotion in psychotherapy.* New York, NY: Lyle Stuart.

Ellis, A. (1995). Rational emotive behavior therapy. In R. J. Corsini & D. Wedding (Eds.), *Current psychotherapies* (5th ed., pp. 162–196). Itasca, IL: Peacock.

Ellis, A. (2011). Rational emotive behavior therapy. In R. J. Corsini & D. Wedding (Eds.), *Current psychotherapies* (9th ed., pp. 196–234). Belmont, CA: Brooks/Cole.

Ellis, H. D. (1992). Graduate education in psychology. Past, present, and future. *American Psychologist, 47,* 570–576. doi:10.1037/0003-066X.47.4.570

Enns, C. Z. (1993). Twenty years of feminist counseling and therapy: From naming biases to implementing multifaceted practice. *Counseling Psychologist, 21,* 3–87. doi:10.1177/0011000093211001

Enns, C. Z. (2004). *Feminist theories and feminist psychotherapies: Origins, themes, and diversity* (2nd ed.). Binghamton, NY: Haworth Press.

Enns, C. Z. (2010). Locational feminisms and feminist social identity analysis. *Professional Psychology: Research and Practice, 41,* 333–339. doi:10.1037/a0020260

Enns, C. Z. (2012a). Feminist approaches to counseling. In E. M. Altmaier & J. C. Hansen (Eds.), *The Oxford handbook of counseling psychology* (pp. 434–459). New York, NY: Oxford University Press.

Enns, C. Z. (2012b). Gender: Women—theories and research. In N. A. Fouad, J. C. Carter, & L. M. Subich (Eds.), *APA handbook of counseling psychology: Vol. 1. Theories, research, and methods* (pp. 397–422). Washington, DC: American Psychological Association.

Enns, C. Z., & Williams, E. N. (Eds.). (2012). *The Oxford handbook of feminist multicultural counseling psychology.* New York, NY: Oxford University Press.

Enns, C. Z., Williams, E. N., & Fassinger, R. E. (2012). Feminist multicultural psychology: Evolution, change, and challenge. In C. Z. Enns & E. N. Williams (Eds.), *The Oxford handbook of feminist multicultural counseling psychology* (pp. 3–23). New York, NY: Oxford University Press. doi:10.1093/oxfordhb/9780199744220.013.0001

Epstein, D., Bell, M. E., & Goodman, L. A. (2003). Transforming aggressive prosecution policies: Prioritizing victims' long-term safety in the prosecution of domestic violence cases. *Journal of Gender, Social Policy, & the Law, 11,* 465–498.

Erikson, E. H. (1950). *Childhood and society.* New York, NY: Norton.

Erikson, E. H. (1959). Identity and the life cycle. *Psychological Issues, 1,* Monograph 1.

Erikson, E. H. (1968). *Identity: Youth and crisis.* Oxford, England: Norton.

Espelage, D. L., & Poteat, V. P. (2012a). Counseling psychologists in schools. In N. A. Fouad, J. A. Carter, & L. M. Subich (Eds.), *APA handbook of counseling psychology: Vol. 2. Practice, interventions, and applications* (pp. 541–566). Washington, DC: American Psychological Association.

Espelage, D. L., & Poteat, P. (2012b). School-based prevention of peer relationship problems. In E. M. Altmaier & J. C. Hansen (Eds.), *The Oxford handbook of counseling psychology* (pp. 703–722). New York, NY: Oxford Press.

Exner, J. E., Jr., & Weiner, I. B. (2003). *The Rorschach: A comprehensive system* (4th ed.). New York, NY: Wiley.

Eysenck, H. J. (1952). The effects of psychotherapy: An evaluation. *Journal of Consulting Psychology, 16,* 319–324. doi:10.1037/h0063633

Eysenck, H. J. (1959). Learning theory and behavior therapy. *Journal of Mental Science, 105,* 61–75.

Eysenck, H. J. (Ed.). (1960). *Behavior therapy and the neuroses.* Oxford, England: Pergamon Press.

Fagan, J., & Shepherd, I. L. (Eds.). (1970). *Gestalt therapy now.* New York, NY: Harper & Row.

Farber, B. A. (2003). Patient self-disclosure: A review of the research. *Journal of Clinical Psychology, 59,* 589–600. doi:10.1002/jclp.10161

Farber, B. A. (2006). *Self-disclosure in psychotherapy.* New York, NY: Guilford Press.

Farber, B. A., & Doolin, E. M. (2011). Positive regard and affirmation. In J. C. Norcross (Ed.), *Psychotherapy relationships that work* (2nd ed., pp. 168–188). New York, NY: Oxford University Press.

Farber, B. A., & Hall, D. (2002). Disclosure to therapists: What is and is not discussed in psychotherapy. *Journal of Clinical Psychology, 58,* 359–370. doi:10.1002/jclp.1148

Farmer, H. S. (1985). Model of career and achievement motivation for women and men. *Journal of Counseling Psychology, 32,* 363–390. doi:10.1037/0022-0167.32.3.363

Fassinger, R. (2000). Gender and sexuality in human development: Implications for prevention and advocacy in counseling psychology. In S. D. Brown & R. W. Lent (Eds.), *Handbook of counseling psychology* (2nd ed., pp. 346–378). New York, NY: Wiley.

Fassinger, R. E. (2004). Centralizing feminism and multiculturalism in counseling. *Journal of Multicultural Counseling and Development, 32,* 344–345.

Fassinger, R. E., & Arseneau, J. R. (2007). "I'd rather get wet than be under that umbrella": Differentiating the experiences and identities of lesbian, gay, bisexual, and transgender people. In K. J. Bieschke, R. M. Perez, & K. A. DeBord (Eds.), *Handbook of counseling and psychotherapy with lesbian, gay, bisexual, and transgender clients* (2nd ed., pp. 19–49). Washington, DC: American Psychological Association. doi:10.1037/11482-001

Fassinger, R. E., & Hensler-McGinnis, N. F. (2005). Multicultural feminist mentoring as individual and small-group pedagogy. In C. Z. Enns & A. L. Sinacore (Eds.), *Teaching and social justice: Integrating multicultural and feminist theories in the classroom* (pp. 143–161). Washington, DC: American Psychological Association. doi:10.1037/10929-009

Fenichel, O. (1945). *The psychoanalytic theory of neurosis.* New York, NY: Norton.

Fisch, R., Weakland, J., & Segal, L. (1982). *The tactics of change: Doing therapy briefly.* San Francisco, CA: Jossey-Bass.

Fischer, A. R., Jome, L. M., & Atkinson, D. R. (1998). Reconceptualizing multicultural counseling. *Counseling Psychologist, 26,* 525–588. doi:10.1177/0011000098264001

Fitzgerald, L. F., Fassinger, R. E., & Betz, N. E. (1995). Theoretical advances in the study of women's career development. In W. B. Walsh

& S. H. Osipow (Eds.), *Handbook of vocational psychology: Theory, research, and practice* (2nd ed., pp. 67–109). Mahwah, NJ: Erlbaum.

Fitzgerald, L. F., & Nutt, R. (1986). The Division 17 principles concerning the counseling/psychotherapy of women: Rationale and implementation. *Counseling Psychologist, 14*, 180–216. doi:10.1177/0011000086141019

Fitzgerald, L. F., & Osipow, S. H. (1986). An occupational analysis of counseling psychology: How special is the specialty? *American Psychologist, 41*, 535–544. doi:10.1037/0003-066X.41.5.535

Flanagan, D. P., & Kaufman, A. S. (2009). *Essentials of WISC-IV assessment.* New York, NY: Wiley.

Flores, L. Y., Hsieh, C., & Chiao, H. (2011). Vocational psychology and assessment with immigrants in the United States: Future directions for training, research, and practice. *Journal of Career Assessment, 19*, 323–332. doi:10.1177/1069072710395538

Flores, L. Y., Rooney, S. C., Heppner, P. P., Browne, L. D., & Wei, M.-F. (1999). Trend analyses of major contributions in *The Counseling Psychologist* cited from 1986 to 1996. *The Counseling Psychologist, 27*, 73–95. doi:10.1177/0011000099271006

Flum, H., & Blustein, D. L. (2000). Reinvigorating the study of vocational exploration: A framework for research. *Journal of Vocational Behavior, 56*, 380–404. doi:10.1006/jvbe.2000.1721

Ford, J. D., Fallot, R., & Harris, M. (2009). Group therapy. In C. A. Courtois & J. D. Ford (Eds.), *Treating complex traumatic stress disorders: An evidence-based guide* (pp. 415–440). New York, NY: Guilford Press.

Foreman, M. E. (1966). Some empirical correlates of psychological health. *Journal of Counseling Psychology, 13*, 3–11. doi:10.1037/h0023052

Forrest, L. (2008). President's report. *Society of Counseling Psychology Newsletter, 29*(2), 1.

Forsyth, D. R., & Strong, S. R. (1986). The scientific study of counseling and psychotherapy: A unificationist view. *American Psychologist, 41*, 113–119. doi:10.1037/0003-066X.41.2.113

Fosha, D. (2000). *The transforming power of affect: A model for accelerated change.* New York, NY: Basic Books.

Fosshage, J. L. (1997). Psychoanalysis and psychoanalytic psychotherapy: Is there a meaningful distinction in the process? *Psychoanalytic Psychology, 14*, 409–425. doi:10.1037/h0079733

Foster, S., & Gurman, A. (1985). Family therapies. In S. Lynn & J. Garske (Eds.), *Contemporary psychotherapies: Models and methods* (pp. 377–418). Columbus, OH: Merrill.

Fouad, N. A. (1997). School-to-work transition: Voice from an implementer. *The Counseling Psychologist, 25*, 403–412. doi:10.1177/0011000097253003

Fouad, N. A. (2002). Cross-cultural differences in vocational interests: Between-group differences on the Strong Interest Inventory. *Journal of Counseling Psychology, 49*, 283–289. doi:10.1037/0022-0167.49.3.282

Fouad, N. A., & Arredondo, P. (2007). *Becoming culturally oriented: Practical advice for psychologists and educators.* Washington, DC: American Psychological Association. doi:10.1037/11483-000

Fouad, N. A., & Bingham, R. B. (1995). Career counseling with racial and ethnic minorities. In W. B. Walsh & S. H. Osipow (Eds.), *Handbook of vocational psychology* (2nd ed., pp. 331–366). Hillsdale, NJ: Erlbaum.

Fouad, N. A., Carter, J. C., & Subich, L. M. (Eds.). (2012). *APA handbook of counseling psychology.* Washington, DC: American Psychological Association.

Fouad, N. A., & Chan, P. M. (1999). Gender and ethnicity: Influence on test interpretation and reception. In J. W. Lichtenberg & R. K. Goodyear (Eds.), *Scientist-practitioner perspectives on test interpretation* (pp. 31–58). Needham Heights, MA: Allyn & Bacon.

Fouad, N. A., Gerstein, L. H., & Toporek, R. L. (2006). Social justice and counseling psychology in context. In R. L. Toporek, L. H. Gerstein, N. A. Fouad, G. Roysircar, & T. Israel (Eds.), *Handbook for social justice in counseling psychology: Leadership, vision, and action* (pp. 1–16). Thousand Oaks, CA: Sage. doi:10.4135/9781412976220.n1

Fouad, N. A., McPherson, R., Gerstein, L., Blustein, D., Elman, N., Helledy, K., & Metz, A. (2004). Houston, 2001: Context and legacy. *The Counseling Psychologist, 32,* 15–77. doi:10.1177/0011000003259943

Fouad, N. A., & Prince, J. P. (2012). Social justice in counseling psychology. In E. M. Altmaier & J. C. Hansen (Eds.), *The Oxford handbook of counseling psychology* (pp. 856–872). New York, NY: Oxford University Press.

Fouts, G., & Burggraf, K. (2000). Television situation comedies: Female weight, male negative comments, and audience reactions. *Sex Roles, 42,* 925–932. doi:10.1023/A:1007054618340

Frank, G. (1998). On the relational school of psychoanalysis: Some additional thoughts. *Psychoanalytic Psychology, 15,* 141–153. doi:10.1037/0736-9735.15.1.141

Franklin, K. (1998). Unassuming motivations: Contextualizing the narratives of antigay assailants. In G. M. Herek (Ed.), *Sexual orientation and stigma: Understanding prejudice against lesbians, gay men, and bisexuals* (pp. 1–23). Thousand Oaks, CA: Sage. doi:10.4135/9781452243818.n1

Franklin, K. (2000). Antigay behaviors among young adults: Prevalence, patterns, and motivators in a non-criminal population. *Journal of Interpersonal Violence, 15,* 339–362. doi:10.1177/088626000015004001

Fredrickson, B. L., & Roberts, T. A. (1997). Objectification theory: Toward understanding women's lived experiences and mental health risks. *Psychology of Women Quarterly, 21,* 173–206. doi:10.1111/j.1471-6402.1997.tb00108.x

Freedman, J., & Combs, G. (1996). *Narrative therapy: The social construction of preferred reality.* New York, NY: Norton.

Fretz, B. R. (1966). Postural movements in a counseling dyad. *Journal of Counseling Psychology, 13,* 335–343. doi:10.1037/h0023716

Fretz, B. R. (1985). Counseling psychology. In E. M. Altmaier & M. E. Meyer (Eds.), *Applied specialties in psychology* (pp. 45–74). New York, NY: Random House.

Fretz, B. R. (1993). Counseling psychology: A transformation for the third age. *The Counseling Psychologist, 21,* 154–170. doi:10.1177/0011000093211010

Fretz, B. R., & Mills, D. H. (1980). *Licensing and certification of psychologists and counselors.* San Francisco, CA: Jossey-Bass.

Freud, A. (1966). The ego and the mechanisms of defense. In *The writings of Anna Freud* (Vol. 2). New York, NY: International Universities Press. (Original work published 1936)

Freud, S. (1938). The interpretation of dreams. In A. A. Brill (Ed.), *The basic writings of Sigmund Freud* (pp. 179–549). New York, NY: Random House. (Original work published 1900)

Freud, S. (1940). An outline of psychoanalysis. *International Journal of Psychoanalysis, 21,* 27–84.

Freud, S. (1953). The ego and the id. In J. Strachey (Ed.), *Standard edition of the complete psychological works of Sigmund Freud* (Vol. 19, pp 3–66). London, England: Hogarth Press. (Original work published 1923)

Freud, S. (1959). The dynamics of transference. In E. Jones (Ed.) & J. Riviere (Trans.), *Collected papers* (Vol. 2). New York, NY: Basic Books. (Original work published 1912)

Freud, S. (1961). The ego and the id. In J. Strachey (Ed. & Trans.), *The standard edition of the complete psychological works of Sigmund Freud* (Vol. 19, pp. 3–66). London, England: Hogarth Press. (Original work published 1923)

Friedlander, M. L., Escudero, V., Heatherington, L., & Diamond, G. M. (2011). Alliance in couple and family therapy. In J. Norcross (Ed.), *Psychotherapy relationships that work* (2nd ed., pp. 92–109). New York, NY: Oxford University Press.

Friedman, M. (1983). *The healing dialogue in psychotherapy.* New York, NY: Aronson.

Frone, M. R. (2003). Work–family balance. In J. C. Quick & L. E. Tetrick (Eds.), *Handbook of occupational health psychology* (pp. 143–162). Washington, DC: American Psychological Association. doi:10.1037/10474-007

Fuertes, J., Mislowack, A., Brown, S., Gur-Arie, S., Wilkinson, S., & Gelso, C. J. (2007). Correlates of the real relationship in psychotherapy: A study of dyads. *Psychotherapy Research, 17,* 423–430. doi:10.1080/10503300600789189

Fuertes, J., Spokane, A., & Holloway, E. (2013). *Specialty competencies in counseling psychology.* New York, NY: Oxford University Press.

Fuertes, J. N. (2012). Multicultural counseling and psychotherapy. In E. M. Altmaier & J. C. Hansen (Eds.), *The Oxford handbook of counseling psychology* (pp. 570–588). New York, NY: Oxford University Press.

Fuertes, J. N., & Gretchen, D. (2001). Emerging theories of multicultural counseling. In J. G. Ponterotto, J. M. Casas, L. A. Suzuki, & C. M. Alexander (Eds.), *Handbook of multicultural counseling* (pp. 509–541). Newbury Park, CA: Sage.

Fuertes, J. N., & Ponterotto, J. G. (2003). Culturally appropriate intervention strategies. In G. Roysircar, P. Arredondo, J. N. Fuertes, R. Toporek, & J. G. Ponterotto (Eds.), *Multicultural competencies 2003: Association for Multicultural Counseling and Development* (pp. 51–58). Alexandria, VA: American Counseling Association.

Fukuyama, M. A. (1990). Taking a universal approach to multicultural counseling. *Counselor Education and Supervision, 30*, 6–17. doi:10.1002/j.1556-6978.1990.tb01174.x

Fuqua, D. R., & Hartman, B. W. (1983). Differential diagnosis and treatment of career indecision. *Personnel and Guidance Journal, 62*, 27–29. doi:10.1111/j.2164-4918.1983.tb00112.x

Fuqua, D. R., Newman, J. L., Anderson, M. W., & Johnson, A. W. (1986). Preliminary study of internal dialogue in a training setting. *Psychological Reports, 58*, 163–172. doi:10.2466/pr0.1986.58.1.163

Gable, S. L., & Haidt, J. (2005). What (and why) is positive psychology? *Review of General Psychology, 9*, 103–110. doi:10.1037/1089-2680.9.2.103

Gadassi, R., Gati, I., & Dayan, A. (2012). The adaptability of career decision-making profiles. *Journal of Counseling Psychology, 59*, 612–622. doi:10.1037/a0029155

Gaddy, C. D., Charlot-Swilley, D. C., Nelson, P. D., & Reich, J. N. (1995). Selected outcomes of accredited programs. *Professional Psychology: Research and Practice, 26*, 507–513. doi:10.1037/0735-7028.26.5.507

Gallessich, J. (1985). Toward a meta-theory of consultation. *The Counseling Psychologist, 13*, 336–354. doi:10.1177/0011000085133002

Garb, H. N. (1994). Judgment research: Implications for clinical practice and testimony in court. *Applied & Preventive Psychology, 3*, 173–183. doi:10.1016/S0962-1849(05)80069-1

Garcia, M. E., Malott, R. W., & Brethower, D. (1988). A system of thesis and dissertation supervision: Helping graduate students succeed. *Teaching of Psychology, 15*, 186–191.

Garfield, S. L. (1985). Clinical psychology. In E. M. Altmaier & M. E. Meyer (Eds.), *Applied specialties in psychology* (pp. 19–44). New York, NY: Random House.

Gaston, L., Marmar, C. R., Thompson, L. W., & Gallagher, D. (1988). Relation of patient pretreatment characteristics to the therapeutic alliance in diverse psychotherapies. *Journal of Consulting and Clinical Psychology, 56*, 483–489. doi:10.1037/0022-006X.56.4.483

Gazzola, N., & Stalikas, A. (2004). Therapist interpretations and client processes in three therapeutic modalities: Implications for psychotherapy integration. *Journal of Psychotherapy Integration, 14*, 397–418. doi:10.1037/1053-0479.14.4.397

Gelso, C. J. (1979a). Research in counseling: Clarifications, elaborations, defenses, and admissions. *The Counseling Psychologist, 8*(3), 61–67. doi:10.1177/001100007900800312

Gelso, C. J. (1979b). Research in counseling: Methodological and professional issues. *The Counseling Psychologist, 8*(3), 7–36. doi:10.1177/001100007900800303

Gelso, C. J. (1985). Rigor, relevance, and counseling research: On the need to maintain our course between Scylla and Charybdis. *Journal of Counseling & Development, 63,* 551–553. doi:10.1002/j.1556-6676.1985.tb00678.x

Gelso, C. J. (1992). Realities and emerging myths about brief therapy. *The Counseling Psychologist, 20,* 464–471. doi:10.1177/0011000092203005

Gelso, C. J. (1993). On the making of a scientist-practitioner: A theory of research training in professional psychology. *Professional Psychology: Research and Practice, 24,* 468–476. doi:10.1037/0735-7028.24.4.468

Gelso, C. J. (1995). A theory for all seasons: The four psychologies of psychoanalysis. *Contemporary Psychology, 40,* 331–333. doi:10.1037/003561

Gelso, C. J. (2005). Introduction to special issue. *Psychotherapy: Theory, Research, Practice, Training, 42,* 419–420. doi:10.1037/0033-3204.42.4.419

Gelso, C. J. (2006). Applying theories in research: The interplay of theory and research in science. In E. T. L. Leong & J. T. Austin (Eds.), *The psychology research handbook* (2nd ed., pp. 455–464). Thousand Oaks, CA: Sage. doi:10.4135/9781412976626.n32

Gelso, C. J. (2009). The real relationship in a postmodern world: Theoretical and empirical explorations. *Psychotherapy Research, 19,* 253–264. doi:10.1080/10503300802389242

Gelso, C. J. (2011). *The real relationship in psychotherapy: The hidden foundation of change.* Washington, DC: American Psychological Association. doi:10.1037/12349-000

Gelso, C. J. (in press). A tripartite model of the therapeutic relationship: Theory, research, and practice. *Psychotherapy Research.*

Gelso, C. J., Betz, N. E., Friedlander, M. L., Helms, J. E., Hill, C. E., Patton, M. A., . . . Wampold, B. E. (1988). Research in counseling: Prospects and recommendations. *The Counseling Psychologist, 16,* 385–406. doi:10.1177/0011000088163006

Gelso, C. J., & Bhatia, A. (2012). Crossing theoretical lines: The role and effect of transference in nonanalytic psychotherapies. *Psychotherapy, 49,* 384–390. doi:10.1037/a0028802

Gelso, C. J., & Carter, J. A. (1985). The relationship in counseling and psychotherapy: Components, consequences, and theoretical antecedents. *The Counseling Psychologist, 13,* 155–243. doi:10.1177/0011000085132001

Gelso, C. J., & Carter, J. A. (1994). Components of the psychotherapy relationship: Their interaction and unfolding during treatment. *Journal of Counseling Psychology, 41,* 296–306. doi:10.1037/0022-0167.41.3.296

Gelso, C. J., & Fassinger, R. E. (1990). Counseling psychology: Theory and research on interventions. *Annual Review of Psychology, 41*, 355–386. doi:10.1146/annurev.ps.41.020190.002035

Gelso, C. J., & Fassinger, R. E. (1992). Personality, development, and counseling psychology: Depth, ambivalence, and actualization. *Journal of Counseling Psychology, 39*, 275–298. doi:10.1037/0022-0167.39.3.275

Gelso, C. J., & Fretz, B. R. (1992). *Counseling psychology*. New York, NY: Harcourt Brace.

Gelso, C. J., & Fretz, B. R. (2001). *Counseling psychology* (2nd ed.). New York, NY: Harcourt.

Gelso, C. J., & Harbin, J. (2007). Insight, action, and the therapeutic relationship. In L. G. Castonguay & C. E. Hill (Eds.), *Insight in psychotherapy* (pp. 293–311). Washington, DC: American Psychological Association. doi:10.1037/11532-014

Gelso, C. J., & Hayes, J. A. (1998). *The psychotherapy relationship: Theory, research, and practice*. New York, NY: Wiley.

Gelso, C. J., & Hayes, J. A. (2007). *Countertransference and the therapist's inner experience: Perils and possibilities*. Mahwah, NJ: Erlbaum.

Gelso, C. J., & Johnson, D. H. (1983). *Explorations in time-limited counseling and psychotherapy*. New York, NY: Teachers College Press.

Gelso, C. J., Kelley, F. A., Fuertes, J. N., Marmarosh, C., Holmes, S. E., Costa, C., & Hancock, G. R. (2005). Measuring the real relationship in psychotherapy: Initial validation of the Therapist Form. *Journal of Counseling Psychology, 52*, 640–649. doi:10.1037/0022-0167.52.4.640

Gelso, C. J., Kivlighan, D. M., Busa-Knepp, J., Spiegel, E. B., Ain, S., Hummel, A. M., . . . Markin, R. D. (2012). The unfolding of the real relationship and the outcome of brief psychotherapy. *Journal of Counseling Psychology, 59*, 495–506. doi:10.1037/a0029838

Gelso, C. J., Kivlighan, D. M., Wine, B., Jones, A., & Friedman, S. C. (1997). Transference, insight, and the course of time-limited therapy. *Journal of Counseling Psychology, 44*, 209–217. doi:10.1037/0022-0167.44.2.209

Gelso, C. J., & Lent, R. W. (2000). Scientific training and scholarly productivity: The person, the training environment, and their interaction. In S. D. Brown & R. W. Lent (Eds.), *Handbook of counseling psychology* (3rd ed., pp. 109–139). New York, NY: Wiley.

Gelso, C. J., & Palma, B. (2011). Directions for research on self-disclosure and immediacy: Moderation, mediation, and the inverted U. *Psychotherapy, 48*, 342–348. doi:10.1037/a0025909

Gelso, C. J., & Samstag, L. W. (2008). A tripartite model of the therapeutic relationship. In S. D. Brown & R. W. Lent (Eds.), *Handbook of counseling psychology* (4th ed., pp. 267–283). Hoboken, NJ: Wiley.

Gelso, C. J., & Woodhouse, S. (2002). The termination of psychotherapy: What research tells us about the process of ending treatment. In G. S. Tryon (Ed.), *Research applications to the process of counseling* (pp. 344–369). Boston, MA: Allyn & Bacon.

Gelso, C. J., & Woodhouse, S. (2003). Toward a positive psychotherapy: Focus on human strength. In W. B. Walsh (Ed.), *Counseling psychology and optimal human functioning* (pp. 171–198). Mahwah, NJ: Erlbaum.

Gendlin, E. T. (1970). Research in psychotherapy with schizophrenic patients and the nature of that "illness." In J. T. Hart & T. M. Tomlinson (Eds.), *New directions in client-centered therapy* (pp. 280–291). Boston, MA: Houghton Mifflin.

Gerstein, L. H., & Shullman, S. L. (1992). Counseling psychology and the workplace: The emergence of organizational counseling psychology. In S. D. Brown & R. W. Lent (Eds.), *Handbook of counseling psychology* (2nd ed., pp. 581–625). New York, NY: Wiley.

Gibson, J., & Brown, S. D. (1992). Counseling adults for life transitions. In S. D. Brown & R. W. Lent (Eds.), *Handbook of counseling psychology* (2nd ed., pp. 285–313). New York, NY: Wiley.

Gilbert, L. A. (1980). Feminist therapy. In A. Brodsky & R. T. Hare-Mustin (Eds.), *Women and psychotherapy* (pp. 245–265). New York, NY: Guilford Press.

Gilbert, L. A., & Rader, J. (2008). Work, family, and dual-earner couples: Implications for research and practice. In S. D. Brown & R. W. Lent (Eds.), *Handbook of counseling psychology* (4th ed., pp. 426–443). Hoboken, NJ: Wiley.

Gilbert, L. A., & Waldroop, J. (1978). Evaluation of a procedure for increasing sex-fair counseling. *Journal of Counseling Psychology, 25,* 410–418. doi:10.1037/0022-0167.25.5.410

Gill, M. M. (1994). *Transitions in psychoanalysis.* Hillsdale, NJ: Analytic Press.

Gilligan, C. (1982). *In a different voice.* Cambridge, MA: Harvard University Press.

Gladding, S. T. (1999). *Group work: A counseling specialty* (3rd ed.). Columbus, OH: Prentice-Hall.

Gladstein, G. A. (1983). Understanding empathy: Integrating counseling, developmental, and social psychology perspectives. *Journal of Counseling Psychology, 30,* 467–482. doi:10.1037/0022-0167.30.4.467

Glick, P., & Fiske, S. T. (1996). The Ambivalent Sexism Inventory: Differentiating hostile and benevolent sexism. *Journal of Personality and Social Psychology, 70,* 491–512. doi:10.1037/0022-3514.70.3.491

Glosoff, H. L., Herlihy, B., & Spence, E. B. (2000). Privileged communication in the counselor–client relationship. *Journal of Counseling & Development, 78,* 454–462. doi:10.1002/j.1556-6676.2000.tb01929.x

Goates-Jones, M. K., Hill, C. E., Stahl, J. V., & Doschek, E. E. (2009). Therapist response modes in the exploration stage: Timing and effectiveness. *Counselling Psychology Quarterly, 22,* 221–231. doi:10.1080/09515070903185256

Goldfried, M. R. (1988). Application of rational restructuring to anxiety disorders. *The Counseling Psychologist, 16,* 50–68. doi:10.1177/0011000088161004

Goldfried, M. R., & Davila, J. (2005). The role of relationship and technique in therapeutic change. *Psychotherapy: Theory, Research, Practice, Training, 42,* 421–430. doi:10.1037/0033-3204.42.4.421

Goldfried, M. R., & Davison, G. C. (1994). *Clinical behavior therapy* (2nd ed.). New York, NY: Wiley Interscience.

Goldman, L. (1961). *Using tests in counseling.* New York, NY: Appleton-Century-Crofts.

Goldman, L. (Ed.). (1978). *Research methods for counselors.* New York, NY: Wiley.

Goldman, L. (1979). Research is more than technology. *The Counseling Psychologist, 8*(3), 41–44. doi:10.1177/001100007900800306

Goodman, L. A., Dutton, M. A., Weinfurt, K., & Cook, S. (2003). The Intimate Partner Violence Strategies Index: Development and application. *Violence Against Women, 9,* 163–186. doi:10.1177/1077801202239004

Goodman, L. A., Koss, M. P., & Russo, N. F. (1993). Violence against women: Physical and mental health effects. *Applied & Preventive Psychology, 2,* 79–89. doi:10.1016/S0962-1849(05)80114-3

Goodman, L. A., Liang, B., Helms, J. E., Latta, R. E., Sparks, E., & Weintraub, S. R. (2004). Training counseling psychologists as social justice agents: Feminist and multicultural principles in action. *The Counseling Psychologist, 32,* 793–836. doi:10.1177/0011000004268802

Goodman, L. A., & Smyth, K. F. (2011). A call for a social network-oriented approach to services for survivors of intimate partner violence. *Psychology of Violence, 1,* 79–92. doi:10.1037/a0022977

Goodman, M. B., & Moradi, B. (2008). Attitudes and behaviors toward lesbian and gay persons: Critical correlates and mediated relations. *Journal of Counseling Psychology, 55,* 371–384. doi:10.1037/0022-0167.55.3.371

Goodyear, R. K. (1990). Research on the effects of test interpretation. *The Counseling Psychologist, 18,* 240–257. doi:10.1177/0011000090182006

Goodyear, R. K., Murdock, N., Lichtenberg, J. W., McPherson, R., Koetting, K., & Petren, S. (2008). Stability and change in counseling psychologists' identities, roles, functions, and career satisfaction across 15 years. *The Counseling Psychologist, 36,* 220–249. doi:10.1177/0011000007309481

Gore, P. A., & Leuwerke, W. C. (2000). Predicting occupational considerations: A comparison of self-efficacy beliefs, outcome expectations, and person–environment congruence. *Journal of Career Assessment, 8,* 237–250. doi:10.1177/106907270000800303

Gormley, B. (2012). Feminist multicultural mentoring in counseling psychology. In C. Z. Enns & E. N. Williams (Eds.), *The Oxford handbook of feminist multicultural counseling psychology* (pp. 451–464). New York, NY: Oxford Press. doi:10.1093/oxfordhb/9780199744220.013.0024

Gottfredson, G. D. (1999). John L. Holland's contributions to vocational psychology: A review and evaluation. *Journal of Vocational Behavior, 55,* 15–40. doi:10.1006/jvbe.1999.1695

Gottfredson, L. S. (1981). Circumscription and compromise: A developmental theory of occupational aspirations. *Journal of Counseling Psychology, 28,* 545–579. doi:10.1037/0022-0167.28.6.545

Gottfredson, L. S. (1996). Gottfredson's theory of circumscription and compromise. In D. Brown, L. Brooks, & Associates. (Eds.), *Career choice and development* (3rd ed., pp. 179–232). San Francisco, CA: Jossey-Bass.

Gottfredson, L. S. (2005). Applying Gottfredson's theory of circumscription and compromise in career guidance counseling. In S. D. Brown & R. W. Lent (Eds.), *Career development counseling: Putting theory and research to work* (pp. 71–100). Hoboken, NJ: Wiley.

Gough, B., Weyman, N., Alderson, J., Butler, G., & Stoner, M. (2008). "They did not have a word": The parental quest to locate a "true sex" for their intersex children. *Psychology and Health, 23,* 493–507. doi:10.1080/14768320601176170

Graff, H., & Luborsky, L. (1977). Long-term trends in transference and resistance: A report on quantitative-analytic methods applied to four psychoanalyses. *Journal of the American Psychoanalytic Association, 25,* 471–490. doi:10.1177/000306517702500210

Graham, J. M., & Kim, Y. (2011). Predictors of doctoral student success in professional psychology: Characteristics of students, programs, and universities. *Journal of Clinical Psychology, 67,* 340–354. doi:10.1002/jclp.20767

Grawe, K. (1997). Research-informed psychotherapy. *Psychotherapy Research, 7,* 1–19. doi:10.1080/10503309712331331843

Green, B. F. (1981). A primer of testing. *American Psychologist, 36,* 1001–1011. doi:10.1037/0003-066X.36.10.1001

Greenberg, J. R., & Mitchell, S. A. (1983). *Object relations in psychoanalytic theory.* Cambridge, MA: Harvard University Press.

Greenberg, L. S. (1983). The relationship in Gestalt therapy. In M. Lambert (Ed.), *Psychotherapy and patient relationships* (pp. 126–153). Homewood, IL: Dow Jones-Irwin.

Greenberg, L. S. (1985). An integrative approach to the relationship in counseling and psychotherapy. *The Counseling Psychologist, 13,* 251–259. doi:10.1177/0011000085132003

Greenberg, L. S. (2002). *Emotion-focused therapy: Coaching clients to work through their feelings.* Washington, DC: American Psychological Association. doi:10.1037/10447-000

Greene, C. H., & Banks, L. M. (2009). Ethical guideline evolution in psychological support to interrogation operations. *Consulting Psychology Journal: Practice and Research, 61,* 25–32. doi:10.1037/a0015102

Greenhaus, J. H., & Beutell, N. J. (1985). Sources of conflict between work and family roles. *Academy of Management Review, 10,* 76–88.

Greenhaus, J. H., & Powell, G. N. (2006). When work and family are allies: A theory of work–family enrichment. *Academy of Management Review, 31,* 72–92. doi:10.5465/AMR.2006.19379625

Greenson, R. R. (1967). *The technique and practice of psychoanalysis, Vol. 1.* New York, NY: International Universities Press.

Greenwald, A. G., & Banaji, M. R. (1995). Implicit social cognition: Attitudes, self-esteem, and stereotypes. *Psychological Review, 102,* 4–27. doi:10.1037/0033-295X.102.1.4

Gregory, R. J. (2011). *Psychological testing: History, principles, and applications* (6th ed.). New York, NY: Pearson.

Grummon, D. L. (1965). Client-centered theory. In B. Stefflre (Ed.), *Theories of counseling* (pp. 30–90). New York, NY: McGraw-Hill.

Guay, F., Senécal, C., Gauthier, L., & Fernet, C. (2003). Predicting career indecision: A self-determination theory perspective. *Journal of Counseling Psychology, 50,* 165–177. doi:10.1037/0022-0167.50.2.165

Gustad, J. W., & Tuma, A. H. (1957). The effects of different methods of test introduction and interpretation on client learning and counseling. *Journal of Counseling Psychology, 4,* 313–317. doi:10.1037/h0041195

Gysbers, N. C. (1997). Involving counseling psychology in the school-to-work movement. *The Counseling Psychologist, 25,* 413–427. doi:10.1177/0011000097253004

Gysbers, N. C., Heppner, M. J., & Johnston, J. A. (2009). *Career counseling: Contexts, processes, and techniques* (3rd ed.). Alexandria, VA: American Counseling Association.

Hackett, G. (1993). Career counseling and psychotherapy: False dichotomies and recommended remedies. *Journal of Career Assessment, 1,* 105–117. doi:10.1177/106907279300100201

Hackett, G., & Betz, N. E. (1981). A self-efficacy approach to the career development of women. *Journal of Vocational Behavior, 18,* 326–339. doi:10.1016/0001-8791(81)90019-1

Hackett, G., & Lent, R. W. (1992). Theoretical advances and current inquiry in career psychology. In S. D. Brown & R. W. Lent (Eds.), *Handbook of counseling psychology* (pp. 419–451). New York, NY: Wiley.

Hackney, H. (1978). The evolution of empathy. *Personnel and Guidance Journal, 57,* 35–38. doi:10.1002/j.2164-4918.1978.tb05091.x

Hage, S. M., & Romano, J. L. (2010). History of prevention and prevention groups: Legacy for the 21st century. *Group Dynamics: Theory, Research, and Practice, 14,* 199–210. doi:10.1037/a0020736

Hage, S. M., Romano, J. L., Conyne, R. K., Kenny, M., Schwartz, J. P., & Waldo, M. (2007). Best practice guidelines on prevention practice, research, training, and social advocacy for psychologists. *The Counseling Psychologist, 35,* 493–566. doi:10.1177/0011000006291411

Haldeman, D. C. (2012). The evolving family. In N. A. Fouad, J. C. Carter, & L. M. Subich (Eds.), *APA handbook of counseling psychology: Vol. 2.*

Practice, interventions, and applications (pp. 105–123). Washington, DC: American Psychological Association.

Haley, A. (1976). *Roots.* Garden City, NY: Doubleday.

Haley, J. (1976). *Problem-solving therapy.* San Francisco, CA: Jossey-Bass.

Hall, C. C. I. (1997). Cultural malpractice: The growing obsolescence of psychology with the changing U.S. population. *American Psychologist, 52,* 642–651. doi:10.1037/0003-066X.52.6.642

Hall, D. A., & Farber, B. A. (2001). Patterns of patient disclosure in psychotherapy. *Journal of the American Academy of Psychoanalysis, 29,* 213–230. doi:10.1521/jaap.29.2.213.17262

Hall, E. T. (1963). A system for the notation of proxemic behavior. *American Anthropologist, 65,* 1003–1026. doi:10.1525/aa.1963.65.5.02a00020

Hambleton, R. K., Merenda, P. F., & Spielberger, C. D. (2005). *Adapting educational and psychological tests for cross-cultural assessment.* Mahwah, NJ: Erlbaum.

Hansen, J. C. (2012). Contemporary counseling psychology. In E. M. Altmaier & J. C. Hansen (Eds.), *The Oxford handbook of counseling psychology* (pp. 917–922). New York, NY: Oxford University Press.

Hansen, J. C., Dik, B. J., & Zhou, S. (2008). An examination of the structure of leisure interests of college students, working-age adults, and retirees. *Journal of Counseling Psychology, 55,* 133–145. doi:10.1037/0022-0167.55.2.133

Hanson, W. E., Claiborn, C. D., & Kerr, B. (1997). Differential effects of two test-interpretation styles in counseling: A field study. *Journal of Counseling Psychology, 44,* 400–405. doi:10.1037/0022-0167.44.4.400

Harbin, J. M., Gelso, C. J., & Pérez Rojas, A. E. (2013). Therapist work with client strengths: Development and validation of a measure. *The Counseling Psychologist.* Advance online publication. doi:10.1177/0011000012470570

Harding, S. (1998). Gender, development, and post-enlightenment philosophy of science. *Hypatia, 13,* 146–167.

Harper, F. D. (2003). Background: Concepts and history. In F. D. Harper & J. McFadden (Eds.), *Culture and counseling: New approaches* (pp. 1–19). Needham Heights, MA: Allyn & Bacon.

Harper, F. D., & Bruce-Sanford, G. C. (1989). *Counseling techniques: An outline and overview.* Alexandria, VA: Douglass.

Harper, M. C., & Shoffner, M. F. (2004). Counseling for continued career development after retirement: An application of the theory of work adjustment. *Career Development Quarterly, 52,* 272–284. doi:10.1002/j.2161-0045.2004.tb00648.x

Hartmann, H. (1958). *Ego psychology and the problem of adaptation.* New York, NY: International Universities Press. (Original work published 1939) doi:10.1037/13180-000

Harvey, V. S. (1997). Improving readability of psychological reports. *Professional Psychology: Research and Practice, 28,* 271–274. doi:10.1037/0735-7028.28.3.271

Haverkamp, B. E., Morrow, S. L., & Ponterotto, J. G. (2005). A time and place for qualitative and mixed methods in counseling psychology research. *Journal of Counseling Psychology, 52,* 123–125. doi:10.1037/0022-0167.52.2.123

Hayes, J. A. (1997). What does the Brief Symptom Inventory measure in college and university counseling center clients? *Journal of Counseling Psychology, 44,* 360–367. doi:10.1037/0022-0167.44.4.360

Hayes, J. A., Gelso, C. R., & Hummel, A. M. (2011). Managing countertransference. *Psychotherapy, 48,* 88–97. doi:10.1037/a0022182

Hayes, J. A., McCracken, J. E., McClanahan, M. K., Hill, C. E., Harp, J. S., & Carozzoni, P. (1998). Therapist perspectives on countertransference: Qualitative data in search of a theory. *Journal of Counseling Psychology, 45,* 468–482. doi:10.1037/0022-0167.45.4.468

Hayes, S. C., Strosahl, K. D., & Wilson, K. G. (1999). *Acceptance and commitment therapy: An experiential approach to behavior change.* New York, NY: Guilford Press.

Healy, C. C. (1990). Reforming career appraisals to meet the needs of clients in the 1990s. *The Counseling Psychologist, 18,* 214–226. doi:10.1177/0011000090182004

Healy, P. M., & Palepu, L. (2003). The fall of Enron. *Journal of Economic Perspectives, 17,* 3–26. doi:10.1257/089533003765888403

Heath, S. R. (1964). *The reasonable adventurer.* Pittsburgh, PA: University of Pittsburgh Press.

Heesacker, M., & Lichtenberg, J. W. (2012). Theory and research for counseling interventions. In E. M. Altmaier & J. C. Hansen (Eds.), *The Oxford handbook of counseling psychology* (pp. 71–94). New York, NY: Oxford University Press.

Held, B. S. (1996). Solution-focused therapy and the post-modern: A critical analysis. In S. D. Miller, M. A. Hubble, & B. L. Duncan (Eds.), *Handbook of solution-focused brief therapy* (pp. 27–43). San Francisco, CA: Jossey-Bass.

Helms, J. E. (1984). Toward a theoretical explanation of the effects of race on counseling: A Black and White model. *The Counseling Psychologist, 12*(4), 153–165. doi:10.1177/0011000084124013

Helms, J. E. (1992). *A race is a nice thing to have.* Topeka, KS: Content Communications.

Helms, J. E. (1994). How multiculturalism obscures racial factors in the therapy process. *Journal of Counseling Psychology, 41,* 162–165. doi:10.1037/0022-0167.41.2.162

Helms, J. E. (1995). An update of Helms's White and people of color racial identity models. In J. C. Ponterotto, J. M. Casas, L. A. Suzuki, & C. M. Alexander (Eds.), *Handbook of multicultural counseling* (pp. 181–198). Thousand Oaks, CA: Sage.

Helms, J. E., & Cook, D. A. (1999). *Using race and culture in counseling and psychotherapy: Theory and process.* Boston, MA: Allyn & Bacon.

Helms, J. E., & Talleyrand, R. M. (1997). Race is not ethnicity. *American Psychologist, 52*, 1246–1247. doi:10.1037/0003-066X.52.11.1246

Henretty, J. R., & Levitt, H. M. (2010). The role of the therapist self-disclosure in psychotherapy: A qualitative review. *Clinical Psychology Review, 30*, 63–77. doi:10.1016/j.cpr.2009.09.004

Heppner, M. J., & Hendricks, F. (1995). A process and outcome study examining career indecision and indecisiveness. *Journal of Counseling & Development, 73*, 426–437. doi:10.1002/j.1556-6676.1995.tb01776.x

Heppner, P. P. (1999). Thirty years of *The Counseling Psychologist:* 1969–1999. *The Counseling Psychologist, 27*, 5–13. doi:10.1177/0011000099271001

Heppner, P. P., & Anderson, W. P. (1985). On the perceived non-utility of research in counseling. *Journal of Counseling & Development, 63*, 545–547. doi:10.1002/j.1556-6676.1985.tb00676.x

Heppner, P. P., Casas, J. M., Carter, J., & Stone, G. L. (2000). The maturation of counseling psychology: Multifaceted perspectives, 1978–1998. In S. D. Brown & R. W. Lent (Eds.), *Handbook of counseling psychology* (3rd ed., pp. 3–49). New York, NY: Wiley.

Heppner, P. P., & Krauskopf, C. J. (1987). An information-processing approach to personal problem solving. *The Counseling Psychologist, 15*, 371–447. doi:10.1177/0011000087153001

Heppner, P. P., Wampold, B. E., & Kivlighan, D. M. (2008). *Research in counseling* (3rd ed.). Belmont, CA: Thompson Brooks/Cole.

Heppner, P. P., Witty, T. E., & Dixon, W. A. (2004). Problem-solving appraisal and human adjustment: A review of 20 years of research using the Problem Solving Inventory. *The Counseling Psychologist, 32*, 344–428. doi:10.1177/0011000003262793

Herek, G. M. (2004). Beyond "homophobia": Thinking about sexual prejudice and stigma in the twenty-first century. *Sexuality Research & Social Policy, 1*, 6–24.

Herek, G. M. (2008). Hate crimes and stigma-related experiences among sexual minority adults in the United States: Prevalence estimates from a national probability sample. *Journal of Interpersonal Violence, 24*, 54–74. doi:10.1177/0886260508316477

Herek, G. M., Gillis, J. R., & Cogan, J. C. (1999). Psychological sequelae of hate crime victimization among lesbian, gay, and bisexual adults. *Journal of Consulting and Clinical Psychology, 67*, 945–951. doi:10.1037/0022-006X.67.6.945

Herman, J. L. (1992). *Trauma and recovery: The aftermath of violence—from domestic to political terror.* New York, NY: Basic Books.

Herr, E. L. (1996). Toward the convergence of career theory and practice. In M. L. Savickas & W. B. Walsh (Eds.), *Handbook of career counseling theory and practice* (pp. 13–35). Palo Alto, CA: Davies-Black.

Hesketh, B. (2000). Prevention and development in the workplace. In S. D. Brown & R. W. Lent (Eds.), *Handbook of counseling psychology* (3rd ed., pp. 471–498). New York, NY: Wiley.

Hiebert, B., Uhlemann, M. R., Marshall, A., & Lee, D. Y. (1998). The relationship between self-talk, anxiety, and counseling skill. *Canadian Journal of Counselling, 32,* 163–171.

Hill, C. E. (1978). The development of a system for classifying counselor responses. *Journal of Counseling Psychology, 25,* 461–468. doi:10.1037/0022-0167.25.5.461

Hill, C. E. (1982). Counseling process research: Philosophical and methodological dilemmas. *The Counseling Psychologist, 10,* 7–19. doi:10.1177/0011000082104003

Hill, C. E. (1985). *Manual for the Hill counselor verbal response modes category system* (rev. ed.). Unpublished manuscript, University of Maryland.

Hill, C. E. (1986). An overview of the Hill counselor and client verbal response modes category systems. In L. S. Greenberg & W. M. Pinsol (Eds.), *The psychotherapeutic process: A research handbook* (pp. 131–160). New York, NY: Guilford Press.

Hill, C. E. (1989). *Therapist techniques and client outcome: Eight cases of brief psychotherapy.* Newbury Park, CA: Sage.

Hill, C. E. (1990). Review of exploratory in-session process research. *Journal of Consulting and Clinical Psychology, 58,* 288–294. doi:10.1037/0022-006X.58.3.288

Hill, C. E. (2004). Immediacy. In C. Hill (Ed.), *Helping skills: Facilitating exploration, insight, and action* (2nd ed., pp. 283–297). Washington, DC: American Psychological Association. doi:10.1037/10624-000

Hill, C. E. (2009). *Helping skills: Facilitating exploration, insight and action* (3rd ed.) Washington, DC: American Psychological Association.

Hill, C. E. (Ed.). (2012). *Consensual qualitative research: A practical resource for investigating social science phenomena.* Washington, DC: American Psychological Association.

Hill, C. E., & Corbett, M. M. (1993). A perspective on the history of process and outcome research in counseling psychology. *Journal of Counseling Psychology, 40,* 3–24. doi:10.1037/0022-0167.40.1.3

Hill, C. E., Gelso, C. J., & Mohr, J. J. (2000). Client concealment and self-presentation in therapy: Comment on Kelly (2000). *Psychological Bulletin, 126,* 495–500. doi:10.1037/0033-2909.126.4.495

Hill, C. E., Helms, J. E., Tichenor, V., Spiegel, S. B., O'Grady, K. E., & Perry, E. S. (1988). The effects of therapist response modes in brief psychotherapy. *Journal of Counseling Psychology, 35,* 222–233. doi:10.1037/0022-0167.35.3.222

Hill, C. E., Knox, S., Thompson, B. J., Williams, E. N., Hess, S. A., & Ladany, N. (2005). Consensual qualitative research: An update. *Journal of Counseling Psychology, 52,* 196–205. doi:10.1037/0022-0167.52.2.196

Hill, C. E., Mahalik, J. R., & Thompson, B. J. (1989). Therapist self-disclosure. *Psychotherapy: Theory, Research, Practice, Training, 26,* 290–295. doi:10.1037/h0085438

Hill, C. E., Nutt-Williams, E., Heaton, K., Thompson, B. J., & Rhodes, R. (1996). Therapist retrospective recall of impasses in long-term psychotherapy: A qualitative analysis. *Journal of Counseling Psychology, 43,* 207–217. doi:10.1037/0022-0167.43.2.207

Hill, C. E., & O' Brien, K. M. (1999). *Helping skills: Facilitating exploration, insight, and action.* Washington, DC: American Psychological Association.

Hill, C. E., O'Grady, K. E., Balinger, V., Busse, W., Falk, D. R., Hill, M., . . . Taffe, R. (1994). Methodological examination of videotape-assisted reviews in brief therapy: Helpfulness ratings, therapist intentions, client reactions, mood, and session evaluation. *Journal of Counseling Psychology, 41,* 236–247. doi:10.1037/0022-0167.41.2.236

Hill, C. E., Thompson, B. J., Cogar, M. C., & Denman, D. W. (1993). Beneath the surface of long-term therapy: Therapist and client report on their own and each other's covert processes. *Journal of Counseling Psychology, 40,* 278–287. doi:10.1037/0022-0167.40.3.278

Hill, C. E., Thompson, B. J., & Williams, E. N. (1997). A guide to conducting consensual qualitative research. *The Counseling Psychologist, 25,* 517–572. doi:10.1177/0011000097254001

Hill, C. E., & Williams, E. N. (2000). The process of individual therapy. In S. D. Brown & R. W Lent (Eds.), *Handbook of counseling psychology* (3rd ed., pp. 670–710). New York, NY: Wiley.

Hill, C. E., & Williams, E. N. (2012). The sample. In C. E. Hill (Ed.), *Consensual qualitative research: A practical resource for investigating social science phenomena* (pp. 71–81). Washington, DC: American Psychological Association.

Hill, R. (2005). *Positive aging: A guide for mental health professionals and consumers.* New York, NY: Norton.

Hills, H. I., & Strozier, A. L. (1992). Multicultural training in APA-approved counseling psychology programs: A survey. *Professional Psychology: Research and Practice, 23,* 43–51. doi:10.1037/0735-7028.23.1.43

Hofmann, S. G. (2011). *An introduction to modern CBT: Psychological solutions to mental health problems.* Chichester, United Kingdom: Wiley-Blackwell.

Holahan, W., & Yesenosky, J. M. (1992). Subgroups within Division 17: Divisiveness or opportunity for cohesion? *The Counseling Psychologist, 20,* 660–676. doi:10.1177/0011000092204010

Holinger, P. C. (1999). Noninterpretive interventions in psychoanalysis and psychotherapy: A developmental perspective. *Psychoanalytic Psychology, 16,* 233–253. doi:10.1037/0736-9735.16.2.233

Holland, J. L. (1985). *The Vocational Preference Inventory.* Odessa, FL: Psychological Assessment Resources.

Holland, J. L. (1994). *Self-Directed Search Form R* (4th ed.). Odessa, FL: Psychological Assessment Resources.

Holland, J. L. (1996). Exploring careers with a typology: What we have learned and some new directions. *American Psychologist, 51*, 397–406. doi:10.1037/0003-066X.51.4.397

Holland, J. L. (1997). *Making vocational choices: A theory of vocational personalities and work environments* (3rd ed.). Odessa, FL: Psychological Assessment Resources.

Holland, J. L. (1998). *Self-Directed Search Form R* (4th ed.). Odessa, FL: Psychological Assessment Resources.

Holland, J. L., Daiger, D. C., & Power, P. G. (1980). *My vocational situation.* Palo Alto, CA: Consulting Psychologists Press.

Holland, J. L., & Holland, J. E. (1977). Vocational indecision: More evidence and speculation. *Journal of Counseling Psychology, 24*, 404–414. doi:10.1037/0022-0167.24.5.404

Holland, J. L., Johnston, J. A., & Asama, N. F. (1993). The Vocational Identity Scale: A diagnostic and treatment tool. *Journal of Career Assessment, 1*, 1–12. doi:10.1177/106907279300100102

Holt, R. (1970). Yet another look at clinical and statistical prediction: Or, is clinical psychology worthwhile? *American Psychologist, 25*, 337–349. doi:10.1037/h0029481

Holzman, L. A., Searight, H. R., & Hughes, H. M. (1996). Clinical psychology graduate students and personal psychotherapy: Results of an exploratory survey. *Professional Psychology: Research and Practice, 27*, 98–101. doi:10.1037/0735-7028.27.1.98

Hood, A. B., & Johnson, R. W. (2007). *Assessment in counseling: A guide to the use of psychological assessment procedures.* Washington, DC: American Counseling Association.

Horne, S. G., & Aurora, K. S. K. (2012). Feminist multicultural counseling psychology in transnational contexts. In C. Z. Enns & E. N. Williams (Eds.), *The Oxford handbook of feminist multicultural counseling psychology* (pp. 240–252). New York, NY: Oxford University Press. doi:10.1093/oxfordhb/9780199744220.013.0013

Horvath, A. O. (2009). How real is the "real relationship"? *Psychotherapy Research, 19*, 273–277. doi:10.1080/10503300802592506

Horvath, A. O., Del Re, A. C., Flückiger, C., & Symonds, D. (2011). Alliance in individual psychotherapy. In J. Norcross (Ed.), *Psychotherapy relationships that work* (2nd ed., pp. 25–69). New York, NY: Oxford University Press.

Horvath, A. O., & Greenberg, L. (1994). *The working alliance: Theory, research, and practice.* New York, NY: Wiley.

Horwitz, L. (1974). *Clinical prediction in psychotherapy.* New York, NY: Aronson.

Horwitz, L. (1986). An integrated, group-centered approach. In I. L. Kutash & A. Wolf (Eds.), *Psychotherapist's casebook: Theory and technique in the practice of modern therapies* (pp. 353–363). San Francisco, CA: Jossey-Bass.

Hoshmand, L. (1989). Alternate research paradigms: A review and teaching proposal. *The Counseling Psychologist, 17*, 3–79. doi:10.1177/0011000089171001

Howard, G. S. (1984). A modest proposal for a revision of strategies for counseling research. *Journal of Counseling Psychology, 31*, 430–441. doi:10.1037/0022-0167.31.4.430

Howard, G. S. (1985). Can research in the human sciences become more relevant to practice? *Journal of Counseling & Development, 63*, 539–544. doi:10.1002/j.1556-6676.1985.tb00675.x

Howard, G. S. (1986). The scientist–practitioner model in counseling psychology: Toward a deeper integration of theory, research, and practice. *The Counseling Psychologist, 14*, 61–105. doi:10.1177/0011000086141006

Howard, G. S. (1992). Behold our creation! What counseling psychology has become and might yet become. *Journal of Counseling Psychology, 39*, 419–442. doi:10.1037/0022-0167.39.4.419

Howard, G. S. (1993). Ecocounseling psychology: An introduction and overview. *The Counseling Psychologist, 21*, 550–559. doi:10.1177/0011000093214002

Huang, P., Lin, C., & Chang, Y. (2010). Current status of fulltime internship training in counseling psychology. *Bulletin of Educational Psychology, 42*, 123–142.

Hudson, J. I., Hiripi, E., Pope, H. G., & Kessler, R. C. (2007). The prevalence and correlates of eating disorders in the National Comorbidity Survey Replication. *Biological Psychiatry, 61*, 348–358. doi:10.1016/j.biopsych.2006.03.040

Humphrey, S. E., Nahrgang, J. D., & Morgeson, F. P. (2007). Integrating motivational, social, and contextual work design features: A meta-analytic summary and theoretical extension of the work design literature. *Journal of Applied Psychology, 92*, 1332–1356. doi:10.1037/0021-9010.92.5.1332

Hunter, M., & Struve, J. (1998). *The ethical use of touch in psychotherapy.* Thousand Oaks, CA: Sage. doi:10.1080/10720169808400156

Internet World Stats. (2011). *The Internet big picture: World Internet users and population stats.* Retrieved from http://www.internetworldstats.com/stats.htm

Israel, T. (2012). Exploring privilege in counseling psychology: Shifting the lens. *The Counseling Psychologist, 40*, 158–180. doi:10.1177/0011000011426297

Ivey, A., Ivey, M., Myers, J., & Sweeney, T. (2005). *Developmental counseling and therapy: Promoting wellness over the lifespan.* Boston, MA: Lahaska/Houghton-Mifflin.

Ivey, A. E. (1979). Counseling psychology—The most broadly-based applied psychology specialty. *The Counseling Psychologist, 8*(3), 3–6. doi:10.1177/001100007900800302

Ivey, A. E. (1986). *Developmental therapy: Theory into practice.* San Francisco, CA: Jossey-Bass.

Ivey, A. E., Ivey, M. B., & Zalaquett, C. P. (2010). *Intentional interviewing and counseling: Facilitating client development in a multicultural society* (7th ed.). Belmont, CA: Brooks-Cole.

Iwakabe, S., Rogan, K., & Stalikas, A. (2000). The relationship between client emotional expressiveness, therapist interventions, and the working alliance: An exploration of eight emotional expression events. *Journal of Psychotherapy Integration, 10*, 375–401. doi:10.1023/A:1009479100305

Jackson, D. D. (1957). The question of family homeostasis. *The Psychiatric Quarterly Supplement, 31*, 79–90.

Jackson, M. L. (1995). Multicultural counseling: Historical perspectives. In J. G. Ponterotto, J. M. Casas, L. A. Suzuki, & C. M. Alexander (Eds.), *Handbook of multicultural counseling* (pp. 3–16). Thousand Oaks, CA: Sage.

Jackson, Z. V., Wright, S. L., & Perrone-McGovern, K. M. (2010). Work–family interface for men in nontraditional careers. *Journal of Employment Counseling, 47*, 157–166. doi:10.1002/j.2161-1920.2010.tb00100.x

Jacob, M. C. (1987). Managing the internship application experience: Advice from an exhausted but contented survivor. *The Counseling Psychologist, 15*, 146–155. doi:10.1177/0011000087151009

Jacobs, L., & Hycner, R. (2009). *Relational approaches in Gestalt therapy.* Santa Cruz, CA: Gestalt Press.

Jacobson, E. (1938). *Progressive relaxation.* New York, NY: Brunner/Mazel.

Jahoda, M. (1958). *Current concepts of positive mental health.* New York, NY: Basic Books. doi:10.1037/11258-000

James, L. (2008). *Fixing hell.* New York, NY: Grand Central.

Jeffrey, T. B., Rankin, R. J., & Jeffrey, L. K. (1992). In service of two masters: The ethical–legal dilemma faced by military psychologists. *Professional Psychology: Research and Practice, 23*, 91–95. doi:10.1037/0735-7028.23.2.91

Jennings, L., & Skovholt, T. M. (1999). The cognitive, emotional, and relational characteristics of master therapists. *Journal of Counseling Psychology, 46*, 3–11. doi:10.1037/0022-0167.46.1.3

Johnson, D. H., & Gelso, C. J. (1980). The effectiveness of time limits in counseling and psychotherapy: A critical review. *The Counseling Psychologist, 9*(1), 70–83. doi:10.1177/001100008000900115

Johnson, S. M. (2004). *The practice of emotionally-focused marital therapy: Creating connections.* New York, NY: Brunner/Routledge.

Johnson, W. B. (2002). Consulting in the military context: Implications of the revised training principles. *Consulting Psychology Journal: Practice and Research, 54*, 233–241. doi:10.1037/1061-4087.54.4.233

Johnson, W. B., & Kennedy, C. H. (2010). Preparing psychologists for high-risk jobs: Key ethical considerations for military clinical supervisors. *Professional Psychology: Research and Practice, 41*, 298–304. doi:10.1037/a0019899

Joint Commission on Mental Illness and Mental Health. (1961). *Action for mental health*. New York, NY: Basic Books.

Jones, D. A., & McIntosh, B. R. (2010). Organizational and occupational commitment in relation to bridge employment and retirement intentions. *Journal of Vocational Behavior, 77*, 290–303. doi:10.1016/j.jvb.2010.04.004

Jones, E. (1953). *The life and works of Sigmund Freud* (Vol. 1). New York, NY: Basic Books.

Jones, E. (1955). *The life and works of Sigmund Freud* (Vol. 2). New York, NY: Basic Books.

Jones, E. (1957). *The life and works of Sigmund Freud* (Vol. 3). New York, NY: Basic Books.

Jones, K. D., & Heesacker, M. (2012). Addressing the situation: Evidence for the significance of microcontexts with the gender role conflict construct. *Psychology of Men & Masculinity, 13*, 294–307. doi:10.1037/a0025797

Jordaan, J. E., Myers, R. A., Layton, W. C., & Morgan, H. H. (1968). *The counseling psychologist*. Washington, DC: American Psychological Association.

Jordan, A. E., & Meara, N. M. (1990). Ethics and the professional practice of psychologists: The role of virtues and principles. *Professional Psychology: Research and Practice, 21*, 107–114. doi:10.1037/0735-7028.21.2.107

Joyce, A. S., Duncan, S. C., & Piper, W. E. (1995). Task analysis of "working" responses to dynamic interpretation in short-term individual psychotherapy. *Psychotherapy Research, 5*, 49–62. doi:10.1080/10503309512331331136

Joyce, N. R., & Rankin, T. J. (2010). The lessons of the development of the first APA ethics code: Blending science, practice, and politics. *Ethics & Behavior, 20*, 466–481. doi:10.1080/10508422.2010.521448

Joyce, P., & Sills, C. (2010). *Skills in Gestalt counselling and psychotherapy* (2nd ed.). Thousand Oaks, CA: Sage.

Juntunen, C. L. (2002). Development, developmental concerns, and counseling. In C. L. Juntunen & D. R. Atkinson (Eds.), *Counseling across the lifespan: Prevention and treatment* (pp. 23–37). Thousand Oaks, CA: Sage. doi:10.4135/9781452231792.n2

Juntunen, C. L. (2006). The psychology of working: The clinical context. *Professional Psychology: Research and Practice, 37*, 342–350. doi:10.1037/0735-7028.37.4.342

Juntunen, C. L., & Even, C. E. (2012). Theories of vocational psychology. In N. A. Fouad, J. A. Carter, & L. M. Subich (Eds.), *APA handbook of counseling psychology: Vol. 1. Theories, research, and methods* (pp. 237–267). Washington, DC: American Psychological Association.

Kabat-Zinn, J. (1990). *Full catastrophe living: Using the wisdom of your body and mind to face stress, pain and illness*. New York, NY: Delta.

Kagan, N., Armsworth, M. W., Altmaier, E. M., Dowd, E. T., Hansen, J. C., Mills, D. E., . . . Vasquez, M. J. T. (1988). Professional practice of counseling psychology in various settings. *The Counseling Psychologist, 16*, 347–365. doi:10.1177/0011000088163004

Kagan, N. I., Kagan, H., & Watson, M. G. (1995). Stress reduction in the workplace: The effectiveness of psychoeducational programs. *Journal of Counseling Psychology, 42*, 71–78. doi:10.1037/0022-0167.42.1.71

Kalbeitzer, R. (2009). Psychologists and interrogations: Ethical dilemmas in times of war. *Ethics & Behavior, 19*, 156–168. doi:10.1080/10508420902772793

Kanfer, F. H. (1977). The many faces of self-control, or behavior modification changes its focus. In R. B. Stuart (Ed.), *Behavioral self-managment* (pp. 1–48). New York, NY: Brunner/Mazel.

Kaschak, E. (1981). Feminist psychotherapy: The first decade. In S. Cox (Ed.), *Female psychology: The emerging self* (pp. 387–400). New York, NY: St. Martin's.

Kashubeck-West, S., & Mintz, L. B. (2001). Eating disorders in women: Etiology, assessment, and treatment. *The Counseling Psychologist, 29*, 627–634. doi:10.1177/0011000001295001

Kashubeck-West, S., Saunders, K. J., & Coker, A. (2012). Body image. In K. L. Goodheart, J. R. Clopton, & J. J. Robert-Mccomb (Eds.), *Eating disorders in women and children: Prevention, stress management, and treatment* (2nd ed., pp. 163–180). Boca Raton, FL: CRC Press.

Kashubeck-West, S., & Tagger, L. (2012). Feminist multicultural perspectives on body image and eating disorders in women. In C. Z. Enns & E. N. Williams (Eds.), *The Oxford handbook of feminist multicultural counseling psychology* (pp. 392–410). New York, NY: Oxford University Press. doi:10.1093/oxfordhb/9780199744220.013.0021

Kaslow, N. J., & Friedman, D. (1984). The interface of personal treatment and clinical training for psychotherapist trainees. In F. W. Kaslow (Ed.), *Psychotherapy with psychotherapists* (pp. 33–57). New York, NY: Haworth.

Kasper, L. B., Hill, C. E., & Kivlighan, D. M., Jr. (2008). Therapist immediacy in brief psychotherapy: Case study I. *Psychotherapy: Theory, Research, Practice, Training, 45*, 281–297. doi:10.1037/a0013305

Keith-Spiegel, P., & Wiederman, M. W. (2000). *The complete guide to graduate school admission: Psychology, counseling, and related professions.* Hillsdale, NJ: Erlbaum.

Kelley, F. A., Gelso, C. J., Fuertes, J. N., Marmarosh, C., & Lanier, S. H. (2010). The Real Relationship Inventory: Development and psychometric investigation of the Client Form. *Psychotherapy: Theory, Research, Practice, Training, 47*, 540–553. doi:10.1037/a0022082

Kelly, A. E. (1998). Clients' secret keeping in outpatient therapy. *Journal of Counseling Psychology, 45*, 50–57. doi:10.1037/0022-0167.45.1.50

Kelly, A. E., & Yuan, K.-H. (2009). Clients' secret keeping and the working alliance in adult outpatient therapy. *Psychotherapy: Theory, Practice, Research, Training, 46*, 193–202. doi:10.1037/a0016084

Kenny, M. E., Bower, M. E., Perry, J. C., Blustein, D. L., & Amtzis, A. T. (2004). *The Tools for Tomorrow Program: Integrating school-to-career psychoeducation into high school curriculum.* Chestnut Hill, MA: Boston College.

Kenny, M. E., & Walsh-Blair, L. Y. (2012). Educational development: Applications. In N. A. Fouad, J. A. Carter, & L. M. Subich (Eds.), *APA handbook of counseling psychology: Vol. 2. Practice, interventions, and applications* (pp. 29–55). Washington, DC: American Psychological Association.

Kernberg, O. (1975). *Borderline conditions and pathological narcissism.* New York, NY: Aronson.

Kerr, M. (1981). Family systems theory and therapy. In A. Gurman & D. Kniskern (Eds.), *Handbook of family therapy* (pp. 226–264). New York, NY: Brunner/Mazel.

Kiesler, D. J. (1971). Experimental designs in psychotherapy research. In A. Bergin & S. Garfield (Eds.), *Handbook of psychotherapy and behavior change* (pp. 36–74). New York, NY: Wiley.

Kim, B. S. K., Carwright, B. Y., Asay, P. A., & D'Andrea, M. J. (2003). A revision of the Multicultural Awareness, Knowledge, and Skills Survey—Counselor Edition. *Measurement and Evaluation in Counseling and Development, 36*, 161–180.

Kinsey, A. C., Pomeroy, W. B., & Martin, C. E. (1948). *Sexual behavior in the human male.* Philadelphia, PA: Saunders.

Kinsey, A. C., Pomeroy, W. B., Martin, C. E., & Gebhard, P. (1953). *Sexual behavior in the human female.* Philadelphia, PA: Saunders.

Kirsch, I. (2005). Placebo psychotherapy: Synonym or oxymoron? *Journal of Clinical Psychology, 61*, 791–803. doi:10.1002/jclp.20126

Kirsh, B. (1974). Consciousness-raising groups as therapy for women. In V. Franks & V. Burtle (Eds.), *Women in therapy: New psychotherapies for a changing society* (pp. 326–354). New York, NY: Brunner/Mazel.

Kiselica, M. S. (1998). Preparing Anglos for the challenges and joys of multiculturalism. *The Counseling Psychologist, 26*, 5–21. doi:10.1177/0011000098261001

Kitchener, K. S. (1984). Intuition, critical evaluation and ethical principles: The foundation for ethical decisions in counseling psychology. *The Counseling Psychologist, 12*(3), 43–55. doi:10.1177/0011000084123005

Kitchener, K. S. (2000). *Foundations of ethical practice, research and teaching in psychology.* Mahwah, NJ: Erlbaum.

Kitchener, K. S., & Anderson, S. K. (2011). *Foundations of ethical practice, research, and teaching in psychology and counseling* (2nd ed.). New York, NY: Taylor & Francis.

Kivlighan, D. M. (2002). Transference, interpretations, and insight: A research-practice model. In G. S. Tryon (Ed.), *Counseling based on process research: Applying what we know* (pp. 166–196). Boston, MA: Allyn & Bacon.

Kivlighan, D. M., Jr., Coleman, M. N., & Anderson, D. C. (2000). Process, outcome, and methodology in group counseling research. In S. Brown & R. Lent (Eds.), *Handbook of counseling psychology* (3rd ed., pp. 767–796). New York, NY: Wiley.

Kivlighan, D. M., Jr., Miles, J. R., & Paquin, J. D. (2010). Therapeutic factors in group counseling: Asking new questions. In R. Conyne (Ed.), *The Oxford handbook of group counseling* (pp. 121–136). New York, NY: Oxford University Press.

Klonoff, E. A., Landrine, H., & Campbell, R. (2000). Sexist discrimination may account for well-known gender differences in psychiatric symptoms. *Psychology of Women Quarterly, 24*, 93–99. doi:10.1111/j.1471-6402.2000.tb01025.x

Knapp, S., & VandeCreek, L. (1997). *Jaffee v. Redmond:* The Supreme Court recognizes a psychotherapist–patient privilege in federal courts. *Professional Psychology: Research and Practice, 28*, 567–572. doi:10.1037/0735-7028.28.6.567

Knapp, S., & VandeCreek, L. (2003). An overview of the major changes in the 2002 APA ethics code. *Professional Psychology: Research and Practice, 34*, 301–308. doi:10.1037/0735-7028.34.3.301

Knapp, S., & VandeCreek, L. (2004). A principle-based analysis of the 2002 American Psychological Association Ethics Code. *Psychotherapy: Theory, Research, Practice, Training, 41*, 247–254. doi:10.1037/0033-3204.41.3.247

Knapp, S. J., Gottlieb, M. C., Handelsman, M. M., & VandeCreek, L. D. (2012). *APA handbook of ethics in psychology.* Washington, DC: American Psychological Association.

Knox, S., & Hill, C. E. (2003). Therapist self-disclosure: Research-based suggestions for practitioners. *Journal of Clinical Psychology, 59*, 529–539. doi:10.1002/jclp.10157

Kohlberg, L. (1984). *Essays in moral development.* New York, NY: Harper & Row.

Kohut, H. (1971). *The analysis of the self.* New York, NY: International Universities Press.

Kohut, H. (1977). *The restoration of the self.* New York, NY: International Universities Press.

Kohut, H. (1984). *How does analysis cure?* Chicago, IL: University of Chicago Press.

Kolden, G. G., Klein, M. H., Wang, C.-C., & Austin, S. B. (2011). Congruence/genuineness. In J. C. Norcross (Ed.), *Psychotherapy relationships that work* (2nd ed., pp. 187–202). New York, NY: Oxford University Press.

Koocher, G. P., & Keith-Spiegel, P. (2008). *Ethics in psychology and the mental health professions* (3rd ed.). New York, NY: Oxford University Press.

Koocher, G. P., & Morray, E. (2000). Regulation of telepsychology: A survey of state attorneys general. *Professional Psychology: Research and Practice, 31*, 503–508. doi:10.1037/0735-7028.31.5.503

Koss, M. P., Goodman, L. A., Brown, A., Fitzgerald, L. F., Keita, G. P., & Russo, N. F. (1994). *No safe haven: Male violence against women at home, at work, and in the community.* Washington, DC: American Psychological Association. doi:10.1037/10156-000

Kovel, J. (1970). *White racism: A psychohistory.* New York, NY: Pantheon.

Kravetz, D. (1978). Consciousness-raising groups in the 1970s. *Psychology of Women Quarterly, 3,* 168–186. doi:10.1111/j.1471-6402.1978.tb00532.x

Krumboltz, J. D. (Ed.). (1966). *Revolution in counseling: Implications of behavioral science.* Boston, MA: Houghton Mifflin.

Krumboltz, J. D. (1968). Future directions for counseling research. In J. M. Whiteley (Ed.), *Research in counseling: Evaluation and refocus* (pp.184–203). Columbus, OH: Merrill.

Krumboltz, J. D. (1979). A social learning theory of career decision making. In A. M. Mitchell, G. B. Jones, & J. D. Krumboltz (Eds.), *Social learning and career decision making* (pp. 19–49). Cranston, RI: Carrol Press.

Krumboltz, J. D. (1988). *Career Beliefs Inventory.* Palo Alto, CA: Consulting Psychologists Press.

Krumboltz, J. D. (1991). *Manual for the Career Beliefs Inventory.* Palo Alto, CA: Consulting Psychologists Press.

Krumboltz, J. D. (1996). Learning theory of career counseling. In M. L. Savickas & W. B. Walsh (Eds.), *Handbook of career counseling theory and practice* (pp. 55–80). Palo Alto, CA: Davies-Black.

Krumboltz, J. D. (2009). The happenstance learning theory. *Journal of Career Assessment, 17,* 135–154. doi:10.1177/1069072708328861

Krumboltz, J. D., & Baker, R. D. (1973). Behavioral counseling for vocational decision. In H. Borow (Ed.), *Career guidance for a new age* (pp. 143–186). Boston, MA: Houghton Mifflin.

Krumboltz, J. D., & Coon, D. W. (1995). Current professional issues in vocational psychology. In W. B. Walsh & S. H. Osipow (Eds.), *Handbook of vocational psychology* (2nd ed., pp. 391–426). Mahwah, NJ: Erlbaum.

Krumboltz, J. D., Mitchell, A. M., & Jones, G. B. (1976). A social learning theory of career selection. *The Counseling Psychologist, 6*(1), 71–81. doi:10.1177/001100007600600117

Krumboltz, J. D., & Mitchell, L. K. (1979). Relevant rigorous research. *The Counseling Psychologist, 8*(3), 50–52. doi:10.1177/001100007900800309

Krumboltz, J. D., & Thoresen, C. E. (1969). *Behavioral counseling.* New York, NY: Holt, Rinehart & Winston.

Kuder, G. E, & Zytowski, D. G. (1991). *Kuder Occupational Interest Survey Form DD: General manual.* Monterey, CA: California Testing Bureau.

Kuhn, T. S. (1970). *The structure of scientific revolutions.* Chicago, IL: University of Chicago Press.

LaFromboise, T., Coleman, H. L. K., & Gerton, J. (1993). Psychological impact of biculturalism: Evidence and theory. *Psychological Bulletin, 114,* 395–412. doi:10.1037/0033-2909.114.3.395

LaFromboise, T. D., Coleman, H. L. K., & Hernandez, A. (1991). Development and factor structure of the Cross-Cultural Counseling Inventory—Revised. *Professional Psychology: Research and Practice, 22,* 380–388. doi:10.1037/0735-7028.22.5.380

Lambert, M. J. (Ed.). (1983). *A guide to psychotherapy and patient relationships.* Homewood, IL: Dow Jones-Irwin.

Lambert, M. J. (Ed.). (2013). *Bergin and Garfield's handbook of psychotherapy and behavior change* (6th ed.). New York, NY: Wiley.

Lambert, M. J., & Bergin, A. E. (1994). The effectiveness of psychotherapy. In A. Bergin & S. Garfield (Eds.), *Handbook of psychotherapy and behavior change* (4th ed., pp. 143–189). New York, NY: Wiley.

Lambert, M. J., & Hill, C. E. (1994). Assessing psychotherapy outcomes and process. In A. E. Bergin and S. L. Garfield (Eds.), *Handbook of psychotherapy and behavior change* (4th ed., pp. 72–113). New York, NY: Wiley.

Lambert, M. J., & Veermersch, D. A. (2008). Measuring and improving psychotherapy outcome in routine practice. In S. Brown & R. Lent (Eds.), *Handbook of counseling psychology* (4th ed., 233–248). New York, NY: Wiley.

Lampropoulos, G. K. (2000). A reexamination of the empirically supported treatments critiques. *Psychotherapy Research, 10,* 474–487. doi:10.1093/ptr/10.4.474

Lampropoulos, G. K., Goldfried, M. R., Castonguay, L. G., Lambert, M. L., Stiles, W. B., & Nestoros, J. N. (2002). What kind of research can we realistically expect from the practitioner? *Journal of Clinical Psychology, 58,* 1241–1264. doi:10.1002/jclp.10109

Lanci, M., & Spreng, A. (2008). *The therapist's starter guide: Setting up and building your practice, working with clients, and managing professional growth.* Hoboken, NJ: Wiley.

Langs, R. J. (1974). *The technique of psychoanalytic psychotherapy, Vol. 1.* New York, NY: Aronson.

Langs, R. J. (1976). *The bipersonal field.* New York, NY: Aronson.

Lapan, R. T., & Jingeleski, J. (1992). Circumscribing vocational aspirations in junior high school. *Journal of Counseling Psychology, 39,* 81–90. doi:10.1037/0022-0167.39.1.81

Lapan, R. T., Turner, S., & Pierce, M. E. (2012). College and career readiness: Policy and research to support effective counseling in schools. In N. A. Fouad, J. A. Carter, & L. M. Subich (Eds.), *APA handbook of counseling psychology: Vol. 2. Practice, interventions, and applications* (pp. 57–73). Washington, DC: American Psychological Association. doi:10.1037/13755-003

Larson, L. M. (2012). Worklife across the lifespan. In E. M. Altmaier & J. C. Hansen (Eds.), *The Oxford handbook of counseling psychology* (pp. 128–178). New York, NY: Oxford University Press.

Larson, L. M., Heppner, P. P., Ham, T., & Dugan, K. (1988). Investigating multiple subtypes of career indecision through cluster analysis. *Journal of Counseling Psychology, 35,* 439–446. doi:10.1037/0022-0167.35.4.439

Larson, L. M., Rottinghaus, P. J., & Borgen, F. H. (2002). Meta-analyses of Big Six interests and Big Five personality variables. *Journal of Vocational Behavior, 61,* 217–239. doi:10.1006/jvbe.2001.1854

Larson, L. M., Wei, M., Wu, T. F., Borgen, F. H., & Bailey, D. C. (2007). Discriminating among educational majors and career aspirations in Taiwanese undergraduates: The contribution of personality and self-efficacy. *Journal of Counseling Psychology, 54,* 395–408. doi:10.1037/0022-0167.54.4.395

Lebow, J. L. (2005). *Handbook of clinical family therapy.* New York, NY: Wiley.

Lebow, J. L. (2008). Couple and family therapy. In J. L. Lebow (Ed.), *Twenty-first century psychotherapy* (pp. 307–346). New York, NY: Wiley.

Lecca, P. J., Quervalú, I., Nunes, J. V., & Gonzales, H. F. (1998). *Cultural competency in health, social, and human services: Directions for the twenty-first century.* New York, NY: Garland.

Lee, D. L., Sheridan, D. J., Rosen, A. D., & Jones, I. (2013). Psychotherapy trainees' multicultural case conceptualization content: Thematic differences across three cases. *Psychotherapy, 50,* 206–212. doi:10.1037/a0028242

Lee, D. Y., Uhlemann, M. R., & Haase, R. F. (1985). Counselor verbal and nonverbal responses and perceived expertness, trustworthiness, and attractiveness. *Journal of Counseling Psychology, 32,* 181–187. doi:10.1037/0022-0167.32.2.181

Lee, K. (2005). Coping with career indecision: Differences between four career choice types. *Journal of Career Development, 31,* 279–289. doi:10.1007/s10871-005-4741-0

Lehavot, K., Barnett, J. E., & Powers, D. (2010). Psychotherapy, professional relationships, and ethical considerations in the MySpace generation. *Professional Psychology: Research and Practice, 41,* 160–166. doi:10.1037/a0018709

Lejuez, C. W., Hopko, D. R., Levine, S., Gholkar, R., & Collins, L. M. (2005). The therapeutic alliance in behavior therapy. *Psychotherapy: Theory, Research, Practice, Training, 42,* 456–468. doi:10.1037/0033-3204.42.4.456

Lent, R. W. (2008). Understanding and promoting work satisfaction: An integrative review. In S. D. Brown & R. W. Lent (Eds.), *Handbook of counseling psychology* (4th ed., pp. 462–480). Hoboken, NJ: Wiley.

Lent, R. W., Brown, S. D., & Hackett, G. (1994). Toward a unifying social cognitive theory of career and academic interest, choice, and performance. *Journal of Vocational Behavior, 45,* 79–122. doi:10.1006/jvbe.1994.1027

Lent, R. W., Brown, S. D., & Hackett, G. (1996). Career development for a social cognitive perspective. In D. Brown, L. Brooks, & Associates. (Eds.), *Career choice and development* (3rd ed., pp. 373–421). San Francisco, CA: Jossey-Bass.

Lent, R. W., Brown, S. D., & Hackett, G. (2000). Contextual supports and barriers to career choice: A social cognitive analysis. *Journal of Counseling Psychology, 47,* 36–49. doi:10.1037/0022-0167.47.1.36

Leong, F. T. L. (1993). The career counseling process with racial-ethnic minorities: The case of Asian Americans. *Career Development Quarterly, 42,* 26–40. doi:10.1002/j.2161-0045.1993.tb00242.x

Leong, F. T. L. (1996). Toward an integrative model for cross-cultural counseling and psychotherapy. *Applied & Preventive Psychology, 5,* 189–209. doi:10.1016/S0962-1849(96)80012-6

Leong, F. T. L., & Santiago-Rivera, A. L. (1999). Climbing the multiculturalism summit: Challenges and pitfalls. In P. Pedersen (Ed.), *Multiculturalism as a fourth force* (pp. 61–72). Philadelphia: Brunner/Mazel.

Lev, A. I. (2007). Transgender communities: Developing identity through connection. In K. J. Bieschke, R. M. Perez, & K. A. DeBord (Eds.), *Handbook of counseling and psychotherapy with lesbian, gay, bisexual, and transgender clients* (2nd ed., pp. 147–175). Washington, DC: American Psychological Association. doi:10.1037/11482-006

Levant, R., & Shlien, J. (Eds.). (1984). *Client-centered therapy and the person-centered approach: New directions in theory, research, and practice.* New York, NY: Praeger.

Levenson, H. (2010). *Brief dynamic therapy.* Washington, DC: American Psychological Association.

Levin, A. S., Krumboltz, J. D., & Krumboltz, B. L. (1995). *Exploring your career beliefs: A workbook for the Career Beliefs Inventory with techniques for integrating your Strong and MBTI results.* Palo Alto, CA: Consulting Psychologists Press.

Levin, M. (1995). Does race matter? *American Psychologist, 50,* 45–46. doi:10.1037/0003-066X.50.1.45

Levinson, D. J. (1980). The mentoring relationship. In M. Morgan (Ed.), *Managing career development* (pp. 117–119). New York, NY: Van Nostrand.

Levitsky, A., & Perls, F. S. (1970). The rules and games of Gestalt therapy. In J. Fagan & I. L. Shepherd (Eds.), *Gestalt therapy now* (pp. 140–149). New York, NY: Harper & Row.

Levitt, M. J., Lane, J. D., & Levitt, J. L. (2005). Immigration stress, social support, and adjustment in the first post-migration year: An intergenerational analysis. *Research in Human Development, 2,* 159–177. doi:10.1207/s15427617rhd0204_1

Levy, K. N., & Scala, J. W. (2012). Transference, transference interpretations, and transference-focused psychotherapies. *Psychotherapy, 49,* 391–403. doi:10.1037/a0029371

Lewin, K. (1935). *A dynamic theory of personality: Selected papers.* New York, NY: McGraw-Hill.

Lewis, J., Arnold, M., House, R., & Toporek, R. L. (2002). *American Counseling Association advocacy competencies.* Alexandria, VA: American Counseling Association.

Lichtenberger, E. O., & Kaufman, A. S. (2013). *Essentials of WAIS-IV assessment* (2nd ed.). New York, NY: Wiley.

Lieberman, M., Yalom, I., & Miles, M. (1973). *Encounter groups: First facts.* New York, NY: Basic Books.

Lietaer, G. (1984). Unconditional positive regard: A controversial basic attitude in client-centered therapy. In R. F. Levant & J. M. Shlien (Eds.), *Client-centered therapy and the person-centered approach* (pp. 41–58). New York, NY: Praeger.

Lightsey, O. R., Jr. (1996). What leads to wellness? The role of psychological resources in wellbeing. *The Counseling Psychologist, 24,* 589–735. doi:10.1177/0011000096244002

Lilienfeld, S. O. (2007). Psychological treatments that cause harm. *Perspectives on Psychological Science, 2,* 53–70. doi:10.1111/j.1745-6916.2007.00029.x

Lindon, J. A. (1994). Gratification and provision in psychoanalysis: Should we get rid of the "rule of abstinence"? *Psychoanalytic Dialogues, 4,* 549–582. doi:10.1080/10481889409539038

Linehan, M. M. (1993). *Cognitive behavioral therapy of borderline personality disorder.* New York, NY: Guilford Press.

Linehan, M. M. (1997). Validation and psychotherapy. In A. Bohart & L. Greenberg (Eds.), *Empathy reconsidered: New directions in psychotherapy* (pp. 353–392). Washington, DC: American Psychological Association. doi:10.1037/10226-016

Linskey, A. (2012, November 7). Voters approve same-sex marriage law. *The Baltimore Sun.* Retrieved from http://articles.baltimoresun.com/2012-11-01/news/bs-md-same-sex-ballot-20121106

Liu, W. M. (2012). Developing a social class and classism consciousness. In E. M. Altmaier & J. C. Hansen (Eds.), *The Oxford handbook of counseling psychology* (pp. 326–345). New York, NY: Oxford University Press.

Liu, W. M., & Pope-Davis, D. B. (2003). Moving from diversity to multiculturalism: Exploring power and its implications for multicultural competence. In D. B. Pope-Davis, H. L. K. Coleman, W. M. Liu, & R. L. Toporek (Eds.), *Handbook of multicultural competencies in counseling and psychotherapy* (pp. 90–102). Thousand Oaks, CA: Sage. doi:10.4135/9781452231693.n6

Llewelyn, S. P. (1988). Psychological therapy as viewed by clients and therapists. *British Journal of Clinical Psychology, 27,* 223–237. doi:10.1111/j.2044-8260.1988.tb00779.x

Lobel, S. A. (1999). Impacts of diversity and work–life initiatives in organizations. In G. N. Powell (Ed.), *Handbook of gender and work* (pp. 453–474). Thousand Oaks, CA: Sage. doi:10.4135/9781452231365.n23

Locke, B. D., Buzolitz, J. S., Lei, P.-W., Boswell, J. F., McAleavey, A. A., Sevig, T. D., . . . Hayes, J. A. (2011). Development of the Counseling Center Assessment of Psychological Symptoms-62 (CCAPS-62). *Journal of Counseling Psychology, 58,* 97–109. doi:10.1037/a0021282

Loftquist, L. H., & Dawis, R. V. (1984). Research on work adjustment and satisfaction: Implications for career counseling. In S. D. Brown & R. W. Lent (Eds.), *Handbook of counseling psychology* (pp. 216–237). New York, NY: Wiley.

Lopez, S. J., & Edwards, L. M. (2008). The interface of counseling psychology and positive psychology: Assessing and promoting strengths. In S. Brown & R. Lent (Eds.), *Handbook of counseling psychology* (4th ed., pp. 86–99). New York, NY: Wiley.

Lopez, S. J., Edwards, L. M., Magyar-Moe, J. L., Pedrotti, J. T., & Ryder, J. A. (2003). Fulfilling its promise: Counseling psychology's efforts to promote optimal human functioning. In W. B. Walsh (Ed.), *Counseling psychology and optimal human functioning* (pp. 171–198). Mahwah, NJ: Erlbaum.

Lopez, S. J., Magyar-Moe, J. L., Petersen, S. E., Ryder, J. A., Krieshok, T. S., O'Byrne, K. K., . . . Fry, N. A. (2006). Counseling psychology's focus on positive aspects of human functioning. *The Counseling Psychologist, 34,* 205–227. doi:10.1177/0011000005283393

Lopez, S. J., Tree, H., Bowers, K., & Burns, M. E. (2004). *KU strengths mentoring protocol.* Unpublished manuscript, University of Kansas.

López, S. R., Barrio, C., Kopelowicz, A., & Vega, W. A. (2012). From documenting to eliminating disparities in mental health care for Latinos. *American Psychologist, 67,* 511–523. doi:10.1037/a0029737

Low, K. S. D., & Rounds, J. (2006). Vocational interests: Bridging person and environment. In D. Segal & J. Thomas (Eds.), *Comprehensive handbook of personality and psychology: Vol. 1: Personality and everyday functioning* (pp. 251–267). New York, NY: Wiley.

Lowe, C. M. (1969). *Value orientations in counseling and psychotherapy: The meanings of mental health.* San Francisco, CA: Chandler.

Lowman, R. (1993). *Counseling and psychotherapy of work dysfunctions.* Washington, DC: American Psychological Association. doi:10.1037/10133-000

Luborsky, L. (1984). *Principles of psychoanalytic psychotherapy: A manual for supportive–expressive treatment.* New York, NY: Basic Books.

Luborsky, L., Singer, B., & Luborsky, L. (1975). Comparative studies of psychotherapies: Is it true that "Everyone has won and all must have prizes?" *Archives of General Psychiatry, 32,* 995–1008. doi:10.1001/archpsyc.1975.01760260059004

Lucas, M. S. (1993). A validation of types of career indecision at a counseling center. *Journal of Counseling Psychology, 40,* 440–446. doi:10.1037/0022-0167.40.4.440

Lyons, H. Z., Brenner, B. R., & Fassinger, R. E. (2005). A multicultural test of the theory of work adjustment: Investigating the role of heterosexism and fit perceptions in the job satisfaction of lesbian, gay, and bisexual employees. *Journal of Counseling Psychology, 52,* 537–548. doi:10.1037/0022-0167.52.4.537

Lyons, H. Z., & O'Brien, K. M. (2006). The role of person–environment fit in the job satisfaction and tenure intentions of African American employees. *Journal of Counseling Psychology, 53*, 387–396. doi:10.1037/0022-0167.53.4.387

Maccoby, E. E. (1980). *Social development: Psychological growth and the parent–child relationship*. San Diego, CA: Harcourt.

MacIsaac, D. S. (1996). Optimal frustration: An endangered concept. In A. Goldberg (Ed.), *Progress in self psychology: Vol. 12. Basic ideas reconsidered* (pp. 3–16). Hillsdale, NJ: Analytic Press.

Madanes, C. (1981). *Strategic family therapy*. San Francisco, CA: Jossey-Bass.

Madrid, P. A., Garfield, R., Jaberi, P., Daly, M., Richard, G., & Grant, R. (2008). Mental health services in Louisiana school-based health centers post-Hurricanes Katrina and Rita. *Professional Psychology: Research and Practice, 39*, 45–51. doi:10.1037/0735-7028.39.1.45

Magoon, T. M., & Holland, J. L. (1984). Research training and supervision. In S. Brown & R. Lent (Eds.), *Handbook of counseling psychology* (pp. 682–715). New York, NY: Wiley.

Maheu, M. M. (2001). Practicing psychotherapy on the Internet: Risk management challenges and opportunities. *Register Report, 27*, 23–28.

Mahler, M. S., Bergman, A., & Pine, F. (1975). *The psychological birth of the human infant: symbiosis and individuation*. New York, NY: Basic Books.

Mallinckrodt, B. (2010). The psychotherapy relationship as attachment: Evidence and implications. *Journal of Personal and Social Relationships, 27*, 262–270. doi:10.1177/0265407509360905

Mallinckrodt, B., & Fretz, B. R. (1988). Social support and the impact of job loss on older professionals. *Journal of Counseling Psychology, 35*, 281–286. doi:10.1037/0022-0167.35.3.281

Mallinckrodt, B., Gelso, C. J., & Royalty, G. M. (1990). Impact of the research training environment and counseling psychology students' Holland personality type on interest in research. *Professional Psychology: Research and Practice, 21*, 26–32. doi:10.1037/0735-7028.21.1.26

Mallinckrodt, B., Porter, M. J., & Kivlighan, D. M. (2005). Client attachment to therapist, depth of session exploration, and object relations in brief psychotherapy. *Psychotherapy: Theory, Research, Practice, Training, 42*, 85–100. doi:10.1037/0033-3204.42.1.85

Maltzman, S. (2012). Process and outcomes in counseling and psychotherapy. In E. M. Altmaier & J. C. Hansen (Eds.), *The Oxford handbook of counseling psychology* (pp. 95–127). New York, NY: Oxford University Press.

Mann, J. (1973). *Time-limited psychotherapy*. Cambridge, MA: Harvard University Press.

Mann, J. (1991). Time-limited psychotherapy. In P. Crits-Christoph & J. P. Barber (Eds.), *Handbook of short-term dynamic psychotherapy* (pp. 17–44). New York, NY: Basic Books.

Marcia, J. E. (1966). Development and validation of ego-identity status. *Journal of Personality and Social Psychology, 3,* 551–558. doi:10.1037/h0023281

Markin, R. D., & Kivlighan, D. M. (2007). Bias in psychotherapy ratings of transference and insight. *Psychotherapy, 44,* 300–315. doi:10.1037/0033-3204.44.3.300

Markin, R. D., & Marmarosh, C. (2010). Application of adult attachment theory to group member transference and the group therapy process. *Psychotherapy: Theory, Research, Practice, Training, 47,* 111–121. doi:10.1037/a0018840

Marmarosh, C. L. (2012). Empirically supported perspectives on transference. *Psychotherapy, 49,* 364–369. doi:10.1037/a0028801

Marmarosh, C. L., Gelso, C. J., Markin, R. D., Majors, R., Mallory, C., & Choi, J. (2009). The real relationship in psychotherapy: Relationships to adult attachments, working alliance, and therapy outcome. *Journal of Counseling Psychology, 56,* 337–350. doi:10.1037/a0015169

Marmarosh, C. L., Markin, R. D., & Spiegel, E. (2013). *Attachment in group psychotherapy.* Washington, DC: American Psychological Association. doi:10.1037/14186-000

Maruish, M. E. (1999). *The use of psychological testing for treatment planning and outcome assessment.* Hillsdale, NJ: Erlbaum.

Maslow, A. (1970). *Motivation and personality* (2nd ed.). New York, NY: Harper & Row.

Maslow, A. H. (1954). *Motivation and personality.* New York, NY: Harper & Row.

Maslow, A. H. (1968). *Toward a psychology of being* (2nd ed.). New York, NY: Van Nostrand Reinhold.

Masten, A. S., Burt, K. B., Roisman, G. I., Obradovic, J., Long, J. D., & Tellegen, A. (2004). Resources and resilience in the transition to adulthood: Continuity and change. *Development and Psychopathology, 16,* 1071–1094. doi:10.1017/S0954579404040143

Matheny, K. B., Aycock, D. W., Pugh, J. L., Curlette, W. L., & Cannella, K. A. S. (1986). Stress coping: A qualitative and quantitative synthesis with implications for treatment. *The Counseling Psychologist, 14,* 499–549. doi:10.1177/0011000086144001

Mathy, R. M., Kerr, D. L., & Haydin, B. M. (2003). Methodological rigor and ethical considerations in Internet-mediated research. *Psychotherapy: Theory, Research, Practice, Training, 40,* 77–85. doi:10.1037/0033-3204.40.1-2.77

May, R. (1967). *Psychology and the human dilemma.* New York, NY: Van Nostrand Reinhold.

Mayotte-Blum, J., Slavin-Mulford, J., Lehmann, M., Pesale, F., Becker-Matero, N., & Hilsenroth, M. (2012). Therapeutic intimacy across long-term psychodynamic psychotherapy: An evidence-based case study. *Journal of Counseling Psychology, 59,* 27–40. doi:10.1037/a0026087

McArthur, C. (1954). Analyzing the clinical process. *Journal of Counseling Psychology, 1,* 203–208. doi:10.1037/h0061275

McCarn, S. R., & Fassinger, R. E. (1996). Revisioning sexual minority identity formation: A new model of lesbian identity and its implications for counseling and research. *The Counseling Psychologist, 24,* 508–534. doi:10.1177/0011000096243011

McCarthy, P. R., & Betz, N. E. (1978). Differential effects of self-disclosing versus self-involving counselor statements. *Journal of Counseling Psychology, 25,* 251–256. doi:10.1037/0022-0167.25.4.251

McCrae, R. R., & Costa, P. T., Jr. (1999). A five-factor theory of personality. In L. A. Pervin & O. P. John (Eds.), *Handbook of personality: Theory and research* (2nd ed., pp. 139–153). New York, NY: Guilford Press.

McCrae, R. R., & Costa, P. T., Jr. (2008). The five-factor theory of personality. In O. P. John, R. W. Robins, & L. A. Pervin (Eds.), *Handbook of personality: Theory and research* (3rd ed., pp. 159–181). New York, NY: Guilford Press.

McCullough Vaillant, L. (1997). *Changing character: Short-term anxiety-regulating psychotherapy for restructuring defenses, affects, and attachment.* New York, NY: Basic Books.

McEwan, J., & Duncan, P. (1993). Personal therapy in the training of psychologists. *Canadian Psychology/Psychologie canadienne, 34,* 186–197. doi:10.1037/h0078766

McGoldrick, M., Giordano, J., & Garcia-Preto, N. (Eds.). (2005). *Ethnicity and family therapy* (3rd ed.). New York, NY: Guilford Press.

McIntosh, P. (1989, July/August). White privilege: Unpacking the invisible knapsack. *Peace and Freedom,* 10–12.

McKee-Ryan, F. M., Song, Z., Wanberg, C. R., & Kinicki, A. J. (2005). Psychological and physical well-being during unemployment: A meta-analytic study. *Journal of Applied Psychology, 90,* 53–76. doi:10.1037/0021-9010.90.1.53

McLeod, J. (2011). *Qualitative research in counselling and psychotherapy.* London, United Kingdom: Sage.

McPherson, R., Pisecco, S., Elman, N., Crosbie-Burnett, M., & Sayger, T. (2000). Counseling psychology's ambivalent relationship with master's-level training. *The Counseling Psychologist, 28,* 687–700. doi:10.1177/0011000000285006

McWhirter, E. H., & McWhirter, B. T. (2007). Grounding clinical training and supervision in an empowerment model. In E. Aldarondo (Ed.), *Advancing social justice through clinical practice* (pp. 417–442). Mahwah, NJ: Erlbaum.

McWilliams, N. (2011). *Psychoanalytic diagnosis: Understanding personality structure in the clinical process* (2nd ed.) New York, NY: Guilford Press.

Meade, C. J., Hamilton, M. K., & Yuen, R. K.-W.(1982). Consultation research: The time has come, the walrus said. *The Counseling Psychologist, 10*(4), 39–51. doi:10.1177/0011000082104009

Meara, N. M. (1990). 1989 Division 17 presidential address: Science, practice, and politics. *The Counseling Psychologist, 18*, 144–167. doi:10.1177/0011000090181012

Meara, N. M. (1996). Prudence and career assessment: Making our implicit assumptions explicit. In M. L. Savickas & W. B. Walsh (Eds.), *Handbook of career counseling theory and practice* (pp. 315–330). Palo Alto, CA: Davies-Black.

Meara, N. M., & Myers, R. A. (1998). A history of Division 17 (Counseling Psychology): Establishing stability amid change. In D. A. Dewsbury (Ed.), *Unification through division: Histories of the divisions of the American Psychological Association* (Vol. III, pp. 9–41). Washington, DC: American Psychological Association.

Meara, N. M., Schmidt, L. D., & Day, J. D. (1996). Principles and virtues: A foundation for ethical decisions, policies, and character. *The Counseling Psychologist, 24*, 4–77. doi:10.1177/0011000096241002

Mednick, M. T., & Urbanski, L. L. (1991). The origins and activities of APA's Division of the Psychology of Women. *Psychology of Women Quarterly, 15*, 651–663. doi:10.1111/j.1471-6402.1991.tb00437.x

Meehl, P. E. (1954). *Clinical versus statistical prediction.* Minneapolis: University of Minnesota Press. doi:10.1037/11281-000

Megargee, E. I. (2001). *A guide to obtaining a psychology internship* (4th ed.). New York, NY: Brunner-Routledge.

Meichenbaum, D. (1977). *Cognitive-behavior modification.* New York, NY: Plenum Press. doi:10.1007/978-1-4757-9739-8

Meichenbaum, D. H., & Deffenbacher, J. L. (1988). Stress inoculation training. *The Counseling Psychologist, 16*, 69–90. doi:10.1177/0011000088161005

Menninger, K., Mayman, M., & Pruyser, P. (1963). *The vital balance: The life process in mental health and illness.* New York, NY: Wiley.

Merluzzi, T. V., & Hegde, K. (2003). Implications of social and cultural influences for multicultural competencies in health psychology. In D. B. Pope-Davis, H. L. K. Coleman, W. M. Liu, & R. L. Toporek (Eds.), *Handbook of multicultural competencies in counseling and psychology* (pp. 420–438). Thousand Oaks, CA: Sage. doi:10.4135/9781452231693.n27

Mermin, G. B. T., Johnson, R. W., & Murphy, D. P. (2007). Why do boomers plan to work longer? *Journals of Gerontology: Series B: Psychological Sciences and Social Sciences, 62*, S286–S294. doi:10.1093/geronb/62.5.S286

Messer, S. B., & Warren, C. S. (1995). *Models of brief psychodynamic therapy.* New York, NY: Guilford Press.

Meyer, G. J., Finn, S. E., Eyde, L., Kay, G. G., Kubiszyn, T., Moreland, K., . . . Dies, R. (1998). *Benefits and costs of psychological assessment in health care delivery: Report of the Board of Professional Affairs Psychological Assessment Work Group, Part I.* Washington, DC: American Psychological Association.

Mintz, L. B., Bartels, K. M., & Rideout, C. A. (1995). Training in counseling ethnic minorities and race-based availability of graduate school resources. *Professional Psychology: Research and Practice, 26*, 316–321. doi:10.1037/0735-7028.26.3.316

Mintz, L. B., & O'Neil, J. M. (1990). Gender roles, sex, and the process of psychotherapy: Many questions and few answers. *Journal of Counseling & Development, 68*, 381–387. doi:10.1002/j.1556-6676.1990.tb02515.x

Mintz, L. B., & Tager, D. (2012). Feminist therapy with male clients: Empowering men to be their whole selves. In C. Z. Enns & E. N. Williams (Eds.), *The Oxford handbook of feminist multicultural counseling psychology* (pp. 322–338). New York, NY: Oxford University Press. doi:10.1093/oxfordhb/9780199744220.013.0017

Minuchin, P. (1985). Families and individual development: Provocations from the field of family therapy. *Child Development, 56*, 289–302.

Minuchin, P., Colapinto, J., & Minuchin, S. (2007). *Working with families of the poor* (2nd ed.). New York, NY: Guilford Press.

Minuchin, S. (1974). *Families and family therapy.* Cambridge, MA: Harvard University Press.

Minuchin, S., Lee, W.-Y., & Simon, G. M. (1996). *Mastering family therapy: Journeys of hope and transformation.* New York, NY: Wiley.

Minuchin, S., & Nichols, M. P. (1993). *Family healing: Tales of hope and renewal from family therapy.* New York, NY: Free Press.

Minuchin, S., Rosman, B., & Baker, L. (1978). *Psychosomatic families.* Cambridge, MA: Harvard University Press.

Mishne, J. M. (1993). *The evolution and application of clinical theory: Perspectives from four psychologies.* New York, NY: Free Press.

Mitchell, K. E., Levin, A. S., & Krumboltz, J. D. (1999). Planned happenstance: Constructing unexpected career opportunities. *Journal of Counseling & Development, 77*, 115–124. doi:10.1002/j.1556-6676.1999.tb02431.x

Mitchell, L. K., & Krumboltz, J. D. (1984). Social learning approaches to career decision making. In D. Brown, L. Brooks, & Associates. (Eds.), *Career choice and development* (pp. 235–280). San Francisco, CA: Jossey-Bass.

Mitchell, L. K., & Krumboltz, J. D. (1996). Krumboltz's learning theory of career choice and counseling. In D. Brown, L. Brooks, & Associates (Eds.), *Career choice and development* (3rd ed., pp. 233–280). San Francisco, CA: Jossey-Bass.

Mitchell, S. A. (1993). *Hope and dread in psychoanalysis.* New York, NY: Basic Books.

Miville, M. L., Adams, E. M., & Juntunen, C. L. (2007). Counseling psychology perspectives on the predoctoral internship supply–demand imbalance: Strategies for problem definition and resolution. *Training and Education in Professional Psychology, 1*, 258–266. doi:10.1037/1931-3918.1.4.258

Monro, F., & Huon, G. (2005). Media-portrayed idealized images, body shame, and appearance anxiety. *International Journal of Eating Disorders, 38,* 85–90. doi:10.1002/eat.20153

Moore, W. E. (1970). *The professions: Roles and rules.* New York, NY: Sage.

Moradi, B., & Funderburk, J. R. (2006). Roles of perceived sexist events and perceived social support in the mental health of women seeking counseling. *Journal of Counseling Psychology, 53,* 464–473. doi:10.1037/0022-0167.53.4.464

Moradi, B., & Huang, Y. (2008). Objectification theory and psychology of women: A decade of advances and future directions. *Psychology of Women Quarterly, 32,* 377–398. doi:10.1111/j.1471-6402.2008.00452.x

Moradi, B., Mohr, J. J., Worthington, R. L., & Fassinger, R. E. (2009). Counseling psychology research on sexual (orientation) minority issues: Conceptual and methodological challenges and opportunities. *Journal of Counseling Psychology, 56,* 5–22. doi:10.1037/a0014572

Moradi, B., & Yoder, J. D. (2012). The psychology of women. In E. M. Altmaier & J. C. Hansen (Eds.), *The Oxford handbook of counseling psychology* (pp. 346–374). New York, NY: Oxford University Press.

Morgan, E. M., & Landrum, R. E. (2012). *You've earned your doctorate in psychology . . . now what? Securing a job as an academic or professional psychologist.* Washington, DC: American Psychological Association.

Morgan, R. D., Kuther, T. L., & Habben, C. J. (Eds.). (2005). *Life after graduate school in psychology: Insider's advice from new psychologists.* New York, NY: Psychology Press.

Morran, D. K. (1986). Relationship of counselor self-talk and hypothesis formulation to performance level. *Journal of Counseling Psychology, 33,* 395–400. doi:10.1037/0022-0167.33.4.395

Morran, D. K., Kurpius, D. J., & Brack, G. (1989). Empirical investigation of counselor self-talk categories. *Journal of Counseling Psychology, 36,* 505–510. doi:10.1037/0022-0167.36.4.505

Morrow, S. L. (2012). Sexual orientations and identity. In E. M. Altmaier & J. C. Hansen (Eds.), *The Oxford handbook of counseling psychology* (pp. 409–433). New York, NY: Oxford University Press.

Morrow, S. L., & Hawxhurst, D. (1998). Feminist therapy: Integrating political analysis in counseling and psychotherapy. *Women & Therapy, 21,* 37–50. doi:10.1300/J015v21n02_03

Morrow, S. L., & Hawxhurst, D. (2012). Political analysis: Cornerstone of feminist multicultural counseling and psychotherapy. In C. Z. Enns & E. N. Williams (Eds.), *The Oxford handbook of feminist multicultural counseling psychology* (pp. 339–357). New York, NY: Oxford University Press. doi:10.1093/oxfordhb/9780199744220.013.0018

Morrow, S. L., & Smith, M. L. (2000). Qualitative research for counseling psychology. In S. D. Brown & R. W. Lent (Eds.), *Handbook of counseling psychology* (3rd ed., pp. 199–230). New York, NY: Wiley.

Munley, P. H., Pate, W. E., II, & Duncan, L. E. (2008). Demographic, educational, employment, and professional characteristics of counseling psychologists. *The Counseling Psychologist, 36,* 250–280. doi:10.1177/0011000006296915

Muran, J. C., Castonguay, L. G., & Strauss, B. (2010). A brief introduction to psychotherapy research. In L. G. Castonguay, J. C. Muran, L. Angus, J. A. Hayes, N. Ladany, & T. Anderson (Eds.), *Bringing psychotherapy research to life: Understanding change through the work of leading clinical researchers* (pp. 3–13). Washington, DC: American Psychological Association. doi:10.1037/12137-001

Murdock, N. L. (2013). *Theories of counseling and psychotherapy: A case approach* (3rd ed.). New York, NY: Pearson.

Murdock, N. L., Alcorn, J., Heesacker, M., & Stoltenberg, C. (1998). Model training program in counseling psychology. *The Counseling Psychologist, 26,* 658–672. doi:10.1177/0011000098264008

Murphy, K. A., Blustein, D. L., Bohlig, A. J., & Platt, M. G. (2010). The college-to-work career transition: An exploration of emerging adulthood. *Journal of Counseling & Development, 88,* 174–181. doi:10.1002/j.1556-6678.2010.tb00006.x

Murphy, K. R., & Dzieweczynski, J. L. (2005). Why don't measures of broad dimensions of personality perform better as predictors of job performance? *Human Performance, 18,* 343–357. doi:10.1207/s15327043hup1804_2

Mussell, M. P., Binford, R. B., & Fulkerson, J. A. (2000). Eating disorders: Summary of risk factors, prevention programming, and prevention research. *The Counseling Psychologist, 28,* 764–796. doi:10.1177/0011000000286002

Myers, R. A., & Cairo, P. C. (1992). Counseling and career adjustment. In S. D. Brown & R. W. Lent (Eds.), *Handbook of counseling psychology* (2nd ed., pp. 549–580). New York, NY: Wiley.

Myers, S. B., Sweeney, A. C., Popick, V., Wesley, K., Bordfeld, A., & Fingerhut, R. (2012). Self-care practices and perceived stress levels among psychology graduate students. *Training and Education in Professional Psychology, 6,* 55–66. doi:10.1037/a0026534

Nathan, P. E. (1998). The *DSM–IV* and its antecedents: Enhancing syndromal diagnosis. In J. W. Barron (Ed.), *Making diagnosis meaningful* (pp. 3–28). Washington, DC: American Psychological Association. doi:10.1037/10307-001

Nathan, P. E. (2007). Efficacy, effectiveness, and the clinical utility of psychotherapy research. In S. G. Hofmann & J. Weinberger (Eds.), *The art and science of psychotherapy* (pp. 69–83). New York, NY: Routledge.

National Center for Educational Statistics. (2010). *Status and trends in the education of racial and ethnic minorities.* Retrieved from http://nces.ed.gov/pubs2007/minoritytrends/chapter3.asp

Neimeyer, G., & Resnikoff, A. (1982). Qualitative strategies in counseling research. *The Counseling Psychologist, 10*(4), 75–85. doi:10.1177/0011000082104015

Neimeyer, G., Saferstein, J., & Rice, K. G. (2005). Does the model matter? The relationship between science-practice emphasis and outcomes in academic training programs in counseling psychology. *The Counseling Psychologist, 33*, 635–654. doi:10.1177/0011000005277821

Neimeyer, G., Taylor, J., Wear, D., & Buyukgoze-Kavas, A. (2011). How special are the specialties? Workplace settings in counseling and clinical psychology in the United States. *Counselling Psychology Quarterly, 24*, 43–53. doi:10.1080/09515070.2011.558343

Neimeyer, R. A. (1993). An appraisal of constructivist psychotherapies. *Journal of Consulting and Clinical Psychology, 61*, 221–234. doi:10.1037/0022-006X.61.2.221

Nevill, D. D., & Super, D. E. (1986). *The Salience Inventory manual: Theory, application, and research*. Palo Alto, CA: Consulting Psychologists Press.

Neville, H. A. (2009). Rationalizing the racial order: Racial colorblindness as a legitimizing ideology. In T. Koditschek, S. K. Cha-Jua, & H. A. Neville (Eds.), *Race struggles* (pp. 115–133). Chicago: University of Illinois Press.

Neville, H. A., Awad, G. H., Brooks, J. E., Flores, M. P., & Bluemel, J. (2013). Color-blind racial ideology: Theory, training, and measurement implications in psychology. *American Psychologist, 68*, 455–466. doi:10.1037/a0033282

Neville, H. A., Heppner, M. J., Louie, C. E., Thompson, C. E., Brooks, L., & Baker, C. E. (1996). The impact of multicultural training on White racial identity attitudes and therapy competencies. *Professional Psychology: Research and Practice, 27*, 83–89. doi:10.1037/0735-7028.27.1.83

Neville, H. A., Lilly, R. L., Duran, G., Lee, R. M., & Browne, L. (2000). Construction and initial validation of the Color-Blind Racial Attitudes Scale (CoBRAS). *Journal of Counseling Psychology, 47*, 59–70. doi:10.1037/0022-0167.47.1.59

Neville, H. A., Spanierman, L., & Doan, B. T. (2006). Exploring the association between color-blind racial ideology and multicultural counseling competencies. *Cultural Diversity and Ethnic Minority Psychology, 12*, 275–290. doi:10.1037/1099-9809.12.2.275

Neville, H. A., Spanierman, L. B., & Lewis, J. A. (2012). The expanded psychosocial model of racism: A new model for understanding and disrupting racism and White privilege. In N. A. Fouad, J. C. Carter, & L. M. Subich (Eds.), *APA handbook of counseling psychology: Vol. 2. Practice, interventions, and applications* (pp. 333–360). Washington, DC: American Psychological Association.

Neville, H. A., Worthington, R. L., & Spanierman, L. B. (2001). Race, power, and multicultural counseling psychology: Understanding White privilege and color-blind racial attitudes. In J. G. Ponterotto, J. M. Casas, L. A. Suzuki, & C. M. Alexander (Eds.), *Handbook of multicultural counseling* (2nd ed., pp. 257–288). Thousand Oaks, CA: Sage.

Newman, M. G., Castonguay, L. G., Borkovec, T. D., Fisher, A. J., & Nordberg, S. S. (2008). An open trial of integrative therapy for generalized anxiety disorder. *Psychotherapy: Theory, Research, Practice, Training, 45*, 135–147. doi:10.1037/0033-3204.45.2.135

Nicholas, D. R., & Stern, M. (2011). Counseling psychology in clinical health psychology: The impact of specialty perspective. *Professional Psychology: Research and Practice, 42*, 331–337. doi:10.1037/a0024197

Nichols, M. (1984). *Family therapy: Concepts and methods.* New York, NY: Gardner Press.

Nichols, M. P. (2010). *Family therapy: Concepts and methods* (7th ed.). Boston, MA: Allyn & Bacon.

Nichols, M. P., & Schwartz, R. C. (1998). *Family therapy: Concepts and methods* (4th ed.). Boston, MA: Allyn & Bacon.

Nickelson, D. W. (1998). Telehealth and the evolving health care system: Strategic opportunities for professional psychology. *Professional Psychology: Research and Practice, 29*, 527–535. doi:10.1037/0735-7028.29.6.527

Niemann, Y. F. (2001). Stereotypes about Chicanas and Chicanos: Implications for counseling. *The Counseling Psychologist, 29*, 55–90. doi:10.1177/0011000001291003

Niles, S. G., & Harris-Bowlsbey, J. (2005). *Career development interventions in the 21st century* (2nd ed.). Upper Saddle River, NJ: Pearson.

Norcross, J. C. (2010). The therapeutic relationship. In B. L. Duncan, S. D. Miller, B. E. Wampold, & M. A. Hubble (Eds.), *The heart and soul of change: Delivering what works in therapy* (2nd ed., pp. 113–141). Washington, DC: American Psychological Association. doi:10.1037/12075-004

Norcross, J. C. (Ed.). (2011). *Psychotherapy relationships that work* (2nd ed.). New York, NY: Oxford University Press.

Norcross, J. C., & Halgin, R. P. (2005). Training in psychotherapy integration. In J. C. Norcross & M. R. Goldfried (Eds.), *Handbook of psychotherapy integration* (2nd ed., pp. 439–458). New York, NY: Oxford University Press.

Norcross, J. C., Kohut, J. L., & Wicherski, M. (2005). Graduate study in psychology, 1971 to 2004. *American Psychologist, 60*, 959–975. doi:10.1037/0003-066X.60.9.959

Norcross, J. C., & Lambert, M. J. (2006). The therapy relationship. In J. C. Norcross, L. E. Beutler, & R. F. Levant (Eds.), *Evidence-based practices in mental health: Debate and dialogue about the fundamental questions* (pp. 208–218). Washington, DC: American Psychological Association. doi:10.1037/11265-000

Norcross, J. C., & Lambert, M. J. (2011). Introduction. In J. Norcross (Ed.), *Psychotherapy relationships that work* (2nd ed., pp. 3–24). New York, NY: Oxford University Press.

Norcross, J. C., & Sayette, M. A. (2011). *Insider's guide to graduate programs in clinical and counseling psychology.* New York, NY: Guilford Press.

Norcross, J. C., Sayette, M. A., Mayne, T. J., Karg, R. S., & Turkson, M. A. (1998). Selecting a doctoral program in professional psychology: Some comparisons among PhD counseling, PhD clinical, and PsyD clinical psychology programs. *Professional Psychology: Research and Practice, 29,* 609–614. doi:10.1037/0735-7028.29.6.609

Norsworthy, K. L., Abrams, E. M., & Lindlau, S. (2012). Activism, advocacy, and social justice in feminist multicultural counseling psychology. In C. Z. Enns & E. N. Williams (Eds.), *The Oxford handbook of feminist multicultural counseling psychology* (pp. 465–482). New York, NY: Oxford University Press. doi:10.1093/oxfordhb/9780199744220.013.0025

Nunnally, J. (1978). *Psychometric theory* (2nd ed.) New York, NY: McGraw-Hill.

Nutt-Williams, E., & Hill, C. E. (1996). The relationship between self-talk and therapy process variables for novice therapists. *Journal of Counseling Psychology, 43,* 170–177. doi:10.1037/0022-0167.43.2.170

O'Leary, K. D., & Wilson, G. T. (1987). *Behavior therapy: Application and outcome* (2nd ed.). Englewood Cliffs, NJ: Prentice Hall.

Olkin, R. (2012). Disability: A primer for therapists. In E. M. Altmaier & J. C. Hansen (Eds.), *The Oxford handbook of counseling psychology* (pp. 460–479). New York, NY: Oxford University Press.

Olson, S. K., Downing, N. E., Heppner, P. P., & Pinkney, J. (1986). Is there life after graduate school? Coping with the transitions to post-doctoral employment. *Professional Psychology: Research and Practice, 17,* 415–419. doi:10.1037/0735-7028.17.5.415

Omer, H. (1997). Narrative empathy. *Psychotherapy: Theory, Research, Practice, Training, 34,* 19–27. doi:10.1037/h0087748

O'Neil, J. M. (1981). Male sex role conflicts, sexism, and masculinity: Psychological implications for men, women, and the counseling psychologist. *The Counseling Psychologist, 9*(2), 61–80. doi:10.1177/001100008100900213

O'Neil, J. M. (2008). Summarizing 25 years of research on men's gender role conflict using the Gender Role Conflict Scale: New research paradigms and clinical implications. *The Counseling Psychologist, 36,* 358–445. doi:10.1177/001000008317057

O'Neil, J. M. (2012). The psychology of men. In E. M. Altmaier & J. C. Hansen (Eds.), *The Oxford handbook of counseling psychology* (pp. 375–408). New York, NY: Oxford University Press.

O'Neill, P. (2002). Tectonic change: The qualitative paradigm in psychology. *Canadian Psychology/Psychologie canadienne, 43,* 190–194. doi:10.1037/h0086915

Orlinsky, D. E., & Rønnestad, M. H. (2005). *How psychotherapists develop: A study of therapeutic work and professional growth*. Washington, DC: American Psychological Association. doi:10.1037/11157-000

Ormerod, A. J., Joseph, D. L., Weitzman, L. M., & Winterrowd, E. (2012). Career issues and challenges viewed through a feminist multicultural lens: Work–life interface and sexual harassment. In C. Z. Enns & E. N. Williams (Eds.), *The Oxford handbook of feminist multicultural counseling psychology* (pp. 277–303). New York, NY: Oxford University Press.

Osborn, D. S., Dikel, M. R., & Sampson, J. P. (2011). *The internet: A tool for career planning* (3rd ed.). Broken Arrow, OK: National Career Development Association.

Osipow, S. H. (1983). *Theories of career development* (3rd ed.). Englewood Cliffs, NJ: Prentice-Hall.

Osipow, S. H. (1987). Counseling psychology: Theory, research, and practice in career counseling. *Annual Review of Psychology, 38*, 257–278. doi:10.1146/annurev.ps.38.020187.001353

Osipow, S. H., Carney, C. C., Winer, J. L., Yanico, B., & Koschier, M. (1980). *The Career Decision Scale* (3rd ed.). Columbus, OH: Marathon Consulting and Press.

Osofsky, J. D. (1995). Perspectives on attachment and psychoanalysis. *Psychoanalytic Psychology, 12*, 347–362. doi:10.1037/h0079699

Pabian, Y. L., Welfel, W., & Beebe, R. S. (2009). Psychologists' knowledge of their states' laws pertaining to Tarasoff-type situations. *Professional Psychology: Research and Practice, 40*, 8–14. doi:10.1037/a0014784

Packard, B. W.-L. (2003). Student training promotes mentoring awareness and action. *Career Development Quarterly, 51*, 335–345. doi:10.1002/j.2161-0045.2003.tb00614.x

Packard, T. (2009). The 2008 Leona Tyler Award Address: Core values that distinguish counseling psychology: Personal and professional perspectives. *The Counseling Psychologist, 37*, 610–624. doi:10.1177/0011000009333986

Palmer, G., & Efron, D. (2007). Emotionally-focused family therapy: Developing the model. *Journal of Systemic Therapies, 26*, 17–24. doi:10.1521/jsyt.2007.26.4.17

Palmore, E. (1969). Predicting longevity. *The Gerontologist, 9*, 247–250. doi:10.1093/geront/9.4_Part_1.247

Palombi, B. J. (2012). Women with disabilities: The cultural context of disability, feminism, able-bodied privilege, and microaggressions. In C. Z. Enns & E. N. Williams (Eds.), *The Oxford handbook of feminist multicultural counseling psychology* (pp. 199–220). New York, NY: Oxford University Press. doi:10.1093/oxfordhb/9780199744220.013.0011

Paniagua, F. A. (1998). *Assessing and treating culturally diverse clients* (2nd ed.). Thousand Oaks, CA: Sage.

Paniagua, F. A. (2005). *Assessing and treating culturally diverse clients* (3rd ed.). Thousand Oaks, CA: Sage.

Parent, M. C., & Williamson, J. B. (2010). Program disparities in unmatched internship applicants. *Training and Education in Professional Psychology, 4,* 116–120. doi:10.1037/a0018216

Parsons, F. (1909). *Choosing a vocation.* Boston, MA: Houghton Mifflin.

Passons, W. R. (1975). *Gestalt approaches to counseling.* New York, NY: Holt, Rinehart & Winston.

Patterson, C. H. (1984). Empathy, warmth, and genuineness in psychotherapy: A review of reviews. *Psychotherapy: Theory, Research, Practice, Training, 21,* 431–439. doi:10.1037/h0085985

Patterson, C. J. (2009). Children of lesbian and gay parents: Psychology, law, and policy. *American Psychologist, 64,* 727–736. doi:10.1037/0003-066X.64.8.727

Patton, M. J. (1984). Managing social interaction in counseling: A contribution from the philosophy of science. *Journal of Counseling Psychology, 31,* 442–456. doi:10.1037/0022-0167.31.4.442

Patton, M. J., Kivlighan, D. M., & Multon, K. D. (1997). The Missouri psychoanalytic counseling research project: Relation of changes in process and outcome. *Journal of Counseling Psychology, 44,* 189–208. doi:10.1037/0022-0167.44.2.189

Patton, M. J., & Meara, N. M. (1992). *Psychoanalytic counseling.* New York, NY: Wiley.

Paul, G. L. (1966). *Insight versus desensitization in psychotherapy.* Stanford, CA: Stanford University Press.

Paul, G. L. (1967). Strategy of outcome research in psychotherapy. *Journal of Consulting Psychology, 31,* 109–118. doi:10.1037/h0024436

Pedersen, P. (Ed.). (1999). *Multiculturalism as a fourth force.* Philadelphia, PA: Brunner/Mazel.

Pepinsky, H. B., Hill-Frederick, K., & Epperson, D. L. (1978). Silver anniversary: The *Journal of Counseling Psychology* as a matter of policies. *Journal of Counseling Psychology, 25,* 483–498. doi:10.1037/h0078070

Pepinsky, H. B., & Pepinsky, P. N. (1954). *Counseling theory and practice.* New York, NY: Ronald Press. doi:10.1037/10631-000

Peräkylä, A. (2010). Shifting the perspective after the patient's response to an interpretation. *International Journal of Psychoanalysis, 91,* 1363–1384. doi:10.1111/j.1745-8315.2010.00323.x

Perls, F. S. (1947). *Ego, hunger, and aggression.* New York, NY: Random House.

Perls, F. S. (1969a). *Gestalt therapy verbatim.* New York, NY: Bantam.

Perls, F. S. (1969b). *In and out of the garbage pail.* Lafayette, CA: Real People Press.

Perls, F. S. (1970). Four lectures. In J. Fagan & J. L. Shepherd (Eds.), *Gestalt therapy now* (pp. 14–38). New York, NY: Harper & Row.

Perls, F. S., Hefferline, R., & Goodman, P. (1951). *Gestalt therapy: Excitement and growth in personality.* New York, NY: Dell.

Perrone, K. M. (2005). Work–family interface for same-sex, dual-earner couples: Implications for counselors. *Career Development Quarterly, 53,* 317–324. doi:10.1002/j.2161-0045.2005.tb00662.x

Persons, J. B. (2008). *The case formulation approach to cognitive-behavior therapy.* New York, NY: Guilford Press.

Peterson, D. R. (2003). Unintended consequences: Ventures and misadventures in the education of professional psychologists. *American Psychologist, 58,* 791–800. doi:10.1037/0003-066X.58.10.791

Phillips, S. D. (1992). Career counseling: Choice and implementation. In S. D. Brown & R. W. Lent (Eds.), *Handbook of counseling psychology* (2nd ed., pp. 513–547). New York, NY: Wiley.

Phinney, J. S. (1996). When we talk about American ethnic groups, what do we mean? *American Psychologist, 51,* 918–927. doi:10.1037/0003-066X.51.9.918

Piaget, J. (1952). *The language and thought of the child.* London, England: Routledge & Kegan Paul.

Pickman, A. J. (1994). *The complete guide to outplacement counseling.* Hillsdale, NJ: Erlbaum.

Pieterse, A. L. & Miller, M. J. (2010). Current considerations in the assessment of adults: A revision and extension of culturally inclusive models. In J. G. Ponterotto, J. M. Casas, L. A. Suzuki, & C. M. Alexander (Eds.), *Handbook of multicultural counseling* (3rd ed., pp. 649–666). Thousand Oaks, CA: Sage.

Pine, F. (1990). *Drive, ego, object, and self: A synthesis for clinical work.* New York, NY: Basic Books.

Pleck, E. H., & Pleck, J. H. (1980). *The American man.* Englewood Cliffs, NJ: Prentice-Hall.

Podsakoff, N. P., LePine, J. A., & LePine, M. A. (2007). Differential challenge stressor–hindrance stressor relationship with job attitudes, turnover intentions, turnover, and withdrawal behavior: A meta-analysis. *Journal of Applied Psychology, 92,* 438–454. doi:10.1037/0021-9010.92.2.438

Polkinghorne, D. E. (1984). Further extensions of methodological diversity for counseling research. *Journal of Counseling Psychology, 31,* 416–429. doi:10.1037/0022-0167.31.4.416

Polster, E., & Polster, M. (1973). *Gestalt therapy integrated: Contours of theory and practice.* New York, NY: Vintage Books.

Ponterotto, J. G. (1988). Racial/ethnic minority research in the *Journal of Counseling Psychology:* A content analysis and methodological critique. *Journal of Counseling Psychology, 35,* 410–418. doi:10.1037/0022-0167.35.4.410

Ponterotto, J. G. (1997). Multicultural counseling training: A competency model and national survey. In D. B. Pope-Davis & H. L. K.

Coleman (Eds.), *Multicultural counseling competencies* (pp. 111–130). Thousand Oaks, CA: Sage.

Ponterotto, J. G. (2005). Qualitative research in counseling psychology: A primer on research paradigms and philosophy of science. *Journal of Counseling Psychology, 52,* 126–136. doi:10.1037/0022-0167.52.2.126

Ponterotto, J. G., Casas, J. M., Suzuki, L. A., & Alexander, C. M. (Eds.). (2001). *Handbook of multicultural counseling* (2nd ed.). Thousand Oaks, CA: Sage.

Ponterotto, J. G., Fuertes, J. N., & Chen, E. C. (2000). Models of multicultural counseling. In S. D. Brown & R. W. Lent (Eds.), *Handbook of counseling psychology* (3rd ed., pp. 639–669). New York, NY: Wiley.

Ponterotto, J. G., Gretchen, D., Utsey, S. O., Rieger, B. P., & Austin, R. (2002). A revision of the Multicultural Counseling Awareness Scale. *Journal of Multicultural Counseling and Development, 30,* 153–180. doi:10.1002/j.2161-1912.2002.tb00489.x

Ponterotto, J. G., & Park-Taylor, J. (2007). Racial and ethnic identity theory, measurement, and research in counseling psychology: Present status and future directions. *Journal of Counseling Psychology, 54,* 282–294. doi:10.1037/0022-0167.54.3.282

Ponterotto, J. G., & Potere, J. C. (2003). The Multicultural Counseling Knowledge and Awareness Scale (MCKAS): Validity, reliability, and user guidelines. In D. B. Pope-Davis, H. L. K. Coleman, W. M. Liu, & R. L. Toporek (Eds.), *Handbook of multicultural competencies: In counseling & psychology* (pp. 137–153). Thousand Oaks, CA: Sage. doi:10.4135/9781452231693.n9

Ponterotto, J. G., Rieger, B. P., Barrett, A., & Sparks, R. (1994). Assessing multicultural counseling competence: A review of instrumentation. *Journal of Counseling & Development, 72,* 316–322. doi:10.1002/j.1556-6676.1994.tb00941.x

Pope, K. S. (2011). Are the American Psychological Association's detainee interrogation policies ethical and effective? Key claims, documents, and results. *Zeitschrift für Psychologie/Journal of Psychology, 219,* 150–158. doi:10.1027/2151-2604/a000062

Pope, K. S., & Tabachnick, B. G. (1994). Therapists as patients: A national survey of psychologists' experiences, problems, and beliefs. *Professional Psychology: Research and Practice, 25,* 247–258. doi:10.1037/0735-7028.25.3.247

Pope, K. S., & Vasquez, M. J. T. (2010). *Ethics in psychotherapy and counseling: A practical guide.* Hoboken, NJ: Wiley.

Pope, K. S., & Vetter, V. A. (1992). Ethical dilemmas encountered by members of the American Psychological Association. *American Psychologist, 47,* 397–411. doi:10.1037/0003-066X.47.3.397

Pope, M., Barret, B., Szymanski, D. M., Chung, Y. B., Singaravelu, H., McLean, R., & Sanabria, S. (2004). Culturally appropriate career counseling with gay and lesbian clients. *Career Development Quarterly, 53,* 158–177. doi:10.1002/j.2161-0045.2004.tb00987.x

Pope-Davis, D. B., Coleman, H. L. K., Liu, W. M., & Toporek, R. L. (2003). *Handbook of multicultural competencies in counseling and psychology.* Thousand Oaks, CA: Sage.

Pope-Davis, D. B., & Dings, J. G. (1995). The assessment of multicultural counseling competencies. In J. G. Ponterotto, J. M. Casas, L. A. Suzuki, & C. M. Alexander (Eds.), *Handbook of multicultural counseling* (pp. 287–311). Thousand Oaks, CA: Sage.

Pope-Davis, D. B., Liu, W. M., Toporek, R. L., & Brittan-Powell, C. S. (2001). What's missing from multicultural competency research: Review, introspection, and recommendations. *Cultural Diversity and Ethnic Minority Psychology, 7,* 121–138. doi:10.1037/1099-9809.7.2.121

Pope-Davis, D. B., Reynolds, A. L., Dings, J. G., & Nielson, D. (1995). Examining multicultural counseling competencies of graduate students in psychology. *Professional Psychology: Research and Practice, 26,* 322–329. doi:10.1037/0735-7028.26.3.322

Potoczniak, D. J. (2007). Development of bisexual men's identities and relationships. In K. J. Bieschke, R. M. Perez, & K. A. DeBord (Eds.), *Handbook of counseling and psychotherapy with lesbian, gay, bisexual, and transgender clients* (2nd ed., pp. 119–145). Washington, DC: American Psychological Association. doi:10.1037/11482-005

Prensky, M. (2001). Digital natives: Digital immigrants. *Horizon, 9,* 1–6.

Prilleltensky, I. (1997). Values, assumptions, and practices: Assessing the moral implications of psychological discourse and action. *American Psychologist, 52,* 517–535. doi:10.1037/0003-066X.52.5.517

Prochaska, J. O., & Norcross, J. C. (1999). *Systems of psychotherapy: A transtheoretical analysis* (4th ed.). Belmont, CA: Brooks/Cole.

Prochaska, J. O., & Norcross, J. C. (2007). *Systems of psychotherapy: A transtheoretical analysis* (7th ed.). Pacific Grove, CA: Brooks/Cole.

Prochaska, J. O., & Norcross, J. C. (2010). *Systems of psychotherapy: A transtheoretical analysis* (7th ed.). Belmont, CA: Brooks/Cole.

Pyant, C. T., & Yanico, B. J. (1991). Relationship of racial identity and gender-role attitudes to Black women's psychological well-being. *Journal of Counseling Psychology, 38,* 315–322. doi:10.1037/0022-0167.38.3.315

Quenk, N. L. (2009). *Essentials of Myers–Briggs Type Indicator assessment* (2nd ed.). New York, NY: Wiley.

Quintana, S. M. (2007). Racial and ethnic identity: Developmental perspectives and research. *Journal of Counseling Psychology, 54,* 259–270. doi:10.1037/0022-0167.54.3.259

Quintana, S. M., & Bernal, M. E. (1995). Ethnic minority training in counseling psychology. *The Counseling Psychologist, 23,* 102–121. doi:10.1177/0011000095231010

Quintana, S. M., Chew, A., & Schell, G. (2012). Counseling psychology theory and research on race and ethnicity: Implications for a psychological science of diversity. In N. A. Fouad, J. C. Carter, & L. M. Subich (Eds.), *APA handbook of counseling psychology: Vol. 1. Theories, research, and methods* (pp. 453–489). Washington, DC: American Psychological Association. doi:10.1037/13754-017

Quirk, M. P., Strosahl, K., Kreilkamp, T., & Erdberg, P. (1995). Personality feedback consultation to families in a managed mental health care practice. *Professional Psychology: Research and Practice, 26*, 27–32. doi:10.1037/0735-7028.26.1.27

Radloff, T. D. L. (2007). Measuring the impact of higher education on racial prejudice and opposition to race-based policy. *New York Sociologist, 2*, 1–15.

Ragusea, A. S., & VandeCreek, L. (2003). Suggestions for the ethical practice of online psychotherapy. *Psychotherapy: Theory, Research, Practice, Training, 40*, 94–102. doi:10.1037/0033-3204.40.1-2.94

Raimy, V. C. (1950). *Training in clinical psychology.* New York, NY: Prentice-Hall.

Raney, S. C., Hwang, B. J., & Douce, L. A. (2008). Finding postdoctoral training and employment in the United States. In N. T. Hasan, N. A. Fouad, & C. Williams-Nickelson (Eds.), *Studying psychology in the United States: Expert guidance for international students* (pp. 131–139). Washington, DC: American Psychological Association.

Raque-Bogdan, T. L., Torrey, C. L., Lewis, B. L., & Borges, N. J. (2013). Counseling health psychology: Assessing health psychology training within counseling psychology doctoral programs. *The Counseling Psychologist, 41*, 428–452. doi:10.1177/0011000012439611

Raskin, N., Rogers, C., & Witty, M. (2011). Client-centered therapy. In R. J. Corsini & D. Wedding (Eds.), *Current psychotherapies* (9th ed., pp. 148–195). Belmont, CA: Brooks/Cole.

Raskin, N. J., & Rogers, C. R. (1995). Person-centered therapy. In R. J. Corsini & D. Wedding (Eds.), *Current psychotherapies* (5th ed., pp. 128–161). Itasca, IL: Peacock.

Ratts, M. J., & Santos, K. (2012). Career counseling without borders: Moving beyond traditional career practices of helping. In D. Capuzzi & M. Stauffer (Eds.), *Career counseling: Foundations, perspectives, and applications* (2nd ed., pp. 111–125). New York, NY: Routledge.

Reardon, R. C., & Lenz, J. G. (1998). *The Self-Directed Search and related Holland career materials: Practitioner's guide.* Odessa, FL: Psychological Assessment Resources.

Remer, P. A., & Oh, K. H. (2012). Feminist therapy in counseling psychology. In C. Z. Enns & E. N. Williams (Eds.), *The Oxford handbook of feminist multicultural counseling psychology* (pp. 304–321). New York, NY: Oxford University Press. doi:10.1093/oxfordhb/9780199744220.013.0016

Rest, J. R. (1984). Research on moral development: Implications for training counseling psychologists. *The Counseling Psychologist, 12*(3), 19–29. doi:10.1177/0011000084123003

Reynolds, A. L. (1995). Challenges and strategies for teaching multicultural counseling courses. In J. G. Ponterotto, J. M. Casas, L. A. Suzuki, & C. M. Alexander (Eds.), *Handbook of multicultural counseling* (pp. 312–330). Thousand Oaks, CA: Sage.

Richardson, M. S. (1996). From career counseling to counseling/psychotherapy and work, jobs, and career. In M. L. Savickas & W. B. Walsh (Eds.), *Handbook of career counseling theory and practice* (pp. 347–360). Palo Alto, CA: Davies-Black.

Richardson, M. S. (2012). Counseling for work and relationship. *The Counseling Psychologist, 40,* 190–242. doi:10.1177/0011000011406452

Richardson, M. S., & Patton, M. J. (1992). Guest editors' introduction to the centennial articles. *Journal of Counseling Psychology, 39,* 3–6. doi:10.1037/h0092604

Ridley, C. R. (1995). *Overcoming unintentional racism in counseling and therapy.* Thousand Oaks, CA: Sage.

Ridley, C. R., Li, L. C., & Hill, C. L. (1998). Multicultural assessment: Reexamination, reconceptualization, and practical application. *The Counseling Psychologist, 26,* 827–910. doi:10.1177/0011000098266001

Ridley, C. R., Mendoza, D. W., & Kanitz, B. E. (1994). Multicultural training: Reexamination, operationalization, and integration. *The Counseling Psychologist, 22,* 227–289. doi:10.1177/0011000094222001

Ridley, C. R., Mendoza, D. W., Kanitz, B. E., Angermeier, L., & Zenk, R. (1994). Cultural sensitivity in multicultural counseling: A perceptual schema model. *Journal of Counseling Psychology, 41,* 125–136. doi:10.1037/0022-0167.41.2.125

Rimm, D. C., & Cunningham, H. M. (1985). Behavior therapies. In S. Lynn & J. Garske (Eds.), *Contemporary psychotherapies* (pp. 221–259). Columbus, OH: Merrill.

Rimm, D. C., & Masters, J. C. (1979). *Behavior therapy: Techniques and empirical findings.* New York, NY: Academic Press.

Rivas-Drake, D., Hughes, D., & Way, N. (2009). A preliminary analysis of associations among ethnic racial socialization, ethnic discrimination, and ethnic identity among urban sixth graders. *Journal of Research on Adolescence, 19,* 558–584. doi:10.1111/j.1532-7795.2009.00607.x

Robbins, S. B. (1989). Role of contemporary psychoanalysis in counseling psychology. *Journal of Counseling Psychology, 36,* 267–278. doi:10.1037/0022-0167.36.3.267

Roberts, D. S., & Geller, E. S. (1995). An "actively caring" model for occupational safety: A field test. *Applied & Preventive Psychology, 4,* 53–59. doi:10.1016/S0962-1849(05)80051-4

Robinson, D. T., & Morris, J. R. (2000). Multicultural counseling: Historical context and current training considerations. *Western Journal of Black Studies, 24,* 239–253.

Robinson, F. P. (1950). *Principles and procedures of student counseling.* New York, NY: Harper.

Robitschek, C., & Woodson, S. J. (2006). Vocational psychology: Using one of counseling psychology's strengths to foster human strength. *The Counseling Psychologist, 34*, 260–275. doi:10.1177/0011000005281321

Rodin, J., Silberstein, L. R., & Striegel-Moore, R. H. (1985). Women and weight: A normative discontent. In T. B. Sonderegger (Ed.), *Nebraska Symposium on Motivation: Psychology and gender* (pp. 267–307). Lincoln: University of Nebraska Press.

Rogers, C. R. (1939). *The clinical treatment of the problem child.* Boston, MA: Houghton Mifflin.

Rogers, C. R. (1942). *Counseling and psychotherapy.* Boston, MA: Houghton Mifflin.

Rogers, C. R. (1951). *Client-centered therapy.* Boston, MA: Houghton Mifflin.

Rogers, C. R. (1957). The necessary and sufficient conditions for therapeutic personality change. *Journal of Consulting Psychology, 21*, 95–103. doi:10.1037/h0045357

Rogers, C. R. (1959). A theory of therapy, personality, and interpersonal relationships, as developed in the client-centered framework. In S. Koch (Ed.), *Psychology: A study of science: Vol. 3. Formulations of the person and the social context* (pp. 184–246). New York, NY: McGraw-Hill.

Rogers, C. R. (1961). *On becoming a person.* Boston, MA: Houghton Mifflin.

Rogers, C. R. (1962). Toward becoming a fully functioning person. In A. W. Combs (Ed.), *Perceiving, behaving, becoming: A new focus for education* (pp. 21–33).Washington, DC: Yearbook Association for Supervision and Curriculum Development. doi:10.1037/14325-003

Rogers, C. R. (Ed.). (1967). *The therapeutic relationship and its impact: A study of psychotherapy with schizophrenics.* Madison: University of Wisconsin Press.

Rogers, C. R. (1973). My philosophy of interpersonal relationships and how it grew. *Journal of Humanistic Psychology, 13*, 3–15. doi:10.1177/002216787301300202

Rogers, C. R. (1975). Empathy: An unappreciated way of being. *The Counseling Psychologist, 5*, 2–10. doi:10.1177/001100007500500202

Rogers, C. R. (1980). *A way of being.* Boston, MA: Houghton Mifflin.

Rogers, C. R., & Dymond, R. (1954). *Psychotherapy and personality change.* Chicago, IL: University of Chicago Press.

Romano, J. L., & Hage, S. M. (2000). Prevention and counseling psychology: Revitalizing commitments for the 21st century. *The Counseling Psychologist, 28*, 733–763. doi:10.1177/0011000000286001

Rønnestad, M. H., & Skovholt, T. M. (2013). *The developing practitioner: Growth and stagnation of therapists and counselors.* New York, NY: Routledge.

Root, M. P. P. (1995). The psychology of Asian American women. In H. Landrine (Ed.), *Bringing cultural diversity to feminist psychology: Theory, research, and practice* (pp. 265–301). Washington, DC: American Psychological Association. doi:10.1037/10501-012

Rosenhan, D. L. (1973, January 19). On being sane in insane places. *Science, 179*, 250–258. doi:10.1126/science.179.4070.250

Rosewater, L. B., & Walker, L. E. A. (Eds.). (1985). *Handbook of feminist therapy*. New York, NY: Springer.

Rosin, H. M., & Korabik, K. (2002). Do family-friendly policies fulfill their promise? An investigation of their impact on work–family conflict and work and personal outcomes. In D. L. Nelson & R. J. Burke (Eds.), *Gender, work stress, and health* (pp. 211–226). Washington, DC: American Psychological Association. doi:10.1037/10467-013

Rottinghaus, P. J., Larson, L. M., & Borgen, F. H. (2003). Theoretical and empirical linkages of self-efficacy and interests. *Journal of Vocational Behavior, 62*, 221–236. doi:10.1016/S0001-8791(02)00039-8

Rowe, J. W., & Kahn, R. L. (1998). *Successful aging*. New York, NY: Pantheon.

Roysircar, G. (2006). Prevention work in school and with youth: Promoting competence and reducing risks. In R. L. Toporek, L. H. Gerstein, N. A. Fouad, G. Roysircar, & T. Israel (Eds.), *Handbook for social justice in counseling psychology: Leadership, vision, and action* (pp. 77–85). Thousand Oaks, CA: Sage. doi:10.4135/9781412976220.n6

Rozee, P. D., & Koss, M. P. (2001). Rape: A century of resistance. *Psychology of Women Quarterly, 25*, 295–311. doi:10.1111/1471-6402.00030

Rude, S. S., Weissberg, N., & Gazda, G. M. (1988). Looking to the future: Themes from the Third National Conference for Counseling Psychology. *The Counseling Psychologist, 16*, 423–430. doi:10.1177/0011000088163008

Ruelas, S. R., Atkinson, D. R., & Ramos-Sanchez, L. (1998). Counselor helping model, participant ethnicity and acculturation level, and perceived counselor credibility. *Journal of Counseling Psychology, 45*, 98–103. doi:10.1037/0022-0167.45.1.98

Rushton, J. P. (1995). Construct validity, censorship, and the genetics of race. *American Psychologist, 50*, 40–41. doi:10.1037/0003-066X.50.1.40.b

Rust, P. C. (2003). Finding a sexual identity and community: Therapeutic implications and cultural assumptions in scientific models of coming out. In L. D. Garnets & D. C. Kimmel (Eds.), *Psychological perspectives on lesbian, gay, and bisexual experiences* (pp. 227–269). New York, NY: Columbia University Press.

Rust, P. C. (2007). The construction and reconstruction of bisexuality. In B. Firestein (Ed.), *Becoming visible: Counseling bisexuals across the lifespan* (pp. 3–27). New York, NY: Columbia University Press.

Ryan, A., Safran, J. D., Doran, J. M., & Muran, J. C. (2012). Therapist mindfulness, alliance and treatment outcomes. *Psychotherapy Research, 22*, 289–297. doi:10.1080/10503307.2011.650653

Rychlak, J. F. (1968). *A philosophy of science for personality theory*. Boston, MA: Houghton Mifflin. doi:10.1037/10535-000

Ryum, T., Stiles, T. C., Svartberg, M., & McCullough, L. (2010). The role of transference work, the therapeutic alliance, and their interaction in reducing interpersonal problems among psychotherapy patients with Cluster C personality disorders. *Psychotherapy: Theory, Research, Practice, Training, 47*, 442–453. doi:10.1037/a0021183

Safran, J. D., & Muran, C. (2000). *Negotiating the therapeutic alliance: A relational treatment guide.* New York, NY: Guilford Press.

Safran, J. D, Muran, C., & Eubanks-Carter, C. (2011). In J. Norcross (Ed.), *Psychotherapy relationships that work* (2nd ed., pp. 224–238). New York, NY: Oxford University Press.

Safran, J. D., Muran, J. C., Samstag, L. W., & Stevens, C. (2001). Repairing alliance ruptures. *Psychotherapy: Theory, Research, Practice, Training, 38*, 406–412. doi:10.1037/0033-3204.38.4.406

Salaway, G., Caruso, J. B., Nelson, M. R., & Ellison, N. B. (2008). *The ECAR study of undergraduate students and information technology, 2008.* Retrieved from http://net.educause.edu/ir/library/pdf/ers0808/rs/ers0808w.pdf

Salk, R. H., & Engeln-Maddox, R. (2011). "If you're fat, then I'm humongous!": Frequency, content, and impact of fat talk among college women. *Psychology of Women Quarterly, 35*, 18–28. doi:10.1177/0361684310384107

Salomone, P. R. (1982). Difficult cases in career counseling: II. The indecisive client. *Personnel and Guidance Journal, 60*, 496–500. doi:10.1002/j.2164-4918.1982.tb00703.x

Sampson, J. P., Jr., Peterson, G. W., Lenz, J. G., Reardon, R. C., & Saunders, D. E. (1996). *Career Thoughts Inventory.* Odessa, FL: Psychological Assessment Resources.

Samstag, L. W., Muran, J. C., & Safran, J. D. (2004). Defining and identifying alliance ruptures. In D. P. Charman (Ed.), *Core processes in brief psychodynamic psychotherapy: Advancing effective practice* (pp. 187–214). Mahwah, NJ: Erlbaum.

Sanders Thompson, V. L., Bazile, A., & Akbar, M. (2004). African Americans' perceptions of psychotherapy and psychotherapists. *Professional Psychology: Research and Practice, 35*, 19–26. doi:10.1037/0735-7028.35.1.19

Savickas, M. L. (1996). A framework for linking career theory and practice. In M. L. Savickas & W. B. Walsh (Eds.), *Handbook of career counseling theory and practice* (pp. 191–208). Palo Alto, CA: Davies-Black.

Savickas, M. L. (2002). Career construction: A developmental theory of vocational behavior. In S. D. Brown & R. W. Lent (Eds.), *Career choice and development* (4th ed., pp. 149–205). San Francisco, CA: Jossey-Bass.

Savickas, M. L. (2003). Toward a taxonomy of human strengths: Career counseling's contribution to positive psychology. In W. B. Walsh (Ed.), *Counseling psychology and optimal human functioning* (pp. 229–250). Mahwah, NJ: Erlbaum.

Savickas, M. L. (2005). The theory and practice of career construction. In S. D. Brown & R. W. Lent (Eds.), *Career development and counseling: Putting theory and research to work* (pp. 42–70). Hoboken, NJ: Wiley.

Savickas, M. L. (2011). *Career counseling*. Washington, DC: American Psychological Association.

Savin-Williams, R. C. (2001). *Mom, Dad, I'm gay: How families negotiate coming out*. Washington, DC: American Psychological Association.

Scarf, M. (1987). *Intimate partners: Patterns in love and marriage*. New York, NY: Random House.

Scheel, M. J., Berman, M., Friedlander, M. L., Conoley, C. W., Duan, C., & Whiston, S. (2011). Whatever happened to counseling in counseling psychology? *The Counseling Psychologist, 39*, 673–692. doi:10.1177/0011000010380278

Scheel, M. J., & Conoley, C. W. (2012). Psychotherapy process and outcome research in counseling psychology. In N. A. Fouad, J. A. Carter, & L. M. Subich (Eds.), *APA handbook of counseling psychology: Vol. 1. Theories, research, and methods* (pp. 203–236). Washington, DC: American Psychological Association. doi:10.1037/13754-008

Scheel, M. J., Davis, C. K., & Henderson, J. D. (2013). Therapist use of client strengths: A qualitative study of positive processes. *The Counseling Psychologist, 41*, 392–427. doi:10.1177/0011000012439427

Scherman, A., & Doan, R. E. (1985). Subjects, designs, and generalizations in Volumes 25–29 of the *Journal of Counseling Psychology. Journal of Counseling Psychology, 32*, 272–276. doi:10.1037/0022-0167.32.2.272

Schiffman, J. B., Delucia-Waack, J. L., & Gerrity, D. A. (2006). An examination of the construct of homophobia: Prejudice or phobia? *Journal of LGBT Issues in Counseling, 1*, 75–93. doi:10.1300/J462v01n01_06

Schlossberg, N. K. (2011). The challenge of change: The transition model and its applications. *Journal of Employment Counseling, 48*, 159–162. doi:10.1002/j.2161-1920.2011.tb01102.x

Schlosser, L. Z., & Gelso, C. J. (2001). Measuring the working alliance in advisor–advisee relationships in graduate school. *Journal of Counseling Psychology, 48*, 157–167. doi:10.1037/0022-0167.48.2.157

Schmidt, C. K., & Nilsson, J. E. (2006). The effects of simultaneous developmental processes: Factors relating to the career development of lesbian, gay, and bisexual youth. *Career Development Quarterly, 55*, 22–37. doi:10.1002/j.2161-0045.2006.tb00002.x

Schmidt, L. (1977). Why has the professional practice of psychological counseling developed in the United States? *The Counseling Psychologist, 7*(2), 19–21. doi:10.1177/001100007700700208

Schneider, B. (2008). The people still make the place. In D. B. Smith (Ed.), *The people make the place: Dynamic linkages between individuals and organizations* (pp. 267–289). New York, NY: Taylor & Francis.

Schneider, B., & Smith, D. B. (Eds.). (2004). *Personality and organization*. Mahwah, NJ: Erlbaum.

Schneider, K. J., & Krug, O. T. (2010). *Existential–humanistic therapy.* Washington, DC: American Psychological Association.

Schultheiss, D. E. P. (2006). The interface of work and family life. *Professional Psychology: Research and Practice, 37*, 334–341. doi:10.1037/0735-7028.37.4.334

Schweizer, K., Brunner, F., Schützmann, K., Schönbucher, V., & Richter-Apelt, H. (2009). Gender identity and coping in female 46, XY adults with androgen biosynthesis deficiency (intersexuality/DSD). *Journal of Counseling Psychology, 56*, 189–201. doi:10.1037/a0013575

Scott, C. W. (1980). History of the division of counseling psychology: 1945–1963. In J. M. Whiteley (Ed.), *The history of counseling psychology* (pp. 25–40). Monterey, CA: Brooks/Cole.

Section on Counseling Health Psychology of Division 17. (2005). *Bylaws.* Retrieved from http://www.apa.org/divisions/div17/sections/health/Bylaws.html

Segal, U., Elliott, D., & Mayadas, N. (Eds.). (2010). *Immigration worldwide: Policies, practices, and trends.* New York, NY: Oxford University Press.

Seligman, M. E. P. (1995). The effectiveness of psychotherapy: The *Consumer Reports* study. *American Psychologist, 50*, 965–974. doi:10.1037/0003-066X.50.12.965

Seligman, M. E. P. (2002). *Authentic happiness.* New York, NY: Free Press.

Seligman, M. E. P., & Csikszentmihalyi, M. M. (2000). Positive psychology: An introduction. *American Psychologist, 55*, 5–14. doi:10.1037/0003-066X.55.1.5

Seligman, M. E. P., Rashid, T., & Parks, A. C. (2006). Positive psychotherapy. *American Psychologist, 61*, 774–788. doi:10.1037/0003-066X.61.8.774

Sell, R. L. (1997). Defining and measuring sexual orientation: A review. *Archives of Sexual Behavior, 26*, 643–658. doi:10.1023/A:1024528427013

Selvini Palazzoli, M., Boscolo, L., Cecchin, G., & Prata, G. (1978). *Paradox and counterparadox.* New York, NY: Aronson.

Sexton, T. L., & Alexander, J. F. (2005). Functional family therapy for externalizing disorders in adolescents. In J. Lebow (Ed.), *Handbook of clinical family therapy* (pp. 164–191). New York, NY: Wiley.

Sexton, T. L., Datchi, C., Evans, L., LaFollette, J., & Wright, L. (2013). The effectiveness of couple and family-based clinical interventions. In M. J. Lambert (Ed.), *Bergin and Garfield's handbook of psychotherapy and behavior change* (6th ed., pp. 587–639). New York, NY: Wiley.

Sharf, R. S. (2006). *Applying career development theory to counseling.* Belmont, CA: Thompson Higher Education.

Shean, G. D. (2012). Some limitations on the external validity of psychotherapy efficacy studies and suggestions for future research. *American Journal of Psychotherapy, 66*, 227–242.

Shedler, J. (2010). The efficacy of psychodynamic psychotherapy. *American Psychologist, 65*, 98–109. doi:10.1037/a0018378

Sheets, R. L., & Mohr, J. J. (2009). Perceived social support from friends and family and psychosocial functioning in bisexual young adult college students. *Journal of Counseling Psychology, 56,* 152–163. doi:10.1037/0022-0167.56.1.152

Shepherd, I. L. (1970). Limitations and cautions in the Gestalt approach. In J. Fagan & I. L. Shepherd (Eds.), *Gestalt therapy now* (pp. 234–238). New York, NY: Harper & Row.

Sherman, M. D., & Thelen, M. H. (1998). Distress and professional impairment among psychologists in clinical practice. *Professional Psychology: Research and Practice, 29,* 79–85. doi:10.1037/0735-7028.29.1.79

Shields, S. A. (2008). Gender: An intersectionality perspective. *Sex Roles, 59,* 301–311. doi:10.1007/s11199-008-9501-8

Shirk, S. R., & Karver, M. S. (2011). Alliance in child and adolescent psychotherapy. In J. Norcross (Ed.), *Psychotherapy relationships that work* (2nd ed., pp. 70–91). New York, NY: Oxford University Press.

Shullman, S. L. (2002). Reflections of a consulting counseling psychologist: Implications of the Principles for Education and Training at the Doctoral and Postdoctoral Level in Consulting Psychology for the Practice of Counseling Psychology. *Consulting Psychology Journal: Practice and Research, 54,* 242–251. doi:10.1037/1061-4087.54.4.242

Shullman, S. L., Celeste, B. L., & Stickland, T. (2006). Extending the Parsons legacy: Applications of counseling psychology in pursuit of social justice through the development of public policy. In R. L. Toporek, L. H. Gerstein, N. A. Fouad, G. Roysircar, & T. Israel (Eds.), *Handbook for social justice in counseling psychology: Leadership, vision, and action* (pp. 499–513). Thousand Oaks, CA: Sage. doi:10.4135/9781412976220.n33

Shultz, K. S., & Wang, M. (2011). Psychological perspectives on the changing nature of retirement. *American Psychologist, 66,* 170–179. doi:10.1037/a0022411

Siegel, L. (1985). Industrial and organizational psychology. In E. M. Altmaier and M. E. Meyer (Eds.), *Applied specialties in psychology* (pp. 207–238). New York, NY: Random House.

Silverman, D. K. (1998). The tie that binds: Affect regulation, attachment, and psychoanalysis. *Psychoanalytic Psychology, 15,* 187–212. doi:10.1037/0736-9735.15.2.187

Silvia, P. J. (2003). Self-efficacy and interest: Experimental studies of optimal incompetence. *Journal of Vocational Behavior, 62,* 237–249. doi:10.1016/S0001-8791(02)00013-1

Simkin, J. S., & Yontef, G. M. (1984). Gestalt therapy. In R. J. Corsini (Ed.), *Current psychotherapies* (3rd ed., pp. 279–319). Itasca, IL: Peacock.

Simon, J., & Osipow, S. H. (1996). Continuity of career: The vocational script in counseling older adults. *Career Development Quarterly, 45,* 152–162. doi:10.1002/j.2161-0045.1996.tb00265.x

Simons, A. D., Padesky, C. A., Montemarano, J., Lewis, C. C., Marakami, J., Lamb, K., . . . Beck, A. T. (2010). Training and dissemination of cognitive behavior therapy for depression in adults: A preliminary examination of therapist competence and client outcomes. *Journal of Consulting and Clinical Psychology, 78,* 751–756. doi:10.1037/a0020569

Skinner, B. F. (1938). *The behavior of organisms: An experimental analysis.* New York, NY: Appleton.

Skovholt, T., Schauble, P., Gormally, J., & Davis, R. (1978). Guest editors' introduction. *The Counseling Psychologist, 7*(4), 2. doi:10.1177/001100007800700401

Skovholt, T. M., & Jennings, L. (2004). *Master therapist: Exploring expertise in therapy and counseling.* Needham Heights, MA: Allyn & Bacon.

Skovholt, T. M., & Ronnestad, M. H. (1992). *The evolving professional self.* New York, NY: Wiley.

Slan-Jerusalim, R., & Chen, C. P. (2009). Work–family conflict and career development theories: A search for helping strategies. *Journal of Counseling & Development, 87,* 492–499. doi:10.1002/j.1556-6678.2009.tb00134.x

Slavin, J. H. (1989). Post-doctoral training for psychologists in psychoanalysis. *Psychologist Psychoanalyst, 9,* 8–11.

Slimp, P. A. O., & Burian, B. K. (1994). Multiple role relationships during internship: Consequences and recommendations. *Professional Psychology: Research and Practice, 25,* 39–45. doi:10.1037/0735-7028.25.1.39

Sloane, R. B., Staples, F. R., Cristol, A. H., Yorkston, N. J., & Whipple, K. (1975). *Psychotherapy versus behavior therapy.* Cambridge, MA: Harvard University Press.

Smith, B. L. (1998). Psychological testing, psychodiagnosis, and psychotherapy. In J. W. Barron (Ed.), *Making diagnosis meaningful* (pp. 227–245). Washington, DC: American Psychological Association.

Smith, E. J. (2006). The strength-based counseling model. *The Counseling Psychologist, 34,* 13–79. doi:10.1177/0011000005277018

Smith, L., Appio, L., & Chang, J. (2012). Feminist multicultural counseling psychology and poverty. In C. Z. Enns & E. N. Williams (Eds.), *The Oxford handbook of feminist multicultural counseling psychology* (pp. 199–220). New York, NY: Oxford University Press. doi:10.1093/oxfordhb/9780199744220.013.0008

Smith, L. C., Shin, R. Q., & Officer, L. M. (2012). Moving counseling forward on LGB and transgender issues: Speaking queerly on discourses and microaggressions. *The Counseling Psychologist, 40,* 385–408. doi:10.1177/0011000011403165

Smith, M. L., & Glass, G. V. (1977). Meta-analysis of psychotherapy outcome studies. *American Psychologist, 32,* 752–760. doi:10.1037/0003-066X.32.9.752

Smith, T. B., Constantine, M. G., Dunn, T. W., Dinehart, J. M., & Montoya, J. A. (2006). Multicultural education in the mental health professions: A meta-analytic review. *Journal of Counseling Psychology, 53,* 132–145. doi:10.1037/0022-0167.53.1.132

Smith, T. S., McGuire, J. M., Abbott, D. W., & Blau, B. I. (1991). Clinical ethical decision making: An investigation of the rationales used to justify doing less than one believes one should. *Professional Psychology: Research and Practice, 22,* 235–239. doi:10.1037/0735-7028.22.3.235

Snowden, L. R. (2012). Health and mental health policies' roles in better understanding and closing African American–White American disparities in treatment access and quality of care. *American Psychologist, 67,* 524–531. doi:10.1037/a0030054

Snyder, C. R., Lopez, S. J., & Pedrotti, J. T. (2011). *Positive psychology: The scientific and practical explorations of human strengths* (2nd ed.). Thousand Oaks, CA: Sage.

Sodowsky, G. R., Taffe, R. C., Gutkin, T. B., & Wise, S. L. (1994). Development of the Multicultural Counseling Inventory: A self-report measure of multicultural competencies. *Journal of Counseling Psychology, 41,* 137–148. doi:10.1037/0022-0167.41.2.137

Solberg, V. S., Howard, K. A., Blustein, D. L., & Close, W. (2002). Career development in the schools: Connecting school-to-work-to-life. *The Counseling Psychologist, 30,* 705–725. doi:10.1177/0011000002305003

Solberg Nes, L., Evans, D. R., & Segerstrom, S. C. (2009). Optimism and college retention: Mediation by motivation, performance, and adjustment. *Journal of Applied Social Psychology, 39,* 1887–1912. doi:10.1111/j.1559-1816.2009.00508.x

Soldz, S. (2008, June 24). The torture trainers and the American Psychological Association. *Counterpunch.* Retrieved from http://www.counterpunch.org/soldz0625008.html

Sophie, J. (1986). A critical examination of stage theories of lesbian identity development. *Journal of Homosexuality, 12,* 39–51. doi:10.1300/J082v12n02_03

Southern Poverty Law Center. (2012). Southern Poverty Law Center report: As election season heats up, extremist groups at record levels. Retrieved from http://www.splcenter.org/get-informed/news/southern-poverty-law-center-report-as-election-season-heats-up-extremist-groups-at

Speight, S. L., Isom, D. A., & Thomas, A. J. (2012). From Hottentot to Superwoman: Issues of identity and mental health for African American women. In C. Z. Enns & E. N. Williams (Eds.), *The Oxford handbook of feminist multicultural counseling psychology* (pp. 115–130). New York, NY: Oxford University Press. doi:10.1093/oxfordhb/9780199744220.013.0006

Speight, S. L., Thomas, A. J., Kennel, R. G., & Anderson, M. E. (1995). Operationalizing multicultural training in doctoral programs and internships. *Professional Psychology: Research and Practice, 26,* 401–406. doi:10.1037/0735-7028.26.4.401

Speight, S. L., & Vera, E. M. (2004). A social justice agenda: Ready, or not? *The Counseling Psychologist, 32,* 109–118. doi:10.1177/0011000003260005

Spengler, P. M. (1998). Multicultural assessment and a scientist–practitioner model of psychological assessment. *The Counseling Psychologist, 26,* 930–938. doi:10.1177/0011000098266004

Spengler, P. M., Strohmer, D. C., Dixon, D. N., & Shivy, V. A. (1995). A scientist–practitioner model of psychological assessment. *The Counseling Psychologist, 23,* 506–534. doi:10.1177/0011000095233009

Spiegler, M. D., & Guevremont, D. C. (2010). *Contemporary behavior therapy* (5th ed.). Pacific Grove, CA: Brooks/Cole.

Spokane, A. R. (1991). *Career intervention.* Englewood Cliffs, NJ: Prentice-Hall.

Spokane, A. R., & Cruza-Guet, M. C. (2005). Holland's theory of vocational personalities in work environments. In S. D. Brown & R. W. Lent (Eds.), *Career development counseling* (pp. 24–41). Hoboken, NJ: Wiley.

Staggs, G. D., Larson, L. M., & Borgen, F. H. (2007). Convergence of personality and interests: Meta-analysis of the Multidimensional Personality Questionnaire and the Strong Interest Inventory. *Journal of Career Assessment, 15,* 423–445. doi:10.1177/1069072707305760

Stanley, S. M., Markham, H. J., & Whitton, S. W. (2002). Communication, conflict, and commitment: Insights on the foundations of relationship success from a national survey. *Family Process, 41,* 659–675. doi:10.1111/j.1545-5300.2002.00659.x

Steenbarger, B. N. (1992). Toward science-practice integration in brief counseling and therapy. *The Counseling Psychologist, 20,* 403–450. doi:10.1177/0011000092203001

Stoltenberg, C. D., Kashubeck-West, S., Biever, J. L., Patterson, T., & Welch, I. D. (2000). Training models in counseling psychology: Scientist-practitioner versus practitioner-scholar. *The Counseling Psychologist, 28,* 622–640. doi:10.1177/0011000000285002

Stone, C., Dew, E., & Sackett, S. (1998, August). *Work experiences and career and job satisfaction of new counseling psychologists.* Paper presented at the American Psychological Association Convention, San Francisco, CA.

Stone, G. L. (1984). In defense of the artificial. *Journal of Counseling Psychology, 31,* 108–110. doi:10.1037/0022-0167.31.1.108

Strauss, B. S. (1997). Treating, teaching, and training: Clinical psychologists in hospitals. In R. J. Sternberg (Ed.), *Career paths in psychology: Where your degree can take you* (pp. 133–150). Washington, DC: American Psychological Association.

Stricker, G. (1997). Are science and practice commensurable? *American Psychologist, 52,* 442–448. doi:10.1037/0003-066X.52.4.442

Strohmer, D. C., & Arm, J. R. (2006). The more things change the more they stay the same: Reaction to Aegisdottir et al. *The Counseling Psychologist, 34,* 383–390. doi:10.1177/0011000005285879

Stromberg, C. (1993, April). Privacy, confidentiality and privilege. *The Psychologist's Legal Update.* Washington, DC: National Register of Health Service Providers in Psychology.

Strong, E. K. (1943). *Vocational interests of men and women*. Palo Alto, CA: Stanford University Press.

Strong, S. R. (1991). Theory-driven science and naive empiricism in counseling psychology. *Journal of Counseling Psychology, 38*, 204–210. doi:10.1037/0022-0167.38.2.204

Strong, T., & Zeman, D. (2010). Dialogic considerations of confrontation as a counseling activity: An examination of Allen Ivey's use of confronting as a microskill. *Journal of Counseling & Development, 88*, 332–339. doi:10.1002/j.1556-6678.2010.tb00030.x

Strupp, H. H., & Binder, J. L. (1984). *Psychotherapy in a new key*. New York, NY: Basic Books.

Sue, D. W. (2001). Multidimensional facets of cultural competence. *The Counseling Psychologist, 29*, 790–821. doi:10.1177/0011000001296002

Sue, D. W., Arredondo, P., & McDavis, R. J. (1992). Multicultural counseling competencies and standards: A call to the profession. *Journal of Counseling & Development, 70*, 477–486. doi:10.1002/j.1556-6676.1992.tb01642.x

Sue, D. W., Bernier, J. E., Durran, A., Feinberg, L., Pedersen, P., Smith, E. J., & Vasquez-Nuttall, E. (1982). Cross-cultural counseling competencies. *The Counseling Psychologist, 10*, 45–52. doi:10.1177/0011000082102008

Sue, D. W., Capodilupo, C. M., Torino, G. C., Bucceri, J. M., Holder, A. M. B., & Esquilin, M. E. (2007). Racial microaggressions in everyday life: Implications for clinical practice. *American Psychologist, 62*, 271–286. doi:10.1037/0003-066X.62.4.271

Sue, D. W., Carter, R. T., Casas, J. M., Fouad, N. A., Ivey, A. E., Jensen, M., . . . Vazquez-Nutall, E. (1998). *Multicultural counseling competencies: Individual and organizational development*. Thousand Oaks, CA: Sage.

Sue, D. W., Lin, A. I., Torino, G. C., Capodilupo, C. M., & Rivera, D. P. (2009). Racial microaggressions and difficult dialogues on race in the classroom. *Cultural Diversity and Ethnic Minority Psychology, 15*, 183–190. doi:10.1037/a0014191

Sue, D. W., Rivera, D. P., Capodilupo, C. M., Lin, A. I., & Torino, G. C. (2010). Racial dialogues and White trainee fears: Implications for education and training. *Cultural Diversity and Ethnic Minority Psychology, 16*, 206–213. doi:10.1037/a0016112

Sue, D. W., & Sue, D. (2003). *Counseling the culturally different: Theory and practice* (4th ed.). New York, NY: Wiley.

Sue, D. W., & Sue, D. (2008). *Counseling the culturally diverse: Theory and practice* (5th ed.). Hoboken, NJ: Wiley.

Sue, D. W., & Sue, D. (2012). *Counseling the culturally different: Theory and practice* (6th ed.). New York, NY: Wiley.

Sue, S., Cheng, J. K. Y., Saad, C. S., & Chu, J. P. (2012). Asian American mental health: A call to action. *American Psychologist, 67*, 532–544. doi:10.1037/a0028900

Sullivan, H. S. (1954). *The psychiatric interview.* New York, NY: Norton.

Sundberg, N. D. (1981). Cross-cultural counseling and psychotherapy: A research overview. In A. J. Marsella & P. B. Pedersen (Eds.), *Cross-cultural counseling and psychotherapy* (pp. 28–62). Elmsford, NY: Pergamon Press.

Sundel, M., & Sundel, S. S. (1999). *Behavior change in the human services* (4th ed.). Thousand Oaks, CA: Sage.

Super, D. E. (1942). *The dynamics of vocational adjustment.* New York, NY: Harper.

Super, D. E. (1953). A theory of vocational development. *American Psychologist, 8,* 185–190. doi:10.1037/h0056046

Super, D. E. (1955). Transition: From vocational guidance to counseling psychology. *Journal of Counseling Psychology, 2,* 3–9. doi:10.1037/h0041630

Super, D. E. (1957). *The psychology of careers.* New York, NY: Harper & Row.

Super, D. E. (1963). Self-concepts in vocational development. In D. E. Super, R. Starishevsky, N. Matlin, & J. P. Jordaan (Eds.), *Career development: Self-concept theory* (pp. 17–32). New York, NY: College Entrance Examination Board.

Super, D. E. (1973). The Work Values Inventory. In D. G. Zytowski (Ed.), *Contemporary approaches to interest measurement* (pp. 189–205). Minneapolis: University of Minnesota Press.

Super, D. E. (1994). A life span, life space perspective on convergence. In M. L. Savickas & R. W. Lent (Eds.), *Convergence in career development theories* (pp. 63–74). Palo Alto, CA: Consulting Psychologists Press.

Super, D. E., & Nevill, D. D. (1986). *The Values Scale.* Palo Alto, CA: Consulting Psychologists Press.

Super, D. E., Thompson, A. S., Lindeman, R. H., Jordaan, J. P., & Myers, R. A. (1981). *Career Development Inventory.* Palo Alto, CA: Consulting Psychologists Press.

Suzuki, L. A., Onoue, M. A., Fukui, H., & Ezrapour, C. (2012). Foundations of counseling psychology: Assessment. In N. A. Fouad (Ed.), *APA handbook of counseling psychology: Vol. 1. Theories, research, and methods* (pp. 167–200). Washington, DC: American Psychological Association.

Suzuki, L. A., & Ponterotto, J. G. (2008). *Handbook of multicultural assessment: Clinical, psychological, and educational applications.* San Francisco, CA: Jossey-Bass.

Suzuki, L. A., Ponterotto, J. G., & Meller, P. J. (Eds.). (2008). *Handbook of multicultural assessment* (3rd ed.). San Francisco, CA: Jossey-Bass.

Šverko, B. (2001). Life roles and values in international perspective: Super's contribution through the Work Importance Study. *International Journal for Educational and Vocational Guidance, 1,* 121–130. doi:10.1023/A:1016929016249

Swanson, J., & Fouad, N. (1999). *Career theory and practice.* Mahwah, NJ: Erlbaum.

Swanson, J. L. (1995). The process and outcome of career counseling. In W. B. Walsh & S. H. Osipow (Eds.), *Handbook of vocational psychology* (2nd ed., pp. 217–259). Hillsdale, NJ: Erlbaum.

Swanson, J. L. (2002). Understanding the complexity of clients' lives: Infusing a truly integrative career-personal perspective into graduate training. *The Counseling Psychologist, 30,* 815–832. doi:10.1177/001100002237756

Swanson, J. L. (2012). Work and psychological health. In N. A. Fouad, J. A. Carter, & L. M. Subich (Eds.), *APA handbook of counseling psychology: Vol. 2. Practice, interventions, and applications* (pp. 3–27).Washington, DC: American Psychological Association.

Swim, J. K., Hyers, L. L., Cohen, L. L., & Ferguson, M. J. (2001). Everyday sexism: Evidence for its incidence, nature, and psychological impact from three daily diary studies. *Journal of Social Issues, 57,* 31–53. doi:10.1111/0022-4537.00200

Szasz, T. S. (1960). The myth of mental illness. *American Psychologist, 15,* 113–118. doi:10.1037/h0046535

Szymanski, D. M., & Hilton, A. N. (2012). Feminist counseling psychology and lesbians, bisexual women, and transgender persons. In C. Z. Enns & E. N. Williams (Eds.), *The Oxford handbook of feminist multicultural counseling psychology* (pp. 131–154). New York, NY: Oxford University Press. doi:10.1093/oxfordhb/9780199744220.013.0007

Szymanski, D. M., & Ikizler, A. S. (2013). Internalized heterosexism as a mediator in the relationship between gender role conflict, heterosexist discrimination, and depression among sexual minority men. *Psychology of Men & Masculinity, 14,* 211–219. doi:10.1037/a0027787

Szymanski, D. M., Kashubeck-West, S., & Meyer, J. (2008). Internalized heterosexism: A historical and theoretical overview. *The Counseling Psychologist, 36,* 510–524. doi:10.1177/0011000007309488

Szymanski, D. M., & Moffitt, L. B. (2012). Sexism and heterosexism. In N. A. Fouad, J. C. Carter, & L. M. Subich (Eds.), *APA handbook of counseling psychology: Vol. 2. Practice, interventions, and applications* (pp. 361–390). Washington, DC: American Psychological Association.

Task Force on the Promotion and Dissemination of Psychological Procedures. (1995). Training in and dissemination of empirically validated psychological treatments. *The Clinical Psychologist, 48,* 3–23.

Tenopyr, M. L. (1997). Improving the workplace: Industrial/organizational psychology as a career. In R. J. Sternberg (Ed.), *Career paths in psychology: Where your degree can take you* (pp. 185–196). Washington, DC: American Psychological Association.

Thompson, A. S., & Super, D. E. (Eds.). (1964). *The professional preparation of counseling psychologists: Report of the 1964 Greyston Conference.* New York, NY: Bureau of Publications, Teachers College, Columbia University.

Thompson, C. E., & Neville, H. A. (1999). Racism, mental health, and mental health practice. *The Counseling Psychologist, 27,* 155–223. doi:10.1177/0011000099272001

Thoresen, C. E., & Eagleston, J. R. (1985). Counseling for health. *The Counseling Psychologist, 13,* 15–87.

Tiedeman, D. B. (1980). Status and prospect in counseling psychology: 1962. In J. M. Whiteley (Ed.), *The history of counseling psychology* (pp. 125–132). Monterey, CA: Brooks/Cole.

Tinsley, D. J., & Schwendener-Holt, M. J. (1992). Retirement and leisure. In S. D. Brown & R. W. Lent (Eds.), *Handbook of counseling psychology* (2nd ed., pp. 627–662). New York, NY: Wiley.

Tinsley, H. E. A., & Bradley, R. W. (1986). Test interpretation. *Journal of Counseling & Development, 64,* 462–466. doi:10.1002/j.1556-6676.1986.tb01166.x

Tokar, D. M., Withrow, J. R., Hall, R. J., & Moradi, B. (2003). Psychological separation, attachment security, vocational self-concept crystallization, and career indecision: A structural equation analysis. *Journal of Counseling Psychology, 50,* 3–19. doi:10.1037/0022-0167.50.1.3

Tolin, D. F., & Foa, E. B. (2006). Sex differences in trauma and post-traumatic stress disorder: A quantitative review of 25 years of research. *Psychological Bulletin, 132,* 959–992. doi:10.1037/0033-2909.132.6.959

Topa, G., Moriano, J. A., Depolo, M., Alcover, C. M., & Morales, J. F. (2009). Antecedents and consequences of retirement planning and decision-making: A meta-analysis and model. *Journal of Vocational Behavior, 75,* 38–55. doi:10.1016/j.jvb.2009.03.002

Toporek, R. L., Gerstein, L. H., Fouad, N. A., Roysircar, G., & Israel, T. (2006). *Handbook for social justice in counseling psychology: Leadership, vision and action.* Thousand Oaks, CA: Sage.

Toporek, R. L., & Liu, W. M. (2001). Advocacy in counseling: Addressing race, class, and gender oppression. In D. B. Pope-Davis & H. L. K. Coleman (Eds.), *The intersection of race, class, and gender in multicultural counseling* (pp. 285–413). Thousand Oaks, CA: Sage.

Town, J. M., Diener, M. J., Abbass, A., Leichsenring, F., Driessen, E., & Rabung, S. (2012). A meta-analysis of psychodynamic psychotherapy outcomes: Evaluating the effects of research-specific procedures. *Psychotherapy, 47,* 276–290. doi: 10.1037/a0029564

Tracey, T. J. G., & Robbins, S. B. (2005). Stability of interests across ethnicity and gender: A longitudinal examination of grades 8 through 12. *Journal of Vocational Behavior, 67,* 335–364. doi:10.1016/j.jvb.2004.11.003

Tuason, M. T. G., Güss, C. D., & Carroll, L. (2012). The disaster continues: A qualitative study on the experiences of displaced Hurricane Katrina survivors. *Professional Psychology: Research and Practice, 43,* 288–297. doi:10.1037/a0028054

Tucker, C. M., Ferdinant, L. A., Mirsu-Paun, A., Herman, K. C., Delgado-Romero, E., van den Berg, J. J., & Jones, J. D. (2007). The roles of counseling psychologists in reducing health disparities. *The Counseling Psychologist, 35,* 650–679.

Tuckman, B. W. (1965). Developmental sequence in small groups. *Psychological Bulletin, 63,* 384–399. doi:10.1037/h0022100

Tunnell, G. B. (1977). Three dimensions of naturalness: An expanded definition of field research. *Psychological Bulletin, 84,* 426–437. doi:10.1037/0033-2909.84.3.426

Tyler, L. (1961). *The work of the counselor.* New York, NY: Appleton-Century-Crofts.

Tyler, L., Tiedeman, D., & Wrenn, C. G. (1980). The current status of counseling psychology: 1961. In J. M. Whiteley (Ed.), *The history of counseling psychology* (pp. 114–124). Monterey, CA: Brooks/Cole.

Tyson, K., Darity, W., Jr., & Castellino, D. R. (2005). It's not "a Black thing": Understanding the burden of acting White and other dilemmas of high achievement. *American Sociological Review, 70,* 582–605. doi:10.1177/000312240507000403

Ullmann, L. P., & Krasner, L. (1965). *Case studies in behavior modification.* New York, NY: Holt, Rinehart & Winston.

Unger, R. K. (1979). Toward a redefinition of sex and gender. *American Psychologist, 34,* 1085–1094. doi:10.1037/0003-066X.34.11.1085

Urofsky, R. I., Engels, D. W., & Engebretson, K. (2009). Kitchener's principle ethics: Implications for counseling practice and research. *Counseling and Values, 53,* 67–78. doi:10.1002/j.2161-007X.2009.tb00114.x

U.S. Census. (2010). *Race and Hispanic origin of the foreign-born population in the United States: 2007* (American Community Surveys ACS-11). Washington, DC: Author.

U.S. Department of Education. (2007). *NIDRR long-range plan for fiscal years 2005–2009: Executive summary.* Retrieved from http://www.ncddr.org/new/announcements/lrp/fy2005-2009/exec-summ.html

U.S. Department of Health and Human Services. (1999). *Mental health: A report of the Surgeon General.* Rockville, MD: Author.

U.S. Department of Health and Human Services. (2001). *Mental health: Culture, race, and ethnicity—A supplement to* Mental health: A report of the Surgeon General. Rockville, MD: Author.

Utsey, S. O., Gernat, C. A., & Hammar, L. (2005). Examining White counselor trainees' reactions to racial issues in counseling and supervision dyads. *The Counseling Psychologist, 33,* 449–478.

Utsey, S. O., Ponterotto, J. G., & Porter, J. S. (2008). Prejudice and racism, year 2008—still going strong: Research on reducing prejudice with recommended methodological advances. *Journal of Counseling & Development, 86,* 339–347. doi:10.1002/j.1556-6678.2008.tb00518.x

Vacha-Haase, T., & Duffy, M. (2012). Counseling psychologists working with older adults. In E. M. Altmaier & J. C. Hansen (Eds.), *The Oxford handbook of counseling psychology* (pp. 480–499). New York, NY: Oxford University Press.

Vacha-Haase, T., Hill, R. D., & Bermingham, D. W. (2012). Aging theory and research. In N. A. Fouad, J. C. Carter, & L. M. Subich (Eds.), *APA handbook of counseling psychology: Vol. 1. Theories, research, and methods* (pp. 491–505). Washington, DC: American Psychological Association.

Vasquez, M. J. T. (2007). Cultural difference and the therapeutic alliance: An evidence-based analysis. *American Psychologist, 62,* 878–885. doi:10.1037/0003-066X.62.8.878

Vasquez, M. J. T. (2012). Psychology and social justice: Why we do what we do. *American Psychologist, 67,* 337–346. doi:10.1037/a0029232

Verquer, M. L., Beehr, T. A., & Wagner, S. H. (2003). A meta-analysis of relations between person–organization fit and work attitudes. *Journal of Vocational Behavior, 63,* 473–489. doi:10.1016/S0001-8791(02)00036-2

Vespia, K. M., Fitzpatrick, M. E., Fouad, N. A., Kantamneni, N., & Chen, Y. (2010). Multicultural career counseling: A national survey of competencies and practices. *Career Development Quarterly, 59,* 54–71. doi:10.1002/j.2161-0045.2010.tb00130.x

Vespia, K. M., & Sauer, E. M. (2006). Defining characteristic or unrealistic ideal: Historical and contemporary perspectives on scientist-practitioner training in counselling psychology. *Counselling Psychology Quarterly, 19,* 229–251. doi:10.1080/09515070600960449

von Bertalanffy, L. (1968). *General system theory: Foundations, development, applications.* New York, NY: Braziller.

von Bertalanffy, L. (1974). General systems theory and psychiatry. In S. Arieti (Ed.), *American handbook of psychiatry* (Vol. 1, pp. 1095–1117). New York, NY: Basic Books.

Vondracek, F. W. (2001). The developmental perspective in vocational psychology. *Journal of Vocational Behavior, 59,* 252–261.

Voydanoff, P. (2005). Social integration, work–family conflict and facilitation, and job and marital quality. *Journal of Marriage and Family, 67,* 666–679. doi:10.1111/j.1741-3737.2005.00161.x

Vygotsky, L. S. (1978). *Mind in society: The development of higher psychological processes.* Cambridge, MA: Harvard University Press.

Wachtel, P. L. (Ed.). (1993). *Therapeutic communication: Principles and effective practice* (pp. 110–134). New York, NY: Guilford Press.

Wachtel, P. L. (2011). *Inside the session.* Washington, DC: American Psychological Association.

Wallerstein, R. (1989). Psychoanalysis and psychotherapy: An historical perspective. *International Journal of Psychoanalysis, 70,* 563–591.

Walsh, W. B. (Ed.). (2003). *Counseling psychology and optimal human functioning.* Mahwah, NJ: Erlbaum.

Walsh, W. B., & Betz, N. E. (2001). *Tests and assessment* (3rd ed.). Englewood Cliffs, NJ: Prentice-Hall.

Walsh, W. B., & Chartrand, J. M. (1994). Emerging directions of person–environment fit. In M. L. Savickas & R. W. Lent (Eds.), *Convergence in career development theories* (pp. 187–195). Palo Alto, CA: Consulting Psychologists Press.

Walsh, W. B., & Heppner, M. J. (Eds.). (2006). *Handbook of career counseling for women* (2nd ed.). Mahwah, NJ: Erlbaum.

Walsh, W. B., & Osipow, S. H. (Eds.). (1983). *Handbook of vocational psychology.* Hillsdale, NJ: Erlbaum.

Walsh, W. B., & Savickas, M. L. (2005). *Handbook of vocational psychology* (3rd ed.). Mahwah, NJ: Erlbaum.

Wampold, B. E. (2001). *The great psychotherapy debate: Models, methods and findings.* Mahwah, NJ: Erlbaum.

Wampold, B. E. (2006). The psychotherapist. In J. C. Norcross, L. E. Beutler, & R. F. Levant (Eds.), *Evidence-based practices in mental health: Debate and dialogue on the fundamental questions* (pp. 200–208). Washington, DC: American Psychological Association.

Wampold, B. E., & Bhati, K. S. (2004). Attending to the omissions: A historical examination of evidence-based practice movements. *Professional Psychology: Research and Practice, 35,* 563–570. doi:10.1037/0735-7028.35.6.563

Wampold, B. E., Lichtenberg, J. W., & Waehler, C. A. (2002). Principles of empirically supported interventions in counseling psychology. *The Counseling Psychologist, 30,* 197–217. doi:10.1177/0011000002302001

Wampold, B. E., Mondin, G. W., Moody, M., Stich, F., Benson, K., & Ahn, H. (1997). A meta-analysis of outcome studies comparing bona fide psychotherapies: Empirically, "all must have prizes." *Psychological Bulletin, 122,* 203–215. doi:10.1037/0033-2909.122.3.203

Wampold, B. W. (2003). Bashing positivism and reversing a medical model under the guise of evidence. *The Counseling Psychologist, 31,* 539–545. doi:10.1177/0011000003256356

Watkins, C. E., & Campbell, V. L. (2000). *Testing and assessment in counseling practice* (2nd ed.). NY: Taylor & Francis.

Watkins, C. E., Campbell, V. L., Hollifield, J., & Duckworth, J. (1989). Projective techniques: Do they have a place in counseling psychology training? *The Counseling Psychologist, 17,* 511–513. doi:10.1177/0011000089173010

Watkins, C. E., Jr., Campbell, V. L., & McGregor, P. (1988). Counseling psychologists' uses of and opinions about psychological tests. *The Counseling Psychologist, 16,* 476–486. doi:10.1177/0011000088163010

Watkins, C. E., Lopez, F. G., Campbell, V. L., & Himmell, C. D. (1986). Contemporary counseling psychology: Results of a national survey. *Journal of Counseling Psychology, 33,* 301–309. doi:10.1037/0022-0167.33.3.301

Watzlawick, P., Beavin, J., & Jackson, D. (1967). *The pragmatics of communication.* New York, NY: Norton.

Watzlawick, P., Weakland, J., & Fisch, R. (1974). *Change: Principles of problem formation and problem resolution.* New York, NY: Norton.

Wechsler, D. (1998). *Wechsler Adult Intelligence Scale* (3rd ed.). San Antonio, TX: Psychological Corporation.

Weinrich, J. D., & Klein, F. (2002). Bi-gay, bi-straight, and bi-bi: Three bisexual subgroups identified using cluster analysis of the Klein Sexual Orientation Grid. *Journal of Bisexuality, 2*(4), 109–139. doi:10.1300/J159v02n04_07

Weiss, D. J., Dawis, R. V., Lofquist, L. V., Gay, E., & Hendel, D. D. (1975). *The Minnesota Importance Questionnaire.* Minneapolis: University of Minnesota, Department of Psychology, Work Adjustment Project.

Welfel, E. R. (1992). Psychologist as ethics educator: Successes, failures, and unanswered questions. *Professional Psychology: Research and Practice, 23,* 182–189. doi:10.1037/0735-7028.23.3.182

Welfel, E. R., & Lipsitz, N. E. (1984). The ethical behavior of professional psychologists: A critical analysis of the research. *The Counseling Psychologist, 12*(3), 31–42. doi:10.1177/0011000084123004

Wellner, A. M. (Ed.). (1978). *Education and credentialing in psychology.* Washington, DC: American Psychological Association.

Wendleton, K. (2007). *The Five O'Clock Club job search workbook.* Independence, KY: Delmar Cengage Learning.

Werner, E. E., & Smith, R. S. (1982). *Vulnerable but invincible: A longitudinal study of resilient children and youth.* New York, NY: McGraw Hill.

Werth, J. L., Kopera-Frye, K., Blevins, D., & Bossick, B. (2003). Older adult representation in the counseling psychology literature. *The Counseling Psychologist, 31,* 789–814. doi:10.1177/0011000003258391

Werth, J. L., Welfel, E. R., & Benjamin, G. A. H. (Eds.). (2009). *The duty to protect: Ethical, legal, and professional considerations for mental health professionals.* Washington, DC: American Psychological Association. doi:10.1037/11866-000

Whalen, M., Lese, K., Barber, J., Williams, E. N., Judge, A., Nilsson, J., & Shibazaki, K. (2004). Counseling practice with feminist-multicultural perspectives. *Journal of Multicultural Counseling and Development, 32,* 379–389.

Whaley, A. L. (2008). Cultural sensitivity and cultural competence: Toward clarity of definitions in cross-cultural counselling and psychotherapy. *Counselling Psychology Quarterly, 21,* 215–222. doi:10.1080/09515070802334781

Whiston, S. C. (2009). *Principles and applications of assessment in counseling* (3rd ed.). Belmont, CA: Cengage Learning.

Whiston, S. C., Campbell, W. L., & Maffini, C. S. (2012). Work–family balance: A counseling psychology perspective. In N. A. Fouad, J. A. Carter, & L. M. Subich (Eds.), *APA handbook of counseling psychology: Vol. 2. Practice, interventions, and applications* (pp. 75–102). Washington, DC: American Psychological Association.

Whiston, S. C., & Rahardja, D. (2008). Vocational counseling process and outcome. In R. W. Lent & S. D. Brown (Eds.), *Handbook of counseling psychology* (4th ed., pp. 444–461). New York, NY: Wiley.

Whitaker, C. (1976). The hindrance of theory in clinical work. In P. Guerin (Ed.), *Family therapy: Theory and practice* (pp. 154–164). New York, NY: Gardner Press.

White, M. (1995). *Re-authoring lives: Interviews and essays.* Adelaide, Australia: Dulwich Centre.

White, R. W. (1973). The concept of the healthy personality: What do we really mean? *The Counseling Psychologist, 4*(2), 3–12. doi:10.1177/001100007300400203

Whiteley, J. N. (Ed.). (1980). *The history of counseling psychology.* Monterey, CA: Brooks/Cole.

Whiteley, J. N. (1984a). Counseling psychology: A historical perspective. *The Counseling Psychologist, 12*(1), 3–109. doi:10.1177/0011000084121001

Whiteley, J. N. (1984b). A historical perspective on the development of counseling psychology as a profession. In S. G. Brown & R. W. Lent (Eds.), *Handbook of counseling psychology* (pp. 3–55). New York, NY: Wiley.

Whiteley, J. N., & Fretz, B. R. (Eds.). (1980). *The present and future of counseling psychology.* Monterey, CA: Brooks/Cole.

Whiteley, J. N., Kagan, N., Harmon, L. W., Fretz, B. R., & Tanney, F. (Eds.). (1984). *The coming decade in counseling psychology.* Alexandria, VA: American Association for Counseling and Development.

Wiens, A. N. (1993). Postdoctoral education-training for specialty practice. *American Psychologist, 48,* 415–422. doi:10.1037/0003-066X.48.4.415

Wiesemann, C. (2011). Is there a right not to know one's sex? The ethics of "gender verification" in women's sports competition. *Journal of Medical Ethics, 37,* 216–220. doi:10.1136/jme.2010.039081

Williams, E. N. (2002). Therapist techniques. In G. S. Tryon (Ed.), *Counseling based on process research: Applying what we know* (pp. 232–264). Boston: Allyn & Bacon.

Williams, E. N. (2003). The relationship between momentary states of therapist self-awareness and perceptions of the counseling process. *Journal of Contemporary Psychotherapy, 33,* 177–186. doi:10.1023/A:1023969502532

Williams, E. N., & Barber, J. S. (2004). Power and responsibility in therapy: Integrating feminism and multiculturalism. *Journal of Multicultural Counseling and Development, 32,* 390–401.

Williams, E. N., Barnett, J. E., & Canter, M. B. (2013). History of Division 29, 1993–2013: Another 20 years of psychotherapy. *Psychotherapy, 50,* 131–138. doi:10.1037/a0030900

Williams, E. N., & Enns, C. Z. (2012). Making the political personal. In C. Z. Enns & E. N. Williams (Eds.), *The Oxford handbook of feminist multicultural counseling psychology* (pp. 485–489). New York, NY: Oxford University Press. doi:10.1093/oxfordhb/9780199744220.013.0026

Williams, E. N., & Fauth, J. (2005). A psychotherapy process study of therapist in session self-awareness. *Psychotherapy Research, 15*, 374–381. doi:10.1080/10503300500091355

Williams, E. N., Hayes, J. A., & Fauth, J. (2008). Therapist self-awareness: Interdisciplinary connections and future directions. In S. D. Brown & R. W. Lent (Eds.), *Handbook of counseling psychology* (4th ed., pp. 303–319). Hoboken, NJ: Wiley.

Williams, E. N., & Hill, C. E. (2001). Evolving connections: Research that is relevant to clinical practice. *American Journal of Psychotherapy, 55*, 336–343.

Williams, E. N., Hurley, K., O'Brien, K., & de Gregorio, A. (2003). Development and validation of the Self-Awareness and Management Strategies (SAMS) Scales for therapists. *Psychotherapy: Theory, Practice, Research, Training, 40*, 278–288. doi:10.1037/0033-3204.40.4.278

Williams, E. N., & Morrow, S. L. (2009). Achieving trustworthiness in qualitative research: A pan-paradigmatic perspective. *Psychotherapy Research, 19*, 576–582. doi:10.1080/10503300802702113

Williams, E. N., Polster, D., Grizzard, B., Rockenbaugh, J., & Judge, A. (2003). What happens when therapists feel bored or anxious: A qualitative study of distracting self-awareness and therapists' management strategies. *Journal of Contemporary Psychotherapy, 33*, 5–18. doi:10.1023/A:1021499526052

Williams, E. N., Soeprapto, E., Like, K., Touradji, P., Hess, S., & Hill, C. E. (1998). Perceptions of serendipity: Career paths of prominent academic women in counseling psychology. *Journal of Counseling Psychology, 45*, 379–389. doi:10.1037/0022-0167.45.4.379

Williams-Nickelson, C., Prinstein, M. J., & Keilin, W. G. (2012). *Internships in psychology: The APAGS workbook for writing successful applications and finding the right fit* (3rd ed.). Washington, DC: American Psychological Association.

Williamson, E. G. (1939). *How to counsel students*. New York, NY: McGraw-Hill. doi:10.1037/13902-000

Wilson, G. T. (2005). Psychological treatment of eating disorders. *Annual Review of Clinical Psychology, 1*, 439–465. doi:10.1146/annurev.clinpsy.1.102803.144250

Wilson, G. T. (2011). Behavior therapy. In R. J. Corsini & D. Wedding (Eds.), *Current psychotherapies* (9th ed., pp. 235–275). Ithaca, IL: Peacock.

Wilson, G. T., Grilo, C., & Vitousek, K. (2007). Psychological treatment of eating disorders. *American Psychologist, 62*, 199–216. doi:10.1037/0003-066X.62.3.199

Wirth, L. (1945). The problem of minority groups. In R. Linton (Ed.), *The science of man in the world crisis* (pp. 346–369). New York, NY: Columbia University Press.

Wolf, E. S. (1991). Advances in self psychology: The evolution of psycho-analytic treatment. *Psychoanalytic Inquiry, 11,* 123–146. doi:10.1080/07351699109533848

Wolpe, J. (1958). *Psychotherapy by reciprocal inhibition.* Stanford, CA: Stanford University Press.

Wong, Y. J. (2006). Strength-centered therapy: A social constructionist, virtues-based psychotherapy. *Psychotherapy: Theory, Research, Practice, Training, 43,* 133–146. doi:10.1037/0033-3204.43.2.133

Woodhouse, S. S., Schlosser, L. Z., Ligiero, D. P., Crook, R. E., & Gelso, C. J. (2003). Client attachment to therapist: Relation to client transference and recollection of parental caregiving. *Journal of Counseling Psychology, 50,* 395–408. doi:1037/0022-0617.50.4.395

Worell, J., & Remer, P. (2003). *Feminist perspectives in therapy: An empowerment model for women* (2nd ed.). Hoboken, NJ: Wiley.

Worthington, E. L., Jr., Hight, T. L., Ripley, J. S., Perrone, K. M., Kurusu, T. A., & Jones, D. R. (1997). Strategic hope-focused relationship-enrichment counseling with individual couples. *Journal of Counseling Psychology, 44,* 381–389. doi:10.1037/0022-0167.44.4.381

Worthington, R. L., & Juntunen, C. L. (1997). The vocational development of non-college-bound youth. *The Counseling Psychologist, 25,* 323–363. doi:10.1177/0011000097253001

Worthington, R. L., & Reynolds, A. L. (2009). Within-group differences in sexual orientation and identity. *Journal of Counseling Psychology, 56,* 44–55. doi:10.1037/a0013498

Worthington, R. L., Soth-McNett, A. M., & Moreno, M. V. (2007). Multicultural counseling competencies research: A 20-year content analysis. *Journal of Counseling Psychology, 54,* 351–361. doi:10.1037/0022-0167.54.4.351

Wrenn, C. G. (1962). The culturally encapsulated counselor. *Harvard Educational Review, 32,* 444–449.

Wrenn, C. G. (1966). Birth and early childhood of a journal. *Journal of Counseling Psychology, 13,* 485–488. doi:10.1037/h0024024

Wright, B. A., & Lopez, S. J. (2002). Widening the diagnostic focus: A case for including human strengths and environmental resources. In C. R. Snyder & S. J. Lopez (Eds.), *The handbook of positive psychology* (pp. 26–44). New York, NY: Oxford University Press.

Yakushko, O. (2009). Xenophobia: Understanding the roots and consequences of negative attitudes toward immigrants. *The Counseling Psychologist, 37,* 36–66. doi:10.1177/0011000008316034

Yakushko, O., Davidson, M. M., & Williams, E. N. (2009). Identity salience model: A paradigm for integrating multiple identities in clinical practice. *Psychotherapy: Theory, Research, Practice, Training, 46,* 180–192. doi:10.1037/a0016080

Yakushko, O., & Morgan, M. L. (2012). Immigration. In N. A. Fouad, J. C. Carter, & L. M. Subich (Eds.), *APA handbook of counseling psychology:*

Vol. 2. Practice, interventions, and applications (pp. 473–495). Washington, DC: American Psychological Association.

Yakushko, O., Watson, M., & Thompson, S. (2008). Stress and coping in the lives of recent immigrants and refugees: Considerations for counseling. *International Journal for the Advancement of Counselling, 30,* 167–178. doi:10.1007/s10447-008-9054-0

Yalom, I. D. (1995). *The theory and practice of group psychotherapy* (4th ed.). New York, NY: Basic Books.

Yalom, I. D., & Leszcz, M. (2005). *The theory and practice of group psychotherapy* (5th ed.). New York, NY: Basic Books.

Yang, E., & Gysbers, N. C. (2007). Career transitions of college seniors. *Career Development Quarterly, 56,* 157–170. doi:10.1002/j.2161-0045.2007.tb00028.x

Yee, A. H., Fairchild, H. H., Weizmann, E., & Wyatt, C. E. (1993). Addressing psychology's problems with race. *American Psychologist, 48,* 1132–1140. doi:10.1037/0003-066X.48.11.1132

Yeh, Y.-J., & Hayes, J. A. (2011). How does disclosing countertransference affect perceptions of the therapist and the session? *Psychotherapy, 48,* 322–329. doi:10.1037/a0023134

Young, R. A., Valach, L., & Collin, A. (2002). A contextual explanation of career. In D. Brown, L. Brooks, & Associates (Eds.), *Career choice and development* (4th ed., pp. 206–250). San Francisco, CA: Jossey-Bass.

Zook, A., & Walton, J. M. (1989). Theoretical orientations and work settings of clinical and counseling psychologists: A current perspective. *Professional Psychology: Research and Practice, 20,* 23–31. doi:10.1037/0735-7028.20.1.23

Zunker, V. G. (1990). *Using assessment results for career development* (3rd ed.). Pacific Grove, CA: Brooks/Cole.

Zwiebach, L., Rhodes, J., & Roemer, L. (2010). Resource loss, resource gain, and mental health among survivors of Hurricane Katrina. *Journal of Traumatic Stress, 23,* 751–758. doi:10.1002/jts.20579

Index

About the Authors

Charles J. Gelso, PhD, is Emeritus Professor in the Department of Psychology at the University of Maryland, College Park. He has published widely in the area of the therapeutic relationship in psychotherapy and the research training environment in graduate education. His most recent books are *The Real Relationship in Psychotherapy: The Hidden Foundation of Change* and *Countertransference and the Therapist's Inner Experience: Perils and Possibilities* (with Jeffrey A. Hayes). He has been the editor of *Psychotherapy* and the *Journal of Counseling Psychology* and has been given many major awards in the field.

Elizabeth Nutt Williams, PhD, is a professor of psychology and dean of the core curriculum at St. Mary's College of Maryland, a public liberal arts honors college. Her most recent book, *The Oxford Handbook of Feminist Multicultural Counseling Psychology* (with Carol Enns), reflects her long-standing interest in the intersections of feminist and multicultural theories and their applications to counseling practice. She has received awards for her teaching as well as for her scholarship in psychotherapy process research from the Society for Psychotherapy Research and from Division 29 (Psychotherapy) of the American Psychological Association

(APA). She has served as president of APA Division 29, as newsletter editor and chair of the Section for the Advancement of Women for the Society of Counseling Psychology, and on numerous editorial boards (including *Psychotherapy, Psychotherapy Research, Psychology of Women Quarterly*, and *The Counseling Psychologist*).

Bruce R. Fretz, PhD, (1939–2012) was a professor in the Department of Psychology at the University of Maryland, College Park, throughout most of his career, and he was the long-standing training director or codirector of the Counseling Psychology Doctoral Program at Maryland. He was also a leader in the field of counseling psychology, having served in many capacities in the Society of Counseling Psychology (Division 17) of the American Psychological Association, including being division president in 1991–1992. He published widely in the major journals in counseling psychology, and was the editor of *The Counseling Psychologist* from 1985–1990. During his career, he was an acclaimed teacher, who loved to teach introductory psychology to university undergraduates as well as advanced doctoral-level courses. Along with Charles Gelso, he was the coauthor of all three editions of *Counseling Psychology*. To learn about his career, read Gelso, Hill, and O'Brien's (2013) "In Memoriam" in *The Counseling Psychologist*.